Nova Scotia

the Bradt Travel Guide

edition

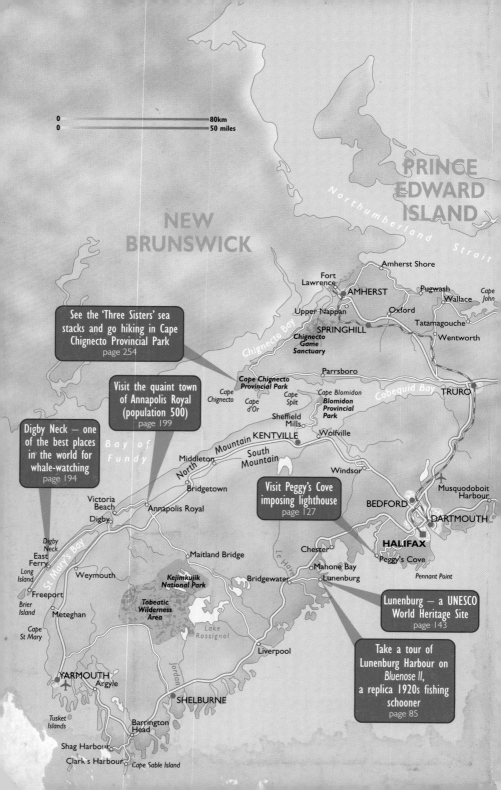

NEW BRUNSWICK

PRINCE EDWARD ISLAND

Northumberland Strait

See the 'Three Sisters' sea
stacks and go hiking in Cape
Chignecto Provincial Park
page 254

Visit the quaint town
of Annapolis Royal
(population 500)
page 199

Digby Neck — one
of the best places
in the world for
whale-watching
page 194

Visit Peggy's Cove
imposing lighthouse
page 127

Lunenburg — a UNESCO
World Heritage Site
page 143

Take a tour of
Lunenburg Harbour on
Bluenose II,
a replica 1920s fishing
schooner
page 85

0 ——— 80km
0 ——— 50 miles

Amherst Shore
Fort
Lawrence
Pugwash
AMHERST
Wallace
Cape
John
Upper Nappan
Oxford
Tatamagouche
Chignecto Bay
SPRINGHILL
*Chignecto
Game
Sanctuary*
Wentworth
Parrsboro
Cobequid Bay
Cape Chignecto
Provincial Park
Cape Blomidon
TRURO
Cape
Chignecto
Cape
d'Or
Cape
Split
*Blomidon
Provincial
Park*
Sheffield
Mills
*Bay of
Fundy*
North Mountain
Wolfville
Middleton
KENTVILLE
South
Mountain
Windsor
Musquodoboit
Harbour
Bridgetown
BEDFORD
DARTMOUTH
Victoria
Beach
Annapolis Royal
HALIFAX
Digby
*Digby
Neck*
East
Ferry
Chester
Peggy's Cove
*Long
Island*
Maitland Bridge
Mahone Bay
Pennant Point
*Brier
Island*
Freeport
Weymouth
*Kejimkujik
National Park*
Bridgewater
Lunenburg
Le Have
Meteghan
*Tobeatic
Wilderness
Area*
St Mary's Bay
Cape
St Mary
*Lake
Rossignol*
Liverpool
Jordan
YARMOUTH
Argyle
SHELBURNE
*Tusket
Islands*
Barrington
Head
Shag Harbour
Clark's Harbour
Cape Sable Island

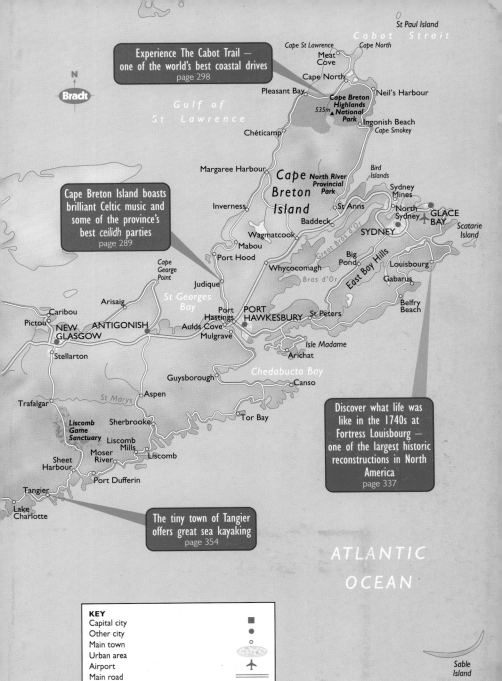

N

Bradt

Gulf of St Lawrence

Cabot Strait

St Paul Island

Cape St Lawrence
Cape North
Meat Cove
Cape North
Pleasant Bay
Neil's Harbour

Experience The Cabot Trail — one of the world's best coastal drives
page 298

Cape Breton Highlands National Park
535m
Ingonish Beach
Cape Smokey

Chéticamp

Margaree Harbour

Cape Breton Island

North River Provincial Park

Bird Islands

Sydney Mines
North Sydney
SYDNEY
GLACE BAY
Scatarie Island

Inverness
St Anns
Baddeck

Cape Breton Island boasts brilliant Celtic music and some of the province's best *ceilidh* parties
page 289

Wagmatcook
Mabou
Port Hood

Great Bras d'Or

Big Pond
Louisbourg
Gabarus

Whycocomagh

Bras d'Or

East Bay Hills

Belfry Beach

Cape George Point

Judique

St Georges Bay

Arisaig

Caribou
Pictou
NEW GLASGOW
ANTIGONISH

Port Hastings
Aulds Cove
Mulgrave

PORT HAWKESBURY
St Peters

Stellarton

Isle Madame
Arichat

Guysborough
Canso

Chedabucto Bay

Trafalgar

St Marys
Aspen

Tor Bay

Discover what life was like in the 1740s at Fortress Louisbourg — one of the largest historic reconstructions in North America
page 337

Liscomb Game Sanctuary
Sherbrooke
Liscomb Mills
Moser River
Liscomb

Sheet Harbour
Port Dufferin

Tangier
Lake Charlotte

The tiny town of Tangier offers great sea kayaking
page 354

ATLANTIC OCEAN

Sable Island

KEY
Capital city	■
Other city	●
Main town	○
Urban area	
Airport	✈
Main road	
Other road	
Railway	
Province boundary	
National/provincial park	
Wilderness area/game sanctuary	

Nova Scotia

Don't miss...

Bluenose II
Take a tour of Lunenburg Harbour aboard this majestic 1920s replica fishing schooner
(NSTB) page 146

Peggy's Cove
Nova Scotia's famous imposing lighthouse
(NSTB) page 127

The Cabot Trail
One of the world's
finest coastal drives
(NSTB) page 298

Whale-watching
Digby Neck is one of
the best places in the
world for sightings
(NSTB) page 194

**Fortress
Louisbourg**
Discover what life
was like in the 1740s
at this historic
reconstruction site
(NSTB) page 337

left Explore Halifax Harbour aboard *Theodore Too* — Nova Scotia's maritime equivalent of Thomas the Tank Engine (NSTB) page 85

below Nova Scotia's seat of government, Province House, was 'a gem of Georgian architecture' according to Charles Dickens (NSTB) page 110

bottom Halifax waterfront at night (NSTB) page 82

above Lunenburg's Old Town — which dates from 1753 — was designated a UNESCO World Heritage site in 1995 (NSTB) page 143

below Mahone Bay's three churches — St James Anglican (l), St John's Lutheran (m) and Trinity United Church (r) — are one of Nova Scotia's iconic sites (NSTB) page 141

left **Discover the native Mi'kmaq culture** (NSTB) page 6

below **Mi'kmaq native, Todd Labrador, with his handmade canoe** (SH)

AUTHOR

David Orkin is a freelance travel writer whose work appears regularly in leading UK publications such as *The Independent*, *Wanderlust* and *Condé Nast Traveller*. He began writing about travel in 2000 after working in the travel industry for over 15 years, including eight years co-running his own successful company. He has travelled extensively since the mid 1970s and first visited Nova Scotia in 2004. Since then he has returned several times, exploring every corner of the province and (when not globetrotting) now spends the majority of the year in Nova Scotia.

AUTHOR'S STORY

When I visited Nova Scotia for the first time I looked for a guidebook to help enhance my experience there, but found that most of them lumped the province with its neighbours, Prince Edward Island and New Brunswick, some also including Newfoundland and Labrador. Fine for an overview of the entire region, but of limited use to anyone wanting to focus solely on Nova Scotia. I turned to Nova Scotia's tourism authorities who produced (and still do) *Doers' & Dreamers'*, a thorough listing of all the province's museums and attractions and virtually all accommodation choices from campgrounds to deluxe resorts, but these are unedited lists.

Each time that I went back to Nova Scotia and explored places – some wonderful, others missable – it became increasingly obvious that there was a need for a more comprehensive, subjective guide. Something to cater to those who wanted to do, those who wanted to dream, and those who wanted to discover the province's highlights, as well as its virtually unknown nooks and crannies. I put a proposal to write a book to the publisher that I thought would be most appropriate for such a guide. Bradt agreed.

Research took place on foot, in canoe and kayak, by ferry, by bike, by coach, and tens of thousands of kilometres by car – and I tried to return everywhere at a different time of year to see how different my impressions were. My recently acquired (Canadian) Permanent Resident status allowed me to spend even more time exploring the province and enjoying long conversations with waiters, fishermen, B&B owners, shopkeepers, park rangers, artists, tourists, birders, musicians and many more – in Nova Scotia it is hard to find someone who doesn't like talking about their fascinating homeland. This guidebook is the collective result of those discussions and explorations.

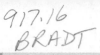

PUBLISHER'S FOREWORD   *Adrian Phillips*

Bradt has built a reputation around publishing guides to destinations off the tourist trail. That can mean places like Rwanda and Ethiopia, of course, but we mustn't forget that there are still areas of mystery and romance in the developed world. As author David Orkin says, despite many visits to Canada over the years, he knew very little about Nova Scotia before going there for the first time – just that it was probably 'cold, wet and windy'. Well, what a land of colour awaited. Who could fail to be enchanted by rugged cliffs, mist-veiled lighthouses and legends of pirates' derring-do? And who could fail to relax in a province where time marches to a slower beat? Nova Scotia – and David's excellent book – is very much in the Bradt mould.

First published December 2009

Bradt Travel Guides Ltd, 23 High Street, Chalfont St Peter, Bucks SL9 9QE, England
www.bradtguides.com
Published in the USA by The Globe Pequot Press Inc, 246 Goose Lane,
PO Box 480, Guilford, Connecticut 06475-0480

Text copyright © 2009 David Orkin
Maps copyright © 2009 Bradt Travel Guides Ltd
Photographs © 2009 Individual photographers
Editorial Project Manager: Emma Thomson

The author and publishers have made every effort to ensure the accuracy of the information in this book at the time of going to press. However, they cannot accept any responsibility for any loss, injury or inconvenience resulting from the use of information contained in this guide.

British Library Cataloguing in Publication Data
A catalogue record for this book is available from the British Library
ISBN-13: 978 1 84162 282 8

Photographs Nova Scotia Tourist Board (NSTB), Peter Gergely (PG), Ron Gallagher (RG), Sherman Hines (SH)
Front cover Lunenburg (SH)
Back cover Cyclists amongst autumn colours (NSTB), Todd Labrador, a native Mi'kmaq resident (SH)
Title page Peggy's Cove lighthouse (PG), Lobster (RG), Whale breaching, Bay of Fundy (NSTB)

Maps Alan Whitaker, Malcolm Barnes (colour map). The Nova Scotia map published by International Travel Maps (❧ +1 604 273 1400; *www.itmb.com*) was used to produce many of the maps in this book. A map published by All 4 One Graphics was used to produce the map of Shelburne.

Typeset from the author's disc by Wakewing, High Wycombe
Printed and bound in India by Nutech Print Services

Acknowledgements

The list could fill a chapter, so I'll try to concentrate on those who have gone way beyond the call of duty. My thanks go to (those I've omitted and) Jo Atherton, Adam Axworthy, Ed Bottrell, Louise Breton, Susan Budd, Lindsay Champion, Harold Clapp, Jill Cruikshank, Scott Cunningham, Trudi Curley, Sebelle Deese, Lee George, Tim Harris, Danny Hennigar, Jason Kannon, Daniel MacKay, Blake Maybank, Kathryn Munro, Dorothy Outhouse, Danny Paul, Sam Stewart, Bria Stokesbury, June Swift, Raymond Taavel, Jason Weickert, and Bill Whitman.

Thanks to everyone at Bradt, particularly Emma Thomson and Adrian Phillips, and to Alan Whitaker for his sterling work in converting my barely legible scribbles into such good maps. Last, but by no means least, special thanks to Vanessa, Oliver and Eleanor for their patience and support.

FEEDBACK REQUEST

Whilst much seems timeless in Nova Scotia, many things relevant to the visitor change frequently. Cafés, restaurants and B&Bs seem to close down, open up or change owners more frequently than elsewhere. Museums move or expand, new tours start up, etc. Even more common are changes to opening hours, days and dates. If you are making a special journey to an attraction or restaurant, call ahead to check it'll be open. I will do my best to keep up with all the changes, but welcome your help. In addition, your tips, ideas, personal reflections – and criticism – will help improve the next edition. Contact me by email at bradtnsguide@yahoo.co.uk, or by post c/o Bradt Travel Guides, 23 High Street, Chalfont St Peter, Bucks SL9 9QE. Thanks! David

Contents

LIST OF MAPS

Introduction

By the time I first visited Nova Scotia I had worked in the travel industry for close to 20 years and considered myself well travelled. I had made numerous long trips to Canada, but other than the fact that its airport (and presumably biggest city) was Halifax, I knew very little about Nova Scotia. If pressed, I would have said that I imagined it was cold, wet and windy.

Since then, I've learnt much about the province. Although it always seemed to be lumped in with its maritime neighbours (New Brunswick, Prince Edward Island and Newfoundland and Labrador), it is large enough (55,300km²) and varied enough (dense forest, countless remote lakes and waterways, a vibrant capital, fabulous music, photogenic fishing villages, towering cliffs and beautiful sandy beaches) to be a popular destination in its own right. Wrapped in 7,400km of coastline and virtually an island, Nova Scotia's culture and heartbeat has always been shaped by the sea. Stories of pirates, buried treasure and ghost-ships abound, and there are stunningly located lighthouses to photograph.

Compared with the UK, it may have relatively cold winters with a fair amount of snow, but Nova Scotia is hardly 'the Frozen North' – the provincial capital, Halifax, is on the same latitude as Bordeaux, France.

When in Nova Scotia, my partner and I liked the contrast of the simple, slow rural lifestyle versus the buzz of Halifax; we were enchanted by the character, comfort – and breakfasts – at the B&Bs; we delighted in the heritage architecture, the music, the seafood, the orchards and the wild flowers; and chatting to the locals – humorous, welcoming and proud of their province – was always entertaining.

We wondered how the kids would enjoy it. Nova Scotia's theme parks are few and far between, and the province's biggest, Upper Clements Park (see page 205), isn't exactly Disneyland. There are only a few cinemas, and – with a couple of exceptions – the museums aren't exactly hi-tech. Apart from the Northumberland Strait (and a few other hotspots) the sea isn't warm enough for swimming.

But they loved watching a blacksmith at work and wool being spun at the living museums, taking a boat trip in search of whales, paddling a canoe, and gorging themselves on berries at a U-pick (pick-your-own) farm. On Cape Breton Island we had moose-spotting competitions, sailed on the Bras d'Or Lake, explored the fortress at Louisbourg and swapped four wheels for two on Isle Madame.

The kids played soldiers at the Halifax Citadel, and rolled down the grassy ramparts at Annapolis Royal's Fort Anne. Ice creams made up for the disappointment of failing to find any fossils or gemstones on the beach at Scots Bay.

After several visits we decided to buy a big souvenir – a house overlooking the sea – and now call Nova Scotia home.

Part One

GENERAL INFORMATION

Name of province Nova Scotia
Country name Canada
Languages English, French
Population 935,000
People Scottish 29%, English 27%, Irish 19%, French/Acadian 12%, German 8%, Mi'kmaq 2%, others 3%
Religion Roman Catholic 37%, United Church 16%, Anglican 13%, Baptist 11%, Presbyterian 3%, Lutheran 1%, Pentecostal 1%, other or no religious affiliation 18%
Canadian Prime Minister Stephen Harper
Nova Scotia Premier Darrell Dexter
Nova Scotia ruling political party New Democratic Party (NDP)
Neighbouring provinces and states Land border with New Brunswick, Canada; nearby Canadian provinces Prince Edward Island and Newfoundland and Labrador. Nearest US state: Maine
Area 55,300km²
Time Atlantic Standard Time Zone (AST). Winter GMT –4; summer GMT –3 (clocks adjusted second Sunday in March and first Sunday in November)
Currency Canadian dollar (CAN$ or CAD)
Exchange rate £1=CAN$1.78, US$1=CAN$1.09, €1=CAN$1.56 (August 2009)
Flag An extended blue cross on a white background superimposed with a shield bearing the Royal Arms of Scotland
Telephone codes Canada + 1 (international code); Nova Scotia 902
Electricity supply 110 volts
Public holidays 1 January (New Year's Day), March/April (Good Friday), March/April (Easter Monday), May (Victoria Day; first Monday after 25 May), 1 July (Canada Day), August (Natal Day; first Monday in Aug), September (Labour Day; first Monday in Sept), October (Thanksgiving Day; second Monday in Oct), 11 November (Remembrance Day), 23 December (Christmas Day), 26 December (Boxing Day).

Background Information

GEOGRAPHY

With an area of 55,300km², Nova Scotia is the second smallest of Canada's 13 provinces and territories – only nearby Prince Edward Island (at 5,660km²) is smaller. For a European comparison Nova Scotia is larger than Denmark (approximately 43,000km²) but much smaller than Scotland (approximately 79,000km²).

Connected to mainland Canada only by a narrow isthmus, it is almost surrounded by the sea. To the south and east is the Atlantic Ocean; to the northeast is the Cabot Strait; to the north the Northumberland Strait; and to the northwest the Bay of Fundy. Although it measures over 550km in length, with an average width of 130km, Nova Scotia has 7,400km of coastline. No point of land is more than 60km from the sea.

The shape of the province has been likened to that of a lobster, with Cape Breton Island to the northeast forming the claws.

Halifax is Nova Scotia's capital and is situated at the head of a huge natural harbour on the southeastern coast of the province. In terms of latitude, Halifax is further south than both Paris and Vienna. In fact, the province lies halfway between the North Pole and the Equator, straddling the 45th parallel.

Thick forests – with pine, spruce, fir, hemlock, birch and maple dominating – dotted with lakes cover 80% of the land, but there are also blossom-covered orchards, blueberry fields, and rolling farmland. Much of the best farmland is found in the Annapolis Valley, sheltered by hills to both the north and south.

In general, elevations do not exceed 200m. The main exception is on Cape Breton Island, where 535m-high White Hill forms the province's highest point.

CLIMATE

Nova Scotia lies within the Northern Temperate Zone. The climate is more typically continental than maritime, although the sea has an attenuating effect on the temperature highs and lows. Cape Breton Island experiences much more extreme weather patterns than mainland Nova Scotia.

WINTER (*early November–mid April*) Winter is moderately cold with high temperatures ranging from an average of -4°C to 5°C. At this time of year, freezing rain is a Nova Scotia speciality. There are a fair number of bright, sunny (albeit cold) days. The Northumberland Strait and Gulf of St Lawrence are ice-covered during much of the winter, cooling down nearby coastal areas.

SPRING (*mid-April–mid-June*) During spring average high temperatures range from 4°C to 14°C and in coastal areas.

SUMMER (*mid-June–mid-September*) Summer temperatures range from daytime highs of 18–25°C (occasionally reaching 30°C) to evening lows of 9–14°C. Further inland, the air is typically about 5°C warmer.

AUTUMN (*mid-September–early November*) Early autumn is often mild, and the warm Gulf Stream extends the season, but days become cooler as winter approaches.

In general, sea temperatures are too low for enjoyable swimming: the main exceptions to this are the coastal waters of the Northumberland Strait and northwest Cape Breton Island, particularly in August.

Annual precipitation averages 1,200mm, falling mainly as rain during autumn and as snow in winter. Boosting the average are the highlands of Cape Breton Island (an average of over 1,600mm of precipitation per year) and the southwest (1,500mm): in comparison, the Northumberland Strait receives less than 1,000mm a year.

The merging of warm, moisture-laden air above the Gulf Stream with the far cooler air above the Labrador Current results in a lot of fog: this can often blanket coastal regions, particularly in the morning between mid-spring and early summer. The good news is that the fog is often localised, and more often than not dissipates by late morning. Some of the foggiest parts of the province are Halifax, Yarmouth, Canso, Sydney and Sable Island.

Although most fizzle out before they reach Nova Scotia, some hurricanes and tropical storms do stay the distance and sweep across the province, uprooting trees, knocking down power lines and washing away bridges. The worst in recent years was Hurricane Juan (September 2003) which caused vast amounts of damage.

Environment Canada's website (*www.weatheroffice.gc.ca/canada_e.html*) offers weather forecasts for over 40 towns across the province. Current weather forecasts can also be obtained by phone (☏ *426 9090*).

TIME

Nova Scotia is in the Atlantic Time Zone. This is four hours behind Greenwich Mean Time (GMT) but like most provinces in Canada, Daylight Saving Time is observed between the second Sunday in March and the first Sunday in November. During this period, the province is three hours behind GMT. The Atlantic Time Zone is one hour ahead of Eastern Standard Time and four hours ahead of Pacific Time.

HISTORY

NB: Nova Scotia was not thus named until 1621, and was not declared a province until 1867. Nevertheless, I have used this designation for history before those dates to save repetition of the phrase 'what is now called'. Similarly, current place names have been used to describe events in areas that were at the time unnamed or known by a different name.

THE FIRST INHABITANTS The earliest evidence of human habitation found in Nova Scotia was discovered in 1948 at Debert, near Truro. Thousands of Paleo-Indian artefacts were later unearthed, and some were radiocarbon-dated to 8,600BC. Paleo-Indians are believed to have crossed to the North American continent from Siberia. Over the years, as temperatures in the region waxed and waned, the inhabitants of the area are likely to have retreated south, returning perhaps a few centuries later: this cycle was probably repeated a few times. The native people living in Nova Scotia were the Mi'kmaq, members of the Algonquian-speaking Abenaki Confederacy.

EARLY VISITORS? There is much speculation – and the occasional shred of evidence – to suggest that various outsiders visited Nova Scotia well before French settlement.

Irish-born St Brendan the Navigator may have stopped by early in the 6th century. Vikings almost certainly visited nearby Newfoundland very early in the 11th century, and there have been several claims that Iceland-born Leif Ericsson stopped at several places on Nova Scotia's southwest coast in 1007.

Some say Prince Henry Sinclair from Scotland landed in 1398, and the Venetian Zeno brothers may have visited soon after. One man claimed to have found ruins of a 15th-century Chinese settlement on Cape Breton Island.

Basque fishermen are certain to have made landfall in Nova Scotia during whaling and cod-fishing trips in the province's waters, possibly as early as the 15th century.

In 1497, John Cabot crossed the Atlantic from England. None of Cabot's own records has survived, but a map drawn 45 years later by his son suggests that Cabot landed at northern Cape Breton Island.

In the early 1520s, the Portuguese probably had a seasonal fishing colony at the site of present-day Ingonish.

THE FRENCH AND ENGLISH In 1603, the French were looking to plant Gallic seeds in the New World. French nobleman Pierre du Gua, Sieur de Mons (sometimes written as 'de Monts'), was awarded a monopoly to trade fur across a vast swathe of North America on the condition that he would establish a colony there.

In 1604, he and Samuel de Champlain established the first permanent European settlement north of St Augustine, Florida, at Port-Royal (see page 210). They were befriended by Mi'kmaq in the area. The French named the entire region 'Acadie', anglicised as Acadia.

At roughly the same time, England began to colonise some of the eastern parts of the United States of America. For over 150 years the English and these settlers were allies: English ships under Samuel Argall from Virginia destroyed the Port-Royal settlement in 1614.

A 1632 treaty returned Acadia to the French who made another attempt to colonise, establishing a settlement on the LaHave River (see page 156), and re-

NEW SCOTLAND

Sir William Alexander, a member of the court of King James I, proposed establishing a New Scotland in North America and put his idea to HRH in 1621. In a generous mood, the king granted Sir William most of the northeast American continent. The land was to be named 'Nova Scotia' and in return, Sir William had to pay 'one penny of Scottish money'.

After failed attempts to get shiploads of immigrants to his land in both 1622 and 1623, he came up with another scheme. In 1624, Sir William persuaded the king to create 150 Baronets of the Kingdom of New Scotland: in return for a substantial amount of money, those so honoured would receive a land grant in the new kingdom, a knighthood, and several other privileges. Barons did not even have to cross the Atlantic to receive their titles – a small patch of Edinburgh Castle's parade ground was declared to be part of Nova Scotia and set aside for the purpose (to this day a little bit of Nova Scotia lies under Edinburgh Castle's Esplanade). Finally, in 1628, he sent his (Baronet) son in command of four vessels to Port-Royal, but soon after, King Charles, who had succeeded James, instructed Sir William to demolish all New Scotland's buildings and remove all his people from it. Sir William complied, but never received the £10,000 compensation promised. He died bankrupt in 1640.

establishing Port-Royal close to its original site. As French presence in – and colonisation of – Acadia grew slowly, one man in particular, Nicolas Denys (see page 323) was instrumental in establishing settlements both on mainland Nova Scotia and on Cape Breton Island.

Treaties between the English and French continued to pass Nova Scotia back and forth, and in the late 1680s, the French in Quebec attacked New England. This

THE MI'KMAQ

Pre-colonisation, Mi'kmaq territory included all of Nova Scotia and Prince Edward Island, and parts of Quebec, New Brunswick and Maine.

The Mi'kmaq practised a religion based on Mother Nature, deeply tied to the land. Mythology also played an important part in spiritual life. They lived in conical birch-bark wigwams; birch bark was also used to make canoes in which to travel the waterways. The Mi'kmaq were also at home on the sea, travelling in ocean-going versions of their light canoes.

For centuries, they lived along the shoreline in summer, fishing, gathering shellfish, and hunting seals and whales. In the winter, most moved inland, setting up settlements in sheltered forested areas. Moose, bear, caribou, and smaller game provided food and clothing, supplemented by wild berries: plants and herbs were used for teas and medicinal purposes.

They respected their environment and only killed, took or used what they needed. When Europeans first settled Nova Scotia, the natural resources were virtually untouched. They befriended the first French settlers, acting as guides, teaching them to live off the land and showing them how to make fish-weirs and eel-traps, how to ice-fish, which wild berries were safe to eat and how to prepare them, how to cure and prevent scurvy, and more.

The Mi'kmaq began to convert to Christianity in 1610, and their way of life underwent other major changes as they abandoned many traditional customs and focused on gathering furs and hides for trade purposes. The French gave them weapons, and both French and English passed on diseases such as smallpox which killed hundreds – if not thousands. Distrustful and fearful, the English and New Englanders saw the Mi'kmaq not as allies but hostile savages, and decided that forceful subjugation and assimilation would be the best course of action. In 1749, Governor Cornwallis put a bounty on the head (or scalp) of every Mi'kmaq, man, woman or child. The amount of the bounty was increased the following year. Although a proclamation by King George III in 1763 promised protection for the Mi'kmaq and their hunting grounds, they suffered a similar fate to that of First Nations people and Native Americans across the continent. Often caught between the French and the English/British power struggle for North America, they were robbed of their land, persecuted, forced to live with virtually no rights, and herded onto reserves. For decades, the federal government actively suppressed Mi'kmaq traditions. For example, in 1885, religious ceremonies were prohibited. In 1927, Canadian government legislation forbade aboriginals in Canada from forming political organisations, as well as practising their traditional culture and language.

In the 19th century, the Mi'kmaq were confined to about 60 locations, both on and off reserve, dotted about the province. In the 1940s, the Canadians implemented a Centralisation Policy, which mandated that they be moved against their will to just two reserves. Young Mi'kmaq children were taken away from their families and taught the 'white-man's ways', to integrate them into mainstream society – and rapidly lose the culture and heritage of their ancient way of life.

See also page 14.

prompted the New Englanders to attack the Acadians, who were far more interested in farming than fighting. Each time the French attacked New England from Quebec or New Brunswick, the New Englanders ransacked a few more Acadian villages in misguided revenge. The Treaty of Utrecht in 1713 gave most of Acadia to the British, but left Cape Breton Island in French hands. Nova Scotia became an official colony, and Annapolis Royal (see page 199) its capital.

LOUISBOURG AND HALIFAX The French decided that they had to build a mighty fort on Cape Breton Island, to protect their fishing interests and help guard Quebec from prospective attacks by the British navy. The chosen site was Louisbourg (see page 333), named for Louis XV.

War broke out again in 1744, and the French attacked Canso (see page 362). Effectively, they now controlled the region's highly lucrative fishing industry. This was not good for the New Englanders who attacked and took the fortress of Louisbourg in 1745: in 1748, a treaty returned it and Cape Breton Island to the French.

Halifax was founded by General Edward Cornwallis in 1749, partly as a secure base from which the British could attack the French. It was declared Nova Scotia's capital. Attempts to increase the population went into overdrive: land, rations, equipment, support and military protection were all promised to those prepared to start a new life in Nova Scotia.

BEYOND HALIFAX Shiploads of new immigrants began to arrive in Halifax, the vast majority foreign Protestants predominantly from German-speaking parts of modern-day France, Switzerland and Germany.

When they reached Halifax, they found that land grants were far smaller than had been advertised, rations and supplies were meagre, and wages were set so low that paying off passages would take a lifetime. The British kept them quiet and created another base by shipping many of the German-speakers to Lunenburg (see page 143).

OATHS OF ALLEGIANCE In general, the Acadians had tried to get on with their lives (whether the land was called Acadia or Nova Scotia), building dykes in order to reclaim the marshlands and wetlands around tidal river estuaries, and farming the fertile results. They planted orchards and the odd vineyard. However, they spoke French, were friendly with the Mi'kmaq – with whom the French were still closely allied – and were not trusted by the British.

Governor Cornwallis had demanded an oath of allegiance from them, but terms were not agreed. When Charles Lawrence became Lieutenant-Governor in 1753, approximately 10,000 Acadians lived in Nova Scotia. In 1755, they were asked to sign another oath of allegiance to the British, this one even stronger, stating that in the case of war, the Acadians could be told to fight with the British against the French. Again, they refused to sign.

LE GRAND DERANGEMENT – THE GREAT UPHEAVAL On 28 July 1755, Lawrence and the rest of the governing council in Halifax called for the deportation of 'French inhabitants'. Orders were sent to the major British forts, and the operation began in mid–August. The Acadians were to be sent off on ships and could take with them only what they could carry: land and livestock would become the property of the Crown.

Almost 3,000 Acadians were deported from one area alone – Grand Pré (see page 223) – and in all around 10,000 were herded onto ships and banished to colonies along the eastern American seaboard, to French colonies in the Caribbean, some even to Europe. In many cases, families became separated in the huge operation. Troops burned all the Acadians' buildings so that they would have nothing to return to.

Some Acadians adapted to their new lives. Some drifted south and reached Louisiana, then under French control. Many others never lost their attachment to their former homeland, and survived from day to day, hoping for an opportunity to return from expulsion.

Another British–French war started in 1756, and the supposedly invincible French fortress at Louisbourg fell again in 1758.

FILLING THE VACUUM The flow of immigrants increased significantly with the signing of the Treaty of Paris in 1763, after which the French were no longer seen as a threat in Nova Scotia.

The Planters In its efforts to repopulate Nova Scotia – and increase and improve the food supply – the government attempted to attract New Englanders with free grants of rich farmland (stolen from the Acadians) and other benefits. The first such land grants were in two dykeland areas near modern-day Wolfville (see page 218) and the first Planters – as these immigrants were called – arrived from Connecticut, Rhode Island, and Massachusetts in 1760.

Returning Acadians From 1763, the British allowed exiled Acadians to return to Nova Scotia. Unable to pay for passage by sea, hundreds returned on foot to find that their old lands had been given away to other immigrants. They walked on and settled eventually in less desirable areas with poor-quality soil, such as the Bay of Fundy coast between Yarmouth and Digby, part of which is still known as the French Shore (see page 186). Many former farmers turned to fishing.

The Scots After the Battle of Culloden in 1746, the British authorities began to stamp out all aspects of Scottish Highland culture. Those that could afford to do so moved away, and many headed for the New World. The major influx to Nova Scotia began in 1763 when the *Hector* sailed into Pictou (see page 273).

Back home, the Highland Clearances forced tens of thousands off the land they had long called home: many followed in the wake of the *Hector* and headed for Pictou.

On arrival, they dispersed along the Northumberland Strait shore (by 1830 there were around 50,000 Scots in Pictou and Antigonish counties) and on to Cape Breton Island, which became part of Nova Scotia in 1820.

The Irish By 1760, the Irish (mostly Catholics) made up about 20–25% of the population of Halifax. This was thanks in large part to Alexander McNutt – born in Londonderry, Northern Ireland – who emigrated to America in the early 1750s, and was stationed in Nova Scotia whilst in the army. Simply by applying to the governor, he received generous (free) land grants on both sides of the Minas Basin, and on the South Shore. He dreamt of turning Nova Scotia into 'New Ireland' and invited primarily Presbyterians from the country of his birth to come over and buy their own plot of land from him. Almost 300 arrived in Halifax from Londonderry in 1761, and another 150 or so followed. The Irish Privy Council didn't want a mass exodus of its citizens and stopped McNutt from emptying (old) Ireland. (Incidentally, McNutt then turned his attention to building a New Jerusalem on the South Shore – but that's another story.)

Economic conditions were not good in Ireland even before the devastation resulting from failed potato crops in the 1840s. North America offered hope, possibilities, dreams, and (sometimes) work. A fair share of the hundreds of thousands of Irish who emigrated across the Atlantic in the 19th century made Nova Scotia their new home.

Loyalists When the American Revolution started in 1775, a good chunk of the population of the colonies preferred to remain loyal to the British Crown, but understandably were far from popular in the United States. From 1783, tens of thousands of 'Loyalists' emigrated, with around 20,000 going to Nova Scotia. Some 10,000 went to Shelburne (see page 165), instantly creating (what was then) North America's fourth-largest city.

Comparatively wealthy – even aristocratic – and well educated, many Loyalists were not best suited to pioneer life and moved on to pastures new. The remainder persevered and, in general, adapted well to Nova Scotia.

Germans The first wave of German immigrants arrived in the early 1750s: after the American Revolution, there was a second wave when soldiers in German regiments hired to fight by the British Crown were offered land and provisions to start a new life in Nova Scotia. These men were mostly from Hesse, Brunswick, Anspach-Bayreuth and Waldeck; many settled between Digby and Annapolis Royal.

Black immigration There were three significant tranches of black immigration to Nova Scotia.

When the Loyalists left the United States in the aftermath of the American Revolution, they were joined by their slaves and former slaves who had fought on the Loyalist side in return for their freedom. About 3,000 blacks came to Nova Scotia, many settling at Burchtown (later Birchtown – see page 170). Some went to Halifax, settling near Dartmouth in Preston – which to this day has a sizeable black population.

In 1796, over 500 Trelawny Maroons (maroons were runaway slaves and/or their descendants) were sent to Halifax from Jamaica.

Another wave of black immigration came during the 1812–15 Anglo-American War: American slaves who deserted to the British side were offered the opportunity to serve with the British military service or go as free settlers to a British colony. In this time, approximately 1,500 former slaves settled in Nova Scotia.

PEACE AND CONFEDERATION After so much conflict, from 1815 Nova Scotia enjoyed a rare long period of peace.

SHIPBUILDING

With Halifax beginning to grow, Governor Cornwallis (see page 7) introduced a bounty for every new vessel built. Vessels were needed for trade, transport, and – in times of war – as privateers (see box on page 10).

Between 1800 and 1875, thousands of vessels were built in hundreds of shipyards all around the province. Nova Scotia had safe harbours and river mouths, plentiful timber and sawmills, and some of the world's best ship designers, craftsmen and shipwrights. However, from the late 1870s onward the demand for wooden ships began to slow down, not helped by use of the new railways and the increasing use of steel in shipbuilding. The Golden Age of Sail was over.

Over the years, nature, time and recycling of building materials have removed most traces of all those shipyards.

In the 1820s, a British company, the General Mining Association (GMA), won control of mining leases in the colonies – and a monopoly over coal mining in Nova Scotia. It invested large sums of money into the mines and the mining infrastructure.

Having been stung by its American colonies, the British government was reluctant to let colonies have too much power, and did its best to ensure that major decisions were always on the lines of what London (rather than the colonists) might want.

PRIVATEERS – OR PIRATES?

War, particularly sea battles, dominated much of Nova Scotia's early history, with almost constant conflict between the colony's 'Anglo' settlers and either (sometimes both) the French and the Americans.

Privateers – privately owned vessels which would attack the enemy's merchant ships, allowing the navies to concentrate on fighting each other – took to the seas. This form of 'legalised piracy', which reached a peak between 1760 and 1815, had strict rules: captains (usually backed by private investors) had to register full details of their vessel and its owners, and a bond was payable. The captain would then receive a *letter of marque*, an official licence to set out to harass the enemy, and capture every enemy vessel ('prize') he could. Privateers often strayed far from Nova Scotia's coastal waters, hunting American ships along the eastern seaboard and seeking out French vessels trading in the Caribbean.

When a prize was captured, it – and at least one member of its crew – would be taken to naval officials. Nova Scotia's privateers were required to take prizes to Halifax's Privateers Wharf where they would be inspected. Legally captured prizes – no enemy men were to be killed in cold blood or inhumanely treated, and the prize had to be an enemy, rather than a neutral, ship – were sold at auction and the money was split between (in descending order) the authorities, the privateer's owners, the captain and his officers – and perhaps a few coins for the rest of the crew. The highest bidders were privateer investors who bought the captured ships to put back to use in their own privateer fleets. Consequently, some vessels changed sides frequently.

Privateers didn't restrict themselves to the sea when seeking bounty, often putting in to feebly defended ports and harbours where armed raiders would rush ashore and strip the settlement of anything of value. Louisbourg (see page 333) was a haven for French privateers, but the Nova Scotia port most associated with privateers was Liverpool (see page 156).

At an auction in 1811, Liverpool-born Enos Collins purchased a captured slave-smuggling schooner, to convert and use as a privateer vessel: he named her the *Liverpool Packet*, and put her under the command of Joseph Barss. The *Liverpool Packet* wreaked havoc on American shipping between 1812 and 1814 and by the end of the conflict had taken over 50 prizes. When he died in 1871, Collins, who had been a shrewd banker, merchant and investor, was said to be the richest man in Canada. Most of those who invested in privateers, however, made little or no money at all.

Privateering was abolished in 1856 by the Declaration of Paris, but its memory lives on – each July Liverpool celebrates 'Privateer Days'.

Nova Scotia is incredibly rich in pirate folklore and it seems that there is a tale of buried treasure for almost every one of the province's multitude of beaches, coves and islands. Most pirate activity took place between the late 17th and mid-18th centuries, but the vast majority of pirate tales told these days are probably better filed under 'fiction' than 'fact'. (See *Geocaching*, page 63.)

In the mid 1860s, conferences were held in Charlottetown (Prince Edward Island), Quebec City and London, England. These gave birth to the British North America Act to which Queen Victoria gave royal assent. The act, which united the Province of Canada with New Brunswick and Nova Scotia to form the Dominion of Canada, came into effect on 1 July 1867: 1 July is still celebrated as Canada Day. The 36 attendees, six of whom were from Nova Scotia, at the historic conferences are known as the Fathers of Confederation.

In 1982, the British Parliament passed the Canada Act which left Canada as part of the Commonwealth, but finally severed all Canada's remaining legislative dependence on the United Kingdom.

However, during the 1830s and 1840s, Joseph Howe, a newspaper owner and politician, led a group of political reformers. Through his efforts, Nova Scotia became the first colony in the British Empire to become self-governing and to achieve responsible government based on parliamentary accountability. Howe later became premier of Nova Scotia from 1860 to 1862.

Nova Scotia had long been only too happy to stand alone politically, but the idea of joining together with neighbouring New Brunswick and Prince Edward Island had begun to sound a lot more attractive. As it turned out, within a few years the Dominion of Canada was created (see box above).

Many people in Nova Scotia were anti-Confederation, but it did bring the province benefits – including a railway connection with the rest of Canada.

Steel was first produced commercially in 1883, and many more coal mines were opening, particularly in Pictou and Cumberland counties, and on Cape Breton Island.

THE 20TH CENTURY The new century brought two tragic events which put Halifax in the news: the aftermath of the sinking of the *Titanic* in 1912 (see page 85), and 1917's Halifax Explosion (see page 86). The latter (in particular) left a big grey cloud over the province, and for many years the people's mood remained sombre. Times continued to be hard, and worsened as Nova Scotia suffered its own elongated Great Depression.

One of the few bright lights shining through those gloomy times came in the unlikely form of a fishing vessel, the *Bluenose* (see page 146). Through a long and difficult period, this racing champion's successes gave the people a reason to be proud, and lifted the spirits of many.

Halifax was a very important port during World War I. In World War II, Halifax was again a crucial part of the Allied war effort as a gathering point for convoys heading across the Atlantic, a 'holding area' for neutral ships, and the departure point for Canadian forces heading out by sea.

The post-war years brought the opening of the Canso Causeway (see page 294) providing a land link between mainland Nova Scotia and Cape Breton Island. In general, though, the economy was in poor shape, and thousands left the province to seek greener grass elsewhere.

In the late 1950s and 1960s, workers left farming and fishing for new jobs in manufacturing and there was a big population shift from rural to urban areas. Coal mining – long a mainstay of the economy – began to die as the cost of obtaining the coal made it uncompetitive compared with oil and gas. Just a few small mines hung on, but most were closed.

Then the fishing industry – a major contributor to Nova Scotia's economy for centuries – hit serious problems. Overfishing had resulted in massive drops in

As the 19th century progressed, the temperance movement had been gaining strength across North America. Prohibition laws were introduced in Canada in 1878, but individual areas could choose to opt out of the legislation.

When the US government introduced (stricter) Prohibition in 1920, Canadian distillers were permitted to export to non-Prohibition nations, the nearest being the French-owned islands of St Pierre and Miquelon (just off the southeast coast of Newfoundland), and vast quantities of alcohol were sent there.

Nova Scotia's coastal waters were the perfect secret sea route between the islands and the east coast of the US, and many fishing-boat owners adapted their vessels to carry liquid contraband. When the US authorities began to use faster craft, the province's boatbuilders designed more efficient purpose-built vessels in which to evade their pursuers.

Ports such as Mahone Bay, Lunenburg, Liverpool, Yarmouth and Meteghan were home to dozens of 'rum-running' vessels. Rum, in fact, was very rarely part of the cargo but was used as a generic term for the alcoholic drinks that were carried.

Sometimes vessels failed to evade the American or Canadian authorities and the boat's captain would normally be jailed, but – until 1933 when prohibition was repealed in the US – Nova Scotia's skilled seafarers enjoyed a very profitable – albeit illegal – period.

catch sizes, and by the early 1990s, tens of thousands of jobs were lost – not just by those who fished for cod and flat-fish, but in the processing plants, boatbuilders, and those who serviced them.

Natural gas was discovered off Sable Island in 1968, but at that time, developing costs were prohibitive. However, oil was discovered in the same region and was drilled from 1992 to 1999 – Canada's first offshore oil project. The first gas was finally shipped to market in December 1999 via the Sable Offshore Energy Project, and production is expected to continue for the next 15 years.

The consequences of Nova Scotia's economic woes through much of the 20th century haven't all been bad. Outside a few urban areas, there has been precious little development. Forests still cover the majority of the land, and – in the main – the coastline is generally unspoilt. Another positive trend is just beginning as former fishermen are beginning to look at tourism as a way to make use of their boats.

GOVERNMENT AND POLITICS

A member of the Commonwealth, Canada is a constitutional monarchy, with Queen Elizabeth II the sovereign and head of state. The queen appoints a governor-general to represent her for a five-year term. Canada's federation of ten provinces and three territories operates under a parliamentary democracy in which power is shared between the federal government, based in Ottawa, and the provincial governments.

THE FEDERAL GOVERNMENT The head of government is the prime minister, who is the leader of the majority party or party coalition in the House of Commons.

The Canadian Parliament comprises two houses: the House of Commons, with 308 members (11 from Nova Scotia), is apportioned by provincial population and elected by plurality from the country's districts; the Senate comprises 105 members (ten from Nova Scotia) appointed by the governor-general on the advice of the prime minister. Legislation must be passed by both houses and signed by the governor-general to become law.

The Federal government has authority over defence, criminal law, trade, banking, and other affairs of national interest.

PROVINCIAL GOVERNMENT Responsible for civil services, health, education, natural resources, and local government, Nova Scotia's Legislative Assembly consists of a one-house legislative body with members elected every four years. Although there is a nominal head of government (the lieutenant-governor, appointed by the Governor-General of Canada), executive power rests with the 52-member Halifax-based Nova Scotia House of Assembly, headed by a premier, the leader of the majority party. At the time of writing, the lieutenant-governor is Mayann E Francis.

For many years, the people of Nova Scotia have been ruled by a minority government. In May 2009, the Nova Scotia Progressive Conservative Party ('Tories') under Rodney MacDonald (who took office in February 2006) lost a vote of confidence over financial policy.

Elections the following month saw a huge swing to the left, with the New Democratic Party (NDP) led by Darrell Dexter sweeping to power and winning 31 of the province's 52 ridings. The Liberals ('Grits') became the official Opposition with 11 seats, and the Tories were reduced to just 10 seats.

The NDP win ended 10 years of Tory rule.

In an effort to reduce bureaucracy, the government did away with incorporated cities in the 1990s forming the Halifax Regional Municipality (HRM) through the amalgamation of the former cities of Halifax and Dartmouth and the town of Bedford and the municipality of Halifax County, and the Cape Breton Regional Municipality (CBRM) by amalgamating the former city of Sydney, six towns and the municipality of the county of Cape Breton.

ECONOMY

Traditionally, Nova Scotia's economy has been based on natural resources. Fishing has been important since the days of pre-European settlement, and the profusion of forest was the basis for a strong lumber industry and shipbuilding. Coal mining took off in the mid 19th century, and flourished for a century – it's said that the province contains more coal fields for its area than any other part of the world. Iron mines were in operation between 1825 and 1920, and the province had a gold rush in the 1860s, though gold mining's best years proved to be from 1885 to 1903.

Gypsum has been mined since the 1770s (the province is now the leading Canadian producer), salt since 1918 (first at Malagash, see page 269, then at Pugwash, see page 266), and barytes – primarily around the Minas Basin – since the 1860s.

In the main, the economy continues to undergo the slow transition from industrial to more service-oriented, and the service industries now employ the largest number of workers in the province.

Overfishing and poor resource management from the 1970s to early 1990s had devastating effects on the region's cod-fishing industry. Fishing bans, quotas and other attempts to turn things around seem to be having little effect. More important to the sector today are shellfish: shrimps, crabs, and scallops – oh, and lobster; Nova Scotia is the world's largest exporter of the crustacean.

The waters off Sable Island (see page 368) are the site of offshore natural gas-drilling platforms. Current production averages 400–500 million cubic feet per day.

Although less than 10% of Nova Scotia's land is arable, agriculture contributes heavily to the economy. Significant crops include apples and wild blueberries, and poultry and dairy products figure strongly. Over two-thirds of the province is covered by productive forest, some of which is harvested for lumber and pulp. Nova Scotia is the world's largest exporter of wild blueberries and Christmas trees. Acadian Seaplants, based in the province, is the world's largest manufacturer of seaweed-based speciality products.

There are both hydro-electric and – harnessing the power of the sea – tidal-power generating plants (see pages 204 and 248 respectively).

Manufacturing is also a major contributor, but it is small businesses that make up over 90% of the province's economy.

Tourism has been a growing contributor, with most visitors entering the province by road through New Brunswick. Air arrivals are increasing, but numbers travelling by ferry have been hit more than most recently by rising fuel costs and a spell of US dollar weakness.

In 2007, Nova Scotia's (nominal) gross domestic product (GDP) was CAN$33.010 billion (real GDP CAN$28.803 billion).

PEOPLE

Nova Scotia is home to approximately 935,000 people: the majority live in urban centres, with approximately 40% living in the Halifax Regional Municipality. This means the province's population density is 18 people/km² (England's is approximately 390 people/km²).

Almost 80% of the population can trace their ancestry to Scotland, England or Ireland; France and Germany are next on the list. Although the highest number of immigrants continue to arrive from the UK and Ireland, arrival numbers from eastern Europe, the Middle East, and southeast Asia and the Far East are not insignificant. Recent years have also seen many Canadians move here from the provinces of Ontario, Alberta and British Columbia: many sold their homes and realised that – in terms of buying property – their dollars will go much further in Nova Scotia.

THE MI'KMAQ IN THE 21ST CENTURY

Today, approximately 16,000 Mi'kmaq (see page 6) live in the province. They are divided into 13 Mi'kmaq First Nation Bands, whose members have usufructuary rights (rights to enjoy and benefit from property that belongs to someone else) to approximately 11,200ha of mostly unproductive land (the title of Reserve Land is held by the Canadian Crown). About 60% live on 32 widely scattered Indian reserves. In recent years, in a few cases the Mi'kmaq have used their Aboriginal Rights, supported by the Royal Proclamation of 1763, to try to reclaim their hunting and fishing rights – albeit to the annoyance of some in the province's heavily regulated mainstream fishing industry.

After centuries of suffering suppression, persecution and attempted genocide, there are attempts to put the historical record straight. Daniel N Paul's *We Were Not the Savages* (www.danielnpaul.com) is a must-read for anyone interested in the history of the province from a Mi'kmaq perspective. The author is also behind a petition (www.petitiononline.com/01101749/petition.html) to rename all the province's public entities named in honour of Governor Edward Cornwallis who founded Halifax in 1749 and who offered bounties for the scalps of Mi'kmaq men, women, and children. A hopeful sign for the future is that many younger Mi'kmaq are rediscovering their language, culture and heritage.

Just occasionally, the visitor may be thrown by an unusual word or expression. A resident of Nova Scotia is a Bluenose (or Bluenoser). There are different versions of the origin: these include the coloured marks left on their noses by fishermen wearing (poorly dyed) blue mittens, and a variety of knobbly potato, blueish in colour, grown in (and exported from) the province early in the 19th century. Nova Scotia's most famous sailing vessel (see page 146) was named the *Bluenose*.

Someone from elsewhere who now lives in the province is a Come-From-Away (CFA). All over Canada a 'looney' (or 'loonie') is a Canadian one-dollar coin (a bird, the loon, has for many years appeared on the tails side of the coin) and a 'twoonie' (or 'tooney' or 'toonie') is a two-dollar coin. Furthermore, a take-away is referred to as a' 'take-out'; and a lookout is called a 'look-off'. Finally, dates are written numerically (MM/DD/YY), so 18 March 2010 would be written 03/18/10.

As is generally the case, life in the big urban centres is lived at a much faster pace than in small towns and rural areas: if you've been exploring the province for a few days, coming back to Halifax can seem like jumping forward a few decades.

Visitors will find most locals approachable, friendly and helpful – 'old timers' in particular love to talk, so if you ask one for directions you may also get their (usually fascinating) life histories.

GENEALOGY There is far more interest in genealogy in Nova Scotia (and North America in general) than in Europe. The Mi'kmaq apart, everyone is – or descends from – an immigrant, and perhaps because people's ancestors only started arriving here in the last four centuries, tracing roots is more manageable. You'll find genealogical research facilities and archives all over the province.

LANGUAGE

Canada is bilingual (English and French) by constitution, but less than 7% of Nova Scotia's residents are bilingual. English is the language of choice for almost 93% of the population, while just under 4% call French their mother tongue. In some places (Pugwash – see page 266 – and Antigonish – see page 281, for example) street signs are in Scottish Gaelic (Gáidhlig), the language brought over by the Scottish Highlanders: in recent years many community name signs on Cape Breton Island have been replaced with signs showing both the English and Scottish Gaelic names.

RELIGION

Church affiliation in Nova Scotia is higher than elsewhere in Canada. Roman Catholics are the largest group, making up almost 37% of the population. Next (in descending order) are the United Church of Canada, Anglicans and Baptists. There are smaller percentages of Lutheran, Presbyterian, Greek Orthodox and other Christian denominations. The province has small populations of Muslims, Hindus, Buddhists and Jews.

EDUCATION

Nova Scotia has more than 440 public (state) schools. These are under the auspices of seven regional school boards, and one school board which is responsible for the province's 20 French-language schools. Private schools include Halifax Grammar and Windsor's Kings Edgehill, and there are Montessori schools (where tuition is based on the child-development theories of Maria Montessori, who advocated that the teacher's role is to introduce children to materials and then remain a silent presence in the classroom, whilst the children direct their own learning in Halifax, Windsor, Wolfville and Sydney.

Children normally begin school in the September following their fifth birthday. Parents are allowed to home school if they wish. The first year is called Primary and the next year is Grade 1 and so on to Grade 12, the final year of high school. There are no equivalents to the UK's Ofsted reports or school 'league tables'.

In addition to 11 universities, the Nova Scotia Community College (NSCC) has 13 campuses around the province.

CULTURE

LITERATURE Although the Mi'kmaq have a long history of oral storytelling, the first recorded written work in the province was scribed by the French at Port-Royal (see page 210) in the first years of the 17th century. Since then, much of the best literature to come out of the province has been historical fiction. Perhaps the most prolific author of this genre was Thomas H Raddall (1903–94), who was born in England but came to Nova Scotia in 1913. He later worked as a wireless operator on Sable Island (see page 368), and in 1923, settled in Liverpool. He wrote a number of historical novels and tales, and history books. *Halifax, Warden of the North*, for example, is an excellent history of the province's capital from its founding to the mid 20th century.

Evelyn Eaton's third novel, *Quietly My Captain Waits* (1940) was set in Port-Royal (see page 210) between 1690 and 1706. Eaton wrote the book – which became a great commercial success – whilst staying at her summer home in Victoria Beach (see page 210).

Most historical fiction (and history) books were written in eras when nobody batted an eyelid when the Mi'kmaq were portrayed as treacherous savages.

Daniel Paul (1938–) is a journalist, activist and lecturer. His First Nations History, *We Were Not the Savages*, offers a Mi'kmaq perspective on the province's history.

Although a man of many talents, in literary terms Thomas Chandler Haliburton (1796–1865) is best known for his political satire – and creating Sam Slick, protagonist of his humorous 'Clockmaker' books (see page 228).

Rita Joe (1932–2007) was born on Cape Breton Island and started writing poetry in her late thirties. *The Poems of Rita Joe* was published in 1978, and other books followed. Known as 'the Poet Laureate of the Mi'kmaq', she was awarded the Order of Canada, the country's highest civilian honour, in 1989.

Born in Massachusetts, poet and writer Elizbeth Bishop (1911–79) spent some of her childhood in Great Village (see page 244). Much of her work was inspired by her time in Nova Scotia. She later became Poet Laureate of the United States and a Pulitzer Prize winner.

ART Helsinki-born William deGarthe (1907–83) lived in Peggy's Cove (see page 127) for almost 30 years and much of his work had a marine theme. His home is now a gallery. Willard M Mitchell (1881–1955) lived in Amherst (see page 259) for about 20 years and is best known for his miniature landscape watercolours. One of Canada's greatest contemporary artists, Alex Colville (1920–) has spent most of his life in Nova Scotia and has lived in Wolfville (see page 218 for the last three decades.

The province has produced some renowned folk artists including Maud Lewis (see box below) and Joe Norris (1924–96). Dotted around, you'll find some excellent folk art galleries, and the genre is celebrated with an annual festival in Lunenburg (see page 143).

MUSIC Music has always been an important part of life in Nova Scotia since the Scots began to pour into Pictou in the 1770s (see page 273).

Whilst a wide variety of musical genres has begun to take off (particularly in the last few decades in Halifax and environs), this has not been at the expense of the popularity of Celtic music: whether traditional or fused with other styles, Celtic music is very much alive, well, and thriving in 21st-century Nova Scotia. Some visitors come primarily for the music; others look back on their time in Nova Scotia and realise what a highlight the music was.

Celtic music The Scottish Highlanders who arrived in the late 18th and early 19th centuries brought their music with them, and all these years later the highest concentration of Celtic music and dancing is to be found in the region where so many of those immigrants settled, Cape Breton Island.

The term 'Celtic music' covers a broad spectrum. Pure traditional tunes are still played, virtually unchanged from when they were learnt in Scotland, but the music has evolved its own identity, too, in forms such as Cape Breton fiddle music. Some musicians add a dollop of other musical influences into the Celtic mix.

You can hear wonderful Celtic music throughout the year on Cape Breton Island, but opportunities increase dramatically in the summer, when there's a

MAUD LEWIS

Born in rural Yarmouth County in 1903, Maud Dowley suffered birth defects that gave her hunched shoulders and pressed her chin into her chest. She was very small and developed rheumatoid arthritis in childhood. Maud had no formal art training and dropped out of school (where she had been teased incessantly) at 14. When her parents died in the late 1930s, their 'estate' was left to their son, and he made no provision for his sister. She answered an advert for a housekeeper and moved to the home of Everett Lewis, a door-to-door fish seller. The two lived in his simple one-room home in Marshalltown (near Digby), and were married soon afterwards. Here, despite worsening arthritis, Maud painted and painted. Every surface in the house became her canvas, as did any scraps of cardboard or wallpaper. Everett sold Maud's paintings of colourful scenes of rural Nova Scotia whilst on his fish rounds, and later to tourists in the area. Most sold for a dollar or two.

In 1965, still living in the tiny hut – Everett didn't want to waste money on running water or electricity – Maud was featured on a television documentary, and soon after, in a Toronto paper. Her fame began to spread rapidly: in 1969, a White House aide commissioned two of her paintings for Richard Nixon (Maud asked for payment in advance). Sadly, her arthritis prevented her from being able to fulfil most of the orders that fame had finally brought.

She died of pneumonia in 1970 and was buried in a pauper's grave. Everett tried forging a few paintings and died in 1979: the Lewis shack was acquired by the Art Gallery of Nova Scotia (see page 108) where it is now on display.

kitchen party or ceilidh (pronounced 'kay-lee' – a Gaelic word which refers to a traditional dance or music gathering) almost every evening somewhere in easy reach. That is definitely the case during October's joyous Celtic Colours Festival (see page 293), timed to coincide with nature's brilliant autumn leaf display. Celtic music aficionados should not miss this festival. Look out for ceilidhs all over the province – they aren't exclusive to Cape Breton Island.

So who are the people to watch out for? The line-up of the Rankins (formerly the Rankin Family) may have changed over the years, but standards haven't dropped at all. The band members also perform solo and/or in non-quartet formations. Gordie Sampson is a multi-award-winning singer-songwriter. Natalie MacMaster is Cape Breton Island's best-known fiddler – one of her cousins is Ashley MacIsaac, also a master of the instrument. Other big names include another fiddler, Jerry Holland, The Cottars and The Barra MacNeils.

Those well–established, but less well-known on the international circuit include Mary Jane Lamond, fiddler Andrea Beaton, Rita and Mary Rankin and Troy MacGillivray. But don't just look for those who have made it – in general, the standard of playing is so high that you're unlikely to be disappointed whoever you see. And where there's music, feet start tapping: step dancing, square dancing, highland dancing – and 'enthusiastic-but-unco-ordinated-tourists-forgetting-inhibitions dancing'.

Classical and choral Nova Scotia has produced one of the greatest contraltos in Canadian music history. Portia White (1911–68) was born in Truro (see page 239) and received international acclaim in the 1950s and 1960s. She was also an inspiration for the province's black community.

Established over a quarter of a century ago, Halifax-based Symphony Nova Scotia (*www.symphonynovascotia.ca*) is the province's top chamber orchestra. Peter Allen is the province's leading classical pianist.

Comprising coal miners from Cape Breton Island, male choral ensemble The Men of the Deeps has been entertaining audiences for over four decades (see page 332).

Country, folk, pop and rock The province has produced some country megastars including Hank Snow (see page 161), Wilf Carter and more recently Anne Murray (see page 257). Born in 1944, folk/country singer Rita MacNeil has been wowing audiences since the 1970s. Folk legend Stan Rogers (who died in a plane crash in 1983, aged just 33) spent many summers in Nova Scotia and is commemorated in an annual festival (see page 363).

Country music is alive today with the flag flown by artists and bands such as George Canyon, Joyce Seamone, Dan Mason and Jesse Beck, but is often blended with roots, folk and rock by bands such as The Guthries and the Moonshine Ramblers. Old Man Luedecke sings fun songs and plays the banjo.

Hot, current rock and pop bands include The Superfantastics, In-flight Safety, Wintersleep, Joel Plaskett Emergency and indie singer Rebekah Higgs. Roots singer-songwriters Dave Gunning, Jenn Grant and Christina Martin are well worth looking out for. J P Cormier plays guitar and dobro (a distinctive resonator guitar), mixing genres including bluegrass. Jeanne (Doucet) Currie, Lennie Gallant and Acadie à la Mode all offer good introductions to Acadian music.

On the jazz and blues front, Steve Dooks plays smooth and easy piano, Shan Arsenault is an excellent jazz guitarist and ERA are a contemporary jazz trio. Thom Swift blends blues with country and folk. Matt Minglewood (whose music also crosses several genres) is also someone to look out for.

Halifax, in particular, has a powerful hip-hop scene. Important artists include Buck 65 and Jamie Sparks.

Born in 1810, Silas Tertius Rand became a Baptist missionary largely by self-education. Rather than go overseas, he lived with the local Mi'kmaq for over 40 years, attempting to show them the way to heaven. He had to master their language and in thus doing, compiled a dictionary and wrote a grammar, and recorded a collection of 80 Mi'kmaq stories and legends. These actions are said to have saved the Mi'kmaq language (and some more of their tales) from oblivion. Much of what we know today about Mi'kmaq traditions is a direct result of his work.

Folklore Long before the Europeans arrived, the Mi'kmaq had their customs, tales – most of which involved Glooscap (sometimes written as 'Kluscap'), a mythical demi-god who slept using Nova Scotia as a bed and Prince Edward Island as a pillow - beliefs and sayings. As a consequence of the trials and tribulations of having to share their land for over four centuries, some of their folklore was lost for ever. The work of people such as Silas Tertius Rand has helped to stop even more being forgotten.

The Europeans – particularly those of Celtic origin – brought their own folklore with them, and over time this has been shaped by their lives and surroundings in Nova Scotia, with the sea perhaps the biggest influence.

Most early immigrants from Scotland and Ireland in particular arrived with a belief in God and the supernatural: they were no strangers to stories of mysterious unworldly creatures inhabiting hills, valleys and dark forests (of which Nova Scotia has many). Sprinkle into the mix the (supposedly hostile) local people who lived in tepees, spoke a strange language and had strange customs. Then add the sea: fog and sea mists, huge tides, howling wind, pirates. The result – an incredibly rich folklore of sea shanties, songs and ballads, proverbs, tales of buried treasure, witches, all manner of superstitions – and so much more.

Much of this has been lost, but Nova Scotia has benefited from the work of some forward-thinking folklorists who realised that records had to be made before it was too late.

According to Mi'kmaq tradition, there were seven stages in the creation of the world (seven is an important recurring number in Mi'kmaq mythology). First there was Kisu'lkw, the Giver of Life, followed by Na'ku'set, the Sun (also called Grandfather). Created by bolts of lightning were both Sitgamu'k, Mother Earth, and the fourth stage of creation, Glooscap, who was later charged with passing on his knowledge to the Mi'kmaq people. He was followed by his Grandmother, Nokami (or Nugumi), with Glooscap's nephew, Netaoansum, and mother, Ni'kanaptekewi'sqw, completing the set.

When it was time for Glooscap to leave his people, he chanted and called for a whale to carry him to a land far to the west. The first whale to respond was rejected as being too small, but one of the desired proportions was the next to appear. Glooscap climbed onto its huge back, and the pair headed off through the sea.

When they reached their destination, Glooscap bade farewell to the whale, and offered the creature a pipe to smoke. The whale put the pipe in its huge mouth and swam off back towards its distant home: Glooscap climbed a hill and watched its progress, smiling as he saw the whale puffing out plumes of smoke at intervals.

Glooscap still lives away to the west: it is hoped that he will return to ease his people's troubles when the time is right.

In Nova Scotia, supernatural warnings of approaching (generally bad) events are most commonly known as 'forerunners'. There are several types, including unexplained knocks-on-doors or walls (typically of bedrooms), or pictures or mirrors suddenly falling down and smashing. There was, for example, a man who lived alone in a fishing shack and regularly complained of hearing screams and moans. Eventually these bothered the man so much that he moved away. Shortly afterwards, a ship was blown onto the rocks near the shack, and despite attempts to rescue those on board, they were thrown from the vessel and dashed against the rocks, their screams of pain and terror being carried on the howling wind to the onlookers. Whilst graves were dug the victims' bodies were placed in a temporary morgue – the very hut where the screams had previously been heard.

Forerunners mostly deal with sound, but visual signs are labelled foresight too. In a typical example, someone would have a vision of a funeral for a particular person before the 'deceased-to-be' had even fallen sick.

Even those who proclaim themselves non-believers in ghosts having no time for that 'stuff-and-nonsense' seem to find it acceptable to believe in forerunners and foresight.

The province's best known folklorist was Dartmouth-native Helen Creighton (1899–1989) who collected folk songs and tales across the province and further afield for over 50 years. She wrote 13 books on the subject and recorded over 15,000 songs and ballads.

In 2008, Bridgewater-based family band Drumlin* (*www.drumlin.ca*) released *Mackerel Skies*, an excellent CD of 12 of the heritage songs collected by Helen Creighton.

Many of her books are collections of tales of ghostly (or at least unexplained) happenings. These tell of 'forerunners' (see box above), phantom ships, ghosts guarding buried treasure, and non-threatening spectres who just pass by also feature. And her material didn't just come from the Scots and Irish: she collected many stories from those of German, Acadian (in the 1830s, a French missionary recorded that some of the Acadians in Yarmouth County used books of spells regularly), Mi'kmaq and English origin.

ARCHITECTURE The history of Nova Scotia's early architecture and town planning is more varied (and complex) than one finds in any other Canadian province, with strong French, British, German/European, pre- and post-revolution American, and Scottish influences. Through time – and British thoroughness in razing everything Acadian to the ground in the 1750s – no Acadian buildings remain from pre-Expulsion, although the Habitation (see page 210) is a pretty accurate reconstruction of the original (1605) French fur-trading post.

Most of the earliest-surviving edifices were built by Loyalists (see page 9) from New England. In some cases, timber frames for the houses were cut in Boston,

Those born (or who lived) in Nova Scotia include: shipping magnate Sir Samuel Cunard, Alexander Graham Bell, actor Donald Sutherland, Pulitzer Prize-winning poet Elizabeth Bishop, singers Anne Murray, Hank Snow, Sarah McLachlan, Sara Vaughan, Rita MacNeil, the Rankin Family, and fiddler Natalie MacMaster.

Massachusetts, and shipped to Nova Scotia where local materials were used to complete the structure: such was the case with St Paul's Church in Halifax (see page 110). The Loyalists also introduced the popular Cape Cod design, a simple wood-frame house with a gabled roof and shingle siding.

Fine mansions were later built from the profits of shipbuilding and shipping. Be sure to visit Lunenburg (see page 143), the best-surviving example of a planned British colonial settlement in North America – though the buildings themselves show a strong European influence. A particular feature to look out for is the Lunenburg 'bump' (see page 145). Liverpool (see page 156), Shelburne (see page 165), Yarmouth (see page 180) and Annapolis Royal (see page 199 should all be included in your itinerary.

Prescott House (see page 223), Province House in Halifax (see page 110) and Uniacke House (see page 115) are all excellent examples of Georgian architecture. Other styles frequently occurring include Queen Anne Revival, Second Empire, Gothic Revival and Victorian Italianate. Amherst (see page 259) has numerous impressive 19th- and early 20th-century public buildings constructed from local sandstone in a variety of styles.

One often hears the term 'century house' in Nova Scotia – this tends to be used when describing houses constructed in the late 1800s (presumably because they are more than 100 years-old).

SHIPWRECKS For centuries, attempting to navigate round the coastal waters, rocky shores and islands of Nova Scotia – especially in darkness, fog, blinding blizzards, and/or raging seas – proved too much for countless vessels. Almost 5,000 wrecks have been recorded (one wonders how many more haven't made it onto the lists).

Some areas in particular have seen alarming numbers of wrecks. Sable Island (see page 368) has long been known as the 'Graveyard of the Atlantic'. St Paul Island (see page 308) the 'Graveyard of the Gulf'. Dozens of vessels have gone down in the Cape Sable Island (see page 172) area, and, in truth, there are few parts of the province's coastline that haven't seen a shipwreck.

Lighthouses, their foghorns and technological improvements were great navigational steps forward, but the boom in the quantity of shipping, particularly in the second half of the 19th century, kept wreck numbers high. The good news was that on many occasions, a higher proportion of those on board survived.

The RMS *Titanic* (see page 85) is closely associated with Nova Scotia, but actually went down over 900km east-southeast of the province. Almost 40 years earlier, however, another White Star Line ship, the SS *Atlantic* (see page 126) met her end near Lower Prospect, with over 560 lives lost: it was at the time the world's worst merchant shipwreck.

In many cases, a ship's unfortunate end brought some good to local residents: valuable cargo was often washed ashore, and salvaging wreckage provided a living in some areas. So much so that there were several cases where ships were lured deliberately onto rocks by those hoping to reap reward from the resulting wrecks. Many of the wrecks now attract recreational divers (see page 63), and there are still those who seek treasure – though legislation was introduced in the 1960s to prohibit salvage work on old shipwrecks without a permit.

NATURAL HISTORY

FLORA The province offers a range of habitats from the Atlantic Coastal Plain to the high plateaux of Cape Breton's northern highlands, and these support a wide variety of flora – including over 1,650 vascular plants. Trees cover close to 80% of Nova Scotia, but aren't just evergreen conifers, something that becomes even more apparent if you visit in the autumn. At this time, hardwoods such as maple, birch, oak, aspen and mountain ash burst into an explosion of brilliant colour. It is a conifer, however, the red spruce (Picea rubens), that has been designated Nova Scotia's provincial tree.

In exposed coastal areas, stunted trees such as black spruce, often bent by the wind, are common as are shrubs such as creeping juniper, common juniper and black crowberry. Sand dunes are usually covered with marram grass (also known as American beach grass). You're also likely to see seaside plantain, beach pea, sea rocket and seaside goldenrod: look out too for the aromatic Northern bayberry and beautiful wild roses.

Nova Scotia's provincial flower is the mayflower, or trailing arbutus, which blooms (with delicately scented pink flowers) in the forest glades in early spring, often amid the last remaining snows of winter. From then until early autumn a range of species will be in bloom – the visitor will often see carpets of colour by the roadside. Stands of lupins, for example, are stunning in June.

Some of the more common summer-flowering species include Queen Anne's lace, ox-eye daisy, pearly everlasting and yarrow. Purple loosestrife may be an aggressive weed, but still contributes to the floral colour show.

Bog plants typically include various mosses, cranberries and liverwort. Many types of orchid can also be seen. Some bogs are also home to insectivorous plants such as sundew, butterwort, pitcher plant and bladderwort.

AUTUMN COLOURS

As summer begins to give way to autumn, days become shorter and nights become cooler. The colour of the leaves of deciduous trees and shrubs, dark green with chlorophyll in summer, also begins to change. Chlorophyll production declines, and the green colour fades. Whilst the leaves of many species turn yellow, the colour pigmentation of red oak, mountain ash, blueberry and huckleberry leaves, for example, turn red, whilst the colour of sugar and red maple leaves runs the range from yellow to purple.

When contrasted with the dark green of the evergreens and the blue (hopefully) of the sky, the result is one of nature's most stunning displays.

In a typical year, the 'leaf-peeping' season runs from the end of September until late October, and is at its height in the second week of October. In season, there's a regularly updated leaf-watch map and blog on the official Tourism Nova Scotia website (*www.novascotia.com/leaf*).

Where are the best viewing areas? A free booklet available from tourist offices lists over 80 possibilities. Personal favourites (if you time it right) are Milton (see page 161), Kejimkujik National Park (see page 205), Bear River (see page 197), Wentworth (see page 269) and Cape George (see page 282). There are many wonderful areas on Cape Breton Island, too – try to time your visit to coincide with the wonderful Celtic Colours Festival (see page 293).

Lupins in the Chebogue region of Yarmouth County are said to be from seeds brought from Holland by a Miss Phoebe Robbins around 1900.

Seaweeds Many of the algae found on the beaches and shores are put to good use. Rockweed is the dominant brown seaweed found intertidally along the province's coast. Hand-harvested, its main use is as a fertiliser. Irish moss has long been harvested for use as a food source: it contains high amounts of carrageenan, used in the manufacture of dairy products, cosmetics and more.

Dulse has reddish-purple, somewhat leathery fronds. Rich in minerals and vitamins and with a high protein content, it is often dried and sold as a snack food (something of an acquired taste which I am yet to acquire!).

FAUNA

Mammals You're too late for the woodland caribou (hunted to extinction here by the 1920s), but Nova Scotia is home to almost 70 different land mammals. The most common large mammal is the white-tailed deer, which, when disturbed, will 'flash' the white underside of its distinctive tail. They are often seen prancing across the road in wooded rural areas, particularly early or late in the day. Other species include: mink, river otter, red fox, coyote (similar to a large, grey-brown fox), red squirrel, seven types of bat, eastern chipmunk (reddish-brown in colour with five distinct black stripes down its back and a member of the squirrel family), and various members of the weasel family including the American marten.

Mammals with which visitors from the UK may be less familiar include the porcupine, common on the mainland. The porcupine – the province's second-largest rodent after the beaver – is an excellent climber. It has strong, short legs with powerful claws and is covered with thousands of sharp quills. They feed on twigs, leaves, buds and the inner bark of trees and are nocturnal. If you travel off the major highways, you're likely to see porcupines, but sadly they will almost always be roadkill (killed by traffic). Kejimkujik National Park is a good place to try and spot a live one.

Another common species is the eastern striped skunk, easily recognised by its long, black fur, long, bushy tail, and two white strips that run along its back. It can grow up to one metre in length. If a skunk turns its back on you and raises its tail, run – or at least cover your eyes: it is about to squirt from its anal glands a particularly malodorous and long-lasting spray.

Raccoons are found throughout the province: excellent climbers and generally nocturnal, they have small pointed ears, greyish fur, a black mask around the eyes and black rings around a long, bushy tail.

Dartmouth-based Acadian Seaplants (☎ 468 2840; www.acadianseaplants.com) has come a long way in a couple of decades. Based near Lower East Pubnico (see page 173), it operates the largest land-based commercial seaweed cultivation facility in the world, and has expanded into the neighbouring provinces of New Brunswick and Prince Edward Island. Rockweed, Irish moss, kelp, bladderwrack and other algae are collected, processed, and used to produce a range of agricultural, beauty and brewing products, including an 'instant seaweed salad' which is very popular in Japan.

Also known as a groundhog, the woodchuck is the largest member of the squirrel family and grows up to 40–50cm in length. It has a stocky build with a flattened head and short tail.

The muskrat is a large (40–50cm) rodent with brown to black fur, webbed feet and a long, scaly tail flattened on both sides. It is an excellent swimmer.

The northern flying squirrel is common throughout the forests of Nova Scotia, the smaller and much rarer southern flying squirrel is thought to be limited to parts of the Gaspereau Valley and Kejimkujik National Park. The squirrels have a pair of skin membranes which enable them to glide (rather than fly) up to 35m.

Approximately 100–500 lynx live on Cape Breton Island, the majority in remote areas of the island's northern highlands. Sometimes mistaken for a bobcat, the lynx has larger paws, longer ear tufts and a totally black-tipped tale. Bobcats have stumpy tails, with a dark tip on top. Their hind legs are noticeably longer than the forelegs, and their coats tend to be more patterned than the lynx.

Having survived the days when their pelts were the mainstay of Nova Scotia's economy, the beaver is common throughout the province, and is Nova Scotia's largest rodent. It is known for its habit of building dams (and dome-shaped lodges) on streams to form ponds.

With the possible exception of the black bear, the land mammal that most visitors want to see is the largest member of the deer family, the moose. Dark brown and awkward-looking, moose have humped shoulders, spindly legs, a drooping muzzle, and a bell – a flap of skin hanging from the throat. An adult male (bull) moose stands approximately two-metres tall at the shoulder and weighs around 500kg. In spring, bulls grow (often huge) antlers that are shed late in winter. Moose can be dangerous if approached too closely, especially during mating season (September–October) or calving season (late May–early June). There are two moose sub-species in the province, the mainland moose and the Cape Breton moose. Approximately 5,000 moose live on Cape Breton Island, which offers the highest chance of a sighting, whereas fewer than 1,000 moose are thought to survive in isolated areas of the mainland.

The black bear is usually – but not necessarily – black and is the only type of bear found in Nova Scotia. Though widespread, it is not often seen by the majority of visitors. Although not true hibernators, bears tend to stay in their dens from mid-November to early spring. During this period, their metabolism slows and they are unconscious but will wake and respond to danger. Adult males stand at about one metre high at the shoulder and can weigh 200kg. They are said to be nocturnal, but I have seen black bears crossing backroads and walking along the edge of woodland in the middle of the day. Whilst undoubtedly dangerous, there have been no records of anyone even being scratched by a bear in Nova Scotia. Don't be the first, though – be aware.

Finally, the only wild horses to be found in Nova Scotia are Sable Island horses, see page 369 for further information.

Reptiles and amphibians Nova Scotia has no poisonous snakes: the largest (though rarely over one metre in length) and most widespread is the maritime garter snake.

Seven species of turtle can be found off Nova Scotia's shores during different periods of the year. During summer, there are sightings of the Atlantic leatherback, Ridley and loggerhead turtles.

Four species of (harmless) salamander live in the province, the rarest of which is the four-toed salamander, which is orange to reddish brown with black spots and is the only white-bellied salamander. In addition, there's just one type

Although (supposedly) hunted to extinction in the province over a century ago, no-one is too sure whether cougars (known elsewhere in North America as mountain lions) exist in Nova Scotia. There are about 100 reported sightings a year (one man alone has claimed five separate sightings between 1991 and 2009), but as yet no physical evidence. The Department of Natural Resources sits on the fence: apparently the animal has been included on the Department's 'protected' list 'just in case'.

of toad (the eastern American) and seven frog species – the largest of which is the bullfrog.

Birds *with Blake Maybank* (e *maybank@ns.sympatico.ca; www.tinyurl.com/canbird*), *editor of* Nova Scotia Birds, *a quarterly magazine published by the Nova Scotia Bird Society* (*www.nsbs.chebucto.org*). Nova Scotia is a superb bird-watching (we call it *birding*) destination. Despite being the second-smallest province in Canada, it boasts the country's third-highest bird species' total; only British Columbia and Ontario – Canada's largest provinces – have more.

While there are no species endemic to Nova Scotia, the province is a reliable and logistically friendly base to seek out certain sought-after birds, including boreal forest specialities (spruce grouse, boreal chickadee, black-backed woodpecker and white-winged crossbill), winter birds from the high arctic (dovekie and black-headed gull), seabirds (Manx shearwater and great skua), and regional specialities (Bicknell's thrush that breeds in the Cape Breton highlands, and the Ipswich race of savanna sparrow, that breeds only on Sable Island).

The province is well situated in all seasons. The surrounding ocean moderates the climate, and the cooler summers mean that northern species can breed –

NOTABLE BIRDING SITES

During the breeding season the best sites are in the interior, where diversity of breeding birds is the greatest. The two national parks, Kejimkujik (see page 205) in the south, and Cape Breton Highlands (see page 303) in the north are both rewarding, with extensive trail systems, visitor facilities, and informed staff. Elsewhere there are dozens of smaller provincial and regional parks, trails, and freshwater marshes. Try, for example, the Uniacke Estate (see page 115), Amherst Point (see page 264), the Fairmont Ridge Trail (see page 282) and the Musquodoboit Trailway (see page 350). For spring and autumn land bird migration the best sites are the Canso Peninsula (see page 362), Hartlen Point (see page 121), Cape Sable Island (see page 172) and Long and Brier islands (see page 194).

Autumn shorebirds are best viewed at Cherry Hill Beach (see page 157), Cape Sable Island (see page 172) and Evangeline Beach near Grand Pré (see page 225). The finest autumn hawk-watching site is on Brier Island (see page 196).

Winter birding is primarily a coastal experience, with popular areas including Halifax Harbour (see page 77), Pictou Harbour (see page 273), Cape Sable Island (see page 172), Canso Harbour (see page 362), Brier Island (see page 196), and Sydney Harbour (see page 325).

If you want to go birding with a guide, try Blake Maybank (✆ 852 2077; e *maybank@ns.sympatico.ca, www.tinyurl.com/canbird*) or Tight Lines (✆ 649 2428; e *flyfish@tightlines.ca, www.tightlines.ca*). Alternatively, consider going out with a local birdwatcher: two or three are usually listed on www.birdingpal.com.

Background Information NATURAL HISTORY

among the 150-plus breeding species are 22 warblers, nine flycatchers and 20 sparrows and finches. The ocean also moderates the winter, with nearly 200 species sighted each year between December and February. And because Nova Scotia lies at the eastern end of the continent, halfway between the Pole and the Equator, many waifs and rarities have visited, comprising more than 35% of the province's impressive total of 470 species.

Visitors are also drawn to the province's birding spectacles. From June to October the Bay of Fundy offers superb whale-watching, and the abundant food that attracts the whales also lures large numbers of seabirds, making Nova Scotia the most affordable and reliable spot in eastern North America to see thousands of shearwaters (greater, sooty and Manx), storm petrels (both Wilson's and Leach's), and phalaropes (red and red-necked), as well as numerous puffins, razorbills, fulmar, jaegers, and occasionally south polar skuas.

Nova Scotia has its own seabird colonies. Atlantic puffins, razorbills and black-legged kittiwakes reign over the Bird Islands in Cape Breton, accessible by daily guided boat tour, and Canada's largest roseate tern colony lies on The Brothers Islands, off the village of Lower West Pubnico in Yarmouth County. Another great avian display is the southward migration of Arctic-nesting shorebirds. Millions of sandpipers refuel in the rich Bay of Fundy mudflats exposed by the world's highest tides. The largest flocks, primarily semi-palmated sandpipers and sometimes in excess of half a million birds, typically occur in the second and third weeks of August. Along the Atlantic coast shorebird flocks are smaller, but contain more species.

Winter offers its own spectacle, when nearly 1,000 bald eagles descend on the Annapolis Valley (see page 219).

The search for bird species and spectacles occurs against a backdrop of uncommon beauty – visiting birdwatchers, especially those from Europe or urban United States, enjoy the absence of crowds, and the freedom to wander almost anywhere the urge takes them. The joy of watching shorebirds on a nearly deserted pristine beach, or listening to warblers sing along well-maintained and secure trails, is an experience rare or absent in much of the world.

MARINE WILDLIFE

Whales Whilst man has been instrumental in wiping out over 90% of the world's whale population in the last couple of centuries, the good news is that Nova Scotia is one of the best places in the world to go whale-watching, both in terms of quantity, and variety – 21 whale species cruise the province's coastal waters. Baleen whales (such as minke, humpback, fin and the critically endangered north Atlantic right whales) are drawn by huge amounts of plankton, krill and schools of small fish, particularly where the cold outflow of the Bay of Fundy meets the warm Gulf Stream waters. Toothed whales (such as pilot, killer (orca) and sperm whales) tend to eat fish and squid and are common in the Gulf of St Lawrence and Cabot Strait. Although it varies from species to species, whale numbers tend to be highest from late July to mid-September.

For many visitors, a tour on a whale-watching boat is a must-do (and highlight) of a summer or early autumn visit to Nova Scotia. Seeing a huge humpback whale breaching at close quarters or watching a huge fluked tail disappear into the sea are memories that will last a lifetime. On many tours, porpoises, dolphins, seals and pelagic seabirds join in the action and are added bonuses.

Although trips are offered from various places in the province, two areas stand out. One is northern Cape Breton Island, but, for me, the best whale-watching trips depart from Westport (see page 196) on Brier Island, and Freeport and Tiverton (see page 196) on adjacent Long Island. Boat trips apart, it is not unusual to spot whales from the land, especially in the areas just mentioned.

The hearty appetites of seals – and overfishing – are two of the reasons most often cited for the incredible decline in Atlantic Canada's cod population. Seal numbers have increased steadily since the moratorium on cod fishing was introduced, and fishermen (and Nova Scotia's Fisheries and Aquaculture Minister) regularly call for a similar increase in the quota of seals which the federal government permits to be 'harvested'. At the time of writing, Nova Scotia has a yearly quota of 12,000 grey seals, but fishermen want this increased to between 20,000 and 25,000 per year. In defending Canada's seal hunts (which have been called 'the largest slaughter of marine mammals on earth'), the Canadian government has said that rules have been laid down so that each seal is killed humanely.

Old habits die hard – there are records of the French clubbing seal pups to death here in the 1670s.

Seals Four seal species are found in the coastal waters of Nova Scotia: The harbour, grey, harp and hooded seal. Don't be surprised to see a harbour seal pop its head out of the water in Halifax Harbour; otherwise good places to see seals include Kejimkujik Seaside (see page 164), Brier Island (see page 196) and northeast Cape Breton Island. Most maritime fishermen blame seals for decimating fish stocks in the region.

Fish, shellfish and molluscs For centuries, incredible quantities of fish – particularly cod – drew fishermen from near and far to the region's waters. As recently as the last few decades, cod numbers have dropped alarmingly (see box above), largely due to overfishing. Dozens of other species live in the province's coastal waters, streams, rivers and lakes: these include Atlantic salmon, mackerel, pollock, haddock, flounder, hake, herring, monkfish, perch, pickerel, trout and eel. Bluefin tuna, porbeagle and blue shark are popular targets for deep-sea sport-fishing.

Despite the (near) death of groundfishing, shellfish and molluscs – particularly lobster, scallop, shrimp, clam and crab – are now the focus of the fishermen's attention, and grace many a table in the province's eateries.

NATIONAL PARKS Nova Scotia boasts two of Canada's 42 national parks: Kejimkujik National Park and Cape Breton Highlands National Park.

Kejimkujik National Park Kejimkujik National Park – or 'Keji' as it is more commonly known – is accessed by Highway 8 which connects Liverpool (see page 156) and Annapolis Royal (see page 199). The largest inland national park in Atlantic Canada draws lovers of the outdoors for hiking, lake swimming, mountain biking, canoeing and kayaking. For more information see pages 205–9.

Cape Breton Highlands National Park Completely different in character from Keji, this national park is situated in northern Cape Breton Island. Boasting magnificent coastal and mountain scenery and superb hiking, it is accessed by a dramatic scenic drive, the Cabot Trail, and is described on pages 303–11.

PROVINCIAL PARKS Nova Scotia also has almost 130 provincial parks (*www.nsparks.ca*) administered by the Parks and Recreation section of the Department of Natural Resources. These vary from parks with a couple of picnic tables and interpretive panels, to magnificent stretches of coastal scenery peppered with hiking trails.

The majority of provincial parks are day-use only and are open between mid-May and mid-October: about 20 others have campgrounds – reservations can be made online or by phone (❧ T/F 1 888 544 3434) and generally shorter seasons. Sadly, some are only open between late June and the beginning of September. When parks are closed for the season, barriers prevent vehicular entry: grounds, trails and roads are not maintained and no services are provided (water is turned off, and toilets locked). However, it is almost always possible to park outside and enter the parks on foot – but be aware that you do so at your own risk.

Admission is charged at just two of the parks: Shubenacadie Provincial Wildlife Park (see page 238), and Cape Chignecto Provincial Park (see page 254). For wonderful coastal hiking, try for example Cape Chignecto, Blomidon (see page 217) or Taylor Head (see page 355): beach fans will enjoy Rissers Beach (see page 156), Summerville (see page 162), Thomas Raddall (see page 164), Mavillette Beach (see page 186), the beach parks of the Northumberland Shore (see pages 265–86), and Martinique Beach (see page 351). Look for moose in the park at Cape Smokey (see page 311).

CONSERVATION

Nova Scotia is a beautiful province, rich in natural resources, waterways, lakes and forests. Traditionally, the province's industry sector drew on this treasure: forestry, mining, fishing, and agriculture were primary employers for many years, and continue to play an important role in the economy of the province. In fact, Nova Scotia has had an interesting duality toward environmental issues: it was an early pioneer in recycling, implemented a moratorium on uranium mining in 1985, and has been a world leader in waste management for over ten years. Yet its main electricity supplier, Nova Scotia Power, relies primarily on coal and oil to generate its power; the Sydney tar ponds on Cape Breton Island are a hazardous waste site created from run-off from the coke ovens at the now-decommissioned steel mill; there are large swathes of clearcut land where old-growth forests once stood; and there are two major harbours that for many years have received the raw sewage outputs of the province's two largest urban centres, Halifax and Sydney. On top of this, Nova Scotia receives acid rain and air pollution from industries to the west.

Recently, however, the government of Nova Scotia created a legislated manifesto that set targets for renewable energy generation, waste reduction, water and public land protection, among others. While not entirely comprehensive, it is a step in the right direction. Furthermore, long-delayed treatment of the tar ponds has begun; harbour cleanup in Halifax has made major strides now that two of three sewage-treatment plants are operational; and stronger air-quality regulations in both the US and Canada have resulted in dramatic improvements in Nova Scotia's air quality. Environmental groups in the province, such as the Ecology Action Centre, continue to advocate for, and educate toward, cleaner air, water, and energy production, and stronger enforcement of conservation and protection laws.

PROTECTED LAND Approximately 30% of land in Nova Scotia is Crown (or public) land. The province has over 30 'Protected Areas' (the largest of which being the Tobeatic Wilderness Area (known as 'The Toby'; see box on page 170), over 15 nature reserves, and two heritage rivers (the Margaree and the Shelburne).

Mining, forestry and the like are prohibited in Protected Areas (except where pre-existing commitments were made), which is all well and good. There are, however, many other areas of public land which concerned citizens believe should be protected from such things as industrial forestry and exploitative mining. In Nova Scotia, game sanctuaries don't protect habitat, they only curtail certain types of hunting activities. By contrast, protected wilderness areas protect habitat and prevent forest harvesting, mining, road building, and other types of development.

UNESCO WORLD HERITAGE SITES Two of Canada's 15 UNESCO World Heritage Sites are found in the province: Old Town Lunenburg (see page 143) and the Joggins Fossil Cliffs (see page 255).

Explore Canada!

Take advantage of the low, competitive rates and great service Dollar Rent A Car provides. With more than 60 locations in Canada, Dollar will be there for you with a wide range of modern, low-mileage vehicles as soon as you arrive.

For reservations, visit one of our International sites:

UK . . . . .www.dollar.co.uk
USA & CANADA . . . . .www.dollar.com
Europe . . . . .www.dollar.de
or contact your travel provider

2

Practical Information

WHEN TO VISIT

Whilst there are reasons to visit Nova Scotia in the winter – a few festivals, some wildlife-spotting opportunities, and some minor ski resorts – there can be a lot of snow and it can get very cold. Most attractions, many eateries and places to stay outside the biggest urban centres are closed. Realistically, those considering a visit to the province should concentrate on the period between May and late October.

May is quiet, though the days are long and the weather is warming up. Later in the month apple blossom covers much of the Annapolis Valley. By the beginning of June the weather is generally good for outdoor activities such as hiking, cycling, swimming, kayaking, etc, though late spring and early summer can be foggy. The golf courses and most provincial parks are open, more attractions are opening by the day, the festival season is well underway, and by the middle of June whale-watching trips have begun.

July, August and early September are relatively busy; everything is open, though high-season pricing is in effect. Those who enjoy swimming in the sea will find that August and early September offer the warmest air and water temperatures. If you will be visiting at these times, book your accommodation well in advance, and bear in mind that things will be busier. You can still find uncrowded beaches – though you'll have to walk away from the parking areas – but bear in mind that a crowded beach by Nova Scotia standards would seem relatively quiet in many other places.

By the second week of September things quieten down: many attractions have already started to close, and kids are back at school. Having said that, if your travel is not restricted to school holidays, it is a good time to visit. The daytime weather generally remains good, though night-time temperatures begin to drop. Another wave of visitors then arrives to enjoy the magnificent autumn colours – and to attend the Celtic Colours Festival (see page 293) on Cape Breton Island.

HIGHLIGHTS

'Something for everyone' is a much-used phrase in guidebooks and destination-based travel articles. Does it apply to Nova Scotia? Almost. But don't come for nightlife (limited) or hi-tech theme parks (the one major theme park doesn't have state-of-the-art rides), and don't come for bustling resorts with beach bars and lines of sun-lounger chairs and parasols on the sand.

CULTURE Nova Scotia is proud of its cultural heritage. Numerous centres and festivals have been established to educate and celebrate Celtic, Gaelic, Acadian and Mi'Kmaq (aboriginal) cultures. In all, there are over 500 festivals, most of which are held during the summer, celebrating everything from rhubarb to the roseate tern, black flies to blueberries.

Celtic music fans should make a beeline for Cape Breton Island Celtic Colours Festival, but a wide variety of musical genres can be heard at music festivals held all over the province (see individual chapters). Halifax has a particularly strong live music scene, which spans the range from rap to classical.

FOLKLORE Dozens of locations, including a university, schools, inns, B&Bs and restaurants, are said to be haunted, and several towns host ghost walk tours – even candlelit graveyard tours – in case you fancy rubbing shoulders with ghouls. Plenty of places sell books of Nova Scotian ghost stories as souvenirs. Shag Harbour (see page 174) was the site of an – as yet unexplained – UFO crash in 1967. Several places are associated with tales of buried treasure too – none more so than Oak Island.

FOOD AND DRINK Long known for sublime seafood – particularly scallops, clams and lobster – the province has developed a good little wine industry. Tour its wineries and sample their produce.

ACCOMMODATION WITH CHARACTER There are a few high-rise hotels in the biggest urban centres, but far better are the delightful B&Bs and inns, many of which occupy beautifully restored century-old houses and mansions.

HISTORICAL SITES Nova Scotia is very rich in historical sites compared with much of North America. The most important sites include: Halifax Citadel, one of the largest British fortresses on the North American continent; Port-Royal, the earliest European settlement in North America north of Florida; Fort Anne, which contains the oldest building in any Canadian National Historic Site; the Alexander Graham Bell National Historic Site; and the Fortress of Louisbourg, one of the largest historic reconstructions in North America. There are numerous lighthouses (including Canada's first), and countless examples of well-preserved Victorian and Georgian architecture. Old Town Lunenburg is a UNESCO World Heritage Site.

NATURAL HISTORY Geologists and fossil fans will want to visit the Joggins Fossil Cliffs – recently designated a UNESCO World Natural Heritage Site – a world-renowned paleontological site with extensive deposits of 300 million-year-old fossils. There are seven other major fossil sites in Nova Scotia (NB: unless you have a Heritage Research Permit (for details see *www.gov.ns.ca/snsmr/paal/tourism/paal157.asp*) you're not allowed to take the fossils away with you). In addition, Parrsboro is home to the Fundy Geological Museum. Some beaches on the Bay of Fundy's shores can be good hunting grounds for those in search of semi-precious stones.

OUTDOOR ACTIVITIES For outdoor types, there is superb hiking, particularly on Cape Breton Island. Waterways in remote parts of the province such as the Tobeatic Wilderness Area and Kejimkujik National Park attract adventurous get-away-from-it-all canoeists.

There are numerous golf courses; two on Cape Breton Island are rated amongst Canada's best.

Choose from over 100 beaches, many beautiful, most almost deserted and with virtually no development.

Water-based activities include world-class sea kayaking, sailing and tidal-bore rafting. Surfing and scuba diving (primarily wreck diving) are also popular.

Fish numbers have dropped, but both deep-sea sport-fishing and freshwater angling continue to be popular, as does (rightly or wrongly) hunting.

The terrain in many parts of Nova Scotia, including the Yarmouth area and Cape Breton Island's Isle Madame, lends itself to cycling holidays. If you prefer four wheels, the province offers several lovely drives, the majority overlooking the sea. One – the Cabot Trail – ranks amongst the world's best coastal drives.

WILDLIFE AND NATURE For wildlife enthusiasts, the Digby Neck in particular offers some of the world's best whale-watching opportunities. In addition, there are several seal colonies just off Brier Island (see page 196).

From the few roads which pass through the province's densely forested interior you may be lucky to spot black bear. If you want to see moose, head for the Cape Breton Highlands National Park.

Birdwatchers are spoilt for choice: bald eagles can be seen around the Bras d'Or Lake in summer and autumn, and in huge numbers near Sheffield Mills in the winter. August is the best time to see the southward migration of Arctic-nesting shorebirds.

New England might be better known for its autumn colours, but they're pretty impressive here, too. Combine leaf-peeping with some of the world's best Celtic music at Cape Breton Island's annual Celtic Colours Festival in October.

SUGGESTED ITINERARIES

As everyone has their likes and dislikes and their own preferred way of travel, use these basic itineraries as starting points and tailor them to your own preferences. Personally, I prefer to spend more time in fewer places, but I appreciate that others may wish to pack as much of the province as possible into their trip.

A WEEKEND Stay in Halifax and take a day trip out to Mahone Bay and Lunenburg.

A WEEK Stay a couple of nights in Halifax, a couple of nights in Lunenburg (visiting Chester and Mahone Bay *en route*), relax on one of the beaches near Liverpool or explore Kejimkujik National Park *en route* to Annapolis Royal: spend two nights there, taking a whale-watching tour from Brier Island, then a night in Wolfville (visiting Grand Pré). Or, stay a couple of nights in Halifax, a night in Antigonish, head to Cape Breton Island and start driving the Cabot Trail clockwise, stay a couple of nights in the Ingonishes, a night in Sydney or Louisbourg and a night on Isle Madame.

TWO WEEKS Combine the two one-week suggestions, replacing two of the Halifax nights with a night in Parrsboro (between Wolfville and Antigonish) and a night in Guysborough (after Isle Madame).

Any extra days will allow you to include Shelburne, Yarmouth, Cape Chignecto, and more of the Eastern Shore. Ideally, take longer and cover less distance. Don't rush Nova Scotia !

TOUR OPERATORS

Any decent travel agent in the UK should be able to book you a flight to Nova Scotia, book rooms at the big hotels and arrange car (or motor-home) hire. There isn't a company that focuses solely on the province, but some know it better than others.

UK Some of the operators mentioned below offer suggested self-drive itineraries around the province, and should also be able to organise a tailor-made itinerary to suit your needs. Note that UK operators don't offer multi-day escorted trips just around Nova Scotia – most combine a few days exploring the province with time also in New Brunswick and Prince Edward Island. Operators – all of whom will tailor-make itineraries for you – with good Nova Scotia content in their programmes include:

Bridge & Wickers 3 The Courtyard, 44 Gloucester Ave, London NW1 8JD; ℡ 020 7483 6555; e sales@bridgeandwickers.com; www.bridgeandwickers.co.uk. 6- & 7-night self-drive Nova Scotia itineraries, plus longer trips combining the maritime provinces.
Canadian Affair ℡ 020 7616 9185; e mail@ canadian-affair.com; www.canadianaffair.com. Especially good for flights on Air Transat & Thomas Cook airlines. 7-night self-drive Nova Scotia itinerary.

Frontier Canada ℡ 020 8776 8709; e canada@frontier-travel.co.uk; www.frontier-canada.co.uk. Tailor-made holidays to Canada. 6-night walking holidays in Nova Scotia, 8- & 14-night self-drive holidays in the province.
Inn Travel Whitwell Grange, near Castle Howard, Yorks YO60 7JU; ℡ 01653 617793; e inntravel@inntravel.co.uk; www.inntravel.co.uk. 5- &11-night Nova Scotia self-drive tours using selected inns & B&Bs in Nova Scotia.

The following companies are strong on Canada, but have more limited Nova Scotia product:

All Canada Holidays (Connections) ℡ 0800 988 5847; www.all-canada.co.uk
Audley Travel New Mill, New Mill Lane, Witney, Oxfordshire OX29 9SX; ℡ 01993 838 700; www.audleytravel.com
1st Class Holidays ℡ 0161 877 0432, 0844 449 0771; e mail@1stclassholidays.com; www.1stclassholidays.com
Independent Traveller Devonshire Hse, Devonshire Lane, Loughborough, Leics LE11 3DF; ℡ 01509 618800; e holidays@uni-travel.co.uk; www.itiscanada.co.uk

Titan HiTours ℡ 0800 988 5823; www.titanhitours.co.uk. Focuses on escorted coach tours.
Travel 2 Bookable only through travel agents.
Travelpack ℡ 0844 493 0402; e canada@ travelpack.com; www.travelpack.com. Offices in Harrow, Middlesex & Glasgow.
World Discovery ℡ 01306 888799; e enquiries@ worlddiscovery.co.uk; www.worlddiscovery.co.uk. Offer self-drive tours.

US

Backroads 801 Cedar St, Berkeley, CA; ℡ 1 510 527 1555; T/F 1 800 462 2848; www.backroads.com. Offers hiking & biking tours.
Caravan ℡ T/F 1 800 227 2826; www.caravan.com
Elderhostel ℡ T/F 1 800 454 5768; www.elderhostel.org. A Boston-based non-profit organisation offering 'learning adventures' & educational tour programmes for those aged 55 or over.

Field Guides ℡ T/F 1 800 728 4953; www.fieldguides.com. Offers tours for birdwatchers, combining Nova Scotia & Newfoundland.
Grand Circle Travel ℡ T/F 1 800 959 0405; www.gct.com. Offers escorted tours with good Nova Scotia content.
Tauck ℡ T/F 1 800 788 7885; www.tauck.com. Offers escorted tours with good Nova Scotia content.

EUROPE The following companies specialise in holidays in North America and can advise on and arrange Nova Scotia itineraries:

Germany

America Unlimited Hanover; ℡ +49 (0) 511 3744 4750; www.america-unlimited.de

Canusa Touristik Hamburg; ℡ +49 (0) 40 227 2530; www.canusa.de

Netherlands

Jan Doets America Tours Heerhugowaard; ℡ +31 (0) 7257 53333; e info@jandoets.nl; www.jandoets.nl

AUSTRALIA Few Australian tour operators know Nova Scotia well, or even include much about the province in their brochures. Probably the best bet is:

Sensational Canada ✎ +61 (0)2 9499 9639, T/F I 800 446 302; e info@sensationalcanada.com; www.sensationalcanada.com

NOVA SCOTIA & CANADA

Ambassatours Gray Line ✎ 423 6242, T/F I 800 565 7173; e tours@ambassatours.com; www.ambassatours.com. Offers day & multi-day coach tours.

Atlantic Canada Nature Safaris ✎ 455 3595, T/F I 877 455 3595; e tours@atlanticcanadasafaris.com; www.atlanticcanadasafaris.com. Offers walking & nature tours.

Explore Travel Group ✎ 405 4900; www.explore.ca, http://novascotiavacations.ca. Offers various packages in Nova Scotia & the maritimes.

Great Earth Expeditions ✎ 223 2409; e ryan@ greatearthexpeditions.com; www.greatearthexpeditions.com. Offers hiking, camping, kayaking & more to out-of-the-way areas.

Maxxim Vacations ✎ T/F I 800 567 6666; e request@maxximvacations.com; www.maxximvacations.com. Offers guided & independent packages.

Nova Scotia Travel ✎ T/F I 888 682 6449; e info@novascotiatravel.ca; www.novascotiatravel.ca. Offers packaged & custom tours.

Scott Walking Adventures ✎ 858 2060, T/F I 800 262 8644; www.scottwalking.com. Offers guided & self-guided hiking trips.

Seacoast Escapes ✎ 889 3662, T/F I 866 771 7178; e info@seacoastescapes.ca; www.seacoastescapes.ca. Offers packaged & custom tours.

Sea Spray Outdoor Adventures ✎ 383 2732; e office@cabot-trail-outdoors.com; www.cabot-trail-outdoors.com. Offers a range of Cabot Trail tours, from trail running in summer to snow-shoeing in winter.

TayMac Tours ✎ 422 4861, T/F I 800 565 8296; e tmt@taymactours.com; www.taymactours.com. Offers guided & independent packages.

You're unlikely to save much money, but you can of course tailor-make your own trip by booking flights through an operator or direct with the airline, vehicle hire through an operator, car-hire broker, or direct with the car-hire (or motorhome) company. Larger hotels can be booked through a travel company or direct with the hotel, but for most inns and B&Bs you'll need to contact the property directly.

Specialist tours Excellent cycle-tour companies offer both guided small group trips and self-guided tours through some of Nova Scotia's prettiest countryside. And you won't be roughing it at night – the companies tend to use some of the province's wonderful B&Bs and inns for overnight accommodation. Some tours are accompanied by a support vehicle to carry luggage (and saddle-weary tour participants). Bike hire is included, or you can use your own. All the following companies also offer sea-kayaking holidays.

Coastal Adventures ✎ 772 2774; www.coastaladventures.com
Freewheeling Adventures ✎ 857 3600, T/F I 800 672 0775; www.freewheeling.ca

Pedal & Sea Adventures ✎ T/F I 877 777 5699; www.pedalandseaadventures.com

i TOURIST INFORMATION

OVERSEAS Nova Scotia has virtually no representation abroad, but recently introduced a freephone number in the UK (✎ 0800 1565 0000), which connects through to tourist information staff in the province. From elsewhere in the world (for North America, see below) you'll need to ring this alternative number (✎ 425

5781). You can also contact Nova Scotia's tourist information department by email (e *info@checkinnovascotia.com*).

The tourism website (*www.novascotia.com*) is also a good source of information and offers some free, useful brochures, maps and leaflets, including the annual *Doers' & Dreamers'* services guide published annually in the early spring.

Canada has tourist offices in about a dozen of the world's major cities, but in my experience these offices provide pretty limited information on Nova Scotia.

IN NOVA SCOTIA Just three provincial visitor information centres are open year–round in Nova Scotia: one at Halifax Airport (see page 39), one on Halifax's waterfront (see page 85), and the other at Amherst (see page 259), near the Nova Scotia–New Brunswick border. Between mid-May and mid-October, dozens more tourist information offices open, and these are listed under the relevant towns later on in the book. Within North America (and, of course, Nova Scotia) you can obtain tourist information and assistance, make reservations and more by phoning ❧ T/F 1 800 565 0000.

RED TAPE

At the time of writing, citizens of the EU, Australia and New Zealand, and many other countries (visit *www.cic.gc.ca/english/visit/visas.asp* for an up-to-date list) do not require a visa to visit Canada. As long as they meet certain criteria (eg: good health, enough money for their stay, ability to satisfy the immigration officer that they will leave Canada at the end of their visit), most visitors are permitted to stay in Canada for up to six months. If you wish to extend your stay once in Canada, you must apply at least 30 days before the stamp in your passport expires. There is a form to complete, and a fee (currently CAN$75) to pay.

Unless you are a citizen of the US (see below), you will need a valid passport to enter Canada and it should be valid for at least as long as your intended period of stay.

If you are a citizen of the US, you do not need a passport to enter Canada (unless arriving in Canada from a third country), but you now need a passport to re-enter the US, and those travelling by land or sea need a passport, or other appropriate secure document like a NEXUS card. If you are a permanent resident of the United States, you must bring your permanent resident card (ie: Green Card) with you. The US Department of State website (*www.travel.state.gov/travel/*) will have the latest information.

Most visitors to Canada are not allowed to work or study in Canada without permission. You must apply for a work or study permit before coming to Canada. If you are visiting Canada and you want to apply to work or study, you must leave Canada and apply from your home country. The Canadian government's Citizenship and Immigration website (*www.cic.gc.ca*) should answer most questions. NB: This information is correct at the time of writing, but rules and practices change: do check the current situation before buying your ticket.

CUSTOMS REGULATIONS Visitors to Nova Scotia (and Canada in general) are permitted to bring in personal items such as clothing, camping and sports

---

WILDE'S WIT

Touring North America in 1882, Oscar Wilde was asked by a customs official if he had anything of value to declare. 'Only my genius' was Wilde's reply.

equipment, cameras, tape recorders and personal computers that will be used during a visit. Gifts (each valued at CAN$60 or less) for friends or family can be brought in duty- and tax-free, but alcohol and tobacco products are not classed as gifts.

Those aged over 18 (19 for alcohol) can bring in the following duty-free: either 1.5 litres of wine or 1.14 litres of liquor (maximum 1.14 litres if you're bringing wine and liquor) or 24 (355ml) cans (maximum 8.5 litres) of beer or ale. Despite the ban on smoking in public places, you can bring in 200 cigarettes, 50 cigars/cigarillos, and 200g of manufactured tobacco duty-free.

There are strict rules concerning the import of numerous things from food products to firearms, plants to prescription drugs. See the regulations at www.cbsa-asfc.gc.ca/publications/pub/rc4161-eng.html#P003 .

Ⓔ EMBASSIES

ABROAD

Australia Commonwealth Av, Canberra, 2600 ACT; ☎ +61 (0)2 6270 4000; e cnbra@international.gc.ca; www.canada.org.au. There is also a Consulate General in Sydney & consulates in Melbourne & Perth.
France 37 Av Montaigne, 75008 Paris; ☎ +33 (0)1 44 43 29 00; e paris@international.gc.ca; www.dfait-maeci.gc.ca/canadaeuropa/france/
Germany Leipziger Platz 17, 10117 Berlin; ☎ +49 (0)30 203 120; e brlin@international.gc.ca; www.dfait-maeci.gc.ca/canada-europa/germany/

Italy Via Zara 30, 00198 Rome; ☎ +39 (0)6 854 441; e rome@international.gc.ca; www.canada.it
UK 38 Grosvenor St, London W1K 4AA; ☎ +44 (0)20 7258 6600; e idn@international.gc.ca; www.london.gc.ca. There are also consulates in Belfast, Birmingham, Cardiff & Edinburgh.
US 501 Pennsylvania Av, NW, Washington, DC, 20001; ☎ +1 202 682 1740; www.canadianembassy.org

There are also about 20 consulate generals and consulates. Visit (*http://w01.international.gc.ca/cra-rce/index.aspx*) for the full list and contact details.

IN NOVA SCOTIA

Germany Suite 1100, Purdy's Wharf Tower 1, 1959 Upper Water St, Halifax, B3J 3R7; ☎ 420 1599
Italy Suite 7, 1574 Argyle St, Halifax, B3J 2B3, ☎ 492 3934, e italconsul@attcanada.ca; 1 Sharple Av, Sydney, B1R 2B7, ☎ 567 2290

UK 1 Canal St, Dartmouth, B2Y 3Y9; ☎ 461 1381
US Suite 904, Purdy's Wharf Tower 2, 1969 Upper Water St, Halifax, B3J 3E5; ☎ 429 2480; www.halifax.usconsulate.gov/content/index.asp

GETTING THERE AND AWAY

Most European visitors arrive into Nova Scotia by air, flying into Halifax Robert L Stanfield International Airport. For those coming from (or going to) other parts of Canada, there are a few other options: one rail connection, and two road crossings from the neighbouring province of New Brunswick (itself connected by road to the Canadian province of Quebec, and to Maine in the United States). There are also ferry connections with Maine, New Brunswick, Prince Edward Island and Newfoundland.

Travellers from the US have the choice of flying, connecting with the train or coach (see page 40), taking one of the ferries from Maine, driving to Saint John (New Brunswick) and taking the ferry from there, or driving through New Brunswick to take the land route into Nova Scotia. Portland, Maine, to Saint John (New Brunswick), is just over 480km by road: Portland to the New Brunswick – Nova Scotia border, near Amherst, is 750km.

Practical Information GETTING THERE AND AWAY 2

✈ BY AIR After improving for a few years, options for those looking to fly to Nova Scotia from Europe suffered a setback in 2008 when low-cost airline Zoom went into administration. Air Canada offers daily non-stop flights between Heathrow and Halifax, and various other companies offer a direct flight or two per week between May and October. Flying time from London to Halifax is around 6½ hours (the Gulf Stream winds mean that the return journey is usually about 45 minutes quicker). If you are having problems finding seats at a competitive fare, it might be worth looking beyond direct flights – more options exist if you are prepared to change planes. However, it's worth comparing any savings in cost against the extra time and inconvenience the stopovers will incur. The most expensive time to fly is in July and August.

If you're coming from elsewhere in Canada, options also exist to fly direct to Sydney (on Cape Breton Island) from Montreal, and in the summer, Toronto.

From the UK

Air Canada ✎ 0871 220 1111; www.aircanada.co.uk. Daily flights between London Heathrow & Halifax. In general, if direct flights are full, it is possible to change planes in Toronto or Montreal for the same fare.
Air Transat and Thomas Cook ✎ 020 7616 9187; www.airtransat.co.uk. Direct flights between London Gatwick & Halifax (late Apr–late Oct, Tue & Thu). You can mix & match Air Transat flights with Thomas Cook flights (eg: use one airline out & the other back) through this company.

Flyglobespan ✎ 0871 271 9028; www.flyglobespan.com. Direct flights between Glasgow & Halifax (late May–mid-Oct, Sat).
Icelandair ✎ 0870 787 4020; www.icelandair.co.uk. No direct flights, but flights 3-times weekly (May–Oct, Mon, Thu & Sat) from Heathrow, Manchester & Glasgow with a plane change in Reykjavik.

From Europe

Air Canada ✎ 0871 220 1111; www.aircanada.com. Daily flights from Paris, Frankfurt, Munich, Rome & Zurich with a change in Toronto or Montreal.
Condor ✎ +49 (0) 180 576 7757 (in Germany); www.condor.com. Twice-weekly direct flights between Frankfurt & Halifax (mid-May–late Oct, Mon & Wed).

Corsairfly www.corsairfly.com. Weekly flights between Paris & Halifax (summer, Wed).
Icelandair ✎ 0870 787 4020; www.icelandair.com. Flights via Reykjavik with a plane change (May–Oct, Mon, Thu & Sat) from Barcelona, Madrid, Paris, Amsterdam, Milan, Munich, Frankfurt, Berlin, Copenhagen, Gothenburg, Stockholm, Helsinki, Oslo & Bergen.

From elsewhere in Canada

Air Canada ✎ T/F 1 888 247 2262; www.aircanada.com. Daily direct flights to Halifax from St John's, Montreal, Toronto, Calgary & Vancouver.
Air Canada Jazz ✎ T/F 1 888 247 2262; www.flyjazz.ca. Daily direct flights to Halifax from Gander, Deer Lake, Moncton, Fredericton, Saint John & Montreal. Also operates a direct Montreal–Sydney service in summer.

Air St Pierre ✎ T/F 1 877 277 7765; www.airsaintpierre.com. Flights between Saint Pierre (St Pierre & Miquelon islands, just south of Newfoundland) & Halifax year-round (Wed & Fri), & Sydney (early Jul–early Sep, Thu & Sun).
Porter Airlines ✎ T/F 1 888 619 8622; www.flyporter.com. Daily flights between Halifax, & both Toronto & Ottawa (end-May–early Sep).

DAYS GONE BY

In 1936, an aircraft crash-landed in a bog near Main-a-Dieu (see page 333) in eastern Cape Breton Island. The shaken pilot climbed out of the cockpit and said 'I'm Mrs Markham: I've just flown from England'. Beryl Markham had just flown for 21 hours, completing the first-ever east-to-west solo flight between England and the American continent.

Sunwing ↘ T/F 1 800 761 1711; www.sunwing.ca. Flights between Toronto & Halifax (summer Tue & Fri). **Westjet** ↘ T/F 1 888 937 8538; www.westjet.com. Flights to Halifax daily year-round from Saint John, Hamilton, Toronto & Calgary, & in the summer to Halifax from Montreal & Edmonton (both daily), & to Sydney from Toronto (Tue, Thu, Sat & Sun).

From the US
In addition to the daily (except where specified) direct flights between US airports and Halifax, if you are prepared to change planes, there are dozens more possibilities. Incidentally, if you are flying directly to the US, Halifax Airport has a US Customs pre-clearance facility allowing you to go through US Customs and Border Protection before your flight – saving quite a bit of time at the other end.

Air Canada Jazz ↘ T/F 1 888 247 2262; www.flyjazz.ca. Direct flights to Halifax from Boston & New York (La Guardia). **American Airlines** ↘ T/F 1 800 433 7300; www.aa.com. Direct flights between New York (JFK) & Halifax. **Continental** ↘ T/F 1 800 231 0856; www.continental.com. Direct flights between Newark & Halifax.

Delta ↘ T/F 1 800 221 1212; www.delta.com. Direct flights between Atlanta, Boston, New York (JFK) & Halifax. **Starlink Aviation** ↘ 1 514 631 7500, T/F 1 877 782 8247; www.starlinkaviation.com. Direct flights between Portland, Maine & Yarmouth. **United** ↘ T/F 1 800 538 2929; www.united.com. Direct flights between Washington DC & Halifax.

From Australia
There are no direct flights between Australia and Nova Scotia. You will have to change planes at least twice. A few airlines offer through fares, eg: **Air Canada** (↘ *1300 655 767; www.aircanada.com/au/en/home.html*), **American** (↘ *+61 (0) 7 3329 6060; www.aa.com*) and **United** (↘ *131 777; www.unitedairlines.com.au*). It is often cheaper to buy a ticket to (say) New York, and a separate ticket New York–Halifax.

Airports
Halifax Robert L Stanfield International Airport
(↘ *873 4422; www.hiaa.ca, www.flyhalifax.com*) Not surprisingly, this tends to be referred to as Halifax Airport or 'the airport': its IATA code is YHZ. Modern and efficient (though if a couple of international flights arrive at the same time, it can take a while to clear immigration) this airport processes some 3.5 million passengers annually. There's a well-stocked tourist information office just outside the arrivals hall, as well as ATMs, bureaux de change, car hire and ground transportation desks, and shops and cafés. A 2,300-space multi-storey car park opened in spring 2009: construction of a new airport hotel has been put on hold on account of the current economic downturn. It is situated just off Exit 6 of Highway 102, approximately 35km from downtown Halifax. In general, the journey to or from the city should take 30–45 minutes, but traffic can be bad going into Halifax between 08.00 and 09.30, and leaving the city between 16.30 and 18.00, so allow perhaps 80 minutes at these times. For details of transport to and from the airport, see page 78. For listings of airport hotels see page 91.

Sydney Airport
(↘ *564 7720; www.sydneyairport.ca*) Sydney airport is 9km from Sydney, Cape Breton Island. The airport's IATA code is YQY. Few flights come and go, but there's a restaurant, ATM and car-hire desks.

Yarmouth (International) Airport
(*310 Forest St;* ↘ *742 6484*) The airport's IATA code is YQI. Approximately 3.5km from downtown Yarmouth, at the time of writing, only 20 scheduled flights per week were using the airport.

2

BY CAR Whether driving from the US or Canada, unless you take The CAT or a ferry (see below) you'll pass through New Brunswick and cross into Nova Scotia near Amherst (see page 259). From there it is 215km/134 miles – about a 2½–3-hour drive – to Halifax. Montreal is about 1,250km/777 miles from Halifax by road, and (again if you don't take a ferry) Boston is 1,120km/700 miles. For more on driving in Nova Scotia, see page 49.

BY COACH

Acadian (✆ T/F 1 800 567 5151; www.smtbus.com) Offers three coach services per day between Halifax (calling at various places in Nova Scotia including Dartmouth, Halifax Airport, Truro and Amherst) and Sackville and Moncton (both in New Brunswick). Halifax to Moncton takes just over four hours and costs CAN$48 one-way, CAN$82 return. From Moncton there are onward connections to Quebec or Maine (US) and thence further afield (on partner coach networks) into Canada or down into the US. Acadian honours Greyhound passes.

PEI Express Shuttle (✆ T/F 1 877 877 1771; www.peishuttle.com) Operates 11-passenger air-conditioned vans daily between Nova Scotia and Prince Edward Island via New Brunswick. The route is Charlottetown–Summerside–Borden (all in Prince Edward Island)–Halifax Airport–Halifax City–Dartmouth. Journey time is approximately four to five hours and the trip costs CAN$60 one-way.

BY TRAIN

VIA Rail (✆ T/F 1 888 842 7245; www.viarail.ca) Operates an overnight train, *The Ocean*, six times a week between Montreal and Halifax. The train leaves Montreal every evening (except Tuesday), travels via Moncton and New Brunswick, arriving in Halifax in mid afternoon. In the other direction, an afternoon departure from Halifax (again daily except Tuesday) reaches Montreal the next morning.

Year-round, the train offers standard economy class, and sleeper class; the latter affords you a bed in private accommodation. Between mid-June and mid-October, you can also travel in sleeper touring class. Extra benefits, instead of standard sleeper class, include on-train presentations with cultural and historical insights to the Maritimes, exclusive access to the train's lounges and panoramic section of the luxurious Park Car, breakfast, lunch and a three-course dinner. Regular fares start at CAN$222 one-way, CAN$444 return in economy class, but early bookers may be able to secure 'supersaver' economy class fares, offering a CAN$100 discount (each way) off regular fares.

BY SEA

Bay Ferries (✆ T/F 1 888 249 7245; www.bayferries.com) Operates four routes: Yarmouth–Portland (Maine, US) (*early–Jul–early–Sep, Wed–Sun; Jun–early–Jul, early–Sep–mid-Oct, Thu–Sun; journey: 5½ hrs; fares from US$99 one-way*); Yarmouth–Bar Harbor (Maine, US) (*mid-Oct , Mon & Tue; journey: just under 3hrs; fares from US$69 one-way*) on The CAT, which carries up to 775 passengers, 250 cars and 14 coaches or RVs; Digby–Saint John (New Brunswick) on the *Princess of Acadia* (*year-round, daily; journey: 3hrs, fares from CAN$30 one-way*); and Caribou (near Pictou)–Wood Island (Prince Edward Island) on NFL Ferries MV *Confederation* and MV *Holiday Island* (*May–mid-Dec, daily; journey: 75 minutes; fares from CAN$30 one-way*).

Marine Atlantic (✆ T/F 1 800 341 7981; www.marine-atlantic.ca) Offers two connections between Nova Scotia's Cape Breton Island and the Canadian province of Newfoundland: North Sydney–Port aux Basques (Newfoundland) (*1–2 trips/day, year–round; journey: 6–7hrs; fares from CAN$29 one-way*); and North

Sydney–Argentia (Newfoundland) (*3 sailings/week, late June–late September; journey: 14hrs; fares from CAN$80 one-way*).

✚ HEALTH with Dr Felicity Nicholson

The standard of public health in Canada is excellent, but very expensive for non-residents. If you become ill in Nova Scotia, for minor ailments, seek out a pharmacy.

If it is something more serious, your next step is to go to one of the few walk-in clinics or to the emergency department of a hospital. You will have to pay at both to use the facilities and to see a doctor, and for any treatment and/or medicines that may be required. It is a similar story for emergency dental work. Consequently, it would be foolhardy to visit Nova Scotia (and anywhere in North America) without comprehensive medical insurance (check that your travel insurance policy includes adequate cover).

If you take prescription medicines to Nova Scotia, make sure that they are in their original packaging (with a label that specifies what they are and that they are being used under prescription). If that is not possible, carry a copy of the prescription or a letter from your doctor. Otherwise, they may be confiscated by customs officials.

No vaccinations are legally required, however, it is always wise to be up to date with routine vaccinations such as diphtheria, tetanus and polio. Tap water is potable and safe to drink.

BLACK FLIES AND MOSQUITOES Tiny, biting black flies appear in the spring and (though everyone says that they go by early–mid-June) may hang around into July. They cannot bite through clothing, but sometimes bite above the hairline, or below the collar line. They don't bite after dark. In rural areas in May and early June, it is not uncommon to see locals who are working outside wearing head nets.

Just before the black flies start to die down for the year, mosquitoes make their appearance, and buzz around until late summer – even longer in swampy areas. Whereas in many places mosquitoes are creatures of the night, in Nova S... are just as evident in the daytime. In theory, coastal areas are less bad... I've seen plenty of evidence to the contrary.

Mosquitoes here do not carry malaria, but there is said to b... Nile virus. However, as of January 2009, no humans hav... having acquired West Nile virus in the province.

Help protect against black flies and mosquitoes by... coloured long-sleeved shirts and trousers and cover e... based insect repellent.

Practical Information HE

Lieke Scheewe (with advice from Gordon Rattray; www.able-travel.com)

Canada, including Nova Scotia, has relatively high accessibility standards. There has been an increasing awareness that many people need special services, from various diet requirements to accessibility arrangements and protection from animal allergies. As such, its beach resorts as well as its wilderness are becoming a joy for everyone.

GETTING THERE AND AROUND Access to Travel (*www.accesstotravel.gc.ca/*) is a comprehensive resource that emerged from a co-operative effort between federal and local governments as well as the private and non-profit sectors. It provides up-to-date information on accessible transportation services across Canada, including information on transportation by bus, rail, air and ferry, local public and private transportation. A few essential services:

By air Halifax International Airport is fully accessible for wheelchair users (including availability of narrow aisle chairs, adapted washrooms, etc) and way-finding is accessible for those with visual impairments (eg: signs have contrasting colours and lifts have tactile markers). A Volunteer Host Program, called the Tartan Team, provides personal assistance. **Need-A-Lift** (🕿 / 902 222 5438) is one of the wheelchair-accessible transportation services that can take you from the airport to your final destination.

By ferry Marine Atlantic (🕿 T/F / 800 341 7981; www.marine-atlantic.ca) operates all its ferries in full compliance with Canadian accessibility legislation. It has, for example, an adapted cabin for persons with limited mobility and appropriate informational signage for those with visual impairments. Make reservations in advance and mention required services. For some of these services proof of disability is required.

By road and rail Acadian Lines (🕿 T/F / 800 567 5151; www.smtbus.com) has eight buses equipped with a wheelchair lift and anchoring systems. Wheelchair users must book their seat 72 hours prior to departure. They are also ready to help you on board if you use a walker, cane, or other mobility device and offer free travel companions for those who need assistance during the trip.

VIA Rail Canada (🕿 T/F / 888 842 7245; www.viarail.ca) offers a wide variety of to those with limited mobility or other disabilities. The services may vary from to another. Book your ticket at least 48 hours in advance and specify which require.

with long grass can be home to ticks, particularly in spring in parts of the province – Bedford, Gunning Cove (near burg area – some black-legged ticks carry the bacteria lisease. Both black-legged and dog (or wood) ticks are va Scotia. If you go walking in tick country, try to avoid as. Wear long trousers tucked into socks, a long-sleeved a DEET-based insect repellent on outer clothing. After xamine yourself all over as soon as it is practical. If you oved with special tick tweezers that can be bought in you can use your fingernails: grasp the tick as close pull steadily and firmly away at right angles to your

ACCOMMODATION Accessible accommodation is not very difficult to find, although the amount of accessible rooms is usually very limited. Travellers with special needs are urged to make their reservations in advance of arrival and to mention any specific arrangements they may require at the time of booking. A few useful resources:

Check In (✆ T/F 1 800 565 0000) can help you locate (partially) accessible, smoke-free and pet-free properties.

The website of **Cottage Portal™** (*www.cottageportal.com*) is very useful in finding wheelchair-accessible accommodation.

Mersey River Chalets and Nature Retreat (✆ 1 902 682 2443; *www.merseyriverchalets.ns.ca*) is a wilderness resort which provides fully accessible accommodation for wheelchair users. In addition, they offer specially designed nature trails and wharfs to allow access to swimming, canoeing and kayaking.

ACTIVITIES Besides Access Guide Canada (see below), other interesting websites for recreational activities are:

www.pc.gc.ca The Parks Canada website has accessibility information on national parks, historic sites and marine conservation areas.
www.acadventures.ca Accessible Canadian Adventures designs, co-ordinates and arranges hunting, fishing and wildlife-photography trips for disabled sportsmen and women.
www.abilities.ca/agc Destination Nova Scotia is a searchable database for restaurants, festivals, and other types of recreation and specifies for (partial) wheelchair accessibility.
www.ns.edining.ca eDining.ca provides listings of restaurants and specifies their wheelchair accessibility.

TRAVEL INSURANCE Most insurance companies will cater for disabled travellers, but it is essential that they are made aware of your disability. Examples of specialised companies in the UK that cover pre-existing medical conditions are **Free Spirit** (✆ 0845 230 5000; *www.free-spirit.com*) and **Age Concern** (✆ 0845 601 2234; *www.ageconcern.org.uk*), who have no upper age limit.

FURTHER INFORMATION The most comprehensive accessibility information website is offered by **Access Guide Canada**, a voluntary programme compiling information on a wide variety of services, from transportation to lodgings and entertainment venues. Start your search by entering your destination province and community within Canada at www.abilities.ca/agc/. Contact the **Nova Scotia League for Equal Opportunities** (*5251 Duke St, Suite 1211, Halifax, NS, B3K 4E1*; ✆ +1 902 455 6942; f +1 902 454 4781; e *nsleo@eastlink.ca*) with enquiries regarding transportation services, access to recreational facilities, or other services and referrals.

skin. The tick will then come away complete, as long as you do not jerk or twist. If possible douse the wound with alcohol (any spirit will do) or iodine. Irritants (eg: Olbas oil) or lit cigarettes are to be discouraged since they can cause the ticks to regurgitate and therefore increase the risk of disease. It is best to get a travelling companion to check you for ticks; if you are travelling with small children, remember to check their heads, and particularly behind the ears. Spreading redness around the bite and/or fever and/or aching joints after a tick bite imply that you have an infection that requires antibiotic treatment, so seek advice.

LEECHES Leeches can occur in still or slow-moving water, such as the shallow edges of lakes. Many locals carry salt shakers with them when going on swimming (or paddling) trips to a lake, and if a leech attaches itself, a sprinkle of salt will usually make the creature dislodge. Leeches do not carry disease but do inject an anti-coagulant agent into the wound, so try to clean the wound, put on a dab of antiseptic cream, and cover with a plaster.

POISON IVY This toxic plant is found here and there in Nova Scotia (and in most of North America): it produces urushiol, an irritant which causes an allergic reaction to most of those who come in contact with it. The reaction takes the form of itching and inflammation and can be severe. I've only seen poison ivy once in Nova Scotia, and there were several big 'Warning! Poison Ivy' signs all around.

SUN Especially with cooling coastal breezes or thin layers of cloud, it is easy to get sunburned in Nova Scotia. Cover up and use sun-damage protection.

SAFETY

Canada is politically stable and one of the world's safer places, and Nova Scotia's crime rates are about average for the country (they have been on a downward trend for the last few years). Rightly or wrongly, many people in rural areas still don't lock their doors.

Violent crimes are infrequent; far more common is petty theft. Some parts of the big urban areas are troubled by youth crime, often drug- or drink-inspired, but probably to a lesser degree than in equivalent cities in Europe or the US.

Outside the urban centres, things seem so laid-back that it is easy to forget common sense. For instance, if you must leave valuable items in your car unattended, keep them out of sight, preferably locked in the vehicle's boot. And wherever you are in the world, carrying large amounts of cash around isn't a great idea.

THE LAW If you steer clear of drugs, you are unlikely to have unsolicited contact with the police in Nova Scotia. Pedestrians should be aware that although in the UK, crossing the road safely is considered a personal responsibility, in Canada and the US jaywalking (crossing a road without regard to traffic regulations) is a crime – albeit one that dozens of people in the province commit regularly, often in view of the police. Once behind a wheel, your chances of attracting the attention of local law enforcers do increase. See *By car*, page 49.

THE POLICE You won't see red-jacketed, horse-riding, Mounties in Nova Scotia – here the Royal Canadian Mounted Police (RCMP) dress less garishly and travel in police cars.

Municipal governments around the province are responsible for policing, and can choose if they want policing to be done by the RCMP or their own force. There are municipal forces in the two major urban centres (the central core of the Halifax Regional Municipality and Cape Breton Regional Municipality) and ten other towns, while the RCMP provides policing elsewhere in the province and in

POWER BEATS TERRORISTS

In 1883, Chief Constable Nicholas Power arrested two men in possession of explosives suspected of planning to blow up the HMS *Canada* in Halifax Harbour. At the time, Prince George, who would later become King George V, was serving on that very ship. Power was awarded the King's Police Medal (the police equivalent of the Armed Forces' Victoria Cross) in 1915.

rural areas. It also performs the vast majority of highway policing. Some communities have their own local numbers on which to contact the police for non-emergencies. These can be found in the phone directory, or online at www.411.ca. The standard number to call for police assistance (and the fire or ambulance service) is 911.

TERRORISM No recent terrorism events have occurred in the province (unlike in 1883 – see box on opposite page), and Canada as a whole has had few problems with terrorists in the last couple of decades.

WOMEN TRAVELLERS Women using their common sense are unlikely to have any problems in Nova Scotia, even if travelling alone. There have been claims that immigration officials give solo female travellers more of a grilling than others. Other than that it's just a case of common sense: don't wander in dodgy areas at night, hitchhike alone, etc.

GAY AND LESBIAN TRAVELLERS Attitudes to gays and lesbians vary across the province. The Halifax Pride Festival (*www.halifaxpride.com*), for example, is Atlantic Canada's largest Pride celebration. On the other hand, in 2007, Truro's mayor and council refused requests to raise the Gay Pride flag at the town hall and opposed a local Gay Pride parade. It takes time for embedded conservative beliefs to change: Truro's officials apart, in general there is greater acceptance in the big urban centres and more tourist-orientated communities.

Look out for *Wayves* magazine (*www.wayves.ca*), published 11-times yearly in Halifax for gays across the Atlantic Canada region.

WHAT TO TAKE

Choose your clothes on the basis that temperatures and weather conditions can change quickly and dramatically even in summer. A sudden sea mist can block out the sun and cause the temperature to drop a number of degrees – dress in layers.

Rain- and wind-proof gear is useful at any time of year, and a sturdy, fold-up umbrella (which doesn't blow inside-out at the first hint of a breeze) can be useful for summer showers, or if the sun gets too strong.

In addition to comfortable walking shoes, hiking boots or shoes (with a good grip) will enable you to better enjoy the many beautiful trails.

Long-sleeved shirts and blouses can help protect against mosquitoes and tiny black flies: insect repellent can be a necessity in some areas at some times of the year, though it can be purchased locally.

Binoculars can be useful for wildlife spotting, and if you're taking electrical goods, or those that operate on rechargeable batteries, see page 46.

Take out comprehensive travel insurance when you book your travel arrangements – this should cover cancellation, lost or stolen baggage, and – most importantly – medical emergencies.

ELECTRICITY Canada's electrical sockets are the same as those found in the US, ie: two flat-pin plugs. Occasionally, some have a third round earth pin. The electrical supply is 110 volts and 60 hertz (cycles per second).

Many, but not all, electrical appliances sold in the UK have dual voltage power supplies and will work happily in Canada once you attach a UK–US/Canada adaptor. If the appliance rating plate on your device does not say something like 'input 100–240V', you may need a transformer or converter and an adaptor: check with an electrical shop to be sure.

UK–US/Canada adaptors are surprisingly difficult to find in Nova Scotia, so take what you'll need with you.

$ MONEY

CASH The Canadian dollar (CAN$) is Canada's official unit of currency. One dollar equals 100 cents. Dollars are issued in banknote denominations of 5, 10, 20, 50 and 100 and coins of 1 (often called a 'looney'; see box on page 15) and 2 dollars (a 'toonie'). Cent coin denominations are 1 (penny), 5 (nickel), 10 (dime), 25 (quarter) and 50.

US dollars are widely accepted, but change (if any) will be given in Canadian dollars, and the exchange rate will almost always be worse than that offered by banks.

In recent years, the Canadian dollar exchange rate has yo-yo'd against both the pound and the US dollar. The current exchange rates are £1=CAN$1.78, US$1=CAN$1.09 and €1=CAN$1.56 (August 2009).

CREDIT AND DEBIT CARDS Virtually all major credit and debit cards are quite widely accepted in Nova Scotia, but some businesses are still cash only. Although you can use your credit card to withdraw cash from an ATM, charges are significantly higher than using a debit card. As is the case in the UK, at some ATMs (for example, those in petrol stations or general stores) there may be a charge for using the machine, in addition to the fee charged by most UK banks each time that a debit card is used abroad. Check with your bank as other fees (for example, exchange-rate loading) may also apply. At the time of writing, Nationwide (*www.nationwide.co.uk*) is the only high-street provider that doesn't charge you commission if you use your card abroad. Using a credit card for purchases and a debit card for getting cash is now the most popular combination for those visiting the province.

It is worth notifying your bank where you will be going and for how long at least a week or so before you leave home: at the same time, make a note of the phone numbers to use if your card(s) are lost or stolen whilst in Nova Scotia.

HARMONIZED SALES TAX (HST)

Most goods and services in Nova Scotia attract Harmonized Sales Tax (HST), currently at 13%. Exceptions include basic groceries (milk, bread, vegetables), but in most cases whenever you see a price in Nova Scotia – on a menu, in a shop, for a hotel room, etc – expect an extra 13% to be added. Until recently, visitors could claim back some (or all) of the HST they had paid when in Nova Scotia, but no longer. Unless stated otherwise, prices shown in this book include HST.

If you have an International Student Card (ISIC), or International Youth Travel Card (IYTC), or are a 'senior', it is always worth asking for a discount at attractions, for tours, even for accommodation. Students, youths and seniors (60+) are entitled to reduced rates on VIA Rail and Acadian coaches.

EXCHANGING CURRENCY AND TRAVELLERS' CHEQUES Currency can be exchanged in banks, credit unions, trust companies, larger hotels, and at currency-exchange bureaux. Check not only the exchange rate, but any commission charges.

Most travellers to Nova Scotia now rely on credit cards, and ATMs (often referred to as ABMs in Nova Scotia) for cash withdrawals with debit cards.

Many businesses in the province will accept travellers' cheques for payment (you're likely to need photo ID such as a passport in support) and give change in cash dollars. Travellers' cheques can only be used by the person who purchased them, and lost or stolen travellers' cheques can be replaced. I'd recommend getting American Express Canadian dollar travellers' cheques. In the UK these can be purchased from the Post Office (*www.postoffice.co.uk*).

PRE-PAID TRAVEL MONEY CARDS These are a relatively recent phenomenon and are designed to give the security of travellers' cheques with the convenience of a plastic debit card. They are offered by banks, the Post Office and some retailers, eg: Tesco. You apply for a card, load it up with funds before you go, and use your card to withdraw cash at the province's ATMs, or to pay at most businesses that accept credit cards. You can even top the card up whilst you are away. The downside is that again there are fees to watch out for. Some providers charge for card applications, ATM withdrawals and top-ups. However, as more players come into the market, it is likely that these cards will become more competitive and user-friendly.

BANKS Banking hours vary, but in general are: 10.00–16.00 Monday–Friday. Some banks stay open later on Fridays, and a few may open on Saturday mornings. In terms of their networks, the province's main banks are **Scotiabank** (*www.scotiabank.com*) and **Royal Bank** (*www.rbcroyalbank.com*). Twenty-four-hour ATMs (often called ABMs) are commonplace (see *Credit and debit cards*, opposite). Larger supermarkets almost always have ATMs, and many offer some banking services.

2

A litre of (regular) petrol	CAN$1.04
A litre of milk	CAN$1.87
A (473ml) bottle of beer (Keiths IPA)	CAN$2.50
A dinner main course (including vegetables) at a reasonable restaurant	CAN$14–19
A bus (or ferry) ticket in Halifax	CAN$2.25
A three–five-hour whale-watching trip from Brier Island (see page 198)	CAN$55.00
A dormitory bed in a backpackers' hostel	CAN$25.00
A daily newspaper (the *Chronicle Herald*)	CAN$1.25

BUDGETING

So how expensive is a holiday in Nova Scotia going to be? Some things are easy to work out – air fares (including all the taxes), car hire (if you pre-pay), whilst others are of course more variable. A lot, too, depends on the vagaries of fluctuating exchange rates.

In general, you'll find grocery prices similar to (or perhaps a tiny bit more than) the UK, and probably a little higher than in the US. Eating out in most cafés and restaurants is significantly cheaper than in the UK, though this is less noticeable at fast-food take-away joints.

Petrol (gas) prices have fluctuated a lot of late, but are usually at least 50% cheaper than the UK (see *www.novascotiagasprices.com*). Compared with provinces (and American states) on the west of the continent, Nova Scotia is quite compact, so driving distances tend to be shorter too.

Although there aren't many youth (or backpacker) hostels, there are plenty of cheap motels, and most B&Bs are very well priced, (especially when you take the quality breakfasts into account), and tend to be cheaper than in many other Canadian provinces. A range of accommodation is available for those who are happy to spend more for more space, better facilities etc.

GETTING AROUND

It is easy to travel around Nova Scotia – if you have a vehicle. Sadly, public transport is limited, and non-existent in some areas.

✈ BY AIR

Air Canada (☎ T/F 1 888 247 2262; *www.aircanada.com*) Offers a few flights a day between Halifax and Sydney, Cape Breton Island, and **Starlink Aviation** (☎ +1 514 631 7500, T/F 1 877 782 8247; *www.starlinkaviation.com*) began operating twice daily flights between Halifax and Yarmouth as of February 2009.

🚗 BY CAR
For the freedom it gives you, the (generally) good roads, and – compared with much of Europe and urban North America – the (generally) very light traffic, driving is by far the best way to get around the province. British motorists, used to driving on the left, will quickly adapt to driving on the right. Most drivers in Nova Scotia are courteous, patient, and observant of speed limits. Outside downtown Halifax, parking is rarely a problem.

Traffic jams are not unheard of, particularly during rush hour on the approaches to and from Halifax and Dartmouth, and the motorway (Highway 102) which links them with the airport.

DRIVING THROUGH HISTORY

In September 1899, The *Halifax Echo* reported the arrival (from Liverpool, England) of a ship carrying the first car ever seen in Nova Scotia.

Until 14 April 1923, driving was on the left-hand side of the road. At that time, teams of oxen (pulling wagons) were common on the province's roads, but it proved almost impossible to retrain them to walk on the other side of the road. So many redundant oxen were sent to the slaughterhouse as a result that there was a dramatic reduction in the price of beef. Horses proved a bit more adaptable: almost nine decades later, it is only the occasional absent-minded driver visiting from the UK who gets it wrong.

Everywhere is well within a day's drive of Halifax. You could easily reach Yarmouth in three–four hours, and Sydney (on the east coast of Cape Breton Island) in four–five hours. But Nova Scotia is not about rushing from A to B: in fact, quite the opposite. Where possible, try to avoid the motorways and aim instead for the smaller, often much more scenic – albeit slower – alternatives. Try to allow far more time than distances on the map might suggest. One of the joys of touring the province is discovering what lies beyond the main roads: making side trips down virtually uninhabited peninsulas, trying to spot whales from a headland, stopping to pick your own strawberries, to wander deserted beaches, take in the view from a look-out, or to watch boats bobbing in the harbour at tiny fishing villages.

If you're a member of an automobile association such as the AAA, AA or RAC, you should be able to take advantage of the services of the **Canadian Automobile Association** (*www.caa.ca*) which has offices in Halifax (✆ *443 5530*) and Dartmouth (✆ *468 6306*). Members of related overseas associations can enjoy many benefits including free maps and guides, travel agency services, and emergency road services.

Roads Nova Scotia has some 23,000km of roads, and 4,100 road bridges. Officially, all named roads in Nova Scotia are 'highways' whether they are (what we would call) motorways or narrow country roads. Limited-access motorways (usually blue or green on road maps, and numbered 100–199) are usually two lanes in each direction, sometimes dual carriageways, but sometimes just a single lane in each direction.

The vast majority of those entering the province by road will do so near Amherst (see page 259) on the Trans Canada Highway (TCH), Highway 104. Between Exits 8 and 10, a toll (from CAN$4) is levied. The TCH heads east to Cape Breton Island (*en route*, a short spur, Highway 106, leads to the Caribou ferry terminal, see page 273) where it connects with Highway 105. Highway 104 continues to St Peter's (see page 322), whereas Highway 105 leads to North Sydney (see page 325).

For those renting a car at Halifax Airport, the airport is off Highway 102, which connects Halifax with the Trans Canada Highway, meeting it near Truro.

Highway 101 runs between Halifax and Yarmouth via the Annapolis Valley, and Highway 103 connects the same end points via the South Shore.

The old (pre-motorway) single-digit main roads tend to run almost parallel with their motorway counterparts (eg: Highway 1 and 101, 2 and 102, etc).

Most other roads are one lane in each direction, with soft (gravel) shoulders. Be prepared for some rough surfaces and pot-holes – a combination of winter weather and the cost of maintaining thousands of kilometres of backroads. In rural areas (much of the province!) watch out for wildlife (eg: deer, porcupine) particularly if driving towards dusk or after dark.

Petrol (gas) is sold by the litre, and you should bear in mind that few rural petrol stations are open 24/7. The (self-explanatory) website www.novascotiagasprices.com may also be of interest.

Licences Full national driving licences from most major countries of the world, including the UK, Australia and the US, are valid in Nova Scotia. If your licence is not in English or French, I'd recommend obtaining an International Driving Permit. UK drivers with new two-part (photocard and paper) licences should take both parts with them, although the paper part is rarely asked for.

Driving laws Wearing of safety belts is compulsory for all passengers, and motorcyclists and any pillion passengers must wear helmets. Infants weighing under 10kg must be strapped into a rear-facing secured approved seat: toddlers weighing 10–18kg must be strapped into an appropriate forward-facing child's seat. Children over 18kg, but under 145cm, must use a booster seat. Those hiring cars can request these seats to be included at extra cost: I've found it easier to take them with me from the UK.

Speed limits are generally 100km/h on the Trans Canada Highway and 100-series roads, 80km/h on other highways, 50km/h in cities and towns, and 30km/h when children are present.

The province's highways are patrolled by the Royal Canadian Mounted Police (RCMP) and by air patrol: substantial fines are imposed for violating speed limits.

Be very careful around yellow, old-fashioned school buses: you must stop at least 20 metres from a school bus, on either side of the road, which is loading or unloading passengers (this will be indicated by flashing red lights, or 'stop flags' on the side of the bus). Do not proceed until the lights are switched off, or flags lifted.

When driving in towns and cities, take great care when you see pedestrians anywhere near the kerb: it is compulsory to stop for pedestrians at a crosswalk (like a zebra crossing but without the Belisha beacons), and some pedestrians have become so used to courteous local drivers stopping and waving them across the road that they may step out into the road without looking.

You must stop completely at a stop sign (traffic police aren't impressed by 'rolling stops'), but – unless signs say otherwise – you are permitted to turn right at a red traffic light, having first stopped and checked that it is safe to do so. When turning left at a junction, turn in front of a car coming from the opposite direction which is also turning left.

In an emergency, pull as far away from the driving lanes as possible, and switch on your hazard lights. If you are involved in a collision, within 24 hours you must notify the RCMP, local police, or the Registry of Motor Vehicles if the accident involves injury, death or damage of more than CAN$1,000.

Authorities in Nova Scotia regard drinking and driving (with a blood-alcohol level of 0.08% or higher), or driving whilst under the influence of drugs, as very serious offences. You could be imprisoned for up to five years even on a first offence.

For further information, see the provincial government-produced *Nova Scotia Driver's Handbook*, downloadable at www.gov.ns.ca/snsmr/rmv/handbook/.

Insurance for US drivers If you are driving your vehicle in Nova Scotia, proof of auto insurance is required. US auto insurance is accepted as long as you are visiting as a tourist. US insurance firms will issue a Canadian insurance card, which should be obtained prior to departure from the US and carried with you when driving in Nova Scotia. You may also be asked to prove vehicle ownership, so it is wise to carry your vehicle registration form.

Car hire Most visitors driving in Nova Scotia will need to hire (or rent) a vehicle. You will need to be 21 or over: most rental companies apply a Young Driver Surcharge for under 25s, present a passport, full driving licence, and – even if you have pre-paid for your vehicle hire – will be asked for a credit card to cover any incidental charges.

All major car-hire companies have outlets at Halifax International Airport and in (or close to) downtown Halifax. For other locations, see below. Most companies will allow you to pick-up in downtown Halifax and drop-off at Halifax International Airport at no extra cost. If, however, you want to pick-up in Halifax and drop-off in, say, Sydney, check for one-way rental surcharges.

When comparing prices, there are numerous factors to take into consideration: check inclusions and exclusions, extra driver charges if more than one of you will take the wheel, taxes and more. All-inclusive pre-paid rates, especially when booked via the internet, are often the best value. Using an internet car broker (eg: *www.carhireexpress.co.uk*, *www.carhire4less.co.uk* or *www.easycar.com*) can save a lot of searching time. Major rental companies (and locations of their depots) include:

Avis ✎ 0844 581 8181; www.avis.co.uk. Halifax & airport, Dartmouth, New Glasgow, Sydney, Bridgewater & Yarmouth.
Budget ✎ 0844 581 2231; www.budget.co.uk. Halifax & airport, Dartmouth, Sydney & Truro.
Dollar ✎ 0800 252 897; www.dollar.co.uk. Halifax & airport.

Enterprise ✎ 0870 350 3000; www.enterprise.co.uk. Halifax & airport, Dartmouth, New Glasgow, Sydney, Bridgewater, Yarmouth, Amherst, Antigonish, Barrington, Lower Sackville, Middleton & New Minas.
Hertz ✎ 0870 844 8844; www.hertz.co.uk. Halifax & airport, Bridgewater, Westville (near Stellarton).
National ✎ 0870 599 4000; www.nationalcar.co.uk. Halifax & airport, Truro, Port Hawkesbury & Sydney.

Tour operators are also worth checking: in the past, I've found **netflights.com** (✎ *0800 747 0000; www.netflights.com*), **Expedia** (*www.expedia.co.uk*) and **Canadian Affair** (✎ *020 7616 9184; www.canadianaffair.com*) to be competitive.

Motorhome rental Another option is to hire a motorhome (campervan) or RV (recreational vehicle) as they're often known in North America. You can then

DAILY ACADIAN COACH SERVICES TO THE NORTH AND EAST

Departure Town Stops	Halifax	Halifax	Halifax	Halifax
	Dartmouth	Dartmouth	Dartmouth	Dartmouth
	Halifax Airport	Halifax Airport	Halifax Airport	Halifax Airport
	Truro	Truro	Truro	Truro
	Amherst	New Glasgow	Antigonish	Wentworth
	New Brunswick	Antigonish		Oxford
		Port Hawkesbury		Springhill
		St Peters		Amherst
		Big Pond		New Brunswick
		Sydney		

Departure Town Stops	Halifax	Halifax	Halifax	Halifax
	Dartmouth	Dartmouth	Dartmouth	Dartmouth
	Halifax Airport	Halifax Airport	Halifax Airport	Halifax Airport
	Truro	Truro	Truro	Elmsdale
	Truro Station	New Glasgow	Amherst	Stewiacke
	Bible Hill	Antigonish	New Brunswick	Truro
	New Glasgow	Port Hawkesbury		Barneys River
	Antigonish	Whycoco		Antigonish
	Monastery	Baddeck		
	Havre Boucher	North Sydney		
	Aulds Cover	Sydney		
	Port Hawkesbury			
	Whycoco			
	Baddeck			
	North Sydney			
	Sydney River			
	Sydney			

Bus operator	Acadian	Acadian	Acadian	Trius
Departure frequency	(Friday only)	(Daily)	(Daily)	(Daily)
Departure town	Halifax	Halifax	Halifax	Halifax
Stops	Dartmouth	Dartmouth	Dartmouth	Hubbards
	Lower Sackville	Lower Sackville	Lower Sackville	Chester
	Falmouth	Falmouth	Falmouth	Mahone Bay
	Wolfville	Wolfville	Wolfville	Lunenburg
	Kentville	Kentville	Kentville	Bridgewater
			Berwick	Mill Village
			Kingston	Brooklyn
			Middleton	Liverpool
			Bridgetown	Summerville
			Annapolis Royal	Port Mouton
			Cornwallis	Port Joli
			Digby	Shelburne
				Birchtown
				Barrington
				Pubnico
				Argyle
				Tusket
				Yarmouth

reduce costs by sleeping (comfortably) and even cooking in your vehicle. Prices aren't particularly cheap, and there are extras to add. Personally, I think western Canada is better suited to motorhome holidays, but it is something to consider.

Canadream ✆ 435 3276, T/F 1 800 461 7368; www.canadream.com. Bookable through Canadian Affair (see page 34) & based in Dartmouth.

Cruise Canada ✆ 865 0639, T/F 1 800 671 8042; www.cruisecanada.com. Bookable in the UK through Travelpack (see page 34) & based in Upper Sackville.

BY COACH With one exception, long-distance coach (usually called 'bus' in Canada and the US) services in the province are operated by **Acadian Lines** (✆ *T/F 1 800 567 5151; www.smtbus.com*). Typical fares are Halifax–Annapolis Royal, CAN$42 one-way; Halifax–Sydney CAN$76 one-way, CAN$129 return.

Various operators have had a go at a service between Yarmouth and Halifax via the South Shore: at the time of writing this is offered once daily in each direction by Prince Edward Island-based **Trius Tours** (✆ *T/F 1 877 566 1567; www.peisland.com/triustours/line.htm*).

Times have been omitted from the boxes on pages 51 and 52 because they change often; call the bus companies or log onto their websites to check for the latest times.

By the 1840s there was a regular stagecoach service between Halifax and Truro. On leaving Halifax, the coach was pulled by six grey horses. However, this was mainly for show: just a few miles after leaving Halifax, the handsome horses were changed and replaced with (less eye-catching) heavier and more powerful beasts. Strength was needed – the road was often axle-deep in mud.

BY SHUTTLE Shuttle services, usually in comfortable minivans, are another option. Most shuttle operators will also do pick-ups/drop-offs at Halifax International Airport. For services between Halifax International airport and downtown Halifax/Dartmouth, see page 78.

Shuttle services

Between Halifax and Yarmouth (daily service; fare approx CAN$75–85 one-way)

Campbell's Shuttle Service ☎ 742 6101, T/F 1 800 742 6101; www.campbell-shuttle-service.com. Via the South Shore.

Cloud Nine Shuttle ☎ 742 3992, T/F 1 888 805 3335; www.thecloudnineshuttle.com. Via the South Shore.

The Green Shuttle ☎ 749 6295; www.greenshuttle.ca. Usually via the South Shore, in fuel-efficient vehicles.

PAB Shuttle Service ☎ 245 1963, T/F 1 888 283 2222; www.pabshuttle.com. Via the Annapolis Valley.

Between Halifax and Mahone Bay, Lunenburg and Bridgewater (daily service by advance reservation)

Kiwi Kaboodle ☎ 531 5494, T/F 1 866 549 4522; www.novascotiatoursandtravel.com. Halifax–Lunenburg CAN$35 one-way.

Try Town Transit ☎ 521 0855, T/F 1 877 521 0855

Between Digby, Yarmouth and Halifax (daily service by advance reservation)

Kathleen's Shuttle and Tours ☎ 834 2024; www.freewebs.com/digbytoursandshuttle/

Between Halifax and Cape Breton Island

Several operators offer daily shuttles between Halifax and Cape Breton Island, primarily Sydney. A one-way trip between Halifax and Sydney will cost approx CAN$60–80. Most will allow pick-ups and drop-offs at Dartmouth, Halifax Airport, Truro, New Glasgow, Antigonish, Port Hastings, Whycocomagh and Baddeck. These include:

Cape Shuttle Service ☎ 539 8585, T/F 1 800 349 1698; www.capeshuttleservice.com

Cheapway Shuttle Service ☎ T/F 1 877 224 1976

Inverness Shuttle ☎ 945 2000; www.invernessshuttle.com. Connects Halifax, Dartmouth & the airport with Judique, Port Hood, Mabou, Inverness & Margaree 5–6 days a week.

Macleod's Shuttle Service ☎ 862 1551, T/F 1 800 471 7775; www.macleodsshuttleservice.com

Scotia Shuttle ☎ 435 9686, T/F 1 800 898 5883; www.scotiashuttle.com

Various shuttle operators/guides will customise tours for you: try for example Digby-based **Kathleen's Shuttle and Tours** (see above) or Halifax-based **Tall Tale Tours** (☎ *830 9179*).

BY BUS Local public bus services cover the most populated parts of the Halifax Regional Municipality (see page 79), the Cape Breton Regional Municipality (see page 325), and the stretch of the Annapolis Valley between Weymouth and Windsor (see page 190).

BY TRAIN Passenger rail travel is very limited, but possible: six days a week, **VIA Rail** (☎ *T/F 1 888 842 7245; www.viarail.ca*) runs a service between Montreal, Quebec and Halifax, and this stops at Amherst, Springhill Junction and Truro.

BY BIKE Cyclists are permitted on all Nova Scotia's roads, including motorways. Helmets must be worn. When riding at night you must use a white front light and

Salty Bear (\ 404 3636, T/F 1 888 425 2327; www.saltybear.ca) offers tours geared towards the backpacker – similar in many ways to Australia's *OZ Experience* bus service, although its network is far more limited and there are fewer departures. Accommodation is usually in dorms, but upgrades to private rooms can normally be arranged. A two-day tour visits Peggy's Cove, Lunenburg, Annapolis Royal (passing Kejimkujik National Park where you can disembark/embark), Cape Blomidon, and the Wolfville area before returning to Halifax. The five-day tour goes via Antigonish to Cape Breton Island then squashes in a quick visit to the neighbouring province of Prince Edward Island before returning to Halifax. There are regular (twice-weekly) departures, and for even greater flexibility, you can get off somewhere *en route* and then get back on a few days later at no extra cost (apart from accommodation for the extra nights). Trips include free (or optional at extra cost) excursions. Bearing in mind the paucity of public transport in the province, Salty Bear's trips are worth considering both as tours and as an alternative method of transport for the car-less.

a red rear reflector (a rear-facing, flashing red light is acceptable). Reflectors and reflective clothing are also advisable.

Most airlines allow bikes as checked baggage, but will have rules as to how the bike should be packed: a handling fee may also apply. Check and re-check before booking your ticket.

For more on cycling in Nova Scotia, see page 63.

HITCHHIKING Hitchhiking is not allowed on 100-series major (controlled-access) motorways. Whilst chances are that all will go well and that you'll meet some interesting people, climbing into a stranger's vehicle always carries some degree of risk. Police may also pull over and chat to hitchers to check that they are not missing persons or runaways. As in much of the world, hitching isn't as easy (or as safe) as it used to be – and the release in 2007 of a remake of a 1986 film, *The Hitcher*, hasn't helped. Storylines of psychopathic, murderous hitchhikers don't exactly encourage drivers to pick up strangers.

ACCOMMODATION

The province offers a range of places to stay, from wilderness campsites through to deluxe hotels and resorts. Virtually all of these are listed on Nova Scotia's official tourism website (*www.novascotia.com*), and appear in the official annual *Doers' & Dreamers'* guide (see page 36). Outside the biggest urban centres, relatively few properties are open year-round: for most, the season runs mid-May–early October.

HOTELS Halifax and Sydney are home to the big-name (relatively) high-rise hotels. Dotted about the province's shoreline are resorts offering everything from standard rooms to three- or four-bedroom private chalets, and numerous activities, which often include a golf course.

MOTELS Motels range from traditional family-owned single-storey buildings (some of which have seen better days) where you can park right outside the door of your room, to brand-new international chains, often with heated indoor swimming pools.

B&BS For me, one of the joys of travelling around Nova Scotia is its B&Bs and small inns. Several are housed in beautifully renovated historic buildings, many of which are heritage properties, and are tastefully decorated with period(ish) antiques. Despite the historical surroundings, amenities are modern and the plumbing works well. Each property is unique and full of character, and good hosts can quickly recognise whether you want your own space, or whether you'd like to sit, chat and perhaps benefit from their local knowledge. Breakfasts are generally superb. A good place to start looking is the website of the **Nova Scotia Association of Unique Country Inns** (*www.uniquecountryinns.com* or *www.bbcanada.com/nova_scotia*).

Bathrooms can be shared, private or ensuite. Occasionally, the terminology can cause confusion: where a property has a shared bathroom, that bathroom is for the use of the occupants of more than one guestroom; a private bathroom is solely for the use of guests in a particular room, but guests will have to go out of their room and across the corridor or down the hall to the bathroom; if a bathroom is ensuite, you will be able to access your own bathroom by opening a door in your guestroom. All (non-camping) accommodation listed in this book offers ensuite or private bathrooms unless otherwise noted.

Also be aware that some inns and B&B owners have pets and there may be dogs or cats on the premises: check before booking if that might bother you.

HOSTELS AND BACKPACKERS These are somewhat limited. There are Hostelling International (HI) hostels in Halifax (see page 90), at South Milford near Kejimkujik National Park (see page 205), at Wentworth (see page 270) and Aberdeen, Cape Breton Island (see page 321). There are also private hostels in Halifax, near Lunenburg/Mahone Bay (see page 143), at Port Mouton (see page 163), just outside Kejimkujik National Park, in Yarmouth (see page 180), Digby (see page 189), on Brier Island (see page 196), Aberdeen (see page 321) and Pleasant Bay (see page 363) on Cape Breton Island. If there are two (or more) of you, a cheap room in a motel or simple B&B often won't cost much more than a couple of dormitory beds would.

RATING THE RATINGS

In the absence of a standard international rating system for hotels, inns, B&Bs and other accommodation, Canada uses a star system under the auspices of **Canada Select** (*www.canadaselect.com*), administered in Nova Scotia by **Quality Visitor Services** (☎ 406 4747; *www.qvs.ca*). The programme is voluntary in Nova Scotia. Accommodations are divided into six categories (Hotel/Motel, Fishing/Hunting Lodge, Inn, Resort, B&B/Tourist Home, Cottage) with several of these having further subdivisions. Properties are evaluated by an inspector who takes several factors (including facilities, services and amenities provided) into account, and a star rating from 1 to 5, in ½-star increments is awarded.

All that is well and good for many of the types of accommodation, but doesn't work very well for B&Bs and inns. Under the rating system for B&Bs, an establishment that chooses to have a TV in a lounge (rather than in each guestroom) drops one star immediately. If it decides not to have a phone in every guestroom, another star disappears. Many people spend a couple of nights at a five-star-rated B&B or inn, then transfer to a three-star and are surprised to find it a lot better. In my mind, the system focuses too heavily on facilities/amenities offered, too lightly on individuality, ambience, charm, service, and quality, and not at all on comfort or the hospitality offered by the hosts. A number of inn and B&B owners agree, and – rather than receive a lower star rating based on a checklist of amenities – have withdrawn from the Canada Select programme. So don't rush to select or omit a property based just on its star rating (or lack thereof).

CAMPING If you're looking to spend your nights under canvas – well, nylon – Nova Scotia has both province-run and privately owned campgrounds. The former are in the two national parks (see page 27) and over 20 provincial parks (see *www.novascotiaparks.ca*) – but note that many provincial parks close in early September. There are about 120 privately owned campgrounds, over 70 of which are listed on the **Campground Owners Association of Nova Scotia** website (*www.campingnovascotia.com*). In addition to standard sites, many campgrounds have serviced sites where those with motorhomes can hook up to water, electricity and a sewer. At the other end of the scale, there are also opportunities for wilderness or back-country camping.

High season (with the highest prices) is July and early–mid-September, but advance reservations are recommended for stays between late June and the end of September (and during the Celtic Colours Festival in Cape Breton in October). Outside these dates, festivals apart, you should be able to find something in the area. If you're stuck, **Check In Nova Scotia** (❧ *T/F 1 800 565 0000; www.checkinnovascotia.com*) is the government-run accommodation reservation service and provides access to over 700 hotels, motels, inns, B&Bs and campgrounds throughout the province. Unless stated otherwise, the prices quoted in this book are high-season rates for a single night's stay in a room for two people. Many properties offer significantly cheaper rates out of season: others may give discounts for stays of more than a couple of nights. In my opinion, it is always worth asking about discounts – they are sometimes given to students, seniors, automobile association members, those wanting more than one room, etc – but don't expect any reductions in high season.

RENTALS Those looking for more space will find a variety of places to rent, from studio apartments to large multi-bedroom houses. Confusingly, these are often referred to as housekeeping units, vacation homes or cottages. They will have equipped kitchens or kitchenettes, and towels and bedding will be provided. How well equipped they are varies from place to place. Often a minimum rental of three or more nights applies, and in summer a minimum of a week is the norm, usually starting on a Saturday.

Many are marketed by **Cottage Connection** (❧ *634 7274, T/F 1 800 780 3682; www.stayinnovascotia.com*). Also try **Sandy Lane Vacations** (❧ *875 2729, T/F 1 800 646 1577; www.sandylanevacations.com*) who focus on the South Shore west of Bridgewater.

HOMESTAYS WITH THE MI'KMAQ As yet, there are no organized programs for those who wish to stay overnight (or longer) with a Mi'kmaq family. However, it may be possible to arrange homestays on an *ad hoc* basis by contacting either the **Bear River First Nation Heritage and Cultural Centre** (see page 199) or the **Wagmatcook Culture and Heritage Centre** (see page 321).

✖ EATING AND DRINKING

William Deer, who lives here, keeps the best of wine and beer, brandy, and cider, and other good cheer. Fish, and ducks, and moose and deer, caught or shot in the woods near here, with cutlets, or steaks, as will appear; If you will stop you need not fear But you will be well treated by William Deer, And by Mrs Deer, his dearest, deary dear!

Sign outside an inn in Preston, Nova Scotia, in the 1850s

FOOD Visitors who enjoy seafood will be in gastronomic nirvana everywhere in Nova Scotia. The price may have crept up over the years, but fish (usually haddock) and chips is almost always done well, freshly cooked and not too greasy. You'll also see a lot of flounder, halibut and salmon: plank (or planked) salmon – where the fish is slow-cooked on a wood (usually cedar) plank – is a highlight.

Then there's the shellfish. Top of the pile is lobster – Nova Scotia is the world's largest exporter of the crustacean, but more than enough remains to grace menus throughout the province. It is usually steamed or boiled in sea water, then served with butter – fancier methods of presentation, such as lobster thermidor or lobster Newburg, are seen less often. The larger supermarkets often have glass lobster tanks – at Sobeys stores (see page 61) you can choose a lobster and have it cooked while you wait, at no extra cost.

But the province's waters offer other treats, too. Enjoy some of the world's most delicious scallops, plus tasty mussels, oysters, crab and clams. Seafood chowder (a thick, chunky creamy seafood soup) can be a meal in itself.

Those who choose not to eat, or want a change from, seafood need not worry. You will usually find a reasonable selection of lamb, chicken, turkey and beef

RESTAURANT PRICE CODES

Restaurant listings are laid out in decreasing price order, under the following categories: Luxury, Upmarket, Mid-range and Budget. The following key (also on the inside front cover) gives an indication of prices. Prices are based on the cost of a main meal (including tax) per person.

$$$$	CAN$35+
$$$	CAN$23–34
$$	CAN$13–22
$	< CAN$13

Practical Information EATING AND DRINKING

2

The province's earliest European settlers left a gastronomic legacy that still lives on. Order Solomon Gundy and you'll be presented with pickled herring; fiddleheads are the unfurled fronds of ostrich ferns, delicious steamed and served with a squeeze of lemon juice and a dab of butter. Dulse is dried, purple seaweed, usually nibbled as a snack. Lunenburg pudding is a kind of meat-based paté. Blueberry grunt is a much-loved summer dessert. Although many dishes focus on seafood, there are several to look out for which are land-based: *chicken fricot* (stew), *tourtiere* (meat pie), *pâte à la rapure* (often called 'rappie pie') and butterscotch pie. Particularly popular with the junk-food crowd are *donair* (a Nova Scotia version of the doner kebab) and *poutine* – chips (fries) topped with cheese curds and brown gravy. Taste buds tingling yet?

SOLOMON GUNDY
Ingredients
6 salt herring (heads and tails removed, cleaned, skinned and deboned)
3 medium onions thinly sliced
2 cups vinegar
2 tablespoons pickling spice
½ cup caster sugar

Directions Cut the herring into approximately 2cm pieces and soak for 24 hours in cold water. Squeeze the water from the herring. Place in jar with slices of onion, in alternate layers. Heat vinegar, pickling spice and sugar, stirring. Allow to cool, pour into jar. Seal jar and keep in fridge for 8–10 days.

BLUEBERRY GRUNT
Fruit mix ingredients
4 cups blueberries
⅔ cup caster sugar
½ cup water
1 tablespoon lemon juice

Dumpling ingredients
2 cups plain flour
4 teaspoons baking powder
1 tablespoon caster sugar
½ teaspoon salt
2 tablespoon butter
Milk

Directions Combine fruit mix ingredients and bring to a boil in a large saucepan. Reduce heat and simmer until berries are soft and sauce begins to thicken, about 5 minutes. Sift flour, baking powder, sugar and salt into a bowl. Cut in butter and stir in just enough milk to make a soft dough. Mix well, then drop spoonfuls of batter onto the simmering berry sauce. Immediately cover saucepan and simmer without removing cover for 15 minutes. Serve warm with whipped cream.

dishes. Upmarket steak restaurants tend to use beef flown in from Alberta, Canada, or the US.

In the summer and autumn, fruit is fresh and plentiful, and apples and blueberries in particular make their way on to many menus – and not just in the dessert section. For example, apple sauce is a perfect accompaniment to roast pork, whilst blueberry sauce works well with red meat.

Outside Halifax and Dartmouth, the university towns of Wolfville and Antigonish, and places that attract a high number of visitors, the majority of restaurateurs still seem to care little about their restaurant's aesthetics or their food's cholesterol levels. Less than a decade ago, those who wanted to avoid deep-fried food were looked upon with bewilderment.

The good news is that recent years have seen some changes. Driven by a combination of factors – the theory of healthy eating slowly filtering through to Nova Scotia, the culinary wishes expressed by visitors, and an increase in new restaurateurs from outside the province – many more establishments have done away with the deep-fryer and use fresh, often organic, locally grown produce. Thought is given to the look of the establishment's interior, and food presentation, and the menus themselves are more varied and creative. Many of the old-style eateries have now begun to join the revolution and will now grill (or at least) pan-fry fish for you – although this may add a dollar or two to the price.

Those who prefer fast and/or junk food need not worry: McDonald's (where the summer menu usually includes a McLobster roll!), KFC, Subway, Dairy Queen, Taco Bell and many other burger chains are well represented, and there are countless pizza joints and take-aways.

Look, too, beyond traditional restaurants, cafés, dining rooms and bistros: community breakfasts and suppers may not offer *haute cuisine* but are almost always excellent value and a great way to meet (and chat to) the locals. Farmers' markets and supermarket deli counters are good places to put a picnic together, and – in season – you can pick your own fresh berries for dessert.

Bear in mind, too, that away from the capital, some of the province's best eateries are actually inn restaurants.

Vegetarians Whilst vegetarian restaurants are few and far between, vegetarian choices are usually offered, although they may not be more exciting than pasta or pizza. In general, the new-wave, more sophisticated cafés, bistros and restaurants will be more vegetarian-friendly.

DRINK You'll find big-name Canadian and American beers everywhere, but even more popular are Nova Scotia-produced brands. Best known (and ubiquitous) is Keith's, but beer fans should also look out for Propeller (ESB and London-style porter are good), Granite (try Peculiar) and Garrison (try Irish Red Ale and Raspberry Wheat), all based in Halifax. There are also a few brewpubs dotted around, for example Rudder's in Yarmouth (see page 184), Paddy's Pub in

---

THE NOBLE GRAPE

In recent years, the province has been climbing a few rungs up the serious wine-producer ladder. Longest established are Domaine de Grand Pré (see page 225) and Jost Vineyards (see page 268).

Nova Scotia excels at crisp, refreshing white wines such as L'Acadie Blanc and Seyval Blanc, and both are terrific with the local fresh seafood. Rich reds such as Marechal Foch and Baco Noir also have great potential as local vintners discover how to get the best from local soils and climate.

Oenophiles may wish to subscribe (free) to Canada's best wine e-newsletter (*www.nataliemaclean.com*). Its author, sommelier and award-winning wine writer Natalie MacLean, believes that the provincial wines now compete on the world stage in terms of quality, but adds that their production is still too small for widespread national or international distribution.

A good time for wine aficionados to visit the province is early September to late October, to tie in with the six-week 'Discover the Wines of Nova Scotia Tour'. For details see the website www.winesofnovascotia.ca.

Practical Information EATING AND DRINKING

2

59

Kentville (see page 215) and Wolfville (see page 218), and the Rare Bird in Guysborough (see page 367).

Another tipple that you should sample is Glen Breton Rare Canadian Single Malt Whisky, distilled on Cape Breton Island (see page 297).

With an abundance of delicious apples, you won't be surprised to hear that very good cider is produced locally. Visitors from the UK may get a surprise when they taste it though: unless called hard cider, it will be nothing stronger than sweet, refreshing apple juice.

The legal drinking age is 19 years. Accompanied children and those under 19 are allowed in licensed restaurants and pubs up to 21.00. Whilst it is generally not as bad as the US (where I – three decades over the minimum drinking age – have often been asked for photo ID to confirm I'm legal to drink), but if you are (or look) young, you may be asked to prove it.

With a few exceptions (eg: vineyard shops) alcohol is only sold at government-licensed liquor stores (see page 61).

A recent change in the provincial law means that licensed restaurants are allowed to operate a 'bring your own wine' policy: some have taken up the opportunity, but many of these charge outrageously for corkage – CAN$25 (or higher) per bottle is not unknown. Licensed restaurants can serve alcoholic drinks from 10.00 to 02.00 daily.

PUBLIC HOLIDAYS AND FESTIVALS

Nova Scotia's calendar has long been packed with all manner of festivals (especially between late spring and autumn) celebrating the province's music, food, arts, heritage, history and more. In fact, Nova Scotia likes the tag 'Canada's Official Festival Province'. In recent years, more festivals have been added, and attempts have been made to hold some of these in traditional off-season periods.

Information on the best regional festivals and events is included under the relevant regional section. The following public holidays are celebrated annually (note that many businesses and shops may close on these days).

1 January	New Year's Day
March/April	Good Friday
March/April	Easter Monday
May	Victoria Day (the Monday preceding 25 May)
1 July	Canada Day

TARTAN TALE

In preparation for an agricultural show in 1953, Bessie Murray, a talented weaver (born in Crewe, England), was asked to make a wall panel depicting the history of sheep rearing in the province. She included a Scottish shepherd in her mural, and dreamt up a new tartan for his kilt. Inspiration came from her memories of the natural colours of the sea, forest and granite outcrops at the coastal community of Terence Bay (see page 125). So much interest was generated by the tiny kilt that Bessie and a friend started a company and began to produce the design on cloth in greater quantities.

Her tartan was officially adopted by the province in 1955, the first provincial tartan in Canada: manufacture and sale of the tartan is now covered by the Nova Scotia Tartan Act and Nova Scotia tartan-makers must be licensed by the government.

August	Natal Day (first Monday in August)
September	Labour Day (first Monday in September)
October	Thanksgiving Day (second Monday in October)
11 November	Remembrance Day
25 December	Christmas Day
26 December	Boxing Day

 SHOPPING

Popular gifts or souvenirs include locally produced wine, especially ice wine (see page 270), whisky (see page 297), maple syrup, Nova Scotia tartan, and all manner of arts and crafts. Recent years have seen a boom in the quantity and quality of artists and artisans in the province. So in addition to cuddly moose, whales and red plastic lobsters all mass-produced in factories on the other side of the world, visitors can take home a locally made individually crafted work of art.

ANTIQUES You'll also see plenty of antique shops – plus those that cross the line that divides antiques and junk. If you are interested in the former, you may find the website www.antiquesnovascotia.com of interest. Yard sales are very popular on weekends between spring and autumn: some are advertised in provincial papers, but in most cases just by hand-written fluorescent signs stuck up around the relevant town or village giving the address and time of the sale. These vary from a family clear-out held in an attempt to earn a few dollars for what they would otherwise throw out, to the disposal of the entire contents of an impressive, well-furnished old house. They can be rich hunting grounds or a waste of time. Get there early for the best stuff.

FOOD SHOPPING For food shopping, self-caterers will probably look to stock up at the huge supermarkets, Atlantic Superstore (*www.superstore.ca/east/*) and Sobeys (*www.sobeys.com*). In general, these are open 07.30–22.00 Monday–Saturday, 10.00–17.00 Sunday, but check specific store hours for early mornings and late evenings. There are also smaller chains (such as Foodland), and a seemingly ever-decreasing number of general stores. Farmers' markets – usually held one morning a week – are well worth visiting, not just for fresh local produce and baked goods, but often too for arts and crafts. Some of the best include those at Halifax (see page 102), Hubbards (see page 133) Wolfville (see page 223) and Annapolis Royal (see page 205).

The summer offers numerous U-pick ('pick-your-own') fruit possibilities.

With a few exceptions (eg: vineyard shops) alcohol is only sold at government-licensed liquor, beer and wine stores – and only to persons aged 19 and above, expect to be asked for photo ID if you're under 40! A list of all Nova Scotia Liquor Commission (NSLC) stores and their opening hours – usually 10.00–21.00 Monday–Saturday, 12.00–17.00 Sunday – can be seen at the 'find a store' section of the website www.thenslc.com.

SHOPPING MALLS Many people head out to the big malls to do their shopping. Apart from plenty of free parking and convenience, these tend to stay open later than downtown shops. Alongside the malls you'll usually find big 'box' stores (such as Canadian Tire and Wal-Mart). With about a dozen locations province-wide, Zellers (*www.zellers.com*) is a popular department store.

For the last few years, Sunday shopping has been legal (though in general it is mainly supermarkets and big mall stores that open on Sundays).

Remember that in most cases, 13% tax will be added to prices (see page 46).

SOUVENIR GOODS Studios and galleries are to be found all over the province, but some areas and communities, such as Bear River (see page 197) and North River on Cape Breton Island (see page 312) are particularly popular with creative types. Often you'll be able to watch artisans creating pottery, working glass, carving wood or painting. A piece of whimsical folk art, a stained-glass sun-catcher, a handcrafted walking stick, or a hooked rug, all make excellent presents or keepsakes. In tourist offices, look out for the (free) Studio Map: produced annually, it lists art and craft studios and galleries all over the province and can also be viewed at www.studiorally.ca.

ARTS AND ENTERTAINMENT

CINEMA The province has just 14 cinemas, all owned by Empire Theatres (*www.empiretheatres.com*), many of which are in and around Halifax. In many towns, films are screened from time to time in theatres or community/cultural centres.

Before films can be screened, they have to be made: Halifax – home to the ten-day Atlantic Film Festival (see page 82) – is the hub of east coast Canada's film industry. Film-making contributes about CAN$100 million annually to the province's economy and employs close to 2,000 people. Film Nova Scotia (\ *424 7177, T/F 1 888 360 2111; www.film.ns.ca*) is the starting point for those wanting to learn more.

MUSEUMS Nova Scotia has well over 100 museums, ranging from little one-room schoolhouses to the Nova Scotia Museum of Industry (see page 280), one of the biggest museums in Atlantic Canada. Many are themed, with subjects covering for example fishing, mining, lighthouses, Acadian history, the Age of Sail, or individuals such as country singer Hank Snow. Popular too are the 'living museums', staffed by costumed interpreters who demonstrate the almost-forgotten skills of the blacksmith, the wool carder, the potter, the wooden boatbuilder and the lobster plug carver.

A total of 27 of the province's museums make up the diverse family of the Nova Scotia Museum (*www.museum.gov.ns.ca*): admission at each varies from CAN$2 to CAN$9. A pass is available covering admission to all 27 museums for CAN$42. At many other of the museums, often community-run and staffed by volunteers, entrance is free, but donations are welcomed.

NIGHTLIFE Nightlife is best in Halifax and environs, and to a far lesser degree Sydney and the university towns of Wolfville and Antigonish. Other than that, you're probably looking at pubs and bars, a disco (if you're very lucky), or stargazing.

THEATRE During their time at Port-Royal (see page 210), one of the French party, lawyer, author and explorer Marc Lescarbot , wrote a play. *Le Theatre de Neptune* had its world première when performed in the shallows between ships and shore in 1607. This was the first recorded dramatic production in Canada. Lescarbot was something of a poet, and in addition wrote at least once weekly on events at the Habitation (see page 210). On this basis, it is said that Canadian drama, verse and prose were first created at Port Royal.

Theatre still plays a big part in the province's arts scene: Halifax, Liverpool, Wolfville and Antigonish are some of the places with annual theatre festivals: calendars of events at theatres in many other communities mix performing arts with film screenings.

CANOEING AND RIVER KAYAKING An abundance of unspoilt (almost untouched) wilderness, lakes, ponds and rivers draw those wishing to explore the inland waters by canoe or kayak. In season, various commercial operators offer hourly rentals: to venture into the back country on a multi-day trip, it is worth consulting a specialist outfit such as **Hinterland Adventures** (🕿 *837 4092, T/F 1 800 378 8177; www.kayakingnovascotia.com*).

CYCLING A good network of largely empty roads and (northern Cape Breton Island apart) low hills means wonderful cycling opportunities. In addition to magnificent and varied coastal scenery, there are fertile valleys and many historic towns to explore.

Either build an itinerary around one of the province's scenic trails or base yourself somewhere such as Hubbards, Lunenburg, Yarmouth, or Wolfville for a few days, head out on day trips and return each evening to your accommodation.

Hundreds of old logging and mining roads and long-forgotten centuries-old footpaths cover much of rural Nova Scotia and provide excellent possibilities for mountain biking.

A few shops and companies around the province hire out road and mountain bikes for anything from an hour or two, allowing you to potter around the local area. These are listed in the following chapters. See also *Getting around, By bike*, page 54.

DIVING The waters around Nova Scotia offer some of the best cold-water wreck diving places in the world (you'll need either a drysuit, or a warm wetsuit). Most diving is done in the summer months, when the winds are down and the water is at its warmest. A few hardy locals dive year-round.

The Atlantic Ocean and the Gulf of St Lawrence offer particularly good underwater visibility and the waters are home to a great variety of marine life and an incredible collection of shipwrecks.

There are a number of diving shops in Halifax/Dartmouth and elsewhere, of which the best is probably **Torpedo Rays** (*625 Windmill Rd, Dartmouth;* 🕿 *481 0444, T/F 1 877 255 3483; www.torpedorays.com*).

FISHING Deep-sea fishing tours in search of blue shark, or the increasingly rare bluefin tuna, are easily arranged on licensed charter boats berthed at many of the province's harbours.

Freshwater anglers try for brook, rainbow and brown trout, Atlantic whitefish, yellow perch, shad, smallmouth bass and – the once-mighty – Atlantic salmon. For much of the past two decades, salmon numbers have been dropping towards critical levels. For more on Atlantic salmon and trout fishing in the province, see the **Nova Scotia Salmon Association's** website (*www.novascotiasalmon.ns.ca*).

If you are thinking of fishing whilst in the province, get clued up on fishing regulations via the **Department of Fisheries and Aquaculture** website (*www.gov.ns.ca/fish/*), where you'll also find a list of fishing guides.

GEOCACHING Geocaching (*www.geocachingnovascotia.ca*) – a type of treasure hunt game using a Global Positioning System (GPS) device – is quite popular in the province. The idea is to find a treasure or cache placed in a specific location using only GPS co-ordinates. Tales of buried treasure abound in the province, and there have been a handful of finds over the centuries. However, I have decided to leave 'metal detector' off the 'what to take' list.

GOLF Nova Scotia now has over 80 golf courses including world-renowned Highland Links (see page 311) and Bell Bay (see page 319), both on Cape Breton Island. Depending on their location, and the weather, the season can start as early as April and run to the end of October. Compared with many places, green fees are very reasonable.

Golf Nova Scotia (\ T/F *1 800 565 0000; www.golfnovascotia.com*) markets over 20 of the province's well-regarded courses, publishes a guide to golf in Nova Scotia, and offers stay-and-play packages.

HIKING AND WALKING With fabulous varied coastal and mountain scenery, inland valleys, pristine rivers, dozens of lakes and waterfalls, wild flowers and abundant wildlife, Nova Scotia is a delight for the hiker.

The trails of the Cape Breton Highlands National Park (see page 303) are justifiably popular, but so many more areas are wonderful to explore on foot. Also on Cape Breton Island, there are a number of superb hikes in the Mabou area (see page 295), whilst on the 'mainland', Cape Chignecto Provincial Park (see page 254) and the Cape Split Trail (see page 217) are hiking highlights. Several sections of the province's old disused railway lines have been converted to multi-use trails.

RAFTING Whilst you won't find organised white-water rafting here, Nova Scotia offers a unique alternative. Several commercial operators take raftloads of (soft) adventure-seekers onto the Shubenacadie River to ride the tidal bore (see page 237).

ROCKHOUNDING The richest areas for rockhounding – looking for rocks, semi-precious stones and minerals in their natural environment – are the beaches of the Minas Basin and the Bay of Fundy. In fact, the annual Gem and Mineral Show, held in August in Parrsboro (see page 250) used to be called the Rockhound Roundup. The region's extreme tides erode cliff faces that may contain jasper, amethyst, agates, zeolites and more, sometimes depositing the semi-precious stones in amongst the other pebbles.

SAILING The waters of Nova Scotia are actively used by a 40,000-vessel fishery and a range of commercial and military vessels. However, the density of boats is low and few spots are busy or crowded. Even in relatively busy harbours and bays, sailors can quickly get away to pristine waters, uninhabited islands and secluded anchorages.

The vast Bras d'Or Lake of Cape Breton Island is a renowned cruising destination for larger sailboats and mega-yachts because of its beauty and its accessibility (north and south) from the ocean. Other noted cruising destinations include Mahone Bay, St Margaret's Bay and Halifax Harbour.

Nova Scotia is still one of the best-kept secrets for sailors, whether out for a day or a cruising adventure.

Whilst there are very few, if any, Nova Scotia businesses that offer bareboat (where you skipper and crew the yacht) charters, sailing and cruising training is readily available. A full range of courses with certified instructors is offered by the **Nova Scotia Yachting Association** (*www.nsya.ns.ca*) lasting from a few hours to a week. Try, for example, **Sou'Wester Adventures** (\ *627 4004, T/F 1 877 665 4004; www.souwesteradventures.com*).

SEA KAYAKING with *Dr Scott Cunningham* (**e** *info@coastaladventures.com; www.coastaladventures.com*) Sea kayaking has become increasingly popular in recent years and Nova Scotia, with its countless harbours and headlands, inlets and islands, offers a world-class destination. The meandering shoreline is extensive, access is easy and the contrasts are exceptional. There is something for paddlers of every taste and skill level. You will find protected day trips for the beginner as well as challenging multi-day routes, and everything in between. And thousands of kilometres of coastline means that you can explore all this in relative solitude.

My favourite realm, and my home, is along the rugged Eastern Shore, where an isolated band of islands stretches from Clam Harbour to Canso. This forgotten wilderness forms a compelling mix of natural and human history. Some of these outposts are just tiny specks, scarcely breathing air at high water, while others are huge forest-covered expanses that dominate the horizon, and beckon to the inquisitive traveller. Explore abandoned lighthouses and shipwrecks, uncover those vanishing signs of our own transient history, or camp on a deserted isle where your only companions are the seals and the seabirds, far from the summer bustle. Tangier is an ideal place from which to start. On the other side of Halifax, the South Shore offers dozens of places to put in and explore, especially the Kejimkujik Seaside, the LaHave Islands, Blue Rocks, and Prospect. Even Halifax, with its eclectic waterfront and harbour islands, merits a visit by kayak.

Further north, on Cape Breton Island, the majestic Highlands rising abruptly from the Gulf of St Lawrence are particularly imposing when viewed from the perspective of a sea kayak. Sea spires, caves and a colourful geology decorate the perimeter, while the Cabot Trail winds out of sight and sound far above. Rich deciduous valleys alternate with barren vertical cliffs, washed by waterfalls and you will certainly spot bald eagles and seals. If lucky you will also paddle with the whales, as I have done many a time. By midsummer the water can warm up considerably, to 20°C, but this is an open coast and experience is advised.

The Bay of Fundy is perhaps the most distinctive region. The highest tides ever recorded on earth wash these shores, sculpting cliffs and inundating massive salt marshes and mud banks with surprising speed. Experience here is essential. Cape Chignecto's long and rich geological history has resulted in a striking melange of colours, textures and forms. The abrupt cliffs, numerous pinnacles and sea caves, combine with tides exceeding 40ft to create a spectacular land/seascape.

If you arrive early in the season when the Atlantic coast may be draped in fog (the best times are early July to October), or if the Highlands and the Fundy are too exposed for your taste, you should try the province's Northumberland Strait shore where you will be treated to the warmest salt water north of the Carolinas. Fog has been banned, and the miles of sandy shores and salt-marsh estuaries offer protected paddling for the entire family. Kayakers are not the only ones who enjoy

TALLY-HO

Be aware that hunting is legal in Nova Scotia, and enjoyed by many. To avoid being mistaken for a black bear, moose or white-tailed deer, wear something brightly coloured if you go walking in the woods between September and mid-December.

Hunting is regulated by the provincial government's Department of Natural Resources (*www.gov.ns.ca/natr/hunt/default.htm*). The following operators all organise hunting trips:

Bears East Adventures ✎ 252 2287; www.geocities.com/bearseastadventures/. On St Mary's River near Sherbrooke (Eastern Shore).
Free Spirit Guide Services ✎ 657 3814; www.klickns.com/guide web files/guideservice.html. Near Tatamagouche & Wallace, Northumberland Strait.
Paradise Kayaks Tours ✎ 733 3244; www.paradisekayaks.com. Based in southeastern Cape Breton Island.

soaking up a few summer rays and this shore has become a mecca for the vacation crowd. However, secluded corners can still be found.

There are many other exciting areas of our coastline to entice you and your sea kayak. A comprehensive guide, *Sea Kayaking in Nova Scotia*, available at most bookstores, will help with detailed descriptions of over 40 routes. Bring your own boat and paddle on your own, or accompany a local outfit who can introduce you to the biology, geology, and human history of this fascinating environment where the land meets the sea. Happy paddling!

SKATING There are ice rinks all over the province, but the majority are only open between late autumn and early spring. Unfortunately, very few offer ice-skate hire. Many locals prefer outdoor skating (on frozen ponds and lakes) to arena rinks.

SKIING AND SNOWBOARDING Winter visitors do have some opportunities to strap on the skis (or a snowboard) and take to the slopes. Whilst vertical rises don't break any records, rentals and lift passes are cheap, and the resort staff – and other skiers – friendly.

PHOTOGRAPHIC TIPS
Ariadne Van Zandbergen

EQUIPMENT Although with some thought and an eye for composition you can take reasonable photos with a 'point and shoot' camera, you need an SLR camera with one or more lenses if you are at all serious about photography. The most important component in a digital SLR is the sensor. There are two types of sensor: DX and FX. The FX is a full size sensor identical to the old film size (36mm). The DX sensor is half size and produces less quality. Your choice of lenses will be determined by whether you have a DX or FX sensor in your camera as the DX sensor introduces a 0.5x multiplication to the focal length. So a 300mm lens becomes in effect a 450mm lens. FX ('full frame') sensors are the future, so I will further refer to focal lengths appropriate to the FX sensor.

Always buy the best lens you can afford. Fixed fast lenses are ideal, but very costly. Zoom lenses are easier to change composition without changing lenses the whole time. If you carry only one lens a 24–70mm or similar zoom should be ideal. For a second lens, a lightweight 80–200mm or 70–300mm or similar will be excellent for candid shots and varying your composition. Wildlife photography will be very frustrating if you don't have at least a 300mm lens. For a small loss of quality, teleconverters are a cheap and compact way to increase magnification: a 300 lens with a 1.4x converter becomes 420mm, and with a 2x it becomes 600mm. NB 1.4x and 2x teleconverters reduce the speed of your lens by 1.4 and 2 stops respectively.

The resolution of digital cameras is improving the whole time. For ordinary prints a 6-megapixel camera is fine. For better results and the possibility to enlarge images and for professional reproduction, higher resolution is available up to 21 megapixels.

It is important to have enough memory space when photographing on your holiday. The number of pictures you can fit on a card depends on the quality you choose. You should calculate how many pictures you can fit on a card and either take enough cards or take a storage drive onto which you can download the cards' content. You can obviously take a laptop which gives the advantage that you can see your pictures properly at the end of each day and edit and delete rejects. If you don't want the extra bulk and weight you can buy a storage device which can read memory cards. These drives come in different capacities.

Keep in mind that digital camera batteries, computers and other storage devices need charging. Make sure you have all the chargers, cables, converters with you. Most hotels/lodges have charging points, but it will be best to enquire about this in advance. When camping you might have to rely on charging from the car battery.

The main downhill resorts are Ski Martock (see page 229) near Windsor, Ski Wentworth (see page 270) between Truro and Amherst, and Cape Smokey (see page 311) and Ski Ben Eoin (see page 325), both on Cape Breton Island. Cross-country skiing is widespread, and snowmobiles are popular for whizzing across the white stuff.

SURFING AND WINDSURFING Nova Scotia ain't Hawaii (at least in terms of weather), but adventure-loving locals – and a few visitors – love to slip into a wetsuit and climb onto a board year-round. The most popular base for surfers is Lawrencetown (see page 346) on the Eastern Shore. In general, the waves are best between September and May.

(MEDIA AND COMMUNICATIONS

PRINT The province's leading newspaper is the independently owned *Chronicle Herald*, which first appeared in 1875. Daily circulation is now close to 115,000, and the Sunday version, the *Sunday Herald*, sells about 80,000 copies. In general, editorial policy tends to be moderate conservative.

DUST AND HEAT Dust and heat are often a problem. Keep your equipment in a sealed bag, and avoid exposing equipment to the sun when possible. Digital cameras are prone to collecting dust particles on the sensor which results in spots on the image. The dirt mostly enters the camera when changing lenses, so you should be careful when doing this. To some extent photos can be 'cleaned' up afterwards in Photoshop, but this is time-consuming. You can have your camera sensor professionally cleaned, or you can do this yourself with special brushes and swabs made for this purpose, but note that touching the sensor might cause damage and should only be done with the greatest care.

LIGHT The most striking outdoor photographs are often taken during the hour or two of 'golden light' after dawn and before sunset. Shooting in low light may enforce the use of very low shutter speeds, in which case a tripod/beanbag will be required to avoid camera shake. The most advanced digital SLRs have very little loss of quality on higher ISO settings, which allows you to shoot at lower light conditions. It is still recommended not to increase the ISO unless necessary.

With careful handling, side lighting and back lighting can produce stunning effects, especially in soft light and at sunrise or sunset. Generally, however, it is best to shoot with the sun behind you. When photographing animals or people in the harsh midday sun, images taken in light but even shade are likely to look nicer than those taken in direct sunlight or patchy shade, since the latter conditions create too much contrast.

PROTOCOL In some countries, it is unacceptable to photograph local people without permission, and many people will refuse to pose or will ask for a donation. In such circumstances, don't try to sneak photographs as you might get yourself into trouble. Even the most willing subject will often pose stiffly when a camera is pointed at them; relax them by making a joke, and take a few shots in quick succession to improve the odds of capturing a natural pose.

Ariadne Van Zandbergen is a professional travel and wildlife photographer specialised in Africa. She runs 'The Africa Image Library'. For photo requests, visit the website www.africaimagelibrary.co.za or contact her direct on e ariadne@hixnet.co.za

The Transcontinental newspaper group publishes the daily *Halifax News* and four other regional dailies, the *Amherst Daily News*, *Cape Breton Post*, *The News* (New Glasgow) and the *Truro Daily News*.

The free *Metro* is published on weekdays and distributed through much of the Halifax Regional Municipality (HRM).

The Coast (also free) is published on Thursday and distributed in Halifax, Dartmouth, and some nearby communities: it focuses primarily on Halifax. There are excellent listings pages, and reviews, including restaurants, music, performing arts and more. Editorial policy tends to be slightly left-wing.

Almost 30 other local newspapers are published weekly including one in French, *Le Courrier*.

Inspired by the UK's *Private Eye*, the fortnightly *Frank* magazine mixes humour, news and satire.

TELEVISION In addition to the Canadian Broadcasting Corporation's CBHT and French-language CBAFT, other terrestrial television stations include CJHT (part of the CTV network) and CIHF Global Maritimes, owned by Canwest. Catch up with the news on CBC at 06.00, noon or at 18.00.

Most tourist accommodations now offer cable/satellite television.

RADIO The Canadian Broadcasting Corporation offers four terrestrial networks (CBC Radio One, CBC Radio 2, and two French-language networks). You can tune in to a range of English and French radio stations in the province, though reception can be poor in some areas.

Some hire cars are equipped with satellite radio, opening up a host of other stations.

Probably the most outspoken talk show is Andrew Krystal's *Maritime Morning*, which airs 09.00–12.00 Monday–Friday on News 95.7FM.

TELEPHONE Public telephones (pay phones) in Nova Scotia can usually be operated by coin or (far more convenient and usually cheaper) phonecard. Sold at newsagents, general stores, petrol stations, post offices and many other places, phonecards come in various denominations (eg: CAN$10 or CAN$20). Some may be better than others depending on your telephonic requirements (eg: if you're likely to make a high proportion of calls to numbers outside the province). I've found the President's Choice cards sold at Atlantic Superstores to be a good all-rounder.

The area code for the whole of Nova Scotia is ☏ 902 and the international access code for Canada, like the US, is ☏ +1. If you're calling overseas from the province other than within Canada, to the US or Caribbean, the outgoing code is ☏ 011 followed by the relevant country code. Some common country codes are: Australia +61, France +33, Germany +49, Ireland +353, UK +44.

Mobile phones Not all mobile phones are enabled for international roaming, and (more important) not all handsets work in Canada. If your phone is enabled and compatible with the Canadian mobile-phone providers, check with your provider for the charges for making and receiving calls and texts. Alternatively, you can buy a pay-as-you-go SIM card either in the UK before you go – try, for example, **Go-Sim** (☏ *0845 658 3410; www.go-sim.com*) – or once in Nova Scotia from Rogers (see the 'store locator' section of www.rogersplus.ca for branches and phone numbers in the province). Mobile-phone reception in some of the province's more far-flung areas isn't always reliable. But think how far we've come since the days of Alexander Graham Bell, inventor of the telephone, who lived near Baddeck on Cape Breton Island.

The vast majority of phone numbers listed in this guide are standard seven-digit numbers. If calling these numbers from anywhere in the province outside the immediate area, Canada or the USA, dial the provincial area code (902) first. You may hear a message telling you to redial, prefixing the 902 with a 1. If dialling from outside these areas, you'll also need to add the international code for North America (00). Numbers listed as T/F (which begin 1 8XX) are (in theory) toll free. Some are toll free from outside North America, but if you try to call others from abroad, you will be intercepted by a message telling you your call is not toll free: you can proceed with the call and should be charged the normal tariff. To call these 1 8XX numbers from outside North America, dial 00 first (eg: 00 1 8XX, etc).

Useful telephone numbers

Fire, police, medical ☎ 911
Operator ☎ 0
Local directory assistance ☎ 411

Long-distance directory assistance ☎ 1 + the area code, if you know it, + 555 1212 (directory assistance is free from a payphone)

POST OFFICES City and town post offices (☎ T/F 1 866 607 6301) are usually open 08.00–17.00 Monday–Friday, whilst rural outlets have varying hours (they may well close for lunch) and some may open on Saturday mornings. To confuse matters, in the biggest urban areas some larger shops have post office counters which operate different hours. Canada Post's website (*www.canadapost.ca*) has a 'find a post office' section which gives each office's location and opening hours.

Postage prices are determined by weight and size of the item, and destination: standard-size letters within Canada cost CAN$0.52, to send to the US it is CAN$0.96, and internationally CAN$1.60.

INTERNET A few internet cafés are to be found in some of the biggest urban centres, and the network of Wi-Fi hotspots is ever-growing. Many accommodations offer wireless internet for those travelling with a laptop, or have a computer terminal for guests' use.

Many public buildings, especially libraries and tourist offices, offer free public internet access: look for a sign saying c@p site or check www.nscap.ca.

MAPS The provincial and regional tourist offices offer a range of free maps that might well be all you need on a holiday in the province. A range of simple regional and community maps can also be found online by looking at the 'Plan a Trip' section of www.novascotia.com and then selecting 'Maps' from the 'Travel Tools' box.

The provincial government's **Service Nova Scotia and Municipal Relations** department (☎ 667 7231; T/F 1 800 798 0706; *www.gov.ns.ca/snsmr/maps/*) produces and sells a range of regional atlases, maps and guidebooks (including 98 1:50,000 topographic maps – with contours at 10m intervals - covering the entire province). These are available online, by phone, or at one of the province's six **Land Registration Offices**: for the Dartmouth address, see page 118; for the others see the website *www.gov.ns.ca/snsmr/offices.asp*

More detailed road atlases, often including New Brunswick and Prince Edward Island, can be purchased at bookshops and petrol stations for about CAN$10.

International Travel Maps (☎ +1 604 273 1400; *www.itmb.com*) publishes a good 1:400,000-scale map of Nova Scotia which has been used to produce several of the maps in this guide.

For shops selling specialised maps in Halifax, see page 102.

BUSINESS

Business etiquette is similar to that in western Europe and the US. Suits are common for men, but staff at many companies dress more casually. Business hours tend to be 08.00–09.00 to 16.00–17.00, with a break of 30–60 minutes at lunch. Many companies offer flexible working hours, and an increasing number of staff work from home. Halifax is a popular place for international business conferences and conventions, and several hotels and resorts around the province endeavour to attract the convention market.

Many global companies are represented in Nova Scotia including EADS (European Aeronautic Defence and Space Company), Composites Atlantic, Michelin and Stora Enso. It is home to world-renowned research facilities such as the National Research Council's Institute for Marine Biosciences and the Bedford Institute of Oceanography. Defence, security and aerospace companies include Lockheed Martin, General Dynamics, IMP Group and Pratt and Whitney. The province is one of North America's leading emerging IT and business process outsourcing (BPO) destinations: AOL, Convergys, Research in Motion (RIM), Unisys and Xerox all have bases here.

A list of all the province's main Chambers of Commerce and Boards of Trade can be found at the **Nova Scotia Chambers of Commerce** website (*www.nschamber.ca*). The UK-based Canada–United Kingdom Chamber of Commerce (*38 Grosvenor St, London W1K 4DP;* ↘ *020 7258 6578; www.canada-uk.org*) might also be of use.

BUYING PROPERTY

Many visitors come to Nova Scotia, happen to glance in an estate agent's (real estate brokerage's) window, and wonder if they are seeing things. Magnificent houses on large acreages can still be found for the sort of price you might expect for a run-down house in rural eastern Europe. People say that Nova Scotia is a Canadian version of New England, but even with the recent house-price crash in the US, prices here are still a fraction of those in Maine, New Hampshire or Connecticut. You can start house hunting long before you leave home: just go to www.realtor.ca.

If you see something you like, or – when in the province – are tempted by a 'For Sale' sign as you drive by a beautiful house on a bluff overlooking the ocean, you can contact the real estate brokerage directly (the phone number will be on the website or sign). However, I would suggest approaching another realtor (real estate broker) at a different company in the same area (for an explanation, see later in this section). You can always try more than one company until you find someone with whom you feel you have a rapport. They will work on your behalf as a purchasing agent, at no cost to you, as all the brokerage companies have access to competitors' listed properties. Give your chosen realtor a list of the properties in which you are interested and they will arrange viewing appointments on any you wish to see. They may also suggest other properties which they feel may interest you. In general, the owners are usually out when you view a house, and your realtor is your guide through as many homes as you wish to view.

They will advise you on some of their pros and cons, and – if something interests you – will negotiate with the seller's realtor on your behalf. They act as the conduit between the buyer and the home owner. That is why I suggest avoiding the situation where your realtor is the listing realtor for the property in which you are interested: rightly or wrongly it is the perception that realtors will work harder for the seller than the buyer in such circumstances (though realtors work under a strict code of ethics, imposed by the Canadian Real Estate Association (CREA), requiring them to follow a set of guidelines when representing both buyer and seller in the same transaction).

If you are considering making an offer well below the asking price, different realtors work in different ways. Some will have an informal chat with the seller's listing realtor or if it is their own listing, directly with the homeowner; whilst others will insist that you make a formal offer in writing. Either way is appropriate.

All Nova Scotia Purchase and Sale agreements now have a pre-written clause making it advisable to contact an experienced property (real estate) lawyer after signing your Agreement of Purchase and Sale and allowing them time to review the fine print and comment or recommend changes to the transaction. Any realtor should be able to point you in the direction of a good lawyer.

Your offer should include certain conditions: these will vary from purchase to purchase. They might relate to timing – don't be rushed as you are likely to need time to arrange financing (and, probably transfer of funds from the UK to Nova Scotia) before you are bound to the contract. It should be made clear that your offer is subject to a satisfactory home inspection (what is called a survey in the UK) and, perhaps a land survey, which confirms that the home is located on the land described in the deed. If the property relies on a well for its water supply and/or a septic tank for sewage disposal – as many do outside cities and towns – you might also want to have those checked as a condition to be included in the agreement.

Another condition might be that the sale is dependent on your being able to obtain insurance for the property: some insurance companies will refuse to insure certain properties, or (more likely) may insist that certain changes are made before the cover that they offer will take effect.

In the vast majority of cases, either prior to making an offer to purchase or upon making the offer to purchase, you will be given a Property Condition Disclosure Statement (PCDS) which the seller has completed. In this, the seller must disclose (to the best of his or her knowledge) information about the property, even if these may be damaging to the sale. Topics covered include recent repairs, water supply, electrical services, plumbing, water leakage issues, rights of way and building restrictions. You will be allowed a certain amount of time to check this through.

It is very important that you go through the PCDS carefully, clarifying anything that is unclear, ambiguous or has been left blank. In my opinion, I think that it is worth ensuring that your home inspector has a copy of the PCDS so that they can also comment on any specific problems that have been noted thereon.

Ensure also that your lawyer sees the PCDS, if available, before you go ahead with the purchase.

Once all has been agreed, on the pre-arranged date you pay the agreed down payment (a negotiated amount, which may be as much as 10% of the sale price) if all the conditions have been met. Note that if you then get cold feet, you will not only lose your deposit but could be sued for damages.

Don't get carried away, and do think things through. How much will the house and grounds cost to maintain? What will happen to the property when you're not using it? Are you thinking of buying to let? Outside Halifax and Wolfville (university towns), the rental season doesn't stretch much beyond July and August. You are likely to need a property manager, or property maintenance company. Bear extra costs – such as legal fees, deed transfer tax, home inspection, adjustments (including your share of property taxes and fuel pre-paid by the seller), all plus 13% Harmonized Sales Tax (HST) – in mind. HST only applies to the purchase price

Thinking of emigrating to Nova Scotia? Before you can become a Canadian citizen, you have to apply for Permanent Residence. To do this, you can be sponsored by a family member who is a Canadian citizen (or Permanent Resident) or apply under one of the following categories:

- Skilled workers and professionals
- Canadian Experience Class (if you have recent Canadian work experience)
- Investors, entrepreneurs and self-employed people

The **Citizenship and Immigration Canada** website (www.cic.gc.ca) has a useful self-assessment test section where you can see if you might have enough points to qualify.

Successful candidates should expect to have to wait two years or more from when they submit their initial application until they receive their Permanent Residence.

A quicker method is likely to be via the **Nova Scotia Nominee Program** (see www.novascotiaimmigration.com). Here you apply to the Nova Scotia Office of Immigration: if you are considered worthy, you will receive a Letter of Nomination. You then apply via the Federal scheme as above, but will hopefully have been 'fast-tracked'.

Either way, there will be fees to pay: CAN$490 for Right of Permanent Residence, then CAN$475–1,050 depending on the category. You'll also have to fork out for a private medical.

Do the paperwork yourself, or engage the services of an immigration lawyer (try, for example, **Cox and Palmer** (421 6262; www.coxandpalmer.com).

of the property if you are buying a new home from a developer – but not if you are buying a home that has been owned/inhabited previously.

Recommended realtors include **Tradewinds Realty Inc** (*www.tradewindsrealty.com*) and **RE/MAX** (*www.remax-oa.com*). For home inspectors, choose a member of the **Canadian Association of Home and Property Inspectors** (*www.cahpi-atl.com*).

CULTURAL ETIQUETTE

TIPPING As in the US, tipping is a common practice in Canada. Taxi drivers are normally tipped 15% of the fare, hairdressers and barbers also 15%, airport/hotel porters CAN$1–2 per bag, and valet parkers CAN$1–2. Tour guides and bus drivers normally receive CAN$3–5 per day. Tipping your server, a dollar or two per round, whether at the bar or at your table, is common in bars.

In cafés and restaurants, you don't need to tip if eating at the counter (but of course you can do if the service is particularly good), but you are expected to tip 15–20% for meals.

SMOKING Smoking is not permitted in indoor public areas, bars and restaurants, or on restaurant and bar patios. It is illegal to smoke in a vehicle with passengers under the age of 19.

VISITING SOMEONE'S HOME Many people in Nova Scotia take their shoes off when they enter their homes: be aware of this, and perhaps ask your host if you should de-shoe.

Canada has many worthy countrywide charities such as the **Canadian Society for the Prevention of Cruelty to Children** (❱ *1 702 526 0214;* e *cspcc@bellnet.ca; www.parentingcourse.net*) and **Help the Aged Canada** (❱ *1 613 232 0727, T/F 1 800 648 1111; www.helptheaged.ca*).

Specific to the province is **Feed Nova Scotia** (*213 Bedford Hwy, Halifax, B3M 2J9;* ❱ *457 1900; www.feednovascotia.ca*), which aims to feed hungry people by providing year-round food deliveries to a network of 150 food banks across the province. The organisation's ultimate aim is to eliminate chronic hunger and alleviate poverty.

For over 250 years, lighthouses helped reduce the high number of wrecked ships in the province's coastal waters. Unfortunately, the majority of the 350-plus lighthouses are now gone or in ruinous states. The **Nova Scotia Lighthouse Preservation Society** (*www.nslps.com*) ploughs time, effort and money to preserve lighthouse heritage.

The **Nova Scotia Nature Trust** (❱ *425 5263; www.nsnt.ca*) works to conserve the province's increasingly threatened ecologically significant lands.

There is a Nova Scotia chapter of the **Canadian Parks and Wilderness Society** (*1099 Marginal Rd, Suite 201, Halifax, B3H 4P7;* ❱ *446 4155; www.cpawsns.org*), Canada's leading grass-roots non-government organisation for wilderness conservation.

The majority of the province's museums are staffed by volunteers and offer free admission – donations are always welcomed.

Part Two

THE GUIDE

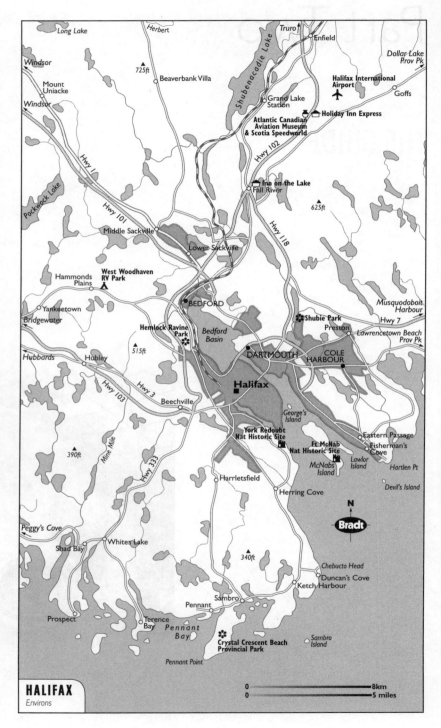

3

Halifax, Dartmouth and Around

Nova Scotia's capital is not a city as such, but a municipality. The cities of Halifax and Dartmouth, the town of Bedford and the municipality of the county of Halifax were dissolved and amalgamated into the Halifax Regional Municipality (HRM) in 1996. The HRM has a population of close to 360,000 and is home to over one third of Nova Scotia's population. Despite the urban consolidation, virtually everyone still talks about the different entities as though nothing has changed.

Halifax – which has the largest component population (approximately 115,000) and is home to the majority of the government buildings and offices – sits at the heart of the HRM. It is here that one finds the majority of the HRM's hotels, restaurants and best museums and attractions.

Dartmouth (with a population of approximately 68,000) is across the harbour from Halifax – a short ride by regular ferry.

At the head of the harbour is Bedford (population approximately 14,000). Visitors should try and head beyond the urban centres to explore areas such as the Northwest Arm (see page 113), the Eastern Passage (see page 121) and the Uniacke estate (see page 115).

Although it stretches as far to the southwest as Hubbards (see page 133) and to the east as Ecum Secum (see page 357), this chapter focuses on the heart of the HRM.

ORIENTATION

Halifax's *raison d'être* was its harbour, and the harbour is still a major part of life for Halifax, Dartmouth and Bedford. At the mouth of the harbour are Chebucto Head on the Halifax side and Hartlen Point on the Dartmouth side. Herring Cove Road and Purcell's Cove Road lead towards the downtown area from Chebucto Head, passing fjord-like Northwest Arm. On the Dartmouth side, Shore Road and Eastern Passage Road run close to the waterfront, with McNab's and Lawlor islands just offshore.

Connected by passenger ferry, downtown Halifax and downtown Dartmouth face each other across the harbour, which then narrows through a stretch called The Narrows, before opening up into the expanse of the 40km² Bedford Basin. Two toll bridges – the MacDonald to the south and MacKay slightly further north – cross the narrows, providing road links between the two communities. Near Bedford, which is at the head of the Bedford Basin, two of the province's major motorways meet. Highway 102 leads southwest to Halifax and northeast to Halifax International Airport, approximately 38km from downtown, and Truro. Highway 101 leads southwest to Dartmouth, and northeast to Windsor, Wolfville and Yarmouth, via the Annapolis Valley.

The region's other major motorway, Highway 103, leads west from Halifax towards Liverpool, Bridgewater and Yarmouth, via the South Shore.

The layout of downtown Halifax is relatively simple, with a series of short streets rising up from the western side of Halifax Harbour towards Citadel Hill. On the waterfront itself, most of the tourist sites are between Casino Nova Scotia to the north, and the cruise ship dock to the south. Lower and Upper Water streets run parallel to the water, with Barrington Street two to three blocks inland.

En route up to Citadel Hill, grassy Grand Parade is bordered by Barrington, Argyle, Duke and Prince streets. Around Citadel Hill are large green areas with individual names, but collectively referred to as The Commons, and bordered by Robie Street. Cogswell Street runs from Barrington Street to Robie Street, continuing on as Quinpool Road before reaching the Armdale Rotary.

Locals tend to refer to everything south of The Commons as the South End, and everything to the north as the North End. The North End – much of which was flattened by the Halifax Explosion in 1917 (see box, page 86) – includes the Hydrostone district, bordered by Young, Agricola, Duffus and Gottingen streets. This European-style district was built in the aftermath of the Halifax Explosion using hydrostone, a special kind of masonry. Completed in 1920, the district includes a market with a collection of shops and eateries.

In the South End (the southernmost part of which is occupied by beautiful Point Pleasant Park) is the city's academic area, site of Dalhousie University, University of King's College and St Mary's University.

GETTING THERE

For international and inter-provincial services, see page 38.

BY AIR Flights connect Halifax with Sydney and Yarmouth (see page 48).

Airport transfers
Halifax/Dartmouth **Airporter** (❭ *873 2091; www.airporter.biz*) provides 20 services each way daily between various Halifax hotels (and Dartmouth) and the airport. The one-way fare is CAN$19.

A taxi or limousine to the centre of Halifax costs CAN$53. You'll see 'ground transportation' booths as you emerge from the arrivals hall.

Other towns Acadian (see page 51) is not permitted to carry passengers solely between the airport and Halifax/Dartmouth, or vice versa, but picks up and drops off at the airport to and from numerous other destinations in the province.

Several shuttle operators will pick up and drop off at the airport on their regular runs. For details, see 'Transportation Information' in the 'Traveler Information' section of www.hiaa.ca.

BY CAR If you are travelling by car from the north and/or the airport, Highway 102 brings you into downtown Halifax via Bayers Road (avoiding the toll bridges). Coming from Dartmouth and/or the Eastern Shore, it makes most sense to take one of the toll bridges.

There are two toll bridges in the HRM: the A Murray MacKay Bridge and Angus L MacDonald Bridge; the latter has pedestrian and bicycle access. The toll is CAN$0.75 and some booths are designated for those without exact change.

Car hire Car-hire companies offer rentals at the airport and other locations including downtown Halifax and Dartmouth. See page 50 for further information.

BY BUS Long-distance bus services arrive and depart from the VIA Rail Station (*1161 Hollis St*), 1km south of downtown. The main carriers are **Acadian** (✆ *T/F 1 800 567 5151; www.smtbus.com*), which has departures from Halifax to various points throughout the province and beyond (see page 51), and **Trius Tours** (✆ *T/F 1 877 566 1567; www.peisland.com/triustours/line.htm*) which offers a daily connection with Yarmouth and points *en route*. For route details, see page 52.

BY TRAIN Don't be fooled by the size and grandeur of the VIA Rail Station. There's just one departure and arrival six days a week, a service which connects Halifax with Montreal, Quebec. Stops in Nova Scotia are at Truro, Springhill Junction and Amherst. For fares and times contact **VIA Rail** (✆ *T/F 1 888 842 7245; www.viarail.ca*).

GETTING AROUND

BY CAR The downtown core of Halifax is quite compact, and parking can be hard to find. Colour-coded parking meters (red: max 30 minutes; grey: max 1 hour; green: max 2 hours; yellow: max 3–5 hours) charge CAN$0.25/10 minutes (CAN$0.25/7.5 minutes at the waterfront meters) and are strictly monitored by a very enthusiastic enforcement team. Downtown Dartmouth only has grey and green meters. Meters are in effect 08.00–18.00 Monday–Friday.

There are several garages (MetroPark [88–9 D4], Scotia Square Mall [88–9 E3] and the Casino [88–9 F1]) which charge from CAN$2.50/hour, and car parks (try Lower Water Street [88–9 G6], or off Spring Garden Road on Queen and Birmingham streets [88–9 C7]), which charge from CAN$1.50/hour. The larger downtown hotels charge guests around CAN$20/day for parking.

By and large, Haligonians drive slowly and considerately: they will allow traffic to merge and often stop at the first sign of a pedestrian near a kerb (you are obliged to stop for pedestrians at crosswalks). There are several one-way streets to watch out for, and the Armdale Rotary – basically just a simple roundabout – often causes locals vast amounts of confusion.

BY TAXI Taxis are easiest to find outside major hotels, shopping malls and the VIA Rail Station [92–3 G4]. You may be able to flag down a cruising taxi. Fares start at CAN$3, with CAN$1.50/km added after that. Each extra passenger is charged CAN$0.50. A ride from the Halifax waterfront to Citadel Hill, for example, will cost about CAN$7.

🚕 **Casino Taxi** ✆ 429 6666
🚕 **Halifax Taxi** ✆ 456 1150
🚕 **Yellow Cab** ✆ 420 0000

BY BUS Metro Transit (✆ *490 4000; www.halifax.ca/metrotransit*) operates public transport in Halifax, Dartmouth and to some other parts of the HRM. The website has schedules, route maps and more. Almost all tickets (including free transfers) cost: adult CAN$2.25, senior and child (aged five–15) CAN$1.50, and under fives free. A book of ten tickets costs CAN$18 (child CAN$13). Conductors prefer exact change only. If you are changing buses, or will be travelling by both bus and ferry, ask for a (free) transfer ticket – valid for 90 minutes.

There is talk of extending the network and introducing new limited-stop services (Metro Express) in the near future. See the website above for the latest.

Bright yellow **Fred** (Free Rides Everywhere Downtown) buses cruise a loop through the downtown (*early Jul–late Oct 10.30–17.00 daily; approximately every*

30min; free). Stops include Pier 21, Water Street, Spring Garden Road and Citadel Hill.

If you're at a stop waiting for a bus, dial 480 followed by the four-digit bus stop number (marked in red at every stop) for real-time information on when the next bus will be arriving.

Almost 20 bus routes use accessible low-floor buses (ALF), and the ferries are also accessible. There is also an Access-A-Bus service providing door-to-door accessible transportation throughout the city. If you might use the service, contact Metro Transit in advance to register.

Need-A-Lift (☎ *222 5438; www.needalift.ca*) offers a wheelchair-accessible bus and taxi service in many HRM areas. Prices start at CAN$29 (plus tax).

BY FERRY Metro Transit also runs the Halifax–Dartmouth ferry (the oldest saltwater passenger service in North America) from the foot of George Street [88–9 G4] to Alderney Drive in Dartmouth [117 C3] (*06.30–23.30 Mon–Sat, 10.30–18.00 Sun*). Not that I want to take business away from Halifax's boat tour operators, but for CAN$2 each way, the eight–ten-minute crossing (*departures every 15–30 minutes*) makes an excellent, cheap harbour ride. There is also a similarly priced ferry service (*weekdays only;* ⊕ *06.30–17.50*) between Halifax and Woodside (on the Dartmouth side).

BY BIKE In recent years, the HRM has made efforts to making the city more bike-friendly, and renting a bike (or riding your own) can be a good way to explore the area (with some steep hills to keep you fit). Best bet for rentals is **Idealbikes** [88–9 E5] (☎ *1678 Barrington St;* ☎ *444 7433; www.idealbikes.ca*). **Pedal and Sea Adventures** (☎ *T/F 1 877 777 5699; www.pedalandseaadventures.com*) is based in Hubbards (see page 35) but offers free delivery to the Halifax area.

ON FOOT The downtown area is easily explored on foot, though Citadel Hill [88–9 B3] and the Public Gardens [88–9 A6] are a long way uphill from the waterfront. In the downtown area, many hotels and shops are connected by covered pedestrian walkways (pedways).

FESTIVALS AND EVENTS

Halifax, Dartmouth and the surrounding communities have an event-packed calendar. Although (not surprisingly) anything with an outdoor focus is held in the summer months, it seems that there is something going on throughout the year. Tickets for some of the bigger events are available through companies such as Ticket Atlantic (☎ *451 1221; www.ticketatlantic.com*) and Ticketpro (☎ *T/F 1 888 311 9090; www.ticketpro.ca*) – phone or see websites for the nearest outlet.

FEBRUARY
Savour Food and Wine (☎ *429 5343, T/F 1 800 665 3463; www.savourfoodandwine.com*) Wine and cheese tastings, seminars on beer, cooking lessons, and – for a ten-day period – special deals at some of the city's best restaurants.

APRIL
Halifax International Writers Festival (*www.halifaxwritersfest.com*) Readings, workshops, etc, over five days in early April.

Halifax Comedy Fest (*www.halifaxcomedyfest.ca*) A week-long festival of laughs. Prices for shows range from free to CAN$40.

MAY

Bluenose Marathon (*www.bluenosemarathon.com*) Marathon, half-marathon and 5km and 10km events.

SuperNova Theatre Festival (*www.easternfront.ns.ca*) In recent years, venues have alternated between Alderney Landing [117 C3] and the Neptune Theatre [88–9 E6]. Tickets CAN$20, CAN$60 for four plays.

JUNE

Catch! Nova Scotia Seafood Festival (*www.catchseafoodfestival.com*) Held in late June.

Greek Festival (*www.greekfest.org*) Very popular even with those who don't have Hellenic roots. Held mid-June.

The Nova Scotia Multi-cultural Festival (*Alderney Gate Complex, Dartmouth;* \ *423 6534; www.multifest.ca*) A three-day Dartmouth waterfront event held in mid-June. Take in the sights, sounds, smells and tastes.

The Scotia Festival of Music (\ *429 9467; www.scotiafestival.ns.ca*) A celebration of chamber music over two weeks in early June. Concert tickets CAN$25, multi-concert tickets available.

JULY

AlFresco Film Festo (\ *422 3456; www.atlanticfilm.com/alfresco/*) This outdoor film festival – held between late July and late August – hosts screenings on the Halifax waterfront behind the Westin Nova Scotian hotel [92–3 G3], with a range of films projected onto a special screen. CAN$5 donation per film suggested.

Atlantic Jazz Festival (\ *492 2225, T/F 1 800 567 5277; www.jazzeast.com*) Held over nine days, this is the largest Canadian music festival east of Montreal, and one of North America's major jazz events. Performances are held in a range of venues – in a variety of music styles. Many of the world's big names come to play, but it is also a reminder of the breadth and depth of local talent. Tickets CAN$15 and up: day passes and festival passes available.

Halifax Pride (*www.halifaxpride.com*) In the words of the organisers: 'a Lesbian, Gay, Bisexual, Transgender and Queer (LGBTQ) Pride Week Festival…accessible to all.' Atlantic Canada's largest Pride celebration.

Nova Scotia International Tattoo (\ *420 1114, T/F 1 800 563 1114; www.nstattoo.ca; tickets CAN$31–62*) Billing itself 'the world's largest annual indoor show', this is a fantastic eight-day mix of marching bands, gymnastics, pageantry, dance, military competitions, music and more held in early July. And the organisers keep trying to push the barriers further. Performers come from the world over, and previous tattoos have seen 20 Swiss Elvis impersonators performing on parallel bars, and regular favourites include the Gun Run. A great – and very popular – family event. Held at the Halifax Metro Centre [88–9 D4], there is one performance daily (either a matinee at 14.30, or in the evening at 19.30).

Shakespeare by the Sea (\ *422 0295; www.shakespearebythesea.ca; admission by donation – CAN$15 suggested*) Between July and early September a selection of the bard's (and other) works performed outdoors in an amphitheatre at an old gun battery in Point Pleasant Park [92–3 H6].

Tall Ships (*www.tallshipsnovascotia.com*) The bad news is that this event – where beautiful sailing ships from around the world join many of Canada's finest sailing vessels in Halifax Harbour – only takes place every four years and it was hosted here in 2009, which means it's not due back until 2013.

AUGUST

International Busker Festival (↘ *430 8413; www.buskers.ca*) Those to whom a busker is just a one-man band covering a 1960s' Bob Dylan song (badly) will have their eyes opened at this ten-day celebration of 'street theatre'. See jugglers, mime artists and fire-eaters from all over the world – and a whole lot more – at six waterfront properties. Free and great fun – even if one of them does break in to 'Blowing in the Wind'.

Natal Day (*www.natalday.org*) The communities of Halifax and Dartmouth come together in early August to celebrate their birthdays with a civic holiday long known as Natal Day. The event is now sponsored by Alexander Keith's brewery, and is known as Alexander Keith's Natal Day Festival. It is held over five days: expect parades, running races, live entertainment, fireworks and more.

SEPTEMBER

Atlantic Film Festival (↘ *422 3456; www.atlanticfilm.com*) This ten-day mid-September celebration of film and video from the Atlantic Provinces, Canada and around the world offers screenings of more than 150 films. These are shown in cinemas in and around town. Tickets cost $10–15 per screening.

Atlantic Fringe Festival (↘ *435 4837; www.atlanticfringe.ca*) A week of 200 performing arts shows held at various downtown venues in early September. Tickets tend to be CAN$4–10 per show.

Great Atlantic Blues and Beyond Festival (*www.atlanticbluesfest.com*) Held over three days, on two stages at the Alderney Landing complex [117 C3].

OCTOBER

Halifax Pop Explosion (↘ *482 8176; www.halifaxpopexplosion.com*) A five-day festival featuring a range of music from folk-rock to hip-hop.

NOVEMBER

Christmas at the Forum (*Halifax Forum, 2901 Windsor St;* ↘ *T/F 1 866 995 7469; www.christmasattheforum.com*) A festival of crafts, antiques, art and food held over three days at the beginning of the month.

Christmas Craft Village (*Exhibition Park; www.atlanticchristmasfair.com*) Another three-day Christmas crafts event.

HALIFAX

The province's most important metropolis was once the major point of entry to Canada for over a million immigrants and refugees (see *Pier 21*, page 106), and the port remains a busy centre for shipping. Much attention focuses on the bustling waterfront, and traffic in the harbour is a mix of ferries, yachts, tugs, container ships, naval vessels and ocean cruisers.

Halifax and Nova Scotia's strong links to the sea are recognised at the absorbing Maritime Museum of the Atlantic [88–9 F5] (see page 106), whilst high up the hill is the impressive Halifax Citadel National Historic Site of Canada [88–9 B3] (see page 105).

A range of museums, galleries and indoor attractions – not to mention shopping, particularly on lively Spring Garden Road [88–9 D7] – will occupy you if the weather isn't at its best, but when the sun comes out and the mercury rises you'll want to wander the beautiful Halifax Public Gardens [88–9 A6] (see page 106) and hike along the seafront at Point Pleasant Park [92–3 H6] (page 109), take a boat on the harbour [88–9 G4], or go for a picnic. Summer is the time for an array of festivals, many of which are free.

Although hills may put some off, the downtown area is easily explored on foot – just as well bearing in mind that parking spots can be hard to find. Try to go beyond the downtown area to sample the shops and eateries of cosmopolitan Quinpool Road [92–3 C4], or the Hydrostone district [92–3 B1] (see page 101).

Whilst first impressions will suggest that Halifax is friendly, charming and relaxed, dig deeper and you'll also find a well-developed music scene, lively pubs, and restaurants and bars to suit most palates and budgets. The two universities keep the atmosphere youthful – but rarely rowdy.

HISTORY Late in the 1740s, the British were looking for a site for a garrison as a base from which to defeat the French at Louisbourg, now back in French hands. They saw the potential of the area known to the Mi'kmaq as Jipugtug ('the great long harbour'), which was later anglicised as Chebucto. On one side of the wonderful harbour was a drumlin on which a fortress could be built. In 1749, Colonel Edward Cornwallis arrived with about 2,500 settlers on 13 ships, and founded a settlement. The Earl of Halifax, President of the Board of Trade and Plantations, had been instrumental in obtaining British government approval for the projected town, and it was named Halifax in his honour.

Immediately, the first fortress was built on the hilltop: this later developed into the Citadel [88–9 B3] (see page 105). St Paul's Church [88–9 E5] (see page 110), Canada's first Anglican sanctuary, was constructed in 1750: that year, more settlers arrived and founded Dartmouth across the harbour. By 1752, the two towns were linked by a ferry system, the oldest saltwater ferry system in North America.

Protestants were recruited from mainland Europe in an attempt to counter the French and Catholic presence in Nova Scotia and between 1776 and 1783, population in the settlement was further boosted with the arrival of thousands of Loyalists from America.

LAME DUC

In an attempt to harass the British and the New Englanders who had taken Louisbourg (see page 333), in 1746, Louis XV sent a huge naval expedition to seek revenge. Under the command of the Duc d'Anville (who had little naval experience), a fleet of over 70 sailing vessels and thousands of men endured an awful ten-week crossing of the Atlantic – including losing ships off Sable Island (see page 368) – before reaching what is now Halifax Harbour. The Duc himself died within a week of the arrival and was buried on George's Island (see page 113). Typhoid continued to claim lives, and when the men went ashore to bury their dead, the disease was passed on to the local Mi'kmaq population with devastating results.

The battered French fleet limped out of the harbour with the intention of sailing round and attacking Annapolis Royal (see page 199) but turned back and headed for home. Less than a fifth of the original party reached France alive.

In days long gone by, criminals were often flogged, then branded on the ball of a thumb. Second offenders often faced the noose. In Halifax, there were central gallows at the foot of George Street [88–9 G4] (near the modern-day ferry terminal) and military gallows in the middle of the Citadel Hill parade ground [88–9 B3].

At the mouth of Halifax Harbour, a small, open cove named Black Rock Beach was the site of one of Halifax's earliest public gallows. Years later, these gallows were dismantled, relocated to McNab's Island and reassembled on a beach there. To this day, that stretch of sand is known as Hangman's Beach.

Realising Halifax's strategic importance, in the years that followed, fortifications went up along the harbour approaches: these included batteries at McNab's Island, a Martello tower at Point Pleasant [92–3 H6], and forts at George's Island [92–3 H3] and York Redoubt [92–3 G7].

St Mary's University [92–3 F5] was established in 1802 and Dalhousie University [92–3 E4] opened in 1818. Alexander Keith's brewing company [88–9 F7] (see page 109) opened in 1820. In 1834, a cholera epidemic killed over 600 people in Halifax.

Native Haligonian Samuel Cunard was the leading figure in the city's shipping business, and in 1840, the Cunard Steamship Company's *Britannia* became the first vessel to offer a regular passenger service between Liverpool, England, and Halifax.

The only North American city founded by the British government (as opposed to British merchants or individuals) was incorporated in 1841, and was connected by rail to Windsor (see page 225) and Truro (see page 239) in 1858.

After Canadian confederation in 1867, the city retained its British military garrison until British troops were replaced by the Canadian army in 1906. The British Royal Navy remained until 1910 when the newly created Royal Canadian Navy took over the Naval Dockyard.

The city leapt into the international spotlight in 1912 when the RMS *Titanic* sank northeast of Nova Scotia (see box opposite).

The harbour, ice-free year-round, had long been recognised as one of the best deep-water ports in all of eastern North America. Opening into the expanse of Bedford Basin, this was a sanctuary where literally hundreds of ships could moor in safety.

During both World Wars, Halifax Harbour sheltered convoys from German U-boat attack before they headed out across the Atlantic. The port city was of great strategic importance both for this reason and as the departure point for Canadian soldiers heading overseas.

The devastating Halifax Explosion (see box on page 86) occurred in December 1917.

Sir Winston Churchill visited Halifax twice during World War II. Having been shown the Public Gardens and Citadel Hill, he told the mayor: 'Now, sir, we know your city is something more than a shed on a wharf.'

By the 1960s, Halifax was looking more than a little run down. Just in time, there was massive investment from federal, provincial, and private sectors: several old buildings were renovated, the waterfront tastefully and imaginatively brought back to life, and many new hotels built. Care was taken to limit the height of high-rise buildings, and to preserve sight-lines.

Recent years saw another disaster, when huge amounts of damage were caused, but (thankfully) only eight people lost their lives. Tens of thousands of trees were knocked down, many in Point Pleasant Park: there was extensive damage to buildings, and many homes had no electricity for a fortnight. All this was a result of Hurricane Juan, which arrived in the early hours of 29 September 2003 and lashed Halifax with sustained wind gusts of over 180km/h. To date, this was the most damaging storm in modern history for Halifax.

TOURIST INFORMATION

Z Tourist Information Scotia Square Mall, 5251 Duke St; ☎ 490 5963; ⊕ year-round 08.30–16.30 Mon–Fri.

Z Tourist Information 1655 Water St; ☎ 424 4248; ⊕ daily late Oct–mid-May 09.00–17.00; mid-

May–Jun & mid-Sep–mid-Oct 08.00–18.00; mid-Jun–mid-Sep 08.00–19.00.

Z Tourist Information 1598 Argyle St (at Sackville St); ☎ 490 4000; ⊕ mid-May–mid-Oct 09.00–18.00 daily.

LOCAL TOUR OPERATORS Biggest of the companies offering sightseeing tours in the HRM and further afield is **Ambassatours/Gray Line** (☎ 423 6242, T/F 1 800 565 7173; www.ambassatours.com).

At 20.30 on certain dark evenings (see website for dates) between July and October, a guided two-hour **Halifax Ghost Walk** (☎ 466 160; www.thehalifaxghostwalk.com; CAN$10) sets off from the Old Town clock. It's interesting – and fun.

A harbour tour is a must, and one company lets you combine land and sea: **Harbour Hopper Tours** (☎ 490 8687; www.harbourhopper.com; ⊕ early May–late Oct) offers 55-minute tours in a brightly coloured amphibious vehicle.

Sailing the harbour in a historic tall ship is very popular. The beautiful **Tall Ship Silva** (☎ 429 9463; www.tallshipsilva.com; ⊕ mid-Jun–mid-Sep) offers three 90-minute sailings daily, plus a two-hour late-night party cruise at 22.30 Thursday–Saturday. The **Bluenose II** (☎ 634 4794, ext 221, T/F 1 866 579 4909 ext 221; www.museum.gov.ns.ca/bluenose/) (see page 146) spends some of the summer season offering two-hour tours of Halifax Harbour. Check the schedule and call or make reservations online.

Murphy's on the Water (☎ 420 1015; www.murphysonthewater.com; ⊕ May-late Oct) offers a wide range of tours on a variety of vessels including the tugboat *Theodore Too*, the Nova Scotia maritime equivalent of Thomas the Tank Engine.

LOCAL TRAVEL AGENTS

Flight Centre Scotia Sq, 5201 Duke St; T/F 1 866 788 5077; www.flightcentre.ca

Maritime Travel Halifax Shopping Centre, 7001 Mumford Rd; ☎ 455 7856; www.maritimetravel.ca

Travel Cuts 1589 Barrington St; ☎ 482 8000, T/F 1 888 359 2887; www.travelcuts.com

RMS *TITANIC*

On 10 April 1912, the White Star Line's RMS *Titanic* – at that time the largest passenger steamship in the world – left Southampton, England, on her maiden voyage to New York, carrying over 1,300 passengers and 900 crew. Just before midnight on 14 April, she struck an iceberg south of Newfoundland, and sunk in less than three hours. Although 706 survivors were rescued, well over 1,500 men, women and children died. Some victims' bodies were recovered and buried at sea: 209 bodies were brought to Halifax. A temporary morgue was established in a curling rink (now an Army Surplus store): 150 victims were buried in three Halifax cemeteries between May and early June (121 in the Fairview Lawn Cemetery, 19 in the Mount Olivet Cemetery, and ten in the Baron de Hirsch Private Cemetery).

The Maritime Museum of the Atlantic (see page 106) has a special section devoted to the *Titanic* disaster and its aftermath.

In winter 1917, Halifax Harbour was alive with activity as heavily armed warships prepared to escort convoys carrying troops, munitions and supplies on the dangerous crossing of the Atlantic, neutral vessels waited at anchor, and the usual shipping traffic buzzed around.

On the morning of 6 December, the French ship *Mont-Blanc* left her anchorage outside the mouth of the harbour to join one of the convoys. She was loaded with hundreds of tons of TNT, picric acid, benzene and other explosives. At the same time, the *Imo*, a Norwegian ship in service of the Belgian Relief, was headed in the opposite direction. To cut a long story (and much speculation) short, the *Imo* struck the *Mont-Blanc* on the bow. Fire immediately broke out on board the *Mont-Blanc* and her terrified captain and crew took to the lifeboats and rowed for their lives to the Dartmouth shore.

The abandoned *Mont-Blanc* drifted toward the Halifax docks. At 09.05, what was at the time the largest manmade explosion in history – unrivalled until the detonation of the first atomic bomb – occurred. About 130ha of the city's North End was flattened, over 10,000 people were wounded (many blinded by glass from shattered windows), and almost 2,000 were killed. Around 8,000 people's homes were destroyed, and tens of millions of dollars of damage done. The shock wave of the blast was felt over 400km away in Sydney on Cape Breton Island.

Fort Needham Memorial Park on Needham Street is home to a memorial carillon dedicated in 1984 to the memory of those who died in the explosion.

Incidentally, in World War II, three other potentially huge explosions involving vessels carrying munitions were narrowly avoided.

 WHERE TO STAY All too often, conventions or major events can fill all hotel beds in and close to downtown. Many of the bigger hotels are geared to business travellers and may offer cheaper rates on Friday and Saturday nights. It is always worth asking for a discount, especially if you're staying out of season or for more than a couple of nights. Many of the larger hotels are also bookable through internet travel companies such as Expedia (*www.expedia.co.uk*) which sometimes offers lower rates than the hotel itself. All accommodation is open year-round unless stated otherwise.

Waterfront and downtown
Luxury

⌂ **Lord Nelson Hotel & Suites** [88–9 A6] (261 rooms & suites) 1515 South Park St; ✆ 423 6331, T/F 1 800 565 2020; e ask@lordnelsonhotel.com; www.lordnelsonhotel.com. On the corner of Spring Garden Rd with many rooms overlooking the Public Gardens, the décor in this grandiose c1928 hotel is contemporary in style: bathrooms are spacious. There's a fitness room, & an on-site traditional-English style pub where food is served. Parking is CAN$20/day, valet parking CAN$25. $$$$

⌂ **Prince George Hotel** [88–9 D4] (189 rooms & 14 suites) 1725 Market St; ✆ 425 1986, T/F 1 800 565 1567; www.princegeorgehotel.com. Close to the Halifax Citadel (& uphill from the centre of downtown), this c1986 property is another good choice for those who like big, comfortable hotels.

There's a business centre, fitness centre & indoor pool, & 2 decent eateries (Terrace & Gio – see page 94). Underground parking CAN$20/day, valet parking offered. $$$$

⌂ **Radisson Suite Hotel Halifax** [88–9 F5] (104 suites) 1649 Hollis St; ✆ 429 7233; T/F 1 800 333 3333; e info@radissonhalifax.com; www.radissonhalifax.com. Don't be put off by the downtown building's former life as an office block – the spacious 1-bedroom suites are comfortable, there's an exercise room, restaurant, & the indoor pool is a bonus. Valet parking is offered at CAN$18.95/day. $$$$

⌂ **Westin Nova Scotian** [92–3 G3] (297 units) 1181 Hollis St; ✆ 421 1000, T/F 1 877 993 7846; e reservations@westin.ns.ca; www.westin.ns.ca. Built by the Canadian Pacific National Railway in 1930 as the Nova Scotian (adjacent to Halifax Railway Station), this grand 11-storey hotel has recently undergone major renovations (using top designers) & is looking good outside & 'urban chic' within. It has all the facilities you'd expect from a top city hotel (tennis court, indoor pool, fitness centre, business centre & more), a stylish bar & more casual

Upmarket

🏠 **Cambridge Suites Hotel Halifax** [88–9 D6] (200 suites) 1583 Brunswick St; ✆ 420 0555, T/F 1 800 565 1263; www.cambridgesuiteshalifax.com. In addition to comfortable, well-equipped suites (all rooms have microwave & fridge) this modern, well-located property has a licensed restaurant, rooftop fitness centre & sundeck. A good choice for families. Indoor parking CAN$15/day. Continental b/fast inc. $$$

🏠 **Delta Barrington** [88–9 E3] (200 rooms) 1875 Barrington St; ✆ 429 7410, T/F 1 800 268 1133; e hal.reservations@deltahotels.com; www.deltabarrington.com. This comfortable hotel has a business centre, indoor pool, fitness centre, decent restaurant & bar. It might look old from the Granville St side but that's just the result of a painstaking restoration of the building's original façade. Valet parking available CAN$19.95/day. $$$

🏠 **Four Points by Sheraton Halifax** [88–9 E7] (159 rooms, 18 suites) 1496 Hollis St; ✆ 423 4444, T/F 1 866 444 9494; www.starwoodhotels.com. This conveniently located modern c2002 7-storey hotel is another good well-equipped choice. There's an indoor pool, fitness room, & the Niche Restaurant, offering live jazz Thu–Sat evenings. Underground parking CAN$17/day. $$$

🏠 **The Halliburton** [92–3 F3] (25 rooms & 4 suites) 5184 Morris St; ✆ 420 0658, T/F 1 888 512 3344; www.thehalliburton.com. Occupying 3 adjoining c1809 properties, the beautifully restored Halliburton successfully blends B&B & boutique hotel. It is elegant & very comfortable, & when the sun comes out the courtyard garden is very pleasant. The on-site restaurant, Stories (see page 95), offers dinner every evening. Free parking. Light buffet b/fast inc. $$$

🏠 **Waverley Inn** [92–3 F3] (34 rooms) 1266 Barrington St; ✆ 423 9346, T/F 1 800 565 9346; www.waverleyinn.com. This delightful c1866 property has included Oscar Wilde amongst its guests. Expect hardwood floors & antiques. As the cheapest (Traditional) rooms are on the small side, you may want to consider upgrading. Rooms on 3 floors (no lifts). Free parking is a bonus. Hot b/fast buffet & snacks inc. $$$

THE COMMUNITY THAT DISAPPEARED

Compared with the thousands of Acadians deported from Nova Scotia for refusing to sign an oath of allegiance to the British (see page 9), the eviction of 400 townsfolk might not seem a lot. But the residents of Africville, a shanty town on the edge of Halifax, weren't turfed out of their homes in the 18th century, but in the 1960s.

Africville was founded in the 1840s by people living in very poor black communities seeking a better life. Railway lines were built right through the centre of the town and later a slaughterhouse, a fertiliser plant, and factories went up immediately adjacent to it.

Although the residents paid taxes, at no stage did the city of Halifax provide basic services such as running water, sewage, or paved roads. The community had a school, post office, and its focus, the church. But in the 1950s, the large, open city dump was moved to within a few hundred metres of Africville.

Then in 1962, the city government announced it was expropriating the land on which Africville stood as part of an Urban Renewal programme. In 1964, rubbish trucks arrived to remove the first residents. Most had no way to prove that they owned the run-down houses that they occupied, and were given CAN$50 as a goodwill compensatory gesture. In 1970, the last property was bulldozed.

Part of the land on which Africville stood is now the Seaview Memorial Park (named in memory of the former community's demolished church), and this was designated a national historic site in 1996. A three-day picnic (www.africville.ca) is held annually on the last weekend in July to commemorate the community.

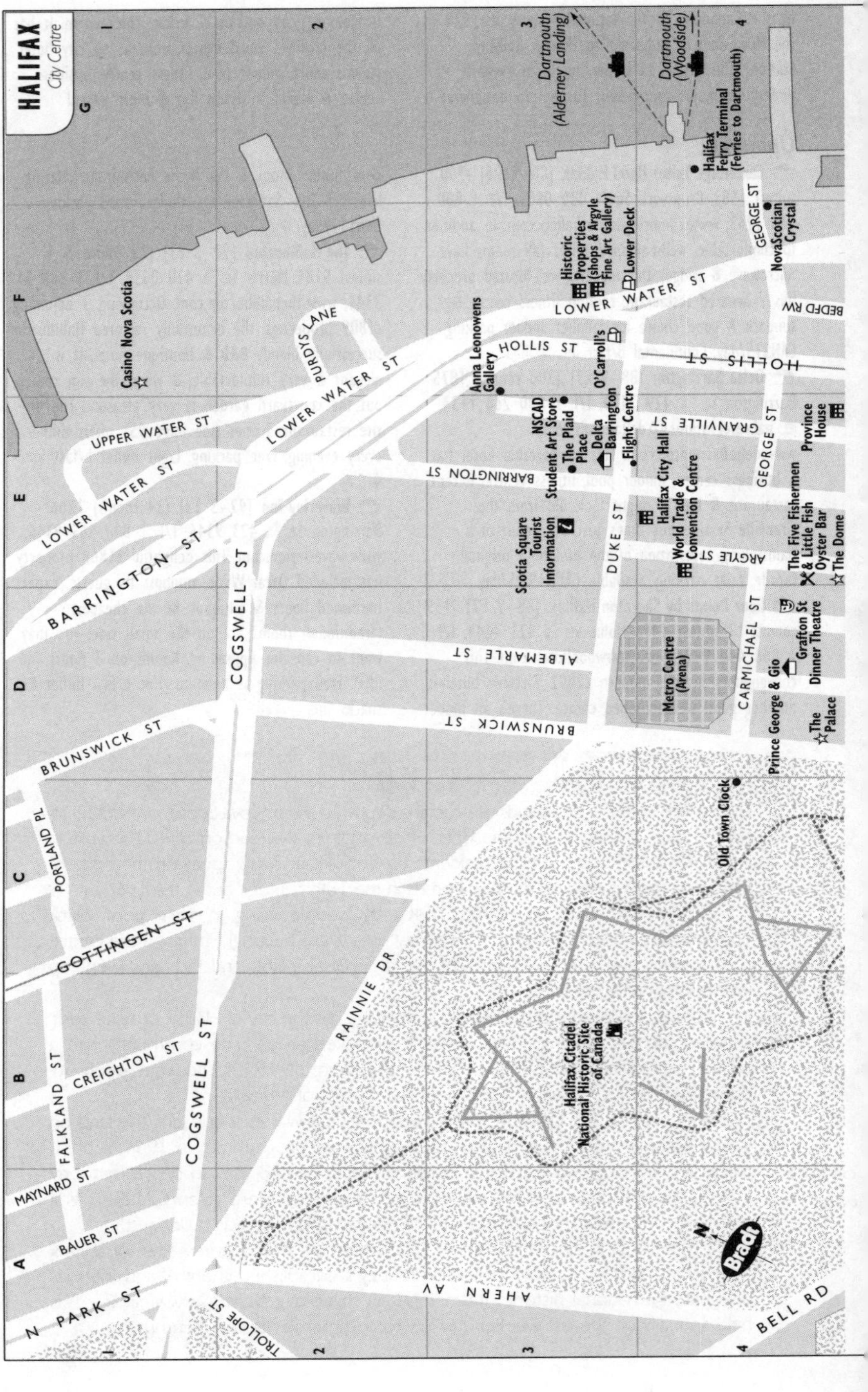

G H I

1

2

3

4

A B C D E F G

Casino Nova Scotia

Dartmouth
(Alderney Landing)

Dartmouth
(Woodside)

Halifax
Ferry Terminal
(Ferries to Dartmouth)

Historic
Properties
(shops & Argyle
Fine Art Gallery)

Lower Deck

GEORGE ST

NovaScotian
Crystal

BEDFD RW

LOWER WATER ST

HOLLIS ST

HOLLIS ST

Anna Leonowens
Gallery

O'Carroll's

UPPER WATER ST

LOWER PURDYS LANE

LOWER WATER ST

NSCAD
Student Art Store

The Plaid
Place

Delta
Barrington

Flight Centre

GRANVILLE ST

Province
House

BARRINGTON ST

BARRINGTON ST

Halifax City Hall

GEORGE ST

The Five Fishermen
& Little Fish
Oyster Bar

The Dome

COGSWELL ST

Scotia Square
Tourist
Information

DUKE ST

World Trade &
Convention Centre

ARGYLE ST

LOWER WATER ST

BARRINGTON ST

ALBEMARLE ST

CARMICHAEL ST

Grafton St
Dinner Theatre

COGSWELL ST

BRUNSWICK ST

Metro Centre
(Arena)

Prince George & Gio

The
Palace

PORTLAND PL

Old Town Clock

GOTTINGEN ST

RAINNIE DR

Halifax Citadel
National Historic Site
of Canada

BRUNSWICK ST

CREIGHTON ST

COGSWELL ST

FALKLAND ST

MAYNARD ST

BAUER ST

N PARK ST

TROLLOPE ST

AHERN AV

BELL RD

N

Bradt

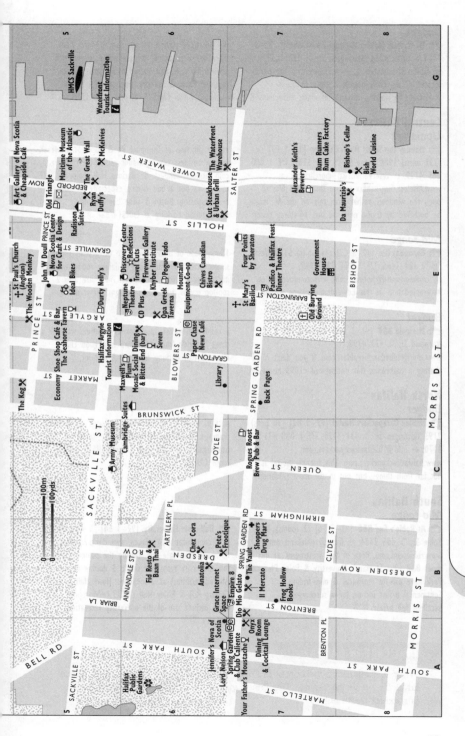

Map labels:

5

6

7

8

G

F

E

D

C

B

A

BELL RD

SACKVILLE ST

Halifax Public Gardens

BRIAR LA

ANNANDALE ROW

SACKVILLE ST

SOUTH PARK ST

Army Museum

Cambridge Suites

BRUNSWICK ST

SACKVILLE ST

The Keg

Economy Shoe Shop Café & Bar, The Seahorse Tavern

PRINCE ST

St Paul's Church (Anglican)
The Wooden Monkey

John W Doull
Ideal Bikes

Durty Nelly's

Halifax Argyle
Tourist Information

Maxwell's Plum

Mosaic Social Dining & Bitter End (bar)

Seven

ARGYLE ST

MARKET ST

BLOWERS ST

GRAFTON ST

Paper Chase News Café

Library

Neptune Theatre

CD Plus

Opa Greek Taverna

Pogue Fado

Discovery Centre
Reflections

Travel Cuts
Fireworks Gallery
Khyber Institute

Mountain Equipment Co-op

Chives Canadian Bistro

GRANVILLE ST

Nova Scotia Centre for Craft & Design

Radisson Suite

PRINCE ST

Old Triangle

Art Gallery of Nova Scotia & Cheapside Café

ROW

BEDFORD ROW

Maritime Museum of the Atlantic

Ryan Duffy's
The Great Wall
McKelvies

HOLLIS ST

LOWER WATER ST

Cut Steakhouse & Urban Grill

SALTER ST

The Waterfront Warehouse

St Mary's Basilica

St Mary's Basilica

BARRINGTON ST

SPRING GARDEN RD

Old Burying Ground

Back Pages

Pacifico & Halifax Feast Dinner Theatre

Four Points by Sheraton

Government House

BISHOP ST

Alexander Keith's Brewery

Rum Runners Rum Cake Factory
Bishop's Cellar
Bish World Cuisine

Da Maurizio's

HMCS Sackville

Waterfront Tourist Information

DOYLE ST

QUEEN ST

Rogues Roost Brew Pub & Bar

MORRIS ST

MORRIS ST

DRESDEN ROW

CLYDE ST

BIRMINGHAM ST

SPRING GARDEN RD

Shoppers Drug Mart

BRENTON ST

Frog Hollow Books

Il Mercato

BRENTON PL

ARTILLERY PL

DRESDEN ROW

Chez Cora
Pete's Frootique

Fid Resto & Baan Thai

Anatolia

Empire 8

Dio Mio Gelato

The Vault

Grace Internet Space

SPRING GARDEN RD

Onyx

Jennifer's Nova of Scotia
Lord Nelson
Spring Garden & Club Caliente

Your Father's Moustache
Dining Room & Cocktail Lounge

SOUTH PARK ST

MARTELLO ST

0 100m

0 100yds

89

Budget

🏠 **HI-Halifax: Halifax Heritage House Hostel** [92–3 F3] (75 beds) 1253 Barrington St; ✆ 422 3863; e halifax@hihostels.ca; www.hihostels.ca. The better located of the city's hostels is close to the waterfront in walking distance of many attractions & the bus/train station. In addition to dorm beds, there are a couple of private/family rooms with private baths & also shared bathrooms, kitchen, common room & laundry. Discounts for YHA/HI members. Dorm CAN$35, private room CAN$57. $

Central Halifax
Upmarket

🏠 **Holiday Inn Select Halifax Centre** [92–3 C3] (232 units) 1980 Robie St; ✆ 423 1161, T/F 1 800 465 4329; e reservations@hihotelhalifax.ca; www.hiselect.com/halifax-centre. Those who like to open the windows, rather than rely on the AC, might be bothered by traffic noise at this 14-storey tower at the junction of Quinpool Rd & Robie St. However, with a business centre, indoor pool, fitness centre, coin laundry, sundeck & spacious well-equipped rooms, it's not a bad choice, especially for the businessperson. Bistro & wine bar on site. Underground parking at CAN$14/day. $$$

Mid-range

🏠 **Commons Inn** [92–3 C2] (41 units) 5780 West St; ✆ 484 3466, T/F 1 877 797 7999; e commonsinn@hotmail.com; www.commonsinn.ca. Accommodation at this Edwardian building within a 15min walk of many downtown attractions includes simple standard rooms, larger deluxe rooms with microwave & fridge, & a suite. There are also 2 rooftop patios. Free parking. Light b/fast inc. $$

Budget

🏠 **Marigold B&B** [92–3 C4] (2 rooms) 6318 Norwood St; ✆ 423 4798; www.marigoldbedandbreakfast.com. If you don't mind sharing a bathroom, this uncluttered c1893 house on a residential street approximately 25mins' walk or a short bus ride from downtown is a good choice. Free off-road parking free. Full b/fast inc. $

North Halifax
Budget

🏠 **Halifax Backpackers Hostel** [92–3 D2] (30 beds) 2193 Gottingen St; ✆ 431 3170, T/F 1 888 431 3170; e info@halifaxbackpackers.com; www.halifaxbackpackers.com. This friendly hostel is not far from things, but not in the most salubrious part of town. A bit run down & dorms are a little cramped. Communal kitchen, laundry, lounge & on-site organic fairtrade café. Dorm CAN$23, private room CAN$58. $

South Halifax
Mid-range

🏠 **At Robie's End B&B** [92–3 F6] (2 rooms) 836 Robie St; ✆ 405 2424; e fran@robiesend.com; www.robiesend.com. Both of the guestrooms at this quiet B&B near St Mary's University & Point Pleasant Park have private entrances & mini-fridges. Continental b/fast inc or, for a surcharge, an excellent full b/fast. $$

🏠 **Dalhousie University** [92–3 E4] ✆ 494 8840; e accommodations@dal.ca; www.dal.ca/confserv; ⊕ early May–late Aug. During the summer break, this university rents out single & double rooms (shared facilities) at 2 locations: Howe Hall (6230 Coburg Rd) & Risley Hall (1233 LeMarchant St). Rates include use of the university recreation facilities. $$

TAKE CARE IN HALIFAX

When walking round the corner of Prince and Barrington streets in 1798, Prince Edward's horse fell heavily. The Prince injured his knee and was sent back to England for treatment.

In 1917, during her husband's time in Amherst (see page 260), Mrs Trotsky and the boys stayed in Halifax, first at the home of the local man who had been assigned as Trotsky's interpreter when he first came ashore, and later at the Prince George Hotel which was on the corner of Sackville and Hollis streets. That hotel burned down a few months after the Trotskys checked out and is connected in name alone with today's Prince George Hotel on Market Street.

Further out

🏠 **Pepperberry B&B** [92–3 A5] (5 rooms) 2688 Joseph Howe Dr; ☎ 479 1700, T/F 1 877 246 3244; e information@pepperberryinn.com; www.pepperberryinn.com. Outside the downtown area (about a 7min drive or a bus ride) near the Armdale Rotary, this elegant, comfortable c1915 house furnished with antiques on a leafy 0.4ha site offers individually decorated rooms. Free off-street parking. Full gourmet b/fast inc. $$$

🏕 **West Woodhaven RV Park** [76] (200 sites) 1757 Hammonds Plains Rd; ☎ 835 2271; www.woodhavenrvpark.com; ⏲ May–Oct. This campsite – 18km from downtown Halifax – is the nearest campground to Halifax or Dartmouth & a good 20min drive away. It has good facilities & a range of serviced & tent camping sites. $

Near the airport Plans to build a new airport hotel adjacent to the terminal were put on ice in 2009 because of the economic outlook. For now, the best options are:

🏠 **Inn on the Lake** [76] (40 units) 3009 Hwy 2, Fall River; ☎ 861 3480, T/F 1 800 463 6465; www.innonthelake.com. With 20 rooms & 20 suites, this establishment just off Hwy 102 Exit 5 offers more than most airport hotels including an outdoor (seasonal) pool & sandy lakeside beach: guests can use canoes & pedal boats. A complimentary airport shuttle is offered 05.00–midnight daily. The pub (⏲ 11.00–22.00 daily) offers food, as does the

rather good licensed Encore Restaurant (⏲ 07.00–22.00 daily). $$
🏠 **Holiday Inn Express Halifax Hotel and Suites** [76] (96 rooms & 23 suites) 180 Pratt & Whitney Drive, Enfield; ☎ 576 7600; www.hiexpress.com. New (2008) & very comfortable, close to Hwy 102 Exit 5A, less than 4km to the terminals. There's an indoor pool & free 24hr airport transfers. Hot b/fast buffet inc. $$

✗ **WHERE TO EAT** In recent years, the food scene in Halifax has seen great and wondrous changes. A new breed of entrepreneur restaurateurs have already made their mark, transforming what wasn't (with the odd exception) a place with the most exciting dining choices in the world.

Today's Halifax (and environs) paints a different story, and one is almost spoilt for choice. Whether you choose to eat in a café, pub, old-style diner or zanily designed trendy upmarket restaurant, in general standards are high and prices reasonable. Multi-cultures also mean a wide range of ethnic restaurants – always a good thing for the adventurous eater. Virtually all of the better restaurants accept reservations – some are so popular that these are a necessity.

Note that many restaurants charge significantly less for the same dish at lunch than in the evening.

Waterfront and downtown
Luxury

✗ **Bear** [92–3 F3] 1241 Barrington St; ☎ 425 2327; www.bearrestaurant.com; ⏲ 17.00–23.00 Mon–Sat. After a successful spell at Gio (see below), chef Ray Bear branched out on his own. In no time

at all, his new venture – offering wonderful modern global cuisine & a stylish but relaxed atmosphere – has become the hottest place in town. $$$$

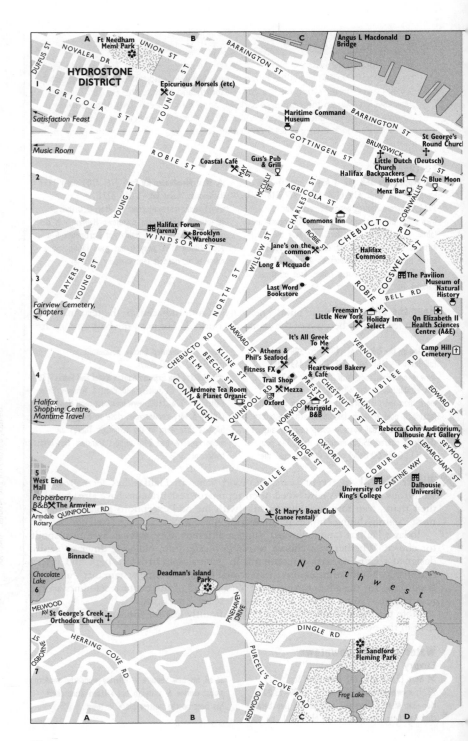

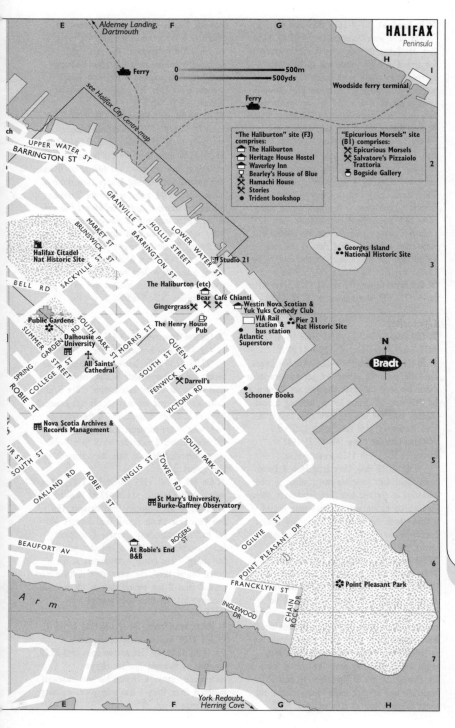

HALIFAX
Peninsula

Alderney Landing, Dartmouth

Ferry

0 ———————— 500m
0 ———————— 500yds

Ferry

Woodside ferry terminal

see Halifax City Centre map

UPPER WATER ST

BARRINGTON ST

"The Haliburton" site (F3) comprises:
- The Haliburton
- Heritage House Hostel
- Waverley Inn
- Bearley's House of Blue
- Hamachi House
- Stories
- Trident bookshop

"Epicurious Morsels" site (B1) comprises:
- Epicurious Morsels
- Salvatore's Pizzaiolo Trattoria
- Bogside Gallery

GRANVILLE ST

MARKET ST
BRUNSWICK ST
HOLLIS STREET
LOWER WATER ST
BARRINGTON ST

Halifax Citadel Nat Historic Site

SACKVILLE ST

Studio 21

Georges Island National Historic Site

BELL RD

The Haliburton (etc)

Bear Café Chianti
Gingergrass

Westin Nova Scotian & Yuk Yuks Comedy Club

Public Gardens

SOUTH PARK ST RD

The Henry House Pub

VIA Rail station & bus station

Pier 21 Nat Historic Site

SUMMER ST

GARDEN

Dalhousie University

MORRIS ST

QUEEN ST

Atlantic Superstore

SPRING GARDEN RD

COLLEGE STREET

All Saints' Cathedral

SOUTH ST

FENWICK ST

Darrell's

N

ROBIE ST

VICTORIA RD

Schooner Books

Bradt

Nova Scotia Archives & Records Management

UR SOUTH ST

INGLIS ST

TOWER RD

SOUTH PARK ST

OAKLAND RD

ROBIE ST

St Mary's University, Burke-Gaffney Observatory

OGILVIE ST

POINT PLEASANT DR

BEAUFORT AV

ROGERS ST

At Robie's End B&B

FRANCKLYN ST

CHAIN ROCK DR

Point Pleasant Park

Arm

INGLEWOOD DR

York Redoubt, Herring Cove

Da Maurizio's [88–9 F8] 1496 Lower Water St; ☎ 423 0859; www.damaurizio.ca; ⊕ 17.00–22.00 Mon–Sat. Before the new wave of exciting places to eat arrived in Halifax, there was da Maurizio's. Specialising in superb north Italian cuisine, this elegant restaurant in the Alexander Keith Brewery complex has more than held its own against some very good competition. Delightful fine-dining. **$$$$**

Ryan Duffy's [88–9 F5] 1650 Bedford Row; ☎ 421 1116; www.ryanduffys.ca; ⊕ 06.30–23.00 Mon–Fri, 07.00–23.00 Sat–Sun. Settled in smoothly in a new location, this old-style upmarket steakhouse still draws discerning & well-heeled steak lovers. There are 2 eating areas, a lounge — which also features a tapas menu — & a more formal dining room: both are simple & elegant. Steak apart, seafood is strongly promoted too, but whether non meat-eaters will enjoy seeing slabs of raw meat carved table-side before being wheeled away to be cooked over charcoal is debatable. **$$$$**

Bish World Cuisine [88–9 F8] 1475 Lower Water St; ☎ 425 7993; www.bish.ca; ⊕ 17.30–22.00 Mon–Sat. Another of the eateries (including Da Maurizio's & Il Mercato — see page 95) owned & run by skilled restaurateurs, this very stylish, upmarket waterfront restaurant offers innovative food, beautifully prepared & presented, though portions aren't huge. The patio is wonderful in summer. **$$$–$$$$**

Cut Steakhouse & Urban Grill [88–9 F6] 5120 Salter St; ☎ 429 5120; www.cutsteakhouse.ca; ⊕ (Grill) 12.00–15.00 daily, (Grill & Steakhouse) 17.00–22.00 daily. There are 2 different dining experiences here: the downstairs Grill is fun & funky with contemporary lighting & large comfortable booths; upstairs the atmosphere in the Steakhouse is relaxed yet luxurious. Both floors offer a fine view of the Halifax waterfront & alfresco dining. The Grill has a light, global menu of tapas-style dishes good for sharing. Upstairs, carnivores prepared to pay for quality can choose from local (well, rural Nova Scotia), prime US, or Kobe beef steaks. There are several non-meat choices too, but this isn't a place for vegetarians. **$$–$$$$**

Upmarket

Café Chianti [92–3 F3] 5165 South St; ☎ 423 7471; www.cafechianti.ca; ⊕ 12.00–14.00 & 17.00–22.00 Mon–Fri, 17.00–22.00 Sat–Sun. Despite the name, the menu includes not just northern Italian dishes, but some Hungarian favourites too. Décor is a bit Hollywood-style Italian for me, including a small roadside patio, but who cares when the food is this good. Particularly good value at lunch. **$$$**

Chives Canadian Bistro [88–9 E6] 1537 Barrington St; ☎ 420 9626; www.chives.ca; ⊕ 17.00–21.30 daily. Chefs Craig Flinn & Darren Lewis adjust their (relatively short) menus to take advantage of the best fresh local ingredients, dishing up Canadian cuisine with a unique twist. Housed in a former bank, the atmosphere is warm & relaxed. Considering the quality of the food, presentation & service, prices are very reasonable. **$$$**

Fid Resto [88–9 B6] 1569 Dresden Row; ☎ 422 9162; www.fidcuisine.ca; ⊕ 17.00–22.00 Tue & Sat–Sun, 11.30–14.00 & 17.00–22.00 Wed–Fri. This modern, minimalist restaurant isn't huge, & the frequently changing menu shorter than many in the city. But, oh, the food! Chef Dennis Johnston blends fresh, predominantly organic, ingredients simply but to stellar effect. On the lunch menu, steak frites might line up alongside green Thai chicken curry. In the evening, the mix of ingredients, eg: beef tenderloin with burdock, might raise eyebrows, but works! Desserts keep up standards, too. **$$$**

The Five Fishermen [88–9 E4] 1740 Argyle St; ☎ 422 4421; www.fivefishermen.com; ⊕ 17.00–22.30 daily. Seafood-lovers should make a beeline for this conveniently located, consistently good restaurant, housed in a historic c1816 building. There are also good non-fishy choices, but beautifully prepared fresh fish & shellfish — & the renowned wine cellar — are the focus. Main courses include unlimited mussels & salad bar which helps make prices more variable — as does the occasional 'early-bird' special. **$$$**

Gio [88–9 D4] 1725 Market St; ☎ 425 1986; www.giohalifax.com; ⊕ 11.00–23.00 Mon–Fri, 17.00–23.00 Sat. Originally from Malaysia, Chef Ben Choo Char blends superb local produce with Far Eastern (particularly Japanese & southeast Asian) touches successfully at this chic, modern, fine-dining — but casual — restaurant at the Prince George Hotel. The menu often includes more unusual meat & fish choices such as elk or *cobia* – a large fish. Far from your average hotel restaurant. **$$$**

Mosaic Social Dining [88–9 D6] 1584 Argyle St; ☎ 405 4700; www.mosaicsocialdining.com; ⊕ 16.00–02.00 Tue–Sat, kitchen open until 22.00 Tue–Wed, to midnight Thu–Sat. Elegant contemporary eatery & cocktail bar with somewhat theatrical décor. Share a few 'small plates' including the flatbread & dips. **$$$**

✘ **Onyx Dining Room & Cocktail Lounge** [88–9 A7] 5680 Spring Garden Rd; ✆ 428 5680; www.onyxdining.com; ◷ 16.30–02.00 Mon–Sat. Elegant, sleek, with a magnificent translucent onyx bar & crystal chandelier, one can't help but be impressed on entry: not a great place to eat alone. The food is Asian-inspired global cuisine with French influences, & there are 2- & 3-course *prix fixé* menus, & a sharing (tapas-type) menu. Sip a cocktail, tuck in to the sublime herb-crusted rack of lamb, & round off with the Onyx turtle. **$$$**

Mid-range

✘ **Anatolia** [88–9 B6] 1518 Dresden Row; ✆ 492 4568; ◷ 11.00–22.00 Mon–Sat, 15.00–22.00 Sun. Whereas the Halifax Regional Municipality has numerous Greek restaurants, Turkish options are very few & far between. Anatolia is very good, & licensed. With tilework, an ornate copper stove-hood & Turkish carpets, the décor is inviting without being too Ali Baba. The food is fresh & tasty, from the range of starters to the charcoal-grilled mains. **$$**
✘ **Baan Thai** [88–9 B6] 1569 Dresden Rd; ✆ 446 4301; www.baanthai.ca; ◷ 17.00–22.00 Sat–Wed, 12.00–14.30 & 17.00–22.00 Thu–Fri. Authentic, high-quality Thai food in pleasant surroundings, plus an outdoor patio which is lovely when the weather obliges. **$$**
✘ **Cheapside Café** [88–9 F5] 1723 Hollis St; ✆ 425 4494; www.agns.gov.ns.ca; ◷ 10.00–17.00 Mon–Sat (to 20.00 Thu), 11.00–17.00 Sun. You don't need to be a culture-vulture to appreciate this excellent café in the Art Gallery of Nova Scotia. The menu is imaginative, & it is the kind of bright, vibrant — but still laid-back place that is just as good for a coffee & scrumptious dessert as something more substantial & if you do like art, you won't be disappointed. **$$**
✘ **Gingergrass** [92–3 F3] 1284 Barrington St; ✆ 425 8555; ◷ 11.30–21.00 Tue–Thu, 11.30–22.00 Fri–Sat. Come for simple, sensibly priced traditional Vietnamese & Thai cuisine that will tingle your taste buds. Friendly & relaxed. **$$**
✘ **Hamachi House** [92–3 F3] 5190 Morris St; 425 7711; www.hamachirestaurants.com; ◷ 11.30– midnight daily. The first of 4 Hamachi restaurants to open in the HRM (see website for the others) is my favourite place in Halifax for Japanese food. The standards are there, of course, but so too are some brave 'fusion' additions. A bento box (Japanese take-away) makes a tasty & healthy lunch. Considering how expensive good Japanese restaurants can be in other parts of the world, treat yourself here! **$$**

✘ **Stories** [92–3 F3] 5184 Morris St; ✆ 444 4400; www.storiesdining.com; ◷ 17.30–21.00 Tue–Sun. Better known for its guestrooms, The Halliburton (see page 87) has a fine-dining winner in Stories. Cuisine is upmarket Canadian, & the menu has a good balance of choices from the land & sea. Presentation & service are impeccable: in winter, enjoy fireside dining, & in summer eat on the patio if the weather permits. **$$$**

✘ **jane's on the common** [92–3 B3] 2394 Robie St; ✆ 431 5683; www.janesonthecommon.com; ◷ 11.00–14.30 & 17.00–21.00 Tue–Fri (to 22.00 Fri), 09.30–14.30 & 17.00–22.00 Sat, 09.30–14.30 & 17.00–21.00 Sun. Quite a few people with very little experience of commercial catering decide to open a restaurant: very rarely do they achieve the ongoing & deserved success of Jane Wright's place. Several gluten-free choices are offered, & weekend brunch is one of many highlights. Building on her achievements, she has added a take-out counter next door (expect gourmet sandwiches, beverages & baked goods). Like the excellent main restaurant, the take-out displays her seeming dislike of capital letters — it is 'jane's next door'. **$$**
✘ **The Keg** [88–9 D5] 1712 Market St; ✆ 425 8355; www.kegsteakhouse.com; ◷ 16.30–22.00 Mon–Sat, 16.30–21.30 Sun. This Vancouver-based chain now has restaurants all over the country & in 5 US states. Are the steaks as good as at, say, Cut or Ryan Duffy's (see page 94)? No. But the Keg is a lot cheaper, service is friendly & enthusiastic, & few go away disappointed. **$$**
✘ **Little Fish Restaurant & Oyster Bar** [88–9 E4] 1740 Argyle St; ✆ 425 4025; www.littlefishrestaurant.ca; ◷ 11.30–22.00 daily year-round. Located below the Five Fishermen (see page 94), this is a more casual, family-friendly (& cheaper) alternative. Eat on the patio if the weather permits. Those who find Nova Scotia portions too generous can order 'little plates'. Oyster Happy Hour 16.00–18.00 daily. **$$**
✘ **Il Mercato** [88–9 B7] 5650 Spring Garden Rd; ✆ 422 2866; www.il-mercato.ca; ◷ 11.00–23.00 Mon–Sat. The food & atmosphere shout 'Italian trattoria' but the décor is contemporary. From the antipasti to the *zucotto* (a dessert that will banish tiramisu from your mind) it is all good. Filled focaccias & gourmet pizzas, eg: one topped with fontina cheese, duck, roast pumpkin & toasted pecan, & a good wine list round off the menu. Usually

bustling, it might not be the best bet for a quiet evening out. $$

✕ McKelvie's [88–9 F5] 1680 Lower Water St; ☎ 421 6161; www.mckelvies.com; ⏰ 11.30–22.00 Mon–Sat, 16.30–22.00 Sun. The full name is 'McKelvie's delishes fishes dishes' but this isn't some awful themed restaurant where the menu descriptions are peppered (ha) with bad puns. There are decent alternatives that didn't originate underwater, a family-friendly-but-still-formal-enough-for-business-meetings atmosphere, & a decent wine list. Best of all, the fish & shellfish — cooked in a wide variety of ways — are good value & indeed delicious. $$

✕ Opa Greek Taverna [88–9 E6] 1565 Argyle St; ☎ 492 7999; www.opataverna.com; ⏰ 11.00–23.00 Mon–Sat, 16.00–22.00 Sun. If it's cold, wet & foggy out (or even if it is hot & sticky) transport yourself to this lively little bit of sunny Greece. Sit under the olive tree, order a bunch of *mezethes* (starters), &/or the usual — but very well done — Greek specialities. Desserts (not just baklava!) include some delicious non-Hellenic calorific choices. Opa is getting very popular, so get there before portion sizes shrink & prices enlarge. $$

Budget

✕ Chez Cora [88–9 B6] 1535 Dresden Row; ☎ 490 2672; www.chezcora.com; ⏰ 06.00–15.00 Mon–Sat, 07.00–15.00 Sun. What started off in a former snack bar in Montreal has rapidly grown to become a chain of about 100 eateries countrywide. This one, just off Spring Garden Rd, is one of the most convenient. Expect bright, cheery décor, hearty servings of omelettes, waffles, pancakes & crêpes (balanced by lots of fresh fruit). $

✕ Darrell's [92–3 F4] 5576 Fenwick St; ☎ 492 2344; www.darrellsrestaurants.com; ⏰ 11.00–22.00 daily. There are salads, very good pita bread wraps, sandwiches & more, but the burgers are hard to resist (except perhaps for the bizarrely popular peanut butter-smothered one). Attempt to wash it down with a super-thick milkshake. Close to the university & with a downstairs area where sport is shown on a large-screen TV, it is understandably popular with students. $

✕ Dio Mio Gelato [88–9 B7] 5670 Spring Garden Rd; ☎ 492 3467; ⏰ 08.00–21.00 Mon–Fri,

North End and Hydrostone
Mid-range and budget

✕ Brooklyn Warehouse [92–3 B3] 2795 Windsor St; ☎ 446 8181; www.brooklynwarehouse.ca; ⏰ 11.30–15.00 & 17.00–21.00 Mon–Fri,

✕ The Waterfront Warehouse [88–9 F6] 1549 Lower Water St; ☎ 425 7610; www.rcr.ca/restaurants/waterfront-warehouse; ⏰ 11.30–22.00 daily. This warehouse — once a tugboat repair shop scheduled for demolition — is thoroughly enjoying its new life as a nautically themed restaurant with a huge stone fireplace & floor-to-ceiling windows overlooking the Halifax Waterfront. The seafood-dominated menu includes oysters, rather good crab cakes, &, of course, lobster. If the weather allows, dine *al fresco* on one of the patios. $$

✕ The Wooden Monkey [88–9 E5] 1707 Grafton St; ☎ 444 3844; www.thewoodenmonkey.ca; ⏰ 11.30–22.00 Sun–Thu, 11.30–23.00 Fri–Sat. Health-conscious diners will enjoy this eatery where just about everything is organic, macrobiotic, locally grown & very tasty. To such a degree that spring (rather than tap) water is used in food preparation. What I think is also good is that the menu offers vegetarian — plus vegan & gluten-free — & meat options. As they have done since the 1960s, such places attract artists, musicians & other such bohemians. Peace. $$

12.00–18.00 Sat–Sun. How does a place offering (albeit excellent) Italian-style ice cream & sorbets survive year-round in Halifax? By also being a café serving up good coffee, dependable bagels, sandwiches & paninis, & some of the tastiest veggie burgers you're ever likely to find. $

✕ The Great Wall [88–9 F5] 1649 Bedford Row; ☎ 422 6153; www.thegreatwall.ca; ⏰ 11.30–22.00 daily. Everything is made from scratch in this well-established Chinese restaurant. The Sun dim sum session (*11.30–15.00*) is justifiably popular. Flavoursome & good value. $

✕ Pete's Frootique [88–9 B6] 1515 Dresden Row; ☎ 425 5700; www.petesfrootique.com; ⏰ 08.00–20.00 Mon–Fri, 08.00–18.00 Sat–Sun. Pete started his business life running a market stall in Nottingham, England. Although primarily an upmarket grocery store, pop in to Pete's To Go or the Hot Bar Action Station for delectable healthy sandwiches & more. $

10.00–15.00 & 17.00–21.00 Sat, 10.00–15.00 Sun. This relatively new addition to the North End dining scene hit the ground running. The team of chefs use

fresh local ingredients in a varied menu which blends & twists North American classics, hints of Asia, & touches of the Mediterranean. No reservations. **$$**
✖ **Coastal Café** [92–3 B2] 2731 Robie St; ☎ 405 4022; www.thecoastal.ca; ⏰ 08.00–15.00 Tue–Sat, 10.00–15.00 Sun. Whilst the HRM has no shortage of food joints offering uninspired but adequate (generally unhealthy) breakfasts & lunches, this is a place in the North End for those looking for higher standards. Unusually for a place that doesn't do dinner, it's run by an excellent chef. Choose, eg: Eggs Camden – scrambled, with smoked salmon, Havarti cheese & chives. **$$**
✖ **Epicurious Morsels** [92–3 B1] 5529 Young St; ☎ 455 0955; www.epicuriousmorsels.com; ⏰ 11.30–15.00 & 17.00–20.00 Tue–Fri, 10.30–14.30 & 17.00–21.00 Sat, 10.30–14.30 & 17.00–20.00 Sun. This is an interesting little place in the Hydrostone, tastefully decorated & comfortable – romantic even. Chef Jim Hanusiak's menu isn't overlong, but whether you're there for the excellent weekend brunch, or a dinner of French–

Mediterranean-inspired dishes & a glass or two of wine, I think you'll be impressed. Be sure to try some in-house-smoked Atlantic salmon. **$$**
✖ **Salvatore's Pizzaiolo Trattoria** [92–3 B1] 5541 Young St; ☎ 455 1133; www.salvatorespizza.ca; ⏰ 11.30–23.00 Tue–Sat, 16.00–22.00 Sun–Mon. It is hard for a pizzeria to stand out from a multitude of others without a gimmick or extreme toppings. The best in town shines bright for the thin-crust bases & quality of ingredients. With 20 toppings to choose from, build your own, or order from the menu – I like to keep it simple & stick to the roasted garlic & sautéed mushrooms. **$$**
✖ **Satisfaction Feast** [92–3 A1] 3559 Robie St; ☎ 422 3540; ⏰ 10.00–20.00 Tue, Thu & Sun, 10.00–15.30 Wed, 10.00–21.00 Fri–Sat. In a new North End location, the oldest vegetarian & vegan restaurant in Halifax isn't resting on its laurels. With a menu including French toast, wraps, curries, burgers (veggie of course), samosas & lasagne, there's something for just about everyone. Try the 'neat' loaf. **$**

Quinpool Road
If you find downtown/waterfront prices too high, or fancy a wander past a varied selection of ethnic and/or budget eateries, head along Quinpool Road. Here are a few highlights:

✖ **Mezza** [92–3 C4] 6386 Quinpool Rd; ☎ 444 3914; www.mezzarestaurant.com; ⏰ 11.30–22.00 Tue–Sun (to 23.00 Fri–Sat). Contemporary & stylish Lebanese fine-dining. For many, a selection of authentic hot & cold starters make a meal in themselves: others need to move on to grilled meat or seafood before an ambrosial dessert not that well known in Beirut – Bailey's cheesecake. **$$$**
✖ **The Armview** [92–3 A5] 7156 Chebucto Rd; ☎ 455 4395; www.thearmview.com; ⏰ 11.00–23.00 Mon–Wed, 08.30–23.45 Thu–Sun. The décor is late 1950s, the menu long and varied, the service friendly, and the food – diner meets *haute cuisine* – superb. Near the Armdale Rotary. **$$–$$$**
✖ **Heartwood Bakery & Café** [92–3 C4] 6250 Quinpool Rd; ☎ 425 2808; www.heartwoodbakeryandcafe.ca; ⏰ 10.00–20.00 Mon–Sat. With a menu that is predominantly vegetarian, vegan & gluten-free, it is good to know that this restaurant uses unprocessed whole grains, fresh fruit & veg, & unrefined oils & sweeteners. Pop in for a bite – rather appetising soups, dips, salads, pastas, etc – or just to grab a decadent-looking but apparently healthy hazelnut brownie or other treat. **$$**

✖ **It's All Greek To Me** [92–3 C4] 6196 Quinpool Rd; ☎ 406 3737; www.allgreektome.com; ⏰ 11.00–22.00 Mon–Sat. This is a bright, fashionable, well-designed upmarket Greek restaurant. Importantly, the food is very good too, from the dips & appetisers to the fish, grilled meat & oven-baked mains. Incidentally, the **Athens** [92–3 C4] (6303 Quinpool Rd; ☎ 422 1595; ⏰ 09.00–22.00 Sun–Thu, 08.00–23.00 Fri–Sat) is another good Greek choice. **$$**
✖ **Ardmore Tea Room** [92–3 B4] 6499 Quinpool Rd; ☎ 423 7523; ⏰ 05.00–20.00 daily. The Ardmore – going for over half a century – just keeps on dishing out the all-day breakfasts & more. Come for huge, cholesterol-packed portions & low prices – not décor or linen tablecloths. Small & ever-popular. **$**
✖ **Freeman's Little New York** [92–3 C3] 6092 Quinpool Rd; ☎ 455 7000; www.freemanspizza.ca; ⏰ 11.00–05.00 daily. Nightbirds who feel like something to eat in the wee small hours best off at this Quinpool Rd institution. Pizzas, burgers, pastas, nachos & more. **$**
✖ **Phil's Seafood** [92–3 C4] 6285 Quinpool Rd; ☎ 431 3474; ⏰ 11.30–20.00 daily. A great fish & chip shop especially if you prefer lots of fish to lots of batter. There are scallops, shrimps & more, too – & it doesn't have to be fried. Good value. **$**

ENTERTAINMENT AND NIGHTLIFE

Pubs It is often said that Halifax has more pubs/bars per capita than anywhere else in Canada.

Several of the region's better pubs serve good-value, sometimes quite upmarket, pub food, and many of the following could be listed just as easily in the *Where to eat* section.

Halifax's most famous brewery is Alexander Keith's (see page 109): within that complex is the Stag's Head Tavern. You'll visit it if you do the brewery tour, but can also just pop in for (for example) a glass of Keith's celebrated India Pale Ale. The atmosphere is friendly, but rarely raucous. Halifax has other brewpubs worth visiting:

Durty Nelly's [88–9 E5] Corner Argyle & Sackville sts; \ 406 7640; www.durtynellys.ca; ⊕ 11.30–02.00 daily. This place prides itself so much on being authentic that it was designed & built in Ireland, shipped to Halifax & put together piece by piece. New (2009), but already a hit.

The Henry House Pub [92–3 F4] 1222 Barrington St; \ 423 5660; www.henryhouse.ca; ⊕ 11.30–midnight Mon–Thu, 11.30–01.00 Fri–Sat, 11.30–23.30 Sun. In a lovely historic 1834 building, this is a must-visit for fans of traditional British pubs. The main dining area upstairs turns out well above average old-style dishes, supplemented by Maritime favourites. Amongst many other tipples, 6 locally brewed British-style ales are offered – sample the Peculiar.

Lower Deck [88–9 F3] 1869 Upper Water St; \ 425 1501; ⊕ 11.30–01.00 daily. Another well-patronised place with regular generally high-quality live music & entertainment. Good food helps make this one of the waterfront's most popular venues.

Maxwell's Plum [88–9 D6] 1600 Grafton St; \ 423 5090; www.themaxwellsplum.com; ⊕ 11.00–02.00 daily. One of the largest selections of on tap beers in the country, plus dozens of bottled varieties. A good place to try the produce of microbreweries, local & otherwise. 4 large-screen TVs, so often lively.

O'Carroll's [88–9 F3] 1860 Upper Water St; \ 423 4405; www.ocarrolls.com; ⊕ 11.00–01.30 daily. As the name might suggest, an Irish pub offering a good range of beer & whiskies. The pub fare isn't bad at all, & there's a more upmarket restaurant part. Live music most nights.

Old Triangle Irish Ale House [88–9 F5] 5136 Prince St; \ 492 4900; www.oldtriangle.com; ⊕ 11.30–midnight Sun–Wed, 11.00–02.00 Thu–Fri, 11.30–02.00 Sat. Equally good for a bite to eat, a drink, or live music. The sweet potato fries may be less authentic than, say, the Irish stew, but boy are they good.

Pogue Fado [88–9 E6] 1581 Barrington St; \ 429 6222; www.poguefado.com; ⊕ 11.00–02.00 daily. Friendly, lively Irish pub with more than adequate food & live music.

Rogue's Roost Brew Pub & Grill [88–9 C7] 5435 Spring Garden Rd; \ 492 2337; www.roguesroost.ca; ⊕ 11.00–02.00 daily. A brewpub, restaurant & live music venue. Try the Oatmeal Stout, & Raspberry Wheat Ale. Service & food are both good.

Bars

Bitter End [88–9 D6] 1572 Argyle St; \ 425 3039; www.bitterend.ca; ⊕ 11.30–02.00 Mon–Fri, 11.00–02.00 Sat–Sun. Warm & comfortable Martini bar & restaurant with wood floors, lots of exposed brickwork, table & booth seating. With 30 types of Martini, plus a wide range of cocktails & more.

Economy Shoe Shop Cafe and Bar [88–9 E5] 1661–3 Argyle St; 423 7463; ⊕ 11.00–01.30 daily. Once word got out that 'the Shoe' was very much in focus with the burgeoning film industry in Halifax, it rapidly became a place to celebrity spot & see-&-be-seen. Food standards seem to rise & drop (a couple of starters are usually a better bet than a main),

TRAILER PARK BOYS

This TV 'mockumentary' about ex-convicts and other residents of a fictional Halifax trailer park ran for seven seasons and spawned 'specials' and full-length films. Fans of the show will want to visit Halifax Bar, Bubbles Mansion (*5287 Prince St;* \ 405 4505; www.bubblesmansion.com), named after one of the main characters.

but eating & drinking seem of secondary importance in this unusual tangle of eclectically decorated rooms. Fashions can change quickly, so you might come away with your autograph book empty. Live jazz on Mon evenings.

♀ **Seven** [88–9 D6] 1579 Grafton St; ☎ 444 4777; www.sevenwinebar.com; ⏰ 16.00–02.00 Mon–Sat, 17.00–23.30 Sun. The upper part of a former fire station houses an elegant restaurant that is well

worth a try: downstairs is a stylish wine bar with one of the best selections in the city. Over two-dozen choices are available by the glass.

♀ **Your Father's Moustache Pub & Eatery** [88–9 A7] 5686 Spring Garden Rd; ☎ 423 6766; www.yourfathersmoustache.ca; ⏰ 10.00–midnight Sun–Wed, 10.00–01.00 Thu–Sat. Restaurant, live music venue, bar & more. When the weather's kind, the rooftop deck overlooking the town is a delight.

Gay bars
♀ **Blue Moon** [92–3 D2] 2099 Gottingen St; ☎ 446 3644; www.thebluemoon.biz

♀ **Menz Bar** [92–3 D2] 2182 Gottingen St; ☎ 446 6969; www.seadogs.ca/menzbar/

Live music Far and away the best source of information for live music listings of all genres is the weekly free newspaper, *The Coast*, (*www.thecoast.ca*), also available in an online format. Many of the eateries, pubs and bars already mentioned host live music: here are some other possibilities:

Downtown
♀ **Bearly's House of Blues & Ribs** [92–3 F3] 1269 Barrington St; ☎ 423 2526; www.bearlys.ca. The best of blues both from within the province & further afield.

♀ **The Pavilion** [92–3 C3] 5816 Cogswell St; www.halifaxpavilion.com. Performances two to three evenings a week in this brick building near the pool & skate park on Halifax Common.

♀ **The Seahorse Tavern** [88–9 E5] 1665 Argyle St; ☎ 423 7200; www.theseahorse.ca. Located below the Economy Shoe Shop (see page 98) this great venue hosts everything from R&B to *klezmer* (Jewish folk/jazz).

North End
♀ **Gus's Pub and Grill** [92–3 C2] 2605 Agricola St; ☎ 423 7786. Small & cramped, but one of the best rock venues in town.

Nightclubs Like restaurants and bars, nightclubs come and go and fall in and out of fashion.

☆ **The Dome** [88–9 E4] 1726 Argyle St; ☎ 422 6907; ⏰ 22.00–03.30 Wed–Sun. Often referred to as the 'liquor dome', there are actually 4 clubs under one roof.

☆ **Pacifico** [88–9 E7] 1505 Barrington St; ☎ 422 3633; www.pacifico.ca; ⏰ 21.00–02.00 Thu–Sat. Come here on a Fri–Sat & you'll feel out of place if you're not wearing something bright & shiny!

☆ **The Palace** [88–9 D4] 1721 Brunswick St; ☎ 420 0015; www.thenewpalace.com; ⏰ 22.00–03.30 Wed–Sun.

☆ **Reflections** [88–9 E6] 5184 Sackville St; ☎ 422 2957; www.reflectionscabaret.com; ⏰ summer 20.00–04.00 daily; winter 20.00–04.00 Thu–Mon. Formerly known as a gay venue, now everyone comes here to dance & party.

Theatre
♕ **Neptune Theatre** [88–9 E6] 1593 Argyle St, Halifax; ☎ 429 7070, T/F 1 800 565 7345; www.neptunetheatre.com. Atlantic Canada's largest professional regional theatre incorporates the main auditorium of the Strand Theatre, built on this site (on the corner of Sackville Street) in 1915. The

theatre group was founded in 1962. Normally, the season runs mid-September–May: 6 mainstream productions are staged in the 485-seat Fountain Hall, whilst the intimate Studio Theatre is home to more innovative productions. Fountain Hall ticket prices tend to be CAN$30–45.

Dinner theatre Pay one price for a meal and theatrical production. We're not talking Shakespeare and Michelin star-cuisine but a fun evening with better than average food.

🖰 **Grafton Street Dinner Theatre** [88–9 D4] 1741 Grafton St, Halifax; ☎ 425 1961; www.graftonstdinnertheatre.com; ⏱ 18.45 Tue–Sun. A 3-act production & 3-course meal for CAN$48.

🖰 **Halifax Feast Dinner Theatre** [88–9 E7] 1505 Barrington St, Halifax; ☎ 420 1840; www.feastdinnertheatre.com; ⏱ 18.30 daily. A 2-act musical comedy & 3-course meal for CAN$48.

Comedy
🖰 **Yuk Yuks Comedy Club** [92–3 G3] Westin Nova Scotian, 1181 Hollis St, Halifax; ☎ 429 9857; www.yukyuks.com/location.aspx?LocationID=36; ⏱ 20.30 Tue–Thu, 19.30 & 22.30 Fri–Sat

Cinemas All of the HRM's main cinemas are part of the Empire (☎ 422 2022; www.empiretheatres.com) group. In addition to the Oxford (see below) art-house films might be shown at venues such as the Rebecca Cohn Auditorium (see below).

🖷 **Empire 8** [88–9 B7] Park Lane 5657 Spring Garden Rd, Halifax; ☎ 423 4860. Eight screen cinema
🖷 **Oxford** [92–3 C4] 6408 Quinpool Rd, Halifax; ☎ 423 7488. Although part of the Empire group, this lovely old Art-Deco cinema with balcony has yet to be chopped up into a multi-screen. Generally, the programme sticks to art-house films, but sometimes new blockbusters slip in.

Classical music, ballet and opera Symphony Nova Scotia (www.symphonynovascotia.ca), one of Canada's finest chamber orchestras, is renowned for its versatility; it's equally at home whether performing anything from Baroque to jazz. The orchestra is based at the **Rebecca Cohn Auditorium** [92–3 D5] (*Dalhousie Arts Centre, 6101 University Av;* ☎ 494 3820, T/F 1 800 874 1669; www.artscentre.dal.ca/box.html). The same venue hosts ballet performances by such groups as the **Halifax Ballet Theatre** [92–3 D5] (☎ 420 1647; www.halifaxballettheatre.org), and big-name concerts. Opera and ballet are also performed at the Dalhousie University Arts Centre's **Sir James Dunn Theatre** [92–3 D5] (*Dalhousie Arts Centre, 6101 University Av;* ☎ 494 3820, T/F 1 800 874 1669; www.artscentre.dal.ca/box.html).

A great place to listen to chamber music is the **Music Room** [92–3 A2] (*6181 Lady Hammond Rd;* ☎ 429 9467; www.scotiafestival.ns.ca) a new purpose-built 110-seat venue with superb acoustics.

The downtown **Halifax Metro Centre** [88–9 D4] (*1800 Argyle St;* ☎ 451 8000; www.halifaxmetrocentre.com) hosts major sporting events and concerts, and in the last year or two, the waterfront Casino Nova Scotia (see below) has begun to offer a stronger programme of regular entertainment.

Casino
Casino Nova Scotia [88–9 F1] (*1983 Upper Water St;* ☎ 425 7777, T/F 1 888 642 6376; www.casinonovascotia.com; ⏱ 10.00– 04.00 daily) Over 19s with money to burn can enjoy table games, slot machines and more at one of the province's two casinos – the other is in Sydney, Cape Breton Island (see page 325). There are a couple of dining options, the Trapeze Grille and Bar and Paradise Buffet, and a couple of entertainment venues, the Schooner Showroom and the smaller Harbourfront. If you don't gamble all your money away, Stay and Play packages (which include meal vouchers, parking and gaming lessons) can be good value.

SHOPPING Spring Garden Road [88–9 D7] is a good place to start, and now features a number of upmarket shopping arcades (such as City Centre Atlantic

[88–9 B7], Spring Garden Place [88–9 A6] and Park Lane [88–9 B7]) housing most of Canada's best-known retail chains – and some good independents. The area also has a great selection of cafés and bistros. There are also boutiques, bars and restaurants in the **Historic Properties** [88–9 F3] on Upper Water Street, a group of restored warehouses. The adjoining Granville Mall [88–9 F3] is also worth a wander. **Barrington Place** [88–9 F3] is a collection of smaller, specialised stores and shops. Down on the waterfront, the relatively new **Bishop's Landing** [88–9 F8] development also houses upmarket shops and places to eat and drink.

Away from the centre, the **Hydrostone Market** [92–3 B1] has a number of boutiques, whilst nearby **Agricola Street** [92–3 A1] is home to many stores that tread that fine line between antique and junk.

The big shopping malls are outside the downtown area. In Halifax, near the Armdale Rotary are the **Halifax Shopping Centre** [92–3 A4] (✆ 453 1752; www.halifaxshoppingcentre.com), and, across the road, the **West End Mall** [92–3 A5] (✆ 455 4101).

Many people head up to Exit 2A of Highway 102 and the big stores of Bayer's Lake's Chain Lake Drive.

Arts and crafts

Bogside Gallery [92–3 B1] 5527 Young St, Hydrostone Market; ✆ 453 3063; ⊕ 10.00–18.00 Mon–Fri. Intricate stained-glass pieces & much more.

Celtic Traditions [88–9 A6] 5640 Spring Garden Rd; ✆ 492 3390; ⊕ 09.30–18.00 Mon–Wed, 09.30–21.00 Thu–Fri, 09.30–17.30 Sat. Ideal for kilts and Celtic paraphernalia.

Fireworks Gallery [88–9 E6] 1569 Barrington St; ✆ 420 1735, T/F 1 800 720 4367; www.fireworksgallery.com; ⊕ 10.00–17.30 Mon–Sat. High-quality jewellery shop selling an extensive range by local & regional artisans.

Jennifer's of Nova Scotia [88–9 A6] 5635 Spring Garden Rd; ✆ 425 3119; www.jennifers.ns.ca; ⊕ 09.30–17.30 Mon–Sat, 11.00–17.00 Sun, Apr–Oct until 21.00 Wed–Fri. A range of quality crafts from all over the province plus a small selection of the best from other parts of the Maritimes.

Nova Scotia Art Gallery Shop [88–9 F5] 1712 Hollis St; ✆ 424 7542; www.agns.gov.ns.ca; ⊕ winter 10.00–17.00 Tue–Sun (to 21.00 Thu); summer 10.00–17.00 daily (to 21.00 Thu). A fine range of local art, crafts & folk art.

NovaScotian Crystal [88–9 F4] 5080 George St; ✆ 492 0416, T/F 1 888 977 2797; www.novascotiancrystal.com; ⊕ call for hours. Canada's only crystal glass maker. Watch master craftspeople using techniques & tools that haven't changed for centuries.

NSCAD Student Art Store [88–9 E3] 1871 Granville St; ✆ 494 8301; ⊕ 11.00–18.00 Tue–Sat. Unique pieces created by students at Nova Scotia's visual arts school.

The Plaid Place [88–9 E3] 1903 Barrington St; ✆ 429 6872, T/F 1 800 563 1749; www.plaidplace.com; ⊕ 09.30–17.30 Mon–Fri, 10.00–17.00 Sun. Ideal for kilts and Celtic paraphernalia.

Studio 21 [92–3 F3] 1223 Lower Water St; ✆ 420 1852; www.studio21.ca; ⊕ 11.00–18.00 Tue–Fri, 10.00–17.00 Sat, 12.00–17.00 Sun. Work from top contemporary artists from all over Canada.

The Vault [88–9 B7] 5640 Spring Garden Rd; ✆ 425 3624; ⊕ 09.30–18.00 Mon–Wed, 09.30–21.00 Thu–Fri, 09.30–17.30 Sat, 12.00–17.00 Sun. Created by women for women, it showcases designer jewellery collections from all over the world.

Books

Chapters [92–3 A3] Bayers Lake Power Centre, 188 Chain Lake Dr; ✆ 450 1023; www.chapters.indigo.ca; ⊕ 10.00–22.00 Mon–Sat, 11.00–21.00 Sun. Nova Scotia's biggest book and music retailer.

Frog Hollow Books [88–9 B7] 1459 Brenton St; ✆ 429 3318; ⊕ Mon–Wed & Sat 10.00–18.00, Thu–Fri 10.00–20.00, Sun 11.00–16.00. An excellent independent bookshop. In a new location since June 2009 (now just off Spring Garden Rd).

Halifax is also blessed with some excellent second-hand bookshops:

Back Pages [88–9 D7] 1526 Queen St; ☏ 423 4750; ☉ 09.30–17.30 Mon–Sat, 12.00–17.00 Sun
John W Doull [88–9 E5] 1684 Barrington St; ☏ 429 1652, T/F 1 800 317 8613; www.doullbooks.com; ☉ Jul–Sep 09.30–21.00 Mon–Fri, 10.00–21.00 Sat, Oct–Jun 09.30–18.00 Mon–Tue, 09.30–21.00 Thu–Fri, 10.00–21.00 Sat

The Last Word Bookstore [92–3 B3] 2160 Windsor St; ☏ 423 2932; ☉ 10.00–17.30 Mon–Sat, 12.00–17.00 Sun
Schooner Books [92–3 G4] 5378 Inglis St; ☏ 423 8419; www.schoonerbooks.com; ☉ 09.30–17.30 Mon–Thu & Sat, 09.30–18.00 Sat
Trident [92–3 F3] 1256 Hollis St; ☏ 423 7100; www.tridenthalifax.com; ☉ 08.00–17.30 Mon–Fri, 08.30–17.00 Sat, 11.00–17.00 Sun. A fun place which dishes up excellent coffee.

Food and wine

Bishop's Cellar [88–9 F8] 1477 Lower Water St; ☏ 490 2675; www.bishopscellar.com; ☉ 10.00–22.00 Mon–Thu, 10.00–midnight Fri, 08.00–midnight Sat, 12.00–20.00 Sun. Knowledgeable staff & with a huge selection. One of the top wine stores in the country.
Pete's Frootique [88–9 B6] (see page 96) An excellent upmarket food emporium.

Planet Organic [92–3 B4] 6487 Quinpool Rd; ☏ 425 7400; www.planetorganic.ca; ☉ 09.00–21.00 daily. Friendly staff who understand organic/health foods & supplements.
Rum Runners Rum Cake Factory [88–9 E7] 1479 Lower Water St; ☏ 421 6079, T/F 1 866 440 7867; www.rumrunners.ca; ☉ Jul–Sep 09.00–21.00 Mon–Sat, 10.00–18.00 Sun, Oct–Jun 10.00–18.00 daily. Delicious rum — & whisky — cakes which make great gifts.

Maps The tourist office has quite a good range of free maps. Standard driving maps and road atlases are sold at most bookshops and the larger petrol stations. If you're looking for something more specialised, try:

Binnacle [92–3 A6] 15 Purcell's Cove Rd; ☏ 423 6464, T/F 1 800 224 3937; www.binnacle.com; ☉ 09.00–18.00 Mon–Fri, 09.00–17.00 Sat. Nautical charts.

Maps and more [88–9 F6] 1601 Lower Water St; ☏ 422 7106; www.maps-and-ducks.com; ☉ 10.00–18.00 Mon–Sat (Jun–Sep until 19.00).
Trail Shop [92–3 C4] 6210 Quinpool Rd; ☏ 423 8736; www.trailshop.com; ☉ 09.00–18.00 Mon–Wed & Sat, 09.00–21.00 Thu–Fri.

Markets The excellent **Halifax Farmers' Market** (*1869 Upper Water St;* ☏ *492 4438;* ☉ *07.00–13.00 Sat*), which includes food, produce, local crafts and much more, has for many years been held in the courtyard beside Alexander Keith's Brewery. At the time of writing, plans are underway to change the venue to Pier 20, further along the waterfront.

If flea markets are more your thing, head for the **Halifax Forum** (*2901 Windsor St;* ☏ *490 4614*) on a Sunday morning.

Music

CD Plus [88–9 E6] 1592 Barrington St; ☏ 422 1559; www.cdplus.com; ☉ 09.30–20.00 Mon–Fri, 09.30–18.00 Sat, 12.00–18.00 Sun. The best place for new music for those who still buy CDs, DVDs — and vinyl!. Prices are competitive & the staff know their stuff.
Halifax Folklore Centre [88–9 D6] 1528 Brunswick St; ☏ 423 7946; ☉ 11.00–17.30 Mon–Wed, 11.00–19.00 Thu–Fri, 11.00–17.00 Sat. A good spot for Celtic music & instruments.

Long and Mcquade [92–3 B3] 6065 Cunard St; ☏ 496 6900; www.long-mcquade.com; ☉ 10.00–18.00 Mon–Thu, 10.00–20.00 Fri, 10.00–17.00 Sun. If hearing all the wonderful Celtic music has inspired you to go & buy yourself a fiddle or other instrument, this is a good place to start.
Taz Records [88–9 D6] 1593 Market St; ☏ 422 5976; www.tazrecords.com; ☉ 10.30–19.00 Mon–Fri, 10.30–18.00 Sat, 12.00–17.00 Sun. Ideal if you want to try to track down second-hand music.

Outdoor and camping gear

Mountain Equipment Co-op [88–9 E6] 1550 Granville St; ✆ 421 2667; www.mec.ca; ⊕ mid-Jun–early-Sep 09.30–21.00 Mon–Fri, 09.00–18.00 Sat, early-Sep–mid-Jun 09.30–19.00 Mon–Wed, 09.30–21.00 Thu–Fri, 09.30–18.00 Sat.

Coast Mountain Sports [92–3 A4] Halifax Shopping Centre, 7001 Mumford Rd; ✆ 455 2528; www.coastmountain.com; ⊕ 09.30–21.00 Mon–Sat 12.00–17.00 Sun.

The Trail Shop [92–3 C4] 6210 Quinpool Rd; ✆ 423 8736; www.trailshop.com; ⊕ 09.00–18.00 Mon–Wed & Sat, 09.00–21.00 Thu–Fri.

SPORT For spectator sports, head to the Halifax Metro Centre to see the Halifax Mooseheads play ice hockey (September–March) and the Halifax Rainmen play basketball (January–March). Tickets can be purchased from the Ticket Atlantic Box Office (✆ *451 1221; www.ticketatlantic.com*) at the Halifax Metro Centre (*1800 Argyle St*). Prices to see the Mooseheads start from CAN$14.50, and the Rainmen from CAN$18. Possibilities for those who wish to participate include:

Canoeing and kayaking

St Mary's Boat Club [92–3 C5] 1641 Fairfield Rd; ✆ 490 4688. On the Northwest Arm. Hourly canoe rental on summer weekends (CAN$8/hr).

Diving The water isn't warm, but there are numerous shipwrecks to keep divers happy, and some good diving companies too, both here and in Dartmouth (see page 119).

Divers World [off map] 11–12 Lakeside Park Dr, Lakeside; ✆ 876 0555; www.diversworld.ns.ca. 10mins' drive from Armdale Rotary.

Nautilus Aquatics [92–3 C4] 6164 Quinpool Rd; ✆ 454 4296, T/F 1 866 423 0007; www.nautilusaquatichobbies.com

Golf Golfers will find over a dozen nine- and 18-hole courses within easy reach of Halifax and Dartmouth. Here are four of the best full-length courses. Granite Springs Golf Club (see page 127) is another good option.

Eaglequest Grandview [off map] Golf & Country Club, 431 Crane Hill Rd, Westphal; ✆ 435 3278; www.eaglequestgolf.com. A challenging (particularly the forested back 9) 6,475yd course just outside Dartmouth off Hwy 7. Green fees CAN$63.

Glen Arbour [off map] 40 Clubhouse Lane, Hammonds Plains; ✆ 835 4053. A lovely, well-designed 6,800yd championship course with natural ponds, streams & mature trees. Not cheap in summer, but a great challenge for the serious golfer. Off Hammonds Plains Rd, 1km west of Bedford. Green fees CAN$155.

Hartlen Point Forces Golf Club [76] Shore Rd; ✆ 465 4653; www.hartlenpoint.com. This 18-hole 5,862yd, par 71 course has beautiful views overlooking the eastern entrance to Halifax Harbour (& almost constant winds). Green fees CAN$55.

Lost Creek Golf Club [off map] 310 Kinsac Rd, Beaver Bank; ✆ 865 4653; www.lostcreek.ca. A beautiful, forested lakeside 5,876yd course. Reach it by taking Beaverbank Rd for 9km from Exit 2 of Hwy 101. Green fees CAN$47.

Gyms and fitness centres Many of the bigger hotels have some sort of fitness facilities for their guests, ranging from a small room with a few machines to large areas with state-of-the-art equipment. If your accommodation doesn't have suitable facilities, try the following:

Fitness FX [92–3 C4] 6330 Quinpool Rd; ✆ 422 1431; www.fitnessfx.ca. Day pass CAN$10.

South Park YMCA [88–9 A6] 1565 South Park St; ✆ 423 9622; www.ymcahrm.ns.ca. By the Halifax Public Gardens. Day pass CAN$11.

The Tower [92–3 F5] Saint Mary's University, 920 Tower Rd; ☎ 420 5555; www.smuhuskies.ca. Excellent facilities plus squash courts. Day pass CAN$9.

Horseriding

Hatfield Farms Adventures [76] 1840 Hammonds Plains Rd; ☎ 835 5676; www.hatfieldfarm.com. Offers trail rides for all levels from CAN$30, plus some 'dude ranch' type packages.

Spas Spas offer a wide range of services. Expect to pay CAN$60–80 for a 60-minute facial.

Spirit Spa [88–9 F7] 5150 Salter St #200; ☎ 431 8100; www.spiritspa.ca

The Summit Day Spa [88–9 A6] 5657 Spring Garden Rd; ☎ 423 3888; www.summitspa.ca

Swimming Some hotels have pools, and hardy souls may like to brave the sea at one of the region's beaches. Freshwater swimming is popular, try Chocolate Lake [92–3 A6] near the Armdale Rotary.

Otherwise, try the **Centennial Pool** [92–3 C2] (*1970 Gottingen St;* ☎ *490 7219; www.centennialpool.ca*) and the **South Park YMCA** [88–9 A6] (see *Gyms and fitness centres*, page 103).

Winter sports When the snow is on the ground, some of the HRM's walking trails are popular with cross-country skiers. The nearest downhill skiing is at Ski Martock (see page 229).

You can ice-skate indoors year–round in Dartmouth (see page 119) in season (mid-October–March) there are several possibilities in Halifax, including the **Halifax Forum** [92–3 B2] (*2901 Windsor St,* ☎ *490 4500;* e *www.halifaxforum.ca; CAN$2.50/session*).

For outdoor ice-skating conditions, check the Halifax Regional Municipality website (*www.halifax.ca*). Several lakes in Halifax are great for skating, including Chocolate Lake [92–3 A6], but you'll rarely find facilities, and skate rental is even harder to come by. It might be worth investing in a second-hand pair.

OTHER PRACTICALITIES

Banks You won't have a problem finding a bank or ABM (ATM) in Halifax or Dartmouth. Many hotels offer currency-exchange services – though the rate may be less competitive – as does the Casino Nova Scotia [88–9 F1] (see page 100).

$ **Royal Bank** 5855 Spring Garden Rd; ☎ 421 8177; ⊕ 09.30–17.00 Mon–Tue & Fri, 09.30–20.00 Wed–Thu, 10.00–15.00 Sat.

$ **TD Canada Trust** 1785 Barrington St; ☎ 420 8040; ⊕ 08.00–18.00 Mon–Wed, 08.00–20.00 Thu–Fri, 08.00–16.00 Sat.

Health The only medical emergency department in the HRM is located at the **Queen Elizabeth II Health Sciences Centre** [92–3 C3] (*1796 Summer St, Halifax;* ☎ *473 3383*). The most central walk-in clinic is the **Family Focus Medical Clinic** [92–3 E4] (*5991 Spring Garden Rd;* ☎ *420 6060;* ⊕ *08.30–21.00 Mon–Fri, 11.00–17.00 Sat–Sun*).

Shoppers Drug Mart [88–9 B7] (*5524 Spring Garden Rd, Halifax;* ☎ *429 2400*) has a 24-hour pharmacy.

Internet Public internet access is free at libraries (see page 105) and at Community Access Program (CAP) sites. For a list of CAP sites in the HRM see www.hrca.ns.ca/find/geo.htm or call ☎ T/F 1 866 569 8428.

Internet cafés tend to come and go quite frequently, but the following have been around for a while:

📧 **Paper Chase News Café** [88–9 D6] 5228 Blowers St; ✎ 423 0750; ⊕ 08.00–21.00 Mon–Sat, 09.00–21.00 Sun; closing times depend on how busy the café is. Has a good selection of newspapers & magazines downstairs, & rather good wholesome food. Internet costs CAN$0.13/min.

📧 **Spring Garden Internet Café** [88–9 A6] 5681 Spring Garden Rd; ✎ 423 0785; ⊕ 06.00–23.30 daily. Internet CAN$0.10/min, packages available.

📧 **Grace Internet Space** [88–9 B6] 5675 Spring Garden Rd; ✎ 405 1357; ⊕ 09.00–22.30 Mon–Fri, 11.00–22.30 Sat–Sun. Internet CAN$2/20min, packages available.

Laundromats Coin-operated laundries in Halifax include:

Kwik Wash [88–9 B7] 5506 Clyde St; ✎ 429 2023
Murphy's [92–3 C2] 6023 North St; ✎ 454 6294

Spin & Tumble [92–3 G4] 1022 Barrington St; ✎ 422 8099

Libraries Halifax Public Libraries (*www.halifaxpubliclibraries.ca*) has ten branches close to the downtown area; the largest and most central is the **Spring Garden Road Memorial Public Library** [88–9 D6] (*5381 Spring Garden Rd;* ✎ *490 5700;* ⊕ *year-round 10.00–21.00 Tue–Thu, 10.00–17.00 Fri–Sat, winter only 14.00–17.00 Sun*). All libraries offer internet-accessible computers.

Police For emergencies ✎ 911; for non-emergency business ✎ 490 5020.

Post offices The main post office is at 1680 Bedford Row [88–9 F5] (✎ *T/F 1 800 267 1177;* ⊕ *07.30–17.15 Mon–Fri*). However, many standard post office services are now offered at a variety of other stores, eg: some branches of Shoppers Drug Mart and Lawton Drugs, and these tend to be open on Saturdays and later in the evening.

WHAT TO SEE AND DO Halifax has something of a reputation for being foggy. In an average year, over 100 days will be foggy at some time or other. Mid-spring to early summer tends to be particularly bad. Keep your fingers crossed because when the sun shines, the outdoor attractions, gardens, parks and waterfront are delightful, as is McNab's Island [76].

The unmissables

Halifax Citadel National Historic Site of Canada [88–9 B3] (*Sackville St;* ✎ *426 5080; www.pc.gc.ca/halifaxcitadel;* ⊕ *early May–Oct 09.00-17.00 daily (to 18.00 Jul–Aug); grounds open year-round but no services available Nov–early May; admission Jun–mid-Sep CAN$11.70, May & Oct CAN$7.80, Nov–Apr free, inc 45–60min guided tour*) The first fortifications were constructed on what was then called Signal Hill in 1749. A three-storey octagonal blockhouse was added in 1776, and during the Duke of Kent's time in Halifax (1794–1800) he implemented major changes. In the 1820s, previous fortifications were levelled, and the height of the hill reduced – the earth moved was used to construct ramparts. The huge, star-shaped, Vauban-style Citadel that is seen today was constructed between 1828 and 1856. Officially known as Fort George and built to reduce the threat of a land attack by American forces, it was one of the largest British fortresses on the American continent, the hilltop setting providing a commanding view of the city and harbour. The Citadel continued its watch over Halifax until the end of World War II. For today's visitor, from below one gets the impression just of a huge grassy mound. But once you've climbed the hill, crossed the plank bridge over the moat and gone through the arched entrance to the inner courtyard, you'll appreciate the full scale of the site.

There are good audio-visual presentations, moats, barrack rooms, garrison cells, tunnels and ramparts to explore, and plenty of cannons – one of which is fired daily at noon. Throughout the summer, students dressed in the uniform of the 78th Highland Regiment (MacKenzie tartan kilts and bright red doublets) enact the drills of 1869, marching to a bagpipe band. This is Halifax's major attraction and one of the most visited National Historic Sites in Canada.

Upstairs in the Cavalier Building is the **Army Museum** (❧ *422 5979; www.pc.gc.ca/lhn-nhs/ns/halifax/edu/edu1_e.asp; opening hours as above, admission included in Citadel fee*), which presents hundreds of artefacts reflecting Atlantic Canada's military heritage and displays on military events in which Canadian forces played a significant role. There's a café downstairs.

To reach Citadel Hill on foot from the waterfront, follow George Street (which later becomes Carmichael Street) uphill.

Halifax Public Gardens [88–9 A6] (*Main entrance on the corner of South Park St and Spring Garden Rd;* ❧ *490 4000; www.halifaxpublicgardens.ca;* ⊕ *early May–early Nov 08.00–dusk daily; admission free*) The Nova Scotia Horticultural Society was formed in 1836, and in the early 1840s began to lay out flower beds and vegetable plots. A civic garden opened in 1867 and has evolved into what many consider to be the finest original formal Victorian public garden in North America. In addition to magnificent floral displays (in late May and June, the tulips are stunning), there are beautiful fountains, ponds with ducks and geese, winding pathways, shady benches and an ornate, red-roofed bandstand which dates from Queen Victoria's Golden Jubilee and is the site of free Sunday afternoon concerts in July and August. The 7ha park, across Sackville Street from the Citadel grounds, is enclosed by a wrought-iron fence with a magnificent set of ornamental gates at the main entrance. Hurricane Juan wrought havoc on the trees in September 2003, but since then much sterling work has been done and the gardens are looking magnificent again.

Maritime Museum of the Atlantic [88–9 F5] (*1675 Lower Water St;* ❧ *424 7490; www.museum.gov.ns.ca/mma;* ⊕ *Nov–Apr 09.30–20.00 Tue, 09.30–17.00 Wed–Sat, 13.00–17.00 Sun; May & Oct 09.30–17.30 Mon–Sat (to 20.00 Tue), 13.00–17.30 Sun; Jun–Sep 09.30–17.30 daily (to 20.00 Tue); admission May–Oct CAN$8.75, Nov–Feb & Apr CAN$4.75, Mar CAN$8.25*) Almost everything about Nova Scotia is linked to the sea, and if you only visit one museum in the province, make it Canada's oldest and largest maritime museum.

Housed in a well-designed purpose-built c1982 structure which incorporates an early 20th-century chandlery at the heart of the city's waterfront, the museum commemorates Nova Scotia's seafaring heritage, traditions and history. Many visitors come for an excellent collection of *Titanic*-abilia, and are not disappointed with the Titanic: The Unsinkable Ship and Halifax Gallery. But even more powerful is Halifax Wrecked, a gallery that recounts the devastating effects of the 1917 Halifax Explosion (see *History*, page 86). See, too, displays on three centuries of shipwrecks, the Golden Age of Sail and the Steam Age, some fabulous scale models of all manner of sea-going vessels, and much more, too.

Between May and October the admission charge will also allow you to board the CSS *Acadia*, moored on the waterfront by the museum. Built in Newcastle-upon-Tyne, England, in 1913, she was Canada's longest-serving survey vessel, and the only surviving ship to have served the Royal Canadian Navy during both world wars.

Pier 21 [92–3 G4] (*1055 Marginal Rd;* ❧ *425 7770; www.pier21.ca;* ⊕ *May–late Nov 09.30–17.30 daily; late Nov–Mar 10.00–17.00 Tue–Sat; Apr 10.00–17.00 Mon–Sat;*

admission CAN$8.50) Focusing on Canadian immigration and nation-building, this inspirational, award-winning interactive interpretive centre is housed in the last remaining ocean immigration shed in Canada, through which – between 1928 and 1971 – well over a million immigrants began new lives in Canada – and 500,000 Canadians departed to World War II military service. For those who know New York, this is Canada's Ellis Island. Be sure to watch the poignant *Oceans of Hope*, a 30-minute multi-media presentation that tells the history of Pier 21 from the late 1920s, through the depression, war and post-war years. The library/resource centre is popular with those whose ancestors passed through the building, and there's a café on site. The attraction has been recognised as one of the Seven Wonders of Canada by the Canadian Broadcasting Corporation (CBC).

Other museums

Discovery Centre [88–9 E6] (*1593 Barrington St;* ✆ *492 4422; www.discoverycentre.ns.ca;* ⊕ *year-round 10.00–17.00 Mon–Sat, 13.00–17.00 Sun; admission CAN$7.50*) This hands-on science centre tries to attract people of all ages, but will be of most worth to those with kids. Not a bad place to keep them happy if it is pouring outside.

Maritime Command Museum [92–3 C1] (*Admiralty Hse, 2725 Gottingen St;* ✆ *721 8250; www.pspmembers.com/marcommuseum;* ⊕ *early Jan–mid-Dec 10.00–15.30 Mon–Fri; admission free*) Housed in a stately c1840s Georgian mansion on the grounds of Canadian Forces Base Halifax, this museum focuses on the history and development of the Canadian navy since its inception in 1910: there are also displays on almost two centuries of Royal Navy presence in – and influence on – Halifax.

Museum of Natural History [92–3 C3] (*1747 Summer St;* ✆ *424 7353; www.museum.gov.ns.ca/mnh/;* ⊕ *Jun–mid-Oct 09.30–17.30 Mon–Sat (to 20.00 Wed), 13.00–17.30 Sun; mid-Oct–May 09.00–17.00 Tue–Sat (to 20.00 Wed), 12.00–17.00 Sun; admission CAN$5.75*) Despite an uninspiring exterior, enter and you'll find not just the expected, eg: galleries of botanical exhibits, stuffed animals and birds, whale skeletons – but plenty more, too. The Archaeology Gallery tells of 11,000 years of human life, the Geology Gallery has 200 and 300 million-year-old fossils, and centuries-old Mi'kmaq craftwork is on show in the Ethnology Gallery. There are also live exhibits in the Marine Gallery's tide tanks and the Nature Centre. In summer, the butterfly house is a bonus. A good introduction to the natural wonders of the province.

Other historical sites

Government House [88–9 E7] (*1451 Barrington St;* ✆ *424 7001*) The official residence of the Lieutenant-Governor of Nova Scotia was built between 1800 and 1805 for Governor Sir John Wentworth. It is not open to the public.

Historic Properties [88–9 F3] (*1869 Upper Water St;* ✆ *429 0530; www.historicproperties.ca*) On the waterfront between the casino and the ferry terminal is a group of Canada's oldest surviving warehouses dating from the early 19th century. Nearly lost to 'urban renewal' in the early 1960s, the solid wood and stone structures – including the c1813 Privateers' Warehouse, built to store the privateers' booty (see page 10) – were painstakingly restored and now house pubs, bars, restaurants and boutiques.

HMCS Sackville: Canada's Naval Memorial [88–9 G5] (*Sackville Landing;* ✆ *429 2132; www.hmcssackville-cnmt.ns.ca;* ⊕ *Jun–Sep 10.00–17.00 daily; admission CAN$4*) Explore the world's last surviving Flower-class corvette which saw much World War II action escorting convoys across the Atlantic, now restored as a memorial to all those who served in the Canadian navy. Between October and May, the vessel is usually moored elsewhere in Halifax: ☎ 427 2837 for location and opening hours.

Old Town Clock [88–9 C4] (*Citadel Hill just off Brunswick St*) Sometimes simply called the Town Clock, this three-tiered tower atop a rectangular building, which was originally used as a guard room and residence for the caretaker, is one of Halifax's most famous landmarks. Prince Edward, Duke of Kent, bothered by poor punctuality at the Halifax garrison, commissioned a clock before his return to England in 1800. The original mechanism, crafted in London, England, and wound twice a week, has been going strong since 1803. Unfortunately, when it originally arrived from England, there were no accompanying instructions, and it lay for some time unused and untouched near the (completed) clock building. Finally, a newly arrived soldier who had worked as a clock-maker did the trick.

Galleries and arts centres

Anna Leonowens Gallery [88–9 F3] (*NSCAD University, 1891 Granville St;* ☎ *494 8223; www.nscad.ca/students/gallery_intro.php;* ⊕ *early Jan–late Aug & mid-Sep–mid-Dec 11.00–17.00 Tue–Fri, 12.00–16.00 Sat; admission free*) In an elegant Italianate building, the gallery displays contemporary art, craft and design: weekly exhibitions focus on the renowned Nova Scotia College of Art and Design (NSCAD) students' work. Occasional shows by visiting artists and curators. See box below for further information.

Argyle Fine Art [88–9 F3] (*1869 Upper Water St;* ☎ *425 9456; www.argylefa.tk;* ⊕ *12.00–17.00 Mon, 10.00–18.00 Tue–Sat; admission free*) One of Halifax's most progressive galleries, with an exciting range of contemporary art.

Art Gallery of Nova Scotia [88–9 F5] (*1723 Hollis St;* ☎ *424 7542; www.agns.gov.ns.ca;* ⊕ *winter 10.00–17.00 Tue–Sun (to 21.00 Thu); summer 10.00–17.00 daily (to 21.00 Thu); tours are offered at 14.30 Tue–Sun & at 19.00 Thu; admission CAN$10*) Atlantic Canada's largest (and finest) art collection is divided between two mid-1860s buildings separated by a cobbled courtyard. The majority has been displayed in the Dominion Building (Gallery North) since 1988: ten years later the collection expanded onto two floors of the Provincial Building. The permanent collection includes contemporary and historic provincial, Canadian and international art: there's a wonderful folk-art section which includes the Maud Lewis House (see page 17). To round it off, the gallery has a good shop, and the excellent Cheapside Café (see *Where to eat*, page 95).

Dalhousie Art Gallery [92–3 D5] (*Dalhousie Arts Centre, 6101 University Av;* ☎ *494 2403; www.artgallery.dal.ca;* ⊕ *year-round 11.00–17.00 Tue–Sun; admission free*) Established in 1953, the oldest public art gallery in Halifax has a permanent

ANNA LEONOWENS

The building at 1740 Argyle St once housed The Victoria College of Art and Design, founded and run by Anna Leonowens (1831–1915). Her time as governess and tutor to the King of Siam's 67 children was later filmed, first as *Anna and the King of Siam* (1946), then as a musical, *The King and I* (1951), and then again as *Anna and The King* (1999). Leonowens lived in Halifax for 19 years and was an active supporter of education and the arts. Her name and memory live on in an art gallery connected to the school she began.

collection of over 1,000 works, changing exhibitions and a programme of lectures, films and artists' presentations.

Khyber Institute for Contemporary Arts [88–9 E6] (*1588 Barrington St;* ℡ *422 9668; www.khyberarts.ns.ca;* ⊕ *12.00–17.00 Tue–Sat; admission free*) Housed in a splendid c1888 edifice, this artist-run centre presents contemporary art in a range of mediums. In recent years, the centre also had a good café/live music venue, but this is closed at the time of writing.

Nova Scotia Centre for Craft and Design [88–9 E5] (*1061 Marginal Rd;* ℡ *492 2522; www.craft-design.ns.ca;* ⊕ *10.00–17.00 Mon–Sat (to 20.00 Thu), 12.00–17.00 Sun; admission free*) Exhibitions of local, national and international fine crafts at the centre's May E Black Gallery. Outside the summer months, the centre offers courses in pottery, jewellery, metal and woodworking, and textiles.

Other sights
Alexander Keith's Nova Scotia Brewery [88–9 E7] (*1496 Lower Water St;* ℡ *455 1474, T/F 1 877 612 1820; www.keiths.ca;* ⊕ *tours Jun–Oct 12.00–20.00 Mon–Sat, 12.00–17.00 Sun; Nov–Apr 17.00–20.00 Fri, 12.00–20.00 Sat, 12.00–17.00 Sun; May 12.00–17.00 Sun–Thu, 12.00–20.00 Fri–Sat; admission CAN$15.95*) Somewhat theatrical, but entertaining, 55-minute tours are offered of one of the oldest working breweries in North America, which opened in 1820 in this huge ironstone and granite building. Although most brewing operations were moved elsewhere years ago, the brewery still produces seasonal brews using traditional techniques. Costumed performers, dressed à la 1860s, tell of the brewery's history, often breaking into song (and dance). Fun, slightly camp, and a bit overpriced in my opinion, even with a couple of beers thrown in, rather than educational. Incidentally, Keith's India Pale Ale (IPA) is Nova Scotia's best-selling beer.

Burke-Gaffney Observatory [92–3 F5] (*Loyola Bldg, Saint Mary's University, Robie St;* ℡ *496 8257; www.ap.smu.ca/bgo; free public tours on alternate Sat evenings, in summer every Sat*) The largest of the observatory's telescopes is 41cm in diameter.

Halifax City Hall [88–9 E4] (*1841 Argyle St;* ℡ *490 4000; www.halifax.ca/community/HalifaxCityHall/; free guided tours Jul–Sep 09.00–12.00 & 13.00–17.00 Mon–Fri*) This c1888 Second Empire-style building at the opposite end of the Grand Parade from St Paul's Church is the seat of government for the Halifax Regional Municipality.

Point Pleasant Park [92–3 H6] (*Point Pleasant Dr; www.pointpleasantpark.ca;* ⊕ *06.00–midnight daily*) This 75ha park at South End Halifax suffered devastation when Hurricane Juan struck in 2003 (see *History*, page 85). More than 75% of the 100,000 trees were destroyed: the cleanup closed the park for nine months. Over five years later, remnants of the destruction are still there, but so too are plenty of positive signs of the work done by Mother Nature (and the park authorities) to repair the damage.

The park is criss-crossed by tens of kilometres of walking and biking trails (bikes permitted Monday–Friday only, but not on statutory holidays), and a waterfront trail which is very popular with joggers leads along the Halifax Harbour side to the point, then back along the Northwest Arm shoreline (approximately 2km each way). In the park are ruins of several forts and fortifications, including the c1796–97 **Prince of Wales Martello Tower National Historic Site of Canada** (↘ *426 5080; www.pc.gc.ca/lhn-nhs/ns/prince/;* ⊕ *Jul–early Sep 10.00–18.00 daily; admission free*) built by order of Prince Edward, Duke of Kent, to help protect British gun batteries in Halifax. It was the first of its type in North America.

Park signage is plentiful but there is a paucity of maps: the only one that I've found is at the Tower Road entrance at Point Pleasant Drive. Smoking is not permitted in the park.

Occupying such a strategically important position, the park is officially on British territory. In 1866, the (then) city of Halifax agreed to rent the site from the British government for one shilling (five pence, about ten cents Canadian) a year, on a 999-year lease.

To get to the park, take South Park Street south from Sackville Street: South Park becomes Young Avenue, and this leads to Point Pleasant Drive. Tower Road and Marginal Road also lead here. Those using public transport should take bus #9 from Barrington Street.

Province House [88–9 E4] (*1726 Hollis St;* ↘ *424 4661; www.gov.ns.ca/legislature/;* ⊕ *Jul–Aug 09.00–17.00 Mon–Fri, 10.00–16.00 Sat–Sun; Sep–Jun 09.00–16.00 Mon–Fri; admission free*) Opened in 1819 and constructed of Wallace sandstone (see page 86) this fine Palladian-style building is the seat of the Nova Scotia government, which was Canada's oldest provincial legislative assembly. Visiting Halifax in 1842, Charles Dickens called it 'a gem of Georgian architecture'. Call ahead to ask about guided tours.

Nova Scotia Archives and Records Management [92–3 E5] (*6016 University Av;* ↘ *424 6060; www.gov.ns.ca/nsarm/;* ⊕ *year-round 08.30–16.30 Mon–Fri (to 21.00 Wed), 09.00–17.00 Sat; admission free*) A splendid resource for genealogists.

Churches and cathedrals
St Paul's Anglican Church [88–9 E5] (*1749 Argyle St;* ↘ *429 2240; www.stpaulshalifax.org;* ⊕ *09.00–16.00 Mon–Fri; tours offered Jun–Sep*) Built in 1750, white, wooden St Paul's is the oldest Anglican church in Canada and the oldest surviving building in Halifax. The church – at the edge of the Grand Parade – was modelled on a c1722 church in London, England's Vere Street: the timbers were cut in Boston, Massachusetts, and shipped to Halifax. Many important colonial figures are buried in the crypt, including Bishop Charles Inglis (1734–1816) who was a driving force towards the construction of many of the province's churches. As a consequence of the Halifax Explosion (see page 267) a piece of window frame was embedded (and can still be seen) in the interior wall of the narthex (entry lobby area). The blast also damaged one of the windows, creating what looks a bit like the silhouette of a historical figure: the Explosion Window is on the upper level, and is the third from the back of the building.

Cathedral Church of All Saints [92–3 E4] (*5732 College St;* ↘ *423 6002; www.cathedralchurchofallsaints.com;* ⊕ *for services, plus year-round 09.00–16.00 Mon–Fri; guided tours mid-Jun–mid-Aug Mon–Fri*) Constructed from local stone, the church opened in 1910, and many events are planned for 2010, its centenary year. There are beautiful stained-glass windows, and fine woodcarvings.

Little Dutch (Deutsch) Church [92–3 D2] (*Brunswick St at Gerrish St;* ✆ *423 1059; www.roundchurch.ca;* ⊕ *for services, mid-Jun–late Sep, check website for times*) In 1756, some German settlers moved a house to this location and adapted it to be Halifax's second church, after St Paul's, and first Lutheran church. Other locals confused 'Deutsch' ('German') with 'Dutch', and the church became known as the Little Dutch Church. Towards the end of the 19th century, the church attracted a growing non-Lutheran congregation – in numbers larger than it could cope with.

St George's Round Church [92–3 D2] (*2222 Brunswick St;* ✆ *423 1059; www.roundchurch.ca;* ⊕ *to visit during services*). Built in 1799–1800 to accommodate the growing congregation of the Little Dutch Church (see above), this is an excellent example of a circular wooden Palladian church. Up until 1827 it functioned as a German-speaking church, but then became an Anglican parish. In 1994, more than a third of the building – including the dome – was destroyed by fire. The church was restored using traditional 19th-century building techniques.

St Mary's Basilica [88–9 E7] (*1508 Barrington St;* ✆ *423 4116; www.stmarysbasilica.ns.ca; guided tours Jun–Aug at 10.00 & 14.00*) The Roman Catholic Church was not permitted to build a house of worship in Nova Scotia until 1784, when a small church was built on this site. Construction on what was to become the second Catholic cathedral in Canada began in 1820 and shipwrights were hired to build the roof. The first mass was celebrated in 1829 and St Peter's Church was renamed St Mary's Cathedral in 1833. Major renovations began in 1860, giving the building a far more Gothic appearance. The cathedral had beautiful stained-glass windows, most of which were destroyed in the Halifax Explosion: these were replaced with equally impressive ones made in Munich, Germany. The title 'Basilica' was bestowed by Pope Pius XII who visited in 1950.

Cemeteries and burial grounds

Fairview Cemetery [92–3 A3] (*3720 Windsor St;* ✆ *490 4883;* ⊕ *dawn–dusk daily*) Those fascinated by the story (and film) of the *Titanic* (see box on page 85) will want to visit this cemetery, the final resting place of 121 *Titanic* victims. Some graves just have numbers, but where identification was possible, a name accompanies the number.

Ah, the power of Hollywood: most visited grave is that of J Dawson, #227. Leonardo DiCaprio played Jack Dawson in the 1997 film. Incidentally, the film's writer and director, James Cameron, said he had thought up the character's name and was not aware that there had been a J Dawson on board.

The cemetery also contains the graves of many victims of the Halifax Explosion (see box on page 86). Too far to walk from downtown for most people, to get here take Windsor Street north from Quinpool Road. The cemetery is near the junction with Connaught Avenue.

Old Burying Ground [88–9 E7] (*Barrington St and Spring Garden Rd;* ✆ *429 2240;* ⊕ *Jun–Sep 09.00–17.00*) The first burial ground in Halifax was in use from 1749 to 1844. Interpretive signs indicate gravestones of historic significance. Despite the busy surrounds, this graveyard is a tranquil place to wander and reflect.

Camp Hill Cemetery [92–3 D4] (*Robie and Sackville sts*) In 1844, this cemetery, located to the west of the Public Gardens (see page 106), replaced the Old Burying Ground: amongst provincial big names interred here are statesman Joseph Howe, privateer Enos Collins, Abraham Gesner (inventor of kerosene) and brewer Alexander Keith.

MCNAB'S AND LAWLOR ISLANDS PROVINCIAL PARK Two islands lie at the mouth of Halifax Harbour. The smaller, Lawlor Island, is just off Fisherman's Cove (see page 121): an important bird nesting site, it is not currently open to the public.

McNab's Island, on the other hand, is not only easy to visit, but one of the HRM's hidden gems. Approximately 5km long and up to 1.5km wide, this 400ha island offers a combination of historical and natural features which will delight hikers, birdwatchers, and those with an interest in (particularly military) history.

Deer, coyote and other animals inhabit the island, and over 200 bird species, including nesting raptors such as osprey, have been documented here. Walk some of the many trails through the woods and past tidal pools, explore several former military installations and gun batteries, see some of the old residential houses, relax on sandy Mauger's Beach, and enjoy a wonderful view of the mouth of Halifax Harbour. If the weather is kind, this is a great place to spend a few hours or more.

History Evidence, including a 1,500-year-old shell midden, indicates a Mi'kmaq presence on McNab's Island long before the Europeans. The French used the island as a fishing camp during the 1690s, and in 1782, a Peter McNab purchased it. Around the turn of the 19th century, the British Admiralty built a gallows on what became known as Hangman's Beach, and used it to hang deserters. The bodies were left suspended as a warning to other sailors.

Fortifications were added, and in 1866 the island was forced into use as a makeshift quarantine area when a cholera epidemic struck on the *England*, a steamship *en route* from Liverpool to New York. Around 200 of the 1,200 on board are thought to have been buried on the island.

In the 1860s, the British Admiralty established defences including Ives Point Battery, Fort McNab and the Hugonin Battery.

Between the 1870s and 1920s, the island was a popular recreational destination for the people of Halifax and Dartmouth: thousands came to visit the fairgrounds, bath houses and tea rooms and for picnics or socials.

In both world wars, defences and fortifications were enhanced, and the island anchored one end of a submarine net across the harbour. In 1974, the province began acquiring land for the creation of a provincial park: today, less than 3% of the island is privately owned.

Getting there The island is a 10-minute boat trip from Eastern Passage (see page 121). **McNab's Island Ferry** (❋ *465 4563, T/F 1 800 326 4563; www.mcnabsisland.com; round-trip fare CAN$12*) departs from Fisherman's Cove. **Taylor Made Tours** (❋ *465 6272; www.taylormadetours.ca*) also offers trips across from its private wharf at 1425 Eastern Passage Road. See the Friends of McNab's Island Society website (*www.mcnabsisland.ca*).

No services are available on the island, so remember to bring your own food and water. Be prepared too for changeable weather.

DEVIL'S ISLAND Approximately 12ha in size, Devil's Island is situated about 2km southeast of McNab's Island.

Originally granted to a Captain John Rous in 1752, the first permanent settlement was in 1830, and in 1900 there were about 20 families living on the island.

There are many explanations of how the island earned its current name. Historians say it was briefly owned and occupied by a man named 'Duval', and that with time his name was corrupted. Others say that some Haligonians visited the island for what was supposed to be a day trip, but – owing to a sudden weather deterioration – were stuck there for several days, describing it on their return as somewhere only the devil would live. There were many reports of shepherds (sheep were pastured on the island after the aforementioned fire) and passing sailors seeing ghosts there.

One of the most unusual stories is from the turn of the 20th century: a man reported that when out fishing, a halibut had popped its head out of the water, announced itself as the Devil, and told him that he would die the next day. On the morrow, the man was found dead in his boat near the spot where he claimed to have seen the satanic halibut: examinations showed that – even though he was found sitting in his boat, hands on oars and bone dry – he had drowned. Members of the dead man's family moved into his house on the island, and their baby died within a day or two with no obvious cause of death. There were also reports of the footsteps of a fisherman's boots walking the corridors.

Some claim that unexplainable lights and fires on the island are still seen from the mainland. A supposedly bottomless pit on the island is said to be either a hiding place for pirate treasure or a gateway to hell.

In 2006, psychic medium Alan Hatfield spent a night on the island with a camera crew filming a two-part television documentary entitled *The Ghosts of Devil's Island*. He claims to have recorded several clear and audible spirit voices on audio tape, and an apparition on infra-red video.

Devil's Island can be visited, but there are no scheduled boat services (try the McNab's Island operators). Only small vessels can safely navigate into the only landing area, and then only if sea conditions are perfect. If you get there, you'll find it hard to imagine that the island once boasted 18 houses and a small school.

GEORGE'S ISLAND (☏ 426 5080; *www.pc.gc.ca/lhn-nhs/ns/georges/*) Forming a vital part of Halifax Harbour's defence system since 1750, this island close to downtown Halifax and Dartmouth is of most interest to fans of military history. It had not been open to the public but visits were permitted on one mid-June weekend in 2008, so it might be worth checking for the latest news.

THE NORTHWEST ARM, HERRING COVE AND SAMBRO This is a fascinating excursion of less than 65km in total, especially for those who won't have time to explore much beyond the capital. It starts at the Armdale Rotary, at the west end of Quinpool Road. From here, take Herring Cove Road but then bear left at the top of the hill onto Purcell's Cove Road.

Look out for the impressive **St George's Greek Orthodox Church** (*38 Purcell's Cove Rd;* ☏ *830 3377;* ☉ *Sunday morning for services, otherwise by appointment*): this and the adjacent community centre are the focus for Halifax's Greek community of approximately 400.

Pass the Armdale Yacht Club on Melville Island (formerly the site of a military prison), shortly after which a sign will indicate the turn-off (on the left) to **Deadman's Island Park**. During the war of 1812, thousands of (mainly American) soldiers and sailors were held prisoner close by. Many died in captivity, and almost 200 were buried in unmarked graves on this site. In 2005, the US government erected a plaque to commemorate the men interred here.

You can walk from here to the **Sir Sandford Fleming Park** (*Dingle Rd;* ☏ *490 4000;* ☉ *08.00–dusk daily*), but it is probably better to continue on Purcell's Cove Road, then follow Dingle Road to the car park. This 38ha largely forested park has extensive water frontage with lovely views over the yacht-dotted Northwest Arm, and two main trails. Always popular is the walk along the waterfront, but worthwhile too is the trail through the forest to Frog Pond.

The park's distinctive c1912 ten-storey tower, The Dingle, was commissioned by Sir Sandford Fleming (see box below) to commemorate 150 years of representative government in Nova Scotia. In theory, the tower is open in summer and early autumn (if it is open, climb the winding staircase for fabulous views) but this seems a bit hit or miss.

Continuing on Purcell's Cove Road, you'll pass North America's oldest sailing club, the Royal Nova Scotia Yacht Squadron, which dates from 1837.

Originally built in 1793, most of the fortifications you see today at **York Redoubt** (*Purcell's Cove Rd;* ✆ *426 5080; www.pc.gc.ca/lhn-nhs/ns/york/;* ☉ *daily Nov–Mar 08.00–17.00, Apr–mid-May & Oct 08.00–18.00, mid-May–Aug 08.00–20.00, Sep 08.00–19.00; admission free*) date from more recent times, including tunnels, huge muzzle-loading guns, searchlights, and a Martello tower. The site was chosen for its commanding view over the entrance of Halifax Harbour, and has long been a key element in Halifax's defences. Paths lead downhill to the water, and if the weather is kind, the park makes a fine picnic spot.

York Redoubt is the terminus of bus #15 which runs hourly along Purcell's Cove Road from the terminal in the Halifax Shopping Centre on Mumford Road.

Next stop is the traditional fishing village of **Herring Cove**, built on the rocks around a long narrow inlet. You won't find souvenir shops or restaurants, but places like this and Sambro (see below) are far closer to the real Nova Scotia than, for example, Fisherman's Cove (see page 121). Herring Cove is the terminus for bus #20 which runs every 30 minutes from downtown (Barrington Street and Duke Street).

From Herring Cove, turn left onto Highway 349, Ketch Harbour Road. Look for the sign to the left to **Chebucto Head** and Duncan's Cove. A paved and albeit not terribly well-maintained road leads to a military communications complex at Chebucto Head. The car park is right by the c1967 lighthouse. Come here in August and September and you may be able to see whales from this spot high above the ocean.

Take a quick look at **Duncan's Cove** where houses are grouped around a small sandy cove, then return to Highway 359 and turn left.

Just before you reach **Sambro**, take Sandy Cove Road to the left. After 1.4km, stop just before the Agricultural Research Station. This spot offers the best views of Sambro Island and its lighthouse, the oldest standing and operating lighthouse in the Americas, commissioned in 1758.

Photogenic Sambro, at the head of the eponymous harbour, is the largest fishing village on this route. From here, follow signs to **Crystal Crescent Beach**. Short trails lead down from the car parks to three secluded coves with – if the sun's out – turquoise-blue water, white-sand beaches and beautiful natural surroundings. If such things offend you, be aware that the furthest beach is unofficially 'clothing optional'.

A gorgeous trail of approximately 11km return leads south along the shoreline, bending into the woods from time to time, to Pennant Point. Although this area

SIR SANDFORD FLEMING

Born in Kirkcaldy, Fife, Scotland, Sandford Fleming (1827–1915) came to Canada in 1845. He designed Canada's first postage stamp, proposed, surveyed and engineered Canada's first railway line, and created Standard Time Zones (though these were not fully implemented until many years after his death). He was knighted by Queen Victoria in 1897, and – having lived in Halifax for a number of years – deeded his land (now the park that bears his name) to the city in 1908.

can often be foggy, if it is clear you'll see plentiful seabirds, lovely coastal scenery, perhaps some seals, and views over to Sambro Island.

From here, head back to Sambro from where Highway 306 will whisk you back to Halifax via Harrietsfield.

NEAR THE AIRPORT
Atlantic Canada Aviation Museum (*20 Sky Bd;* ✆ *873 3773; www.atlanticcanadaaviation.com;* ☉ *mid–May–mid–Oct 09.00–17.00 daily; admission free*) See over two-dozen aircraft, from 'home-builds' to supersonic jets, plus an extensive collection of artefacts and exhibits depicting Atlantic Canada's aviation history.

Scotia Speedworld (*Bell Bd;* ✆ *873 2277; www.scotiaspeedworld.ca;* ☉ *late May–mid-Sep; races Fri–Sat evenings; tickets CAN$12–40*) Watch the motors running at the premiere stock-car racing facility in eastern Canada.

Getting there Both attractions are on the other side of Highway 102 from the approach road to Halifax International Airport. Take Exit 6 from Highway 102, 38km from Halifax.

THE UNIACKE ESTATE (*758 Hwy 1;* ✆ *866 0032; www.museum.gov.ns.ca/uemp/;* ☉ *Jun–mid-Oct 09.30–17.30 Mon–Sat, 11.00–17.30 Sun; admission CAN$3.25*) Situated on a 930ha estate is a large colonial-style country home, Uniacke House was built between 1813 and 1815. Now a museum, the house is an all-too-rare example of a 19th-century Georgian estate intact with its original furniture. There are several kilometres of trails to wander – be sure to take the Lake Drumlin Field loop which offers a fantastic view of the main house. The grounds are open year-round but are not maintained out of season.

Getting there Uniacke is on Highway 1, approximately 35km from Halifax.

Directly opposite downtown Halifax, Dartmouth is a ten-minute ferry ride, or relatively quick drive over a toll bridge, across the harbour. Haligonians love to say that the best thing about Dartmouth is that it offers a great view of Halifax: Halifax may have been founded a year earlier and have the lion's share of attractions, but – views back across the water apart – there are some good (and diverse) reasons to visit this side of the harbour.

While it continues to be a bedroom community for Halifax, Dartmouth also stands on its own feet. It is home to **Burnside** [117 A4], already the largest industrial/business park north of Boston and east of Montreal, and continuing to expand. Relatively new, too, is the Dartmouth Crossing shopping mall and entertainment complex. What is to be applauded is that development has shown some sensitivity to the environment: 23 bodies of water were reason enough for Dartmouth to be called the 'City of Lakes'. Although no longer a city (but part of the HRM), Dartmouth is still very popular with nature lovers and outdoor types for its trails, and kayaking, windsurfing, canoeing and swimming in places such as Lake Banook.

Waterfront boardwalks stretch out on both sides of the ferry terminal, providing visitors with excellent views of McNab's and George's islands, the harbour bridges – oh, and of course the Halifax skyline.

Right by the ferry terminal are the World Peace Pavilion (see page 120), and Alderney Landing, home to a Saturday morning farmers' market and a theatre. In easy walking distance are the Dartmouth Heritage Museum, the Quaker House, and the Christ Church.

Further afield are two contrasting don't-miss attractions, the Bedford Institute of Oceanography and the Black Cultural Centre for Nova Scotia (see page 119).

HISTORY Founded in 1750, a year after Halifax, Dartmouth later began to develop as a big whaling town. Many of the whalers were Quakers, originally from New England's Nantucket Island. At the end of the American Revolution, over 150 ships were engaged in the whaling business. Whale oil's uses included lighting and lubrication: whale bone – used in the manufacture of items including corsets and umbrellas – brought high prices. For several years, Dartmouth prospered with the profits of the whaling business, before the entire fleet moved to Milford Haven, Wales, in 1792. Soon after, Loyalists moved in and occupied the whalers' old homes.

Vehicle and passenger ferries regularly criss-crossed the water between Dartmouth and Halifax, but it was the opening of the Angus L MacDonald Bridge in 1955 which ushered in an unprecedented development boom in Dartmouth.

GETTING THERE To reach Dartmouth from Halifax, visitors can drive over the harbour on either the Angus L MacDonald Bridge [92–3 C1] or the A Murray MacKay Bridge [off map]. Others may wish to take the longer scenic route around the harbour through Bedford, or – best of all – cross the harbour by ferry. For further details see page 80.

TOURIST INFORMATION [117 C3] (*2 Ochterloney St, Alderney Landing, Dartmouth;* \ *490 4000;* ⊕ *mid-May–mid-Oct 09.00–18.00 daily*).

 WHERE TO STAY

🏠 **Best Western Dartmouth Hotel and Suites** [117 C1] (143 units) 15 Spectacle Lake Dr; \ 463 2000, T/F 1 800 780 7234; www.bestwestern.com/ca/. This

new (Sep 2008) 4-storey property is available if facilities are more important than character. Away from downtown but close to shopping malls, there's

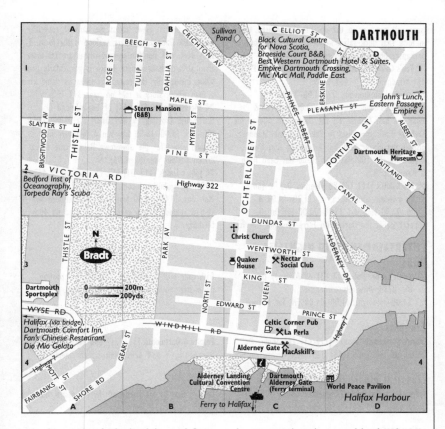

an on-site restaurant & wine bar, indoor pool, fitness centre & business centre. Rooms have fridges. Hot buffet b/fast inc. $$$

Dartmouth Comfort Inn [117 A4] (80 rooms) 456 Windmill Rd; ✆ 463 9900, T/F 1 800 228 5150; www.choicehotels.ca. Decent-sized well-maintained motel rooms at this 2-storey property near Hwy 111. Good continental b/fast inc. $$

Sterns Mansion B&B [117 B1] (4 rooms) 17 Tulip St; ✆ 465 7414, T/F 1 800 565 3885; www.sternsmansion.com. Housed in a charming,

elegant century home in a central location, the larger rooms are particularly good. Gourmet full b/fast & sweet snacks inc. $$

Braeside Court B&B [117 C1] (2 rooms or 2-bedroom suite) 34 Braeside Court; ✆ 462 3956, T/F 1 866 277 8138; e braeside@ns.sympatico.ca; www.braesidecourtbandb.ca. Open-plan, spacious modern townhouse close to a lake & good for hiking trails. Away from downtown. Full b/fast inc. $

✖ WHERE TO EAT

✖ **La Perla** [117 C3] 73 Alderney Dr; ✆ 469 3241; www.laperla.ca; ⏰ 11.30–21.30 Mon–Fri, 17.00–21.30 Sat. Housed in a historic building in downtown Dartmouth, this upmarket north Italian restaurant has an intimate, romantic dining room with a lot of exposed brick, & views over the harbour to the Halifax skyline. If the weather's nice, try to eat on the patio. As usual, lunches are better value than dinners. $$$

✖ **Nectar Social House** [117 C3] 62 Octerloney St; ✆ 406 3363; www.nectardining.com; ⏰ 11.30–14.30 & 17.00–21.00 Tue–Fri, 10.30–14.30 & 17.00–22.00 Sat, 10.30–14.30 & 17.00–21.00 Sun. This stylish, contemporary new addition to the Dartmouth dining scene has hit the ground running. Enjoy a *Nectarini* (raspberry vodka & peach schnapps mixed with orange & pineapple juices) at the lounge/bar, and while eating on the (seasonal) patio or in the upstairs dining area, tuck in to a Thai duck salad, wonderful seared halibut, or perhaps rabbit braised in curry. $$$

✕ **Fan's Chinese Restaurant** [117 A4] Shannon Plaza, 451 Windmill Rd; ↘ 469 9165; www.fansrestaurant.com; ⊕ 11.00–14.00 & 17.00–22.00 Mon–Sat, 17.00–22.00 Sun. Far & away the best Chinese on the Dartmouth side of the harbour, Fan's specialises in Peking cuisine. Standout dish is the ginger beef, but everything that I've tried from the 100-plus item menu has been fresh & flavourful. $$

✕ **MacAskill's** [117 C3] 88 Alderney Dr; ↘ 466 3100; www.macaskills.ns.ca; ⊕ 11.30–14.00 & 17.00–22.00 Mon–Fri, 17.00–22.00 Sat On the upper floor of the Dartmouth Ferry Terminal, this is a great spot for views across the harbour, especially after dark. Panoramas apart, seafood is the focus, & it is done well: non-fish/seafood dishes are far more than an afterthought here. Lunch is particularly good value. Incidentally, the restaurant takes its name from a man whose story is told on page 314. $$

✕ **Dio Mio Gelato** [117 A4] 21 Logiealmond Cl; Dartmouth Crossing; ↘ 469 0187; ⊕ 08.00–21.00 Mon–Fri, 12.00–18.00 Sat–Sun. A relatively new second venue for the downtown Halifax café & ice cream parlour (see page 96). $

✕ **John's Lunch** [117 D1] 352 Pleasant St; ↘ 469 3074; www.johnslunch.com; ⊕ 10.00–21.00 Mon–Sat, 11.00–21.00 Sun. This unpretentious fish & chip & seafood eatery recently celebrated its 40th birthday. $

ENTERTAINMENT AND NIGHTLIFE
Pubs
⊟ **Celtic Corner Pub** [117 C3] 69 Alderney Dr; ↘ 464 0764; www.celticcorner.ca; ⊕ 11.00–midnight, 11.00–01.00 Fri–Sat. A good

Irish pub with a wonderful harbour-view rooftop patio, live music & a Celtic brunch menu.

Cinemas
Empire Dartmouth Crossing [117 C1] 145 Shubie Dr, Dartmouth Crossing; ↘ 481 3251. Multi-screen cinema.

Empire 6 Dartmouth [117 D1] 650 Portland St, Dartmouth; ↘ 434 4200. Multi-screen cinema.

Classical music, ballet and opera
Alderney Landing Cultural Convention Centre [117 C3] Ochterloney St; ↘ 461 4698; www.alderneylanding.com.

Located next to the Dartmouth ferry terminal, hosts theatre, concerts, & more.

SHOPPING The best shopping malls are the **Mic Mac Mall** [117 C1] (↘ *466 2056; www.micmacmall.com*) and the relatively new **Dartmouth Crossing** [117 C1] (↘ *445 8883; www.dartmouthcrossing.com*).

Books
Mic Mac Mall [117 C1] 41 Mic Mac Bd, Dartmouth; ↘ 466 1640

Maps
Land Registration Office [117 A4] 3rd Fl, 780 Windmill Rd, Dartmouth; ↘ 424 4083;

www.gov.ns.ca/snsmr/maps/. Has detailed government-produced maps of the province & its regions.

Markets The **Dartmouth Farmers' Market** [117 C3] (*Alderney Landing; www.dartmouthfarmersmarket.com;* ⊕ *mid–Apr–Oct 07.00–13.00 Sat; Nov–mid-Apr 08.00–13.00 Sat*) is located on the Dartmouth waterfront next to the Ferry Terminal.

SPORT
Canoeing and kayaking
Paddle East [117 C7] Suite 113, 300 Prince Albert Rd, Dartmouth; ↘ 477 1718, T/F 1 866 665 6638; www.paddleeast.ca. Right by Lake Banook on the

outskirts of Dartmouth, this company rents canoes & kayaks & offers lessons. One hour's canoe rental from CAN$20.

Diving

Torpedo Ray's Scuba [117 A2] 625 Windmill Rd, Dartmouth; ✆ 481 0044, T/F 1 877 255 3483; www.torpedorays.com. Shore dives from a range of sites around the harbour; PADI Open Water dive courses from CAN$330); tank & regulator rental from CAN$24/day.

Gyms and fitness centres

Dartmouth Sportsplex [117 A3] 110 Wyse Rd, Dartmouth; ✆ 464 2600; www.dartmouthsportsplex.com. Just by the MacDonald Bridge. Day pass CAN$10. Facilities include cardio theatre, weight room, lifestyle centre, walking & running track, swimming pool, ice rink & squash courts.

Swimming YMCA (*21 Woodlawn Rd;* ✆ *469 9622; www.ymcahrm.ns.ca*), and the **Dartmouth Sportsplex** (see *Gyms and fitness centres* on page 103).

Winter sports For outdoor ice skating, Dartmouth maintains groomed surfaces at Lake Charles. There is no charge, but don't expect facilities or skate rental.

OTHER PRACTICALITIES

Libraries The most convenient is the **Alderney Gate Public Library** [117 C3] (*60 Alderney Drive;* ✆ *490 5745;* ⊕ *year-round 10.00–21.00 Mon–Thu, 10.00–17.00 Fri–Sat, winter only 14.00–17.00 Sun*), on the waterfront right by the ferry terminal. All libraries offer internet-accessible computers.

WHAT TO SEE AND DO

Bedford Institute of Oceanography [117 A2] (*1 Challenger Dr;* ✆ *426 4306; www.bio.gc.ca;* ⊕ *May–Aug Mon–Fri by appointment only; free guided tour available 09.00–16.00 by appointment*) Don't be put off by the uninspiring exterior of this building in the shadow of the A Murray MacKay Bridge: a tour of Canada's largest oceanographic research centre will bring you a new understanding of what goes on in the nooks and crannies of the ocean floor. Learn about salvage work on the *Titanic*, and techniques used to find aircraft wreckage. Then get up close and personal with marine creatures in the touch tank. To get there from downtown Halifax, take the MacKay Bridge, take the Shannon Park exit immediately after the toll gates, turn right at the Stop sign and then first left. From downtown Dartmouth, take Windmill Road to Shannon Park, or take bus #51 from Dartmouth's Bridge Terminal.

Black Cultural Centre for Nova Scotia [117 C1] (*1149 Main St;* ✆ *434 6223, T/F 1 800 465 0767; www.bccns.com;* ⊕ *Jun–Aug 09.00–17.00 Mon–Fri, 10.00–15.00 Sat; Sep–May 09.00–17.00 Mon–Fri; admission CAN$6*) The first site of its kind in Canada, this museum, cultural and education centre preserves and promotes Nova Scotia's black history and culture. The centre represents black communities across the province and displays tell the story of the black Loyalists who fled the American Revolution, the Maroons who came from Jamaica in 1796, and the American slaves who arrived after the war of 1812. It is a fascinating experience for anyone interested in black and/or Nova Scotia history. Located in Dartmouth's eastern outskirts at the junction of Main Street and Cherry Brook Road, to get there go 6km east along Main Street (Highway 7) from Exit 6 of Highway 111. Take bus #68 from Dartmouth's Bridge Terminal.

Dartmouth Heritage Museum [117 D2] (*26 Newcastle St;* ✆ *464 2300; www.dartmouthheritagemuseum.ns.ca;* ⊕ *year-round 10.00–17.00 Tue–Fri, 10.00–13.00 & 14.00–17.00 Sat (in summer also Sun 10.00–13.00 & 14.00–17.00); admission CAN$2*) This restored c1867 downtown building, also known as Evergreen

3

House, was the home of Dr Helen Creighton, Nova Scotia's best-known folklorist (see page 20). A good first stop for those interested in Dartmouth's history.

Quaker House [117 C3] (*57 Ochterloney St;* ↘ *464 2300; www.dartmouthheritagemuseum.ns.ca;* ⊕ *Jun–early Sep 10.00–13.00 & 14.00–17.00 Tue–Sun; admission CAN$2*) A charming restored c1785 house furnished in period style – one of the oldest known residences in the area – built by Quaker whalers. Your visit is enhanced by tales told by costumed guides.

Christ Church [117 C3] (*50 Wentworth St;* ↘ *466 4270; www.christchurchdartmouth.ns.ca;* ⊕ *for services & by appointment*) This is the oldest church in Dartmouth. The weather vane atop its steeple depicts Halley's Comet. Close by is **Sullivan Pond** (*Prince Albert Rd*) a great place to see and feed ducks, geese and swans.

World Peace Pavilion [117 C3] (*Ferry Terminal Park;* ↘ *490 4000; www.halifax.ca/ attractions/peacepav/index.html;* ⊕ *daily May–Oct 08.00–dusk; admission free*) Opened in 1995 by visiting foreign ministers at the G7 summit, every country that had representation in Canada was asked to contribute something to represent 'our planet and efforts to shape our future'. Over 70 countries responded, and artefacts inside the triangular pavilion include pieces from two walls (the Great one in China, and the old Berlin one), a plaque made from ammunition fragments from Slovakia and part of a dismantled nuclear missile silo from the US.

Shubie Park [76] The park takes its name from the Shubie Canal (see box below), and trails lead through the woods along the old canal banks. The stretch between Lake Micmac and Lake Charles has been restored, complete with one of the original locks. Many visitors take to the water in canoes and kayaks, paddling from the main day-use area to Lake Charles. The **Fairbanks Interpretive Centre** (*54 Locks Rd;* ↘ *462 1826;* ⊕ *late May–early Sep 09.00–20.00 Mon–Fri, 13.00–17.00 Sat–Sun; admission free*) has visitor information and displays on the canal's history. The park is best accessed by taking Braemar Drive north from Exit 6 of Highway 111.

THE SHUBIE CANAL PROJECT

Soon after Halifax was founded, the idea to use the string of seven lakes and the Shubenacadie River between Dartmouth and Truro (see page 239) as the basis for a canal linking Halifax Harbour and the Bay of Fundy had been discussed. Seemingly endless feasibility studies and surveys were done, and construction began in July 1826. Within five years, the construction company went bust.

Construction started again in 1854, and despite financial problems, the project was completed in 1861. Nine locks and two inclined planes connected the lakes and river. Steam vessels hauled barges laden with goods along the 115km canal system.

Within a few years, problems arose. Gold was discovered at one of the lakes and a dispute arose over the validity of the title of the lands on which the canal was built. Somewhat unhelpfully, fixed bridges (rather than drawbridges or swing-bridges) were built across the canal at a couple of points, meaning that most canal shipping couldn't pass under them. These factors, plus the advantages offered by the newly booming railways put paid to the canal, and it closed in 1870.

Although it fell into disrepair, some parts of the canal have recently been restored for recreational pursuits, and these are best seen at Shubie Park.

THE EASTERN PASSAGE From downtown Dartmouth, head south down Pleasant Street (Highway 322): you'll pass big oil refineries just after Woodside. If you continue following Shore Road, you leave the harbour and come to the open sea, with good views out to Devil's Island (see *Islands*, page 112) before the road dead-ends about 3km from Fisherman's Cove at Hartlen Point Forces Golf Club (see page 103). If you prefer birds to birdies, there are shore and water birds on the beach here year-round, and in spring and autumn Hartlen Point is one of the best areas to see migrants.

Getting there Bus #60 leaves Dartmouth's Bridge Terminal roughly every 30 minutes from 06.00 to 21.00 (fare CAN$2.25) and stops near the Aviation Museum and Fisherman's Cove.

Tourist information (*200 Government Wharf Rd, Fisherman's Cove;* ↘ *465 8009;* ⊕ *mid–May–mid–Oct 09.00–18.00 daily*).

✗ Where to eat

✗ **Boondocks** 200 Government Wharf Rd; Fisherman's Cove; ↘ 465 3474; www.boondocksdining.ca; ⊕ 11.00–20.00 daily. Bearing in mind it is located at a very popular summer tourist draw & that it has alfresco dining & a fine view (over the Eastern Passage and McNab's Island), prices are quite reasonable & quality quite high. Fish can be deep-fried or pan-fried, there are numerous shellfish choices, & gastronomic landlubbers don't miss out either. $$

✗ **Emma's Eatery** 31 Cow Bay Rd, Eastern Passage; ↘ 406 0606; www.emmaseatery.ca; ⊕ 07.00–15.00 daily. Tucked in amongst a row of shops a short hop from the tourists at Fisherman's Cove is this fun little diner. Bountiful, mouthwatering, comforting all-day breakfasts, good salads, & tasty sandwiches, sensible prices – oh, & serving staff wearing 'Eat Fish Cakes' T-shirts. 'What's not to like?' as the saying goes. $

What to see and do

Fisherman's Cove (↘ *465 6093; www.fishermanscove.ns.ca;* ⊕ *May–mid–Dec; admission free*) The Eastern Passage's biggest attraction is this restored 200-year-old fishing village set around a picturesque harbour. Although many residents still make their living from fishing (primarily haddock, herring, tuna and lobster) the present-day version (which opened in 1996) is primarily a row of 15 craft shops (including pewter, fudge and souvenirs) and a handful of cafés and restaurants. To help you get the feel of the sea, there is a Marine Interpretive Centre (⊕ *Jun–Sep 12.00–19.00 Tue–Sun; admission CAN$1*) with small salt- and freshwater aquaria, displays on seabirds, some interactive exhibits, and an extensive seaside boardwalk. In season, boat trips leave for McNab's Island (see page 112).

Shearwater Aviation Museum (*13 Bonaventure Av, Shearwater Airport;* ↘ *720 1083; www.shearwateraviationmuseum.ns.ca/;* ⊕ *Apr–May & Sep–Nov 10.00–17.00 Tue–Fri, 12.00–16.00 Sat; Jun–Aug 10.00–17.00 Tue–Fri, 12.00–16.00 Sat–Sun; Dec–Mar by appointment only; admission free*) Just off Highway 322 on the site of a former military airport, the museum chronicles Canadian Maritime military aviation from 1918. Highlights include an airworthy 1943 Fairey Swordfish HS469 biplane, and a Sikorsky HO4S-3 'Horse' helicopter operational between 1955 and 1970. Always popular is the flight simulator, which allows you to 'fly' one of a variety of aircraft from the Canadian, British and US armed forces. There are also scale models of an aircraft carrier and a helicopter-carrying destroyer, library, and obligatory gift shop.

BEDFORD

Bedford wraps around the head of Halifax Harbour. Sailors gravitate to the Bedford Basin Yacht Club: also on the waterfront, Admiral DeWolf Park is pleasant for a wander.

Admiral's Cove Park at the south end of Shore Drive was popular with rock climbers and hikers: in recent years it has also been popular with Lyme disease-carrying black-legged ticks, so is best avoided.

GETTING THERE Take Highway 2 from Halifax, then Highway 7 from Dartmouth, or take bus #2 or #4 from Barrington Street to the Lacewood Terminal, then bus #89. Buses #2 and #4 each leave every half hour and the journey time is approximately 30 minutes; bus #89 also leaves every half hour but takes a shorter 25 minutes; the fare is CAN$2.25 (ask for a free transfer).

TOURIST INFORMATION *(920 Bedford Hwy;* ↘ *490 4000;* ⊕ *mid-May–mid-Oct 09.00–18.00 daily).*

✖ WHERE TO EAT AND DRINK

✖ **Il Mercato** Sunnyside Mall, 1595 Bedford Hwy; ↘ 832 4531; www.il-mercato.ca; ⊕ 11.00–22.00 Mon–Fri, 17.00–22.00 Sat. See page 95, for details. **$$**

✖ **Finbar's Irish Pub** Sunnyside Mall; 1595 Bedford Hwy; ↘ 832 9170; www.finbars.ca; ⊕ 11.00–22.00 Mon–Thu, 11.00–01.00 Fri–Sat, 11.00–21.00 Sun. One of the most authentic Irish menus in the province, a well-chosen bunch of beers, & usually excellent live music. **$–$$**

✖ **The Chickenburger** 1531 Bedford Hwy; www.thechickenburger.com; ⊕ 09.00–22.00 daily (to 23.00 Thu–Sat). Whereas some places try to recreate the style of an old-fashioned diner, here you can eat in one that (they tell me) hasn't changed all that much since it opened in 1940. Come for (you guessed it) chickenburgers, (fresh Nova Scotia) beefburgers, fresh, never frozen haddock & chips, irresistible milkshakes – & a jukebox. **$**

✖ **Pete's Frootique** Sunnyside Mall; 1595 Bedford Hwy; ↘ 835 4997; www.petesfrootique.com; ⊕ 08.00–21.00 Mon–Fri, 08.00–18.00 Sat–Sun. A second location for the food emporium with a good take-out counter, Pete's To Go. **$**

WHAT TO SEE AND DO

Hemlock Ravine Park *(Kent Av;* ↘ *490 4000;* ⊕ *year-round; admission free)* This wonderful, rugged 75ha tract of dense old-growth forest (see box on page 123) lies beside the western side of the Bedford Basin between the Bedford Highway and Highway 102. Some of the five interconnecting walking trails (see the map by the

---

TALLAHASSEE

In August 1864, during the American Civil War, the badly damaged Confederate blockade-runner, *Tallahassee*, limped into Halifax Harbour (a neutral port) for repairs.

Two enemy (Union) cruisers anchored off Chebucto Head, waiting for her to leave the sanctuary of the harbour. The *Tallahassee*'s captain's only chance of escape was to navigate a route through the Eastern Passage, long considered too shallow, narrow and dangerous a channel for a ship of the *Tallahassee*'s size.

All lights extinguished and with a skiff going ahead to check the depth and best course to follow, the *Tallahassee* set off under cover of darkness. Miraculously, the vessel reached the open seas undetected, and was well on her way to Wilmington before the enemy learnt of her escape.

When Edward, Duke of Kent, arrived in Halifax in 1794 to serve as commander-in-chief of the Halifax Garrison, he was accompanied by his French mistress, Julie de St Laurent. The two lived on Citadel Hill, but Julie was less than impressed with the view – which took in the military gallows in the middle of the parade ground. She demanded a residence with a more pleasant aspect, and Edward had an elaborate estate built, incorporating a magnificent wooden mansion (long gone), the delightful pathways that you see in Hemlock Ravine Park today, and something else that has survived – the heart-shaped Julie's Pond. The only remaining building from the original estate is the Rotunda, a round music room on a knoll overlooking the water. Supposedly one of Julie's favourite places, it is not open to the public. Edward and Julie left Nova Scotia in 1800.

Because of his royal position, Edward was unable to marry his mistress, though rumours persist that the couple had several children together. He tied the knot with a German princess and their only child became Queen Victoria. Julie lived for a while in a Paris convent, before tying the knot with a Russian–Italian nobleman.

Incidentally, the park is said to be haunted by the ghost of the loser of a duel fought in 1795 between a colonel and a naval officer. The two were said to have over-imbibed at a grand reception hosted by Prince Edward. If you want to discuss what went wrong tactically with the colonel's ghost, he is said to (re)appear from time to time at the site of the fatal fight – near the cove south of the Rotunda – most commonly at 02.00.

car park) lead through towering trees to the hemlock-filled ravine, and can be slippery when wet. By the car park is a heart-shaped pond. To reach the park, take the Bedford Highway and turn onto Kent Avenue 1km north of the Kearney Lake Road junction.

Scott Manor House (*15 Fort Sackville Rd;* ☎ *832 2336; www.scottmanorhouse.ca;* ⊕ *Jul–Aug 13.00–16.00 daily; admission free*) This c1770 gambrel-roofed Dutch Colonial mansion is furnished with period antiques. The tea room (⊕ *Jul–Aug 14.00–16.00 daily*) is a bonus.

Refresh your senses.

This is how it should feel.™

THE WESTIN
NOVA SCOTIAN
HALIFAX

1181 Hollis St.   westin.ns.ca   1-877-993-7846

4

South Shore

The province's beautiful South Shore coastline is deeply indented, with many long, narrow bays, once the haunt of privateers and pirates. With lovely sandy beaches, beautiful coastal provincial parks, pretty fishing villages, towns steeped in history and a mysterious treasure island, this region is also well served with plenty of good places to stay. Some of Nova Scotia's best restaurants – and some excellent low-budget eateries – will satisfy your hunger.

You can drive the 300km-length of Highway 103 – which links Halifax and Yarmouth – in under four hours. Follow this motorway which cuts across the base of numerous peninsulas and you'll see a lot of forest, the odd lake, and (occasionally) the sea off in the distance. Like much of the province, getting the most from the South Shore is not about speeding from town to town by the fastest route, but by giving yourself plenty of time to enjoy the historic streetscapes and what lies along – and off – the countless scenic backroads.

With time, you can go birding on Cape Sable Island or kayak between hundreds of beautiful islands in Mahone Bay. Sip a coffee and mingle with the yachting crowd in a Chester café. Wander the hilly streets of absorbing Lunenburg, established in 1753 and the best-surviving example of a planned British colonial settlement in North America. Rent a bike to explore the surrounding forested peninsulas and inlets. Join the throngs at Peggy's Cove – or other pretty fishing villages that see virtually no visitors. Soak up the sun and breeze on magnificent sandy beaches, particularly around Liverpool, or take a ferry back in time to the Tancook Islands. Experience Acadian life past and present in the Pubnicos, and take to the dance floor at Hubbards' Shore Club. Whereas the majority of the sites and attractions are found on – or close to – the coast, heading inland on Highway 203, just west of Shelburne, leads to the huge expanse of the remote Tobeatic Wilderness Area, a dream come true for experienced back-country explorers.

TERENCE BAY, LOWER PROSPECT AND PROSPECT

These working fishing villages have very few services and, unlike Peggy's Cove (see page 127), see very few visitors. To me, places like Prospect – where the only business in 'town' is a lovely B&B near the end of the peninsula – epitomise the real Nova Scotia. Just before you reach Prospect, a right turn, Indian Point Road, offers parking on the left. From the end of this short road, is an old Mi'kmaq trail which leads 3km along the coast offering wonderful views.

GETTING THERE These communities are off Highway 333 on either side of Prospect Bay, both 32km from Halifax. Terence Bay, to the east, is 17km from Prospect. No public transport serves Terence Bay and the Prospects.

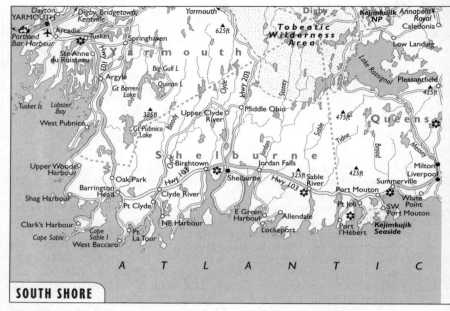

WHERE TO STAY

Prospect Village B&B (4 rooms) 1758 Prospect Bay Rd; ☏ 850 1758, T/F 1 877 850 1758; www.prospectvillagebb.ca; ⊕ year-round; off-season by reservation. Housed in a Victorian former convent, this lovely B&B is a great choice for those wanting to be away from it all, but still have home comforts & easy access to Halifax, Peggy's Cove & the area. Bedrooms have ocean views, the b/fast (made with local/organic ingredients) is a great way to start the day, & the hosts present live local music & stories in the evening. $$

WHAT TO SEE AND DO
SS Atlantic Heritage Park and Interpretation Centre (*180 Sandy Cove Rd, Terence Bay;* ☏ *852 1557; www.ssatlantic.com;* ⊕ *(park) year-round, (centre) mid-May–early Oct 10.00–17.00; admission free*) Set in a beautiful oceanfront park (with picnic tables, a monument marking the mass grave of victims of the SS *Atlantic* tragedy (see box below), and a boardwalk and trail with interpretive panels) is a centre with display panels, personal belongings from some of those on board and artefacts from the ship.

East Coast Outfitters (*2017 Lower Prospect Rd, Lower Prospect;* ☏ *852 2567, T/F 1 877 852 2567; www.eastcoastoutfitters.net;* ⊕ *May–Oct*) This company offers guided sea-

---

SS *ATLANTIC*

In 1873, almost 40 years before the RMS *Titanic* disaster, another White Star vessel was involved in what was at that time the greatest loss of life in a single north Atlantic tragedy. *En route* from Liverpool, England, to New York, the SS *Atlantic* ran aground on Mar's Head, just off Lower Prospect, on 1 April 1873. Although 390 of the 952 people on board survived, all but one (12-year-old John Hindley, from Lancashire) of the 156 women and 189 children on board lost their lives. At least half of the victims are believed to have been interred in a mass grave at Terence Bay.

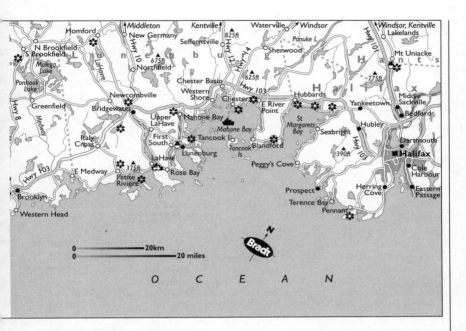

kayak trips (two hours–multi-day) to explore the region's beautiful coastline. It can also customise a camping or B&B-based trip for you. Kayak, canoe and bike rental.

Granite Springs Golf Club (*4441 Prospect Rd, Bayside;* \ *852 4653; www.granitespringsgolf.com*) A 6,460yd course which winds through mature forest and between granite outcrops. Green fees CAN$69.

PEGGY'S COVE (*Population: 120*)

Indubitably, Peggy's Cove is a very picturesque fishing village with an incredibly photogenic octagonal lighthouse overlooking a perfect little harbour. The white c1914 lighthouse, which now houses a seasonal post office (⊕ *mid-May–mid-Sep 10.00–17.00 Mon–Sat*), stands atop granite worn smooth by thousands of years of mighty waves. Just below it, weathered fishing shacks on stilts, stacks of lobster pots and piles of fishing nets line the tiny cove where colourful fishing boats bob in the water. Bright green vegetation on the banks above contrasts with the blue of the sea. The lapping of the waves, rustle of the wind, and squawking seagulls provide the soundtrack.

So what's not to like? The problem is that this is no 'off-the-beaten-track' secret. T Morris Longstreth wrote in 1934's *To Nova Scotia*: 'I am afraid that Peggy's Cove will meet a tragic end. She will be thrown to the tourists.' In summer the same pleasure one gets from thinking how quiet, unspoilt and (relatively) tourist-free the rest of Nova Scotia is can be soured by having to share the beauty of this little village with hordes of other visitors, many of whom arrive by the busload. That doesn't mean that the place is swamped with tacky souvenir shops or rip-off bars, restaurants and hotels: on the contrary, services are limited. There's an interesting gallery, a restaurant, ice-cream shop, one B&B – and a lot of visitors.

To escape the worst of the crowds – and perhaps take advantage of the most beautiful light – get here early, or stay late – the busiest times are between about

4

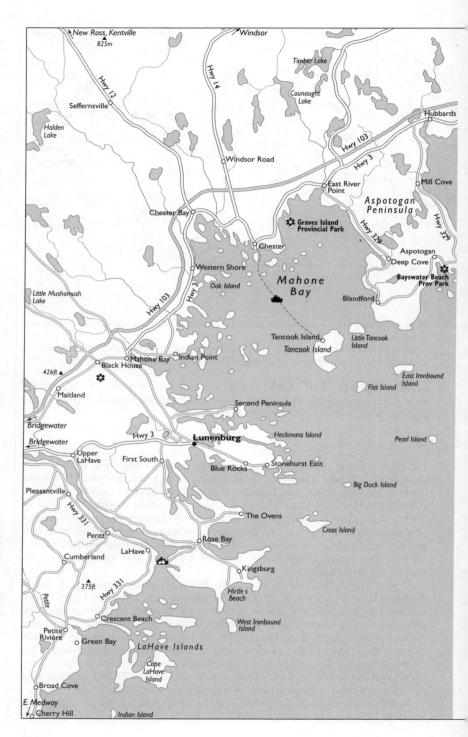

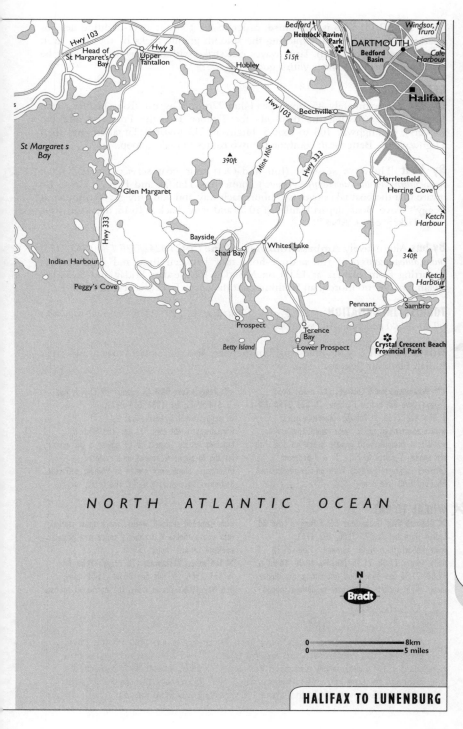

NORTH ATLANTIC OCEAN

N

Bradt

0 ——————— 8km
0 ——————— 5 miles

HALIFAX TO LUNENBURG

08.30 and 17.15. This is, of course, easier to do if you're over-nighting here or nearby. Take great care if exploring the smooth granite rocks by the sea – even when things appear calm, large waves can strike without warning. It might be worthwhile bringing shoes with a good grip.

GETTING THERE

By car Approximately 45 minutes (44km/27miles) by car from Halifax. Take Highway 333 (passing the turn-offs for Terence Bay, the Prospects and the Dovers), or Highway 103 to Exit 5, Highway 213 towards Tantallon, and then Highway 333. Better still: combine the two routes to make a loop.

By boat There's a seasonal (Jun–mid-Oct) tour boat service (\ *422 4200;* *www.murphysonthewater.com/peggyscove/*) connecting Halifax and Peggy's Cove. Be aware that the boat takes over two hours each way, and you only get 90 minutes at Peggy's Cove. Boats depart Halifax at 10.00 and arrive back at 16.15; departure days vary. Tickets cost CAN$79.

By bus Alternatively, **Ambassatours/Gray Line** (\ *423 6242, T/F 1 800 565 7173;* *www.ambassatours.com*) run a three-hour tour between June and mid-October departing from Halifax at 13.00 on Monday, Wednesday, Friday and Saturday. Again, you get no more than 90 minutes at the cove. Tickets cost CAN$48.

TOURIST INFORMATION (*109 Peggy's Point Rd;* \ *823 2253;* ⊕ *mid-May–Oct 09.00–17.00 daily; Jul–Aug to 19.00*)

🏠 **WHERE TO STAY** Try the following, but there are also more places to stay and eat at Indian Harbour (less than 5km away).

🏠 **Oceanstone Inn & Cottages** (17 units) 8650 Peggy's Cove Rd, Indian Harbour; \ 823 2160, T/F 1 866 823 2160; e info@oceanstone.ns.ca; www.oceanstone.ns.ca; ⊕ year-round. Lovely quiet waterfront complex with private beach on 8ha with inn rooms, 5 suites & 7 1-, 2- & 3-bedroom cottages in pretty gardens. With on-site restaurant, Rhubarb Grill (see below). $$

🏠 **Peggy's Cove B&B** (5 rooms) 19 Church Rd; \ 634 4543, T/F 1888 634 8973; e peggyscovebb@eastlink.ca; www.peggyscovebb.com; ⊕ Apr–Oct. With a fabulous setting (expect to be paying a bit extra for the location) & housed in a restored fisherman's home once owned by William deGarthe. Bedrooms have private decks. Full b/fast inc. $$

✖ **WHERE TO EAT**

✖ **Rhubarb Grill** Oceanstone 8650 Peggy's Cove Rd, Indian Harbour; \ 821 3500, 402 3163; www.rhubarbgrill.com; ⊕ summer 17.00–21.30 daily; winter 17.00–21.30 Thu–Fri, 10.00–14.00 & 17.00–21.30 Sat–Sun. Good fine-dining: the dinner menu might include Angus beef tenderloin topped with flambéed seafood, whilst French toast stuffed with goat's cheese & cranberry sauce is a popular weekend brunch choice. $$$

✖ **Sou'wester Restaurant** 178 Peggy's Point Rd; \ 823 2561; ⊕ Jun–Sep 08.00–21.00 daily; Oct–May 10.00–sunset daily. The hordes of tourists

WHO WAS PEGGY?

Around 1845, a schooner *en route* from England was wrecked off the cove. Everyone was swept overboard and lost except a child who was washed ashore, taken in by a local family and given the name Margaret. Eventually she married a local and became known as 'Peggy of the Cove'. Incidentally, the couple are later said to have moved to North Dakota, USA – a long way from the sea!

Over the centuries, countless lives have been lost in shipwrecks off Nova Scotia's coast. But in September 1998, it was an aircraft crashing into the Atlantic that resulted in the loss of 229 lives. There were no survivors from Swissair Flight 111 *en route* from New York to Geneva: the crash was said to have been caused as a result of a spark from a damaged wire igniting insulation material in the aircraft's in-flight entertainment system. The aircraft went down approximately 9km out to sea. Two memorials were erected. One is just off Highway 333, just 2km west of Peggy's Cove (and offers a magnificent view back towards the village): the other is just off Highway 329, 100m past Bayswater Beach Provincial Park (see page 133).

need to be fed, & this huge licensed restaurant makes a valiant attempt to do the job – though it can get very busy during the day. The menu features traditional dishes (eg: Solomon Gundy), good pan-fried haddock & an interesting baked beans & fish hash. Dessert fans should try the homemade gingerbread served warm with ice cream (or go to Dee Dee's!). **$$**

✗ **Tea & Treasures Restaurant** 8369 Peggy's Cove Rd, Indian Harbour; ☎ 823 1908; www.tea-treasures.com; ⊕ May–Oct 08.00–20.00 daily.

Nothing too sophisticated, but prices are reasonable & the food (sandwiches, soup, burgers, seafood dinners) is usually reliable. **$**

✗ **Dee Dee's Ice Cream** 110 Peggy's Point Rd; ☎ 221 6614; ⊕ mid-Jun–Aug 11.00–18.00 (or later) daily; May–mid-Jun & Sep weather dependent. Delectable ice cream emanates from a window in one of the village's original houses. Buttered almond, chocolate, Nova Scotia berry, & banana cardamom are all superb!

WHAT TO SEE AND DO

deGarthe Gallery (☎ *823 2256;* ⊕ *mid-May–mid-Oct 09.00–17.00 daily; CAN$2*) Born in Finland, William deGarthe (1903–83) settled in Peggy's Cove in 1955. His former home now houses over 60 of his paintings and sculptures, most nautically themed. In the 1970s, he began carving a frieze on a granite outcropping on his property. Although he died before completing the project, the 30m memorial to the local fishermen and their families is still very impressive.

HUBBARDS

If you're looking for a base from which to explore Peggy's Cove, Lunenburg, and even Halifax (about a 50-minute drive away), Hubbards – 'the playground of St Margaret's Bay' – isn't a bad choice. Whilst there are no real sights here, the atmosphere is relaxed, there are good (and varied) places to stay and eat, quite a bit going on in summer, and several beaches within easy reach. By far the busiest of these is Queensland Beach: the beach at Cleveland tends to be quieter, and Hubbards itself has a large, popular, white-sand beach with relatively warm water.

GETTING THERE

By car Hubbards is on Highway 3, less than 2km from Highway 103 Exit 6. It is 50km from Halifax and 50km from Lunenburg.

By bus The Trius Tours coach stops here *en route* between Halifax and Yarmouth (see page 52)

TOURIST INFORMATION (*103 Highway 3;* ☎ *857 3249;* ⊕ *late May–mid-Oct 09.00–17.00 daily*). There is also a tourist office further east in Upper Tantallon (*5210 Hwy 3;* ☎ *490 4000;* ⊕ *mid-May–mid-Oct 09.00–18.00 daily*) near the junction of Highways 3 & 333.

South Shore HUBBARDS

4

WHERE TO STAY AND EAT

Dauphinee Inn (6 rooms) 167 Shore Club Rd; 857 1790, T/F 1 800 567 1790; e stay@dauphineeinn.com; www.dauphineeinn.com; May–Oct. In a beautiful waterfront setting, away from the main road, offering rooms decorated with period antiques. The licensed dining room (*mid-Jun–early Oct 16.00–21.00 daily; Jul–Aug 10.00–14.00 Sat–Sun; $$*) is fine but the waterside deck is far better, especially for sunset. The seafood is always good, but a big draw is 'Hot Rock dining'. Super-heated granite rocks are brought to your table for you to cook your meat, poultry or fish main course. Continental b/fast inc, full b/fast at extra cost. $$

Hubbards Beach Campground & Cottages (8 units) 226 Shore Club Rd; 857 9460; www.hubbardsbeach.com; mid-May–Sep. Rustic but comfortable 1–3-bedroom cottages, (many on the lagoon front). The campground has 129 sites with full-service motorhome sites & water-only tent sites.

All in walking distance of one of the best sandy beaches in the region. There's a laundromat too. $$

Shore Club Lobster Suppers 250 Shore Club Rd; 857 9555; www.lobstersupper.com; mid-May–mid-Oct 16.00–20.00 Wed–Sun. Held in the huge, historic Shore Club Dance Hall (see box below). Choose from 3 sizes of lobster, steak, chicken & a vegetarian pasta dish. Price includes salad bar, unlimited mussels, dessert & coffee/tea. Licensed. Complete meal CAN$23–38.

Trellis Café 22 Main St (Hwy 3); 857 1188; www.trelliscafe.com; year-round 08.00–21.00 daily. The seafood is fresh & very good – whether as chowder, fishcakes or pan-fried haddock – & the chicken fajitas are also recommended. Baked goods – such as bumbleberry crisp, coconut cream pie, or huge cinnamon buns – & bread are homemade & very tasty. Sit in or out. Licensed; regular live music. $$

FESTIVALS

May
Lobster Festival No prizes for guessing what's cooking at this weekend event.

July
Canada Day Ceilidh on the Cove Music, Irish dancing, a family barbecue and fireworks at dusk.

End July–early August
World Tuna Flat Races A 'tuna flat' is a cumbersome boat: teams of four rowers compete in the waters of Hubbards Cove to a backdrop of music and barbecues.

October
Pumpkinfest A day of pumpkin-related activities, plus competitions (some more sophisticated than others) such as pumpkin-seed spitting.

OTHER PRACTICALITIES

$ **Scotiabank** Hubbards Shopping Centre, Hwy 3; 857 3333; 10.00–15.00 Mon–Wed, 10.00–17.00 Thu–Fri

JD Shatford Memorial Library 10353 St Margaret's Bay Rd, Hwy 3; 857 9176;
11.00–17.00 Tue, 15.00–21.00 Wed, 18.00–21.00 Thu, 10.00–13.00 Fri, 10.00–14.00 Sun

Post office 10369 St Margaret's Bay Rd, Hwy 3; 08.00–17.30 Mon–Fri, 08.30–12.30 Sat

---

KEEP ON DANCIN'

In August 1946, a dance was held to mark the opening of the newly built Shore Club. Was it a success? Well, dances have been held there every summer Saturday night since. Nova Scotia's last dance hall is still going strong, and a real fun experience. The building is also the location of another Maritime institution, the Lobster Supper (see *Where to stay and eat*, above).

WHAT TO SEE AND DO

Farmers' Market (*Hubbards Barn & Community Park, 57 Hwy 3;* \ *229 1717; www.hubbardsfarmersmarket.com;* ⊕ *May–late Oct 08.00–12.00 Sat (Jul–Aug also 10.00–12.00 Sun)* This market is well worth a visit: less than 2km to the east and just off Highway 3, Bishop's Park is a good picnic spot.

ASPOTOGAN PENINSULA

Just past Hubbards, consider a detour from Highway 3: Highway 329 takes you around the rugged, beautiful **Aspotogan Peninsula** which separates St Margaret's Bay from Mahone Bay. The drive around the peninsula is approximately 44km. You'll pass fishing villages (of which **Northwest Cove** is the prettiest), lovely **Bayswater Beach**, another memorial to Swissair Flight 111 (see box on page 131), and more wonderful ocean views.

Near **Blandford**, the largest community on the peninsula, and the former home of a whaling station, there are views across to East Ironbound Island (see box, page 135).

✖ **WHERE TO EAT** Blandford's **The Deck** (*9 Firehall Rd;* \ *228 2112;* ⊕ *year-round 06.00–21.00 Mon–Fri, 09.00–21.00 Sat–Sun;* $), a general store and licensed café, is your best bet for a bite to eat.

CHESTER (Population: approx 1,200)

On the waterfront at the northern head of beautiful island-dotted Mahone Bay, Chester enjoys a delightful setting. Whilst specific sights are limited to one museum, it's a great place to take in a performance at the theatre, enjoy the Front Harbour waterfront and browse the trendy upmarket shops, watch the yachts on the beautiful bay, play golf, wander the shady, quiet, tree-lined residential streets past elegant (and particularly expensive) mansions, admire the beautifully kept gardens, or just unwind with a coffee and pastry.

Chester has long been popular with Americans: with all the shiny, sleek yachts replacing the usual rugged fishing boats, it feels more sophisticated – and American – than most of the province's seafront communities. The town's population almost doubles during the summer months.

HISTORY Chester was first settled in 1759, predominantly by New England Planters. A blockhouse – with 20 cannons on the roof – was erected soon after to deter hostile Mi'kmaq from entering the settlement. Two of the original mid-18th century cannons are now mounted outside the Legion Hall. It is recorded that porcupine and baked beaver were two dishes popular with early settlers.

The village prospered, initially as a result of fishing. Chester's first hotel was built in 1827, and several more followed. In the mid 19th century, John Wister, an American from Philadelphia, stopped here *en route* between Yarmouth and Halifax and fell in love with the place. He built a summer home – and a yacht, invited his

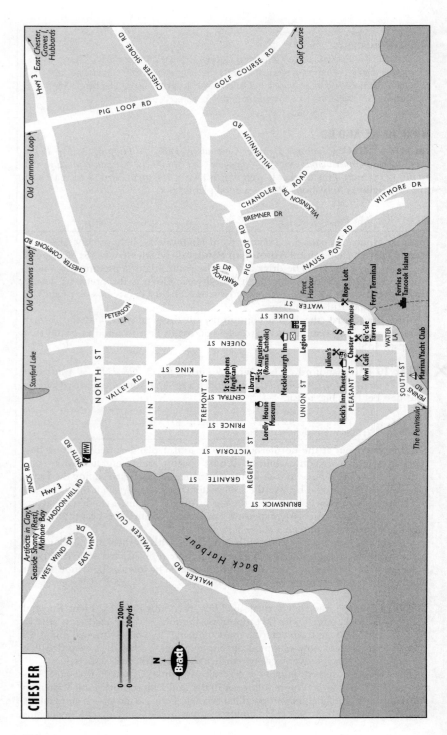

CHESTER

friends over, and they did the same. From such simple beginnings, Chester became known as the 'American town'.

GETTING THERE

By car Chester is on Highway 3, and about 5km from Highway 103 Exit 8. It is 67km from Halifax and 31km from Lunenburg.

By bus The Trius Tours coach stops in Chester (Exit 7 from Highway 103) *en route* between Halifax and Yarmouth (see page 52).

By ferry A ferry service connects Chester with the Tancook Islands (see page 137).

TOURIST INFORMATION (*3996 North St;* ✎ *275 4616;* ⊕ *Jun 10.00–17.00 daily; Jul–Aug 09.00–19.00 daily; Sep 10.00–17.00 daily; Oct–May 11.00–16.00 Thu–Sun*) Housed in the old train station just off Hwy 3 on the south side of town.

WHERE TO STAY

🏠 **Mecklenburgh Inn** (4 rooms) 78 Queen St; ✎ 275 4638; www.mecklenburghinn.ca; ⊕ May–Dec. A shipwright-built, eclectically decorated c1902 hillside property with fine sea views and a bar. There's a self-serve bar, & the covered balconies are a popular gathering place. Full gourmet b/fast inc (the hostess is a Cordon Bleu chef). $$
🏠 **Nicki's Inn Chester** (3 suites) 28 Pleasant St; ✎ 275 4342; www.aco.ca/nickis.html; ⊕ Apr–mid-

Dec. 2 suites have small balconies. B/fast inc, at Julien's or the Kiwi Café (both just a hop away). Also try the food in Nicki Butler's restaurant (see below). $$
🏕 **Grave's Island Provincial Park Campground** (84 sites) Hwy 3; www.novascotiaparks.ca/parks/gravesisland.asp; ⊕ mid-Jun–early Sep. A pleasant campground with open & wooded sites. $

✘ WHERE TO EAT AND DRINK

✘ **Nicki's Inn Chester** 28 Pleasant St; ✎ 275 4342; www.aco.ca/nickis.html; ⊕ 18.00–21.00 Thu–Sun (Jul–Sep Wed–Sun). Nicki Butler's elegant but inviting restaurant offers traditional English Sun lunch – on Sun evenings. On other nights, the regularly changing menu might include chargrilled

beef tenderloin with mushroom ragout, or homemade gnocchi with Gorgonzola cream sauce. Tented outdoor patio (with a heater); short but well-chosen wine list. $$$
✘ **Rope Loft** 36 Water St; ✎ 275 3430; www.ropeloft.com; ⊕ May–Oct 11.30–22.00 daily

South Shore CHESTER

4

(pub until midnight). Restaurant & pub with great location right by the ferry wharf on Front Harbour. Good pub food with a Chester twist (eg: lobster & shrimp pizza). $$–$$$

✗ **Seaside Shanty** 5315 Hwy 3; ☎ 275 2246; ⊕ May–Oct 11.30–20.00 daily (Jul–Aug until 21.00). With a shaded deck right by the water, this licensed understated restaurant has excellent fresh seafood, including very good chowder. $$

✗ **Julien's** 43 Queen St; ☎ 275 2324; ⊕ 08.00–17.00 Tue–Sun. A French-style café very popular for pastries, desserts & fresh bread. Good brunch spot. $–$$

✗ **Kiwi Café** 19 Pleasant St; ☎ 275 1492;

www.kiwicafechester.com; ⊕ year-round 08.30–16.00 daily (earlier opening in summer). Bright, welcoming, even a bit funky, this friendly licensed café has a fire for cool winter days & an outdoor eating area in warmer months. Local & natural produce used where possible. Breakfasts, soups, sandwiches, more substantial meals & baked (including gluten-free) goodies are all worthwhile. $

✗ **Fo'c'sle Tavern** 42 Queen St; ☎ 275 1408; ⊕ from 11.00 daily (from 12.00 Sun). Nova Scotia's oldest rural tavern: wood floors, decent food, good beer selection, occasional live music. Closing time varies from 19.30 on a quiet winter day to 02.00 on a summer weekend.

EVENTS Under the auspices of the Chester Yacht Club, the big event of the year is the **Chester Race Week** (*www.chesterraceweek.com*), the largest keel-boat regatta in Atlantic Canada, held in mid-August. The first documented regatta was held here in 1856 and attracted crowds of over 3,000. These days, the parties and events are every bit as important as the races. A must for sailors and socialites.

OTHER PRACTICALITIES

$ **Scotiabank** 2 Pleasant St; ☎ 275 3540; ⊕ 10.00–17.00 Mon–Fri

✉ **Post office** 76 Queen St; ⊕ 08.30–17.00 Mon–Fri, 08.00–12.00 Sat

WHAT TO SEE AND DO

Lordly House Museum and Park (*133 Central St; ☎ 275 3842; www.chesterbound.com/lordly/LordlyHouse.htm; ⊕ late May–mid-Oct 10.00–17.00 Tue–Sat, 13.00–17.00 Sun; admission free*) This fine c1806 Georgian-style house became the home of Charles Lordly, the district's first municipal clerk. It has survived virtually unchanged with many original features intact. In addition to displays on Lordly and family, there is a section on the *Butterbox Babies* (see box below) and a genealogy research section.

Artifacts in Clay (*4138 Hwy 3; ☎ 275 4271; www.artifactsns.com; ⊕ year-round: mid-Jun–mid-Sep 09.00–17.30 Mon–Sat, 12.00–17.30 Sun; off-season by chance or appointment; admission free*) A purpose-built centre with interpretive area, work studio and shop, focusing on ancient and local ceramic history. There is also a working studio where you can observe the production of ceramics, including forming the clay with a press and 'jolly jigger' wheel, decorating and glazing.

BUTTERBOX BABIES

In the late 1920s, Lila and William Young started up a maternity home in east Chester. Most of those using their services were unwed mothers who paid the Youngs to adopt and care for their babies. The Youngs set up what was effectively a black market for babies: those who could pay thousands of dollars could have their pick of the babies in the Youngs' care. But there was an even more disturbing twist: many babies were deemed 'undesirable', and on these, the Youngs had no desire to waste time or resources. It is thought that hundreds of tiny tragic victims were slowly starved to death and their bodies disposed of in wooden boxes used for packing butter.

In 1813, American privateer ships regularly threatened marine traffic off Nova Scotia's shores. One such vessel, *Young Teazer*, was chased into Mahone Bay by a British ship and was trapped. But rather than be captured, one of the crew threw a flaming brand through the magazine hatch. The resulting explosion was felt and seen by hundreds of people around the bay and most on board were killed instantly. Almost 200 years later, there are regular reports of supposed sightings of the ghost of the *Young Teazer* sailing through Mahone Bay before exploding into a ball of fire.

Chester Playhouse (*22 Pleasant St;* ↘ *275 3933, T/F 1 800 363 7529; www.chesterplayhouse.ns.ca*) This small theatre hosts a range of music, theatre and more between early spring and late autumn.

Chester Golf Course (*Golf Course Rd, Prescott Pt;* ↘ *275 4543; www.chestergolfclub.ca*) Nova Scotia has many beautiful, scenic golf courses, and this 6,080yd course is one of the best. When the sun is out, magnificent views of the bay and islands will either inspire your game or make you lose concentration. Green fees CAN$67.

Grave's Island Provincial Park (*Hwy 3; www.novascotiaparks.ca/parks/gravesisland.asp;* ⊕ *mid-Jun–early Sep*) A pretty, often breezy park 3km east of Chester, reached by a short causeway. Good picnic spot, small beach, playground, trails and campground (see page 135).

AROUND CHESTER

TANCOOK ISLANDS Take a trip back in time to the two Tancook Islands at the mouth of Mahone Bay, a 55-minute ferry ride from Chester. Both islands offer walking trails, good birding, and peace and quiet. The passenger ferry makes between one and four crossings a day (⊕ *times vary: they are posted at the ferry terminal or check with the Chester tourist information office; CAN$5 return*). If you're thinking of visiting, www.tancook.ca is a valuable resource.

Where to stay and eat Little Tancook has no services, but the larger island (approximately 4.5km long and 1.5km wide) offers eat-in or take-out at **Carolyn's Restaurant** (*656 Tancook Island Rd;* ↘ *228 2749;* ⊕ *Jun–Oct 11.30–21.00 daily; $–$$*). For overnighters, accommodation choices are wilderness camping or one bedroom at **Backalong B&B** (*785 Big Tancook Island Rd;* ↘ *228 2088; www.tancookbandb.com;* ⊕ *mid-May–Oct; $$*).

NEW ROSS New Ross – located approximately 31km inland from Chester – is worth a short detour so you can visit **Ross Farm** (*4568 Hwy 12, New Ross;* ↘ *T/F 1 877 689 2210; www.museum.gov.ns.ca/rfm/;* ⊕ *May–Oct 09.30–17.30 daily; Nov–Apr 09.30–16.30 Wed–Sun; admission CAN$6*). Located on 25ha well inland, this living museum aims to remind people that – in addition to the sea – the land played an important part in shaping Nova Scotia's past. Costumed interpreters demonstrate typical farm activities, heritage skills and crafts common 100–175 years ago. Oxen teams work the fields, there are heritage breeds of farm animals, early 19th-century buildings, a nature trail, several activities and special events throughout the year. Good for children.

In 1795, Daniel McGinnis rowed across to Oak Island on a hunting and fishing expedition. Once there, his eyes were drawn to some unusual marks on one of the lower branches of one of the oak trees. Beneath the branch was a depression in the soil almost 5m in diameter. It appeared as though the old vegetation covering this depression had been cut down or removed, as there was only light, new growth. Putting these two things together, the youth assumed that the marks had been made by a block and tackle pulley system which had been used to lower heavy objects into a now filled-in hole. Having been brought up on a diet of tales of wicked pirates sailing the waters of Mahone Bay and burying treasure chests in secret places, he returned the next day with two friends – and shovels and picks.

When they started to dig, the young men found a layer of flagstones just over 1m underground. Having removed these, they dug on and found three layers of oak planks at 3m intervals. Even for three strong and determined young men, this was slow, hard work. Winter drew near and they were forced to suspend their search.

It was nine years before the boys returned: at first, the pattern continued, with more oak plank layers found at 3m intervals. Some of the oak layers were covered in coconut fibre. It is said that unusual (or at least, non-local) stones were found, some bearing inscriptions indecipherable to the diggers.

The team took a day's break and on their return, found most of the shaft flooded. All attempts to bail or pump out the salt water failed. Tunnels were driven in from all angles, but the water menace proved impossible to conquer. Channels were then discovered leading from the sea towards the site, but even after (what looked like successful) attempts had been made to block them, the water problems continued.

Since then, despite countless groups of hopeful searchers, digging, damming, diverting, drilling and blasting haven't done the trick. Even Franklin D Roosevelt (later to become the President of the USA) was part of a 1909 expedition here.

Was 'treasure' buried here? If it was, who buried it? Almost as many theories have been put forward as attempts made to find it. The list of suspects includes Captain Kidd, Sir Francis Drake, Sir Francis Bacon, Sir Henry Morgan, Edward 'Blackbeard' Teach, Acadians uprooted from their homes, Incas who fled the Spaniards, rogue Spaniards diverting Central American booty, Knights Templar, and (of course) aliens. Clue-wise, in 1965, an electromagnetic search of the site by students from Massachusetts found a late 16th-century Spanish coin.

Getting there New Ross is on Highway 12, between Chester (31km/19 miles) and Kentville (43km/27 miles). Take Exit 9 from Highway 103, or Exit 13 from Highway 101.

MAHONE BAY

Apart from Peggy's Cove, Mahone Bay's three churches is one of *the* iconic tourist images of Nova Scotia.

But there's far more to do in this charming and prosperous town than take a photo and move on. There are several studios and galleries to investigate, a museum to visit, the bay and its islands to explore, and some excellent eateries to try.

Behind the tourist information office is the atmospheric old cemetery. Architecture-buffs will find faithfully preserved buildings in a variety of styles including Italianate and Gothic Revival: many of these now house B&Bs, restaurants, and shops. Whilst it may not have anything like the range of accommodation offered in Lunenburg (see page 143), it isn't a bad choice for a base from which to explore the region.

Over the years, several expedition members have reported seeing scary apparitions on the island. One 'regular' is said to be a man in a red frock coat: he leaves no footprints in the sand…

More recent searches, studies and excavations suggest that an incredibly sophisticated series of tunnels and pits connected to the sea lies underground: thus far, modern science and techniques is still losing out to the as yet unidentified engineering genius who designed and constructed it several centuries ago. By 1995, treasure hunters had managed to dig almost 60m underground: the treasure – if there is any – still has not been found.

Well over 200 years have now passed since McGinnis made his find: six treasure hunters have lost their lives, including four who died of carbon monoxide poisoning and/or drowning on a 1965 expedition. Ironically, regardless of whatever lies buried under Oak Island, literally millions of dollars have been spent trying to find it.

And what of the island in recent times? The 58ha island is now connected to the mainland by a causeway. It is now owned by Oak Island Tours Inc, a somewhat secretive treasure-seeking consortium, and excavations continue, though at the time of writing the group was awaiting renewal of a Treasure Trove Licence.

The Oak Island mystery has inspired hundreds of articles, dozens of books and numerous documentaries: in more recent times, two good websites (www.oakislandtreasure.co.uk) and that of the Oak Island Tourism Society (OITS) (www.oakislandscociety.ca) keep those fascinated by the story up to date.

PRACTICALITIES At least three days each year the public can visit the island: sign up for Explore Oak Island Days in June (contact Oak Island Tourism Society for details, see above). That apart, there are views of the island from Western Shore's Wild Rose Park, and Oak Island Road takes you to the beginning of the causeway.

WHERE TO STAY The nearest place to stay and eat is the **Oak Island Resort** (118 units; 36 Treasure Dr, Western Shore; ✆ 627 2600, T/F 1 800 565 5075; www.oakislandresortandspa.com; dining $$–$$$; $$–$$$). The resort is not on the famous island, but overlooks it. The resort and island are just off Highway 3, about 17km west of Chester.

In recent decades, the beautiful setting and relaxed way of life have attracted artists, artisans and musicians, and a number of galleries and studios are dotted along Main Street. Worryingly, the first condominiums have begun to spring up and more may be on their way. Hopefully, this motel/huge supermarket shopping mall-free town won't begin to lose its character.

HISTORY Known to the Mi'kmaq as *Mushamush* and one of their favourite camping grounds, the town was founded in 1754. The majority of the early settlers were European (specifically German, French, and Swiss) Protestants, enticed by the British government's offer of free land, farm equipment, and a year's provisions. A few decades later there was a large influx of New Englanders. Mills were built at the head of the bay, and from 1850 to the early 20th century, shipbuilding thrived along the waterfront. With over 350 islands offering plenty of hiding places, the area has long been connected with pirates – a *mahone* was a low-lying craft used by buccaneers.

GETTING THERE
By car Mahone Bay is on Highway 3 (take Exit 10 from Highway 103), 86km/53 miles from Halifax.

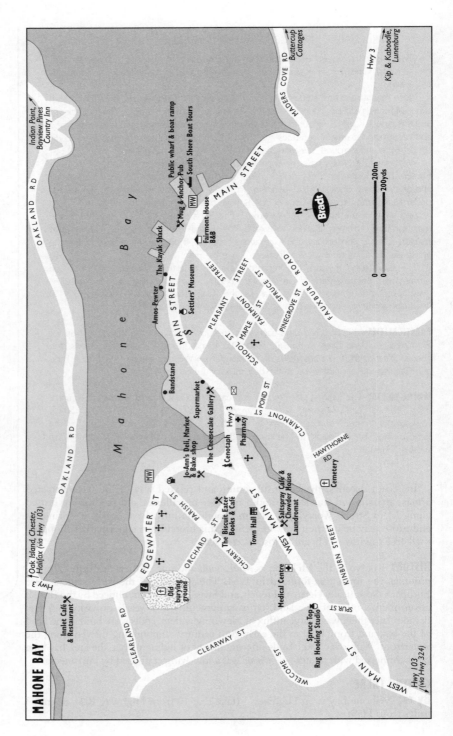

MAHONE BAY

Mahone Bay

Oak Island, Chester,
Halifax (via Hwy 103)

Hwy 3

Innlet Café
& Restaurant ✖

CLEARLAND RD

OAKLAND RD

Indian Point,
Bayview Pines
Country Inn

Old
burying
ground

EDGEWATER ST

PARISH ST

ORCHARD ST

CHERRY LA

CLEARWAY ST

WELCOME ST

SPUR ST

Spruce Top
Rug Hooking Studio

Medical Centre

The Biscuit Eater
Books & Café ✖

Town Hall

WEST MAIN ST

Saltspray Café &
Chowder House ✖

Laundromat

KINBURN STREET

WEST MAIN ST

Hwy 103
(via Hwy 324)

Jo-Ann's Deli, Market
& Bake shop ✖

Supermarket

The Cheesecake Gallery ✖

Cenotaph Hwy 3

Pharmacy

POND ST

CLAIRMONT ST

HAWTHORNE RD

Cemetery

Bandstand

Amos-Pewter

The Kayak Shack

Settlers' Museum ✖

MAIN STREET

SCHOOL ST

PLEASANT STREET

MAPLE ST

FAIRMONT STREET

SPRUCE ST

PINEGROVE ST

FAUXBURG ROAD

STREET

Fairmont House
B&B

Mug & Anchor Pub ✖

Public wharf & boat ramp

South Shore Boat Tours

MAIN STREET

MADERS COVE RD

Buttercup
Cottages

Hwy 3

Kip & Kaboodle,
Lunenburg

N Bradt

200m
200yds

140

By bus Trius Tours stop in Mahone Bay (Exit 10 of Highway 103) *en route* between Halifax and Yarmouth. Tickets are available from the Circle K/Irving garage at Highway 103, Exit 11. Tickets to or from Halifax cost CAN$23 one way, and to or from Yarmouth CAN$48. The journey between Mahone Bay and Halifax, or vice versa, takes one hour 20 minutes, and between Mahone Bay and Yarmouth, or vice versa, three hours 40 minutes.

TOURIST INFORMATION *(165 Edgewater St; 624 6151, T/F 1 888 624 6151; late May–Jun 10.00–17.00 daily; Jul–Aug 09.00–19.00 daily; Sep–early Oct 10.00–17.00 daily)*

WHERE TO STAY

Bayview Pines Country Inn (8 rooms, 2 apts) 678 Oakland Rd, Indian Point; 624 9970, T/F 1 866 624 9970; www.bayviewpines.com; May–Oct; off-season by reservation. An old farmhouse & converted barn on 5.7ha overlooking the bay & islands, approximately 6km from town. Full b/fast inc in room (but not apt) rates. $$

Buttercup Cottages (3 cottages) 410 Herman's Island Rd, Sunnybrook; 634 8199; www3.ns.sympatico.ca/buttercup; May–Oct. Simple but comfortable 2- & 3-bedroom waterfront cottages overlook Echo Bay on the quiet 'backroad' between Mahone Bay & Lunenburg: either town can be reached in a 7min drive. Bikes available for guest use. $$

Fairmont House B&B (3 rooms) 654 Main St; 624 8089; www.fairmonthouse.com; year-round. Built by a shipbuilder, this outstanding c1857 Gothic Revival home still has the original curved staircase – held together with wooden pegs rather than nails or screws – in the entry hall. En-suite bathrooms. Full b/fast inc. $$

Kip & Kaboodle Tourist Accommodation 9466 Hwy 3; 531 5494, T/F 1 866 549 4522; www.kiwikaboodle.com; Apr–Oct. A small backpacker hostel 3km from the town centre on the road to Lunenburg, with bunk beds in 2 mixed rooms: 2 bathrooms, communal kitchen & common room. Seasonal outdoor pool, bikes & kayaks to rent. Private double rooms may be available in adjacent cottage. Linen & light b/fast inc. Dorm CAN$25, cottage CAN$75. $

WHERE TO EAT

The Cheesecake Gallery 533 Main St; 624 0579; Jan–mid-May 16.00–20.00 Thu–Fri, 11.00–20.00 Sat, 11.00–15.00 Sun; mid-May–late Oct 11.00–21.00 daily. Don't be fooled by the name: yes, the walls are adorned with art, & yes, most of the desserts are fantastic cheesecakes, but this bright restaurant offers a range of well-cooked and well-presented bistro food. $$

The Innlet Café 249 Edgewater St; 624 6363; www.innletcafe.com; year-round 11.30–21.00 daily. A 10min waterfront walk round the bay from the town centre, this busy – sometimes too busy –

THE THREE CHURCHES

The classic view of the Mahone Bay skyline – with its three churches reflected in the bay's still water – has become one of the most photographed scenes in Nova Scotia.

The white church with a tower on the right is the Trinity United Church. The oldest of the three, it dates from 1861 and was formerly Knox Presbyterian. Originally located further back, it was dragged to its present location by teams of oxen in 1885. The middle church is St John's Lutheran built in 1869, and the newest church, the high Victorian Gothic Revival-style St James Anglican Church sits on the left and was built in 1887.

Music at the three churches (531 2248; www.threechurches.com) is a series of classical concerts held fortnightly on Friday evenings between early July and early September. Tickets cost CAN$15.

licensed restaurant has an outdoor dining area with great views of the town. Stir-fries & pasta dishes are both good, & the mud cake a real treat. **$$**
✕ The Biscuit Eater 16 Orchard St; ☎ 624 2665; www.biscuiteater.ca; ⊕ 08.30–16.00 Wed–Sat, 10.00–16.00 Sun. This new & used bookshop is also home to a great café, with excellent soups, sandwiches & mouthwatering (if slightly pricey) cakes. No artificial ingredients are used. There is a busy calendar of lectures, discussions & music too. **$**
✕ Jo Ann's Deli 9 Edgewater St; ☎ 624 6305; www.joannsdelimarket.ca; ⊕ May–Oct. 09.00–18.00 daily. There are just a couple of tables outside this tempting deli/grocery store/bakery/greengrocer. Order

a salad, sandwich or grab ingredients for a gourmet picnic: the baked goods are particularly hard to resist. **$**
✕ Mug & Anchor 643 Main St; ☎ 624 6378 ⊕ year-round 11.30–midnight daily. Nice ambience, a deck, good pub food & regular live music. **$**
✕ Saltspray Café 436 Main St; ☎ 624 0457; ⊕ year-round 08.00–22.00 daily. Forced to move from the waterfront after the old venue burned down (it wasn't their fault), in its new c1860 home the Saltspray continues to offer few frills, but good-value home cooking. The pan-fried haddock, for example, is very good. **$**

FESTIVALS

May
Mussel Festival A weekend of mussel (and wine) tasting and mussel farm tours.

End July–early August
Wooden Boat Festival (☎ 624 0348; www.woodenboatfestival.org) Held annually (on the weekend closest to 1 August), this is one of Nova Scotia's best events – with the added benefit of free admission. As the name suggests, it is all about the town's boat and shipbuilding past. There are workshops and demonstrations, sailing races, music and a lot more.

October
Scarecrow Festival and Antique Fair Three days of music, illuminated hand-carved pumpkins, quilting workshops – not to mention scarecrows and antiques.

OTHER PRACTICALITIES
$ BMO Bank of Montreal 562 Main St; ☎ 624 8355; ⊕ 10.00–16.00 Mon–Wed, 10.00–17.00 Thu–Fri

✉ **Post office** 534 Main St; ⊕ 08.00–17.30 Mon–Fri, 09.00–12.00 Sat

WHAT TO SEE AND DO
Amos Pewter (*589 Main St;* ☎ *624 9547, T/F 1 800 565 3369; www.amospewter.com;* ⊕ *May–Dec 09.00–17.30 Mon–Sat, 10.00–17.30 Sun; Jan–Apr 09.00–17.00 Mon–Sat*) Watch and learn about the pewter-crafting process, or get interactive and produce your own piece (CAN$7).

The Kayak Shack (*617 Main St;* ☎ *531 0101; www.thekayakshack.ca;* ⊕ *Jun–Sep*) Right in the middle of town you can rent a canoe, kayak or join a sea kayak tour of the beautiful bay and its hundreds of islands. Bike rental is also available.

Mahone Bay Settlers' Museum (*578 Main St;* ☎ *624 6263; www.settlersmuseum.ns.ca;* ⊕ *Jun–early Sep 10.00–17.00 Tue–Sat, 13.00–17.00 Sun (check locally for the rest of Sep–early Oct); admission free*) In addition to displays on the town's history (focusing – as the name suggests – on the early settlers and their backgrounds), there is a fine collection of ceramics and antiques. The museum building is c1847.

South Shore Boat Tours (☎ *543 5107; www.southshoreboattours.com/tours.html;* ⊕ *Jun–Oct*) Daily two-hour tours on a 38ft boat to see dolphins, seabirds, seals, etc;

four-hour trips in search of whales and Pearl Island's puffins in season (CAN$35–50).

Spruce Top Rug Hooking Studio (*255 West Main St;* ☎ *624 9312, T/F 1 888 784 4665; www.sprucetoprughookingstudio.com;* ⊕ *year-round 10.00–16.00 Mon & Wed–Sat, 12.00–16.00 Sun; admission free*) This studio claims to have the largest collection of hooked rugs in Atlantic Canada. Regular classes are held, and you may be able to see new works being created.

LUNENBURG

Established in 1753, the original town layout has been maintained and many original wooden buildings preserved, with eight dating back to the 18th century. As the best-surviving example of a planned British colonial settlement in North America, Lunenburg's Old Town section was designated a national historic district by the Canadian government, and in 1995 it was declared a UNESCO World Heritage Site, one of only two in North America (the other is Quebec City).

The Old Town sits on a steep hillside overlooking the harbour. As you drive – or better still, walk – through you'll realise just how steep some of the narrow streets are. A guided walking tour should satisfy those wishing to dig deeper, and if walking is not for you, you can even see the sights by horse and carriage.

Many of the well-preserved brightly painted historical buildings now house inns, cafés, restaurants, shops and a seemingly ever-increasing number of galleries.

Today, the fishing industry may have dried up here, but the marine traditions and its seafaring heritage live on proudly. The Fisheries Museum of the Atlantic (see page 149) will help you understand not just Lunenburg, but coastal communities throughout the province. A dory shop on the waterfront has been making these small wooden fishing boats since 1895, and traditional methods are still used. The town is the homeport of the *Bluenose II* (see box on page 146), and tall ships often grace the picturesque harbour.

Long ago, as it prospered and grew, the town spread beyond the original grid. In residential streets a few minutes' walk away are more magnificent homes, this time on much bigger plots of land. Some – with large lawns and beautiful gardens – are now B&Bs or inns.

In the Old Town area, most of the shops, museums and services are in the rectangle bounded by the waterfront, Lincoln, Cornwallis and Hopson streets.

Whilst Old Town Lunenburg is on a relatively steep hillside, the areas surrounding town are relatively flat and the heavily indented coastline and peninsulas beautiful. This is an ideal area to swap four wheels for two. You can take

THE BACK ROAD TO LUNENBURG

From Mahone Bay, the main route to Lunenburg is along Highway 3. A more interesting route – delightful on a sunny day – is to leave Mahone Bay towards Lunenburg on Highway 3 then turn left onto Maders Cove Road. Bear left onto Sunnybrook Road, then turn left onto Herman's Island Road. Bear left onto Princes Inlet Drive. At the fork, either bear right to rejoin Highway 3 (turn left to continue to Lunenburg) or, for another scenic side-trip, bear left along Second Peninsula Road. Go this way and you'll eventually have to turn back and retrace your steps, but you'll have passed some tranquil, delightful waters, and Second Peninsula Provincial Park. If you're doing this route in reverse, from Lunenburg, turn right from Highway 3 onto Second Peninsula Road.

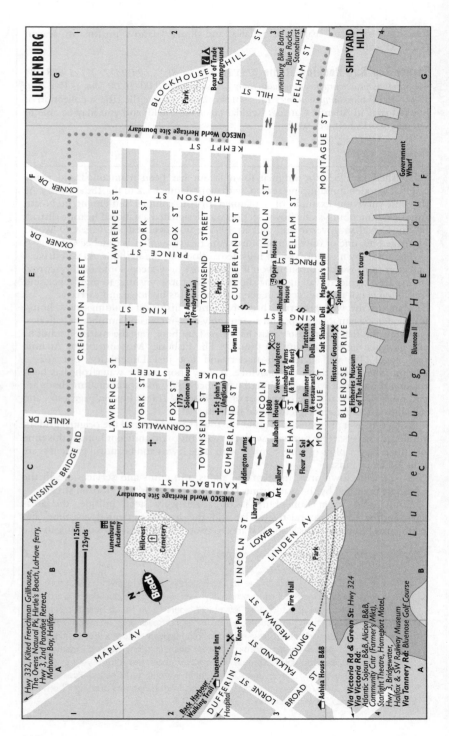

Not a ghost story or a dance, but a unique architectural feature seen in a number of forms in the Old Town, and occasionally elsewhere in the province, is the Lunenburg bump. Inspired by the five-sided Scottish dormer, the Lunenburg bump is a central dormer extended out and down from the roof, thereby creating an overhang – or 'bump' – above the main entrance. If historical architecture is one of your interests, visit the tourist office, and pick up an informative architectural walking tour guide to the town.

a horse and buggy trip round the Old Town, but for a fascinating look deeper into Lunenburg's past, consider a guided walking tour. In addition to the Historic Town tour, one walk takes an in-depth look at Hillcrest Cemetery, whilst another explores Lunenburg by candlelight.

Within an easy drive or cycle ride are several beautiful small forested peninsulas and two tiny photogenic fishing villages well worth exploring. All in all, Lunenburg – roughly equidistant from Halifax and Shelburne – is one of Nova Scotia's most interesting and appealing towns.

HISTORY Early in 1753, a fleet of over a dozen ships from Halifax landed on the site of the Mi'kmaq village of *Merligueche* – 'Milky Waters'. The incomers were mostly Protestants from German-speaking parts of Europe. Land was cleared, defences built, and parcels of land dealt out. The settlement was laid out on what had become a standard plan for new coastal towns, in a compact grid with seven north–south streets intersected by nine east–west streets. It was named for King George II, Duke of Brunschweig-Lunenburg.

In the early years, the Mi'kmaq proved a threat to the settlers, several of whom were killed or taken prisoner until peace was agreed between government officials and Mi'kmaq chiefs in 1762. The next threat came from the sea. In 1782, privateer ships arrived without warning and about 100 armed men rushed ashore, plundering and burning at will.

The early settlers were far more familiar with farming than fishing, but many quickly began to take advantage of the seemingly inexhaustible bounty of the sea. As a consequence, they also became skilled shipbuilders. As the years passed, this port – on a splendid harbour protected by long peninsulas – became home to a huge fishing fleet.

At the turn of the 20th century, Lunenburg's schooner fleet sailed the Grand Banks, competing with the fleets of New England to bring home the abundance of cod. Fishing – especially in the treacherous seas around Nova Scotia – was a dangerous pursuit, and over the years hundreds lost their lives at sea.

GETTING THERE

By car Lunenburg is on Highway 3 and 14km from Highway 103 Exit 11, 100km/62 miles from Halifax, 19km/12 miles from Bridgewater and 11km/7miles from Mahone Bay.

By bus If you just want a quick visit from Halifax, Ambassatours (see page 85) runs a six-hour Lunenburg and Mahone Bay sightseeing tour June–mid–October on Sundays, Tuesdays and Thursdays at 10.00. Tickets cost CAN$105.

TOURIST INFORMATION [144 G2] (*11 Blockhouse Hill Rd;* ☎ *634 8100, T/F 1 888 615 8305;* ⊕ *late May–mid-Oct 09.00–19.00 daily, 20.00 Jul–Aug*)

There had long been competition between fishing fleets from Lunenburg and Gloucester, Massachusetts. So keen was their rivalry that in 1920, the *Halifax Herald* sponsored an annual race for deep-sea fishing schooners from the two fleets. When the Americans won, Canadian pride was hurt: a superior vessel had to be built in time for the next year's competition.

They came up with *Bluenose*, which not only regained the trophy, but it won it for 18 years in succession until World War II loomed, and the race was suspended. New steel-hulled trawlers were rendering wooden fishing vessels redundant and in 1942, the *Bluenose* was sold to carry freight in the Caribbean. Four years later, she foundered and was lost on a Haitian reef.

For many years, this undefeated champion was featured on the back of the Canadian dime (10 cent piece): she is still remembered on Nova Scotia licence plates.

In 1963, the replica *Bluenose II* was built to the original plans by many of the original workers in the same shipyard as the original. Since 1971, she has sailed countless thousands of miles as Nova Scotia's floating ambassador.

If you're lucky, she'll be in port, moored by the Fisheries Museum. Her schedule can be checked – and a two-hour harbour cruise booked, at (☎ 634 4794, T/F 1 866 579 4909; www.museum.gov.ns.ca/bluenose/).

 WHERE TO STAY In Lunenburg, it seems as though the wishes of everyone who ever dreamt of owning a centuries-old house and running it as a B&B have come true. There are dozens, many in the Old Town and several in the quiet tree-lined residential streets less than ten minutes' walk away. Lunenburg is a very popular base for visitors to the South Shore: despite the quantity of places to stay, many only have two or three rooms so it makes sense to book in advance for July and August stays.

Food-wise, it is hard to go wrong with fresh seafood, or try local specialities such as Lunenburg pudding (a type of pork sausage) and sauerkraut.

The businesses listed below are open year-round unless otherwise stated.

Upmarket

🏠 **2nd Paradise Retreat** [144 A1] (2 cottages) Second Peninsula Rd; ☎ 634 4099; www.secondparadise.ns.ca. A lovely Second Peninsula location 6km (10mins' drive) from Lunenburg. Two 2- bedroom eco-friendly cottages set on 11ha of protected oceanfront with private beach. Reservations required. $$$

Mid-range

🏠 **1775 Solomon House** [144 D2] (3 rooms) 69 Townsend St; ☎ 634 3477; f 634 3298; www.bbcanada.com/5511.html. On a quiet street across from St John's Church, this character-filled c1775 Provincial Heritage property is furnished with period antiques. Imaginative & delicious b/fast inc. $$

🏠 **1880 Kaulbach House Historic Inn** [144 D3] (6 rooms) 75 Pelham St; ☎ 634 8818, T/F 1 800 568 8818; www.kaulbachhouse.com; ⏱ May–Dec; off-season by reservation. An elegant, c1880 property in the Old Town with sea views from most of the rooms. Gourmet b/fast inc. $$

🏠 **Addington Arms** [144 C3] (4 rooms) 27 Cornwallis St; ☎ 634 4573, T/F 1 877 979 2727; www.addingtonarms.com; ⏱ year-round. Well-equipped suites (all with sea &/or harbour view) above shops in this c1890 building in the Old Town. 3 suites have en-suite steam rooms. Full b/fast inc. $$

🏠 **Alicion B&B** [144 A4] (3 rooms) 66 McDonald St; ☎ 634 9358, T/F 1 877 634 9358; www.alicionbb.com. Elegant, spacious eco-friendly rooms with huge bathrooms in this quiet c1911 former senator's house a 10min walk from the Old Town. Free use of bikes available. Gourmet b/fast inc. $$

🏠 **Ashlea House B&B** [144 A3] (6 rooms) 42 Falkland St; ✆ 634 7150, T/F 1 866 634 7150; www.ashleahouse.com. A beautiful c1886 house just outside the Old Town with 2nd-floor deck & widow's walk (a railed observation platform) offering fine views. There is a family suite with interconnecting rooms. Full country-style b/fast inc. $$

🏠 **Atlantic Sojourn B&B** [144 A4] (4 rooms) 56 Victoria Rd; ✆ 634 3151, T/F 1 800 550 4824; e atlanticsojourn@eastlink.ca; www.atlanticsojourn.com; ◷ mid-Apr–mid-Nov; off-season by chance. In this recently redecorated very comfortable c1904 house less than 10mins' walk to the Old Town hostesses Sebelle & Susan pride themselves on 'thinking of everything to make your stay more enjoyable' & do a pretty good job. Full b/fast inc. $$

🏠 **Lunenburg Arms Hotel** [144 D3] (24 units) 94 Pelham St; ✆ 640 4040, T/F 1 800 679 4950; www.lunenburgarms.com. This is an excellent Old Town choice for those who prefer a larger hotel. Standard rooms, suites & 2-level suites, all with AC.

Budget

🏠 **Homeport Motel** [144 A4] 167 Victoria Rd; ✆ 634 8234, T/F 1 800 616 4411; www.homeportmotel.com. A 10–15min walk from the Old Town, in addition to standard motel rooms – with fridge, microwave & toaster – there are simple 1- and 2-bedroom suites & laundry facilities on site. $

✗ WHERE TO EAT

Luxury

✗ **Fleur de Sel** [144 C3] 53 Montague St; ✆ 640 2121; www.fleurdesel.net; ◷ Apr–Jun 17.00–20.30 Fri–Sun; Jun–mid-Oct 17.00–21.30 daily; mid-Oct–Christmas 17.00–20.30 Fri–Sun; Apr–Christmas 10.00–14.00 Sun brunch. Housed in a beautiful old

Upmarket

✗ **Tin Fish** [144 D3] 94 Pelham St; ✆ 640 4040, T/F 1 800 679 4950; www.lunenburgarms.com; ◷ 12.00–14.00 & 17.00–21.00 daily. Part of the Lunenburg Arms Hotel, this licensed restaurant offers rather good casual fine-dining. Try, for example, the breast of duck with orange & lemongrass reduction. The restaurant's whimsical décor is not for those who like neutral colours. $$$

Mid-range

✗ **Kilted Frenchman Grillhouse** [144 A1] 3017 Hwy 332; ✆ 764 3000; www.kiltedfrenchman.com; ◷ late Jun–early Sep 17.00–21.30 Tue–Sun; rest of the year

Many overlook the harbour. Full-service Aveda spa is also available. See below for the hotel's Tin Fish Restaurant. $$

🏠 **Lunenburg Inn** [144 A2] (7 rooms) 26 Dufferin St; ✆ 634 3963, T/F 1 800 565 3963; www.lunenburginn.com; ◷ Apr–Nov. A fine c1893 building just outside the Old Town with 5 bedrooms & 2 suites. Victorian-style décor & covered veranda, sundeck, private bar. Gourmet b/fast, eg: strawberry-stuffed French toast inc. $$

🏠 **Rum Runner Inn** [144 D3] (13 rooms) 66–70 Montague St; ✆ 634 9200, T/F 1 888 778 6786; www.rumrunnerinn.com. Overlooking the harbour & golf course, 4 of the bright, spacious modern-looking rooms have private glassed-in verandas. See page 148 for their restaurant. Continental b/fast inc. $$

🏠 **Spinnaker Inn** [144 E4] (4 units) 126 Montague St; ✆ 634 4543, T/F 1 888 634 8973; www.spinnakerinn.com. 2 rooms & 2 split-level suites in this c1850 waterfront property. There's also a large sun-deck. Bedrooms have beautiful wood floors & flat-screen TVs. $$

🏕 **Lunenburg Board of Trade Campground** [144 G2] (55 sites) 11 Blockhouse Hill Rd; ✆ 634 8100, T/F 1 888 615 8305; ◷ mid-May–mid-Oct. Look down over the front & back harbours from this open campground next to the tourist office. Serviced & tent sites. $

sea captain's home with a garden terrace, this award-winning restaurant offers intimate & elegant fine-dining. Try cod tongues & cheeks, butter-poached lobster or local game – or the 7-course surprise tasting menu with wine pairings. $$$–$$$$

✗ **Trattoria Della Nonna** [144 D3] 9 King St; ✆ 640 3112; www.trattoriadellanonna.ca; ◷ summer 11.30–14.00 & 17.00–21.00 Tue–Sat; winter 17.00–21.00 Tue–Wed & Sat, 11.30–14.00 & 17.00–21.00 Thu–Fri. Relatively new, upmarket & stylish (for Nova Scotia). More seafood choices than are normally seen in an Italian restaurant, but plenty of other options. Short but well-chosen wine list. $$$

17.00–21.00 Thu–Sun. Excellent steak/rib restaurant a 15min drive from Lunenburg, with cosy booths by the fireplace, & a wrap-around patio for alfresco dining.

Starters include good seafood chowder & tempura prawns. Beer-lovers should try the house brew. There are plans to open for lunch in the summer. $$
✗ **Magnolia's Grill** [144 E4] 128 Montague St; ↘ 634 3287; ☉ Apr–Nov 11.00–22.00 daily. Recently expanded but often still too small for the demand, Magnolia's is laid-back & informal in terms of décor & ambience, but bright & lively in terms of its regularly changing menu. Particular favourites

include spicy peanut soup (trust me!), fishcakes & sublime (authentic) Key lime pie. If there's a criticism, it might be over some portion sizes – oh, & the fact that it's not always easy to get a table! $$
✗ **Rum Runner Inn** [144 D3] 66–70 Montague St; ↘ 634 8778; www.rumrunnerinn.com; ☉ May–Oct 11.00–21.00 daily. The inn's licensed restaurant has a German chef & offers nautical flair. Try the 'Flaming Seafood Dinner for Two'. $$

Budget

✗ **Historic Grounds** [144 D4] 100 Montague St; ↘ 634 9995; www.historicgrounds.com; ☉ Jun–mid-Sep 07.30–21.30 daily (from 08.00 Sat–Sun); mid-Sep–May 07.30–17.30 daily. A good spot for not just coffee but also light meals. $
✗ **Knot Pub** [144 A3] 4 Dufferin St; ↘ 634 3334; ☉ 12.00–21.30 daily (later in season). This dark but lively pub isn't just a good spot to share a drink with the locals, but the pub grub is pretty good too. No surprises on the menu – but burgers, club sandwiches, fish & chips & the like are well made & well priced. $

✗ **Salt Shaker Deli** [144 E4] 124 Montague St; ↘ 640 3434; www.saltshakerdeli.com; ☉ 11.00–21.00 Tue–Sat, 11.00–15.00 Sun. Nibbles, pizzas, sandwiches, plus more imaginative/eclectic choices such as Pad Thai or shrimp in hoisin sauce. Eat on the deck overlooking the harbour. $
✗ **Sweet Indulgence** [144 D3] 242 Lincoln St; ↘ 640 3399; www.sweetindulgence.ca; ☉ 07.30–18.00 daily (from 09.00 Sat–Sun). Yes, the cakes & desserts are excellent, but don't overlook this casual café for a light lunch – the soups, sandwiches & salads won't disappoint. $

ENTERTAINMENT For live performances, check the schedules at the **Starlight Theatre** [144 A4] (*37 Hall St;* ↘ *634 1987; www.pearltheatre.com*) and **Lunenburg Opera House** [144 E3] (*290 Lincoln St;* ↘ *640 6500; www.lunenburgoperahouse.com*).

FESTIVALS This is a town with a full calendar of festivals and events. For more details, see www.lunenburgns.com/festivals-and-events/. Some of the best are:

June
Summer Opera Festival Performances by the Maritime Concert Opera, the province's only concert opera company.

August
Lunenburg Folk Harbour Festival (↘ *634 3180; www.folkharbour.com*) This excellent four-day event features performances of traditional and contemporary folk and roots music at a variety of venues in the town from pubs to churches, with a main stage in a tent on Blockhouse Hill [144 G2].

Nova Scotia Folk Art Festival (↘ *640 2113; www.nsfolkartfestival.com*) The good news is that this colourful event draws the best proponents of the genre from all over the province: the downside is that – lasting just four hours – it gets too busy.

September
Seafood Festival A weekend of seafood cooking demonstrations, dory boat races and live music, plus a chowder competition & beer tent.

End November–early December
Once Upon a Lunenburg Christmas Market Something to warm the hearts of locals and winter visitors: dozens of decorated Christmas trees, Santa arriving by trawler and lots of jingling bells.

OTHER PRACTICALITIES

$ **BMO Bank of Montreal** 12 King St; ☏ 634 8875; ◷ 09.30–16.30 Mon–Fri

$ **TD Canada Trust** 36 King St; ☏ 634 8809; ◷ 08.00–18.00 Mon–Wed, 08.00–20.00 Thu–Fri, 08.00–16.00 Sat

✚ **Fishermen's Memorial Hospital** 14 High St; ☏ 634 8801

☷ **Lunenburg Library** 19 Pelham St; ☏ 634 8008; ◷ 10.00–17.00 Mon–Wed & Fri–Sat, 10.00–20.00 Thu, 12.00–16.00 Sun

✉ **Post office** 242 Lincoln St; ◷ 08.30–17.00 Mon–Fri

WHAT TO SEE AND DO

Fisheries Museum of the Atlantic [144 D4] (*68 Bluenose Dr;* ☏ *634 4794; www.museum.gov.ns.ca/fma/;* ◷ *(in season) mid-May–mid-Oct 09.30–17.30 daily (Jul–Aug until 19.00 Tue–Sat); admission CAN$10; (off-season) mid-Oct–mid-May 09.30–16.00 Mon–Fri; admission CAN$4*) Appropriately located on the waterfront, the complex includes two dockside vessels (a restored schooner and a steel-hulled trawler), an aquarium with Maritime species and touch-tank, demonstrations of marine-related skills, and three floors of exhibits. Learn about rum-running, traditional Mi'kmaq fishing methods, whales and whaling history – and much more. Absorbing. Parts of the museum complex are open in the off-season (*mid-Oct–mid-May, 09.30–16.00 Mon–Fri; admission CAN$4.00*).

Knaut-Rhuland House [144 E3] (*125 Pelham St;* ☏ *634 3498; www.lunenburgheritagesociety.ca;* ◷ *early Jun–Sep 12.00–18.00 Mon–Sat, 12.00–16.00 Sun; admission CAN$2*) Dating from c1793, this house is one of the best-preserved examples of Georgian architecture in the country.

Halifax and Southwestern Railway Museum [144 A4] (*11188 Hwy 3;* ☏ *634 3184; www.hswmuseum.ednet.ns.ca/;* ◷ *year-round: May–Oct 10.00–17.00 Mon–Sat, 13.00–17.00 Sun; off-season 10.00–17.00 Sat, 13.00–17.00 Sun; admission CAN$6*) The story of the H&SW with a replica 1940s' stationmaster's office, large S-gauge model railway based on the old line, and much more. Just outside town.

St John's Anglican Church [144 D2] (*81 Cumberland St;* ☏ *634 4994; www.stjohnslunenburg.org;* ◷ *mid-Jun–mid-Sep 10.00–17.00 Mon–Sat, 12.00–19.00 Sun*) Originally built in 1754, this was the second-oldest Protestant church in Canada after St Paul's in Halifax. I say 'was' because the church was destroyed by fire late in 2001. Previously one of Canada's best examples of the 'carpenter Gothic' architectural style (wherein features traditionally rendered in stone are interpreted in wood), it was faithfully restored and reopened in 2005. There are displays on the history, fire and restoration of the church. Tours offered in summer.

In addition to St John's church, look out for **St Andrew's Presbyterian** (*Townsend St*) which dates from 1828 but was 'Gothicised' in 1879. Atop the steeple, a large copper cod indicates the wind's direction.

Bluenose Golf Course [144 A4] (*18 Cove Rd;* ☏ *634 4260; www.bluenosegolfclub.com;* ◷ *late Apr–Oct*) A short nine-hole course with stunning views over the town and harbour. Green fees CAN$28.

Lunenburg Farmers' Market [144 A4] (*Community Centre car park, Victoria Rd and Green St; www.lunenburgfarmersmarket.com;* ◷ *May–Oct 08.00–12.00 Thu*) Definitely worth a visit is this market, with plants, flowers, fresh produce, baked goods and much more.

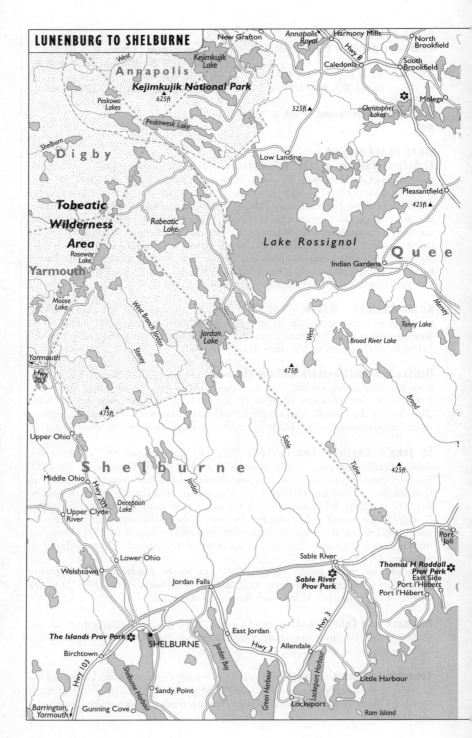

LUNENBURG TO SHELBURNE

New Grafton
Annapolis Royal
Harmony Mills
North Brookfield

West

Kejimkujik Lake

A n n a p o l i s

Kejimkujik National Park
625ft ▲

Hwy 8

Caledonia
South Brookfield

525ft ▲

Christopher Lakes
Molega

Peskowa Lakes

Peskowesk Lake

Low Landing

Shelburn

D i g b y

Pleasantfield
425ft ▲

Tobeatic

Rabeatic Lake

L a k e   R o s s i g n o l

Q u e e

Wilderness

Area
Roseway Lake

Indian Gardens

Yarmouth

West

Moose Lake

Toney Lake

West Branch Jordan

Broad River Lake

Stoney

Jordan Lake

Brood

Yarmouth
Hwy 203

475ft ▲

Sable

Upper Ohio

425ft ▲

S h e l b u r n e

Tidne

Middle Ohio
Hwy 203

Jordan

Upper Clyde River

Deception Lake

Port Joli

Lower Ohio

Sable River

Thomas H Raddall Prov Park
East Side
Port l'Hébert

Welshtown

Jordan Falls

Sable River Prov Park

Port l'Hébert

The Islands Prov Park

Jordan Bay

East Jordan

Allendale

Hwy 3

Hwy 3

Little Harbour

Birchtown

SHELBURNE

Green Harbour

Lockeport Harbour

Hwy 103

Shelburne Harbour

Sandy Point

Barrington, Yarmouth
Gunning Cove

Lockeport

Ram Island

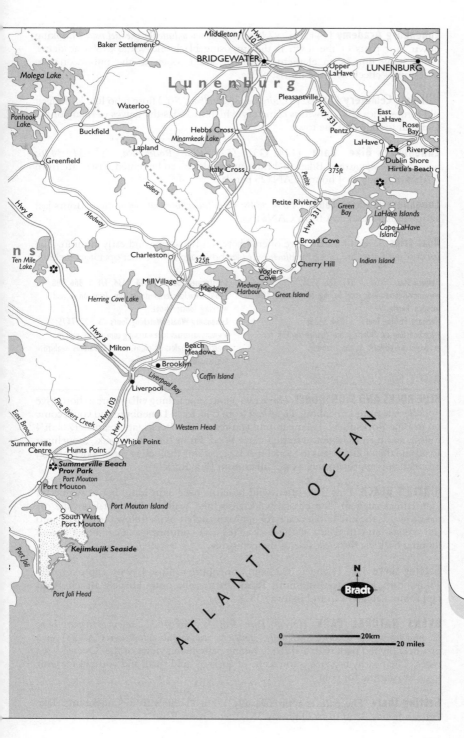

Lunenburg Academy [144 B1] (*97 Kaulbach St; www.lunenburg.ednet.ns.ca*) Looking down over parts of the town is the imposing black-and-white c1894 academy, which now houses an elementary school and is open to the public on rare occasions – check with the tourist office.

Hillcrest Cemetery [144 B2] (*Unity La, off Kaulbach St*) Those who like looking at old tombstones will enjoy this cemetery which includes the graves of many of the German founders of the town.

Lunenburg Bike Barn [144 G3] (*579 Blue Rocks Rd;* ➘ *634 3426; www.bikelunenburg.com*) Bikes (hybrids) and tandems can be rented. Prices are from CAN$18 for up to 4 hours, CAN$25 per day.

Lunenburg Walking Tours (➘ *634 3848; www.lunenburgwalkingtours.com*) Tours last about an hour and cost from CAN$15.

Boat trips Several boat trips are offered between late spring and early autumn. The most sought after are those on *Bluenose II* (see box, page 146). Other operators include:

Eastern Star ➘ T/F | 877 386 3535; www.novascotiasailing.com. Sailing tours on a 48ft wooden ketch.

Heritage Fishing Tours ➘ 634 3535; www.boattour.ca. Offering the chance to fish for mackerel or pollock in the harbour.

Lobstermen Tours ➘ 634 3434, T/F | 866 708 3434; www.lobstermentours.com. Trips on a real working lobster boat.

Lunenburg Whale Watching Tours ➘ 527 7175; www.novascotiawhalewatching.com. Head out in search of whales: dolphins, seals & various seabirds are usually seen.

AROUND LUNENBURG

BLUE ROCKS AND STONEHURST These two photogenic fishing villages are a short drive or cycle ride from Lunenburg. Head east from Old Town Lunenburg and you'll come on to Blue Rocks Road. Follow it until you reach Blue Rocks (approximately 6km/4 miles), and turn right onto Herring Cove Road. From Blue Rocks, take Stonehurst Road and then follow signs to Stonehurst East, parking just before the wooden bridge. Stonehurst is approximately 4km/2 miles from Blue Rocks.

HIRTLE'S BEACH This fine, often wild beach is over 3km long. For a wonderful (sometimes rugged) 7km coastal wilderness hike, walk to the right from the car park towards the end of the beach for approximately 1.5km, follow the path up into the woods, and turn left at the fork. The trail continues to Gaff Point before looping back via the west side of the peninsula.

Getting there Take Highway 332 from Lunenburg to Rose Bay for approximately 15km, turn left onto Kingsburg Road, then right onto Hirtle's Beach Road (approximately 8km from Highway 332).

OVENS NATURAL PARK (*Ovens Park Rd;* ➘ *766 4621; www.ovenspark.com;* ⊙ *mid-May–Sep 09.00–21.00 daily, trails* ⊙ *year-round; admission CAN$8*) is a privately owned park with a cliffside hiking path giving views of the 'Ovens' – sea caves. The nearby beach was the scene of an 1861 gold rush, and you can try your hand at panning for gold.

Getting there The park is approximately 17km/11 miles from Lunenburg. Take Feltzen South Road from Highway 332, then Ovens Road.

Where to stay There is a 174-site cliff-top campground, nine cabins, a swimming pool and a restaurant (⊕ *late Jun–early Sep*; $–$$). The park's owners (the Chapins) had a celebrated sibling, singer/songwriter Harry Chapin (remember 'Cat's in the Cradle' and 'WOLD'?) who was killed in a car crash in 1981. Various family members and local musicians sing and play every evening in July and August.

LUNENBURG COUNTY WINERY (*813 Walburne Rd, nr Newburne*; ☎ *644 2415; www.canada-wine.com*; ⊕ *mid-Jun–mid-Oct daily 09.00–21.00, mid-Oct–mid-Jun 09.00–17.00 Mon–Sat*) Nova Scotia's only winery specialising in fruit (rather than grape) wines is situated on a 40ha blueberry farm. Take Clearland Road from Lunenburg (it later becomes Woodstock Road) and after 21km turn left at Walburne Road and follow it for 4km.

BRIDGEWATER

Straddling the LaHave River, Bridgewater is the major commercial and service centre between Halifax and Yarmouth: the largest shopping mall on the South Shore sits on the river's eastern bank. The area's major employer, Michelin, has a plant in the Industrial Park.

The old downtown area was destroyed by fire in 1899 and isn't particularly attractive. The town has a couple of golf courses and museums and some nice riverside parks: on some tree-lined residential streets stand stately homes which have withstood the test of time.

Outdoorsy types shouldn't miss Riverview Park, and the shared-use 8km Centennial Trail following the old rail bed is worth a wander.

Actor Donald Sutherland grew up and went to school in Bridgewater in the late 1940s.

GETTING THERE

By car Bridgewater is on Highway 3, just off Highway 103 (Exits 12 or 13). It is 100km/62 miles from Halifax, 20km/12 miles from Lunenburg and 45km/28 miles from Liverpool.

By bus The Trius Tours coach stops here *en route* between Halifax and Yarmouth (see page 52).

TOURIST INFORMATION
This has changed venues a couple of times in recent years, closed down completely in 2009, and the 2010 location is yet to be decided. See www.town.bridgewater.ns.ca for the latest developments.

 WHERE TO STAY AND EAT

🏠 **Days Inn** (70 rooms) 50 North St; ☎ 543 7131; T/F 1 877 543 7131; www.daysinn.com; ⊕ year-round. The c1970s Wandlyn Inn was totally renovated in 2008 when taken over by the Days Inn chain. Comfortable if characterless rooms. Indoor pool & a restaurant ($$). Some rooms have fridges. $$
🏠 **Fairview Inn** (24 rooms) 25 Queen St; ☎ 543 2233; www.thefairviewinn.ca; ⊕ year-round. On a quiet lane, Nova Scotia's oldest continually operating inn has been welcoming guests since 1863. Gracious & beautifully restored, with lovely hardwood floors & lots of antiques. Outdoor pool (seasonal). On site is

Cranberry's (⊕ year-round 07.00–11.00, 11.30–14.00 & 17.00–21.00 daily; $$) which in recent years has been Bridgewater's best restaurant by a country mile. The b/fast menu includes gingerbread pancakes with an orange & cranberry syrup & whipped cream, the lunch menu excellent salads, gourmet burgers, etc, & for dinner think 'casual fine-dining' & enjoy, eg: Indian Point mussels, chicken *cordon rouge* & sticky toffee pudding. Healthy light b/fast inc, full b/fast available at extra cost. $$

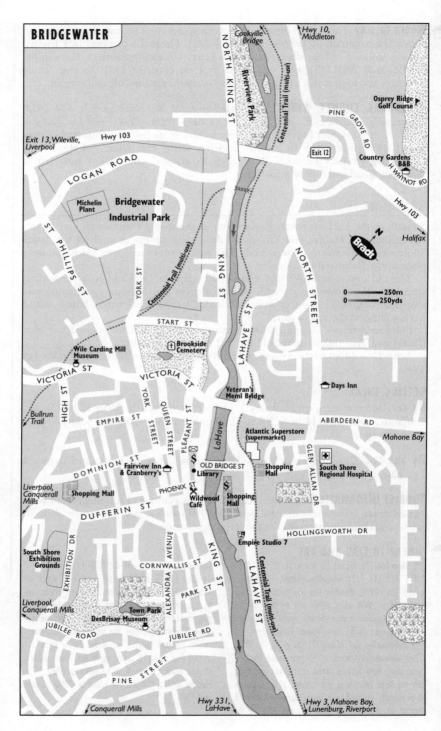

BRIDGEWATER

Exit 13, Wileville, Liverpool

Hwy 103

Cookville Bridge

Riverview Park

Centennial Trail (multi-use)

Hwy 10, Middleton

NORTH KING ST

PINE GROVE RD

Osprey Ridge Golf Course

Exit 12

Country Gardens B&B

H WHYNOT RD

Hwy 103

Halifax

LOGAN ROAD

Michelin Plant

Bridgewater Industrial Park

ST PHILLIPS ST

YORK ST

Centennial Trail (multi-use)

KING ST

LAHAVE ST

NORTH STREET

0 — 250m
0 — 250yds

START ST

Wile Carding Mill Museum

Brookside Cemetery

VICTORIA ST

VICTORIA ST

YORK STREET

Days Inn

High St

Bullrun Trail

EMPIRE ST

QUEEN STREET

PLEASANT ST

Veteran's Meml Bridge

LaHave

ABERDEEN RD

Mahone Bay

DOMINION ST

Fairview Inn & Cranberry's

Library

OLD BRIDGE ST

Atlantic Superstore (supermarket)

Shopping Mall

GLEN ALLAN DR

South Shore Regional Hospital

Liverpool, Conquerall Mills

Shopping Mall

PHOENIX ST

Wildwood Café

Shopping Mall

DUFFERIN ST

EXHIBITION DR

HOLLINGSWORTH DR

Empire Studio 7

South Shore Exhibition Grounds

CORNWALLIS ST

ALEXANDRA AVENUE

KING ST

Centennial Trail (multi-use)

LAHAVE ST

Liverpool, Conquerall Mills

Town Park

PARK ST

DesBrisay Museum

JUBILEE ROAD

JUBILEE RD

PINE STREET

Conquerall Mills

Hwy 331, LaHave

Hwy 3, Mahone Bay, Lunenburg, Riverport

🏠 **Country Gardens B&B** (3 rooms) 527 Harold Whynot Rd, Oak Hill; ☎ 543 6434; www.bbcanada.com/4446.html; ⊕ mid-May–mid-Oct. A welcoming old farmhouse opposite the Osprey Hills Golf Course outside the town centre. Hearty b/fast inc. $

✕ **Wildwood Café** 425 King St, ☎ 530 2011; ⊕ Apr–Sep 09.00–20.00 Mon–Fri, 09.00–16.00

Sat, Oct–Dec, Feb–Mar 09.00–16.00 Mon–Sat. Comfortable, busy new café with vibrant décor & local artists' work on display. The imaginative menu has clear Spanish/Mexican influences, the food is fresh & tasty. Burritos, tacos, quesadillas, salads & excellent paninis. $

ENTERTAINMENT

◄ **Empire Studio 7** 349 Lahave St; ☎ 527 4025; www.empiretheatres.com. 7-screen cinema complex.

FESTIVALS
August
Hank Snow Tribute Four-day tribute to the country-music great born in nearby Brooklyn.

OTHER PRACTICALITIES

$ **Royal Bank** 565 King St; ☎ 543 0184; ⊕ 10.00–17.00 Mon–Fri

$ **Scotiabank** 421 LaHave St; ☎ 543 8155; ⊕ 10.00–17.00 Mon–Wed & Fri, 10.00–20.00 Thu, 09.00–13.00 Sat

✚ **South Shore Regional Hospital** 90 Glen Allan Dr; ☎ 543 4603

📖 **Bridgewater Library** 547 King St; ☎ 543 9222; ⊕ 10.00–17.00 Mon–Wed & Fri–Sat, 10.00–20.00 Thu

✉ **Post office** 613 King St; ⊕ 08.30–17.00 Mon–Fri

WHAT TO SEE AND DO

DesBrisay Museum (*130 Jubilee Rd;* ☎ *543 4033; www.desbrisaymuseum.ca;* ⊕ *Jul–Sep 09.00–17.00 Mon–Sat, 13.00–17.00 Sun; Oct–Jun 13.00–17.00 Wed–Sun; admission CAN$3.50, Sat free*) Encompassing the collection of Judge Mather Byles DesBrisay (1828–1900), the exhibits focus on the natural history, early settlement, cultural and industrial growth of Bridgewater and Lunenburg County from the early 17th century. Look out for the beautiful hooded cradle covered with birch-bark panels and porcupine quills made in the 1860s by Mi'kmaq artist Mary Christianne Morris. Set in the 8ha Bridgewater Woodland Gardens, with picnic areas and walking trails through the woods.

Wile Carding Mill Museum (*242 Victoria Rd;* ☎ *543 8233; www.museum.gov.ns.ca/wcm/;* ⊕ *Jun–Sep 09.30–17.30 Mon–Sat, 13.00–17.30 Sun; admission CAN$3.50 adult*) This c1860 water-powered mill automated the wool-carding process (the process where wool is 'combed' – usually by hand – to separate the fibres prior to spinning).

THE BIG EX

Agricultural fairs are big in Nova Scotia, and the **South Shore Exhibition** (☎ *543 3341; www.thebigex.com; end Jul*) is one of the province's biggest and best. Held at Bridgewater's Exhibition Grounds at 50 Exhibition Drive, farming methods used in days gone by are not forgotten, with the International Ox-Pull a big draw. The event, which includes arts and crafts, food, entertainment and an amusement park, attracts over 50,000 people.

South Shore **BRIDGEWATER**

4

Osprey Ridge Golf Course (*Harold Whynot Rd;* ☏ *543 6666; www.ospreyridge.ns.ca*)
A 6,607yd, par-72 championship course: 10 holes have water in play. Green fees
CAN$58.

LIVERPOOL

If you approach Liverpool past shopping malls or heavy industry, don't be too
put off. Similarly, when you reach Main Street and see a row of fairly run-of-
the-mill shops and services, don't give up. Dig deeper and this town at the
mouth of the Mersey River will reward you. Go further along Main Street to the
town's most desirable area (if house prices are anything to go by), Fort Point,
and you'll find several fine and prestigious homes, a pleasant little park, lovely
water frontage, and a wonderful view – albeit of the Bowater Mersey Paper
Company mill across the river. Eyesore it may be, but the mill has long been
vital to the town's economy.

Wander the residential areas behind Main Street and admire the grand houses
and their gardens. Enjoy the architecture – on Church Street, for example, the
c1854 Court House is one of the province's finest examples of the American Greek
Revival movement. There are interesting museums to explore, an Old Burial
Ground (Main Street at Old Bridge Street) to wander, a couple of good eateries,
and, if you're really not in the mood for things urban, wonderful beaches nearby.

SUGGESTED DETOUR – HIGHWAY 331

From Bridgewater, Highway 331 follows the west bank of the LaHave River for about
20km to LaHave. This is the western terminus for a car ferry which makes frequent
crossings of the river to East LaHave (on Highway 332). The cable ferry (CAN$5) runs
every 30 minutes. Just past the ferry dock, a 100-plus year-old former chandlery now
houses the justifiably popular **LaHave Bakery** (*Highway 331;* ☏ *688 2908;* ☺ *summer
09.00–18.30 daily; winter 09.00–16.30 daily;* $). In addition to baking traditionally bread
made from additive-free and locally grown ingredients and tempting cakes and squares,
there are sandwiches and a couple of hot items (perhaps pizza). There are only a few
tables, so if the weather's nice, order 'to go' and walk down for a riverside picnic by the
museum where Isaac de Razilly, a French nobleman and explorer, established Fort Ste-
Marie-de-Grace here in 1632. This was one of the first permanent European settlements
in Canada, and – from 1632 to 1636 – the first capital of New France. Razilly died in
1636 and his successor decided to move his headquarters to Port-Royal (see page 210).
The settlement was destroyed by fire in the early 1650s. On its site, in a former
lighthouse-keeper's house, is **Fort Point Museum** (*100 Fort Point Rd,* ☏ *688 1632;
www.fortpointmuseum.com;* ☺ *Jun–Sep 10.00–17.00; off-season by appointment; park
☺ year-round; admission free*) which presents 400 years of local history including the
Mi'kmaq, early French settlement and Foreign Protestant settlers. There are fine views
from a third-floor viewing platform, picnic tables and a replica lighthouse. The adjacent
cemetery is also worth a wander.

Continuing on Highway 331, in less than 10km from LaHave you'll reach **Crescent
Beach** where a causeway shelters a fine, long, sandy beach. Drive or cycle across the
causeway to reach the LaHave Islands. The **LaHave Islands Marine Museum** (*100
LaHave Islands Rd;* ☏ *688 2973; www.lahaveislandsmarinemuseum.ca;* ☺ *Jun–Aug
10.00–17.00 daily; admission free*) – housed in a former Methodist church – apart, there
are no services for the visitor.

Back on Highway 331 it is just 1km to **Rissers Beach Provincial Park** (*Hwy 331;
www.novascotiaparks.ca/parks/rissers.asp;* ☺ *mid-May–mid-Oct*). In addition to a long,

HISTORY When Sieur de Mons arrived in 1604 *en route* to Port-Royal he was surprised to find a French fur trader already here. De Mons named the port after the trader, calling it Port Rossignol: the Mi'kmaq called it *Ogumkiqueok*, 'a place of departure'. A group of New Englanders, most of whom were said to be direct descendants of the Pilgrim Fathers, founded Liverpool in 1759.

A shipbuilding and shipping industry developed, but during the American Revolution several ships from the port were seized by American privateers. This stung the port's mariners who built new ships and set off to do their own privateering (see page 10).

Most of what went on in the town at that time was faithfully recorded by an early settler, Simeon Perkins, who built a fine home on the town's main street – and kept a detailed diary. Perkins records, for instance, that smallpox ravaged Liverpool until the people submitted to an ordeal called 'vaccination'. The vaccine was yet to be perfected and Perkins says that as many died of the vaccination as did from smallpox.

With the cessation of hostilities, Liverpool settled into a long period of prosperity centred on shipbuilding and lumbering.

Many of the downtown buildings were destroyed by a great fire in 1865.

GETTING THERE

By car Liverpool is on Highway 3, just off Highway 103 Exit 19; 147km/91 miles from Halifax and 69km/43 miles from Shelburne.

---

sand beach, a boardwalk leads across a marsh. When you reach its end, turn left along the bank of the Petite Rivière and walk back along the beach to complete a loop. The park's 98-site campground offers open and wooded sites, some (the first to be reserved) virtually on the beach.

Again it's about 1km from the park to the village of **Petite Rivière**: cross the bridge and turn left off Highway 331 onto Green Bay Road. The community of **Green Bay** has a couple of lovely (generally sheltered) little beaches, several holiday homes and **Macleod's Canteen** (*542 Green Bay Rd;* ✆ *688 2866;* ⏰ *late Jun–early Sep 11.00–18.00 daily;* $): eat in, out, or take your fish and chips to the beach across the road.

Retrace your steps to Petite Rivière and, back at the crossroads, turn left back onto Highway 331. After about 300m, look out for the **Old Burial Ground** on the left almost opposite the Crousetown turn-off: graves date from the very early 19th century. If you turn onto Petite Rivière Road and follow it to Italy Cross Road, 4km from the aforementioned crossroads you'll find the **Petite Rivière Vineyards** (*1300 Italy Cross Rd;* ✆ *693 3033; www.petiteriverewines.ca;* ⏰ *summer 12.00–17.00 Sat–Sun*). Back on Highway 331, you see forest rather than the sea for the next 7km before reaching picturesque **Broad Cove**: on your right, sophisticated but relaxed **Best Coast Coffee** (*7070 Hwy 331;* ✆ *935 2031;* ⏰ *mid-Jun–mid-Oct 09.30–16.00 Tue–Sun;* $) offers not only good coffee, but gourmet sandwiches and tempting baked goodies.

5km further on at **Cherry Hill**, it's easy to miss the turn-off to another fine, long, and usually very quiet beach. Coming from Broad Cove on Highway 331, turn left onto Henry Conrad Road by the Fire Department.

As you pass East Port Medway 9km further on, for jewellery, pottery, painted mirrors and more, stop at **Glorious Mud Studio Gallery** (*1314 Hwy 331;* ✆ *677 2899; www.gloriousmud.net;* ⏰ *by chance or appointment*). It's about 6km between here and Highway 103 Exit 17 from where it is 30km to Bridgewater or 17km to Liverpool. You'll have driven approximately 60km from Bridgewater.

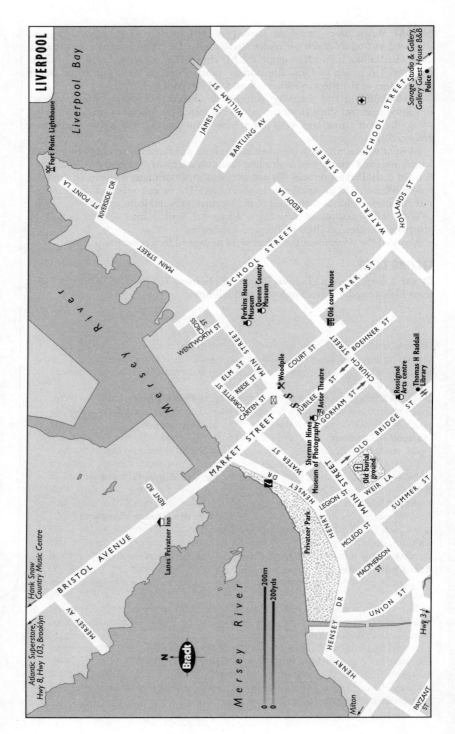

LIVERPOOL

Liverpool Bay

Fort Point Lighthouse

Liverpool Bay

Mersey River

RIVERSIDE DR

FT POINT LA

MAIN STREET

WILLIAM ST

JAMES ST

BARTLING AV

KEDDY LA

SCHOOL STREET

WATERLOO STREET

SCHOOL STREET

HOLLANDS ST

Savage Studio & Gallery,
Gallery Guest House B&B
Police ●

SCHOOL STREET

Perkins House Museum
Queens County Museum

PARK ST

Old court house

BOEHNER ST

WENTWORTH ST

CROSS ST

ELM ST

REESE ST

MAIN STREET

Woodpile

COURT ST

CHURCH STREET

Rossignol Arts centre

Thomas H Raddall Library

CARTEN ST

CORVETTE ST

JUBILEE ST

Astor Theatre

GORHAM ST

ST

ST

Sherman Hines Museum of Photography

MARKET STREET

WATER ST

HENSEY DR

HENRY LEGION STREET

MAIN STREET

OLD BRIDGE ST

Old burial ground

WEIR LA

SUMMER ST

RENT RD

BRISTOL AVENUE

Lanes Privateer Inn

Privateer Park

MCLEOD ST

MACPHERSON ST

UNION ST

HENSEY DR

HENRY

PAYZANT ST

Milton

Hwy 3

Hank Snow
Country Music Centre

Atlantic Superstore,
Hwy 8, Hwy 103, Brooklyn

MERSEY AV

Mersey River

N

Bradt

0   200m
0   200yds

158

By bus The Trius Tours coach stops at Exit 19 of Highway 103 *en route* between Halifax and Yarmouth. The journey between Halifax and Liverpool (or vice versa) takes three hours and ten minutes; the trip between Liverpool and Yarmouth an hour less (see page 52)

TOURIST INFORMATION (*28 Henry Hensey Dr;* ☏ *354 5421;* ⊕ *mid-May–Jun & Sep–mid-Oct 09.30–17.30 daily; Jul–Aug 09.00–19.00 daily*)

🏠 **WHERE TO STAY AND EAT** Fast food apart, Liverpool doesn't have a huge choice of places to eat, although the two I mention are both excellent. A short drive to Brooklyn or Milton (see page 161) adds other options.

🏠 **Lanes Privateer Inn** (27 rooms) 27 Bristol Av; ☏ 354 3456, T/F 1 800 794 3332; www.lanesprivateerinn.com; ⊕ year-round. A Mersey River waterfront inn. Some guestrooms have balconies. There's a pub (⊕ 10.30–22.00 Tue–Thu, 10.00–midnight Fri–Sat, food served until 21.00) & a very good restaurant (⊕ 07.00–20.00 daily; $$) with a varied menu. In particular, the haddock cakes & bread & butter pudding with orange whisky sauce receive many plaudits. Continental b/fast inc, full b/fast for a surcharge. $$

🏠 **Gallery Guest House B&B** (2 rooms) 611 Shore Rd, Mersey Point; ☏ 354 5431; www.bbcanada.com/galleryguesthouse; ⊕ year-round.

Both guestrooms at this charming oceanfront B&B approximately 4km from the town centre on the same premises as the Savage Gallery (see page 161) have private entrances & decks overlooking Liverpool Bay. Breakfast (cheeses, cold cuts, good bread & much more) is brought to your door on a trolley at a pre-arranged time. $

✖ **Woodpile** 181 Main St; ☏ 354 4495; www.woodpilecarvings.com; ⊕ year-round 08.00–17.00 Mon–Fri, 09.00–16.00 Sat. Combined café/woodcarving workshop/gallery (local artists). Ideal for soup, a salad, a sandwich or just a coffee/dessert. Everything is homemade from scratch. $

ENTERTAINMENT

🎭 **Astor Theatre** 59 Gorham St; ☏ 354 5250; www.astortheatre.ns.ca; ⊕ year-round. Built in 1902 as part of the Town Hall, this is the province's oldest-surviving performing arts venue.

Originally an opera house, as film became more popular the emphasis shifted. About 30 years ago, live performances began to regain in popularity, and the Astor now has a varied calendar.

FESTIVALS
May
International Theatre Festival (*www.litf.ca*) Five-day amateur theatre festival held every two years (even years) at the historic Astor Theatre.

June
Country Music Festival (*www.hanksnow.com*) 10 hours of country music and a barbecue held on the grounds of the Hank Snow Country Music Centre (see page 160)

July
Privateer Days (☏ *354 4500; www.privateerdays.ca*) The town's big festival (five days over the first weekend in July) is a lot of fun, with battle re-enactments, town walking tours led by guides in period costume, candlelit graveyard tours, boat races, fireworks and much more.

October
International Ukulele Ceilidh (*www.ukuleleceilidh.ca*) Ukulele concerts and workshops.

OTHER PRACTICALITIES

$ **Royal Bank** 209 Main St; ✆ 354 5717;
⏰ 10.00–16.00 Mon–Wed, 10.00–17.00 Thu–Fri
$ **Scotiabank** 183 Main St; ✆ 354 3431;
⏰ 10.00–16.00 Mon–Wed, 10.00–17.00 Thu–Fri
✚ **Queens General Hospital** 175 School St; ✆ 354 3436

≋ **Thomas H Raddall Library** 145 Old Bridge St;
✆ 354 5270; ⏰ 10.00–17.00 Tue–Wed & Fri,
10.00–20.00 Thu, 10.00–14.00 Sat
✉ **Post office** 176 Main St; ⏰ 08.30–17.00
Mon–Fri

WHAT TO SEE AND DO

Sherman Hines Museum of Photography (*219 Main St;* ✆ *354 2667; www.shermanhinesphotographymuseum.com;* ⏰ *mid-May–mid-Oct 10.00–17.30 Mon–Sat (Jul–Aug 12.00–17.30 only Sun); admission CAN$4, inc free admission to Rossignol Centre*) Liverpool native Sherman Hines, one of Canada's most renowned landscape and portrait photographers, donated his extensive collection of photographic equipment to this museum which also features work by important past and contemporary Canadian photographers. There's much more besides, including displays on holograms and camera obscura, all housed in Liverpool's c1901 former Town Hall.

Rossignol Arts Centre (*205 Church St;* ✆ *354 3067; www.rossignolculturalcentre.com;* ⏰ *mid-May–mid-Oct 10.00–17.30 Mon–Sat (Jul–Aug 12.00–17.30 only Sun); admission CAN$4, inc free admission to Photography Museum*) Liverpool's old high school (and grounds) now house an interesting hotch-potch of exhibits including an outhouse museum, folk art, various mounted birds and animals, and an art gallery. Recently, the chance to 'stay overnight in a museum exhibit' has been offered: choose from a Mongolian tent, Indian tepee, settler's log cabin or British blockhouse. See website for details.

Perkins House Museum (*105 Main St;* ✆ *354 4058; www.museum.gov.ns.ca/peh/;* ⏰ *mid-May–mid-Oct 09.30–17.30 Mon–Sat, 13.00–17.30 Sun; admission CAN$2*) This c1766 New England-style house was built for Simeon Perkins, a prominent Liverpool citizen best known for the diaries which he kept. Perkins lived here until his death in 1812. There are plans to use 'interactive ghosts' to guide you round the house.

Queens County Museum (*109 Main St;* ✆ *354 4058; www.queenscountymuseum.com;* ⏰ *year-round: Jun–mid-Oct 09.30–17.30 Mon–Sat, 13.00–17.30 Sun; mid-Oct–May 09.00–17.00 Mon–Sat; admission CAN$2*) It might look much older, and that was the idea when this interesting museum next door to the Perkins House was built in 1980. The interior is jam-packed with a whole variety of things from Mi'kmaq tools to model railways. Pride of place goes to the Perkins diaries. Genealogists will want to visit the research centre (fee charged).

Hank Snow Country Music Centre (*148 Bristol Av;* ✆ *354 4675; T/F 1 888 450 5525; www.hanksnow.com;* ⏰ *mid-May–mid-Oct 09.00–17.00 Mon–Sat,*

DRINKING SPIRITS

At the end of Main Street just before Fort Point, the building which is now 5 Riverside Drive was built in 1763, and operated as Dexter's Tavern. In the late 18th century, Simeon Perkins (see above) was a regular patron. It is said to be haunted by a tiny, uniformed, mischievous – but so far, benign – ghost. Incidentally, part of another house at the opposite end of Main Street was also an 18th-century tavern and is also supposed to be haunted. Both former taverns are now private residences.

12.00–17.30 Sun; mid-Oct–mid-May 09.00–16.00 Mon–Fri; admission CAN$3) Clarence Eugene 'Hank' Snow (1914–99) was born close by and became a country music legend, recording over 100 albums and selling over 70 million records. See a wealth of 'Yodelling Ranger' material, including his 1947 Cadillac and his stage suits. The centre shares Liverpool's former train station with the Nova Scotia Country Music Hall of Fame.

Fort Point Lighthouse (*Park 21, Fort Point Lane;* ☎ *354 5741;* ⊕ *mid-May–early Oct; admission free*) This park on the waterfront at the end of Main Street is said to be the spot where de Mons landed in 1604: today you'll find cannon and an unusually shaped wooden lighthouse, constructed in 1855. Shut down in 1989 with talk of demolition, Nova Scotia's fourth-oldest surviving lighthouse was saved and opened as a small museum in 1997.

Savage Studio and Gallery (*611 Mersey Point Rd;* ☎ *354 5431; www.savagegallery.ca;* ⊕ *Jul–Aug 10.00–19.00 daily; off-season by chance or appointment*) Art lovers who appreciate land (and especially sea) scapes should visit Roger Savage's gallery a five-minute drive from town.

AROUND LIVERPOOL

BEACH MEADOWS This wonderful long, sandy beach approximately 8km east of Liverpool is one of the best on the South Shore. There are two parking areas from which boardwalks lead to it through the sand dunes. There are views of Coffin Island (named after Peleg Coffin, one of the first settlers), with a lighthouse and abandoned fishing shanties.

BROOKLYN Just across the bay from Liverpool, Brooklyn was originally known as Herring Cove, and the ubiquitous Nicolas Denys had a fishery here in 1634. It has a pretty marina and waterfront park which hosts many summer events. The setting is not, however, helped by the monstrous – but economically important – Bowater Mersey Pulp and Paper Mill, probably the largest employer in the area.

 Where to stay and eat

🏠 **Motel Transcotia** (22 rooms) 3457 Hwy 3; ☎ 354 3494; f 354 3352; ⊕ year-round. Step back a decade or three at this traditional-style motel. The licensed dining room (⊕ 06.00–20.00 daily; $–$$) offers simple, good-value home cookin'. $

🏠 **Best Western Liverpool Hotel & Conference Center** (65 rooms) 63 Queens Pl Dr, off Hwy 3 near Exit 19 of Hwy 103; ☎ 354 2377; www.bestwesternliverpool.com. Brand new (summer 2009) hotel with indoor pool & fitness centre. Reliable choice for those happy with chain hotels. Continental b/fast inc. $$

Festivals
August
Queens County SeaFest (*www.queenscountyseafest.ca*) Three-day festival with a fishing competition, live entertainment, food stalls and family activities.

MILTON Just 4km from Liverpool, either by Highway 8 or by following Main St away from town, Milton is a pretty village on the Mersey River. There are photogenic churches, good birding, and, in late spring, magnificent rhododendrons beneath the white pines at the 22ha Pine Grove Park, and Tupper Park has a picnic area overlooking the Milton Falls. You can also visit a restored c1903 blacksmith shop (⊕ *mid-Jun–Aug 09.30–16.00 Mon–Fri; admission CAN$1*).

Where to stay and eat

🏠 **Mersey Lodge** (5 rooms) 2537 River Rd; 📞 354 5547; f 354 3035; e merseylodge@ns.sympatico.ca; www.merseylodge.com; ⊕ year-round. This rustic but comfortable lodge is well off the beaten track, approx 10km from Milton mostly on an unpaved road. Fish, swim or canoe on the river. Full b/fast inc. $$

🏠 **Morton House Inn B&B** (4 rooms) 147 Main St (Hwy 8); 📞 354 2908, T/F 1 877 354 2908; www.mortonhouseinn.com; ⊕ year-round; off-season by reservation. Located in the village, this c1864 Empire-style mansion is just across the road from the river, & beautifully decorated with antiques. Cheaper rooms are also available. Full b/fast inc in B&B rate. $

WHITE POINT Visitors are drawn here for the family resort and golf course. Hunt's Point, a couple of kilometres further along Highway 3, has a popular take-away.

Getting there White Point is off Highway 3, 9–12km from Liverpool.

Where to stay and eat

🏠 **White Point Beach Resort** White Point; 📞 354 2711, T/F 1 800 565 5068; e greatday@ whitepoint.com; www.whitepoint.com; ⊕ year-round. This long-established, popular family resort has a range of accommodation choices from standard rooms to 3-bedroom log cottages. There's a restaurant & lounge, spa, golf course (see below), 1km of private beach, indoor & outdoor (seasonal) pools & the usual resort extras – oh, & large friendly rabbits roaming the grounds. $$

🏕 **Fisherman's Cove RV & Campground** (22 sites) 6718 Hwy 3, Hunt's Point; 📞 683 2772; www.fishermanscoverv.netfirms.com; ⊕ May–Oct. Small store & laundry facilities.$

✗ **Seaside Seafoods** 6943 Hwy 3, Hunt's Point; 📞 683 2618; ⊕ late Mar–Oct 11.00–21.00 daily. Simple but much-loved fastfood & seafood eatery. The deep-fried clams are fantastic, plus there's the usual selection of fish & chips, burgers & soft ice cream. Picnic tables outside. $

What to see and do Very close to the resort on a small peninsula with majestic ocean views, is the nine-hole **White Point Golf Club** (📞 T/F 1 866 683 2485; ⊕ mid-Apr–early Nov). Played as 18 holes (with separate tees for the back nine) the course is 6,200yds long. Ask about packages if staying at the resort. Green fees for 18 holes CAN$48.

SUMMERVILLE BEACH This long (over 1km) stretch of whitish sand is one of the best and most accessible of the South Shore beaches. Backed by sand dunes and a salt marsh, it has been designated a Provincial Park. Sunbathe, play beach volleyball, swim in the bracing waters or picnic.

Getting there

By car The beach is 17km/11 miles from Liverpool, just off Highway 3, 1.5km from Exit 20 of Highway 103.

By bus The Trius Tours coach stops in Summerville *en route* between Halifax and Yarmouth (see page 52). If you are travelling from Port Mouton or Port Joli, you must call Trius Tours (📞 T/F 1 877 566 1567) a day or two in advance as these are 'request' stops. Cost to or from Halifax is CAN$41 one way, and to or from Yarmouth CAN$33. The journey from Port Mouton or Port Joli to Halifax, or vice versa, takes three hours 10 minutes, and from Port Mouton or Port Joli to Yarmouth, or vice versa, one hour 50 minutes.

Where to stay

🏠 **Quarterdeck Beachside Villas and Grill** (13 units) 7499 Hwy 3, Summerville Centre; 📞 683 2998, T/F 1 800 565 1119; e quarterdeck@eastlink.ca; www.quarterdeck.ns.ca; ⊕ year-round. Accommodation includes 1-bedroom suites, villas (2-storey, 2-bedroom apts, is a better description), each well equipped with a deck & balcony overlooking the sea. Kayak, bike, surfboard rentals. The restaurant (⏰ May–Oct 11.30–late; $$–$$$) has one of the province's best locations, especially the covered deck under which the waves lap (for which you'll need to book a table in advance). The food is good, too: considering the quality, you're not paying too much extra for the setting. Start perhaps with coconut shrimp, & move on to baked halibut. Desserts are worth leaving room for. $$$

PORT MOUTON

This village on the bay of the same name has a couple of places to stay, including a backpackers' hostel and a restaurant, and is well placed for exploring the region's beautiful parks and beaches. Several uninhabited islands dot the bay.

HISTORY Port Mouton was named by Champlain in 1604: when his ship was at anchor in the bay, a sheep jumped into the sea. There were a couple of attempts at settlement (by Scots in the 1620s and English around 1770) but the first lasting attempt was made in 1783 by disbanded soldiers who had served under Sir Guy Carleton. Quickly, they built over 200 houses and called their settlement Guy's Borough. The following year a fire destroyed most of their houses. This – combined with the fact that the region's soil wasn't great for farming – caused the settlers to uproot *en masse*. They headed east, and settled in what is now Guysborough (see page 367).

GETTING THERE

By car Port Mouton is on Highway 103, 19km/12 miles southwest of Liverpool and 48km/30 miles from Shelburne.

By bus The Trius Tours coach stops in both Port Mouton and Port Joli *en route* between Halifax and Yarmouth (see page 52).

 WHERE TO STAY AND EAT

🏠 **Port Mouton Bay Cottages & Seascape Restaurant** (5 cottages) 8403 Hwy 103; 📞 683 2020, T/F 1 866 933 2020; e pmbcottages@ eastlink.ca; www.cottagesinnovascotia.com; ⏰ year-round. Simple, spacious, well-equipped 2-bedroom cottages. $$

BEACH BEAUTY

At the time of writing, Carters Beach is a prime contender for the 'Most Beautiful Beach in Nova Scotia' title – and, amazingly, it's still a relatively well-kept secret. It's being realistic rather than pessimistic to wonder how long it will stay unspoilt.

When you first see the beaches – there are actually three – and the island-dotted bay, you might think that you're in the Mediterranean, especially if the sun is out. The sand is golden, the crystal-clear water has a slight turquoise hue, and huge, smooth black boulders, and sometimes colourful sea kayakers, give the scene depth.

Walk along the first beach and you'll find a stream blocking your way. Depending on the tide and other factors, you may be able to ford it by wading across, or it may be safer to head upstream for about ten minutes and cross there. The second beach is broad and straight, and the third another pretty crescent which ends at high sand dunes well worth climbing for the view.

To reach Carters Beach turn onto Central Port Mouton Road from Highway 103 at Port Mouton. Continue for about 4km until you see a sign to the left to Carters Beach. There's a tiny parking area but no other facilities, and a short (less than 100m) path through the trees down to the beach.

⌂ **Port Mouton International Hostel** (30 beds) 8100 Hwy 103; ☎ 683 2262; e pmhostel@ eastlink.ca; www.wqccda.com/PMhostel; ⏰ year-round. Housed in a c1961 former school, this friendly backpackers' hostel has 1 large & 4 small dorms, with most of the beds bunks. There's a big kitchen & common room, & if you don't feel like cooking, the Seascape (see below) is just across the road. Linen/bedding inc. Dorm CAN$20. $

✕ **Seascape Restaurant** 8426 Hwy 103; ☎ 683 2626; ⏰ early Apr–mid-May & Sep–mid-Nov 11.00–19.00 Tue–Sun; mid-May–Aug 11.00–20.00 daily. Under the same ownership as Port Mouton Bay Cottages & just across the road, this restaurant ain't *haute cuisine* but the fish & chips are very good & you won't go hungry. $

WHAT TO SEE AND DO
Kejimkujik Seaside (*St Catherine's Rd;* ☎ *682 2772; www.pc.gc.ca/kejimkujik;* ⏰ *mid-Apr–Nov; admission CAN$3.90, charged May–Oct*) Confusingly, this is a separate part of Kejimkujik National Park (see page 205), which is approximately 100km inland. Kejimkujik Seaside protects 22km² of wilderness on the Port Mouton Peninsula including pristine white-sand beaches, turquoise waters, coastal bogs, an abundance of wild flowers, rich lagoon systems, and coastal wildlife.

Most easily reached by an 8km unpaved road from Highway 103, this is one of the least disturbed shoreline areas on the south coast of Nova Scotia. No camping is permitted.

From the car park, an easy trail (5.3km return) leads through the trees, on boardwalks over marshy areas, and on to the beach at Harbour Rocks. Here you are likely to see seals basking on the rocks or bobbing about in the water – take binoculars. You can continue along the beach before retracing your steps. A longer (8.8km return from the car park) option is to branch off the first trail and take in Port Joli Head on a coastal loop. Some sections of the beach close between late April and July to protect piping plover nesting sites.

Mosquitoes may cause annoyance, even on the beach. Don't forget repellent.

Rossignol Surf Shop (☎ *354 7100; www.surfnovascotia.com;* ⏰ *May, Jun & Sep 10.00–18.00 Sat–Sun, Jul–Aug 10.00–18.00 daily*) In addition to renting surfboards and wetsuits and advising on the best surfing spots, the company offers guided three-hour and all-day kayak tours around Port Joli and Port Mouton bays. The shop may be moving to White Point Beach Resort (see page 162).

Thomas Raddall Provincial Park (*East Port I'Hebert Rd, Port Joli;* ☎ *683 2664; www.novascotiaparks.ca/parks/thraddall.asp;* ⏰ *mid-May–mid-Oct*) The 678ha park, 3km off Highway 103, 9km west of Port Mouton, has over 11km of trails, some multi-use, and an 82-site wooded campground. The best stretches of sand are Camper's Beach and Sandy Bay Beach. The park has a good selection of animal and birdlife.

LOCKEPORT

The quaint town of Lockeport is well worth exploring for its lovely old homes and fine beaches (five in all). The beautiful 1.5km-long Crescent Beach, not to be confused with a beach of the same name near the LaHave Islands (see page 156), is hard to miss, on the southern edge of the thin strip of land between the 'mainland' and the 'island'.

Beaches apart, the town also boasts the province's only Registered Historic Streetscape. This comprises five houses built by descendants of town founder Jonathan Locke between 1836 and 1876. The houses offer an interesting cross-section of historical architecture with excellent examples of Colonial, Georgian and Victorian styles.

A walking-tour guidebook should be available at the tourist office or museum (see below).

Those with children shouldn't miss the excellent marine-themed playground (⊕ *mid-May–Oct*) in Seacaps Memorial Park.

Beach lovers should be aware that there are at least another dozen good beaches in the area: locals will be happy to direct you to their favourite.

HISTORY The town was founded in 1755 by settlers from Plymouth, Massachusetts, led by a Jonathan Locke. Several other Planters followed and were joined by British settlers – and a few Icelanders.

Although in the early stages of the American Revolution residents were sympathetic to American privateers, sometimes offering them aid and even helping American prisoners who had escaped, that all changed in 1778 when whale boats from Rhode Island arrived and raided their homes for food and valuables.

Since its founding, Lockeport has been a fishing community, and shipbulding began in the 1880s.

GETTING THERE Lockeport is on Highway 3, 18km from Highway 103 Exit 23, 17km from Highway 103 Exit 24.

TOURIST INFORMATION (*157 Locke St;* ✎ *656 3123;* ⊕ *late Jun–mid-Sep 09.00–18.00 daily*). At Crescent Beach, adjacent to the canteen (which serves good ice cream), changing rooms and showers. The upstairs look-out offers fine views.

 WHERE TO STAY AND EAT

⌂ **Ocean Mist Cottages** (6 cottages) 1 Gull Rock Rd; ✎ 656 3200; e info@oceanmistcottages.com; www.oceanmistcottages.com; ⊕ year-round. With a fabulous location less than 20m from Crescent Beach, these fully equipped & quiet 2-bedroom cottages are spacious & comfortable. $$$

✗ **The Parrot's Pins Candlepin Café** 10 Beech St; ✎ 656 2695; ⊕ year-round 11.00–20.00 Wed–Sun.

Housed in a 4-lane bowling alley & decorated with a range of crafts from all over the globe, the good news is that the food – 'international eclectic' – works. It helps that everything is fresh, homemade & mostly local. Try the Bluenoser Martini, a glass of scallops poached in vermouth served with pasta with a creamy vodka lemon sauce. The desserts keep up the standard. A real treat. $$

FESTIVALS
August
Sea Derby (*www.lockeportseaderby.ca*) Weekend fishing tournament.

OTHER PRACTICALITIES

$ **Royal Bank** 25A Beech St; ✎ 656 2212; ⊕ 10.00–15.00 Mon–Wed & Fri, 10.00–17.00 Thu
≋ **Lillian Benham Library** 35 North St; ✎ 656 2817; ⊕ May–Sep 14.30–17.00 & 18.00–19.30 Tue, 10.30–13.00 & 14.30–17.00 Wed, 14.30–17.00 & 18.15–19.30 Thu, 14.30–17.00 Fri,

10.00–12.00 Sat; Oct–Apr 14.30–17.00 & 18.00–19.30 Tue, 10.30–13.00 & 15.00–17.00 Wed, 14.30–17.00 & 18.00–19.30 Thu, 14.30–17.00 Fri, 10.00–12.00 Sat.
✉ **Post office** 30 Beech St; ⊕ 08.15–17.00 Mon–Fri, 08.30–12.30 Sat

SHELBURNE (*Population: 2,250*)

The town of Shelburne sits at the innermost end of what is said by many to be the third-finest harbour in the world (after Sydney, Australia, and Havana, Cuba). Much of what there is to be seen lies within the area bounded by Water Street (the main street), Dock Street and King Street. Within this area are four museums and over 30 original late 18th-century Loyalist homes, most of which are in good condition.

History aside, the waterfront is a pleasant place for a stroll. Bearing in mind that the choices for both dining and accommodation are limited, if you're visiting at the weekend and/or in peak season, it would be wise to book ahead.

HISTORY In the aftermath of the American War of Independence, the newly formed colonies were not a good place to be for those who had been loyal to the British flag. When offered passage, land under protection of the British flag, provisions and tools, many jumped at the chance. Early in 1783, 18 ships loaded with mostly aristocratic Loyalists and a large number of their black slaves sailed into Port Roseway (Shelburne's early name).

Trees were felled, land was cleared, streets were laid out and houses were built quickly. The settlement was renamed Shelburne, in honour of Lord Shelburne, Secretary of State for the Colonies. Thousands more Loyalists arrived later in the year, and Shelburne quickly (but only briefly) become the largest urban centre in British North America, having a population of over 15,000 in 1785.

Then things went sour: the government stopped providing rations and financial assistance. Race riots broke out. Many began to move away, properties were abandoned, houses were torn down for fuel, and still more allowed to fall into ruin and decay. By 1818, the population had dropped to 300.

In time, people began to move back. Shipbuilding started up again, and soon it prospered. New homes were built over the old cellars. The population tripled, and Shelburne became renowned for the building of schooners and brigantines. Late in the 19th century, when steel-hulled steam-powered ships began to replace wooden sailing vessels, Shelburne's economy fell back on fishing: boatbuilding continued on a much smaller scale: this time yachts were the speciality.

Life continued quietly and without great incident until the 1990s when a couple of Hollywood films were shot here (see box below).

GETTING THERE

By car Shelburne is on Highway 3, just off Highway 103 Exit 25 (southbound) or Exit 26 (northbound). It is 210km/130 miles from Halifax, 98km/61 miles from Yarmouth and 67km/42 miles from Liverpool.

By bus The Trius Tours coach stops at Exit 25 or Exit 26 of Highway 103 *en route* between Halifax and Yarmouth (see page 52).

TOURIST INFORMATION *(31 Dock St; ☏ 875 4547; ⊕ daily late May–Jun 10.00–17.00; Jul–Aug 10.00–19.00; Sep–late Oct 09.00–17.00)*

⌂ WHERE TO STAY

⌂ **Boulder Cove Cottages** (5 cottages) 321 Shore Rd, Churchover; ☏ 875 1542, T/F 1 866 732 7867; www.bouldercove.com; ⊕ year-round. Lovely setting on the Birchtown Bay waterfront a 10min drive from Shelburne. Very comfortable 1- & 2-bedroom cottages. Laundry room, walking trail, bikes & boats for guest use. $$

⌂ **Cooper's Inn** (8 rooms) 36 Dock St; ☏ 875 4656, T/F 1 800 688 2011; www.thecoopersinn.com; ⊕ Apr–Oct. Historic charm & modern convenience

HOLLYWOOD HISTORY

Much of *Scarlet Letter*, a 1990s' Hollywood flop, was filmed in Shelburne. Wanting to make the location more authentic, the film company built over a dozen 'old' structures. Most were removed after filming, but some remain, including the 'historic' (c1994!) cooperage on the waterfront across from the Cooper's Inn.

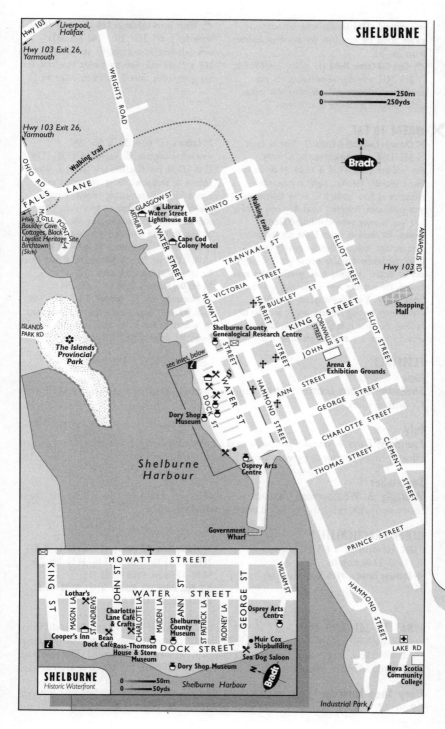

Hwy 103 → Liverpool, Halifax

Hwy 103 Exit 26, Yarmouth

Hwy 103 Exit 26, Yarmouth

WRIGHTS ROAD

Walking trail

OHIO RD

FALLS LANE

Hwy 3, GILL POINT Boulder Cove Cottages, Black Loyalist Heritage Site, Birchtown (5km)

ISLANDS PARK RD

The Islands Provincial Park

GLASGOW ST

ARTHUR ST

WATER STREET

MOWATT STREET

Library
Water Street
Lighthouse B&B

Cape Cod Colony Motel

MINTO ST

Walking trail

TRANVAAL ST

VICTORIA STREET

HARRIET ST

BULKLEY ST

Shelburne County
Genealogical Research Centre

WATER ST

DOCK ST

Dory Shop Museum

KING STREET

CORNWALLIS STREET

ELLIOT STREET

Hwy 103

ANNAPOLIS RD

Shopping Mall

JOHN STREET

Arena & Exhibition Grounds

ELLIOT STREET

ANN STREET

HAMMOND STREET

GEORGE STREET

CHARLOTTE STREET

CLEMENTS STREET

THOMAS STREET

Shelburne Harbour

Osprey Arts Centre

Government Wharf

PRINCE STREET

HAMMOND STREET

LAKE RD

Nova Scotia Community College

Industrial Park

0 — 250m
0 — 250yds

N

Bradt

SHELBURNE
Historic Waterfront

KING ST

MASON LA

Lothar's

ST ANDREWS

Cooper's Inn

JOHN ST

Bean Dock Café

Ross-Thomson House & Store Museum

MOWATT STREET

WATER STREET

CHARLOTTE LA

Charlotte Lane Café & Crafts

MAIDEN LA

ANN ST

ST PATRICK LA

Shelburne County Museum

DOCK STREET

Dory Shop Museum

RODNEY LA

GEORGE ST

WILLIAM ST

Osprey Arts Centre

Muir Cox Shipbuilding

Sea Dog Saloon

0 — 50m
0 — 50yds

N

Bradt

Shelburne Harbour

South Shore SHELBURNE

4

in a restored c1784 Loyalist home with courtyard garden across the road from the waterfront. Gourmet b/fast inc. $$

🏠 **Cape Cod Colony Motel** (23 rooms) 234 Water St; ☎ 875 3411; www.capecodmotel.ns.ca ⏲ year-round. Standard traditional-style motel with coffee-maker, fridge & microwave in each room. $

🏠 **Water Street Lighthouse B&B** (3 rooms) 263 Water St; ☎ 875 2331; T/F 1 888 875 2331; www.shelburnelighthouse.com; ⏲ year-round. Friendly B&B a 15min walk from the historic waterfront. The airy guest rooms share 2 bathrooms. B/fast inc. $

✗ WHERE TO EAT

✗ **Charlotte Lane Café & Crafts** 13 Charlotte Lane; ☎ 875 3314; www.charlottelane.ca; ⏲ early May–mid-Dec 11.30–14.30 & 17.00–20.00 Tue–Sat. This is probably the most highly recommended restaurant in Nova Scotia, & — in my experience — with justification. Discerning locals & visitors travel a long way to enjoy owner-chef Roland Glauser's cooking. The menu is varied & changes seasonally: start, perhaps, with the Bluenose spinach salad. To follow, the lobster & scallop brandy gratin is superb, and for dessert the sticky toffee pudding takes some beating. The extensive wine list includes a Nova Scotia section, & a different special cocktail is offered every evening. Although housed in a heritage building, the décor is bright, with funky local artworks. There is a small garden patio. $$

✗ **Lothar's** 149 Water St; ☎ 875 3697; www.lothars-cafe.com; ⏲ year-round 11.30–14.00 & 17.00–20.00 Thu–Mon. This new (2008) & welcome addition to Shelburne's dining scene offers well-cooked European (particularly German) meat & poultry choices in addition to Nova Scotia seafood standards. The Sun brunch is good, too. $$

✗ **Bean Dock Café** Dock St (corner with John St); ☎ 875 1302; ⏲ year-round 08.30–16.00 Mon–Fri, 10.00–14.00 Sat. Friendly, laid-back & a good choice for coffee, light lunches & desserts. $

✗ **Sea Dog Saloon** 1 Dock St; ☎ 875 2862; www.theseadog.com; ⏲ mid-Apr–Dec 11.00–21.00 daily. The pub's large outside deck is a great place for a drink or bite in the sunshine. A glass of Keith's IPA makes a good accompaniment. $

FESTIVALS

June
Shelburne County Lobster Festival Enjoy crustacean creations at various Shelburne County venues.

July
Founders' Days (*www.shelburnenovascotia.com/foundersdays/*) Look round a Loyalist encampment occupied by volunteers in period military costume.

September
Whirligig & Weathervane Festival (*www.whirligigfestival.com*) See the waterfront festooned with brightly coloured wind-catching devices.

OTHER PRACTICALITIES

$ **CIBC** 146 Water St; ☎ 875 2388; ⏲ 10.00–17.00 Mon–Fri

✚ **Roseway Hospital** 1606 Sandy Point Rd; ☎ 875 3011

📖 **McKay Memorial Library** 17 Glasgow St; ☎ 875 3615; ⏲ 12.30–17.00 & 18.00–20.00 Tue–Thu, 10.00–17.00 Fri, 10.00–14.00 Sat

✉ **Post office** 162 Mowatt St; ⏲ 08.30–17.30 Mon–Fri, 08.30–12.30 Sat

WHAT TO SEE AND DO One CAN$8 ticket (available at any of the individual museums) will gain you entry to four Shelburne museums which normally charge CAN$3 each: they are the Ross-Thomson House and Store, Dory Shop, Shelburne County Museum and Muir-Cox Shipbuilding Interpretive Centre.

Dory Shop Museum (*Dock St;* ☎ *875 3219; www.museum.gov.ns.ca/dory;* ⏲ *Jun–Sep 09.30–17.30 daily; admission CAN$3*) There was something of a revolution in the

Grand Banks fishing industry when someone came up with the idea of loading a schooner with small, light, stackable wooden boats (dories), sailing out to the fishing grounds, lowering them into the water and then letting fishermen try their luck. Dories made in Shelburne were renowned for their strength. In 1983, this c1880 former dory shop was opened as a museum by Prince Charles and Diana, Princess of Wales.

Muir-Cox Shipbuilding Interpretive Centre (*Dock St;* ☏ *875 2483; www.historicshelburne.com/muircox.htm;* ⊕ *Jun–Sep 09.30–17.30 daily; boatshop* ⊕ *year-round 08.00–16.00 Mon–Fri; admission CAN$3*) In near continuous operation from the 1820s until 1984, this is one of the oldest vessel-building locations in Atlantic Canada. Now operated as a museum, the centre depicts the history of shipbuilding in Shelburne from square-rigged barques to internationally acclaimed yachts. Boats are still restored and built in the open boatshop.

Osprey Arts Centre (*107 Water St;* ☏ *875 2359; www.ospreyartscentre.com;* ⊕ *year-round; gallery* ⊕ *09.00–16.00 Mon–Fri*) A performing arts centre which also houses the Coastline Gallery, featuring local artists' work.

Ross-Thomson House and Store Museum (*9 Charlotte Lane;* ☏ *875 3141; www.museum.gov.ns.ca/rth/;* ⊕ *Jun–mid-Oct 09.30–17.30 daily; admission CAN$3*) This c1785 house was the workplace of brothers George and Robert Ross, from Aberdeen, Scotland. The highlight is an authentically stocked 18th-century store and chandlery. The garden is laid out and planted in late 18th-century style.

Shelburne County Genealogical Research Centre (*168 Water St;* ☏ *875 4299;* ⊕ *summer 09.00–16.30 Mon–Sat (check winter hours); CAN$5/day*) An excellent resource for genealogists tracing the roots of Loyalists and Shelburne's other early settlers.

Shelburne County Museum (*20 Dock St;* ☏ *875 3219; www.historicshelburne.com/scm.htm;* ⊕ *year-round: Jun–mid-Oct 09.30–17.30 daily; mid-Oct–May 10.00–12.00 & 14.00–17.00 Mon–Fri; admission CAN$3*) Housed in a c1787 Loyalist building, this is a good place to get an overview of the town's fascinating history. Be sure to see the Newsham firepumper (one of two early 'fire engines' imported from Boston in 1740) and a good exhibit on black Loyalist history.

AROUND SHELBURNE

THE ISLANDS PROVINCIAL PARK (*Hwy 3; www.novascotiaparks.ca/parks/theislands.asp;* ⊕ *mid-May–early Sep*) Huge granite boulders – deposited by melting glaciers 10,000 years ago – dot this pleasant park and open and wooded campground (62 sites) 5km west of Shelburne which offers fine views over Shelburne Harbour. The picnic area is joined to the rest of the park by a short causeway, and there's a rocky beach.

BLACK LOYALIST HERITAGE SITE (*Old Birchtown Rd; Birchtown;* ☏ *875 1310, T/F 1 888 354 0772; www.blackloyalist.com;* ⊕ *site year-round; museum & gift shop Jun–Aug; admission: site free, museum CAN$2.50*) At the time of writing, this site, 9km west of Shelburne on Highway 3, is a work in progress: there are plans to add to the existing museum, interpretive walking trail, old burial ground and gift shop. New projects include a botanical garden, library, and educational/entertainment centre, utilising the site's St Paul's Church building.

BURCHTOWN TO FREETOWN

Amongst the Loyalists who arrived in Port Roseway (Shelburne) in 1783 were over 1,000 blacks: some were slaves, others former slaves, who had sought protection under the British and served the Loyalist cause against the Americans during the War of Independence. Many of the freed were given land a few kilometres to the west of Shelburne in what became known as Burchtown (and, with time, Birchtown).

For a short while, Birchtown was the largest settlement of free blacks in North America – the population in 1784 was over 1,500 – but this was no paradise. Many blacks had been granted infertile land, there was little or no employment and poverty was commonplace. Those who could find work received about a quarter of the wage received by a white doing the same job. Nova Scotia winters were incredible shocks to systems, particularly as with no money to build houses, many lived in what were effectively roofed-over holes on hillsides. In 1791, things were so bad that an emissary was sent to raise the community's concerns with the Secretary of State in England.

As it happened, in addition to colonising Nova Scotia, the English government had similar plans for west Africa, and came up with an ironic proposal. Any adult male who wished would be given free passage to Sierra Leone where he would receive 20 acres of land (plus ten acres for his wife, and five each for any children). Many agreed to the terms, and in 1792, a fleet of 15 vessels left Halifax for west Africa. On board were over 500 from Birchtown alone.

Many of those who left had led or inspired the community: after their departure there was another exodus from Birchtown, this time to other parts of Nova Scotia. Today, fewer than 200 black Nova Scotians live in Shelburne County.

TOBEATIC WILDERNESS AREA

The pristine Tobeatic Wilderness Area (known as TWA or 'The Toby') is vast, covering 104,000ha, and is roughly three-times the size of Kejimkujik National Park (see page 205) which borders it to the east. Spreading over five of the province's counties, this is the largest remaining wild area in the Maritimes. Within its boundaries are the headwaters of nine river systems including the Sissiboo, Roseway, Clyde and Tusket rivers. The nearest communities include Bear River to the north, Weymouth to the northwest and Kemptville to the west.

Barrens (areas of rocky heathland with dwarf shrub and/or lichen vegetation), bogs, wetlands and remote woodland make for superb, virtually undisturbed wildlife habitat: white-tailed deer, porcupine, snowshoe hare and beaver are common. There's a healthy population of black bear, and – rare other than in the Cape Breton Highlands – a few moose. Bird species include loon, warblers, waterfowl and pileated woodpecker, and you may hear the screech of a great horned owl at night. Forest wild flowers (including orchids) are plentiful in late spring and summer. There are several pockets of old-growth forest and the network of rivers, streams and lakes make for outstanding wilderness canoeing, camping and hiking for those with experience – there are no developed campsites and no regularly maintained trails. No vehicle travel – including by ATV or motorboat – is permitted.

Early spring and autumn are probably the best times to visit: water levels are high enough for wilderness canoeing without too many long portages, there are fewer biting insects, and daytime temperatures are more moderate – but be prepared for extreme weather at any time of year.

THE TOBY AND BEYOND One of Nova Scotia's few cross-province roads heads north from just west of Shelburne. After passing the Ohios (Lower, Middle and Upper) and crossing and recrossing the pretty Roseway River, Route 203 skirts one edge of the vast Tobeatic Wilderness Area (see box below). The road travels further inland to East Kemptville (nearby is one of the province's few luxury eco-lodges, Trout Point Lodge – see below) and then meets Route 340 where a left turn will take you towards Yarmouth (see page 180) and a right turn towards Weymouth (see page 188).

BARRINGTON

With a lovely setting at the northeast of Barrington Bay, the community has a museum complex and tourist office. Most services (supermarkets, fast food, etc) are located 8km away at Barrington Passage, which is also the gateway to Cape Sable Island (see page 172). Also worth visiting in the area are beautiful Sandy Hills Beach Provincial Park (*Highway 309, approximately 6km from Barrington*) and the lighthouse at Baccaro Point (*Baccaro Rd, off Highway 309, 18km from Barrington*), a good – if breezy – spot for a picnic, and popular with birdwatchers.

HISTORY One of the oldest communities on the South Shore, this area (including Cape Sable Island) is one of the few parts of Nova Scotia where Quakers settled. Originally from Nantucket, they were whalers. Arriving in 1762, most moved on to Dartmouth (see page 116) in 1784 after being harassed repeatedly by American privateers.

In more recent times, fishing – particularly for lobster – became the mainstay of the community.

This is true, remote wilderness, most of which has no mobile-phone reception: if you overstretch yourself – and/or are unlucky – an exciting adventure could easily turn into disaster. Even if you have experience in this kind of travel, consider using the services of a guide or outfitter.

 WHERE TO STAY AND EAT If you don't like wilderness camping, there are some alternatives:

Trout Point Lodge 189 Trout Point Rd, East Kemptville; ✎ 482 8360, 761 2142; www.troutpoint.com. The best base for exploring the western part of The Toby, Trout Point Lodge is right on the edge of the protected wilderness. It offers a variety of accommodation including cottages & 2 lodges (one – which offers B&B – is open year-round).

Great Lodge ⊕ mid-May–late Oct. If you can afford it, stay at this remote property, which occupies over 40ha at the convergence of the Tusket & Napier rivers. In addition to woodland trails, there is river & lake swimming, canoeing, kayaking, mountain bikes, & catch-and-release fishing. The dining room (⊕ mid-May–late Oct; one sitting at 19.30) serves a creative blend of Creole & Mediterranean cuisine – & an extensive wine list. The fixed-price dinner costs CAN$105 per couple. In my opinion, this is the province's best upmarket wilderness lodge. $$–$$$

ACTIVITIES
Hinterland Adventures ✎ 837 4092, T/F 1 800 378 8177; www.kayakingnovascotia.com. Weymouth-based, this company offers canoe tours into the TWA.
Blake Milbury ✎ 467 3242. Based in Bear River, this company will also guide canoe-based tours.

GETTING THERE

By car Barrington is on Highway 103, 40km/25 miles from Shelburne and 67km/42 miles from Yarmouth.

By bus The Trius Tours coach stops in Barrington *en route* between Halifax and Yarmouth (see page 52).

TOURIST INFORMATION *(2517 Hwy 3; ↘ 637 2625; ⊕ late May–late Sep 08.30–17.00 daily)*

⌂ WHERE TO STAY AND EAT

⌂ **Old School House Motel and Restaurant** (14 units) 3412 Hwy 3, Barrington Passage, 8km from Barrington; ↘ 637 3770; e oldschol@klis.com; www.atyp.com/oldschoolhouse/; ⊕ year-round.

Choose between chalets (each with separate living room) or standard motel rooms. The restaurant (⊕ *07.00–21.00 daily; $–$$*) is unlikely to surprise you, but is usually reliable. $

OTHER PRACTICALITIES

$ **Royal Bank** 3525 Hwy 3, Barrington Passage; ↘ 637 2040; ⊕ 09.30–17.00 Mon–Fri

≋ **Barrington Municipal Library** 3588 Hwy 3, Barrington Passage; ↘ 637 3348; ⊕ 12.30–17.00 & 18.00–20.00 Wed–Fri, 10.00–14.00 Sat

⊠ **Post office** 2398 Hwy 3, Barrington; ⊕ 08.00–17.00 Mon–Fri, 09.00–12.00 Sat

FESTIVALS

July

Nova Scotia Marathon *(www.barringtonmunicipality.com/rec.htm)* A combination of full and half marathons run in late July.

WHAT TO SEE AND DO

Barrington Museum complex (↘ *637 2185; www.capesablehistoricalsociety.com; ⊕ Jun–Sep 09.30–17.30 Mon–Sat, 13.00–17.30 Sun; admission CAN$3/museum)* This group of four museums and a genealogical centre (for which a CAN$10 research fee is charged).

Most popular is the Seal Island Light Museum, a half-height copy of the lighthouse that stood on remote Seal Island. There's a great view over Barrington Bay from the top. At the c1882 water-powered Barrington Woollen Mill, wool was washed, carded, spun, dyed and woven. The Old Meeting House Museum was built in 1765 by Planters. It is Canada's oldest nonconformist Protestant house of worship. Behind the building is the region's oldest cemetery.

The Western Counties Military Museum, housing exhibits ranging from 16th-century cannonballs to coins brought back from the Middle East by Canadian soldiers on peacekeeping duty, shares Barrington's c1843 Old Courthouse with the Cape Sable Historical Society Centre.

CAPE SABLE ISLAND

Not to be confused with Sable Island (see pages 368–71), Cape Sable Island has also seen more than its fair share of shipwrecks. There are few services, but ubiquitous are lobster pots and the smell of the sea. Small communities such as Centreville, Newellton, West Head – and comparatively bustling Clark's Harbour – dot the island.

GETTING THERE The causeway to the island leads off Highway 3 at Barrington Passage, 8km/5miles west of Barrington.

Cape Sable Island is the most southerly accessible point in Atlantic Canada, and one of the province's best spring and autumn migration birding sites for waders. The coast around South Side Inlet and south and west of The Hawk are particularly rich viewing areas and tens of thousands of semipalmated sandpipers and short-billed dowitchers can usually be seen. In late winter and early spring thousands of Brant congregate on the flats of Hawk Channel: seeing the geese take to the skies is a highlight of the annual **Birding and Nature Festival** (❨ 875 1542; www.discovershelburnecounty.com/birdfestival.html; late Mar).

TOURIST INFORMATION (2634 Hwy 330, Clark's Harbour; ❨ 745 2586; ⊕ early Jun–late Sep 09.00–17.00 Mon–Fri)

WHERE TO STAY AND EAT Self-caterers should stock up on the mainland and – with the exception of Sea View (see below) – travellers should expect to go to Barrington or beyond to eat out. Best of the limited accommodation choices are:

Cape Sable Cottages (5 cottages) 37 Long Point Rd, Newellton; ❨ 745 0168; www.capesablecottages.com; ⊕ year-round. The décor in these well-equipped 2-bedroom cottages might not be to everyone's taste, but they are good for those looking to get away from it all. Canoes, kayaks & bikes are available. $$

✕ Sea View ❨ 745 1322 ⊕ Apr–late Sep 10.00–20.00 daily. Located just by the wharf at West Head, this place offers take-out & is a favourite of the local fishermen – always a good sign. $

FESTIVALS
August
Island Days Clark's Harbour. A day of dory races in the middle of the month.

WHAT TO SEE AND DO The island has four main beaches: seals are sometimes seen at Stoney and South Side beaches, and Northeast Point Beach is popular with sunbathers. The wild expanse of Hawk Beach – named for a vessel once shipwrecked here and closest to the c1923 Cape Lighthouse, Nova Scotia's tallest – is great for solitude, proximity to nature and birding.

Archelaus Smith Museum (915 Hwy 330; ❨ 745 3361; www.archelaus.org; ⊕ mid-Jun–late Sep 09.30–17.30 Mon–Sat, 13.30–17.30 Sun; admission free) Named for an early 1760s' settler, see displays on local history, island life, lobster fishing and shipbuilding. The most interesting exhibit is a 'wreck chair' made from wooden pieces salvaged from over 20 shipwrecks.

Clark's Harbour Colourful boats bob in the harbour of this busy little fishing town, and the shore is lined with fish plants and boatbuilding yards. There's a petrol station, general store and a bank. A c1895 edifice constructed by shipbuilders houses the **Seaside Heritage Centre** (2773 Main St; ❨ 745 0844, ⊕ Jun–Sep).

THE PUBNICOS

Highway 3 follows the pretty east shore of Pubnico Harbour passing Lower East, Centre East, Middle East and East Pubnico. At Pubnico, a turn onto Highway 335 takes you along the Pubnico Peninsula past Upper West, West, Middle West and

Lower West Pubnico before fizzling out just before Pubnico Point. The region is well worth exploring by car or bike.

The Pubnico Peninsula is far busier and more prosperous than you might expect, and the reason is that this is the heart of one of the world's richest and most productive lobster-fishing areas. Rich too is the region's Acadian tradition, and you're more likely to hear French spoken than English. Whilst there is no official tourist information office in the Pubnicos, locals will be only too happy to try and help.

Turn off Highway 335 towards Dennis Point and follow the road all the way to the wharf area, usually buzzing with fishing boats; not surprising, seeing that this is one of Canada's largest commercial fishing ports. Around 120 boats call it home, over two-thirds of which concentrate on lobster. The others try for haddock, cod, pollock and swordfish.

At the southern end of Highway 335 is the Pubnico Point Wind Farm: the road becomes unpaved but it's worth persevering. Park and wander between the 17 immense turbines, all named after women.

HISTORY In 1653, Sieur Philippe D'Entremont was awarded the Baronnie de Pombomcoup, a region covering most of the land between modern-day Shelburne and Yarmouth. Pombomcoup (which became Pubnico) is derived from the Mi'kmaq *Pogomkook* meaning 'land cleared for cultivation'.

D'Entremont built a chateau here, and when he moved away transferred his title to his eldest son. Fish were plentiful, the land was good, and a prosperous settlement grew.

The Pubnico Acadians escaped deportation in 1755, but weren't so lucky three years later. The chateau and their buildings were destroyed, the surrounding land torched. The Acadians were exiled but eight years later began to return, and unlike those in most other places, were permitted to regain their old lands.

This is the province's oldest Acadian community still inhabited by the descendants of its founder. One 18th-century house still survives, now as a private residence, at the end of Old Church Road in West Pubnico.

GETTING THERE

By car Pubnico is on Highway 3, just off Exit 31 of Highway 103, 29km/18 miles from Barrington (via Highway 103), 31km/19 miles from Shag Harbour and 4km/2 miles from west Pubnico.

By bus The Trius Tours coach stops at Exit 31 of Highway 103 *en route* between Halifax and Yarmouth (see box on page 52).

⌂ WHERE TO STAY AND EAT

⌂ **Argyle By The Sea B&B** (3 rooms) 848 Argyle Sound Rd, Argyle Sound; ✆ 762 2759; www.bbcanada.com/8457.html; ⊕ May–Oct. Rooms with private or shared bath in this quiet B&B by the ocean. Full b/fast inc. $

⌂ **Red Cap Motel & Restaurant** (12 rooms) 1034 Hwy 335, Middle West Pubnico; ✆ 762 2112; e redcaprestaurant@ns.aliantzinc.ca; www.redcapmotel-rest.com; ⊕ year-round. Traditional motel with recently renovated rooms. Licensed restaurant (⊕ 08.00–21.30 daily; $$) specialises in seafood & Acadian dishes. $

⌂ **Yesteryear's B&B** (3 rooms) 2775 Hwy 3, Pubnico; ✆ 762 2969; www.yesteryears.ca; ⊕ year-round; off-season by reservation. A Victorian house with spacious bedrooms & a good crafts shop on the premises. Substantial b/fast inc. $

▲ **La Baronnie Campground** (10 sites) 1207 Hwy 335, Middle West Pubnico; ✆ 762 3388; ⊕ year-round. Tent sites & 2 serviced sites near the sea, with a laundromat. $

✗ **Dennis Point Café** Dennis Point, Lower West Pubnico; ✆ 762 1220; www.dennispointcafe.com; ⊕ year-round 05.30–21.00 daily. There's an extensive menu at this busy restaurant just across from the wharves where the latest catches are unloaded. They have a deep-fryer but fish can also be broiled or pan-fried. The seafood platters are recommended. $$

✗ **Harbour's End Restaurant** 2567 Hwy 3, Pubnico; ✆ 762 0609; ⊕ daily year-round 11.00–20.00 (until 21.00 summer). Once again, an uninspiring exterior disguises good-value, simple food, all homemade. The emphasis is on seafood, but there are other options, too. The broccoli salad is good, as are the seafood crêpes. Licensed. $

FESTIVALS

June
Tern Festival Birdwatchers will be interested in this (roseate) tern festival, held over three days in late June.

August
Festival chez nous à Pombcoup A big summer draw is this week-long festival, celebrating all things Acadian.

OTHER PRACTICALITIES

$ **Royal Bank** 968 Hwy 335, West Pubnico; ✆ 762 2205; ⊕ 10.00–15.00 Mon–Fri

☞ **Pubnico Branch Library** 35 Hwy 335, Pubnico; ✆ 762 2204; ⊕ May–Sep 15.00–17.30 & 18.15–20.00 Tue, 10.00–13.00 & 15.00–17.30 Wed, 15.00–17.30 & 18.00–20.00 Thu, 15.00–17.00 Fri, 10.00–12.00 Sat; Oct–Apr 15.00–17.30 & 18.00–20.00 Tue, 10.00–13.00 & 15.00–17.30 Wed, 15.00–17.30 & 18.00–20.00 Thu, 15.00–17.00 Fri, 10.15–12.00 Sat.

✉ **Post office** 15 Church St, Middle West Pubnico; ⊕ 09.00–17.30 Mon, 09.30–17.00 Tue–Fri, 09.00–11.30 Sat

WHAT TO SEE AND DO

Le Village Historique Acadien (Historic Acadian Village) (*Old Church Rd, West Pubnico;* ✆ *762 2530, T/F 1 888 381 8999; www.museum.gov.ns.ca/av/;* ⊕ *early Jun–mid-Oct 09.00–17.00 daily; admission CAN$4*) Several old Acadian buildings have been moved to this pretty 7ha site overlooking Pubnico Harbour. Costumed interpreters demonstrate traditional work methods and tell of Acadian life pre-1920. On-site café.

Musée Acadien (*898 Hwy 335, West Pubnico;* ✆ *762 3380; www.museeacadien.ca;* ⊕ *mid-May–mid-Oct 09.00–17.00 Mon–Sat, 12.30–16.30 Sun; admission CAN$3*) Occupying six rooms of a two-storey c1864 house furnished in traditional Acadian style and a modern annexe, the collection displays the history of the Acadians in Pubnico from 1653 to recent times. See a traditional Acadian garden growing plants and vegetables of the type that 17th-century Acadians would have had access to. A good research centre for genealogists.

West Pubnico Golf and Country Club (*Greenwood Rd;* ✆ *762 2007; www.pubnicogolf.ca*) This popular 6,052 yard par 72 course has a long playing season, often opening in late March. Green fees CAN$38.

THE ROAD TO YARMOUTH

Highway 3 provides a more scenic (and slower) alternative to the motorway (Highway 103) between Pubnico and Yarmouth. There's some beautiful coastal scenery and a number of little-visited, sleepy, remote peninsulas (with few services) to explore.

GETTING THERE

By car On Highway 3. Lower Argyle is 6km/4 miles from Pubnico, Sainte-Anne-du-Ruisseau 23km/14 miles, and Tusket 28km/17 miles from Pubnico and 15km/9 miles from Yarmouth.

By bus The Trius Tours coach stops in Argyle and Tusket between Halifax and Yarmouth (see box on page 52).

 WHERE TO STAY AND EAT

Ye Olde Argyler Lodge (6 rooms) 52 Ye Olde Argyler Rd, Lower Argyle; ✆ 643 2500, T/F 1 866 774 0400; www.argyler.com; ⊕ mid-May–Oct. 4 rooms in this comfortable Old English-style lodge right on Lobster Bay have ocean views. The licensed restaurant (⊕ mid-May–mid-Oct 11.00–14.00 &

17.00–21.00 Wed–Sun; $$$) is housed in a modern lodge-style building & serves up gourmet 'New American' cuisine using local ingredients. Try the root beer baby back ribs or seared scallops, & for dessert, chocolate rhapsody. Alfresco dining when the weather permits. Full b/fast inc. $$

In the days of stagecoaches, there were numerous inns between Shag Harbour and Yarmouth. The limited menu at the McDonald Inn in Clyde focused on two of the cheapest foods of that period: mutton and eels.

✗ **Marco's Grill and Pasta House** Hwy 308, Tusket; ✎ 648 0253; www.marcosgrill.com; ⊕ Mar–Dec 11.00–20.00 Sun–Thu, 11.00–21.00 Fri–Sat. Marco's has a long & varied menu including burgers, beef, chicken & seafood — & of course, pasta. Good value. Licensed. **$**

WHAT TO SEE AND DO

Sainte-Anne-du-Ruisseau Sainte-Anne-du-Ruisseau is home to the magnificent c1900 **Eglise Ste-Anne** (*Church of Saint Anne; Hwy 3;* ✎ *648 2315;* ⊕ *year-round*) a black-and-white Gothic-style structure with two towers, high, vaulted ceilings featuring beautiful paintings, and ornate stained glass windows. In July, the **Festival Acadien** is held in the town.

Tusket Here you can visit the oldest standing courthouse in Canada, the (c1802) **Argyle Township Court House and Gaol** (*8168 Hwy 3;* ✎ *648 2493; www.argylecourthouse.com;* ⊕ *May–Jun & Sep–Oct 08.30–12.00 & 13.00–16.30 Mon–Fri; Jul–Aug 09.00–17.00 daily; admission CAN$2*) On the ground floor you can see the guards' quarters and the cells, whilst upstairs are the courtroom and judge's chambers.

5

Yarmouth, French Shore & the Annapolis Valley

This region runs from the port of Yarmouth to Windsor, just 66km northwest of Halifax, taking in the Bay of Fundy coast and the fertile Annapolis Valley. The valley lies between two ridges, the North Mountain and South Mountain. Between Yarmouth and Digby a string of Acadian coastal communities makes up the French Shore.

Close to Digby, renowned for its scallops, and terminus for a year-round car ferry service to Saint John, New Brunswick, the wild and wonderful Digby Neck stretches out into the Bay of Fundy: geologically it is a continuation of the North Mountain ridge. A trip along the narrow peninsula takes you to the departure point for some of North America's best whale-watching experiences.

The Annapolis River empties into the Annapolis Basin: on the basin's north shore is the site of Port-Royal, the first permanent European settlement north of Florida. Close by is the charming historic town of Annapolis Royal, where the streets ooze history.

Inland from the south shore of the basin, the funky, pretty artists' community of Bear River is worth a visit.

Highway 8, one of Nova Scotia's few cross-province roads, connects Annapolis Royal with Liverpool (see page 156), and gives access to Kejimkujik National Park – perhaps the best place to explore the lakes and forests of the interior.

Although best known for its apple orchards, particularly beautiful when in blossom in late May, many other crops are grown in the valley, and in summer smaller roads parallel to Highways 101 and 1 are dotted with U-pick farms where (depending on the time of year) you can pick your own punnets of strawberries, raspberries, blueberries and more.

Towards its northeastern end, the valley becomes busier and more densely populated (relatively speaking). Here you'll find Kentville, the region's commercial centre, and the shopping malls of New Minas. On the Bay of Fundy coast to the north, Capes Split and Blomidon offer high cliffs and magnificent hiking.

RUNIC RUMOURS

In 1812, what became known as the Yarmouth runic stone was brought to public notice by a retired Army surgeon. It had been found near a church between Yarmouth and Cape Forchu (see page 186), weighed around 400lb and had 13 characters carved into its flat face. Some experts suggested that the characters were runes (Viking symbols), claiming this proved suggestions that Leif Ericsson visited Yarmouth in AD1007 (see page 5). However, several reputable scholars have said that the characters now visible were chiselled much closer to 1812 than 1007, and that they are not recognisable as runic. Judge for yourself – the stone is on display at the Yarmouth County Museum (see page 185).

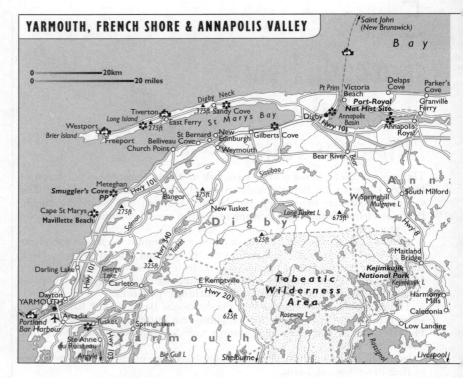

Also close to Kentville is the lively university town of Wolfville, and just 5km further, the emotive Grand Pré National Historic Site.

Highway 101 is the motorway running between Yarmouth and Halifax, passing close to all the region's major communities. Highway 1 runs through the heart of many of the towns, and parallel roads such as Highways 201 and 221 provide quiet, pastoral alternatives.

Digby and Kingston/Greenwood are the major shopping centres between Yarmouth and Kentville. There are backpacker hostels in Yarmouth, Digby, at Brier Island on the Digby Neck, and at South Milford (between Annapolis Royal and Kejimkujik National Park).

FESTIVALS
Late May–early June
Apple Blossom Festival (*www.appleblossom.com*) Events forming part of this apple-focused celebration are held at various Annapolis Valley locations including Middleton (see page 213), Kentville (see page 215) and Berwick (see page 214).

YARMOUTH (Population: 7,200)

Located on the eastern side of Yarmouth Harbour, Yarmouth is the largest urban centre in western Nova Scotia and has long been one of Nova Scotia's most important ports and communities. The region's largest seaport is the gateway for ferries to Maine, USA, and early in 2009 the dust covers were taken off the local airport when flights between Yarmouth and both Portland, Maine, and Halifax

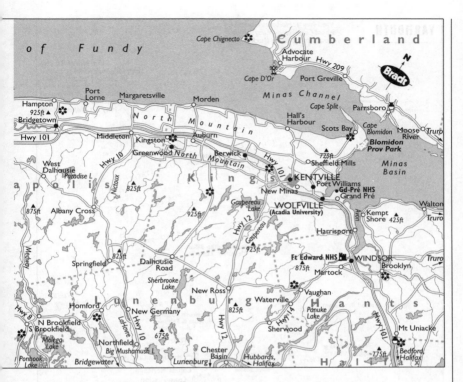

were introduced. Shipping (primarily lumber products), and fishing (especially herring) are major contributors to present-day Yarmouth's economy.

Whilst the town's tourism officials, hoteliers, restaurateurs and shopkeepers appreciate the flow of arrivals and departures on the ferry, the CAT (see page 39) and new flights, they are also frustrated that potential money-spenders pass through Yarmouth almost without stopping, usually *en route* to or from eating or overnighting elsewhere in the province.

Whilst it is no Lunenburg (see page 143) or Annapolis Royal (see page 199), there are some good museums, restaurants and places to stay, a restored waterfront with pleasant waterfront park, and many beautiful Victorian mansions – particularly within the Collins Heritage Conservation District, which encompasses parts of Alma, Carleton, Clements and Collins streets. Yarmouth makes a good base from which to explore the lovely peninsulas and quiet backroads – ideal for cycling – to the southwest, and the French Shore.

ORIENTATION Water Street runs along the waterfront with Main Street parallel to it just up the hill. The ferry terminal is at the junction of Water and Forest streets, and the airport 3.5km away at the other end of Forest Street. Highway 1 becomes Main Street and Highway 3 Starrs Road – where most of the big shopping malls are found – as they come into town: Highways 103 (from Halifax via the South Shore) and 101 (from Halifax via the Annapolis Valley) lead on to Starrs Road.

HISTORY The Mi'kmaq called the area *Kespoogwit*, meaning 'the end of the earth': Samuel de Champlain (see page 5) landed in 1604, naming it Cap Forchu (or Fourchu) for its two-pronged cape.

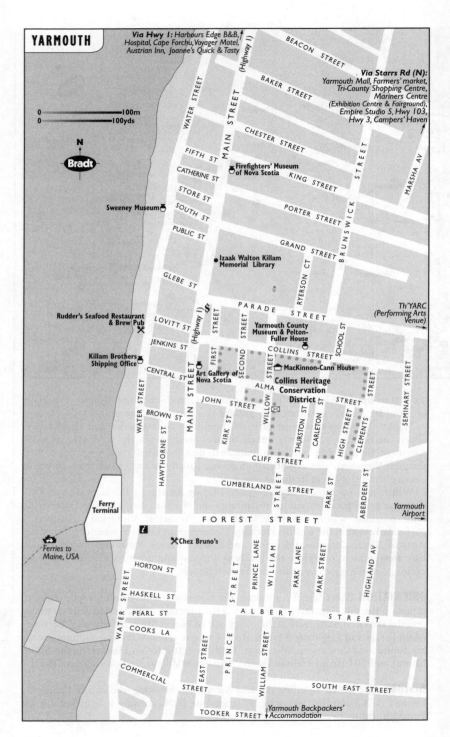

YARMOUTH

Via Hwy 1: Harbours Edge B&B,
Hospital, Cape Forchu, Voyager Motel,
Austrian Inn, Joanne's Quick & Tasty

BEACON STREET

Via Starrs Rd (N):
Yarmouth Mall, Farmers' market,
Tri-County Shopping Centre,
Mariners Centre
(Exhibition Centre & Fairground),
Empire Studio 5, Hwy 103,
Hwy 3, Campers' Haven

BAKER STREET

0 ⊢———┤ 100m
0 ⊢———┤ 100yds

N
Bradt

WATER STREET

MAIN STREET

CHESTER STREET

FIFTH ST

CATHERINE ST

Firefighters' Museum
of Nova Scotia

KING STREET

BRUNSWICK STREET

MARSHA AV

STORE ST

Sweeney Museum

SOUTH ST

PORTER STREET

PUBLIC ST

GRAND STREET

Izaak Walton Killam
Memorial Library

GLEBE ST

RYERSON CT

PARADE STREET

Th'YARC
(Performing Arts
Venue)

Rudder's Seafood Restaurant
& Brew Pub

LOVITT ST

(Highway 1)

FIRST STREET

SECOND STREET

Yarmouth County
Museum & Pelton-
Fuller House

SCHOOL ST

JENKINS ST

Killam Brothers
Shipping Office

CENTRAL ST

Art Gallery of
Nova Scotia

COLLINS STREET

MacKinnon-Cann House

WATER STREET

MAIN STREET

ALMA STREET

Collins Heritage
Conservation
District

SEMINARY STREET

JOHN STREET

KIRK ST

WILLOW STREET

THURSTON ST

CARLETON ST

HIGH STREET

CLEMENTS STREET

STREET

BROWN ST

HAWTHORNE ST

CLIFF STREET

CUMBERLAND STREET

PARK ST

ABERDEEN ST

Yarmouth
Airport

Ferry
Terminal

FOREST STREET

i

Chez Bruno's

Ferries to
Maine, USA

WATER STREET

HORTON ST

HASKELL ST

PEARL ST

COOKS LA

EAST STREET

PRINCE STREET

PRINCE LANE

WILLIAM STREET

PARK LANE

PARK STREET

HIGHLAND AV

ALBERT STREET

COMMERCIAL STREET

WILLIAM STREET

SOUTH EAST STREET

TOOKER STREET

Yarmouth Backpackers'
Accommodation

182

After Expulsion, Yarmouth's first families arrived from Cape Cod, Massachusetts, in 1762. There were no roads to connect the site with anywhere else, but wood was plentiful. Boats were needed for fishing, transportation and trade, and so Yarmouth's long history of shipbuilding began.

Peaking in the late 1870s, when Yarmouth ranked as the world's fourth-largest port of registry and possessed more tonnage per capita than any other seaport in the world, shipbuilding then began a rapid decline.

From the 1850s, regular steamship services connected Boston and New York with Yarmouth. The railway arrived in the 1880s, increasing the importance of this port as one of Nova Scotia's main gateways. Yarmouth remains a significant port, fishing centre and international gateway.

GETTING THERE

By air Starlink Aviation (\ *514 631 7500, T/F 1 877 782 8247; www.starlinkaviation.com*) began operating twice-daily flights between Portland, Maine and Halifax via Yarmouth in February 2009. The airport is 3km east of town at the end of Forest Street. Taxi fares into town cost in the region of CAN$7.

By car Two of the province's major motorways, Highway 101 and 103, converge at Yarmouth. Halifax is approximately 300km/186 miles away via Highway 103 (through the South Shore), and 340km/211 miles away via Highway 101 (through the Annapolis Valley and Windsor). From Yarmouth it is 123km/76 miles to Shelburne (via Highway 103) and 105km/65 miles to Digby via Highway 101.

By bus Trius Tours runs a coach once daily from Yarmouth to Halifax via the South Shore. For travel from Yarmouth, tickets are available from the Rodd Colony Harbour Inn (*6 Forest St*). See page 52 for further information.

By ferry Two ferry services (see page 39) cross the Gulf of Maine, connecting Yarmouth with Bar Harbor and Portland (both in Maine, USA). The ferry terminal is very central, at the western end of Forest Street.

TOURIST INFORMATION (*228 Main St;* \ *742 5033;* ⊕ *early Jun–early Oct 09.00–17.00 daily, 19.00 mid–Jul–Aug*)

🏠 WHERE TO STAY

🏠 **MacKinnon-Cann House Historic Inn** (7 rooms) 27 Willow St; \ 742 9900, T/F 1 866 698 3142; www.mackinnoncanninn.com; ⊕ year-round. Each guest room at this beautifully renovated c1887 Italianate mansion is decorated in the style of a different 20th-century decade: décor in the public rooms is late 19th-century Victorian. The mix works. A lovely place to stay — & eat (see page 184). Full b/fast inc. $$$

🏠 **Harbour's Edge B&B** (4 rooms) 12 Vancouver St; \ 742 2387; www.harboursedge.ns.ca; ⊕ year-round. A c1864 house with a delightful waterfront location & friendly hosts. Full b/fast inc (eg: French toast with orange & locally smoked bacon). $$

🏠 **Voyageur Motel** (17 rooms) 518 Lakeside Dr; \ 742 7157, T/F 1 800 565 5026; www.nsonline.com/voyageur; ⊕ year-round. An early

1990s' single-storey motel on Hwy 1, 4km from Yarmouth. B/fast not inc, but available. $

🏠 **Yarmouth Backpackers' Accommodation** (3 rooms) 6 Trinity Pl; \ 749 0941; www.yarmouthbackpackers.com; ⊕ year-round; off-season by reservation. Housed in a c1880s Italianate-style home with twin, double or 4-bed (bunks) dorm. 2 shared bathrooms, full kitchen. Linen & blankets inc. Dorm CAN$22, private room CAN$50. $

⚊ **Campers' Haven Campground** (192 sites) 9700 Hwy 3, Arcadia; \ 742 4848; ⊕ late May–Sep. Large lakeside campground with open & wooded serviced & unserviced sites approx 6km from downtown. Heated pool (in season), hot tub, laundromat. $

✕ WHERE TO EAT

✕ MacKinnon-Cann House Historic Inn Willow St; ☎ 742 9900, T/F 1 866 698 3142; www.mackinnoncanninn.com; ⊕ Jun–Sep 17.30–20.30 Wed–Sat. The elegant licensed dining room at this beautifully renovated Italianate mansion has a short but interesting menu: cuisine is continental. Reservations recommended. **$$$**

✕ Austrian Inn Hwy 1, Dayton; ☎ 742 6202; ⊕ daily mid-Jun–mid-Sep 11.00–22.00; Mar–mid-Jun & mid-Sep–Dec 11.00–21.00. The menu is a mix of Nova Scotia seafood & typical Austro-German specials. By the lake in Dayton, just outside Yarmouth. **$$**

✕ Chez Bruno's 222 Main St; ☎ 742 0031; www.chezbrunocafe.com; ⊕ year-round Oct–Jun 11.00–20.00 Tue–Sat; Jul–Sep 11.00–20.00 daily. Ignore the exterior – this relatively new, casual Mediterranean-style bistro offers a new dimension to Yarmouth's dining scene. Cuisine is hard to define, a combination of traditional Acadian & French fusion. Start perhaps with the calamari, and move on to the perfect rack of lamb. Licensed. **$$**

✕ Rudder's Seafood Restaurant & Brew Pub 96 Water St; ☎ 742 7311; www.ruddersbrewpub.com; ⊕ year-round 11.00–late daily. Very popular waterfront eatery, pub & microbrewery with wooden floors & beams, & large patio. Good food – start with bacon-wrapped scallops, move on to haddock fishcakes or maritime lobster sandwich, & leave room for the carrot cake or over-the-top chocolate desserts. Wash it down with a Rudder's Red or Yarmouth Town Brown. **$$**

✕ Joanne's Quick & Tasty Hwy 1, Dayton; ☎ 742 3467; ⊕ year-round 07.30–20.30 daily. Another of the province's nothing-to-look-at-but-good-value-food spots. Lots of deep-frying, big portions of clams, scallop, lobster & chicken, & pies topped with mounds of whipped cream. **$–$$**

FESTIVALS

July

Seafest (*www.seafest.ca*) 11 days of varied events – many marine-related.

Sou'Wester International Bike Rally (*www.souwestbikers.com*) Loads of leather and throbbing engines as motorbikes take over town for three days.

End July–early August

Western Nova Scotia Exhibition (*www.westernnovascotiaexhibition.webs.com*) What started out as an agricultural exhibition has developed into six days of concerts, events and activities for all the family.

CHURCHILL CHANGES

One of my favourite places to stay and eat in the entire province, the wonderful Churchill Mansion Country Inn, was sold in spring 2009. The inn – set on a hillside overlooking a lake 16km from Yarmouth – was built in 1891 by Aaron Flint Churchill, an international sea hero, who later became very wealthy in the shipping industry of Savannah, Georgia. The exterior had long been in need of more than 'TLC' but the inn had an abundance of 'ageing grandeur', and the guest and public rooms simply oozed atmosphere. I'm not saying that the Churchill was haunted, but it was certainly a popular spot with those with an interest in the paranormal. The outgoing owner, Bob Benson, enhanced guests' experiences with his fascinating tales over splendid seafood buffet dinners. This used to be an experience not to be missed and worth going out of your way for. Closed in 2009 for major renovations, it is due to re-open in July 2010 as the Churchill Mansion Inn (*44 Old Post Rd, Darling Lake;* ☎ 649 2818, T/F 1 888 470 2818; *www.churchillmansion.com*), with restored Georgian-Victorian décor and six guest rooms (all 'luxury ensuite'). Rates are expected to include a gourmet breakfast and the dining room will be open for dinner each evening. Check the website for the latest.

End August–early September

Yarmouth Cup Ocean Races (*www.yarmouth cup.com*) Yacht race between Falmouth, Maine (USA) and Yarmouth.

September

Nova Scotia International Air Show (*www.nsairshow.ca*) In recent years, bad weather, changing venues and runway resurfacing have all conspired against what should be a thrilling event with both ground and aerial displays. Yarmouth has hosted the NSIAS since 2008.

OTHER PRACTICALITIES

$ **Scotiabank** 389 Main St; ✆ 742 7116; ⊕ 10.00–17.00 Mon–Fri

◼ **Empire Studio 5** (Cinema) 136 Starrs Rd; ✆ 742 7489; www.empiretheatres.com

✚ **Yarmouth Regional Hospital** 60 Vancouver St; ✆ 742 3541

▤ **Izaak Walton Killam Memorial Library** 405 Main St; ✆ 742 5040; ⊕ 10.00–20.00 Mon–Thu, 10.00–17.00 Fri, 10.00–16.00 Sat

⊠ **Post office** 15 Willow St; ⊕ 08.00–17.30 Mon–Fri

🚕 **Yarmouth Town Taxi** ✆ 742 7801

WHAT TO SEE AND DO

Fire-fighters' Museum of Nova Scotia (*451 Main St; ✆ 742 5525; www.museum.gov.ns.ca/fm/; ⊕ year-round: Jun & Sep 09.00–17.00 Mon–Sat; Jul–Aug 09.00–21.00 Mon–Sat, 10.00–17.00 Sun; Oct–May 09.00–16.00 Mon–Fri, 13.00–16.00 Sat; admission CAN$4*) With an extensive collection of fire-fighting equipment from days of yore, this museum is much more interesting than it sounds – and one the kids will enjoy, too.

Yarmouth County Museum and Archives and Pelton-Fuller House (*22 & 20 Collins St; ✆ 742 5539; www.yarmouthcountymuseum.ednet.ns.ca; ⊕ Jun–mid-Oct 09.00–18.00 Mon–Sat, 13.00–18.00 Sun; mid-Oct–May 14.00–17.00 Mon–Sat; admission CAN$3 each or CAN$5 for both museum & Pelton-Fuller House*) This excellent museum in a restored granite former c1893 church contains one of Canada's largest collections of ship paintings and one of the province's largest costume collections. Whilst the collection focuses on Yarmouth's seafaring history and heritage, the complex also includes the largest community archives in Nova Scotia, and another wing with transportation-related exhibits and art galleries. Be sure to see the runic stone (see box on page 179), the 1860s' stagecoach and the early lens from the Cape Forchu light (see page 186). The gift shop is also one of the better ones of the genre.

Next door is the antique-packed Italianate (c1895) Pelton-Fuller House, once the summer residence of Alfred Fuller who made a fortune in the US selling brushes and houseware, becoming known throughout North America as the *Fuller Brush Man*. The house has attractive flower gardens.

Art Gallery of Nova Scotia (*Western Branch; 341 Main St; ✆ 742 7279; ⊕ late May–mid-Oct 10.00–17.00 daily; rest of the year 12.00–17.00 Fri–Sun; admission CAN$5*) The only branch of Halifax's Art Gallery of Nova Scotia (see page 108) is housed in a former bank.

Th'YARC (*76 Parade St; ✆ 742 8150; www.thyarc.ca*) A performing arts complex including a 350-seat theatre and art gallery.

Killam Brothers Shipping Office (*90 Water St; ✆ 742 5539; www.yarmouthcountymuseum.ednet.ns.ca; ⊕ Jun–Aug 09.00–18.00 daily; admission free*) A

19th-century building housing Canada's oldest shipping office: the Killam family were directly involved with many aspects of shipping for almost two centuries.

Sweeney Museum (*112 Water St;* ☎ *742 3457; www.sweeneyfisheriesmuseum.ca;* ⊕ *mid–May–mid-Oct 10.00–18.00 Mon–Sat; admission CAN$3*) A scaled-down reproduction (including a coastal freighter) of part of Yarmouth's old working waterfront, built using original materials.

Cape Forchu (*Hwy 304;* ☎ *742 4522; www.capeforchulight.com;* ⊕ *May–mid-Oct; admission free*) Adjacent to the 23m lighthouse – one of the highest (23m) and most photogenic in the province – the original lightkeeper's quarters house a small museum, tea room (good sandwiches and tasty baked goods) and gift shop. Near the car park, a trail leads down to Leif Ericsson Picnic Park. Take care on the smooth rocks which can be very slippery. To get there, follow Main Street north and turn left at the golden horse fountain onto Vancouver Street. Just past the hospital complex, turn left onto Highway 304 and follow it to its end, approximately 11km from the centre of Yarmouth.

Farmers' market On Saturday mornings (*Jul–Sep*) a farmers' market is held at the Canadian Tire car park (*120 Starrs Rd*).

THE FRENCH SHORE

Officially part of the Municipality of Clare, those in surrounding areas call this string of over a dozen adjoining Acadian villages The French Shore, whilst to most of the residents it is La Ville Française.

The Acadian flag (known as the *stella maris*), flies everywhere. The 'longest main street in the world' is an interesting alternative to the motorway (Highway 101).

HISTORY Post-expulsion (see page 7), returning Acadians who found their old lands taken over by others kept walking until they found land that no one else was interested in. Despite the harsh climate and poor quality of the soil, they persevered. In time, fishing and boatbuilding developed. Mink farms were, and – rightly or wrongly – still are, another money spinner.

FESTIVALS
End July–early August
Festival Acadien de Clare (*www.festivalacadiendeclare.ca*) For a fortnight at the end of July, residents (and many visitors) celebrate the oldest Acadian festival in Canada, with music, food, parades, competitions and raucous fun.

MAVILLETTE The main reason for coming here is to visit Mavillette Beach Provincial Park, a 2km wide gently curving stretch of sand backed by marram grass-covered dunes. Behind the dunes, a large salt marsh is home to avian year-rounders and spring and autumn migrators.

Follow Cape St Mary's Road to its end. You might see seals basking on the rocks below, and the coastal views from this point high above the sea are superb.

⌂ Where to stay
⌂ **A la Maison d'Amitie** (3 rooms) 197 Baseline Rd, Mavillette; ☎ 645 2601; e carol@ houseoffriendship.ca; www.houseoffriendship.ca; ⊕ year-round. With one of the province's great settings – high on the cliffs of St Mary's Bay – & awesome views, the accommodation in this modern home is up to standard, too. Full b/fast inc, & afternoon tea & home-baked goodies. $$$

Cape View Motel and Cottages (15 units) 124 John Doucette Rd, Mavillette; ☎ 645 2258, T/F 1 800 876 1960; www.capeviewmotel.ca; ⊕ Jun–Sep. 10 motel rooms and 5 1- & 2-bedroom cottages in a good setting & across the road from the Cape View Restaurant (see below). Continental b/fast inc. $

SMUGGLERS COVE PROVINCIAL PARK Smugglers Cove is 9km north of Mavillette. Interpretive panels tell of the rum-running past, paths lead to clifftop coastal views, and steep, wooden steps descend through the trees to a sheltered cove with a pebble beach and (apparently) a sea cave 5m high and 18m deep. I have visited the park three times, but couldn't actually find the cave!

METEGHAN Meteghan, 3.5km past Smugglers Cove, is the French Shore's largest community, busiest port and commercial hub (though the total population is less than 1,000). The port is home to several types of fishing boat and the main wharf is a hive of activity throughout the day. Meteghan River, 4.5km north of Meteghan, is Nova Scotia's largest wooden-shipbuilding centre.

Where to stay and eat

☗ **L'Auberge au Havre du Capitaine** (18 rooms) 9118 Hwy 1, Meteghan River; ☎ 769 2001; www.havreducapitaine.ca; ⊕ year-round. A nice inn with traditional Acadian feel (rooms have hardwood floors & are decorated with antiques – though bathrooms are modern). The licensed dining room (⊕ 07.00–21.00 daily; $$) focuses on seafood & Acadian dishes & can be a bit hit or miss.

Reservations recommended for non-guests. $–$$

✗ **Cape View Restaurant** 157 John Doucette Rd, Mavillette; ☎ 645 2519; ⊕ mid-May–Jun & Sep–early Oct 11.00–20.00 daily; Jul–Aug 07.30–21.00 daily. Wonderful views of the beach, good breakfasts, traditional (eg: fish & chips) & Acadian (eg: rappie pie) dishes. $$

Other practicalities

$ **Royal Bank** Hwy 1, Meteghan; ☎ 645 2410; ⊕ 10.00–17.00 Mon–Wed & Fri, 10.00–18.00 Thu

✉ **Post office** 8198 Hwy 1, Meteghan; ⊕ 08.00–17.00 Mon–Fri, 08.30–11.30 Sat

CHURCH POINT (POINTE DE l'EGLISE) A further 15km north, Church Point is the home of Université Sainte-Anne, founded in 1891 and Nova Scotia's only French-language university. The university is the Acadian cultural centre for the entire Clare region. On the campus is grey-shingled Eglise de Sainte-Marie, the largest wooden church in North America. Constructed between 1903 and 1905, it seats almost 1,800 people.

Where to stay and eat

 ⋏ **Belle Baie Park Campground** (146 sites) 2135 Hwy 1, Church Point; ☎ 739 3160; www.bellbaiepark.com; ⊕ early May–late Sep. Serviced & unserviced sites at this St Mary's Bay-

'YOUR FISH OR YOUR LIVES'

In August 1918, *The New York Times* reported that when on one of her regular trips out of Yarmouth in search of halibut, the Nelson A and her crew found themselves face to face with a German U-boat. At gunpoint, they were told to load dories with all their fish and approach the surfaced submarine.

In return for the fish, the men were given food and water – and told to row away from their boat as fast as possible. Following these instructions, moments later they heard a huge boom: both the submarine and – within minutes – the Nelson A disappeared beneath the surface. The crew rowed for shore, and, two days later, arrived back on dry land exhausted but alive.

front campground. Heated pool (in season), laundromat. $

✕ **Chez Christophe** 2655 Hwy 1, Grosses Coques; ☎ 837 5817; www.chezchristophe.ca; ⊕ year-round 11.30–14.00 & 16.30–20.00 Tue–Sun. Located a few kilometres north in the village of Grosses Coques, this cosy, home, restaurant in a century-old Acadian house is probably the region's best. The limited menu includes delicious simply cooked traditional Acadian dishes (such as fricot), prawns, or the excellent seafood lasagne: unimaginative vegetables are the only disappointment. Dessert (eg: coconut cream pie, or a berry crumble) is worth saving room for. There is live Acadian music every Thu evening. Reservations recommended, especially for music evenings. You can bring your own wine & (a real rarity in Nova Scotia) there's no corkage charge. $$

✕ **Rapure Acadienne** 1443 Hwy 1, Church Point; ☎ 769 2172; ⊕ year-round 08.00–17.30 daily. If you only try Acadian speciality rappie pie (see page 58) once in Nova Scotia, try it here, served – as it should be – with a 'side' of butter & molasses. There's 1 table inside & picnic tables outside. $

What to see and do

Acadian Centre Archives (☎ 769 2114; www.centreacadien.usainteanne.ca; ⊕ 08.30–12.00 & 13.00–16.00 Mon–Fri; admission free) Those interested in genealogy won't want to miss this resource at the university.

BELLIVEAU COVE (L'ANSE-DES-BELLIVEAU) Belliveau Cove is 7km north of Church Point. It has a wharf, at the end of which is a pretty c1889 lighthouse, a seasonal tourist information office (see below) and a 5km coastal interpretive trail.

Tourist information (3239 Hwy 1, Belliveau Cove; ☎ 837 7100; ⊕ Jul–Aug 09.00–19.00 Mon–Fri, 09.00–17.00 Sat–Sun; Sep–mid-Oct 10.00–17.00 Mon–Fri, 09.00–13.00 Sat)

Festivals
August
Annual Festival Joseph et Marie Dugas This one-day festival features food, music, games, an arts and crafts sale and a flea market.

What to see and do
Farmers' market (Parc Joseph et Marie Dugas; May–Oct 08.30–12.00 Sat) Come to this park by the wharf for the freshest local fruit, vegetables and baked goods.

ST BERNARD St Bernard marks the end of the French Shore. Its church (☎ 837 5687; ⊕ Jun–Sep) has wonderful acoustics and hosts a series of classical music concerts in the summer.

WEYMOUTH

This former shipbuilding and lumber centre near the mouth of the Sissiboo River has a few services. Like many coastal communities in the province, today's Weymouth is a much quieter place than it would have been a century ago.

GETTING THERE
By car Weymouth is on Highway 1, just off Highway 101 Exit 28, 4km/2 miles from St Bernard, 76km/47 miles from Yarmouth and 35km/23 miles from Digby.

By bus Weymouth is also on the bus route to Bridgetown (see box on page 190).

TOURIST INFORMATION (4575 Hwy 1; ☎ 837 4715; ⊕ early May–Jun 10.00–17.00 Mon–Fri, 11.00–15.00 Sat; Jul–Aug 09.00–18.00 Mon–Fri, 10.00–18.00 Sat, 13.00–18.00 Sun; Sep 10.00–15.00 Mon–Sat; Oct 10.00–15.00 Mon–Fri)

⌂ WHERE TO STAY AND EAT

⌂ **Baie Ste-Marie Ocean Front Cottages** (3 cottages) 5–9 Riverside Rd, New Edinburgh; ✆ 769 0797, T/F 1 866 769 0797; www.nsoceanfrontcottages.com; ⊕ year-round. 3 themed c2003 2-bedroom cottages in a wonderful setting less than 7km from Weymouth on St May's Bay at the mouth of the Sissiboo River. Very well equipped, these make an excellent base from which to visit the whole of southwest Nova Scotia. Min stay 2 nights. $$$

⌂ **Goodwin Hotel** (10 rooms) 4616 Hwy 1; ✆ 837 5120; www3.ns.sympatico.ca/goodwinhotel; ⊕ year-round. Choose between a room with private or shared bath at this simple old-style hotel, an inn since 1890. Food in the licensed dining room (⊕ *summer 07.00–09.00, 11.30–13.30 & 17.00–19.00 Sun–Fri; winter same hours but Mon–Fri; $*) is dependable but won't surprise you. $

OTHER PRACTICALITIES

$ **Royal Bank** Hwy 1; ✆ 837 5136; ⊕ 10.00–15.00 Mon–Fri

☙ **Weymouth Branch Library** 4609 Hwy 1; ✆ 837 4596; ⊕ 13.30–16.30 & 18.00–20.00 Tue & Fri, 13.30–16.30 Wed, 12.30–16.30 Thu, 10.00–13.00 Sat

✉ **Post office** 4659 Hwy 1; ⊕ 08.30–17.00 Mon–Fri, 08.30–12.30 Sun

WHAT TO SEE AND DO

Hinterland Adventures (*Weymouth;* ✆ *837 4092, T/F 1 800 378 8177; www.kayakingnovascotia.com*) This excellent company offers a range of canoe and kayak tours both along the coast and into the wilderness. It also rents equipment.

GILBERT'S COVE

The only site of interest here is **Gilbert's Cove Lighthouse** (*Lighthouse Rd;* ✆ *837 5584; www.gilbertscovelighthouse.com;* ⊕ *mid-Jun–mid-Sep 10.00–16.00 Mon–Sat, 12.00–16.00 Sun; admission free*). Reached by a short unpaved road, the c1904 lighthouse now serves as a museum, tea room and craft shop. Climb the tower for wonderful views over the cove, St Mary's Bay and Digby Neck. There are picnic tables on the grass above the beach.

GETTING THERE Gilbert's Cove is 1km off Highway 101, 11km from Weymouth and 24km from Digby.

DIGBY (Population: 2,320)

This working town 5km from the terminal for ferries to and from Saint John, New Brunswick, has a fine setting at the south end of the vast Annapolis Basin. Since

---

SIGOGNE

Abbé Jean Mande Sigogne (1763–1844) – a French priest who fled his homeland for England during the French revolution – arrived in Nova Scotia in the late 1790s. His mission stations extended from the Pubnicos (see page 173) to Annapolis Royal (page 199) and Bear River (page 197). Much loved by his people, the Abbe was a strong influence in the education of the Acadians, and helped inspire them in their farming, fishing and trading. A terrible fire swept through the region in 1820 destroying the St Bernard church and much else, and again the Abbe was a rock in helping rebuild both the communities' morale and their fire-destroyed buildings. He supervised the construction of many churches in southwest Nova Scotia and died in 1844: his tomb stands outside the university.

commercial scallop fishing began here late in the 1920s, the mollusc (see box on page 191) has been the mainstay of Digby's economy.

A fire in 1899 destroyed over 40 buildings in the small downtown area. Today, Water Street is lined with shops, cafés, and restaurants, behind which a boardwalk makes a pleasant place for a wander. One of the province's few resorts – with a top-class golf course – lies between the town and the ferry terminal.

HISTORY The Mi'kmaq name for the area is *Te'Wapskik*, meaning 'flowing between high rocks', a reference to the Digby Gut. Originally called Conway (after a former secretary of state), the current name is in honour of Admiral Robert Digby, who sailed up the Fundy on the *Atlanta* in 1783 and settled the place with 1,500 Loyalists from New England.

GETTING THERE

By car Digby is just off Highway 101 Exit 26, 105km/65 miles northeast of Yarmouth and 235km/146 miles west of Halifax.

By bus Digby is on the Weymouth–Bridgetown bus route (see box above) and linked to Halifax by a daily Acadian coach (see page 51).

By ferry The terminus for the ferry (see page 39) to Saint John, New Brunswick, is 5km from town. Walk there, or take a taxi. Digby Cabs (see page 193) charge CAN$10.

TOURIST INFORMATION

🄵 Tourist information 110 Montague Row, downtown; 🖉 245 5714, T/F 1 888 463 4429; ⊕ daily late May–Jun & mid-Sep–early Oct, 09.00–17.00; Jul–mid-Sep, 09.00–18.00.

🄵 Tourist information 237 Shore Rd, near the ferry terminal; 🖉 245 2201; ⊕ daily 9–31 May & 18–31 Oct, 09.00–17.00; Jun–17 Oct, 08.30–18.30

WHERE TO STAY

⌂ Digby Pines Golf Resort & Spa (116 units) 103 Shore Rd; 🖉 245 2511, T/F 1 800 667 4637; www.digbypines.ca; ⊕ mid-May–early Oct. With 79 rooms & 6 suites in the c1929 main lodge & 31 well-dispersed 1–3-bedroom cottages (each with a sitting room with working stone fireplace, & covered veranda), this casually elegant old-fashioned resort sits on a hillside overlooking the Annapolis Basin outside the town centre. New Aveda spa, superb 18-hole golf course, heated outdoor pool, tennis courts, fitness centre, children's playground, croquet, & walking/cycling trails. There are 2 bars (1 serving food & overlooking the golf course), & a main dining room (see below). Full b/fast inc in most rates. $$$

🏠 **Montague Row B&B** (3 units) 66 Montague Row; 🕿 245 6039, T/F 1 866 905 7755; www.montaguerow.com; ☼ May–Oct. Choose between a room or suite at this quiet, comfortable, delightful c1880s Victorian Gothic house overlooking the sea. There's also an adjacent modern 2-storey guest home (sleeps 4). Full b/fast inc. $$

🏠 **Thistle Down Country Inn** (12 rooms) 98 Montague Row; 🕿 245 4490, T/F 1 800 565 8081; e thistledown@ns.aliantzinc.ca; www.thistledown.ns.ca; ☼ May–Oct. 6 rooms in a c1904 main building &, tucked behind, a 2-storey modern addition with 6 more. Garden directly on

waterfront. Dinner by reservation. Full b/fast inc. $$

🏠 **Bayside Inn B&B** (11 rooms) 115 Montague Row; 🕿 245 2247, T/F 1 888 754 0555; e info@baysideinn.ca; www.baysideinn.ca; ☼ year-round. A c1885 building just across the road from the waterfront. Cheaper rooms have shared bathrooms. Full b/fast inc. $–$$

🏠 **Digby Backpackers Inn** (12 beds) 168 Queen St; 🕿 245 4573; www.digbyhostel.com; ☼ year-round (Nov–Apr by reservation). Comfortable, friendly new hostel in a Dutch Colonial-style house with 2 4-bed dorms & a private room. Shared bathrooms, communal kitchen, sun room, garden & deck. There are plans to offer bike rental. Dorm CAN$25, private room CAN$60. $

🅧 **Digby Campground** (49 sites) 230 Victoria St; 🕿 245 1985; ☼ mid-May–mid-Oct. Sites at this terraced campground a few blocks up from the seafront are a little bit close together, but you are in walking distance of the town centre. Laundromat & outdoor pool (seasonal). $

✖ WHERE TO EAT

✖ **Digby Pines Golf Resort and Spa** 103 Shore Rd; 🕿 245 2511; www.digbypines.ca; ☼ mid-May–early Oct 18.00–21.00 daily; mid-Jun–mid-Sep 11.00–14.00 Sun brunch. The main dining room of this resort is the grand Annapolis Room. The fine-dining menu focuses on seafood – Digby scallops appear frequently – but carnivores don't miss out, with very good roast beef, & rack of lamb. $$$

✖ **Boardwalk Café** 40 Water St; 🕿 245 5497; www.boardwalkcafe.netfirms.com; ☼ Mar–May & Oct–Dec 11.00–14.00 Mon–Fri; Jun–Sep

11.00–14.00 & 17.00–20.00 Mon–Sat. An excellent, relaxed, licensed café/restaurant. A deck overlooks the wharf & Annapolis Basin. Everything is homemade: the scallops are delicious, as are the desserts – especially the pecan pie & carrot cake. No deep-fryer! $$

✖ **Captain's Cabin** 2 Birch St; 🕿 245 4868; ☼ May–Oct 11.00–22.00 daily. Seafood is the focus. Not the most imaginative of menus, but it isn't all deep-fried – fish is also served poached, grilled or pan-fried. $$

DIGBY SCALLOPS

In Nova Scotia – and further afield – the word 'scallops' is almost always preceded by 'Digby': the town is home to the world's largest inshore scallop fleet.

Scallops are marine molluscs, bivalves with two hard, rounded shells with scalloped edges and a soft body. The shells are opened and closed by the adductor muscle. This is the 'meat', the only part of the scallop that is usually eaten. Unlike many other bivalve molluscs, they do not bury themselves in the sand, but live on the soft sea bed.

Scallops are harvested by 'draggers', specially rigged boats which drag huge metal mesh bags along the sea bed. The cages are emptied into the boats, and the scallops opened (or shucked) by hand. The meat is placed in containers and put on ice until the boats return to shore.

Conditions in the sea off Digby (in particular, the year-round, fairly steady cool water temperatures, and nutrient-rich sea) combine to produce scallops that – cooked well – are a gastronomic treat.

5

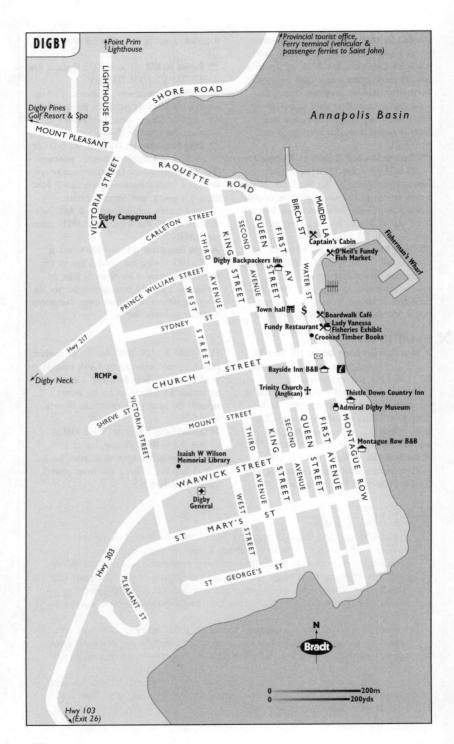

✕ **Fundy Restaurant** 34 Water St; ☎ 245 4950; www.fundyrestaurant.com/fundy.shtml; ⊕ mid-Jun–mid-Sep 07.00–22.00 daily; mid-Sep–mid-Jun 11.00–21.00 daily. A large, casual restaurant overlooking the wharf. Sit inside in the main dining room, in the large solarium, or out on the deck. Local scallops dominate the menu: have them for breakfast in an omelette, in chowder, with pasta – you get the idea. **$$**

✕ **O'Neil's Fundy Fish Market** Prince William St; ☎ 245 6528; ⊕ 09.00–17.00 Mon–Fri, 10.00–17.00 Sat. No view & cafeteria décor but a good-value eatery for simple scallop dishes (deep or pan-fried), fish & chips & the like. Or – if you're self-catering – buy fresh seafood to prepare 'chez vous'. **$**

NIGHTLIFE Nightlife consists of the **Club 98 Lounge** in the Fundy Restaurant (see *Where to eat*), or the lounge bar at the **Digby Pines Resort** (⊕ *mid-May–early Oct 17.00–22.00*).

FESTIVALS
July
East Coast Celebrity Golf Classic (*www.eastcoastclassic.org*) Watch 38 teams (with 'celebrity' captains) play the course at the Digby Pines Golf Resort and Spa over four days.

August
Digby Scallop Days Festival (*www.digbyscallopdays.com*) Five days of music, races, parades and food – including, of course, Digby scallops!

End August–early September
Annual Wharf Rat Rally (*www.wharfratrally.ca*) Atlantic Canada's largest motorcycle rally hits town for six days.

OTHER PRACTICALITIES
$ **Royal Bank** 51 Water St; ☎ 245 4771; ⊕ 09.30–17.00 Mon–Fri
⊜ **Crooked Timber Books** 17 Water St; ☎ 245 1283; www.crookedtimber.com.; ⊕ Apr–Dec 10.00–17.00 Mon–Sat. A good used bookstore with a special interest in Irish literature.
✚ **Digby General Hospital** 75 Warwick St; ☎ 245 2501

⊜ **Isaiah W Wilson Memorial Library** 84 Warwick St; ☎ 245 2163; ⊕ 12.30–15.00 & 18.00–20.00 Tue–Thu, 10.00–17.00 Fri, 10.00–14.00 Sat
✉ **Post office** 9 Water St; ⊕ 08.30–17.15 Mon–Fri
⇌ **Digby Cabs** ☎ 245 6162

WHAT TO SEE AND DO
Trinity Anglican Church (*Queen St;* ☎ *245 6744; www.trinitydigby.ca*) This c1878 church is thought to be one of the few churches in Canada built entirely by shipwrights. Visit the handful of sites listed below and then finish the day looking out across the water at the scallop fleet, watching the action at the wharf, then tucking in to plump, fresh, juicy scallops in one of the waterfront restaurants.

Lady Vanessa Fisheries Exhibit (☎ *245 4950; www.fundyrestaurant.com;* ⊕ *mid-May–mid-Oct; admission CAN$2*) On the waterfront by the Fundy Restaurant, look round this locally built fully restored 30m wooden scallop dragger. Interpretive panels and a 30-minute video describe the scallop-fishing process.

Admiral Digby Museum (*95 Montague Row;* ☎ *245 6322; www.admuseum.ns.ca;* ⊕ *mid-Jun–Aug 09.00–17.00 Tue–Sat; 13.00–17.00 Sun; Sep–mid-Oct 09.00–17.00 Tue–Fri; mid-Oct–mid-Jun 09.00–16.30 Wed & Fri; admission free*) In a mid-1800s Georgian house, with themed (eg: Marine and Costume) period rooms displaying artefacts in permanent and temporary exhibits. An extensive genealogy research facility (fee charged).

Digby Pines This very challenging 18-hole 6,222yd course on the Digby Pines Resort (see page 190) was designed by Stanley Thompson (1894–1953), one of Canada's most celebrated golf course architects. 'Stay & play' packages are popular. Green fees CAN$76.

Point Prim Lighthouse Worth a short drive at any time, but particularly towards sunset, is this lighthouse on the Bay of Fundy side of **Digby Gut**, the narrow opening through which the huge Bay of Fundy tides pour into the Annapolis Basin. From here, there are fine views across the Gut to the remote wooded coastline north of **Victoria Beach** (see page 210). To get there, head towards the ferry terminal but instead of turning onto Shore Road, take the next right onto Lighthouse Road. Follow Lighthouse Road to the end (about 7.5km).

DIGBY NECK

Close to Digby, what looks on a map like a thin, skeletal finger (the last two 'bones' are actually islands) stretches for almost 75km and separates the Bay of Fundy from St Mary's Bay.

Geologically, the Digby Neck, rarely more than 3km wide, is a continuation of North Mountain, which separates the Annapolis River valley from the Bay of Fundy. Both Brier and Long islands are made up of Jurassic basalt lava. As the lava cooled, it sometimes formed vertical polygonal columns such as Balancing Rock (see page 196).

The pace of life in Nova Scotia is generally pretty relaxed, but if you want to slow down even more, enjoy natural splendour, and take a holiday from your holiday, this beautiful area is worth some time.

There are few services, but just enough: pretty villages and good hiking, some of the province's best birding opportunities (see box on page 198) – and what may well be the best whale-watching opportunities along the entire east coast of North America. Although the majority of visitors drive straight to their whale-watching trip and (when it is over) drive back again, try to allow yourself more time to explore this beautiful region.

The wild flowers are out between mid-May and late June, mid-July brings wild blueberries, and soon after, humpback whales. July and August can be foggy, September and October are usually beautiful, though late October can be windy.

GETTING THERE From Digby, Highway 217 runs down the centre of the peninsula for approximately 50km to East Ferry, from where a five-minute car ferry (CAN$5 return, at half past the hour westbound) crosses to Tiverton on Long Island. Highway 217 continues along Long Island for 18km to Freeport, from where another car ferry (ten minutes, CAN$5 return) crosses to Westport on Brier Island. Ferries are timed so that if you're going straight through, you can drive directly from one ferry to the next without too much waiting.

TOURIST INFORMATION Located inside the Islands Museum (see page 196).

THE MAINLAND The first dozen kilometres along Highway 217 – a road also labelled the 'Digby Neck and Islands Scenic Drive' – is an unremarkable inland drive, but before too long there are views over St Mary's Bay and opportunities to make short side trips – for example to the Bay of Fundy shore by taking Trout Cove Road from Centreville. Gulliver's Cove-based **Fundy Adventures** (*685 Gulliver's Cove Rd;* ↘ *245 4388; www.fundyadventures.com*) organises a range of customised experiences for those looking to learn more about the Fundy Shore.

As you continue on Highway 217 along the peninsula, a pretty provincial park on the waterfront at Lake Midway offers picnic tables and freshwater swimming. Highlight of this part of Digby Neck is delightful Sandy Cove. Another worthwhile short detour is to turn onto Little River Road at Little River, and follow it to the St Mary's Bay shore.

Sandy Cove Sandy Cove, 31km from Digby, is one of the province's prettiest communities. The main part of the village is concentrated round the St Mary's Bay side of the Neck, but a short drive through the hills along Bay Road leads to a long, quiet, sandy beach on the Fundy shore. This is a fine spot from which to watch the sun set.

For a magnificent view of Sandy Cove, it is worth heading up nearby **Mount Shubel** which can be reached by a relatively easy 15–20-minute trail. The trailhead is accessed by turning off Highway 217 a few hundred metres northeast of Sandy Cove onto an unpaved road (turn right if you're coming from the Digby side, left if coming from Sandy Cove itself). There's a small parking area a short distance along the unpaved road. This road isn't named or signed, so ask a local for directions if it is not immediately obvious.

East Ferry The mainland ends at East Ferry 46km from Digby, perched atop a cliff overlooking the swirling waters of Petite Passage, and the lighthouse on Long Island.

Where to stay and eat

⌂ **Pioneer Retreat** (3 cottages) 8020 Hwy 217, Centreville; ↘ T/F 1 888 839 2590; www.digbyneck.com; ⊕ May–Dec. Come for peace & quiet on this secluded property. These 1- & 2-bedroom cottages – all with wonderful St Mary's Bay views – are comfortable with fully equipped kitchens, but don't expect TVs or phones. $$

⋏ **Whale Cove Campground** (25 sites) 50 Whale Cove Rd, Whale Cove; ↘ 834 2025; www.whalecovecampground.com; ⊕ May–Oct. Located in Whale Cove, 6km south of Sandy Cove. Some sites at this open campground with laundromat overlooking the Bay of Fundy have electricity & water hook-ups. $

JEROME

One evening in 1863, a ship was seen close to the Bay of Fundy shore at Sandy Cove. In the morning, the vessel had gone, but a strange young man sat on the sand. Although well dressed in fine linen, he was very pale: both his legs had recently been amputated above the knees. The only word he would say was 'Jerome', indicating that that was his name. Doctors, police and ministers came to question him, but he was no more loquacious. After a while, the government paid a family in Meteghan (see page 187) to take him in: Jerome spent the rest of his long life there, never uttering any other words. He died in 1912 and was buried in Meteghan parish cemetery. His story continues to fascinate.

✕ Petit Passage Café 3450 Highway 217, East Ferry; ☎ 834 2226; ⊕ May–Oct 08.30–18.00 daily. A rustic café with deck overlooking Petit Passage. The seafood chowder, soups & scallop rolls are all good, as is the blueberry pie. $

LONG ISLAND

TIVERTON A traditional fishing village with a couple of whale-watching companies (see box on page 198). The nearby Boar's Head Lighthouse is a great place to gaze out over the Bay of Fundy and try to spot whales.

What to see and do
The Islands Museum (*Hwy 217, approximately 2km from Tiverton;* ☎ *839 2853;* ⊕ *daily Jul–late Aug 09.00–18.00, late Aug–late Sep 09.00–16.00; admission free*) Exhibits on life on Long and Brier islands in days gone by, including display boards on Joshua Slocum (see box on page 197).

Balancing Rock Approximately 3.5km past Tiverton is the parking area and trailhead to Balancing Rock. The first part of the trail is relatively flat, with boardwalks over the wettest parts. You then descend over 200 steps on wooden staircases (slippery when wet) down to the cliffs from where there is a perfect view of a 9m pinnacle of basalt rock balanced on a seemingly far too narrow base. The route is approximately 1.5km each way.

FREEPORT Try and allow some time on the way or way back to explore beautiful Freeport. Although most people stay on Highway 217, instead, take the first left immediately after the church and follow Overcove Road, which eventually leads past the fishing wharves, to the end. Park and follow the trail towards Dartmouth Point. A lovely new trail (part-opened at the time of writing) leads up to a look-off and over the hill from just behind the Freeport Development Office (*243 Hwy 217*).

Where to stay and eat
🏠 Summer Solstice B&B (4 rooms) 325 Overcove Rd, Freeport, Long Island; ☎ 839 2170; www.summersolstice.ca; ⊕ mid-May–mid-Oct. Rooms with private or shared bathrooms. The breakfast room of this bright, recently renovated century house overlooks the sea. There's a rooftop balcony offering glorious views, & great hiking in walking distance. $

✕ Lavena's Catch Café 15 Hwy 217, Freeport, Long Island; ☎ 839 2517; ⊕ mid-May–early Oct 11.30–20.00 daily; off-season 11.30–18.00 usually Fri–Sun. Food at my favourite Digby Neck restaurant is freshly made: the steamed clams, seafood chowder, scallops & pan-fried haddock are all excellent. The 'chicken' bit of the chickenburger is a grilled breast, & room should be saved for one of Aunt Heather's desserts! $–$$

BRIER ISLAND

And so to the highlight of Digby Neck. For some, whale-watching apart, there will be nothing to do on 6.5km by 2.5km Brier Island. But it won't disappoint those who enjoy the atmosphere of a community little changed by the passing decades, or are just content to watch the swirling sea and pounding waves. If you're into birdwatching, wild flowers, or even just like walking, cycling or beachcombing, you won't want to leave. Virtually everyone lives in **Westport**: though the village has paved roads, only unpaved roads and walking trails cross the rest of the island.

The squat c1965 **Grand Passage Lighthouse** can be reached via Northern Point Road. Just to the west, as the name suggests, **Seal Cove** is a good place to try and spot seals. On the island's southwest side is the concrete **Brier Island Lighthouse**, one of the most photogenic in the province. To get there, take Wellington Street from Westport, then turn left onto Western Light Road. Or turn left onto Water Street from the ferry and follow the road just a few hundred metres to the end. Park, sit on the rocks and watch seabirds ride the swirling currents, with Peter Island and its 1909 lighthouse as a beautiful backdrop.

Relatively low-lying, the island has far less forest cover than most of the province. This sensitive ecological treasure has sedge and sphagnum bogs, and rare and unusual plants including eastern mountain aven, pitcher plant, dwarf birch, curly-grass fern and several types of orchid. Late spring and summer brings a profusion of wild flowers such as Queen Anne's lace, lady's slipper, blue iris, and many types of wild rose. And even those who couldn't tell an orchid from an Orkin will enjoy the abundance of wild strawberries.

Quite apart from anyone else, the island – on the Atlantic Flyway – is a must-visit for birdwatchers. Over 320 species have been noted here, and a wide variety of birds can be seen easily at all times of the year, including many rarities. Autumn is one of the best times, with the hawk migration a highlight.

 **Where to stay**

Brier Island Lodge and Restaurant (40 rooms) 557 Water St, Westport, Brier Island; ☎ 839 2300, T/F 1 800 662 8355; www.brierisland.com; ⊕ May–late Oct. Approximately 1.5km north of the village centre in a fine location on a bluff overlooking Westport & Grand Passage. Most of the rooms are in 2 modern 2-storey buildings, & these are better bets than rooms 2–10 in the main building. The upstairs rooms have the best views! In the licensed dining room (⊕ mid-Jun–mid-Oct

07.00–10.00 & 18.00–21.30 daily; $$) stick to fresh local seafood. $–$$
Brier Island Backpackers Hostel (12 beds) 225 Water St, Westport, Brier Island; ☎ 839 2273; www.brierislandhostel.com; ⊕ year-round. With 3 rooms (including 1 family room), bunk beds, shared bathrooms, good cooking facilities & a sun deck overlooks the harbour. Comfortable, friendly, & right by the well-stocked general store which has a café (⊕ early Jun–late Sep). Dorm CAN$18. $

BEAR RIVER

Don't take too much notice of tourist literature calling it 'The Switzerland of Nova Scotia', but this interesting little laid-back community with an inland riverside setting is well worth a visit. Pretty throughout the year, it is stunning in autumn when the hardwood trees blaze their colours.

Once a major shipbuilding centre, many of the village's riverside buildings are built on stilts – twice a day, those high Bay-of-Fundy tides make their way into the Annapolis Basin and up the river.

Bear River has long been renowned for its cherries, and hosts a June cherry festival (see page 198). It is said that cherry trees were brought over from England in the 18th century by one William Sutherland.

Yarmouth, French Shore and the Annapolis Valley BEAR RIVER

5

GETTING THERE Bear River is 17km/11 miles from Digby, 29km/18 miles from Annapolis Royal and 7km/4 miles from Highway 101 Exit 24.

TOURIST INFORMATION (*100 Wharf Rd;* ☎ *467 3200;* ⊕ *Jul–Aug 09.00–17.00 daily; Sep 10.00–16.00 Wed–Sun*). Housed in a windmill built by a Dutch immigrant for his homesick wife and set in a small riverside park just off Clementsvale Road.

⌂ WHERE TO STAY AND EAT

⌂ **Vineyard Haven B&B** (3 rooms) 111 Chute Rd; ☎ 467 0434; www.vineyardhaven-ns.com; ⊕ May–Oct. Century farmhouse next to a winery in hills just above the village. AC rooms share a bath. Full gourmet country b/fast (eg: lobster, eggs Benedict served with homemade home fries) & complimentary afternoon tea with home-baked treats inc. $

✗ **The Bear River Café** 1870 Clementsvale Rd; ☎ 467 0241: ⊕ May–Oct 11.00–20.30 Tue–Sun

(to 22.00 Fri–Sat); Nov–Apr 11.00–14.00 & 16.00–20.00 Tue–Thu & Sun, 11.00–21.00 Fri–Sat. Healthy homemade food with an emphasis on fresh, healthy locally grown ingredients in a stilted riverside building with lovely views. New in 2009, licence applied for. $

✗ **Changing Tides Diner** 1882 Clementsvale Rd; ☎ 467 0173; ⊕ Feb–Nov 07.30–19.30. Dependable (if not overexciting) tucker. $

FESTIVALS
Mid-June
Cherry Carnival This one-day event includes a parade, flea market, races, competitions – and lots of sweet cherries for sale.

August
Digby County Exhibition Four-day agricultural show with fairground rides, food and arts & crafts.

WHALE WATCHING ON THE BAY OF FUNDY

The warm Gulf Stream water colliding with the cold outflow from the Bay of Fundy, combined with the tremendous tidal influence on the waters in this area, produces some of the most plankton-rich waters in the world. This attracts whales, particularly baleen whales – the largest animals on earth.

Smaller species such as finback and Minke whales and harbour porpoises are plentiful early in the season, and numbers of huge humpback whales increase as June goes on. White-sided dolphins are another possibility, and in August you might see a very rare right whale. Seals are sometimes sighted, and pelagic seabirds abundant.

Most operators offer two–five-hour boat trips from June to mid-October for approximately CAN$50 (many offer a 'no whales – try again free' guarantee). It's a good idea to make reservations well in advance, especially between July and early September. The main operators are:

Brier Island Whale and Seabird Cruises Westport; ☎ 839 2995, T/F 1 800 656 3660; www.brierislandwhalewatch.com
Freeport Whale and Seabird Tours Freeport; ☎ 839 2177, T/F 1 866 866 8797
Mariner Cruises Westport; ☎ 839 2346, T/F 1 800 239 2189; www.novascotiawhalewatching.ca.
Ocean Explorations Tiverton; ☎ 839 2417, T/F 1 877 654 2341; www.oceanexplorations.ca. Uses small high-speed Zodiac (or similar) inflatable boats. Special trips, eg: dedicated to seabirds, on request. CAN$65.
Petite Passage Whale Watch East Ferry; ☎ 834 2226; www.ppww.ca
Pirate's Cove Whale Cruises Tiverton; ☎ 839 2242, T/F 1 888 480 0004; www.piratescove.ca

WHAT TO SEE AND DO Houses and churches on winding streets peer through the trees on the steep hills on both sides of the river. Be sure to stroll some of these streets to see some of the beautiful old houses, and historic churches, such as the **United Baptist Church** (*37 Pleasant St*).

Many artists and craftspeople – some very talented – now call the village home, and there are several galleries dotted all over the community including three or four on the short main street.

Longest established – and the best – is **The Flight of Fancy** (*1869 Clementsvale Rd;* \ *467 4171, T/F 1 866 467 4171; www.theflight.ca*), close to the bridge. Just around the corner, **Oddacity Designs** (\ *467 0268;* ⊕ *mid-Jun–mid-Sep 10.00–17.00 daily*) has 'wearable art' and more.

Worth seeing, too, is the atmospheric **Old Baptist/Loyalist cemetery** on Lansdowne Road near the junction with Riverview Road.

Grapes are grown on some of the hillsides and tastings are offered at **Bear River Vineyards** (*133 Chute Rd;* \ *467 4156; www.wine.travel;* ⊕ *Jun–Sep 12.00–17.00 Tue–Sun; tours offered at 14.00 & 16.00*).

Bear River Heritage Museum (*River Rd;* \ *467 0902;* ⊕ *Jul–early Sep 10.00–16.00 Mon–Sat; admission free*) Local history museum in a riverside former warehouse.

Riverview Ethnographic Museum (*18 Chute Rd;* \ *467 4321;* ⊕ *year-round 10.00–17.00 Tue–Sat; admission CAN$2*) Six rooms of authentic folk costumes and artefacts from around the globe – and Bear River.

Bear River First Nation Heritage and Cultural Centre (*194 Reservation Rd;* \ *467 0301; www.bearriverculturalcenter.com;* ⊕ *mid-May–mid-Oct 10.00–18.00 Tue–Sat (Jul–Aug daily); off-season by appointment; admission CAN$5*) Portraits of former Mi'kmaq chiefs and elders, local Mi'kmaq artefacts (some dating back 2,500–4,000 years), historical arts and crafts and a handmade authentic birch-bark canoe. Medicine Trail (1km) with medicinal trees and plants.

ANNAPOLIS ROYAL (Population: approx 500)

It is hard not to like Annapolis Royal. First, it has a delightful setting on the Annapolis Basin shore – and wonderful views across the water to the pretty village of Granville Ferry from a boardwalk with benches, picnic tables and a lighthouse. The town has a tree-lined main street, one end of which is lined with gracious mansions, many of which help make up what is the largest concentration of heritage buildings in Nova Scotia, with over 120 municipally registered properties, 20 provincial heritage properties and five federally designated properties. Several of these house some of the province's best inns and B&Bs.

You'll find lovely gardens to stroll through, and waterside trails to wander. You can also visit North America's first tidal power generating plant. There are galleries and a theatre with a good year-round programme. You can visit a historical site dating back four centuries, a museum housed in a 300-year-old building, and an early 18th-century cemetery. All of these (and more) can be reached easily on foot. A short drive will take you to the site of one of the earliest permanent European settlements in North America, a good golf course, a beautiful hiking trail to the Bay of Fundy shore, or Nova Scotia's biggest theme park.

Despite all this, Annapolis Royal only gets really busy during some of the bigger festivals.

Don't come to 'Canada's birthplace' for the nightlife (though there is a friendly little pub), but do come to soak up the history and unique atmosphere.

HISTORY Although the first Port-Royal was destroyed in 1613 (see page 210), in the early 1630s, the French built a new version 11km away, this time on the south shore of the Annapolis Basin. Things were relatively calm for a couple of decades but after that the settlement changed hands backwards and forwards between the French and British.

Back under British control in 1710, the town was renamed 'Annapolis Royal' in honour of their queen, and the fort that had seen so much fighting – and had changed hands so many times – renamed 'Fort Anne'. This time – despite almost countless French attacks – the British flag was raised to stay. Annapolis Royal served as Nova Scotia's first capital until 1749 (when it was succeeded by Halifax).

Annapolis Royal prospered and during the Great Age of Sail was a bustling town with several industries and over 3,000 inhabitants. Shipbuilding reached its peak in 1874 and was centred on Hog Island, which now forms part of the causeway crossing the Annapolis River.

Its job done, Fort Anne was abandoned in the 1850s and fell into disrepair. Following a campaign by locals to have the site preserved and maintained, Fort Anne became Canada's first administered National Historic Site in 1917.

In the late 1970s Annapolis Royal was in a state of decline. The population had dwindled and the council had no money to spend on upkeep. However, a citizen-led group formed the Annapolis Royal Development Commission and lobbied both the provincial and federal governments to inject funds to preserve the town's unique heritage. Their efforts paid off, over CAN$2 million was spent on restoration projects, and in 2004, the town was designated the 'World's Most Liveable Small Community'. The following year, the town was listed as one of five Cultural Capitals of Canada.

GETTING THERE

By car If you're coming from Highway 8, which leads to town from Exit 22 of Highway 101, as it enters town the road becomes St George Street. This continues past many beautiful houses and the Historic Gardens to a traffic light and crossroads. As you continue straight (passing the old Courthouse and Fort Anne on your left, St George Street curves downhill to the shopping district and the wharf. If you're coming from Bridgetown on Highway 1, you'll cross the causeway over the Annapolis River, passing the Tidal Generating Station and tourist office on your left, and arrive at the crossroads and traffic light, the junction with St George Street.

By bus Annapolis Royal is on the Weymouth–Bridgetown Kings County bus route (see page 190) and on the Digby–Halifax Acadian bus route (see page 52).

TOURIST INFORMATION

Annapolis Royal Visitor Information Centre 236 Prince Albert Rd (Hwy 1); 532 5454; ⊕ mid/end May & early/mid-Sep 10.00–16.00 daily; Jun–Aug 09.00–19.00 daily. In the tidal power plant on the north side of town.

 WHERE TO STAY See also Granville Ferry (see page 209), less than 2km away.

Queen Anne Inn (14 rooms) 494 Upper St George St; 532 7850, T/F 1 877 536 0403; www.queenanneinn.ns.ca; ⊕ May–Nov. A striking c1865 grey & white Heritage mansion with a magnificent sweeping mahogany staircase. 10 large bedrooms in main building & 2 2-bedroom suites in Carriage House. There is also a restaurant (see page 203). Grand, but the atmosphere is relaxed. Full b/fast inc. $$$

At the Turret B&B (4 rooms) 372 St George St; 532 5770; T/F 1 866 717 0067; e turretinfo@attheturret.com; www.attheturret.com; ⊕ year-round. A centrally located (turreted!) c1900s' property with original woodwork, stained

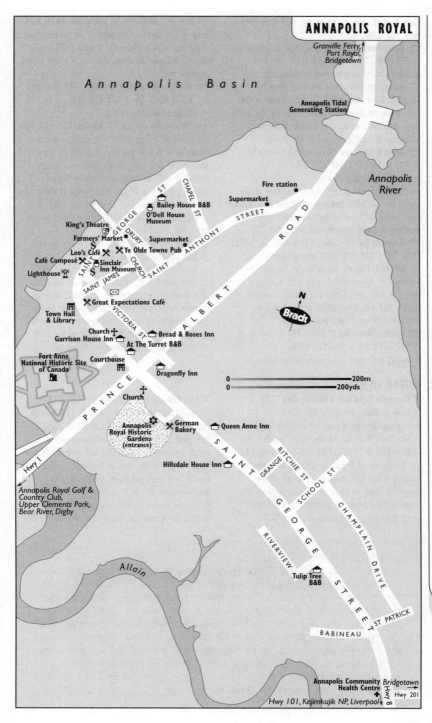

ANNAPOLIS ROYAL

Granville Ferry,
Port Royal,
Bridgetown

Annapolis Basin

Annapolis Tidal
Generating Station

Annapolis
River

Fire station

Supermarket

Bailey House B&B

O'Dell House
Museum

King's Theatre

Farmers' Market

Supermarket

Leo's Café

Ye Olde Towne Pub

Café Composé

Sinclair
Inn Museum

Lighthouse

Great Expectations Café

Town Hall
& Library

Church

Bread & Roses Inn

Garrison House Inn

At The Turret B&B

Fort Anne
National Historic Site
of Canada

Courthouse

Dragonfly Inn

Church

Annapolis
Royal Historic
Gardens
(entrance)

German
Bakery

Queen Anne Inn

Hillsdale House Inn

Tulip Tree
B&B

Annapolis Royal Golf &
Country Club,
Upper Clements Park,
Bear River, Digby

Hwy 1

Allain

Annapolis Community Health Centre

Bridgetown

Hwy 201

Hwy 101, Kejimkujik NP, Liverpool

N

Bradt

0   200m
0   200yds

glass, & large veranda, across the road from Fort Anne. Full b/fast inc. $$

⌂ **Bailey House B&B** (4 rooms) 150 St George St; ✆ 532 1285, T/F 1 877 532 1285; e info@baileyhouse.ca; www.baileyhouse.ca; ⏰ year-round. Just across the road from the Annapolis Basin, this c1770 Georgian home is the best choice for those who want to be by the water. Large bedrooms, en-suite or private bathrooms, waterfront & back gardens. Full b/fast inc. $$

⌂ **Bread & Roses Inn** (9 rooms) 82 Victoria St; ✆ 532 5727, T/F 1 888 899 0551; e rosesinn@ns.aliantzinc.ca; www.breadandroses.ns.ca; ⏰ Apr–Nov. One of the town's few old brick buildings in Queen Anne Revival style from c1882 with large bedrooms, superb wood panelling & lovely gardens. Full b/fast inc. $$

⌂ **Dragonfly Inn** (9 rooms) 124 Victoria St; ✆ 532 7936, T/F 1 877 943 2378; www.dragonflyinn.ca; ⏰ Apr–Nov. 3 lovely rooms in the main c1870 building (⏰ Apr–mid-Oct only), with 6 cheaper rooms in the Coach House just behind. Centrally located. Full b/fast inc (B&B) or, Jul–Sep only, continental b/fast (Coach House). $$

⌂ **Garrison House Inn** (7 units) 350 St George St; ✆ 532 5750, T/F 1 866 532 5750; e info@garrisonhouse.ca; www.garrisonhouse.ca;

⏰ May–Oct; off-season by reservation. Facing Fort Anne & the Garrison cemetery is this purpose-built c1854 inn with 6 bedrooms, 1 suite (with large jacuzzi) & period furniture. A la carte b/fast offered at extra cost. $$

⌂ **Hillsdale House Inn** (13 rooms) 519 St George St; ✆ 532 2345, T/F 1 877 839 2821; e info@hillsdalehouseinn.ca; www.hillsdalehouseinn.ca; ⏰ Apr–Nov. Set back from the street on a 5ha estate with manicured lawns, stately trees & fine gardens. 11 rooms in the c1859 main house & 2 more in the adjacent Carriage House, all individually decorated with antiques. Former guests include the then Prince of Wales (who went on to become King George V) in 1884, & author John Buchan in 1937. Licensed bar (guests only). Full b/fast inc. $$

⌂ **Tulip Tree B&B** (3 units) 683 St George St; ✆ 532 0151, T/F 1 866 532 1051; e reservations@tuliptree.ca; www.tuliptree.ca; ⏰ year-round. A gracious 100-year-old Georgian-style home set in landscaped gardens. 2 bedrooms in main house, plus comfortable, spacious 1-room (plus en-suite) cottage. Breakfast choices might be, eg: salmon quiche with croissant, or waffles with caramelised apples & cranberries. B/fast inc. $$

✖ WHERE TO EAT

✖ **Annapolis Royal Golf & Country Club** 3816 Highway 1, Allains Creek; ✆ 532 2064; www.annapolisroyalgolf.com; ⏰ mid-May–Sep 11.00–20.00 Mon–Sat, 11.00–18.00 Sun; Oct–May 11.00–14.00 & 17.00–19.30 Tue–Sat, 11.00–18.00 Sun. British-owned & run: in addition to scallops, haddock & the like, don't be surprised to see bangers & mash or steak pie. Choose between the casual bar/restaurant or intimate, candlelit fine-dining (reservations required). Licensed. $$

✖ **Café Composé** 235 St George St; ✆ 532 1251; ⏰ mid-May–mid-Oct 11.30–14.30 & 17.00–20.00 Mon–Sat, mid-Oct–mid-May 11.30–14.30 Mon–Sat. This good European-style café/restaurant/bistro is stylish, (relatively) sophisticated and centrally located in the large building next to the little Lighthouse. The food is very good (schnitzels, scallops & more) & the deck a delight. Pop in even if you just want a coffee & piece of strudel to keep you going. There are plans to open for dinner Thu–Sat in the off-season. $$

OF MOOSE AND MEN

It is said that in the 1790s, Prince Edward, Duke of Kent (and father of Queen Victoria), was surprised embracing an attractive serving girl at the c1708 deGannes-Cosby House at 477 George Street, now a private residence and the oldest documented wooden structure in Nova Scotia. Incidentally, the house is said to be haunted, but only by a quiet, well-mannered old lady who never bothers anyone. During the same visit the duke attended a ball held at what later became known as the Bailey House. In the 1830s, the house's owner, 'Marm' Bailey, was renowned for her 'moose muffle soup' (the muffle is the nose and the pendulous, overhanging upper lip of the moose). The Bailey House is now an elegant B&B (see above). Moose muffle soup is not on the breakfast menu.

✕ Garrison House Inn 350 St George St; ✆ 532 5750, T/F 1 866 532 5750; e info@garrisonhouse.ca; www.garrisonhouse.ca; ⏰ mid-May–late Oct 17.00–21.00 daily. The restaurant has 3 intimate rooms, a screened, heated veranda facing Fort Anne & the best choice in the area for fine-dining, especially when owner/chef Patrick Redgrave is cooking. The eclectic menu draws on high-quality fresh local & organic produce. Start, perhaps, with the cold applewood-smoked salmon plate before moving on to lobster risotto with shiitake mushrooms, or perhaps steamed Digby scallops with roasted tomato, feta cheese & tarragon, tossed in rotini pasta. The wine list is relatively short, but well chosen. Reservations recommended. **$$**

✕ Queen Anne Inn 494 Upper St George St; ✆ 532 7850, T/F 1 877 536 0403; www.queenanneinn.ns.ca; ⏰ May–Oct 17.00–21.00 Tue–Sat. The licensed dining room of this heritage mansion has an eclectic menu offering local fare with a global influence – lobster, scallops, free-range chicken, organic beef & more. Alfresco dining Fri–Sat, weather permitting. **$$**

✕ Ye Olde Towne Pub 9–11 Church St; ✆ 532 2244; ⏰ year-round 11.00–23.00 Mon–Fri, 10.00–23.00

Sat, 12.00–20.00 Sun. This pub in a c1884 former bank has a popular outside deck. Generally, food is good & reasonably priced – particularly the daily specials. **$$**

✕ German Bakery & Garden Café 441 St George St; ✆ 532 1990; ⏰ mid-May–mid-Oct 10.00–18.00 daily. Accessed via the car park of the Annapolis Royal Historic Gardens, this café offers a simple lunch/snack menu (sandwiches, bratwurst, schnitzel, etc). The bakery itself (⏰ 09.00–18.00 daily) has a range of relatively pricey bread, rolls, & baked goods. **$**

✕ Great Expectations 302 St George St; ✆ 532 0120; ⏰ May–Dec 10.00–17.00 daily, Jan–Apr 10.00–17.00 Fri–Sat. Part used bookshop, part antique shop, part handmade-chocolate seller, & part café (excellent coffee, iced tea, lemonade, a few snacks) located opposite the library. **$**

✕ Leo's Café 222 St George St; ✆ 532 7424. Located in the c1712 Adams-Ritchie House, this is Annapolis Royal's best spot for a light lunch (salads, soup, wraps, gourmet sandwiches, etc), fantastic cakes & sublime cinnamon rolls. **$**

ENTERTAINMENT

🎭 **King's Theatre** 209 St George St; ✆ 532 7704; www.kingstheatre.ca. This c1921 theatre has an art

gallery on site, and a varied programme (year-round) including theatre, films and live music.

FESTIVALS
August
Natal Days A street parade, community events such as pancake breakfasts, and family activities in and around town.

December
Victorian Christmas Some of the town's magnificent old houses (and their gardens) are decorated and illuminated for the festive season. Parade, craft market, carol concerts.

OTHER PRACTICALITIES

$ Royal Bank 248 St George St; ✆ 532 2371; ⏰ 10.00–15.00 Mon–Wed, 10.00–17.00 Thu–Fri

$ Scotiabank 219 St George St; ✆ 532 2393; ⏰ 10.00–17.00 Mon–Fri

✚ Annapolis Community Health Centre 821 St George St; ✆ 532 2381

📖 **Annapolis Royal Library** 285 St George St; ✆ 532 2226; ⏰ 14.00–17.00 & 18.30–20.30 Mon, 10.00–17.00 Wed & Fri, 10.00–17.00 & 18.30–20.30 Thu, 10.00–14.00 Sat

✉ **Post office** 50 Victoria St; ⏰ 08.00–17.00 Mon–Fri, 09.00–12.00 Sat

WHAT TO SEE AND DO Out-of-season visitors will find many things closed, but the population is less seasonal than in some towns and there's still a little bit of life.

Annapolis Royal Historic Gardens *(441 St George St; ✆ 532 7018; www.historicgardens.com; ⏰ mid-May–Jun & Sep–mid-Oct 09.00–17.00 daily; Jul–Aug 08.00–dusk daily; admission CAN$8.50)* These 7ha gardens opened in 1981 and were

designed to reflect the various periods of local history through a gardening perspective. The Annapolis Valley climate allows a real diversity of plants to be grown: highlights include a Victorian garden, Governor's garden, innovative garden and rose collection – with around 2,000 bushes of more than 240 cultivars. See too the replica of a 1671 Acadian house, complete with thatched roof and an Acadian garden. A wonderful resource for heritage gardening enthusiasts. On-site café.

Annapolis Tidal Generating Station
(*Hwy 1;* ✎ *532 5454;* ⊕ *mid-May–mid-Oct 09.00–17.00 daily (Jul–Aug to 20.00); admission free*) Situated on the causeway across the Annapolis River is the first tidal power plant in the western hemisphere. The plant generates over 30 million kWh of electricity per year, enough to power over 4,000 homes.

Fort Anne National Historic Site of Canada
(*St George St;* ✎ *532 2321; www.pc.gc.ca/fortanne;* ⊕ *daily mid-May–mid-Oct 09.00–17.30 (Jul–Aug to 18.00); off-season weekdays by appointment; site & grounds* ⊕ *year-round; admission CAN$3.90 museum – grounds free*) One of Canada's most important historic sites (see *History*, page 200). Beside the car park and opposite the old parade ground is the distinctive c1797 officers' quarters built by the British which now houses a museum telling the story of the fort and the Acadians in the area.

Be sure to see the 2.4m x 5.5m Heritage Tapestry, which depicts four centuries of European settlement in Annapolis Royal. Over 100 volunteers worked on the project, and even the Queen – on a 1994 state visit to Nova Scotia – chipped in with a few stitches. Outside, see the restored c1708 French gunpowder magazine, and another gunpowder magazine which was later used as a dungeon. The fort's earthworks are the best-surviving example of a Vauban fort in North America: expansive grassy ramparts and grounds overlook the Annapolis Basin and the mouths of the Annapolis and Allain rivers, and lead right down to the water's edge. Even if you're not interested in history, come for a wander, the views, a picnic, or just to let the kids roll down the slopes.

Part of the site is the Garrison Cemetery. Originally the burial grounds for the French military forces here, it later served both the British military and the local parish. The earliest tombstone still in place dates from 1720. Between June and mid-October, an entertaining candlelight graveyard tour is offered by the local Historical Society on Sunday, Tuesday and Thursday evenings.

O'Dell House Museum
(*136 Lower St George St;* ✎ *532 7754; www.annapolisheritagesociety.com;* ⊕ *year-round; hours vary; admission CAN$3*) The c1869 former home and tavern of Corey O'Dell, once a rider on the Pony Express run (see page 211). The downstairs rooms reflect a house of the 1870–1900 period. Upstairs is an Age of Sail display. The museum offers a genealogical centre and archival research facilities.

Sinclair Inn Museum
(*232 St George St;* ✎ *532 7754; www.annapolisheritagesociety.com;* ⊕ *Jun–Aug 09.00–17.00 Mon–Sat, 12.30–17.00 Sun; Sep–mid-Oct 09.00–17.00 Tue–Sat; admission CAN$3*) One of the most significant buildings in Canada, this structure, the front part of which was built in 1710, offers a fascinating insight into the construction techniques of the Acadians – where clay and straw were forced into the wall cavities as insulation – to the (relatively) modern. The building and town's history is brought to life by a series of ten projected 'ghosts', each representing a person who lived or worked in the building from its construction through to the 1950s.

Annapolis Royal Golf and Country Club (*3816 Hwy 1;* \ *532 2064; www.annapolisroyalgolf.com;* ⊕ *approximately Apr–Oct*) A short 5,417yd course, but worth playing, not least for the wonderful views. Weekends apart, you shouldn't need to book a tee time. Green fees CAN$39.

Upper Clements Park (*2931 Hwy 1, Upper Clements;* \ *532 7557, T/F 1 888 248 4567; www.upperclementspark.com;* ⊕ *late Jun–early Sep 11.00–18.45 daily*) Disneyland it isn't, but very few come away from the province's largest theme park disappointed.

There is a whole host of rides and things to do and see, from mini-golf and pedal go-karts to giant waterslides and a rollercoaster. Live entertainment and fireworks Sat evenings from mid-July to late August. Best value (from a range of admission possibilities) is a CAN$26.55 Premium bracelet. Admission includes entry to the wildlife park. The park may close if thunderstorms are forecast.

Just across the road is the **Upper Clements Wildlife Park** (⊕ *May–Oct 10.00–17.00 daily (late Jun–early Sep to 19.00); admission CAN$5*). Take the trail through the forest to see a range of the province's indigenous wildlife, including black bear, deer, moose, wild cats and Sable Island horses.

Both parks are on Highway 1, 7km from Annapolis Royal, and are on the Weymouth–Bridgetown bus route (see page 190).

Farmers' Market (⊕ *mid-May–mid-Oct 08.00–13.00 Sat (plus Jul–Aug Wed pm)*) Offering both produce and crafts.

KEJIMKUJIK NATIONAL PARK

Highway 8 running south from Annapolis Royal presents the quckest route to visit Nova Scotia's beautiful Kejimkujik National Park and National Historic Site (*Hwy 8;* \ *682 2772; www.pc.gc.ca/pn-np/ns/kejimkujik; adult park entry fee CAN$5.80/day*). It is made up of two geographically separate sections, the smaller of which – Kejimkujik Seaside – is described on page 164.

Those familiar with some of North America's national parks might not 'get' Keji, at 38,000ha the Maritimes' largest inland national park. Don't come here expecting magnificent sweeping panoramas, soaring mountains, towering waterfalls or vast canyons – this is a place of woodlands, lakes studded with islands, rivers and streams, best viewed not from a car window but on foot, from the saddle of a mountain bike, or, best of all by staying for a few nights, camping and travelling along the waterways by canoe – as the Mi'kmaq did for so long.

HISTORY The Mi'kmaq inhabited – or at least regularly passed through – this area for thousands of years, travelling by canoe and foot, hunting, fishing and camping. Some Mi'kmaq petroglyphs/pictographs dating from the 18th and 19th centuries have survived: these depict scenes of Mi'kmaq family life, hunting and fishing. Their locations are normally closed to public access, but on occasions they can be viewed on guided walks led by Mi'kmaq guides.

THE ROAD TO KEJI

Highway 8 leads south from Annapolis Royal, under Exit 22 of Highway 101 and on to Kejimkujik National Park (see above) 47km away, and then on to Liverpool (see page 156) 115km away. Just off Highway 8, 27km from Annapolis Royal, the **Raven Haven South Milford HI-Hostel** (*4 beds; Virginia Rd, West Springhill;* \ *532 7320;* ⊕ *mid-Jun–Aug;* $) is on the shore of Sandy Bottom Lake.

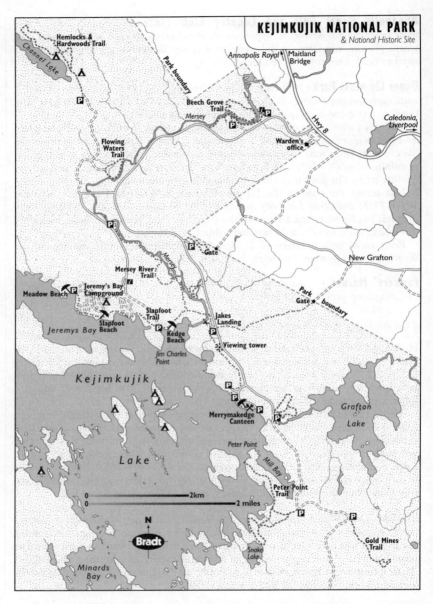

KEJIMKUJIK NATIONAL PARK
& National Historic Site

Almost half of the land that the park occupies was farmed by European settlers, and the whole park area was logged at some stage since the early 17th century.

Prospectors established three small (ultimately unproductive) gold mines at the end of the 19th century – the remains of one can be visited on one of the hiking trails.

In more recent times, the region became popular with hunters and anglers: to accommodate them, lodges were built around Kejimkujik Lake. The national park was established in 1967.

GEOGRAPHY AND GEOLOGY The last glaciation, which began approximately 90,000 years ago and ended 11,000 years ago, was responsible for the erratics (glacier-transported rock fragments), eskers (long winding ridges deposited by meltwater from glaciers), drumlins (hills carved by receding glaciers), shallow lakes, streams and rivers seen today.

Although fresh water covers some 12% of the park, hard rock such as slate, granite and quartzite yields precious few natural minerals to the rivers and streams, meaning that waters are low in the nutrients required to support large quantities of aquatic life. The park's waters have always had a relatively high acidity, but the effects of acid rain, the vast majority of which results from airborne chemical pollutants emitted from factories outside the province, hasn't helped. However, the colour of the water – generally brown – is not a sign of pollution: it is stained by tannin from plants.

FLORA AND FAUNA Black bears are present throughout the park, though sightings are rare and tend to be in the park's southern and western reaches. Beaver lodges and dams can be seen on many waterways, and white-tailed deer, muskrat, otter and porcupine are common. The coyote was first sighted in the park in 1985, and is still rare, as are the American marten and southern flying squirrel (see page 24).

The park is home to five snake species, including the rare Eastern ribbon snake, and three turtles, one of which, the Blanding's turtle, is on the Endangered list. The chances of spotting salamanders and frogs are very good.

Six species of woodpecker, including the pileated woodpecker and the rare black-backed woodpecker, and 20 species of warbler contribute to the park's 200 or so bird species. Most common of the owls is the great barred owl, and the call of the common loon delights many campers after dark. Rarities include the scarlet tanager, great crested flycatcher and the wood thrush.

Kejimkujik's vascular plant count is close to 550 including 90 species of woody plants, over 20 ferns, 15 orchids, and almost 40 aquatic species. Wild flowers are at their best between late May and the end of June.

The park's forest cover is representative of the Atlantic Uplands forest region, including a mix of coniferous and deciduous species. Whilst most areas have been logged over the centuries, some stands of old growth Eastern hemlock and sugar maple-yellow birch can still be found.

The 12 fish species include white and yellow perch, brown bullhead (one of the catfish family), eel, and brook trout.

GETTING THERE

By car The park's entrance is off Highway 8, which connects Liverpool – and Highway 103 Exit 19 – with Annapolis Royal – and Highway 101 Exit 22. It is approximately 70km/43 miles from Liverpool and 48km/30 miles from Annapolis Royal, and 160km/99 miles from Halifax via Highways 103 and 8.

By bus The only regular public transport is the hop-on hop-off tour offered by Salty Bear (see page 54).

WHERE TO STAY AND EAT Overnighting within the park's boundaries means camping – the best way to truly experience Kejimkujik. **Jeremy's Bay Campground** (514 335 4813, T/F 1 877 737 3783; www.pccamping.ca; ⊕ May–Oct; $) has over 350 sites. In season, there are washrooms, sinks for dishwashing and a shower block (but no electrical or sewage hook-ups): between November and April you'll have to manage with pit toilets. Reservations are recommended.

For those looking for more solitude, 46 backcountry campsites are situated in beautiful wilderness settings, scattered along hiking trails and canoe routes. Each individual site has a fire box, picnic table, pit toilet, firewood, and a food storage device. For reservations for wilderness camping (✆ 682 2772).

You can grab a bite at the **Merrymakedge canteen** (⊕ *Jul–Aug 10.00–20.00 daily*), located at the supervised swimming beach.

Outside, less than 4km from the park entrance road is the c1912 **Whitman Inn** (*8 units; 12389 Hwy 8, Kempt;* ✆ *682 2226, T/F 1 800 830 3855; www.whitmaninn.com;* ⊕ *year-round;* $) has good facilities, such as a nice heated indoor pool and sauna, and a well-regarded dining room open for breakfast (*08.00–09.30*) and dinner (*18.00–20.00; Oct–Jun by reservation only;* $$).

Also very convenient, the **Mersey River Chalets** (*16 units; 315 Mersey River Chalets Rd, Maitland Bridge;* ✆ *T/F 1 877 667 2583; www.merseyriverchalets.com;* ⊕ *year-round;* $$) has a nice setting and offers rooms in a lodge, two sizes of chalet (all very comfortable), and – for the more adventurous – five *tipis* (Native American-style tents). There's a good restaurant (⊕ *May–Sep & Jul–Aug 08.00–10.00 & 18.00–20.00 daily; call for days/times May, Jun & Sep;* $$).

At 24km north of the park entrance, the long-established **Milford House Lakeside Cabins** (*27 cabins; 5296 Hwy 8, South Milford;* ✆ *532 2617, T/F 1 877 532 5751; www.milfordhouse.ca;* ⊕ *late Jun–mid-Oct;* $$) offers rustic but comfortable cabins in wooded surroundings. Activites include lake swimming, tennis, croquet and pedal boats. The dining room (⊕ *late Jun–mid-Oct 18.00–20.00; by reservation only for non-guests;* $$) dishes up good food: the menu is short but always features salads: main courses include a seafood and a vegetarian option.

Almost directly opposite the park entrance is a great little eatery, unpretentious, friendly and well-priced, **M & W Restaurant and Variety Store** (*644 Hwy 8, Maitland Bridge;* ✆ *682 2189;* ⊕ *mid-May–mid-Oct 08.00–21.00 daily;* $–$$).

Camping apart, the budget option is in Caledonia, 15km from the park entrance. The **Caledonia Country Hostel** (*8 beds; 9960 Hwy 8, Caledonia;* ✆ *682 2955;* e *sharon_dan@hotmail.com ; www.caledoniacountryhostel.com;* ⊕ *year-round;* $) offers two mini-dorms each with three beds, and a private double room. Bedding is provided, and there is a communal kitchen and deck (with barbecue), and a lounge. If you don't have your own transport the hostel can arrange to pick you up/drop you off or recommend a shuttle company. Dorm CAN$25, private room CAN$60.

Caledonia has a grocery shop, liquor store (off licence), and a couple of fast-food restaurants. There's also a **tourist office** – **Caledonia VIC** (✆ *682 2470; www.caledoniavic@piczo.com;* ⊕ *early Jun–early Oct 10.00–17.00 daily*). A **Farmers' Market** (*May–Oct; Sat*) offers local produce.

ACTIVITIES For the day visitor, there are 15 designated hiking trails to explore, ranging from a 300m loop to a 3.5km each-way riverside wander. The trails are generally pretty flat, so hiking here is more about enjoying the forest, waterways, and animal, bird and plant life than gazing out over far-reaching panoramas. They might not be the giant redwoods of California, but the 300-year-old stand of towering hemlock is pretty impressive: view these and other hardwoods on the aptly

---

WHAT'S IN A NAME?

Few dispute the fact that the derivation of the name Kejimkujik is from a Mi'kmaq word or expression. However, many translations are bandied about, including 'swollen waters' and 'attempting to escape'. Call me juvenile, but my favourite is 'swelled private parts' – puzzlingly said to be in reference to the effort required to row across the park's largest lake. Just about everyone calls the park 'Keji'.

Nova Scotia is probably at its prettiest in autumn, when the province's forests are a blaze of yellow-, auburn- and rust-coloured leaves (SH) page 22

top Cheticamp's Museum of the Hooked Rug includes the Elizabeth LeFort Gallery — her exquisite rugs now grace the walls of Buckingham Palace, the White House, and the Vatican
(NSTB) page 302

left Joe's Scarecrows — near Belle Cote on the Cabot Trail — have been attracting tourists since 1946
(NSTB) page 301

bottom Book a tour of the UNESCO-listed Joggins Fossil Cliffs at the Joggins Fossil Centre — home to 300-million-year-old fossils
(NSTB) page 256

above left   29% of Nova Scotians hail from Scottish ancestry and Celtic traditions are upheld with relish: caber toss competition at Antigonish's Festival of the Tartans (NSTB) page 280

above right   Celtic Colours Festival: a nine-day Celtic music event held every October (NSTB) page 293

below left   Farmers' market selling home-grown produce and crafts, Annapolis Royal (NSTB) page 205

below right   Gorge yourself on scallops at the Digby Scallop Days Festival (NSTB) page 193

above   **Nova Scotia's terrain lends itself well to cycling, particularly Yarmouth and Cape Breton Island** (NSTB) page 63

left   **Tidal bore-rafting on the Shubenacadie River** (NSTB) page 237

below   **Take to the slopes at Wentworth** (NSTB) page 270

top   Hiking trails can be found all over the province, but some of the best are to be found in Cape Chignecto Provincial Park and Cape Split (NSTB) page 64

above   Carters Beach is unspoilt perfection and a prime contender for the 'Most Beautiful Beach in Nova Scotia' title (DO) page 163

right   Surfers should head for Lawrencetown — home to the province's most consistent waves (NSTB) page 347

above left   Look for bald eagles around Bras d'Or Lake in summer and Sheffield Mills in winter (NSTB) page 33

above right   White-tailed deer can be seen wild across much of the province (NSTB) page 170

below   Grey seals: one of four species in Nova Scotia blamed by fishermen for decimating fish stocks (NSTB) page 27

above Moose are solitary creatures, but come together during September and October for the mating season (NSTB) page 24

below Lynx can only be found in the northern highlands of Cape Breton Island (SH) page 24

Kayaking at White Point, Cape Breton Island (NSTB) page 309

named 6km Hemlocks and Hardwoods loop. The 3km return **Gold Mines Trail** leads – as you might have guessed – to an old gold mine (see *History*, page 205). For a good overview of woodlands and riverside, I would recommend combining the **Mersey River Trail** (3.5km one way) with the 3.2km **Slapfoot Trail**.

Mountain bikers will want to try the 4km **Peter Point Trail** and the 18km **Fire Tower Road Trail**. Bikes can be hired at **Jake's Landing** (↘ *682 5253;* e *jakes@ns.sympatico.ca; www.friendsofkeji.ns.ca/jakes/;* ⊕ *mid-May–mid-Oct*): this is also the place to rent canoes and kayaks (from CAN$7.75/hour).

Canoeing has always been the best way to explore Kejimkujik. There are spectacular routes for a wilderness camping trip, or for a day paddle: at very least rent a canoe for an hour or two. The dark, warm waters are also great for swimming.

The fishing season (for which a special licence is required) runs from April to August.

A range of interpretive activities (free with park admission) include canoe events, hikes, children's programmes, concerts and tours to see Mi'kmaq petroglyphs.

Autumn brings a blaze of colours as a backdrop for camping, canoeing, and hiking: winter means conditioned ski trails – and hot apple cider at the visitor centre.

GRANVILLE FERRY

There are fine views across the water to Annapolis Royal, especially in the afternoon – when the sun is further west, and several more elegant old houses nearby at the pretty, laid-back village of Granville Ferry, just across the causeway from Annapolis Royal. If the weather's clement, it's a pleasant walk or easy cycle ride.

GETTING THERE

By car Granville Ferry is on Highway 1, just 1km/0.6 miles from Annapolis Royal and 22km/14 miles from Bridgetown, 9km/6 miles from Exit 22 of Highway 101.

By bus Granville Ferry is on the Weymouth–Bridgetown bus route (see page 190).

WHERE TO STAY AND EAT

⌂ **A Seafaring Maiden** (3 rooms) 5287 Granville Rd, ↘ 532 0379, T/F 1 888 532 0379; www.aseafaringmaiden.com; ⊕ year-round. This beautifully decorated c1881 home has a veranda overlooking Annapolis Royal, Fort Anne & the Annapolis River basin. Full gourmet b/fast inc. $$

Å **Dunromin Waterfront Campground** (207 sites) 4618 Hwy 1; ↘ 532 2808; www.dunromincampsite.com; ⊕ May–mid-Oct. Open & wooded sites, serviced & unserviced, on the bank of the Annapolis River. Laundry, grocery store, café (see below), pool, activities including boat rental & kayak lessons/trips. $

✖ **Sweet Secret Restaurant** 4784 Hwy 1; ↘ 532 0909; ⊕ mid-Apr–mid-Oct 18.30–21.00 daily. Another slightly unprepossessing location, but this licensed restaurant serves reliable seafood & European cuisine (for example, schnitzel). $$

✖ **Stone Horse Café** 4616 Hwy 1; ↘ 532 5554; ⊕ May–mid-Oct 11.30–19.30 daily. Not a deep-fryer in sight, just good healthy, tasty homemade food at this simple unpretentious café. Soups, salads & sandwiches at lunch, more substantial fare in the evening. Garden patio for warmer weather. $

WHAT TO SEE AND DO

North Hills Museum (*5065 Granville Rd;* ↘ *532 2168; www.museum.gov.ns.ca/nhm/;* ⊕ *Jun–mid-Oct 09.30–17.30 Mon–Sat, 15.00–17.30 Sun; admission CAN$3*) Having crossed the causeway, take the first left onto Granville Road. The museum is on the right, 4km past the centre of the village. Housed in a charming, superbly restored c1764 salt box-style farmhouse with Georgian décor. Inside is a wonderful collection of antiques including 18th-century paintings, furniture, ceramics, and glassware.

Kayaking If you feel like getting out on the water, kayaking introduction and tours (two–eight hours) exploring the Annapolis Basin are offered by Dunromin Waterfront Campground (see page 209).

Port-Royal National Historic Site *(Granville Rd;* ☎ *532 2898; www.pc.gc.ca/portroyal;* ⊕ *daily mid-May–mid-Oct 09.00–17.30 (Jul–Aug to 18.00); admission CAN$3.90)* Offers a fascinating look into the life of early European settlers in the New World, and is one of the most historically important sites in not just Canada, but the whole of North America. Accessible toilets are located by the car park.

History In 1604, Sieur de Mons and Samuel de Champlain (from France) established a permanent camp, naming it 'Port-Royal': their Habitation was the first permanent European settlement north of St Augustine, Florida. To keep morale high, in 1606, de Champlain set up North America's first social club, *L'Ordre de Bon Temps* (usually translated as the 'Order of Good Cheer'). Fine food and drink helped distract the settlers from the hardships of life in this remote outpost.

De Champlain established fine gardens with reservoirs and canals, and he built a summer house among trees. The gardens are marked clearly on his 1607 map, the original of which is at the Congress Library in Washington, DC.

The French settlers got on very well with the area's original residents, the Mi'kmaq, and when Sieur de Mons's monopoly was revoked in 1607, the habitation was left in the care of Mi'kmaq chief Membertou. The Mi'kmaq chief did a fine job, and when the French returned in 1610, De Mons's successor, Jean, Sieur de Poutrincourt encouraged Membertou and the Mi'kmaq to convert to Catholicism. A force commissioned to expel all Frenchmen from territory claimed by England, led by Samuel Argall from Virginia, arrived in 1613 whilst the inhabitants were away up the river. The habitation was looted and destroyed.

In 1939–40, the Canadian government built a reconstruction of the c1605 French fur-trading post based on de Champlain's drawings. Where possible, 17th-century construction techniques were used. The buildings form a rectangle around a courtyard and are fortified by a stockade, with two cannon platforms at the southerly corners. A well dug by de Champlain is in the centre of the courtyard. See a blacksmith's shop, kitchen, communal dining room, guardroom, artisans' quarters and more: costumed interpreters are on hand to provide more details.

Getting there The site is 10km/6 miles from Granville Ferry and 12km/7 miles from Annapolis Royal.

VICTORIA BEACH

Rather than turning back after visiting Port-Royal, if time allows consider making a pleasant side trip to Victoria Beach. As you drive, there are fine views over the Annapolis Basin and the narrow, turbulent currents and whirlpools of the **Digby Gut**. Victoria Beach doesn't have a beach to speak of, or much to see other than a large wharf, a colourful collection of boats and a small lighthouse. It does, however, have a storied past and numerous ghost stories emanate from the community. Tales of the sounds of vessels docking but no visible signs of ships, of men dressed in clothes from bygone days who greet people on the path and then disappear into thin air, of a sailor who had died at sea returning each night to stand on the doorstep of his house leaving a puddle of seawater and seaweed, of several sightings of the Grey Lady (see page 348), and even a sea serpent with a huge head and eyes which reared up out of the water.

In the 1940s, the village was the home of historical novelist Evelyn Eaton, best known for *Quietly My Captain Waits*.

GETTING THERE Victoria Beach is at the western end of Granville Road, 25km/16 miles from Granville Ferry and 27km/17 miles from Annapolis Royal. The road ends in uninhabited coastline at this point and you will have to go back along Granville Road to return to Port-Royal or head north towards Delap's Cove.

DELAP'S COVE

The only reason to head out to this remote area is to hike the Delap's Cove Wilderness Trails (see below). There's a rustic loo at the trailhead parking area, but no other services.

GETTING THERE Either take Parkers Mountain Road from Highway 1, just east of Granville Ferry, or (a bit quicker) take the unpaved Hollow Mountain Road from Granville Road just east of Port-Royal. Either way, turn left at the T-junction and follow Shore Road West. Look for a sign on the left to Delap's Cove Wilderness Trail. It's approximately 17km from Granville Ferry by the shorter route.

WHAT TO SEE AND DO
Bohaker Loop Wilderness Trail This remote area, off Shore Road West, offers good hiking. The best trail is the 2.2km Bohaker Loop which leads from the trailhead car park through softwoods and hardwoods to the rocky Bay of Fundy shore, onto a fascinating rock cove jammed with driftwood, flotsam and a wrecked boat. The sure-footed can descend to the cove via steep natural basalt steps (watch out for the incoming tide). On the other side of the cove, Bohaker's Brook drops over the cliff edge as a 12m waterfall. There's a look-off right by the top of the cascade, and the trail follows the brook upstream before curving back to the parking area.

PARKER'S COVE

On the Bay of Fundy shore over North Mountain from Granville Ferry, less than 10km from Granville Ferry and Annapolis Royal, Parker's Cove is a working fishing village with a lobster pound where the crustacean can be purchased live or cooked.

PONY EXPRESS

Early in 1849, six American news organisations clubbed together to finance a *pony express*. A steamer arrived in Halifax from England bringing newspapers from Europe. These were transported by a relay team of horseback couriers from Halifax to Digby Gut, whence they were shipped to the telegraph station at Saint John, New Brunswick. From there, the news items were relayed by telegraph to the press of the American seaboard cities. The Halifax Express covered the 232km in an average time of eight hours. Riders were changed at Kentville, but horses (not ponies) were changed every 19km. As the rider passed through Annapolis Royal, a cannon was fired to signal a steamship waiting at Victoria Beach to prepare to depart. Operating between February and November 1849, this successful system was superseded by the extension of the telegraph to Halifax.

A monument to the Pony Express is found on the seaward side of the road a little before you get to the Victoria Beach wharf area.

GETTING THERE The cove can be reached by taking Parkers Mountain Road from Highway 1 just east of Granville Ferry.

 WHERE TO STAY

⌂ **Mountain Top Cottages** (17 units) 888 Parker Mountain Rd; ☎ 532 2564, T/F 1 877 885 1185; www.mountaintopcottages.com; ⊕ May–Oct. Simple 1- & 2-bedroom cottages set in the woods overlooking a lake on an 80ha property. All cottages have a fridge, microwave & stove. Heated outdoor pool (seasonal), hiking & biking trails & watercraft for use on the lake. $$
⌂ **Lobster Wharf B&B** (3 rooms) 4311 Shore Rd West; ☎ 532 2858, T/F 1 877 942 7322;

www.bbcanada.com/lobsterwharfbb; ⊕ year-round. A renovated c1882 house with shared bathrooms, laundry facilities, a library & solarium. B/fast inc. $

Å **Cove Oceanfront Campground** (90 sites) 4405 Shore Rd West; ☎ 532 5166; www.oceanfront-camping.com; ⊕ May–mid-Oct. Open serviced & unserviced sites in a lovely Bay of Fundy shore setting, with a pool. $

BRIDGETOWN *(Population: 970)*

This pretty riverside town of wide tree-lined streets and grand heritage homes makes a nice wander. Pick up a Cyprus Walk leaflet from the tourist office, or see it at www.town.bridgetown.ns.ca.

GETTING THERE

By car Bridgetown is on Highway 1 and just off Highway 101 (Exits 20 and 21), 26km from Annapolis Royal and 23km from Middleton.

By bus Bridgetown is the terminus for bus routes west to Weymouth and east to Greenwood (see page 190), and is also on the Digby–Halifax Acadian bus route (see page 52).

TOURIST INFORMATION *(232 Granville St W; ☎ 665 5150; ⊕ mid-Jun–Sep 09.00–16.00 Mon–Fri)*

 WHERE TO STAY AND EAT

⌂ **Bridgetown Motor Inn** (28 rooms) 396 Granville St East; ☎ 665 4403, T/F 1 888 424 4664; www.bridgetownmotorinn.ca; ⊕ year-round. Dependable motel with spacious rooms, laundry facilities & outdoor pool (seasonal). B/fast available at extra cost. $
⌂ **Harrington House B&B** (2 rooms) 325 Granville St; ☎ 665 4938, T/F 1 866 360 4513; www.harringtonhouse.ca; ⊕ May–mid-Nov. A c1896 house with large gardens. 1 room has en suite, the other a private bathroom. B/fast inc. $
Å **Annapolis River Campground** (75 sites) 56 Queen St; ☎ 665 2801; ⊕ Apr–Oct. Serviced & unserviced riverside sites; laundry service & canoe rentals. $

Å **Valleyview Provincial Park Campground** (30 sites) 960 Hampton Rd; ☎ 665 2559; www.novascotiaparks.ca/parks/valleyview.asp; ⊕ late Jun–mid-Oct. Small park 6km from town offering wooded sites, panoramic views over the Annapolis Valley & the province's remote forested interior. Take Hampton Mountain Rd from Granville St to get there. $
✕ **End of the Line Pub** 73 Queen St; ☎ 665 5277; www.endofthelinepub.com; ⊕ year-round 10.00–21.30 Mon–Sat, 12.00–20.30 Sun. In the former train station across the road from the bookshop (see below), this pub offers over 20 types of beer & food brighter than its lighting. $–$$

WHAT TO SEE AND DO **Endless Shores Books** *(160 South St; ☎ 665 2029)* is a good used bookshop well worth browsing. Pop into the c1835 **James House Museum** *(12 Queen St; ☎ 665 4530; ⊕ mid-May–early Oct 10.00–16.00 daily; admission free)*. Pleasant **Jubilee Park** is on the Annapolis River.

The self-labelled 'Heart of the Valley', Middleton has a couple of contrasting museums, and a fascinating mix of architecture, especially on Main, School and Commercial streets and Gates Avenue.

One of this part of Nova Scotia's few cross-province roads, Highway 10, connects Middleton with Liverpool (see page 156).

GETTING THERE

By car Middleton is on Highways 1 and 10, and just off Highway 101 Exit 18.

By bus Middleton is on the Bridgetown–Greenwood bus route (see page 190) and the Digby–Halifax Acadian bus route (see page 52).

TOURIST INFORMATION *(8 Bridge St;* ☎ *825 4100;* ⊕ *09.00–17.00 Jun; Jul–Aug 08.00–18.00 daily)*

WHERE TO STAY AND EAT

⌂ **Mid Valley Motel & Restaurant** (58 rooms) 121 Main St; ☎ 825 3433, T/F 1 866 332 3433; www.midvalleymotel.com; ⊕ year-round. One of the area's largest accommodations with rooms laid out in traditional motel drive-up style also has a large licensed restaurant (⊕ 08.00–21.00 daily; $$). There are no surprises on the reasonably priced menu. $$

⌂ **Century Farm Inn** (4 rooms) 10 Main St; ☎ 825 6989, T/F 1 800 237 9896; www.centuryfarminn.com; ⊕ Jun–Sep; off-season by reservation. This c1886 farmhouse is backed by 45ha

on the Annapolis River. Rooms are simply decorated. Full b/fast inc. $

✕ **Pasta Jax** 300 Main St; ☎ 825 6099; ⊕ year-round 11.30–14.00 & 16.30–19.30 Mon–Fri, 17.00–20.00 Sat. Don't worry about the name, it's the food that counts. Both cuisine & décor can best be described as 'rustic contemporary'. Start with artichoke dip, follow perhaps with ribs or seafood pasta, & be sure to leave room for dessert – especially if you're a cheesecake fan. Wash it down with a Sleeman's Honey Brown beer, or a bottle of wine. Reservations recommended for dinner. $–$$

OTHER PRACTICALITIES

$ **Scotiabank** 293–301 Main St; ☎ 825 4894; ⊕ 10.00–17.00 Mon–Fri

✚ **Soldiers Memorial Hospital** 462 Main St; ☎ 825 341

⬱ **Rosa M Harvey Middleton and Area Library** 45 Gates Av; ☎ 825 4835; ⊕ 14.00–17.00 &

18.30–20.30 Tue & Fri, 14.00–17.00 Wed, 10.00–17.00 Thu, 10.00–14.00 Sat

✉ **Post office** 275 Main St; ⊕ 08.30–17.00 Mon–Fri

WHAT TO SEE AND DO On Commercial Street, by the Church Street junction next to the Town Hall, see North America's first water-run town clock. At dusk throughout the summer months, watch out for hundreds of swifts entering the big chimney of the Middleton Regional High School at 18 Gates Avenue.

Old Holy Trinity Church *(49 Main St; www.oldholytrinitychurch.ca;* ⊕ *Jul–Aug – or by appointment)* The church was consecrated in 1791 and is one of only five remaining Loyalist churches in North America.

SAUPON

In days of yore, one Bridgetown hotel – now long gone – was renowned for its signature dish, *saupon*. Cornmeal was boiled in milk for several hours at an even heat. By dinner time, it had thickened, and was served with sugar.

Yarmouth, French Shore and the Annapolis Valley MIDDLETON

5

Annapolis Valley MacDonald Museum (*21 School St;* ✆ *825 6116;* *www.macdonaldmuseum.ca;* ⊕ *mid–Jun–Sep 09.00–17.00 Mon–Sat, 13.00–17.00 Sun; Oct–mid–Jun 10.30–17.00 Mon–Fri; admission CAN$3*) This grand museum is housed in a big red-brick building from c1903 which was the first consolidated school in Canada. Varied exhibits include an old schoolroom, a recreation of a 1930s' general store, the Nova Scotia Museum's clock and watch collection, and much more.

Memory Lane Railway Museum (*61 School St;* ✆ *825 4611;* ⊕ *year-round 09.00–17.00 Mon–Fri, 10.00–14.30 Sat; admission free*) Close to the MacDonald Museum is a complete contrast which is every bit as interesting. Housed in the old railway station (in use 1917–90) is a dusty but worthwhile collection of bits and pieces from days gone by. Trains are the focus and there are both indoor and outdoor working model train tracks.

KINGSTON AND GREENWOOD

The main attractions of these two communities for visitors are a tourist office – and an Atlantic Superstore very close by – in Kingston, and a huge enclosed shopping mall (and the largest air force base on Canada's east coast) in Greenwood. Self-caterers should also bear in mind that there are no other big supermarkets in the 125km between here and Digby (see page 189). There are better restaurants in Middleton and Berwick: your choice here is fast food at one of the malls, or the restaurant at the Aurora Inn (see below).

GETTING THERE

By car Kingston is on Highway 1, 11km/7 miles east of Middleton and 40km/25 miles west of Kentville.

By bus At 2.5km away, Greenwood is the terminus of bus routes west to Bridgetown and east to Wolfville. Kingston is on the Greenwood–Wolfville bus route (see page 190) and the Digby–Halifax Acadian bus route (see page 52).

TOURIST INFORMATION (*510 Main St (Hwy 1), Kingston;* ✆ *765 6678;* ⊕ *daily mid–end May & Sep–early Oct 10.00–17.00; Jun–Aug 09.00–18.00*)

WHERE TO STAY AND EAT

⌂ **Best Western Aurora Inn** (23 units) 831 Main St, Kingston; ✆ 765 3306; www.bestwesternatlantic.com; ⊕ year-round. Few surprises at this single-storey motel-style hotel with spacious rooms. 65-seat licensed restaurant (⊕ 07.00–10.30, 11.00–14.00, 16.30–19.30 daily; $$) $$

OTHER PRACTICALITES

$ **CIBC** 655 Main St, Kingston; ✆ 765 3351
$ **Scotiabank** 963 Central Av, Greenwood; ✆ 765 6383; ⊕ 10.00–15.00 Mon–Wed, 10,00–17.00 Thu–Fri

🕮 **Kingston Library** 671 Main St, Kingston; ✆ 765 3631⊕ 14.00–17.00 & 18.30–20.30 Tue, 10.00–17.00 & 18.30–20.00 Thu, 18.30–20.30 Fri, 10.00–14.00 Sat

BERWICK

This busy town calls itself the 'Apple Capital of Nova Scotia', the reason for the giant apple perched outside the Town Hall. Apple orchards occupy swathes of the surrounding countryside. Commercial Street – which links Highway 101 and Highway 1 – is where you'll find the majority of the shops and services.

GETTING THERE Berwick is just off Highway 101 Exit 15, 20km/12 miles west of Kentville and 21km/13 miles east of Kingston.

WHERE TO STAY AND EAT

⌂ **Hidden Gardens** (2 rooms) 274 Main St; ☎ 538 0813, T/F 1 866 299 0813; e hiddengardens@ns.sympatico.ca www.bbcanada.com/hiddengardens; ⊕ year-round. Choose the 'Sunrise' or 'Sunset' room at this lovely old home. Seasonal outdoor pool. Rate inc enhanced cont b/fast. $

✗ **Kellock's** 160 Commercial St; ☎ 538 5525; www.kellocks.ca; ⊕ year-round 11.30–14.30 & 16.30–20.30 Mon–Fri, 10.30–21.30 Sat. Located in a 125-year-old house ringed by towering elms, with stained-glass windows, tin ceilings & hardwood floors offers relaxed, upmarket dining. Particularly

good deals are weekday lunch buffets. Try the applewood-smoked chicken. $$

✗ **Union Street Café & The Wick Pub** 183 Commercial St; ☎ 538 7787; www.unionstreetcafe.ca; ⊕ year-round 11.00–20.00 Sun–Thu, 11.00–22.00 Fri–Sat. Cosy, colourful & inviting café-restaurant with an eclectic menu. The chicken & roasted vegetable focaccia is a lunchtime favourite: in the evening try ginger maple sesame salmon, followed by chocolate truffle tart. Live music (often high-quality) in the adjoining pub on Fri–Sat evenings. $$

KENTVILLE (Population: 5,700)

The largest community in – and commercial hub of – the Annapolis Valley, Kentville has some lovely old homes, a good museum in the old courthouse, and some pleasant walking trails both by the riverside and on the bed of old railway tracks. The grounds of the **Kentville Agricultural Centre** (see page 216) are beautiful in late spring.

Incidentally, **New Minas**, less than 3km east along Highway 1, is worth visiting only if you like side-by-side shopping malls, fast-food outlets and petrol stations.

GETTING THERE

By car Kentville is on Highways 1 and 12, the latter of which crosses the province down to Chester (see page 137), and off Highway 101 Exits 12–14, 11km/7 miles from Wolfville, 74km/46 miles from Chester and 105km/65 miles from Annapolis Royal.

Yarmouth, French Shore and the Annapolis Valley **KENTVILLE**

5

By bus Wolfville is on the Greenwood–Wolfville bus route (see page 190) and on the Digby–Halifax Acadian bus route (see page 52).

TOURIST INFORMATION *(125 Park St; ↘ 678 7170; ☉ late May–early Oct, 09.30–17.30; 19.30 in Jul–Aug)*

WHERE TO STAY AND EAT

⌂ **Allen's Motel** (12 rooms) 384 Park St; ↘ 678 2683; e allensmotel@ns.sympatico.ca; www.allensmotel.ns.ca; ☉ Apr–Nov. What was a traditional motel set on a 1.2ha property has had renovations & additions, including 2 upstairs rooms. Coin laundry. $

⌂ **Grand Street Inn** (3 rooms) 160 Main St; ↘ 679 1991, T/F 1 877 245 4744; www.grandstreetinn.com; ☉ year-round. Nice rooms in lovely, quiet c1870 Queen Anne Revival home on spacious grounds. Outdoor pool (seasonal) & hot tub. Full b/fast inc. $

⚑ **South Mountain Park Family Camping Resort** (200 sites) 3022 Hwy 12, South Alton; ↘ 678 0152, T/F 1 866 860 6092;

www.southmountainparkcampground.com; ☉ mid-May–mid-Oct. A facility-packed 44ha campground 9km south of Exit 13 of Hwy 101. Open & wooded serviced & tent sites. $

✗ **King's Arms Pub** 390 Main St; ↘ 678 0066; www.kingsarmspub.ca; ☉ year-round 11.00–20.00 Sun–Mon, 11.00–21.00 Tue–Wed, 11.00–22.00 Thu–Sat. A British-style pub with relaxing atmosphere and decent well-priced food. In summer, the patio is nice. $

✗ **Paddy's Brew Pub & Rosie's Restaurant** 42 Aberdeen St; ↘ 678 3199; www.paddyspub.ca; ☉ year-round 11.00–midnight daily. For details, see Wolfville, page 222. $

FESTIVALS
October
Harvest Festival Wagon rides, music, food – and people dressed as pumpkins!

OTHER PRACTICALITIES

$ **Royal Bank** 63 Webster St; ↘ 679 3850; ☉ 10.00–17.00 Mon–Fri

$ **Scotiabank** 47 Aberdeen St; ↘ 678 2181; ☉ 10.00–17.00 Mon–Fri

✚ **Valley Regional Hospital** 150 Exhibition St; ↘ 678 7381

▤ **Kentville Library** 95 Cornwallis St; ↘ 679 2544; ☉ 10.00–17.00 Mon & Wed & Fri, 14.00–17.00 & 18.30–20.30 Tue, 10.000–17.00 & 18.30–20.30 Thu, 10.00–14.00 Sat

✉ **Post office** 495 Main St; ☉ 08.00–17.00 Mon–Fri

WHAT TO SEE AND DO

Kentville Agricultural Centre *(32 Main St; ↘ 679 5333; grounds ☉ year-round; admission free)* The huge (well over 200ha) grounds of this government facility – one of the most modern and sophisticated research centres in Canada – are planted with crops and orchards – there's also a magnificent rhododendron garden. The Kentville Ravine Trail leads from the car park along a river and through old growth forest.

Kings County Museum *(37 Cornwallis St; ↘ 678 6237; www.okcm.ca; ☉ year-round Sep–Apr 09.30–16.30 Tue–Fri; May–Jun 09.30–16.00 Mon–Fri; Jul–Aug 09.30–16.30 Mon–Fri, 11.30–16.30 Sat; admission free)* Housed in the three-storey former c1904 courthouse – with the original courtroom on the top floor a must-see – there's a good display on New England Planters, and a large collection of primarily Victorian textiles. Archives for genealogical research (CAN$3 fee).

Searching the beaches for semi-precious stones Contact: Rob's Rocks *(677 West Main St; ↘ 678 3194; www.robsrockshop.com)*.

Golf The 6,300yd Ken-Wo Golf Course (*9514 Commercial St;* ✆ *681 5388; www.ken-wo.com*) might sound pseudo-Japanese, but got its name because it lies halfway between Kentville and Wolfville. Green fees are CAN$58.

HALL'S HARBOUR

This pretty working fishing village is named after Captain Samuel Hall, an early 19th-century American privateer who terrorised those living in the region with frequent raids to pillage and plunder. Locals say that every seven years in winter, a phantom ship's lights are seen going up the Bay of Fundy.

Above the harbour, steep cliffs are capped with groves of hardwoods and softwoods: the cobble beach is popular for rockhounding (when the tide's out), and there's a 2km forest and coastal eco-trail. Several artists have studios in the village.

GETTING THERE Hall's Harbour is on Highway 359, 18km/11 miles from Kentville.

✕ **WHERE TO EAT** A rustic restaurant (*1157 West Hall's Harbour Rd;* ✆ *679 5299;* ⊕ *daily mid-May–Jun & Sep–mid-Oct 12.00–19.00; Jul–Aug 11.30–20.30;* $–$$) is attached to the **Halls Harbour Lobster Pound** and is a popular lunch spot – choose your clawed lunch and eat it at a wharf-front table.

CAPE SPLIT AND CAPE BLOMIDON

At almost 8km each way, the trail to Cape Split can be a long walk for the inexperienced hiker, but is well worth the effort. The trailhead is at the end of Scots Bay Road, approximately 30km from Exit 11 of Highway 101.

Once you're on your way, you'll have to decide whether to take the more difficult coastal trail (which stays close to the clifftops and is not for those who don't like heights) or the more straightforward inland route which initially leads through mixed forest and which is easier going: later on the trail, the forest is more deciduous: ferns cover much of the forest floor, and lichens and mosses cling to the trees. As you near the end of the cape, the trees end and you arrive at a grassy area high above the water, with the sea on three sides. If it is not misty or foggy, the views are fantastic.

Take particular care here close to the cliff edges. Allow a minimum of 4.5 hours for the return hike.

There are more spectacular views – and a network of over 14km of hiking trails – on the other (eastern) side of the peninsula at **Blomidon Provincial Park** (*Pereaux Rd www.novascotiaparks.ca/parks/blomidon.asp;* ⊕ *mid-May–early Sep*). This 759ha park, the entrance of which is 25km from Highway 101 Exit 11, is largely forested with sugar maple, beech, white spruce and yellow birch, includes 180m-tall red sandstone cliffs and looks out over the Bay of Fundy. At low tide, wander

---

> **LOCAL BOY BECOMES BIG TURK**
>
> Hall's Harbour was the boyhood home of one Ransford D Bucknam (1866–1915). He went to the United States, came to the notice of the Sultan of Turkey, and later became *Bucknam Pasha*, Grand Admiral of the Ottoman Fleet. In June 1912, however, the *Illustrated London News* reported: 'Hamidiye's captain…Bucknam Pasha, has recently been noticed spending more time frequenting waterfront nightclubs than he has pacing Hamidiye's quarterdeck.'

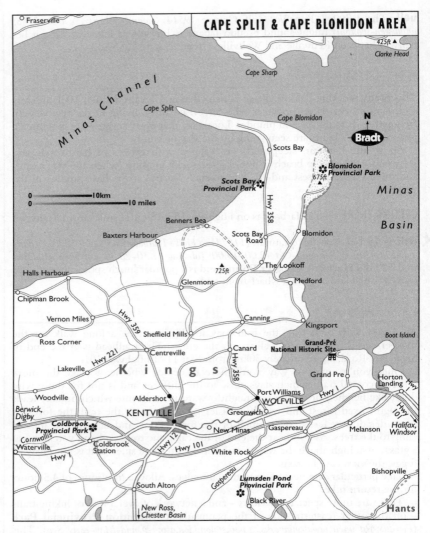

CAPE SPLIT & CAPE BLOMIDON AREA

the beaches where you might be lucky enough to find amethysts or agates. There are four official interconnecting walking trails, from the 1.6km Look-off Trail to the spectacular 6km Jodrey Trail. The 3.5km Borden Brook Trail leads through white spruce forest to a series of waterfalls. The park has a 70-site campground (⏱ *mid-May–early Sep*) with open and wooded sites.

As the home of their demi-god Glooscap, the Cape Blomidon area has great spiritual significance for the Mi'kmaq.

WOLFVILLE

With a prosperous feel and a pleasant climate, Wolfville may not have the history of, say, Annapolis Royal (see page 199), but this charming town has a popular and highly regarded university, several excellent restaurants, and no shortage of beautiful heritage homes or interesting historic architecture. I mention the university because it brings a clear vitality to the town: in general, the large student population is well mannered and enhances the atmosphere, rather than overpowering it.

Highway 1 runs through town as Main Street, and (as you'd expect) this is where most shops, eateries and accommodations are found. To the east of the town centre, Main Street is lined with majestic trees.

Although not immediately obvious, Wolfville does have a waterfront, and its appropriately named Waterfront Park (which opened in 2000) hosts several outdoor events and offers fine views of Cape Blomidon. The park at the junction of Front Street and Harbourside Drive, the extension of Gaspereau Avenue offers totally different views at high and low tide: interpretive panels tell of the area's history of shipping and shipbuilding.

The land reclaimed by the 17th-century Acadian dykes is a good spot for a walk or cycle ride: hillier, the scenic hiking trail through the 12ha Reservoir Park is also a good choice.

I can't say that the new Railtown by the Harbour condominium development right by the park completed in 2008 is to my taste – but at least they didn't knock down the old railway station which now houses the town's library.

HISTORY Originally known to the Mi'kmaq as *mtaban* ('muddy catfish-catching place'), European settlement began with Acadians in the mid- to late-17th century (some of their dykes can still be seen). After the Expulsion, New England Planters settled here, naming it 'Mud Creek' – a small harbour was connected to the Cornwallis River by a narrow, twisting stretch of water, virtually impassable at low tide. Despite problems with navigation caused by the tide, and sandbars, a busy little port was established, and ships were built here.

One of the community's most important residents was Judge Elisha DeWolf (1756–1837) and it was in his honour that the town was renamed.

In 1911, Wolfville became the first town in Nova Scotia with a paved main street.

GETTING THERE

By car Wolfville is on Highway 1 and between Exits 10 and 11 of Highway 101, 90km/56 miles from Halifax, 27km/17 miles from Windsor and 117km/73 miles from Annapolis Royal.

By bus Wolfville is the terminus of bus routes west to Greenwood and south to Windsor (see page 190). It is also on the Digby–Halifax Acadian bus route (see page 52).

TOURIST INFORMATION (*11 Willow St;* ✆ *542 7000;* ⊕ *daily mid–Apr–Jun & Sep–mid–Dec 09.00–17.00; Jul–Aug 10.00–18.00*)

EAGLE-EYED

This part of the Annapolis Valley has the largest overwintering population of bald eagles in eastern North America with hundreds of the majestic avians in the area from late November to early March. The community of Sheffield Mills hosts a couple of annual Eagle Watch weekends (*www.eaglens.ca; late Jan/early Feb*) with food put out to attract the birds.

WHERE TO STAY

🏠 **Blomidon Inn** (29 rooms) 195 Main St; 542 2291, T/F 1 800 565 2291; www.theblomidon.net; year-round. The main building is a beautifully restored c1882 shipbuilder's mansion, with magnificent interior dark wood features & Italian marble fireplaces: each guest room is individually decorated. It is worth choosing a Superior or above (note that not all rooms are in the original building). Paths through landscaped themed gardens, tennis courts. There is also an inn. Various packages are available. Continental b/fast & afternoon tea inc. $$

🏠 **Harwood House B&B** (3 rooms) 33 Highland Av; 542 5707; T/F 1 877 897 0156; www.harwoodhouse.com; year-round. A tastefully renovated, quiet c1923 home with lovely garden & spacious bedrooms. Full gourmet b/fast incorporating vegetables from the garden & local fruit inc. $$

🏠 **Old Orchard Inn & Spa** (130 units) 153 Greenwich Rd; Greenwich; 542 5751, T/F 1 800 561 8090; www.oldorchardinn.com; year-round (cabins May–Oct). Located 5km from Wolfville, just off Highway 101 Exit 11 with over 100 well-maintained rooms & 29 cabins: indoor pool, sauna, hot tub, spa & tennis court. Includes the excellent Acadian Room Restaurant. $$

🏠 **Victoria's Historic Inn & Carriage House B&B** (16 units) 600 Main St; 542 5744, T/F 1 800 556 5744; www.victoriashistoricinn.com; year-round. The c1893 3-storey main building contains 4 rooms & 5 suites (with jacuzzi & fireplace): 7 rooms are in the adjacent Carriage House. Beautifully restored, the property blends Victorian character & modern comforts. Full b/fast & afternoon tea inc. $$

🏠 **Garden House B&B** (3 rooms) 220 Main St; 542 1703; e gardenhouse@ns.sympatico.ca; www.gardenhouse.ca; year-round. Cosy, friendly B&B in a c1830 house a short walk from the town centre; rooms with shared or private bathroom. B/fast inc. $

WHERE TO EAT

✕ **Blomidon Inn** 195 Main St; 542 2291, T/F 1 800 565 2291; www.theblomidon.net; year-round 11.30–14.00 & 17.30–21.30 daily. The Blomidon is renowned, & reservations are therefore strongly recommended. The Atlantic salmon is a speciality, served in a variety of ways. Lobster, *filet mignon* & game feature too, & the wine list is superb. Weekend brunch is another treat. $$$

✕ **Acton's Grill & Café** 406 Main St; 542 7525; www.actons.ca; year-round 11.30–14.00 & 17.00–21.00 daily. One of the town's top restaurants, the lunches are particularly good value – try, for example, the warm mushroom & apple salad with spinach, pecans & goat's cheese, or for dinner, perhaps veal medallions sautéed with lobster in a sherry garlic sauce served on fettuccini. There's a fire in winter & a terrace for warm summer days. $$–$$$

✕ **Tempest** 117 Front St; 542 0588, T/F 1 866 542 0588; www.tempest.ca; mid-Oct–mid-May 17.30–20.30 Tue–Wed, 11.30–14.30 & 17.30–20.30 Fri–Sun; mid-May–mid-Oct 17.30–22.00 Mon–Wed, 11.30–14.30 & 17.30–22.00 Fri–Sun. Wonderful food, beautifully presented. Chef Michael Howell continues to produce a global range of exciting, delicious & eye-catching dishes. The lunch/brunch menu is a gastronomic bargain & includes a Nova Scotia take on a BLT sandwich (bacon, lobster & tomato) and Vietnamese *pho* (seafood soup). At dinner choose 'small' or 'large' plates of seafood, pasta, Thai curry, steak & more. Tapas menu in summer (served from 20.00). $$–$$$

✕ **Old Orchard Inn & Spa** 153 Greenwich Rd; Greenwich; 542 5751, T/F 1 800 561 8090; www.oldorchardinn.com; 07.00–14.00 &

ACADIA UNIVERSITY

In term-time, over 3,000 students – plus staff – at Wolfville's Acadia University (*www.acadiau.ca*), one of Canada's top learning institutions, double the town's population.

Beginning as Horton Academy in 1828, it became Acadia University in 1891. In addition to a gallery and botanical gardens (see page 223), the university has some magnificent buildings. The oldest is the c1878 Seminary, which displays many Second Empire features and is now home to the School of Education. The Georgian Revival-style Carnegie Hall (a science building) was built with the help of a sizeable donation by American philanthropist Andrew Carnegie. Also of note is the Italianate c1913 Emmerson Hall.

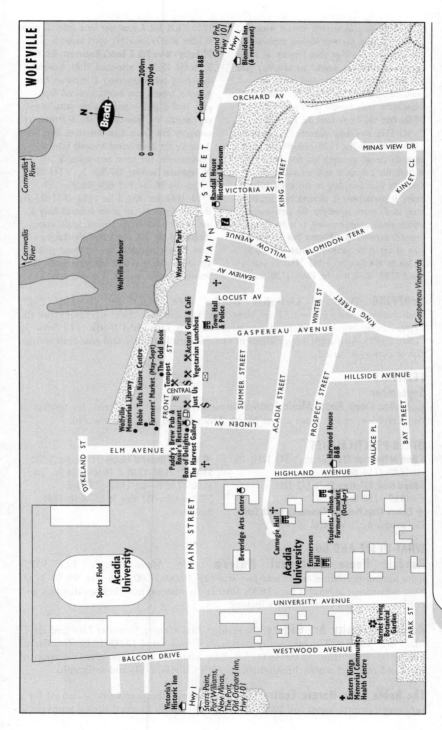

Cornwallis
River

Cornwallis River

WOLFVILLE

N

Bradt

0   200m
0   200yds

Grand Pré,
Hwy 101

Wolfville Harbour

Garden House B&B

ORCHARD AV

MINAS VIEW DR

Biomidon Inn
(& restaurant)

KINLEY CL

Randall House
Historical Museum

Victoria Av

KING STREET

M A I N   S T R E E T

Waterfront Park

BLOMIDON TERR

SEAVIEW AV

WILLOW AVENUE

Gaspereau Vineyards

Wolfville
Memorial Library

Robie Tufts Nature Centre

The Odd Book

LOCUST AV

WINTER ST

KING STREET

Farmers' Market (May–Sept)

Tempest St

Acton's Grill & Café

Town Hall
& Police

Vegetarian Lunchbox

GASPEREAU AVENUE

FRONT
ST

CENTRAL
AV

Just Us

Paddy's Brew Pub &
Rosie's Restaurant

Box of Delights

The Harvest Gallery

SUMMER STREET

ACADIA STREET

HILLSIDE AVENUE

ELM AVENUE

LINDEN AV

PROSPECT STREET

Harwood House
B&B

WALLACE PL

BAY STREET

DYKELAND ST

HIGHLAND AVENUE

Sports Field

Acadia University

M A I N   S T R E E T

Beveridge Arts Centre

Carnegie Hall

Students' Union &
Farmers' market (Oct–Apr)

Acadia
University

Emmerson
Hall

Victoria's
Historic Inn

Hwy 1

Starrs Point,
Port Williams,
New Minas,
The Port,
Old Orchard Inn,
Hwy 101

BALCOM DRIVE

UNIVERSITY AVENUE

PARK ST

WESTWOOD AVENUE

Harriet Irving
Botanical Garden

Eastern Kings
Memorial Community
Health Centre

Yarmouth, French Shore and the Annapolis Valley WOLFVILLE

5

17.00–21.00 daily. An excellent licensed restaurant, the Acadian Room, has wide windows overlooking Cape Blomidon, & a large stone fireplace. To start, the mussels & seafood chowder are both very good, followed by sautéed Digby scallops served with *remoulade*. Local poultry & pork also feature. To follow, warm apple crumble pie is a winner. **$$**
✗ **The Port** 980 Terry's Creek Rd, Port Williams; ✆ 542 5555; www.theportpub.com; ⊕ year-round 11.00–23.00 Sun–Thu, 11.00–midnight Fri–Sat. This nautically themed gastropub less than 7km from Wolfville has a beautiful deck overlooking the Cornwallis River. Everything at this new (2007) eatery & microbrewery is prepared from scratch using locally grown ingredients. The pesto-crusted chicken breast is recommended, as is the Porter chocolate brownie. Sip a Planters Pale beer or a glass of one of the carefully selected wines. **$$**
✗ **Just Us** 450 Main St; ✆ 542 7731; ⊕ year-round 07.00–20.30 Mon–Fri, 08.00–17.30 Sat,

10.00–16.30 Sun. A good spot for a coffee or snack in lobby of a former c1911 opera house. **$**
✗ **Paddy's Brew Pub & Rosie's Restaurant** 460 Main St; ✆ 542 0059; ⊕ year-round 11.00–midnight daily. Lively pub, microbrewery & restaurant. Atrium, glassed-in brewery, cosy booths, hardwood floors, patio. Food is good – seafood, pizza, pasta, burgers etc, especially the home-smoked ribs, & desserts (eg: outrageous Irish Cream Bash Cheesecake). Beer lovers should try the house-brewed Annapolis Valley or Gaspereau ales. Live music most nights. **$**
✗ **Vegetarian Lunchbox** 420 Main St; ✆ 542 1887; ⊕ Jun–Sep 08.30–19.30 daily; Oct–May 09.00–16.00 Mon–Wed & Sat, 09.00–18.30 Thu–Fri. The only vegetarian café in the Annapolis Valley & one of only a few in the province. Salads, wraps, smoothies & the like, plus a regularly changing menu of more substantial fare (eg: African ground nut stew) including at least one vegan option. Most desserts are vegan, too. Eat in or take-away. **$**

SHOPPING Box of Delights Books (*466 Main St;* ✆ *542 9511; www.boxofdelightsbooks.com*). This shop has a good collection of books on the province: for used books, head one street back to **The Odd Book** (*112 Front St;* ✆ *542 9491*). Although it specialises in out-of-print literature and academic works, the selection is varied.

FESTIVALS
September
Canadian Deep Roots Music Festival (*www.deeprootsmusic.ca*) Three-day festival of modern roots music from across North America and around the world.

OTHER PRACTICALITIES
$ **Bank of Montreal** 424 Main St; ✆ 542 2214; ⊕ 10.00–17.00 Mon–Fri
$ **Royal Bank** 437 Main St; ✆ 542 2221; ⊕ 10.00–17.00 Mon–Fri
✚ **Eastern Kings Memorial Community Health Centre** 23 Earnscliffe Av; ✆ 542 2266

⬚ **Wolfville Memorial Library** 21 Elm Av; ✆ 542 5760; ⊕ 11.00–17.00 & 18.30–20.30 Tue–Thu, 11.00–17.00 Fri–Sat, 13.00–17.00 Sun
✉ **Post office** 407 Main St; ⊕ 08.30–17.00 Mon–Fri

WHAT TO SEE AND DO
Randall House Historical Museum (*259 Main St;* ✆ *542 9775; www.wolfvillehs.ednet.ns.ca;* ⊕ *mid-Jun–mid-Sep 10.00–17.00 Mon–Sat, 13.30–17.00 Sun; admission CAN$2*) This c1800s former farmhouse now houses displays and collections on the community's history.

Acadia University Art Gallery (Beveridge Arts Centre (*corner of Highland Av & Main St);* ✆ *585 1373; www.gallery.acadiau.ca;* ⊕ *year-round 12.00–16.00 Tue, Wed & Fri, 12.00–20.00 Thu, 13.00–16.00 Sat–Sun; admission free*) Fine-arts collection of local and regional works, highlighted by Alex Colville's oils and serigraphs.

The Robie Tufts Nature Centre (*Front St*) Despite the grand title – named for a renowned ornithologist and Wolfville resident – this is a roofed shelter supporting a high stack that is home to numerous chimney swifts. Around dusk on summer evenings, watch as the birds swoop down through the chimney top for the night.

Harriet Irving Botanical Gardens (*32 University Av;* ✆ *585 5242; www.botanicalgardens.acadiau.ca;* ⊕ *Apr–Dec dusk–dawn daily; admission free*) 2.5ha of gardens showcase flora from the Acadian Forest Region. See a Nova Scotia take on a Victorian British walled garden, a bog area (with Venus fly-traps) and a medicinal and food garden. Even for non-botanists, these gardens make a pleasant wander.

L'Acadie Vineyards (*310 Slayter Rd, Gaspereau;* ✆ *542 8463; www.lacadievineyards.ca;* ⊕ *May–Oct 11.00–17.00 daily, Nov–Dec 12.00–17.00 Sat–Sun*) Nova Scotia's first certified organic winery and vineyard is 6km from Wolfville. Follow Gaspereau Avenue to Slayter Road.

Gaspereau Vineyards (*2239 White Rock Rd;* ✆ *542 1455; www.gaspereauwine.com;* ⊕ *mid-May–Dec 09.00–18.00 daily; free tours mid-May–mid-Oct 12.00, 14.00 & 16.00*) 14ha of vineyards overlooking the Gaspereau Valley 3km from Wolfville were planted in 1996 on a former apple orchard.

The Harvest Gallery (*462 Main St;* ✆ *542 7093; www.harvestgallery.ca;* ⊕ *year-round 10.00–17.00 Tue–Sat (Jul–Oct also Mon), 11.00–17.00 Sun*) An interesting selection of local arts and crafts.

Prescott House (*1633 Starr's Point Rd, Starr's Point;* ✆ *542 3984; www.museum.gov.ns.ca/prh/;* ⊕ *Jun–mid-Oct 09.30–17.30 Mon–Sat, 13.00–17.30 Sun; admission CAN$3.50*) Situated 10km from Wolfville, one of the province's best-surviving examples of Georgian architecture was completed in 1814 by Charles Ramage Prescott, a businessman and horticulturist. In addition to period furnishings, see Prescott's granddaughter's collections of oriental rugs and hand-stitched samplers.

Farmers' Market (*www.wolfvillefarmersmarket.com;* ⊕ *year-round 08.30–13.00 Sat mornings*) Between May and September this excellent market is held outdoors at the Robie Tufts Nature Centre, Front Street, whilst the rest of the year it occupies two floors of the Acadia Student Union Building, Highland Avenue.

GRAND PRÉ

Grand Pré's pastoral landscape, dyked lands, and air of tranquillity broken only by a steady stream of tour buses give little clue as to its part in one of the most heart-rending events in Canadian history. Nearby, the **Covenanters' Church** (*1989 Grand Pré Rd*) is set on a hill. Constructed between 1804 and 1811 to replace an earlier log structure, this pretty church was built in the style of a New England Meeting House. The tower and steeple were 1818 additions.

HISTORY Grand Pré (French for 'great meadow') was first settled in the early 1680s by a couple of Acadian families from Port-Royal (see page 210). More came to join them, and through hard work and clever use of dykes to reclaim tidal marshlands, created rich farmland. Life was not problem-free: in 1704, for example, the settlement was attacked by New Englanders who broke dykes and burned crops. But the real battle occurred in the winter of 1746/47 when a French force surprised almost 500 soldiers from New England, who had arrived to establish a blockhouse at Grand Pré, and killed over 70 before a ceasefire was agreed.

By the 1750s, Grand Pré had become the largest of all the Acadian communities around the Bay of Fundy.

In 1755, when the Acadians refused to sign an oath of allegiance to the British Crown, and the governor ordered them to be deported (see page 7), Grand Pré was one of the first communities selected.

On 5 September 1755, a Colonel Winslow gathered the men of Grand Pré in the church and informed them that they and their families were to be deported and their lands confiscated. The village buildings were burnt to the ground, and on 29 October a fleet of a dozen ships sailed away with 2,921 Acadians on board.

GETTING THERE Grand Pré is just off Highways 1 and 101, 1.5km/0.9 miles east of Wolfville, or Exit 10 from Highway 101, 21km/13 miles from Windsor.

⌂ WHERE TO STAY AND EAT

⌂ **Evangeline Inn & Motel** (23 rooms) 11668 Highway 1; ☏ 542 2703, T/F 1 888 542 2703; www.evangeline.ns.ca; ⊕ early May–late Oct. The 5-room Inn is housed in the boyhood home of Sir Robert Borden, Prime Minister of Canada 1911–20. The 18-room motel was built in the 1950s (with a 2004 addition): rooms are spacious & pleasant. There is an indoor pool. **Evangeline's Café** (⊕ early May–late Oct 07.00–19.00; $) has a simple menu of cheap breakfasts, salads, sandwiches & burgers. Inn rates inc b/fast. $

⋏ **Land of Evangeline Family Camping Resort** (230 sites) 84 Evangeline Beach Rd; ☏ 542 5309; ⊕ May–Sep. Open & wooded sites, serviced & unserviced, with laundromat. Located near the beach with fine views. $

✕ **Le Caveau Restaurant at Domaine de Grand Pré Winery** 11611 Highway 1; ☏ 542 1753, T/F 1 866 479 4637; www.grandprewines.com; ⊕ mid-Apr–mid-May & Nov–Dec 17.00–20.45 Tue–Sat; mid-May–Oct 11.30–14.00 & 17.00–20.45 daily. Bright, stylish winery restaurant with arched windows, textured walls & rich use of wood. Seasonal local produce with a global flair, accompanied of course by Nova Scotia wines. Citrus-crusted Nova Scotia scallops served with spicy cucumber salad & tamarind glaze are a sumptuous starter, & beef tenderloin served with Chanterelle mushroom ketchup & toasted barley risotto a masterful main. $$$

SHOPPING

Tangled Garden 11827 Hwy 1; ☏ 542 9811; www.tangledgarden.ns.ca; ⊕ mid-Apr–late Dec 10.00–18.00 daily; admission CAN$3. Delicious homemade jams, chutneys, liqueurs, herb jellies & more. Beautiful spiritually inspired herb & sculpture gardens are also worth exploring.

Marchandise 11491 Hwy 1; ☏ 542 4419; ℮ marchandise@ns.sympatico.ca; ⊕ 12.00–18.00 when the owner is there, or by appointment. Crammed full of dusty bric-a-brac antiques, old postcards & used books, including a good selection of Acadiana.

WHAT TO SEE AND DO

Grand Pré National Historic Site of Canada (2242 Grand Pré Rd; ☏ 542 3631, T/F 1 866 542 3631; www.grand-pre.com; ⊕ late May–mid-Oct 09.00–18.00 daily (grounds

EVANGELINE

Almost a century after the events of 1755, Henry Wadsworth Longfellow wrote Evangeline: a tale of Acadie, a poem which immortalised the tragedy that marked the lives of the Acadians. The story of his fictional heroine's search for her lost love through the trials and tribulations of the deportation from Grand Pré became an icon for the indomitable spirit of Acadians and their descendants.

Longfellow never visited Nova Scotia. In 1840, he heard a story about the Expulsion at a dinner party and decided it would make an epic poem. It was published in 1847.

accessible year-round); admission CAN$7.80) Located in what was the centre of the Acadian village (see above), this 5.7ha park commemorates the deportation of the Acadians in 1755.

Paths lead from the modern interpretive centre (display panels, model of Grand Pré in Acadian times) to landscaped formal gardens and a bronze statue of Evangeline, fictional heroine of Longfellow's poem (see box, page 224), and the c1922 Saint Charles church. Inside, the church paintings and stained-glass windows depict the story of the Acadians. With the exception of an Acadian well, nearby dykes and a row of old willow trees, nothing physical remains from the Acadian days, but there are expansive grounds to wander, plus vegetable gardens, a blacksmith shop, orchard, and a look-out over dyked farmland.

Approximately 3km away from the Historic Site, a cross by the sea marks the point from which the fleet carrying the expelled Acadians departed. Ironically, very close by, a monument at Horton Landing commemorates the 8,000-plus New England Planters who came in the 1760s to replace the deported Acadians.

Domaine de Grand Pré (*Contact details as Le Caveau Restaurant above;* ⊕ *late Mar–mid-May & Nov–Dec 11.00–17.00 Wed–Sun; mid-May–Oct 09.00–18.00 Mon–Sat, 11.00–18.00 Sun; 45min winery tours mid-May–Oct 3-times daily for CAN$6*) The current owners, originally from Switzerland, bought this winery (located on former Acadian farmland) in 1994 and have transformed it completely with great success – not only has it produced several award-winning wines, but it is a delightful place to visit. To round things off, there's an excellent restaurant, too (see above).

WINDSOR *(Population: 3,700)*

People are beginning to realise that Windsor is well located, on the Avon River, close to Wolfville and an easy run on Highway 101 to Halifax (or Highway 14 to Chester and the South Shore).

Several beautiful heritage homes are dotted about (though not in the slightly bland downtown area), efforts have been made to regenerate the waterfront, new restaurants and a hotel have opened, and the huge old Nova Scotia Textiles building just outside town is being developed into flats, galleries, shops, eateries and more (see www.millisland.ca).

There are several attractions, most of which are easily reached on foot. In addition, the town is home to Canada's oldest private school, **King's-Edgehill School** (*www.kes.ns.ca*), and, more important for some, claims to be the birthplace of (ice) hockey.

HISTORY Situated at the confluence of the Avon and St Croix rivers, Windsor was known to the Mi'kmaq as *Piziquid* (or *Pesaquid*), 'the meeting of the waters'.

The French began to settle in significant numbers from about 1685. They ploughed fields, planted orchards and built grist mills. By 1748, well over 2,000 Acadians lived in the area. When Halifax was founded in 1749, the decision was made to fortify Piziquid, and a blockhouse was constructed. In 1750, Fort Edward (see page 229) was built. Much of the planning for the expulsion of the Acadians (see page 7) was done here, and many Acadians were held in the fort to await deportation.

After the Expulsion, new settlers began to arrive to replace the Acadians, settling on both sides of the river and renaming it the 'Avon'. In 1764, they named their settlement on the east bank 'Windsor'.

The University of King's College and its secondary school, King's Collegiate School, were founded in 1788–89 by United Empire Loyalists as Anglican academic institutions.

Shipping and shipbuilding prospered here, particularly in the second half of the 19th century. The huge Windsor Cotton Mill opened in the early 1880s, and later became Nova Scotia Textiles.

Huge fires in 1897 and 1924 accounted for much of the downtown, and a 1920 blaze destroyed the university which reopened in Halifax two years later.

With water transport made almost redundant by road and rail travel, a causeway was built across the Avon River in 1970, putting an end to shipping for Windsor.

GETTING THERE

By car Windsor is 26km/16 miles from Wolfville, 66km/41 miles from Halifax (both via Highway 101 or 1), and 134km/83 miles from Truro (via Highways 14 and 102).

By bus From Windsor, buses (see page 190) run to Wolfville and to Brooklyn (see page 232). The closest long-distance bus stop (the Digby–Halifax route) is at Falmouth's Irving Mainway petrol station (2113 Highway 1), a five–ten-minute walk from Windsor's downtown.

TOURIST INFORMATION *(31 Colonial Rd;* ⟍ *798 2690;* ⊕ *daily mid–May–early Oct 09.00–17.00, 19.00 in Jul–Aug)*

WHERE TO STAY AND EAT

⌂ **Clockmaker's Inn** (8 rooms) 1399 King St; ⟍ 792 2573, T/F 1 866 778 3600; www.theclockmakersinn.com; ⊕ year-round. A beautifully restored c1894 Victorian mansion with 4 rooms & 4 suites. Original woodwork, antique furniture, stained-glass windows. Full b/fast & afternoon tea inc. $$

⌂ **Super 8 Motel** (66 rooms) 63 Cole Dr; ⟍ 792 8888, T/F 1 877 513 7666; www.super8motelwindsor.com ⊕ year-round. Just off Hwy 101 Exit 5A, this 3-storey motel opened in 2007. All rooms have fridge & microwave. There is a 12m indoor pool, with 25m waterslide, & a jacuzzi. Continental b/fast inc. $$

⌂ **Woodshire Inn and Cocoa Pesto** (2 rooms) 494 King St; ⟍ 472 3300; e info@thewoodshire.com; www.thewoodshire.com; ⊕ year-round. This 1850s' building was one of the few to survive Windsor's great fire. The 2 luxurious suites feature cedar 4-poster beds, Egyptian cotton linen & modern bathrooms. More suites are planned. Breakfast available for an extra charge. $$

▲ **Hants County Exhibition Trailer Park** (25 sites) 237 Wentworth Rd; ⟍ 798 2011; ⊕ mid-May–early Oct. Serviced & unserviced campsites, go-carts & mini-golf. $

✗ **Cocoa Pesto** Inside Woodshire Inn; www.cocoapesto.com; ⊕ year-round 11.30–14.00 & 17.00–21.00 daily. The colour scheme at Cocoa's might not be to everyone's taste, but the excellent cooking, using fresh, local produce, at this modern, elegant bistro hits the right spot. The home-smoked

GREAT GOURD ALMIGHTY

What do Halloween, Cinderella, hockey and Windsor have in common? Giant pumpkins. When you visit **Howard Dill Enterprises** *(400 College Rd;* ⟍ *798 2728; www.howarddill.com;* ⊕ *year-round)*, don't expect a café serving pumpkin pie or pumpkin soup: the pumpkins cultivated here are grown for size rather than taste and the operation specialises not only in growing enormous gourds but also in developing seeds for others to do the same. One of Dill's seeds grew into a (then) world-record pumpkin weighing 656kg. September and October are the best times to see the field of giants and in October, when Windsor hosts a pumpkin festival and other pumpkin-related events (see *www.worldsbiggestpumpkins.com*).

I mentioned hockey: an iced-over pond on Dill's land is said to have been where ice hockey was first played in Canada. Incidentally, cricket was introduced to Windsor in 1840 but didn't catch on.

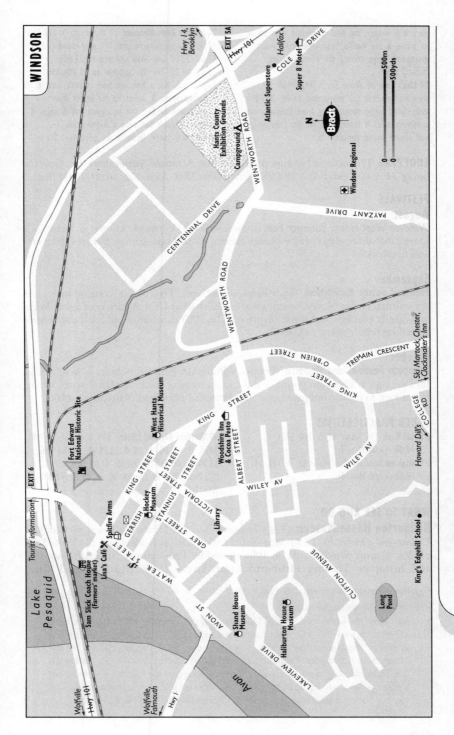

Lake Pesaquid

Wolfville Hwy 101

Wolfville, Falmouth

Hwy 1

AVON

Tourist information

EXIT 6

Sam Slick Coach House (Farmers' market)

Lisa's Café

Spitfire Arms

WATER STREET

AVON ST

GERRISH STREET

KING STREET

Hockey Museum

STANNUS STREET

VICTORIA STREET

GREY STREET

Shand House Museum

LAKEVIEW DRIVE

Haliburton House Museum

CLIFTON AVENUE

Long Pond

King's Edgehill School

Fort Edward National Historic Site

West Hants Historical Museum

KING STREET

Woodshire Inn & Cocoa Pesto

ALBERT STREET

Library

WILEY AV

WILEY AV

KING STREET

O'BRIEN STREET

TREMAIN CRESCENT

COLLEGE RD

Howard Dill's

Ski Martock, Chester, Clockmaker's Inn

CENTENNIAL DRIVE

WENTWORTH ROAD

WENTWORTH ROAD

Hants County Exhibition Grounds

Campground

PAYZANT DRIVE

Windsor Regional

Hwy 14, Brooklyn

EXIT 5A

Hwy 101

Atlantic Superstore

COLE DRIVE

Halifax

Super 8 Motel

N

Bradt

0   500m
0   500yds

pork is a winner, the beef tenderloin lives up to its name, & the vanilla bean cheesecake won't disappoint. Large terrace for alfresco dining. **$$–$$$**

✗ **Lisa's Café** 30 Water St; ☎ 792 1986; www.lisascafe.com; ⏱ year-round 11.00–20.00 daily. Good home cooking; try fried haddock with cranberry salsa & leave room for the fabulous pies and superb bread pudding! **$**

✗ **Spitfire Arms Alehouse** 29 Water St; ☎ 792 1460; www.spitfirearms.com; ⏱ year-round 11.00–23.00 Sun–Wed (kitchen to 21.00), 11.00–01.00 Thu–Sat (kitchen to 22.00). This English pub has a fine selection of both local & imported beers, & dishes up far better than average pub food – not just good fish & chips & bangers & mash but even a Birmingham (vegetarian) curry! Desserts are good too. **$**

SHOPPING The nearest big supermarket is the **Atlantic Superstore** (*11 Cole Dr, just off Hwy 101 Exit 5A;* ☎ *798 9537;* ⏱ *08.00–22.00 Mon–Sat, 10.00–18.00 Sun*).

FESTIVALS
August
Windsor West Hants Summer Fest (*www.samslick.ca*) Formerly known as 'Sam Slick Days', this three-day event includes theatre workshops, games, parades, concerts and fireworks.

September
Hants County Exhibition (*www.hantscountyex.com*) The oldest continuously run agricultural fair in North America was established in 1765. A variety of agricultural and family events – and some surprises. The 2009 exhibition included the biggest travelling reptile show in Canada.

October
Pumpkin Festival and Regatta Windsor's Pumpkin Festival includes a weigh-in to find the region's heaviest gourd, and the excitement of the Pumpkin Regatta, where teams race to paddle hollowed-out and decorated giant pumpkins across a lake.

OTHER PRACTICALITIES
$ **Royal Bank** 111 Water St; ☎ 798 5721; ⏱ 10.00–17.00 Mon–Fri
$ **Scotiabank** Windsor Mall, Water St; ☎ 798 5472; ⏱ 10.00–17.00 Mon–Fri

🕮 **Windsor Regional Library** 195 Albert St; ☎ 798 5424; ⏱ 10.00–17.00 & 18.30–20.30 Tue–Thu, 10.00–17.00 Fri–Sat, 14.00–17.00 Sun
✉ **Post office** 53 Gerrish St; ⏱ 08.30–17.00 Mon–Fri

WHAT TO SEE AND DO
Haliburton House Museum (*414 Clifton Av;* ☎ *798 2915; www.museum.gov.ns.ca/hh/;* ⏱ *Jun–mid-Oct 09.30–17.30 Mon–Sat, 13.00–17.30 Sun; admission CAN$3.25*) A c1830s' elegant wooden villa on 10ha owned by 19th-century author, humourist, and historian Thomas Haliburton (see box below). Much altered since

THOMAS HALIBURTON

Said to be the Father of American Humour, Thomas Chandler Haliburton was born in Windsor in 1796. His most famous creation was a fast-talking, wise-cracking American clock-seller, Sam Slick, who appeared in a regular column in the *Novascotian* newspaper. Many popular sayings are said to derive from Haliburton (via Slick) including 'quick as a wink', 'the early bird gets the worm', 'I wasn't born yesterday,' and 'barking up the wrong tree'. Although seldom read these days, in his day Haliburton was almost as popular as Charles Dickens and Mark Twain.

Haliburton's time (he lived here 1836–56), but still worth a visit. The museum is furnished with period antiques, including Haliburton's desk.

It is said that if you run around Piper's Pond within the grounds near the Clifton Gate House 13 (some say 20) times in an anti-clockwise direction, the ghost of a piper will rise up from the water and play his bagpipes. I haven't tried it.

Shand House Museum (*389 Avon St;* ✆ *798 8213; www.museum.gov.ns.ca/sh/;* ☼ *Jun–mid-Oct 09.30–17.30 daily, 13.00–17.30 Sun; admission CAN$3.25*) A fine c1890 Queen Anne-style mansion built on a hill above the Avon River for a newlywed couple. Beautifully furnished with wonderful interior woodwork, it is one of the first houses in the area fitted with electric lighting and indoor plumbing. There's a good view from the tower, and fascinating bike-related memorabilia – the bridegroom, Clifford Shand, was a champion cyclist (on a penny-farthing).

Windsor Hockey Heritage Centre (*128 Gerrish St;* ✆ *798 1800; www.birthplaceofhockey.com;* ☼ *summer 09.00–17.00 Mon–Sat, 13.00–17.00 Sun; winter 09.00–16.00 Mon–Sat*) Part ice-hockey gear shop, part museum which details Windsor's claim to be the birthplace of ice hockey (called *hockey* in Canada). Displays include old photos of players and teams, and some of the earliest ice-hockey equipment.

Fort Edward National Historic Site (*Fort Edward St;* ✆ *532 2321; www.pc.gc.ca/ lhn-nhs/ns/edward/index_e.asp; grounds* ☼ *year-round: blockhouse* ☼ *late Jun–Aug 10.00–18.00 Tue–Sat; admission free*) Built in 1750 to protect the land route from Halifax to the Annapolis Valley, the site includes the oldest-surviving wooden blockhouse in Canada. The officers' quarters and barracks survived until 1897 when they were destroyed by fire. Between 1903 and 1973 the site was a golf course: the blockhouse apart, there isn't much to see.

West Hants Historical Society Museum (*281 King St;* ✆ *798 4706; www.glinx.com/ ~whhs;* ☼ *late Jun–Aug 10.00–18.00 Tue–Sat; Sep 10.00–16.00 Tue–Fri; admission free*) Displays on the region's history in a former Methodist Church.

Ski Martock (✆ *798 9501; www.martock.com;* ☼ *in season 09.00–21.30 daily, to 22.00 Thu–Sat*) In winter, go downhill skiing a short hop from Windsor (and within an hour's drive of Halifax) at Ski Martock, off Highway 14, approximately 9km from Windsor and 71km from Halifax (take Exit 5 from Highway 101). A quad chair and T-bar rise 183 vertical metres. It's good for beginners and families. A one-day lift pass costs CAN$35.

Farmers' Market (*Sam Slick Coach Hse, waterfront;* ☼ *Jun–Oct 09.00–13.00 Sat*) Organic fruit & veg, baked goods, crafts and buskers – the farmers' market at Wolfville (see page 223) incidentally, is much bigger.

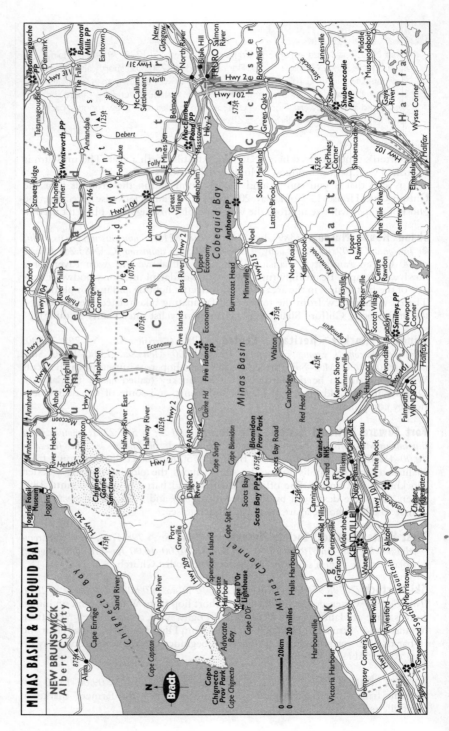

MINAS BASIN & COBEQUID BAY

6

Minas Basin and
Cobequid Bay

Twice a day, the massive tides of the Bay of Fundy pour through the Minas Channel to the Minas Basin, the eastern part of which is Cobequid Bay. Two large rivers, the Shubenacadie (pronounced 'shuben-ACK-addee') and the Salmon, empty into this bay.

This region divides into three main parts. One road, the 125km-long Highway 215, runs along the bay's southern shore (usually called Hants Shore) to – and along – the Shubenacadie River. From the town of Shubenacadie, one of the province's major arteries, Highway 102 (which originates in Halifax) runs north to Truro, third-largest town in Nova Scotia, set on the bank of the Salmon River. From Truro, Highway 2 runs west along the northern shore of Cobequid Bay and the Minas Basin to Parrsboro, from which Highway 209 continues west along the coast to Capes d'Or and Chignecto, before turning north along Chignecto Bay towards Amherst.

Whilst busy Truro has no shortage of services or places to stay and eat, the same cannot be said of the two shorelines, particularly the southern where there is little tourist infrastructure.

The Hants Shore is for those looking to unwind and enjoy a quiet, relaxing drive with lovely views past green fields to the red-sand shores and the water. This is the road less travelled – except perhaps by our feathered friends – it is part of the Western Hemisphere Shorebird Reserve, and serves as a critical feeding and roosting area for huge flocks of migrating shorebirds. You can visit a couple of old lighthouses, one of which – Burntcoat Head (see page 284) – marks the spot of the world's highest tides. The region's fascinating shipbuilding history and a high concentration of wonderful heritage buildings can be seen in Maitland (see page 234). In contrast, a few kilometres away are the thrills and spills of a rather unusual pastime – tidal-bore rafting (see page 236).

Shubenacadie (see page 238) has the province's best wildlife park, and Truro one of the best city parks, plus rare (for Nova Scotia) urban treats such as a seven-screen cinema. There are also huge supermarkets where you can stock up for your onward journey.

The northern shore starts off with a couple of pleasant communities, but as you head west the coastal scenery becomes more dramatic. The Five Islands area (see page 246) is interesting and photogenic, the town of Parrsboro (see page 247) has a few attractions including a good geological museum, and you can stay or eat in a lightkeeper's cottage at Cape d'Or (see page 254). This is a region of soaring cliffs, and the provincial park at Cape Chignecto (see page 255) is nirvana for hikers and also photographers when the weather is clement. The fossil-packed cliffs at Joggins (see page 255) were recently declared a UNESCO World Heritage Site.

You'll find a few more places to stay and eat on this side of the water, but overdeveloped it isn't. Come not for cinemas and supermarkets but solitude and scenery.

A word of caution: the tide changes quietly but quickly: activities such as digging for clams, or fossil/gemstone hunting can make one forget to keep an eye out, and it is easy to get trapped with the only escape route blocked by sheer cliffs. Ignore the tides and you could pay dearly.

HISTORY In the late 1600s, Acadians settled along these shores, constructing extensive dykes to turn the tidal marshlands into fertile fields. After the deportation of the Acadians, the land was resettled, primarily by New England Planters (see page 8).

For well over a century, shipbuilding was the mainstay of the economy for just about every coastal community in this region. Particularly between 1850 and 1890, many of today's tiny, sleepy communities were bustling and prosperous, and home to a couple of shipyards. Very few traces remain.

BROOKLYN

Apart from the provincial park (see below), a petrol station and a Reid's Meats & Clover Farms supermarket (*1034 Hwy 215;* ✆ *757 0701;* ⊕ *08.00–22.00 Mon–Sat, 09.00–22.00 Sun*), there is little reason to stop in Brooklyn.

GETTING THERE Brooklyn is just off Highway 14, 14km east of Windsor take Exit 5 from Highway 101.

 WHERE TO STAY There is a campground ($) in the provincial park, otherwise Windsor (see page 226) is less than 10km away.

WHAT TO DO
Smiley's Provincial Park (*109 Clayton MacKay Rd;* ✆ *757 3131; www.novascotiaparks.ca/parks/smileys.asp;* ⊕ *late Jun–early Sep*) This park on the Meander River takes in forest, farmland and white gypsum cliffs. It is a good picnic spot and you can cool off with a dip in the river. There's a quiet, pleasant 86-site campground with sites in both forest and on farmland.

AVONDALE

You'd never guess that this tiny, quiet community on the Avon River was once home to two thriving shipyards.

GETTING THERE Avondale is 12km/7 miles off Highway 14 (the Mantua turn-off).

WHAT TO SEE AND DO
Avon River Heritage Society Museum (*15-17 Belmont Rd;* ✆ *757 1718; www.avonriver.ca;* ⊕ *late Jun–Sep 10.00–17.00 Tue–Sun; admission free*) The museum – which, like so many, has been struggling to find the money to keep 'afloat' – has

---

SUMMER MUSIC

Kempt Shore, 5km from Summerville, is home to July's **Acoustic Maritime Music Festival** and August's **Annual Kempt Shore Bluegrass and Oldtime Music Festival**: both are held at the 5ha Peterson's Festival Campground (*6055 Hwy 215;* ✆ *633 2535; www.novascotiabluegrass.com*). The 20-site open campground (⊕ *Jun–mid-Oct*) offers views over the Avon River mouth and the Minas Basin.

exhibits on the Age of Sail and traditional shipbuilding skills and displays on the New England Planters. There's a licensed tea room/café with an outdoor deck overlooking the Avon River.

April Great Little Art Show The museum (see above) plays home to both professional and novice artists to display and sell their work in a semi-formal environment.

SUMMERVILLE

Between 1880 and 1937, Summerville was the terminus for a ferry service to Windsor. The pretty community once had a thriving ship building industry. Community suppers are held throughout the year.

GETTING THERE Summerville is on Highway 215, 18km/11 miles from Brooklyn.

 WHERE TO STAY

🏠 **Shipwright Inn** (4 rooms, 1 suite) 1 Wharf Rd; ☎ 633 2860; ⊕ year-round. You can overnight in one of the guest rooms or the suite at this renovated c1870 shipbuilder's home. $–$$

✘ **WHERE TO EAT** Your only option – but a good one – is the **Café Flower Garden** ($–$$), renowned for its seafood chowder, Sunday brunch buffet and Wednesday night music jam sessions, at the Avon Emporium (see below).

WHAT TO SEE AND DO
Avon Emporium (*1 Wharf Rd;* ☎ *633 2860; www.avonemporium.com;* ⊕ *year-round 07.30–20.00 Mon–Sat, 10.00–16.00 Sun*) Most of those who stop these days do so to visit this complex, which includes a gift/craft shop.

WALTON

What – at the time – was the world's largest-known barytes deposit was discovered in the area in 1941. The mineral – the main source of barium, used in industry and for X-ray imaging – was mined until 1978 when flooding halted operations. At one stage the mine accounted for 90% of Canada's barytes production. Concrete silos are the only obvious reminder that not so long ago this sleepy little harbour buzzed with cargo ships.

GETTING THERE Walton is on Highway 215, 46km/29 miles from Brooklyn and 44km/27 miles from Maitland.

 WHERE TO STAY AND EAT

🏕 **Whale Creek Campsite** (50 sites) Hwy 215; ☎ 528 2063; ⊕ late May–early Sep. At the mouth of the Walton River: open & wooded sites. $

✘ **Walton Pub** 39 Shore Rd; ☎ 528 2670; ⊕ 11.00–22.30 Mon–Thu, 11.00–midnight Fri–Sat, 12.00–22.00 Sun. Reliable pub food at sensible prices. $

SHOPPING The **Walton Variety Store** (*39 Hwy 215;* ☎ *528 2051;* ⊕ *09.00–20.00 daily*) is the local general store.

OTHER PRACTICALITIES
✉ **Post office** 4309 Walton Wood Rd; ⊕ 08.00–16.30 Mon–Fri, 09.00–13.00 Sat

WHAT TO SEE AND DO
Walton Lighthouse *(Weir Rd; ✎ 528 2411; www.waltonlighthouse.com;* ⊕ *May–mid-Oct 08.00–19.00 daily)* Inside this c1873 three-storey tower are display panels on the area's history, and a telescope. Outside, picnic tables and a short loop trail through the woods to a coastal look-out.

BURNTCOAT HEAD

Many places claim the record, but most scientists – and the *Guinness Book of World Records* – concur with the claim of the Burntcoat (or is it Burncoat – the debate is ongoing) area as the actual site of the world's highest tides. The maximum tidal range (the difference between high and low tides) recorded here is an astounding 16.8m.

GETTING THERE Burntcoat Head is just off Highway 215, 60km/37 miles from Windsor, 100km/62 miles from Halifax and 50km/31 miles from Truro.

WHERE TO STAY AND EAT
🏠 **Shangri-la Cottages** (3 cottages) 619 Burntcoat Rd; ✎ 369 2050, T/F 1 866 977 3977; e reservations@shangri-lacottages.com; www.shangri-lacottages.com; ⊕ year-round. Bill & Brenda's spacious, quiet, well-equipped & comfortable 1- & 2-bedroom cottages overlook Cobequid Bay & are just a stone's throw from the lighthouse park. **$$$**

✗ **Deanna's Takeout** 4681 Hwy 215, Noel; ✎ 369 2733; ⊕ May–Sep 11.00–22.00 Thu–Sun; Jul–Aug Wed–Sun. A great little take-out with friendly service & generous portions. Grab a club sandwich, fish & chips or just an ice cream & take it to one of the nearby parks to enjoy. **$**

WHAT TO SEE AND DO
Burntcoat Head Park *(611 Burntcoat Rd; ✎ 369 2529;* ⊕ *mid-May-mid-Oct 08.00–dusk daily: lighthouse* ⊕ *Jun–Sep 10.00–18.00 daily; admission free)* This Burntcoat Head lighthouse is a replica of the 1913 version. Set in a pretty picnic park, it serves as an interpretive centre. There is a panoramic view from the tower. A short walking trail leads to the beach which is well worth a visit when the tide is out. Walk on the ocean floor between unique flower-pot-red sandstone formations topped by trees.

MAITLAND

With a lovely location on Cobequid Bay at the mouth of the Shubenacadie River, Maitland was a very important shipbuilding centre in the second half of the 19th century. While no traces of the shipyards remain, the village was designated Nova Scotia's first Heritage Conservation District for its many well-preserved 19th-century homes: styles include Second Empire, Classical Revival and Greek Revival. See, for example, the c1870 Victorian Gothic **Springhurst** *(8557 Hwy 215)*, once the home of Alfred Putnam, one of Maitland's most prominent shipbuilders. Pick up a booklet with a self-guided Historic Homes walking tour at Lawrence House (see page 235). The village also offers a waterfront day-use park with an Acadian dyke and a reconstructed wharf.

HISTORY Present-day Maitland was known to the Mi'kmaq as *twitnook* – 'the tide runs out fast'. Loyalist settlers named it after Sir Peregrine Maitland, Governor of Nova Scotia from 1828 to 1834.

At one time, this was one of the busiest ports in the province, and it was here in 1874 that Canada's largest wooden ship was built by William D Lawrence.

Somewhat unimaginatively, he called it the *William D Lawrence* – its nickname, 'the Great Ship', didn't show much originality either. The vessel was more than twice the size of the usual ocean-going ships of the time.

GETTING THERE Maitland is on Highway 215, 9km/6 miles from Lower Selma, 30km/19 miles from Shubenacadie and 79km/49 miles from Windsor.

WHERE TO STAY AND EAT Two or three of the village's other B&Bs and inns have closed down in recent times, resulting in fewer accommodation choices and even less options for dining. The village is crying out for a good eatery on the short main drag – the best choice for a light, tasty and healthy lunch is the Look-off Café at Riverview Herbs.

Foley House Inn (4 rooms) 9639 Cedar St; 261 2844, T/F 1 888 989 0882; www.foleyhouse.com; May–Oct. Accommodation in this c1830 former shipbuilder's house comprises 3 bedrooms & a suite. Bearing in mind the way places to stay & eat come & go in the village, check ahead that the licensed dining room (*currently* mid-May–mid-Oct 12.00–20.00; $$) will be open for your visit. It specialises in seafood. Full b/fast inc. $

Tidal Life Guesthouse (3 rooms) 9568 Cedar St; 261 2583; e info@thetidallife.ca; www.thetidallife.ca; May–Oct. A c1870 home in over 5ha of grounds. Shared bathroom. Guest lounges. Deluxe continental b/fast inc. $

Millpond Campground (55 sites) 9120 Cedar St, Maitland; 261 2249; www.millpondcampground.com; May–Sep. Open & wooded campground with serviced & unserviced sites: outdoor pool. $

Look-off Café at Riverview Herbs 8907 Hwy 215; 261 2274, T/F 1 866 261 4372; www.riverviewherbs.com; mid-Jun–mid-Sep 10.30–15.00 daily. It has a limited menu of healthy & tasty sandwiches & salads, plus baked goods & aromatic ice cream. $

SHOPPING There are a few shops – antiques and bric-a-brac – and a c1839 general store with an uninspiring take-out on the north side of Highway 215, the main street.

FESTIVALS
September
Launch Day Festival Commemorates the launch of the WD *Lawrence*, the largest wooden-hulled full-rigged vessel ever built in Canada. Held on a Saturday, in late September. Expect a non-motorised procession, a launch re-enactment and a whisky barrel race.

November
Christmas Festival Includes a craft fair, Gentlemen's Tea and Christmas Tree Stroll.

OTHER PRACTICALITIES
Post office 8829 Hwy 215; 07.30–16.30 Mon–Fri, 09.00–12.00 Sat

WHAT TO SEE AND DO
Lawrence House Museum (*8660 Hwy 215;* 261 2628; *www.museum.gov.ns.ca/lh/;* Jun–mid-Oct 09.30–17.30 Mon–Sat, 13.00–17.30 Sun; admission CAN$3.25) This elegant c1870 Classical Revival style building was the home of William D Lawrence, one of Canada's great shipbuilders. It is here, on a hill overlooking the site of his shipyard, that he drew up the plans for construction of Canada's largest wooden ship (see *History*, page 234). Most of the furnishings are original, including furniture and exotic souvenirs collected from around the globe.

Not just for those interested in the history of shipbuilding, Lawrence House also opens a window on Victorian life in the area.

AROUND MAITLAND

EAST HANTS HISTORICAL MUSEUM *(Hwy 215, Lower Selma;* ↘ *369 2261;* ⊕ *Jun–Aug 09.30–17.30 daily)* Housed in a beautifully decorated c1865 former Presbyterian church 9km west of Maitland along Highway 215. There are few surprises here – except perhaps a small *Titanic* display.

ANTHONY PROVINCIAL PARK *(Hwy 215, Lower Selma;* ↘ *261 2947)* A pretty picnic park 9km west of Maitland along Highway 215 and overlooking Cobequid Bay. Wharf-side interpretive displays on the area's history, and beach access at low tide.

GALLERY 215 *(8247 Hwy 215, Selma;* ↘ *261 2151; www.artgallery215.com;* ⊕ *late Jun–early Oct; admission free)* This former c1868 schoolhouse 2km west of Maitland along Highway 215, built by shipbuilding carpenters, reopened in 2006 as a gallery/community centre. The work of around 40 local artists and craftspeople is displayed, and there is a Monday-morning rug-hooking group.

SOUTH MAITLAND

Water is the focus of this small community on the Shubenacadie River, which offers rafting, wetlands birdwatching, and a good opportunity to learn about the Bay of Fundy tides.

GETTING THERE South Maitland can be reached on Highways 215 and 236, 8km/5 miles from Maitland and 22km/14 miles from Shubenacadie.

THE TIDAL BORE EXPLAINED

The Bay of Fundy sees the world's highest recorded tides. Twice daily, one hundred billion tonnes of seawater flows into the funnel-shaped bay. At the end of the bay furthest from its mouth, rivers (such as the Shubenacadie and Salmon) empty into it. The immense force and volume of the incoming tide not only halts these rivers' flows, but reverses them and sends them several kilometres backwards. The first wave caused by the incoming tide reversing the rivers' flows is called the 'tidal bore'.

The highest bores occur around the full and new moons: and although it can move at speeds over 10km/hour, sound travels a lot faster, and you're likely to hear the rush of water before you see it.

But don't be taken in by tourist brochure hype. Many see the tidal bore for the first time and say 'Is that it?'. If you expect a huge tsunami-type wave, you will be very disappointed: what you are likely to see – and hear – is a wave of approximately 25cm moving steadily upriver.

In this area, South Maitland and the nearby Tidal Bore Rafting Park are excellent spots from which to view the phenomenon.

Times for the bore's arrival (generally, pretty accurate) can be found on the Rafting Park's website (see box on page 237) or obtained from local newspapers, accommodations, or tourist offices. Try to arrive at your chosen vantage point a good ten minutes early as nature doesn't always observe the timetable strictly.

On the Shubenacadie, following behind the bore are a series of rapids. These rapids are a vital factor in one of the province's most exciting water-based activities.

For those seeking soaking thrills and spills, Nova Scotia offers its own unique version of white-water rafting.

Things usually start with a gentle boat trip on the Shubenacadie River on which you may see bald eagles.

Near its mouth, rather than a rocky bottom, the river has several sandbars. As the incoming tide rushes up the river, big – but temporary – tidal rapid waves are created over each sandbar. These rapids dissipate after ten to 15 minutes.

Skilled and experienced guides are out to thrill, and pilot motorised inflatable (zodiac-type) boats to hit the waves head-on, lifting the craft and its occupants into the air and crashing them back onto the water. Apart from the splashing and rushing water, expect shrieks and screams of laughter from your fellow passengers.

The boats ride the rapid and have time to turn and do it again two or three times at each sandbar.

Some operators include a break for lunch before you return to the boats for a much calmer trip exploring upriver. Some also throw in mudsliding (voluntary) as a free extra.

The rafting season runs from May to October: the moon and tides determine the expected intensity of the experience (the rafting companies' websites have tide charts to help you choose your level). During lower tides, more time is spent on nature observation.

Wear old, dark clothes that you don't mind getting wet and dirty. Take a towel and extra set of clothes.

Tidal-bore rafting is very popular, especially around the highest tides, so book early to avoid disappointment. Operators include:

Shubenacadie River Adventure Tours 10061 Hwy 215, South Maitland; ☎ T/F 1 888 878 8687; www.shubie.com; ⊕ Jun–Sep. 3hr trips (CAN$78 inc all-you-can-eat BBQ). Mudsliding offered.
Shubenacadie River Runners 8681 Hwy 215, Maitland; ☎ T/F 1 800 856 5061; www.tidalborerafting.com; ⊕ May–Sep. Based in Maitland at the river's mouth, it offers longer trips. Half-day (CAN$67), full day (CAN$89 inc steak barbecue).
Tidal Bore Rafting Park 12215 Hwy 215, Shubenacadie; ☎ 758 4032, T/F 1 800 565 7238; www.tidalboreraftingpark.com; ⊕ May–Oct. 2hr (CAN$71) & 4hr (CAN$89) trips. Mudsliding offered.

TOURIST INFORMATION At the Fundy Tidal Interpretive Centre (see below).

🏠 WHERE TO STAY AND EAT

🏠 **Rafters Ridge Cottages** (13 units) 12215 Hwy 215, Shubenacadie; ☎ 758 4032, T/F 1 800 565 7238; www.tidalboreraftingpark.com; ⊕ year-round; off-season by reservation. Comfortable 1-, 2- & 5-bedroom cabins & chalets set between trees on a hillside overlooking the Shubenacadie River. Discounts are available for those rafting with the company. Even if you're not rafting, this is a pleasant place to stay, with seasonal outdoor pool & walking trails. The rustic pine & cedar licensed restaurant (⊕ May–Oct 08.00–21.00 daily; $–$$) doesn't have a bad menu: soups & pork dishes are usually good, as are the desserts. $$–$$$

WHAT TO SEE AND DO
Fundy Tidal Interpretive Centre (9865 Hwy 236; ☎ 261 2298; www.southmaitlandns.com; ⊕ mid-May–mid-Oct 09.00–17.00 daily; admission free) Behind the centre which explains the Fundy tides and the tidal bore, an observation deck high above the Shubenacadie is a good place to watch the watery action, and the rafters (see box above): time your visit to coincide with the bore arrival.

Very close by, Ducks Unlimited maintains ponds which are home to a variety of waterfowl. Easy walking trails and interpretive boards enhance the birdwatching experience.

SHUBENACADIE

The word 'Shubenacadie' comes from the Mi'kmaq *Segubunakade* meaning 'place where the ground nuts grow' (these ground nuts should not be confused with peanuts - often called 'ground nuts' – but *Apios americana*, a climbing vine and member of the pea family and distantly related to the soya bean). The major attraction is the wildlife park, but it is also worth popping in to the little museum.

GETTING THERE Shubenacadie is on Highway 2, and just off Exit 10 of Highway 102, 66km/41 miles from Halifax and 35km/22 miles from Truro.

WHERE TO STAY AND EAT

⚊ **Wild Nature Camping Ground** (45 sites) 20961 Hwy 2; ☎ 758 1631; ⊕ late May–Sep. Open & wooded serviced & unserviced sites, 1km from Shubenacadie Wildlife Park (see below). $
✗ **Khoury's Restaurant** 2808 Main St; ☎ 758 3715; ⊕ year-round 08.00–20.00 daily. The

restaurant serves up liver & onions, pan-fried haddock & pasta. $
✗ **Yummy's Deli** 2800 Main St; ☎ 758 3811; ⊕ year-round 09.00–18.00 Mon–Sat, 13.00–18.00 Sun. Coffee, soup, sandwiches & simple salads. $

OTHER PRACTICALITIES

$ **Royal Bank** 2824 Main St; ☎ 758 2295; ⊕ 09.30–16.30 Tue–Thu

✉ **Post office** 2770 Hwy 2; ⊕ 08.30–17.00 Mon–Fri, 08.30–12.30 Sat

WHAT TO SEE AND DO

Shubenacadie Wildlife Park (*149 Creighton Rd;* ☎ *758 2040; wildlifepark.gov.ns.ca;* ⊕ *mid–May–mid-Oct 09.00–19.00 daily; mid-Oct–mid-May 09.00–15.00 Sun; admission CAN$4.25 summer, CAN$2.50 winter*) At the busiest and best of the province's wildlife parks, 2km of largely shaded paths lead through 20ha where over 30 species of mammals and over 60 bird species (almost all native to Nova Scotia) can be seen. Species include black bear, moose, Sable Island horses, skunks, groundhogs, beavers and bald eagles. To see the animals out in the open and more sprightly, choose a cooler day or come early in the morning or in the late afternoon.

Tinsmith Shop Museum (*2854 Main St;* ☎ *758 5228; www.tinshopmuseum.ca;* ⊕ *mid–May–mid-Sep 10.00–16.00 Mon–Sat, 12.00–16.00 Sun; O/S by appointment, admission CAN$2*) The shop was built in the 1890s and initially produced tin cans for milk, later branching out to sell all kinds of hardware. The original machinery – installed in 1896 – can still be seen. There's a craft shop and pretty garden.

STEWIACKE

Said to be exactly halfway between the North Pole and the Equator, Stewiacke (the name comes from the Mi'kmaq meaning 'flowing out in small streams' is home to an American-style commercial attraction.

GETTING THERE Stewiacke is on Highway 2, and just off Exit 11 on Highway 102, 68km/42 miles from Halifax, 30km/19 miles from Truro and 7km/4 miles north of Shubenacadie.

TOURIST INFORMATION (*87 Main St West;* ✆ *639 1248;* ⊕ *daily Jan–Mar & Sep–Dec 10.00–7.00 Thu–Mon, daily Apr–Jun 10.00–17.00, daily Jul–Aug 09.00–19.00*)

⌂ WHERE TO STAY AND EAT

⌂ **Nelson House B&B** (3 rooms) 138 Main St East; ✆ 639 1380, T/F 1 866 331 1380; www.thenelsonhousebb.com; ⊕ year-round. A stately c1905 house with a lovely veranda built for the then mayor of Stewiacke. Rooms with en-suite or shared bathrooms. Full b/fast inc (eg: homemade granola with yoghurt & fresh fruit or Belgian waffles with local maple syrup). $$

✗ **Whistler's Pub** 285 George St; ✆ 639 9221; ⊕ 11.00–22.00 daily (food until 20.00, until 21.00 Thu–Sat). The portions are generous & the standard pub food cheap & not too greasy. $

OTHER PRACTICALITIES

$ **Heritage Credit Union** 5353 Hwy 289, Upper Stewiacke; ✆ 671 2647; ⊕ 09.30–17.00 Mon–Thu, 09.30–18.00 Fri

▣ **Stewiacke Branch Library** 295 George St; ✆ 639 2481; 13.00–17.00 & 18.00–20.00 Tue, 10.00–12 noon & 13.00–17.00 &18.00–20.00 Thu, 13.00–16.30 Fri, 13.00–17.00 Sat.

▣ **Post office** 55 Riverside Av; ⊕ 08.30–17.15 Mon–Fri, 09.00–12.00 Sat

WHAT TO SEE

Mastodon Ridge and Showcase Nova Scotia (*Hwy 102 Exit 11;* ✆ *639 2345; www.mastodonridge.com;* ⊕ *mid-May–mid-Oct 10.00–17.00 daily; admission (Showcase Nova Scotia) CAN$4.50*) Not easy to miss – a life-size replica of an 89,000-year-old mastodon, whose bones were unearthed in 1991 in a nearby gypsum quarry, stands outside in full view of Highway 102. With a mini-theatre showing a 12-minute 'best of scenic Nova Scotia' film, 18-hole mini-golf, Showcase Nova Scotia (back through time audio-visual presentation), souvenir shops, and what is said to be the biggest KFC (it used to be called Kentucky Fried Chicken) in Atlantic Canada.

TRURO

Centrally located, situated at the convergence of two of the province's major expressways, on two coach routes and served by VIA Rail, Truro has long been known as the 'Hub of Nova Scotia'. It is the province's third-largest town, with an economy based on shipping, dairy products, and manufacture. Neighbouring Bible Hill has been home to the Nova Scotia Agricultural College (Canada's third-oldest agricultural college) for over a century.

Many of those planning a trip to Nova Scotia get out a map and look for a base from which to make day trips to see all of the province's highlights. Many choose Truro. However, compared with much of the rest of the province, Truro is busy, lacks charm, and doesn't really have the same laid-back small-town feel. Railway level crossings often cause long traffic jams. But if you're happy to do a lot of driving and want somewhere with shopping, services, a good choice of accommodation and eateries from which to visit the capital, the Minas Basin shore, and perhaps the western half of the Northumberland Strait shore, then maybe Truro's for you.

HISTORY The Mi'kmaq named Truro *Cobequid* meaning 'the end of the water's flow' or 'place of rushing water' – a sure sign the tidal bore (see page 236) isn't a new phenomenon.

Pre-Expulsion, Acadian families farmed and traded in this area. A small group of New Englanders made their homes here in 1759, and in the following years, were joined by a number of Irish who Colonel McNutt (see page 8) had brought

6

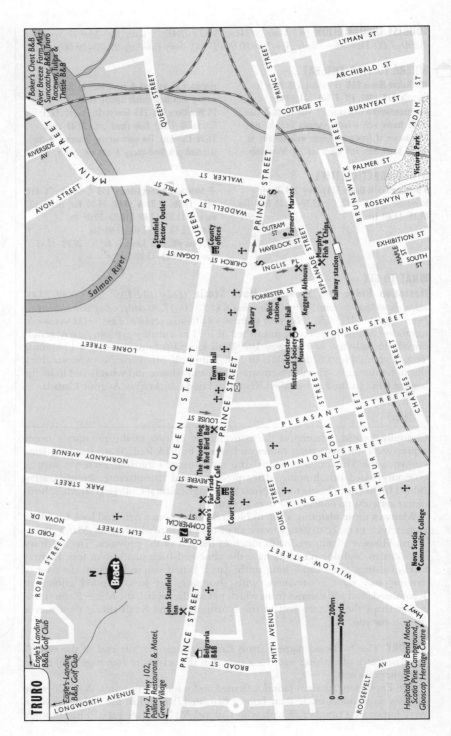

TRURO

Baker's Chest B&B
River Breeze Farm Mkt,
Suncatcher B&B Truro
Raceway, Tulips &
Thistle B&B

RIVERSIDE AV

MAIN STREET

AVON STREET

Salmon River

QUEEN STREET

Stanfield
Factory Outlet

MILL ST

WADDELL ST

WALKER ST

PRINCE STREET

LYMAN ST

ARCHIBALD ST

BURNYEAT ST

COTTAGE ST

BRUNSWICK STREET

PALMER ST

ROSEWYN PL

Victoria Park

ADAM ST

County
offices

QUEEN ST

LOGAN ST

CHURCH ST

OUTRAM
ST

Farmers' Market

HAVELOCK ST

INGLIS PL

EXHIBITION ST

MAPLE ST

SOUTH ST

Murphy's
Fish & Chips

ESPLANADE STREET

LORNE STREET

QUEEN STREET

Library

Police
station

FORRESTER ST

Fire Hall

Kegger's Alehouse

Railway station

Town Hall

PRINCE STREET

Colchester
Historical Society
Museum

YOUNG STREET

CHARLES STREET

NORMANDY AVENUE

The Wooden Hog
& Red Bird Bar

LOUISE ST

PLEASANT STREET

VICTORIA STREET

STREET

PARK STREET

QUEEN STREET

REVERE ST

Fair Trade
Country Café

DOMINION STREET

KING STREET

ARTHUR STREET

FORD ST

NOVA DR

ELM STREET

COURT ST

COMMERCIAL ST

Neenamo's

Court House

DUKE STREET

ROBIE STREET

LONGWORTH AVENUE

Hwy 2, Hwy 102,
Palliser Restaurant & Motel,
Great Village

Eagle's Landing
B&B, Golf Club

Eagle's Landing
B&B, Golf Club

N

Bradt

John Stanfield
Inn

Belgravia
B&B

PRINCE STREET

BROAD ST

SMITH AVENUE

WILLOW STREET

Nova Scotia
Community College

Hospital, Willow Bend Motel,
Scotia Pine Campground,
Glooscap Heritage Centre

Hwy 2

ROOSEVELT AV

0   200m
0   200yds

240

over. They dreaded the 'savage' Mi'kmaq and built a stockaded fort, retiring into it every evening. After some time passed and the Mi'kmaq had failed to display any hostility, the fort was abandoned.

GETTING THERE

By car Truro is on Highway 2, very close to the junction of Highway 104 (the Trans Canada Highway – Exit 15) and Highway 102 Exit 14. It is 117km/73 miles from Amherst, 91km/57 miles from Parrsboro and 100km/62 miles from Halifax.

By bus Two Acadian coach routes stop here: one connects Amherst (and New Brunswick) with Halifax, and the other, Sydney with Halifax (see page 52).

By train Six days a week one train (see page 40) in each direction connects Truro with Halifax, and Amherst (and Montreal). Those travelling from Halifax depart daily (except Tues) at 12.35 and arrive at 14.03 in Truro, while trains travelling from Truro to Halifax depart daily (except Wed) at 14.51 and arrive at 16.23 in Halifax. Tickets start at CAN$23 for a single.

TOURIST INFORMATION

☒ Tourist information Victoria Sq, Court St; ☎ 893 2922; ⊕ May–Jun & Sep–mid-Oct 09.00–17.00 daily; Jul–Aug 08.30–19.30 daily

☒ Tourist information Glooscap Heritage Centre (see page 244) ⊕ mid-May–mid-Oct 08.30–19.30 Mon–Fri, 10.00–18.00 Sat–Sun; mid-Oct–mid-May 08.30–16.30 Mon–Fri

WHERE TO STAY

⌂ Baker's Chest B&B (4 rooms) 53 Farnham Rd; ☎ 893 4824, T/F 1 877 822 5655; www.bakerschest.ca; ⊕ year-round. Century home with lovely gardens, a large indoor jacuzzi, & a fitness room. See page 242 for tea room. Full b/fast inc. $$

⌂ Belgravia B&B (3 rooms) 5 Broad St; ☎ 893 7100, T/F 1 866 877 9900; www.belgravia.ca; ⊕ year-round. A fine c1903 house with many period features & within easy walking distance of the town centre. Hearty full b/fast inc (eg: focaccia with scrambled eggs & smoked salmon, or home-made waffles with fresh blueberry sauce & vanilla yoghurt). $$

⌂ Eagle's Landing B&B (3 rooms) 401 Robie St; ☎ 893 2346, T/F 1 866 893 2346; www.bbcanada.com/10009.html; ⊕ year-round. Comfortable & friendly with garden & nice balcony/deck & an easy walk to the town centre. Gourmet full b/fast & evening snacks inc. $$

⌂ Suncatcher B&B (2 rooms) 25 Wile Crest Av, North River; ☎ 893 7169, T/F 1 877 203 6032;

e suncatcher@eastlink.ca; www.bbcanada.com/1853.html; ⊕ year-round. A comfortable c1970s' B&B about 5km from the town centre with stained-glass studio on premises (weekend workshops offered). Hosts Ruth & Gerry are friendly & knowledgeable about the area. Full b/fast & evening snack inc. $$

⌂ Tulips & Thistle B&B (4 rooms) 913 Pictou Rd; ☎ 895 6141, T/F 1 866 724 7796; www.tulipsandthistlebedandbreakfast.com; ⊕ year-round. Very friendly & comfortable; nice deck, sunroom, pleasant garden. A 9km drive outside town, off Highway104 Exit 17. Full gourmet b/fast inc. $$

⌂ Willow Bend Motel (28 units) 277 Willow St; ☎ 895 5325, T/F 1 888 594 5569; www.willowbendmotel.com; ⊕ year-round. With 15 standard rooms, 6 (larger) deluxe rooms & 7 suites. All have fridges. There is a seasonal outdoor pool & jacuzzi. 'Deluxe' continental b/fast inc. $$

⋏ Scotia Pine Campground (160 sites) Hwy 2, Hilden; ☎ 893 3666, T/F 1 877 893 3666;

ICH BIN EIN BERLINER

A local Truro businessman has loaned the town six sections of the Berlin Wall. These are on display at 867 Prince Street.

www.scotiapine.ca; ⏰ Jun–mid-Oct. Large campground between Truro & Brookfield (take Exit 12 or 13 from Hwy 102); serviced sites for motorhomes, open & wooded tent sites. Pool (in season), sauna & laundromat. $

✕ WHERE TO EAT

✕ **John Stanfield Inn** 437 Prince St; 📞 895 1505, T/F 1 800 561 7666; www.johnstanfieldinn.com; ⏰ year-round 17.00–21.00 daily. 'Fine-dining' in a c1902 Queen Anne period inn. The menu might change frequently, but standards tend to stay high. Choose (for example) rack of Australian lamb with figs & caramelised shallots, or perhaps halibut with mango sticky rice. Good wine list. Reservations recommended. **$$$**

✕ **Neenamo's** 515 Prince St; 📞 843 3131; www.neenamos.wordpress.com; ⏰ year-round 11.00–14.00 & 17.00–21.00 Tue–Fri, 17.00–21.00 Sat. The menu at this relatively new restaurant changes regularly, but includes an interesting mix. Lunch tends to be pastas, paninis, soups & salads, but in the evening you might try Thai seafood curry, or grilled salmon with maple butter cream & risotto cake. Upmarket casual dining. **$$–$$$**

✕ **Kegger's Alehouse** 72 Inglis Pl; 📞 895 5347; www.keggersalehouse.com; ⏰ year-round 16.00–22.00 Mon–Tue, 16.00–midnight Wed–Sat. Offering a fine range of local & international ales; good pub food (eg: steak quesadillas – but the jury is still out on the deep-fried cheesecake), cocktails; lively atmosphere. Live music Wed–Sat evenings. **$$**

✕ **The Wooden Hog** 627 Prince St; 📞 895 0779; ⏰ year-round 09.00–15.00 Mon, 09.00–21.00 Tue–Fri, 11.00–21.00 Sat. A warm, friendly atmosphere in this licensed European-style café. Light lunch includes soups, salads & sandwiches on fresh-baked bread. Evening fare is more substantial with generally good seafood, pasta & chicken dishes. Next door (same ownership) **The Red Bird** (⏰ year-round 16.30–late Wed–Sat; over 18s only) offers the largest selection of spirits (particularly whisky) in the area. **$$**

✕ **Baker's Chest Tea Room** 53 Farnham Rd; 📞 893 4824, T/F 1 877 822 5655; www.bakerschest.ca; ⏰ early May–late Nov 11.00–15.00 Mon–Fri. The bright tea room dishes up freshly made standards – & some Dutch specialities. The seafood chowder & chicken vol-au-vent are recommended, as is the dessert sampler plate. Outdoor patio. **$**

✕ **Fair Trade Country Café** 535 Prince St; 📞 843 3533; www.fairtradecountrycafe.com; ⏰ year-round 07.30–22.00 Mon–Thu, 08.00–23.00 Fri–Sat, 08.00–22.00 Sun. Part coffee shop, part café, part live music venue. Good, healthy (& not so healthy) food, excellent coffee. **$**

✕ **Murphy's Fish & Chips** 88 The Esplanade; 📞 895 1275; www.murphysfishandchips.com; ⏰ year-round 11.00–19.00 Mon–Sat, 12.00–19.00 Sun. An uninspiring location in a little shopping mall, but this family-friendly eatery offers well-cooked, well-priced seafood. **$**

FESTIVALS
July
Nova Scotia Bluegrass & Oldtime Music Festival (*www.downeastgrass.com*) The Provincial Exhibition Grounds in nearby Bible Hill are the new home of this three-day festival.

August
Dutch Mason Blues Festival Three days of blues music, plus a custom motorbike show. See www.dutchmason.com/festival/

Mi'kmaq PowWow Drumming, dancing, Mi'kmaq food and crafts.

Nova Scotia Provincial Exhibition (*www.nspe.ca*) The province's premiere agricultural and industrial fair.

OTHER PRACTICALITIES
$ **Royal Bank** 940 Prince St; 📞 893 4343; ⏰ 10.00–17.00 Mon–Wed & Fri, 10.00–19.00 Thu

$ **Scotiabank** 7 Inglis Pl; 📞 895 0591; ⏰ 10.00–17.00 Mon–Fri

✚ **Colchester Regional Hospital** 207 Willow St; 🕾 893 4321
📚 **Truro Branch Library** 754 Prince St; 🕾 895 4183; ⊕ 10.00–20.00 Tue–Thu, 10.00–18.00 Fri, 10.00–17.00 Sat

✉ **Post office** 664 Prince St; ⊕ 08.00–17.15 Mon–Fri
🚕 **Layton's Taxi** 🕾 895 4471
🚕 **Scotia Taxi** 🕾 883 8093

WHAT TO SEE AND DO In and around the downtown area is some fine architecture (Truro has three designated Heritage Conservation Districts). 'Tree sculptures' (see box below) are another interesting feature. In addition to the **Truro Golf Club** (*86 Golf St; 🕾 893 2508; www.trurogolfclub.com*) there are several other courses within a few minutes' drive of town. The town's *pièce de rèsistance*, though, is the wonderful Victoria Park (see below).

Watch the tidal bore Truro's Salmon River is one of the most accessible places to watch the incoming tide forcing the Salmon River back the wrong way and filling the riverbed. Tidal-bore (see page 236) arrival times are listed in the *Truro Daily News* and at the tourist information office. A good place to bore-watch is by the **Palliser Restaurant and Motel** (*103 Tidal Bore Rd; by Exit 14 of Highway 102*). There's a small interpretation centre and floodlighting for nocturnal visitors.

Colchester Historical Society Museum (*29 Young St; 🕾 895 6284; www.genealogynet.com/colchester/; ⊕ mid-Jun–Aug 10.00–17.00 Mon–Fri, 14.00–17.00 Sat; Sep–mid-Jun 10.00–12.00 & 13.00–16.00 Tue–Fri, 13.00–16.00 Sat; admission CAN$2*) Housed in a c1900 brick building with displays on the town and region's heritage and natural history. The bookshop has a good selection of titles on Truro and the province.

Victoria Park (*Brunswick St & Park Rd; ⊕ Apr–Nov; admission free*) Occupying over 160ha, this is one of the most beautiful natural parks in eastern Canada. The grassy day-use area at the main entrance can get busy on sunny weekends. From there, choose from numerous trails through the woods of red and white spruce, ancient hemlock, and white pine. Head along a deep Triassic gorge and see 2 picturesque waterfalls on Lepper's Brook. Jacob's Ladder is a 175-step wooden staircase up the side of the gorge. For a fabulous view over the surrounding area and the Cobequid Basin, take the trail to the look-off at the top of Wood Street (there is also road access to Wood Street).

River Breeze Farm Market (*660 Onslow Rd; 🕾 895 5138; www.riverbreeze.info; ⊕ year-round 07.00–18.00 daily*) Farm market it may be, but there's usually more going on at River Breeze, such as a petting zoo, U-pick, or (in autumn) Atlantic Canada's largest corn maze.

TREE ART

Truro's tall, beautiful elm trees were ravaged by Dutch elm disease in the 1970s, but in 1999, the town commissioned an artist to carve the base of a diseased tree into a sculpture – of Sir Adams G Archibald, Truro's Father of Confederation (see page 11). This became the first of a series of representations of many of Truro's most prominent residents and historical figures. Dotted about town, these include an Acadian farmer and a bear carrying an ice-hockey stick. A sculpture booklet is available at the tourist office.

Farmers' Market (*Between Outram & Havelock sts; www.trurofarmersmarket.ca;* ⊕ *mid-May–late Oct 08.00–12.00 Sat*) The market has over two-dozen stalls.

Stanfield Factory Outlet (*1 Logan St;* ✆ *895 5406; www.stanfields.com;* ⊕ *09.00–17.00 Tue–Sat*) The UK has M&S, but for Nova Scotia and much of Canada, Truro's Stanfield's – established well over a century ago – is the company most associated with underwear.

AROUND TRURO

TRURO RACEWAY (*Bible Hill Exhibition Grounds, Ryland Av, Bible Hill;* ✆ *893 8075; www.truroraceway.ca;* ⊕ *year–round*) The largest of the province's three harness-racing tracks. To find out what harness racing is all about, head out on a Sunday afternoon.

GLOOSCAP HERITAGE CENTRE (*65 Treaty Trail, Millbrook;* ✆ *843 3496, T/F 1 800 895 1177; www.glooscapheritagecentre.com;* ⊕ *mid-May–mid-Oct 08.30–19.30 Mon–Fri, 10.00–18.00 Sat–Sun; mid-Oct–mid-May 08.30–16.30 Mon–Fri; admission CAN$6*) Just off the motorway (4km from Truro at Exit 13A off Highway 102) and guarded by a 13m statue of Glooscap, this is one of the few museums/centres devoted to the Mi'kmaq. There's a multi-media presentation on Mi'kmaq heritage and Glooscap legends and displays of traditional Mi'kmaq porcupine quillwork, beadwork and clothing. Ask about a couple of short walking trails nearby.

EMPIRE STUDIO 7 (*20 Treaty Trail, Millbrook;* ✆ *895 3456; www.empiretheatres.com*) Multi-screen cinema right by the Glooscap Heritage Centre.

GREAT VILLAGE

This pretty community is associated with Pulitzer Prize-winner Elizabeth Bishop (see box on page 245). Many large Victorian homes are still standing. Great Village was a major shipbuilding area: the first four-masted vessel ever built in Canada, the *John M Blaikie*, was constructed here in the 1880s.

GETTING THERE Great Village is on Highway 2, 27km/17 miles from Truro and 62km/39 miles from Parrsboro.

WHERE TO STAY

🏠 **Blaikie House B&B** (4 rooms) 8 Wharf Rd; ✆ 668 2985; www.blaikiehouse.ca; ⊕ year-round. A beautiful c1870s' Queen Anne Revival house with magnificent curved mahogany staircase, Victorian décor & shared bathrooms. Full b/fast inc. $

⋀ Hidden Hilltop Family Campground (148 sites) 2600 Hwy 4, Glenholme; ✆ 662 3391, T/F 1 866 662 3391; www.hiddenhilltop.com; ⊕ mid-May–mid-Oct. 6km from Great Village, the majority of sites here are serviced, many surrounding a large, open grassy play area. Lots of summer activities, decent-sized outdoor pool (seasonal) & a laundromat. $

WHAT TO SEE AND DO

St James United Church (*corner of Hwy 2 & Lornevale Rd*) St James dates from 1845 but was rebuilt by shipbuilders in 1883 after a fire the previous year: the ceiling resembles an inverted ship's keel.

Joy Laking Studio Gallery (*6730 Hwy 2, Portaupique;* ✆ *647 2816, T/F 1 800 565 5899; www.joylakinggallery.com;* ⊕ *Jun–Sep 09.00–17.00 Mon–Sat, 13.00–17.00*

Sun, or by appointment; admission free) Contemporary art fans will want to pop in to see watercolours and serigraphs – including works in progress – made by one of the province's top contemporary painters at this gallery 10km west of Great Village.

Farmers' Market (*Held in the St James United Church Jun–mid-Sep; Sat mornings*)

The village also has three antique shops.

ECONOMY AND AROUND

There are few services in the village or environs, but great natural beauty. Worth a visit is **Thomas's Cove Coastal Preserve** off Economy Point Road, an almost completely enclosed tidal estuary. Hike the three trails (the longest is 4km), explore tidal mud flats (watch out for the incoming tide) and see the effects of the Bay of Fundy tides on the sandstone coastal landscape. Look out too for blue heron, cormorants, raptors and belted kingfisher.

Several wonderful hiking trails run along and around the **Economy River**, from less than 1km (Economy Falls) to a spectacular 18km hike (Kenomee Canyon), much of it in wilderness.

To reach the trailheads, turn inland from Highway 2 onto River Phillip Road. Even if you're not hiking, it's worth a drive along this road for the views from the roadside look-off.

GETTING THERE Economy is on Highway 2, 52km/32 miles from Truro and 36km/22 miles from Parrsboro.

WHERE TO STAY

Four Seasons Retreat (11 cottages) 320 Cove Rd, Upper Economy; ☎ 647 2628, T/F 1 888 373 0339; www.fourseasonsretreat.ns.ca; ⊕ year-round. Comfortable, well-equipped 1-, 2-, & 3-bedroom cottages are spread out & tucked between the trees. Fine views over Cobequid Bay. Beach access, (seasonal) outdoor heated pool. $$

FESTIVALS
August
Clam Festival The bivalve mollusc is celebrated over three days.

6

In 1860, the Fulton brothers built a sawmill near the Bass River mouth and began making furniture. From 1885, they concentrated solely on chairs. In 1903, the operation became the Dominion Chair Company.

What had become known as 'Bass River chairs' (though the name was never registered) are renowned throughout the province and further afield for their distinctive style and quality. Chair manufacture in Bass River ceased in 1989 when the factory burnt down.

OTHER PRACTICALITIES
✉ **Post office** 2676 Hwy 2; ⊕ 08.00–17.00 Mon–Thu, 08.00–12.00 Fri–Sat

WHAT TO SEE AND DO
That Dutchman's Farm *(112 Brown Rd, Upper Economy;* ☎ *647 2751; www.thatdutchmansfarm.com;* ⊕ *year-round 09.00–18.00 daily (Dec–Apr ring ahead to check))* A traditional Dutch-style farm making cheese off Highway 2. Gouda, both natural and flavoured, is the most popular, but look out for more experimental varieties such as Dragon's Breath. Gardens, trails, farm animals to pet. Café (⊕ *mid-Jun–early Sep 11.00–16.00*) with a limited menu, eg: cheese or ham rolls, apple tart, ice cream, hot drinks.

Cobequid Interpretive Centre *(3246 Hwy 2;* ☎ *647 2600;* ⊕ *Jun–Sep 09.00–17.00 daily)* Displays on the geology, history and culture of this stretch of Cobequid Bay coastline, and information on local hiking trails. Climb the steep stairs up the World War II coastal watchtower for fine views of the mud flats below.

FIVE ISLANDS

Mi'kmaq legend has it that Glooscap (see page 19) created the Five Islands when he threw pebbles at Beaver (who had built a dam and flooded Glooscap's medicine garden).

More recent tales tell of ghosts and buried treasure, though no-one has yet reported finding anything. The power of the water has worn a sea arch or tunnel through Long Island, the third in the chain.

GETTING THERE Five Islands is on Highway 2, 24km/15 miles from Parrsboro and 67km/42 miles from Truro.

🏠 WHERE TO STAY AND EAT
🏠 **Five Islands Retreat** (3 rooms, 3 cabins) ☎ 254 2628, T/F 1 707 363 6464; www.fiveislandsretreat.com; ⊕ early Apr–mid-Sept. In 2003, Dick Lemon, a lawyer & winery entrepreneur, bought Long Island, 1 of the 5 islands. Although topped by a relatively flat plateau, the island is encircled by sheer cliffs. A 194-step staircase was constructed, with building supplies brought in by helicopter. The island sleeps 12 (in a 3-bedroom main house & 3 cabins – 1

a replica lighthouse and 1 boat-shaped). It is rented out in its entirety, from CAN$450 per night. $$$$
⋏ **Five Islands Ocean Resort & Campground** (105 sites) 482 Hwy 2, Lower Five Islands; ☎ 254 2824, T/F 1 66 811 3716; www.fiveislands.ca; ⊕ mid-May–mid-Oct. Lovely coastal views, sea-view outdoor pool, laundromat, canteen, playgrounds. $
⋏ **Five Islands Provincial Park Campground** (90 sites) (For contact details, see page 247); ⊕ late

Jun–early Sep. Open & wooded sites. A beautiful location. $

✕ Diane's Restaurant 874 Hwy 2; ✆ 254 3190; ⏰ May & Oct 11.00–19.00 Fri–Sun; Jun–Sep 11.00–21.00 daily. Linked to a clam factory, so those molluscs are a good choice. So too are fishburgers, seafood chowder & more. If you're here in blueberry season, save room for dessert. B/fast served Sat–Sun. Licensed. $

✕ Granny's 1193 Hwy 2, Lower Five Islands; ✆ 254 3399; ⏰ early May–mid-Sep 11.00–21.00. Another good (although again high cholesterol) choice. Generous portions of fish & chips or clams & chips; ice cream also available. Ask about the charity 'fish wall'. $

FESTIVALS

July
Not Since Moses Races See box below.

WHAT TO SEE AND DO

Five Islands Provincial Park (*Bentley Branch Rd, off Hwy 2;* ✆ *254 2980; www.novascotiaparks.ca/parks/fiveislands.asp;* ⏰ *late Jun–early Sep; admission free*) On the side of Economy Mountain, this 637ha park is a must for hikers, fossil hunters, beachcombers, geologists and those who enjoy magnificent coastal scenery.

The park lies on red sandstone deposited over 225 million years ago. Much of the sandstone and basalt was removed by erosion over the next 180 million years. When the Ice Age ended, flooding rapidly eroded more of the remaining sandstone, creating the 90m cliffs. The sea stack known as the Old Wife, and the protective caps of the five islands themselves, are examples of basalt, more resistant to erosion than the soft sandstone.

Keep your eyes open on the beach (not just for the incoming tide): not only are agate, amethyst, jasper and stilbite sometimes found, but also fossils.

Hikers can enjoy the 4km Estuary Trail along the shore of East River's tidal estuary, the 5km Economy Mountain Trail, which follows an old logging road, passing through stands of maple, birch, beech, and white spruce, and – if they're lucky – the wonderful 4.5km Red Head Trail. This has been closed (owing to erosion) over the last couple of seasons but if the authorities have reopened it in time for your visit, don't miss it! Although it is the most difficult – with a few ups and downs and a long uphill section – of the park's trails, it gives access to ten look-offs, some of which are spectacular. Look out over the magnificent sandstone cliffs, rock formations and sea stacks such as the Old Wife – and, of course, the five islands. The trail can be walked in an hour or two, but allow a lot more time to enjoy the look-off side-trips.

The park has a pleasant campground and two picnic areas.

PARRSBORO (Population: 1,400)

Thanks to its population, Parrsboro is easily the largest community along the north shore of the Minas Basin. The town leapt into the limelight – at least for those interested in palaeontology – in the mid 1980s when two Americans

---

NOT SINCE MOSES

The owner of Five Islands Retreat (see page 246) established this event consisting of 5km and 10km charity runs across the ocean floor – at low tide – between the 'mainland' beach and the five islands in July 2007, and it has already proved a runaway hit. For more, see www.notsincemoses.com.

unearthed one of the biggest and most important fossil finds in North America at nearby **Wasson's Bluff**. The cliffs yielded more than 100,000 fossilised bone fragments, all dating from shortly after the mass extinction some 200 million years ago that marked the end of the Triassic period and the beginning of the Jurassic.

Since then, Parrsboro has become a base for fossickers and rockhounds, and every August the town hosts the **Gem and Mineral Show** (previously called the 'Rock Hound Roundup'). But don't come expecting fossil-themed commercialisation – this is Nova Scotia!

Located at the head of a tidal river, the town has some services, a couple of modest supermarkets and some magnificent old houses – some of which are now inns – built by those who prospered during Parrsboro's glory days. In addition, there are a couple of good museums, an interesting (summer) theatre, and a golf course. It is an obvious base from which to explore the region.

Feasibility and environmental impact studies have been carried out with regard to constructing the province's second tidal power project (the first is at Annapolis Royal – see page 199). The exact location has not been finalised but it is thought that it could be near Partridge Island (see page 251).

HISTORY Rockhounding is nothing new in this area: Samuel de Champlain (see page 5) was the first recorded European visitor in 1607, collecting amethysts from the beach.

Named in 1784 in honour of Lieutenant-Colonel John Parr, Governor of Nova Scotia, from the late 18th to the early 20th centuries, Parrsboro was a busy mercantile centre, an important transport hub, and the focus of a vast shipbuilding region.

GETTING THERE Parrsboro is on Highway 2 and Highway 209, 65km/40 miles from Amherst, 97km/60 miles from Truro and 193km/120 miles from Halifax.

TOURIST INFORMATION At the Fundy Geological Museum (see page 250).

⌂ WHERE TO STAY

⌂ **Gillespie House Inn** (7 rooms) 358 Main St; ☎ 254 3196, T/F 丨 877 901 3196; www.gillespiehouseinn.com; ⊕ year-round; off-season by reservation. Conveniently located & housed in a gracious c1890 eco-friendly home. Peaceful, charming & tastefully decorated. Wholesome full b/fast inc. **$$**

⌂ **Maple Inn** (9 rooms) 2358 Western Av; ☎ 254 3735, T/F 丨 877 627 5346; www.mapleinn.ca; ⊕ year-round. 2 adjacent c1893 Victorian Italianate-style properties were converted to create this B&B. 7 comfortable rooms, 1- & 2-bedroom suites. Full b/fast & evening refreshments inc. **$$**

⌂ **Riverview Cottages** (18 cabins) 3575 Eastern Av; ☎ 254 2388, T/F 丨 877 254 2388; www.riverviewcottages.ca; ⊕ May–mid-Oct. Clean cabins in a peaceful setting on the Aboiteau River. Most cabins have simple kitchenettes but don't expect TVs or Wi-Fi. Free use of canoes. **$**

Å **Glooscap Campground & RV** (73 sites) 1300 Two Islands Rd; ☎ 254 2529; www.town.parrsboro.ns.ca/glooscapcampground.html; ⊕ mid-May–Sep. 6km from the town centre, with sea views, sandy beach & open & wooded sites. **$**

✕ WHERE TO EAT

✕ **Bare Bones Café & Bistro** 151 Main St; ☎ 254 2270; www.ghostinthekitchen.com; ⊕ May–early Oct 11.00–21.00 Tue–Sun. Modest portions, but the menu at this relatively new bistro includes salads, sandwiches & pasta: a good choice if you can't face deep-fried food. **$$**

✕ **Harbour View Restaurant** 476 Pier Rd; ☎ 254 3507; ⊕ May–mid-Oct 07.30–20.00 daily. Popular seafood restaurant by the water. The usual suspects (scallops, clams, lobster, seafood chowder, haddock), plus flounder. Deep-fried is the norm, but grilling or pan-frying may be available on request. Reasonable prices, generous portions. **$$**

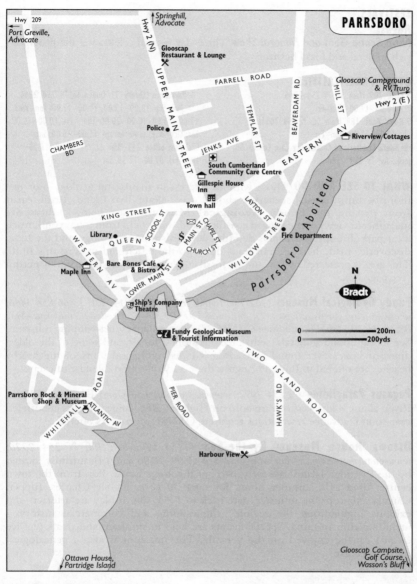

Hwy 209
Port Greville,
Advocate

↑Springhill,
Advocate

Hwy 2 (N)

Glooscap
Restaurant & Lounge

FARRELL ROAD

UPPER MAIN STREET

Police

CHAMBERS BD

JENKS AVE

TEMPLAR ST

BEAVERDAM RD

MILL ST

Glooscap Campground
& RV, Truro

Hwy 2 (E)

Riverview Cottages

EASTERN AV

South Cumberland
Community Care Centre

Gillespie House
Inn

Town hall

KING STREET

SCHOOL ST

MAIN ST

CHAPEL ST

LAYTON ST

CHURCH ST

Library

QUEEN ST

WESTERN AV

Bare Bones Café
& Bistro

Maple Inn

LOWER MAIN ST

Ship's Company
Theatre

WILLOW STREET

Fire Department

Parrsboro Aboiteau

N

Bradt

Fundy Geological Museum
& Tourist Information

0 ————— 200m
0 ————— 200yds

TWO ISLAND ROAD

ROAD

PIER ROAD

HAWK'S RD

Parrsboro Rock & Mineral
Shop & Museum

WHITEHALL

ATLANTIC AV

Harbour View

Ottawa House,
Partridge Island

Glooscap Campsite,
Golf Course,
Wasson's Bluff

✕ **Glooscap Restaurant & Lounge** 758 Main St;
📞 254 3488; ⏰ 11.00–20.00 daily (summer to

21.00). Uninspiring location & décor, but hearty
portions (even if the food isn't over heart-friendly). $

ENTERTAINMENT

Ship's Company Theatre 18 Lower Main St.; 📞 254
3000, T/F 1 800 565 7469; www.shipscompany.com;
⏰ Jul–Sep, main stage performances 19.30 Tue–Sun
& 14.00 Sun; tickets CAN$26. A highly acclaimed &
innovative professional company: the repertoire

focuses on new works from Atlantic Canadian
playwrights. The company staged its first production
aboard the shell of a disused 1924 ferry: when a
new theatre was built in 2004, the remains of the
vessel were incorporated into the lobby.

FESTIVALS

August

Nova Scotia Gem and Mineral Show Three-day festival celebrating the province's rich mineral and fossil heritage.

OTHER PRACTICALITIES

$ CIBC 209 Main St; ☎ 254 2066; ⏱ 10.00–17.00 Mon–Fri

$ Royal Bank 188 Main St; ☎ 254 2051; ⏱ 10.00–17.00 Mon–Fri

✚ South Cumberland Community Care Centre 50 Jenks Av; ☎ 254 2540

☏ Parrsboro Library 91 Queen St; ☎ 254 2046; ⏱ Jun–Sep 10.00–13.00, 14.00–17.00 Tue–Wed, 13.00–16.00, 18.00–20.00 Thu– Fri, 10.00–15.00 Sat; Oct–May, same except 11.00–16.00 Sat.

⊠ Post office 247 Main St; ⏱ 08.30–17.00 Mon–Fri, 09.00–12.30 Sat

WHAT TO SEE AND DO Those with an interest in fossils and geology – or just more beautiful coastal scenery – should drive along Two Islands Road. Apart from passing the **Fundy Geological Museum** (see below), there are magnificent views of the rugged coastline, and about 6km from town you'll reach a car park. Interpretive panels describe the area's unique geology, and the fossil discoveries made here. A trail leads down to the beach and to Wasson's Bluff. This area is protected by law, and no fossil collecting is allowed, except by permit (see page 32).

Fundy Geological Museum (*162 Two Islands Rd;* ☎ *254 3814, T/F 1 866 856 3466; www.museum.gov.ns.ca/fgm/;* ⏱ *Jun–mid-Oct 09.30–17.30 daily; mid-Oct–May 08.30–16.30 Mon–Fri; admission CAN$6.25*) An excellent award-winning museum. See locally found minerals, semi-precious stones, fossils, and some of the oldest dinosaur bones ever found in Canada. Guided geological tours of the nearby beaches are offered in July and August: there's a year-round calendar of events.

Pegasus Paragliding (☎ *254 2972; www.pegasusparagliding.com*) Based in Diligent River, about 10km west of Parrsboro on Highway 209. Tandem flights are offered year-round (advance reservations required, CAN$113): courses offered.

Ottawa House Museum By-the-Sea (*1155 Whitehall Rd;* ☎ *254 2376; www.ottawahouse.org;* ⏱ *late May–mid-Sep 10.00–18.00 daily*) Beautifully located by the Partridge Island causeway, parts of this huge house 3km from the town centre, used as a summer home for over 30 years by Sir Charles Tupper, Canada's sixth prime minister, date back to 1765. On display are artefacts and exhibits highlighting the region's shipbuilding and commercial history – including rum running. Special events are held in summer, and treats (eg: ice cream) can be enjoyed on the veranda. The museum is also a genealogical research centre.

FOSSIL FINDER

Eldon George was born in Parrsboro around 1930 and began collecting minerals and fossils when he was eight. A year later he put a 'Rocks For Sale' sign in the window of the family house. In 1984, he discovered the world's smallest dinosaur footprints as he sheltered from a hailstorm whilst fossicking at Wasson's Bluff.

He has been collecting, displaying and selling rocks and minerals for almost 60 years but is now close to 80: at the time of writing, his shop/museum, house and entire collection are on the market.

Parrsboro Rock and Mineral Shop and Museum (*349 Whitehall Rd;* ✆ *254 2981*) A wide variety of rocks and minerals can be seen, plus a gallery/museum (*admission free*) of rare fossils of prehistoric dinosaurs, reptiles, and amphibians: these include the world's smallest dinosaur footprint. Prospector supplies, books and maps – and some of the fossils and minerals – are on sale (see box on page 250).

Parrsboro Golf Course (*Greenhill Rd;* ✆ *254 2733; www.parrsboro.com/golf.htm;* ◷ *mid-May–mid-Oct*) A 9-hole 2,343yd clifftop course with above-par views. Green fees CAN$19.30 for 9 holes, CAN$28 for 18 holes.

Partridge Island Mi'kmaq legend has it that Glooscap created Partridge Island – a sandy natural causeway appeared in 1869 after freak weather, connecting it to the mainland – from a disobedient partridge. Archaeological evidence points to Mi'Kmaq occupation 10,000 years ago. Various trails start from the end of the causeway, most rewarding of which is the Look-Off Trail which climbs to a look-out offering panoramic views in all directions. Reach the causeway by continuing on Whitehall Road past Ottawa House (see page 250). The island is less than 5km from Parrsboro.

GREVILLE BAY

The major points of interest along the next section of coastline are the village of Port Greville, and the tiny community of Spencer's Island.

PORT GREVILLE Another pleasant little community which would now show few indications of its ship-building glory days were it not for the fascinating Age of Sail Heritage Centre.

Getting there Port Greville is 22km/14 miles from Parrsboro and 82km/51 miles from Joggins.

 Where to stay and eat

Ebb Tide B&B (2 rooms) 8614 Hwy 209; ✆ 348 2011, T/F 1 877 505 5750; e ebbtide@ns.sympatico.ca; www.ebbtide.ca; ◷ year-round. This welcoming B&B with shared bathroom is in an elegantly restored c1898 home with nice gardens. Full b/fast inc. $

What to see and do
Age of Sail Heritage Centre (*Hwy 209;* ✆ *348 2030; www.ageofsailmuseum.ca;* ◷ *Jun–mid-Oct 10.00–18.00 Thu–Mon (Jul–Aug daily); admission CAN$3*) Considering Nova Scotia's worldwide importance during the 'Age of Sail', there

are precious few signs left of such an important part of the province's history. This centre does a good job at addressing that. Housed in a former c1854 Methodist church are audio-visual and panel displays, and thousands of artefacts which bring life to the history of shipbuilding along this shore. The centre comprises a two-storey main building, blacksmith shop, band-saw shed and a c1907 lighthouse. There is a café (⊕ *early Jun–early Oct*) and play area.

SPENCER'S ISLAND At the western end of Greville Bay, this isn't actually an island but takes its name from a real one just off nearby Cape Spencer. That island is said to have been formed by mythical Mi'kmaq hero Glooscap when he upturned his large stone cooking pot.

The community became another important shipbuilding centre in the second half of the 19th century: the first large vessel to be launched was the *Amazon*, built in 1861 (see box on page 253).

Getting there Spencer's Island is 1.2km from Highway 209, 40km/25 miles from Parrsboro.

Where to stay and eat

⌂ **Spencer's Island B&B** (3 rooms) 789 Spencer's Beach Rd; ☎ 392 2721; e spencebb@yahoo.ca; ⊕ Jul–Aug. Close to the beach & well located for exploring the region: pity the season is so short. 3 guest rooms share 2 bathrooms. Full b/fast inc. $
▲ **Old Shipyard Beach Campground** (26 sites) 774 Spencer's Beach Rd; ☎ 392 2487; www.oldshipyardbeachcampground.com; ⊕ Jun–Sep

26. Open serviced & unserviced beachfront sites. Laundromat. Kayak tours available. $
✗ **Spencer's Island Beach Café** Right on the beach; ☎ 392 2390. Chefs seem to change each year here, as do the opening times. However, standards are normally far higher than the words 'beach café' might suggest. It is usually open Jun–Sep for lunch and dinner, but call ahead to check. $$

What to see and do In summer, the c1904 beachfront lighthouse is sometimes open to the public: beside it is a picnic park.

ADVOCATE HARBOUR

Many people rush through in a hurry to get to nearby Cape Chignecto Provincial Park, but try to make time to explore this beautiful area on Advocate Bay, tucked between the towering cliffs of Cape d'Or and Cape Chignecto, and backed by forested mountains.

A 5km-long natural barrier pebble beach – always piled high with driftwood – almost closes off the harbour entrance, especially when the tide is out. Grey seals are sometimes seen (their rookery is 20km out to sea, on Isle Haute). The easiest beach access is from West Advocate. Dykes built centuries ago by the Acadians to reclaim farmland from the sea are still visible, and make for pleasant walks. The sunsets are magnificent.

WHERE TO STAY AND EAT

⌂ **Driftwood Park Retreat** (5 units) 49 Driftwood Lane; ☎ 392 2008, T/F 1 866 810 0110; www.driftwoodparkretreat.com; ⊕ Apr–Oct. Choose from 4 2-bedroom chalets & a 1-bedroom chalet with loft. All are fully equipped, comfortable & very close to the seafront. A great get-away-from-it-all spot within a couple of kilometres of the entrance to the provincial park. $$

⌂ **Lightkeeper's Kitchen & Guest House** (4 rooms) Cape d'Or; ☎ 670 0534; www.capedor.ca; ⊕ May–mid-Oct. This former lighthouse provides the only opportunity to stay in a lightkeeper's cottage in Nova Scotia. It has a spectacular setting with the pounding tides on one side & basalt cliffs behind. Rooms are with en-suite, private or shared bathroom & there are fabulous views & a common room. Note that the lighthouse's foghorn is an important navigation aid: if the fog rolls in, the horn is called into action – regardless of whether or not guests might be sleeping. The attached licensed restaurant (🕒 May–mid-Oct for lunch & dinner daily; $$) has similar panoramas. Reservations are recommended & payment accepted only in cash. Light lunches (eg: salads, sandwiches, fishcakes, seafood chowder) and imaginative evening meals are served, using fresh local ingredients where possible). The guesthouse & restaurant are a few mins' walk downhill from the car park. $

🏠 **Reid's Tourist Home** (4 units) 1391 West Advocate Rd, West Advocate; ☎ 392 2592; www.reidstouristhome.ca; 🕒 Jun–late Sep. 3 simple guest rooms & 2-bedroom cottage on a working cattle farm. $

OTHER PRACTICALITIES

📖 **Advocate Harbour Library** 93 Mills Rd; ☎ 392 2214

✉ **Post office** 3727 Hwy 209

WHAT TO SEE AND DO

NovaShores Adventures (☎ *392 2761, T/F 1 866 638 4118; www.novashores.com*) An Advocate Harbour-based sea kayaking company offering tours from two hours to multi-days. A great way to explore the region's natural splendour – recommended. Prices from CAN$55.

THE MYSTERY SHIP

When the first vessel was built at Spencer's Island, few would have believed that 150 years later, she would still fascinate the world at large. Around 1860, Joshua Dewis built a brigantine designed to carry lumber as her main cargo, and named her *Amazon*.

On her maiden voyage, the captain died of a heart attack within 24 hours of setting sail. Other bumps and tangles included the *Amazon* grounding in the English Channel. After suffering severe damage in a storm off the coast of Cape Breton Island, she was sent to a New York marine scrap yard. Sold at auction and made seaworthy again, she was relaunched and renamed *Mary Celeste*. On 5 November 1872, she departed New York, bound for Genoa, Italy, with a hold full of alcohol. On board were a well-respected captain, his wife and two-year-old daughter, and a crew of seven.

A month later, she was spotted by another ship's crew floating aimlessly near the Azores. Their calls unanswered, they boarded the silent vessel finding it fully provisioned with the sails set and nothing out of place. There were hints that those on board had left in a hurry – the single lifeboat was gone, the child's toys strewn on deck. None of those who had been on board the *Mary Celeste* were ever seen again.

A board of inquiry concluded that piracy or foul play was unlikely, and, while her true fate will never be known, theories abound as to why the captain and crew abandoned ship. The most plausible of these suggests that, although very experienced, the captain had never carried crude alcohol on any of his ships. When the alcohol casks began to leak, he may have feared that the vapour might ignite and explode, and may have ordered a hasty evacuation. Their lifeboat could have drifted for days before perhaps capsizing and sent to a watery grave by a big wave.

After the inquiry she continued sailing for years, but, beset by more troubles, was sold and resold 17 times. In 1884, the *Mary Celeste* was finally scuttled off Haiti for insurance reasons and rediscovered by a team of Canadian divers in 2001.

During the late 1800s, crewless ships left to founder were not unheard of, and rarely attracted media attention. But in 1884, a budding writer penned a short story closely based on the *Mary Celeste* mystery. The author – who changed the name of the ship to the *Marie Celeste*, and added a few other bits of fiction – was Arthur Conan Doyle.

Cape d'Or At East Advocate, signs lead you towards Cape d'Or. The road soon becomes unpaved. One Samuel de Champlain named the cape in 1604, but the metal he saw glittering in the sunlight wasn't gold – it was copper. At **Horseshoe Cove** – located down a left turn about 4.5km after the crest of the hill – a copper-mining community thrived during the late 19th century, and to this day pure copper nuggets are sometimes found on the beach, as too are agates and other semi-precious stones.

Cape d'Or provides the only opportunity in Nova Scotia to stay in a lightkeeper's cottage. The c1965 **Cape d'Or Lighthouse**, manned until 1989, is now automated, but the cottages – built late in the 1950s – now house a restaurant and guesthouse (see page 252). The lighthouse and foghorn warn those at sea of the **Dory Rips**, or riptides: three separate tides converge, resulting in incredibly treacherous, turbulent waters. If the mist starts to roll in during your visit, prepare yourself: the modern-day foghorn – which sounds every 60 seconds – will make you jump.

The main unpaved road continues to a car park with interpretive boards and a replica lighthouse. Trails lead along the cliffs to spectacular viewpoints, or down to the (real) lighthouse. Going down is fine but not everyone enjoys the steep, steady 1km trek back up.

Getting there Cape d'Or is on Highway 209, 44km/27 miles from Parrsboro and 59km/37 miles from Joggins.

CAPE CHIGNECTO PROVINCIAL PARK

Covering 4,200ha, Cape Chignecto Provincial Park (*West Advocate Rd;* ☎ *392 2085; www.capechignecto.net & www.novascotiaparks.ca/parks/capechignecto.asp;* ⊕ *early May–Oct; admission CAN$5 day pass*) is Nova Scotia's largest provincial park and should not be missed by lovers of the wild outdoors. It is located on an arrow-shaped headland pointing into the Bay of Fundy, flanked by Chignecto Bay and the Minas Basin.

Although encompassing 29km of pristine coastline, much of the park sits high above the huge tides, with some of the sheer cliffs reaching 185m. In the water below, nature has created a range of natural sculptures, such as the Three Sisters, huge misshapen sea stacks.

The park has no roads, and to stay within its boundaries you'll have to camp. Partly for these reasons – and the somewhat 'out-of-the-way' location – Cape Chignecto has been something of a hidden gem. But the secret has begun to get out and the opening of a second entrance and day-use area in 2009 will bring more publicity.

Ten marked trails give access to the natural highlights. These range from quick jaunts to the beach from the Red Rocks visitor centre, or the Three Sisters look-out from Eatonville Beach visitor centre to challenging all-day hikes which should only be attempted by experienced hikers, such as the spectacular Red Rocks visitor

CAPE CIRCUIT

The 49km circumnavigation of Cape Chignecto is one of Nova Scotia's – and eastern North America's – great coastal hikes. Although it can be hiked in two to three days, this is not a hike to be rushed. Accommodation is a choice of remote hike-in campsites, and two wilderness cabins near Arch Gulch and Eatonville: reservations are required. Sections of the trail are strenuous with steep ascents and descents. This is a fantastic trail, but should only be attempted by self-sufficient, experienced hikers – who have a good head for heights.

centre–Refugee Cove trail. The big one is a multi-day circuit of the Cape (see box, page 254). The longer hikes are all likely to involve climbing steep slopes and following vertiginous cliffside paths. The wonderful nature, magnificent scenery and spectacular views are a just reward.

Expect to see yellow birch, American beech, Eastern hemlock, balsam fir, sugar maple and white and red spruce. For much of the summer, you'll also see wild flowers. Whilst the peninsula is home to bobcats, moose and black bear, these are very rarely encountered. Far more common are whitetail deer, rabbit and hare. Grey seals can often be seen in late summer, basking on rocks in the coves.

Hiking apart, the park's stunning shoreline, secluded coves and beaches are a wonderful area for sea kayaking (see NovaShores Adventures in the *Advocate Harbour* section, page 253).

The established entrance is very close to Advocate Harbour. The new entrance, due to open in spring/summer 2009, is at Eatonville, and will be accessed via the West Apple River Road. Near both entrances are visitor centres and picnic tables.

GETTING THERE Access to the park is via Red Rocks Road from the village of West Advocate on Highway 209, 46km/29 miles from Parrsboro, or by West Apple River Road 13km/8 miles further northwest along Highway 209.

WHERE TO STAY The park has 31 well-spread walk-in campsites between 75m and 300m from the car park, and almost 60 beautifully located backcountry hike-in sites, but no drive-up camping. There are also a couple of wilderness cabins. Reservations (T/F 1 888 544 3434) are required for hike-in campsites and cabins, and recommended for walk-in campsites.

JOGGINS

Although noted for its coal mining – there are records of coal from Joggins being sold in Boston as early as 1720 – what gives Joggins a prominent position on the 21st-century map goes back much further.

At the head of the bay, Joggins's 15–30m-high sea cliffs stretch for 15km and – twice daily – feel the force of the Bay of Fundy's huge tides. Over time this has eroded the cliff face to reveal thousands of fossils. The exposed alternating grey and reddish-brown cliff faces date from the Carboniferous period.

These fossil cliffs were first brought to public attention in 1852 when geologists found tiny fossilised bones of *Hylonomous lyelli*, one of the world's first reptiles. This was the first evidence that land animals had lived during the Coal Age.

Since then, the cliffs – labelled the 'Coal Age Galapagos' – have revealed a wealth of other important discoveries and are recognised as a world-class palaeontology site, with many experts believing that they preserve the most complete record of life in the Pennsylvanian Period (341 to 289 million years ago) anywhere in the world. This was declared a UNESCO World Heritage Site in the summer of 2008.

Although you can access the beach below the cliffs from several points, you will gain far more from your experience if you precede your exploration with a visit to the Joggins Fossil Centre (see page 256).

You can wander the rock strewn beach at the cliff base and search for fossils which have fallen from the cliff face, but can't take any fossils away with you without a permit (see page 32). The cliff site has picnic tables and interpretive signage. Most of the rocks on the beach have fallen from the cliff face, so proceed with caution – and pay attention to the tides, which come in very quickly.

Visitor services are limited in Joggins – but at least the Fossil Centre (see below) has a café!

GETTING THERE Joggins is on Highway 242, 55km/34 miles from Advocate Harbour, 35km/22 miles from Amherst and 45km/28 miles from Parsborro.

TOURIST INFORMATION At the Joggins Fossil Centre (see below).

✗ WHERE TO EAT

✗ **Roundhouse Café** At Joggins Fossil Centre, see below; ◷ May–Oct 10.00–16.00 daily. Fair-trade, organic coffee & tea, wholesome, homemade food, salads, sandwiches, cakes & cookies. $

WHAT TO SEE AND DO

Joggins Fossil Centre (*100 Main St;* ✆ *251 2727, T/F 1 888 932 9766; www.jogginsfossilcliffs.net;* ◷ *May–Oct 09.30–17.30 daily; off-season by appointment; admission CAN$8, CAN$16 inc 90–120min guided tour*) Exhibits at this c2008 purpose-built environmentally friendly interpretive centre, with gift shop & café, include displays of 300 million-year-old fossils – including insects, amphibians, plants and trees. Guided tours of Joggins Fossil Cliffs can be booked through the centre (phone or see website for schedule).

SPRINGHILL

Not the prettiest of towns in the province, Springhill is a coal-mining town. The mines – which brought happiness, prosperity, and tragedy – are long closed, but still benefit the community. Since they were shut down, the shafts filled with water that has been heated by the surrounding earth to an average temperature of 18°C. Recently, technology has allowed businesses in Springhill's industrial park to use the heated water to reduce their winter heating bills substantially. There are plans to include a geothermal display at the Miners' Museum (see page 257). The town is home to the province's largest 'correctional facility'. Other than visiting inmates, there are two contrasting attractions (see page 257).

GETTING THERE

By car Springhill is on Highway 2, 7km from Exit 5 of the Trans Canada Highway (Highway 104), 25km/16 miles from Amherst and 50km/31 miles from Parrsboro.

By bus Springhill is on the Acadian coach route between Amherst and Halifax (see page 52).

TOURIST INFORMATION In the Anne Murray Centre (*36 Main St;* ◷ *Jul–Aug 09.00–17.00 daily*)

⌂ WHERE TO STAY AND EAT

⌂ **Sugar Maple B&B** 886 Rodney Rd; ✆ 597 2551; www.sugarmaplebb.ca ; ◷ year-round. This modern, bright, friendly & spacious single-storey home approx 7km south of Springhill offers good value. Rate includes hearty country b/fast. $

✗ **JB's Steakhouse** 30 Main St; ✆ 597 2888; ◷ year-round 11.00–21.00 Sun–Tue,11.00–23.00 (or later) Wed–Sat. Don't expect fine-dining or too refined an atmosphere, but the food (not just steaks, but pizza, pasta, burgers, etc) is OK & the prices reasonable. $

FESTIVAL

June
Irish Festival Irish music, food, dancing and a street parade: held over three days.

In 1891, an underground mine explosion claimed 125 lives, including over a dozen boys. In 1956, several railcars broke loose from a mine train and rolled backwards down into the mine, derailing and then hitting a power line. The resulting blast killed 39 miners. Rescuers with no breathing equipment were able to rescue 88 survivors.

Less than two years later, an underground earthquake (or 'bump') occurred in a mine, killing many miners instantly and trapping numerous others underground with no food and water and a dwindling air supply. Mine officials, workers, volunteers and local doctors risked their lives and rescued 104 trapped miners: 74 others were not so lucky. The dead are remembered in the Miners' Memorial Park on Main Street.

Incidentally, the disaster had been predicted by Mother Coo, a fortune teller from Pictou, who also gave advance notice of other mining tragedies including the disasters at Westville's Drummond Mine (59 dead) and Stellarton's Foord Pit (50 dead) in 1873 and 1880 respectively.

Rather than being seen as a human early-warning system, Mother Coo was regarded as a pariah and driven from the area.

OTHER PRACTICALITIES

$ **CIBC** 41 Main St; ✎ 597 3741; ⏲ 10.00–17.00 Mon–Fri

✚ **All Saints Springhill Hospital** 10 Princess St; ✎ 597 3773

☙ **Springhill Library** 75 Main St; ✎ 597 2211; ⏲ 12.00–18.00 Tue & Fri, 10.00–17.00 Wed–Thu

✉ **Post office** 68 Main St; ⏲ 08.30–17.00 Mon–Fri

WHAT TO SEE AND DO

Springhill Miners' Museum (*145 Black River Rd;* ✎ *597 3449;* ⏲ *Jun–Sep 09.00–17.00 daily; admission CAN$5, tours CAN$3*) Two years after the Syndicate Mine closed in 1970, this museum opened on the site. Mining artefacts, the miners' washhouse and their lamp cabin are quite interesting but the highlight is the mine tour: don overalls, hard hats and rubber boots and descend 100m underground: most guides are former coal miners. There's even a chance to dig out some coal to take back with you. Note – the tour is not for the claustrophobic or those not keen on the dark.

Anne Murray Centre (*36 Main St;* ✎ *597 8614; www.annemurray.com;* ⏲ *mid-May–mid-Oct 09.00–17.00 daily; admission CAN$6*) Anne Murray was born in Springhill in 1945. Some 25 years later, she released a song called 'Snowbird' and this went on to become one of North America's most played songs of 1970. Over the years, she has racked up more gold and platinum albums, Grammy awards and country music awards than any other Canadian and sold close to 50 million albums. Exhibits range from a lock of hair from her first haircut to glittering stage costumes and her plentiful gold/platinum albums.

Minas Basin and Cobequid Bay **SPRINGHILL**

6

7

Northumberland Shore

Mainland Nova Scotia's north shore fronts the Northumberland Strait and stretches from the provincial border with New Brunswick to the west, to Aulds Cove, from where the Canso Causeway leads to Cape Breton Island to the east. The shortest and quickest way to get between the two points is on Highway 104, the Trans Canada Highway (TCH), a drive of 265km. However, Highway 104 runs well inland, and just about everything of interest in the region is away from the motorway, on or within a few kilometres of the waterfront. So once again it is best not to rush things, but to take the smaller, quieter, far more scenic roads through quaint communities such as Pugwash, Oxford and Tatamagouche.

Paddle the coastal inlets in a sea kayak, enjoy a scenic round of golf, or hike beautiful trails high above Antigonish Harbour. Or go for a dip: this region of rolling hills and pastoral landscapes is renowned for its beaches, most of which are within provincial parks, and summer swimming is a pleasure – the slogan 'warmest water north of the Carolinas' is oft heard. The average sea temperature between July and late September is over 22°C. To the west, the tide recedes from the red sand beaches to expose vast mud flats: further to the east the stretches of sand at Melmerby and Pomquet beaches are not to be missed.

Scottish Heritage is a big draw for many – from 1773, Pictou was the gateway to Nova Scotia for thousands of Scottish Highlanders, and their history and culture lives on through much of the region.

Those who enjoy things urban should like the pleasant towns of Amherst, Pictou and Antigonish (home to the St Francis Xavier University) but as Amherst, the biggest of the three, has a population of just under 10,000, we're not talking about vast built-up sprawl. Stellarton's vast and impressive Museum of Industry is an ideal rainy-day choice (see page 280).

AMHERST *(Population: 9,000)*

On higher ground than the surrounding marshland and overlooking the Bay of Fundy, Amherst is the land gateway between Nova Scotia and all points west, and the largest town in Cumberland County. The historic downtown – with many magnificent well-preserved sandstone buildings and beautiful old homes on Victoria Street East – is relaxing and pleasing on the eye. Large, colourful murals bring the community's heritage to life, and more continue to be added. One of the most impressive is the **Signature Mural** on the corner of Havelock Street and Victoria Street East, depicting the downtown area during a big parade in 1910.

HISTORY The town of Amherst was founded in 1764 near the site of a British fort destroyed in 1755. It was named for General Jeffrey Amherst, one of the leaders in the victory over the French at Louisbourg in 1758. Many of the early settlers originated in Yorkshire, England.

259

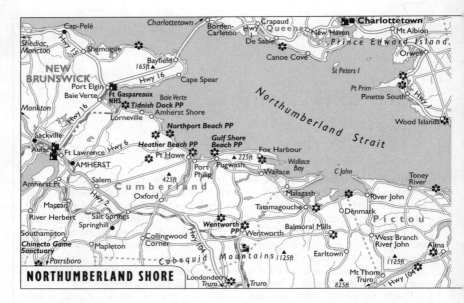

NORTHUMBERLAND SHORE

Centrally located on the only land route between Nova Scotia and the 'mainland', Amherst prospered between the mid 1800s and the early 20th century. The town became renowned for its diverse and active economy, including mining and manufacturing, and was labelled 'Busy Amherst'. Textiles, footwear and even pianos were just some of the items produced here, and in 1908, no other town in the Maritimes had a higher industrial manufacturing output. It was during this period that many of the town's largest and most impressive buildings and homes – many of which still stand – were built.

GETTING THERE AND AROUND

By car Amherst is just off Highway 104 (TCH), via Exits 2–4. It is 4km/2 miles from the New Brunswick border, 117km/73 miles from Truro, 207km/129 miles from Halifax, 183km/114 miles from Pictou and 231km/144 miles from Antigonish.

By bus Acadian coaches stop in Amherst three times a day (each way) *en route* between Moncton (New Brunswick) and Halifax (see page 52).

THE COMMUNIST CONNECTION

In 1916, socialist Leon Trotsky was deported to the US. The following year, when revolution overthrew Tsar Nicholas II, the door was open for him to return to Russia, and he departed New York on the SS *Kristianiafjord*. The ship docked in Halifax, where Canadian and British naval personnel arrested Trotsky, and took his wife and young sons into custody. After a short time at the Citadel in Halifax, Trotsky was transferred to an internment camp in Amherst, which contained around 800 German prisoners, many of them sailors from submarines, where he stayed for almost a month. He aired his political views to the inmates at every opportunity, and it is said that when he left, it was to the sound of the international Socialism anthem *Internationale* being sung by cheering German prisoners. The Trotsky family left Nova Scotia from Halifax a few days later, *en route* to Copenhagen.

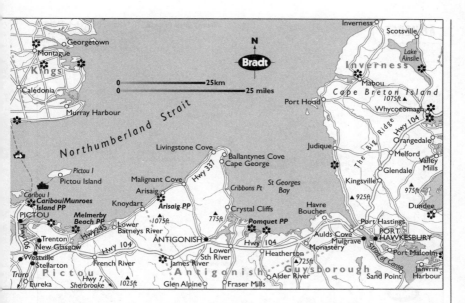

By train Amherst is also on the VIA Rail line (see page 53) between Montreal and Halifax. Six days a week, one train a day in each direction stops *en route* at Amherst's impressive century-old sandstone station at Station Street.

TOURIST INFORMATION

The Provincial Welcome Centre Exit 1, Hwy 104 (TCH); ☎ 667 8429; ⏱ daily early Nov–Apr 08.30–16.30; May–Oct 08.30–17.00 or later, eg:

21.00 in Jul–Aug. Houses a local tourist office (☎ 667 9523; ⏱ Jun–Aug 09.00–17.00).

WHERE TO STAY
Amherst

Amherst 8 Motel (50 rooms) 40 Lord Amherst Dr; ☎ 660 8888; T/F 1 888 561 7666; www.super8amherst.com; ⏱ year-round. A 2-storey c2005 motel with indoor pool but lacking in character, but with decent rooms which have microwaves, mini-fridges & coffee makers. Continental b/fast inc. $$

Regent B&B (4 rooms) 175 Victoria St East; ☎ 667 7676; T/F 1 866 661 2861; www.theregent.ca; ⏱ year-round (Mar by reservation only). A lovely Georgian house with stained & leaded glass window & hand-carved woodwork & sun deck in garden. Formal full b/fast served on fine china inc. $$

Brown's Guest Home B&B (3 rooms) 158 Victoria St East; ☎ 667 9769; e dnallen@istar.ca; www.brownsguesthome.ca; ⏱ May–Oct. A c1904 house very close to the town centre with shared bathrooms. Included in the price is a continental b/fast buffet (rather than the full works). $

Å Gateway Parklands RV campground (127 sites) 1434 Fort Lawrence Rd; ☎ 667 1106; www.gatewayparkland.ca; ⏱ mid-May–mid-Oct. Although geared to those with motorhomes, there are also open & wooded tent sites & a laundromat at this campground approximately 5km from Amherst, by Exit 1 of Hwy 104. $

Lorneville Rather than overnight in Amherst, some people prefer to stay on the Northumberland Strait shore, where you can also camp at the Amherst Shore Provincial Park (see *Around Amherst*, page 264).

Amherst Shore Country Inn (11 units) 5091 Hwy 366; ☎ 661 4800, T/F 1 800 661 2724;

www.ascinn.ns.ca; ⏱ Jan–Oct & Dec. A lovely inn on 8 seaside hectares with gardens, lawns & a long

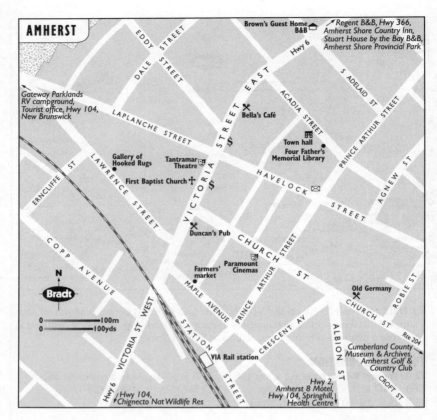

Gateway Parklands
RV campground,
Tourist office, Hwy 104,
New Brunswick

EDDY STREET

DALE STREET

LAPLANCHE STREET

Brown's Guest Home
B&B

Regent B&B, Hwy 366,
Amherst Shore Country Inn,
Stuart House by the Bay B&B,
Amherst Shore Provincial Park

Hwy 6

STREET EAST

S ADELAID ST

ACADIA STREET

Bella's Café

PRINCE ARTHUR STREET

Town hall
Four Father's
Memorial Library

AGNEW ST

Gallery of
Hooked Rugs

ERNCLIFFE ST

LAWRENCE STREET

Tantramar
Theatre

First Baptist Church

VICTORIA STREET

HAVELOCK

STREET

Duncan's Pub

CHURCH STREET

COPP AVENUE

N

Bradt

0   100m
0   100yds

VICTORIA ST WEST

STATION STREET

MAPLE AVENUE

Farmers'
market

Paramount
Cinemas

PRINCE ARTHUR ST

ARTHUR ST

CHURCH ST

Old Germany

ROBIE ST

CHURCH ST

Rte 204

ALBION ST

CRESCENT AV

VIA Rail station

Cumberland County
Museum & Archives,
Amherst Golf &
Country Club

CROFT ST

Hwy 6   Hwy 104,
Chignecto Nat Wildlife Res

Hwy 2,
Amherst 8 Motel,
Hwy 104, Springhill,
Health Centre

private beach owned & run by members of the Laceby family (see *Blomidon Inn*, page 220) & offering 2 rooms, 6 suites & 3 cottages. Various packages available combining accommodation & dining. The inn's restaurant (⊕ for b/fast (inn guests only) & dinner May–Oct daily; Dec–Apr Fri–Sat only, reservation only, dinner (set meal: CAN$45) served at 19.30) has wonderful sea views. The fixed-price menu comprises a soup, a salad, a choice of 2 entrées & choice of 2 desserts. Dinner at the inn

has long been considered one of the province's gastronomic treats & there are no signs of standards slipping. $$
🏠 **Stuart House by the Bay B&B** (3 rooms) 5472 Hwy 366; 📞 661 0750, T/F 1 888 661 0750; www.stuarthousebedandbreakfast.com; ⊕ Jun–Aug (May & Sep–Oct by reservation). A late 19th-century home close to the beach. The bedrooms aren't huge – biggest is the Grand Stuart Room. Full b/fast inc. $

✕ WHERE TO EAT
✕ **Duncan's Pub** 49 Victoria St West; 📞 660 3111; www.duncanspub.ca; ⊕ year-round 11.00–23.00 Mon–Sat, 12.00–22.00 Sun. The town's best pub has a relaxed atmosphere, a good selection of drinks (including cocktails) & good live entertainment Thu–Fri evenings. The food's good too: scallop-stuffed mushroom caps & seafood chowder stand out – & that's just for starters. Book in advance if you're dining. $$
✕ **Old Germany** 80 Church St; 📞 667 2868; ⊕ Feb–Dec 11.00–20.30 Wed–Sun. Homely décor &

hearty food: think Goulash soup, Wiener schnitzel & German sausages – a little bit of northern Europe in Amherst. Try the *sauerbraten* (spiced, marinated roast beef) with red cabbage & sauerkraut washed down with a glass of cherry schnapps. $$
✕ **Bella's Café** 117 Victoria St East; 📞 660 3090; ⊕ year-round 08.30–16.00 Mon–Tue, 08.30–18.00 Wed–Thu, 09.00–20.00 Fri. A popular, sometimes busy, lunch spot offering tasty snacks & light meals & good music; art on display. $

ENTERTAINMENT

➤ Paramount Cinemas 47 Church St; ☎ 667 7791; www.empiretheatres.com
♨ Tantramar Theatre Dominion Bldg, 98 Victoria St East; ☎ 667 7002; www.tantramartheatre.ca. This

c1935 Greek-temple style edifice is home to the Tantramar Theatre Society, with live performances (July and August) including dinner theatre and the 'brown bag theatre' – a lunch box and a show.

OTHER PRACTICALITIES In the main, the many practicalities (services, department stores, supermarkets and shopping malls) are out of the centre along uninspiring South Albion Street.

$ Royal Bank 103 Victoria St East; ☎ 667 7275; ⊕ 10.00–17.00 Mon–Fri
$ Scotiabank 79 Victoria St East; ☎ 667 3328; ⊕ 10.00–17.00 Mon–Fri
✚ Cumberland Regional Health Care Centre 19428 Hwy 2; ☎ 667 3361. Just outside town in Upper Nappan.

☙ Four Fathers Memorial Library 21 Acadia St; ☎ 667 2549; ⊕ 10.00–17.00 Mon & Thu–Fri, 10.00–20.00 Tue–Wed, 10.00–13.00 Sat
⊠ Post office 38 Havelock St; ⊕ 08.30–17.00 Mon–Fri
⇌ M&J Taxi ☎ 661 2560
⇌ D&J Taxi ☎ 667 8288

WHAT TO SEE AND DO

First Baptist Church (*66 Victoria St East;* ☎ *667 2001;* ⊕ *09.00–16.00 daily*) This red sandstone church, built in Queen Anne Revival style in 1846, is worth a visit. A lunchtime concert series featuring local musicians (Wednesday and Friday) runs through the summer months.

Cumberland County Museum and Archives (*150 Church St;* ☎ *667 2561; www.creda.net/~ccmuseum/;* ⊕ *Feb–mid-Dec 09.00–17.00 Tue–Fri, 12.00–17.00 Sat; admission CAN$3*) South of Amherst's main historic district, the museum is housed in the c1838 Grove Cottage, home of Father of Confederation (see page 11) Robert B Dickey. See articles and documents relating to Trotsky's time in Amherst (see box on page 260), a player piano, a wonderful Victorian c1870 staircase and art gallery, plus beautiful gardens, popular for weddings. A well-stocked research library and archives.

The Gallery of Hooked Rugs (*19 Lawrence St;* ☎ *667 0988;* ⊕ *year-round 12.00–16.00 Wed–Fri & Sun; admission CAN$4*) Owned and operated from her own

THE AMHERST MYSTERY

Amherst made the front pages late in the 19th century when an 18-year-old local girl, Esther Cox, began experiencing strange poltergeist-like phenomena: little fires, voices, and rapping noises.

Doctors called to treat her also noted bizarre happenings: inexplicable movements under the bedclothes, inanimate objects moving about the room, and sudden banging noises.

The disturbing happenings continued unabated, and when a neighbour's barn (where Esther had been working) was destroyed by a mysterious fire, she was arrested, charged and convicted of arson. She spent a month in jail but during her trial had met a man with whom she became smitten.

On her release, her fiancé took her to a Mi'kmaq medicine man who performed a type of exorcism on her. The happy couple moved to Massachusetts and she was troubled no more by evil spirits.

In 1888, a best-selling book was written about Esther's experiences. Her house on the town's Princess Street is long gone, but *The Great Amherst Mystery* lives on.

c1872 home by Avis Chapman, with displays of hooked rugs from all over North America.

Farmers' Market (*Maple Ave & Electric St;* ⊕ *May–Dec 10.00–14.00 Fri*)

AROUND AMHERST

AMHERST SHORE PROVINCIAL PARK (*42 sites; Hwy 366;* ⊕ *late Jun–mid-Oct*) A woodland campground close to a lovely beach (see box on page 265).

AMHERST GOLF AND COUNTRY CLUB (*John Black Rd;* ✆ *667 1911; www.amherstgolfclub.com;* ⊕ *Jun–late Oct*) A 6,347yd course to the east of town, with lush fairways, fast greens – and, more often than not, strong winds to contend with. Green fees CAN$47.

CHIGNECTO NATIONAL WILDLIFE RESERVE (*Southampton Rd;* ⊕ *24hrs year-round; admission free*) The 1,670ha reserve encompasses the Amherst Point Migratory Bird Sanctuary and is best known for its variety of waterfowl, both breeding and migratory; the wetlands are among the best waterfowl-breeding grounds in the province. Some 8km of trails wind through a diverse landscape of woodlands, fields, ponds and marshes, offering several bird-viewing sites. To get there follow Victoria Street West to the southwest, cross Highway 104, then continue for 3km.

OXFORD

The Oxford region produces over half of the country's total blueberry harvest each year, earning the town the title of 'Wild Blueberry Capital of Canada'. Approach from Highway 104 and you'll be greeted by a giant smiling blueberry. The town is also a centre for products made from the sap of the region's thousands of maple trees. Oxford's rivers are popular with anglers trying for

TRAINS AND BOATS

Ships travelling between the Gulf of St Lawrence and New England had to make a long and arduous journey around Nova Scotia. To save well over 1,000km of sailing, the construction of a canal across the 27km Isthmus of Chignecto (which separates the Northumberland Strait from the Bay of Fundy) had long been suggested. In 1881, Henry Ketchum, a Scottish-born engineer, proposed the Chignecto Marine Transport Railway. His plan was for hydraulic lifts to be built to raise ships onto 'cradles' which would then be pulled by locomotives along a special railway track. The line was to run between Fort Lawrence on the Bay of Fundy coast and Tidnish Dock on the Northumberland Strait. After years of negotiations and feasibility studies, Canada's federal government agreed to subsidise the railway's construction in 1888 – subject to the railway's completion within an agreed timescale.

The timescale was too tight, especially considering the marshy nature of much of the land, and in 1892, when the line wasn't completed by the deadline agreed, the government withdrew its financial support.

At Tidnish Dock Provincial Park (Hwy 366) a few remains can still be seen, such as the railbed, a stone culvert over the Tidnish River, and remnants of the dock. The park, 25km from Amherst, has interpretive panels and a short walking trail alongside the old rail track.

Along Highway 366, three provincial parks – Amherst Shore, Northport Beach and Heather Beach – offer beach access and more. The beaches are visually striking, with lush green vegetation contrasting with both the red sandstone cliffs (over 10m high in many places) and the blue of the sea. At low tide, the tidal flats often extend well over 1km. The park at Amherst Shore, 36km from Amherst and 27km from Pugwash, has a campground (see page 264) and walking trails: at Northport Beach, 42km from Amherst and 21km from Pugwash, sandbars keep the sea shallow and the water even warmer, whilst Heather Beach, 50km from Amherst and 14km from Pugwash, is usually the busiest of the three.

salmon and trout, and for those with canoes. The surrounding forests are home to abundant wildlife – this attracts hunters in the autumn, so wear something bright if you're out leaf-peeping.

GETTING THERE

By car Oxford is 1.5km off Highway 104 Exit 6. If you're approaching from Highway 6, take Highway 301 south for 16km/10 miles from Port Howe. The road follows the wooded banks of the River Philip and passes through verdant farmland for 16km/10 miles to Oxford. To return to Highway 6, cross the river and follow Highway 321 north. This circuit is beautiful when the autumn colours are blazing.

By bus Oxford is on the Acadian coach line between Amherst and Halifax (see page 52).

TOURIST INFORMATION In the Wild Blueberry Centre (see below)

WHERE TO STAY AND EAT

Parkview Family Restaurant and Inn (10 rooms) 4670 Main St; ↘ 447 2258; ⊕ year-round. The inn offers old-fashioned motel-style accommodation. Old-fashioned also describes the food in the restaurant (⊕ 07.00–20.00 daily; $). Generous portions of diner food, such as liver & onions or fish & chips. Cheap & cheerful. $

FESTIVALS

August

Cumberland County Exhibition and Blueberry Festival (*www.cumberlandcountyexhibition. canadianwebs.com*) Six-day agricultural festival (at the end of August–early September) which includes dances, concerts, kids events and craft displays.

OTHER PRACTICALITIES

✉ **Post office** 5152 Main St; ⊕ 08.00–17.15 Mon–Fri, 08.00–12.00 Sat

WHAT TO SEE AND DO

Wild Blueberry and Maple Centre (*105 Lower Main St;* ↘ *447 2908, T/F 1 877 922 6362; www.town.oxford.ns.ca;* ⊕ *mid-May–mid-Oct 10.00–18.00 daily; admission free*) The centre is located in pleasant grounds on the banks of the Black River and tells you all you need to know about the region's two major agricultural products – cultivation, harvesting, production and more. There is a gift shop & café with a selection of wild blueberry and maple treats.

PUGWASH

This quaint community is located on a pretty harbour at the mouth of the Pugwash River. Across the river from downtown, Pugwash's salt mine isn't easy to miss. Each year, the mine produces over one million tonnes of salt. No tours are offered, but you can watch vast quantities of sodium chloride being loaded onto cargo ships. Whilst this operation spoils an otherwise idyllic riverside, it brings a much-needed boost to the local economy.

Scottish heritage is strong, here, and street signs are in both Gaelic and English.

Durham Street, part of Highway 311, is the main street: the waterfront walkway in Eaton Park makes for a pleasant wander.

GETTING THERE Pugwash is on Highway 6, 50km/31 miles east of Amherst and 37km/23 miles west of Tatamagouche.

TOURIST INFORMATION In the Heritage Centre (see page 267)

WHERE TO STAY AND EAT

Eaton-Webb Guest House (3 units) 236 Water St; 243 3203; e eatonwebb@ns.sympatico.ca; www.freewebs.com/eatonwebbguesthouse; year-round. There are 2 guest rooms in the main house, plus an adjacent little 1-bedroom cottage. Gallery/gift shop also on site, & pretty gardens. $

Hillcrest Motel & Restaurant (8 rooms) 11054 Hwy 6; 243 2727; www.hillcrestmotelandrestaurant.ca/hillcrest/; year-round. A traditional single-storey motel with simple rooms & on-site restaurant (year-round 07.00–20.00 daily; $) offers well-priced local standards, including lobster. $

Gulf Shore Provincial Park (50 sites) 2367 Gulf Shore Rd; 243 2389;

www.gulfshorecampingpark.com; mid-Jun–mid-Sep. In the provincial park. A grassy, open campground on the seafront. $

Sandpiper Restaurant 8244 Hwy 6, Port Philip; 243 2859; Apr–Nov 11.00–19.00 daily (summer to 20.00). A licensed, good-value place approximately 8km west of Pugwash specialising in seafood. $$

Chatterbox Café 10163 Durham St; 243 4059; Jul–Aug 09.30–18.00 daily (or later); off-season hours vary. Welcoming & relaxing with a library, secondhand books for sale, fair-trade organic coffees, speciality teas, soups, salads & sandwiches. Live entertainment Fri–Sat evenings in summer. $

SHOPPING

Seagull Pewter 9926 Durham St; 243 3850, T/F 1 888 955 5551; www.seagullpewter.com; Jun–Oct 09.00–17.00 Mon–Sat, 12.00–17.00

Sun; off-season 10.00–17.00 Thu–Sat. A long-established operation creating, designing and handcrafting pewter. Tours offered in season.

THE BRAIN GAME

In 1955, Albert Einstein called for a conference to discuss the dangers of a nuclear war. Pugwash-born millionaire, Cyrus Eaton, offered to sponsor the event here. Part of his sales pitch was that the beauty of the Pugwash area would produce clarity of thought. And so in 1957, 13 nuclear scientists, including three from the Soviet Union, met on the Pugwash foreshore at Eaton's large but otherwise unremarkable residence (which became known as the Thinkers' Lodge).

It was the first of many such gatherings, now known as the Pugwash Conferences on Science and World Affairs (www.pugwash.org), which take place annually in some of the world's greatest metropolises, London, Washington, Rome, Tokyo – and, as recently as 2007 – Pugwash.

Today the Thinkers' Lodge is owned by the Pugwash Parks Commission. Tours may be offered – check with the tourist office.

The name 'Pugwash' comes from the Mi'kmaq word *pagweak*, meaning 'deep water'.

Incidentally, this Pugwash did not provide the inspiration for the surname of one of the UK's favourite cartoon characters. John Ryan created Captain Horatio Pugwash in 1950 when he was an art teacher in Middlesex, England. Seven years later, he was surprised to hear that a gathering of great minds (see page 266) was being held in a previously virtually unknown Nova Scotia town which shared his captain's name.

FESTIVALS
July
Gathering of the Clans Highland Festival Over the 1 July Canada Day holiday, Pugwash hosts this festival, with highland games, traditional music and dancing.

OTHER PRACTICALITIES
$ Scotiabank Water St; ✆ 243 2541; ⊕ 10.00–17.00 Mon–Fri

☞ Pugwash Library 10222 Durham St; ✆ 243 3331;⊕ Jun –Sep 14.00–19.00 Mon & Thu, 11.00–13.00 & 14.00–17.00 Tue–Wed,

13.00–18.00 Fri, Sat closed; Oct–May, same except 09.00–12.00 Sat.

⊠ Post office 10154 Durham St; ⊕ 08.00–17.15 Mon–Fri, 08.30–12.00 Sat

WHAT TO SEE AND DO
Pugwash Heritage Interpretive Centre (*10222 Durham St;* ✆ *243 2449;* ⊕ *late Jun–Aug 10.00–18.00 daily; admission free*) Interpretive panels on community history, including the salt mine and Thinkers' Lodge (see box on page 266).

Gulf Shore Provincial Park (see page 266) Picnic areas and a nice red sand beach 4km from Pugwash.

Northumberland Links (*1776 Gulf Shore Rd;* ✆ *243 2808, T/F 1 800 882 9661; www.northumberlandlinks.com;* ⊕ *late Jun–mid-Oct*) A very scenic 6,160yd links course, 9km from Pugwash. Green fees CAN$62.

WALLACE

For almost two centuries, this community on the shore of beautiful Wallace Bay has been renowned for its sandstone, which exists as a result of geological activity 300 million years ago. The first quarry opened in 1811, and several others followed. Wallace sandstone was used in the construction of many important buildings both in and outside Nova Scotia: these include the Nova Scotia Legislature in Halifax, the Peace Tower of the Canadian Parliament buildings in Ottawa and the Montreal Stock Exchange.

The stone is still quarried here, but this picturesque seaside village now depends primarily on fishing, farming, and lumbering for its livelihood. The bay's salt marshes and tidal inlets attract a whole range of birdlife, and Wallace's public wharf is a popular spot from which to watch the sun rise and set.

GETTING THERE Wallace is on Highway 6 and Highway 307, 19km/12 miles from Tatamagouche and 17km/11 miles from Pugwash.

WHERE TO STAY AND EAT

🏠 **Fox Harb'r Golf Resort & Spa** (72 suites) 1337 Fox Harbour Rd; ☎ 257 1801, T/F 1 866 257 1801; www.foxharbr.com; ⏲ Jun–Sep. Approximately 9km from Wallace, each of the 12 modern 'guesthouses' contains 6 deluxe suites. The resort has its own marina & private airstrip, & incorporates a private gated community, spa & wellness centre, & seaside tennis courts. Other activities include clay-pigeon shooting &, of course, golf. Guests can take a swing at the fabulous Graham Cooke-designed private 7,253yd par-72 course. $$$$

🏠 **Jubilee Cottage Inn** (3 rooms) 13769 Hwy 6; ☎ 257 2432, T/F 1 800 481 9915; e jubileecottage@ns.sympatico.ca; www.jubileecottage.ca; ⏲ year-round. Comfortable inn in a tastefully restored c1912 home with several period features. Set on 1.2ha on Wallace Bay –

kayaks available for guest use. The Qi Sera Restaurant (⏲ year-round, lunch 11.30–13.30 Mon–Fri, 10.30–14.00 Sun brunch, dinner 17.30–21.30 daily; reservations required for brunch & dinner; $$; 4-course dinner CAN$38) offers light lunches, a good set-menu Sun brunch & an innovative set-menu-themed dinner (which might include eg: butternut & coconut soup, & pan-seared maple trout with turnip-apple compote). Local organic ingredients used where possible. You can bring your own wine (corkage CAN$5 per bottle). Gourmet b/fast inc. $–$$

⛺ **D&D Bayview Campground** (15 sites) 3323 South Shore Rd, Malagash Centre; ☎ 257 2209; ⏲ mid-May–mid-Oct. Delightful views over Tatamagouche Bay from the open campsites: 6km off Hwy 6. $

SHOPPING

Collector Canes 659 Ferry Rd; ☎ 257 2817; www.auracom.com/zperry/; ⏲ by appointment. Doug & Zella Perry hand-carve each cane from

Nova Scotia hardwoods. Walking sticks, hiking sticks & shepherd's crooks can be customised.

FESTIVALS Wallace is the ideal base for these Malagash festivals.

May

Dandelion Festival Events at this new festival include crafts stalls, photography competitions, and a lawn-mowing competition.

July

Summer Festival Malagash's Jost Vineyards (see below) plays host to a Saturday afternoon of music, food and winery tours.

August

Malagash Blueberry Festival Enjoy all things blueberry at Jost Vineyards.

Art & Jazz Festival A Saturday afternoon of music, food and displays of work by local artists held at Jost Vineyards.

September

Jost Vineyards Grape Stomp Teams of four stomp grapes for charity.

OTHER PRACTICALITIES

✉ **Post office** 3872 Hwy 307; ⏲ 08.00–17.00 Mon–Fri, 09.00–13.00 Sat

WHAT TO SEE AND DO

Wallace Bay National Wildlife Area (Aboiteau Rd; ⏲ 24hrs year-round; admission free) This 585ha reserve just west of Wallace encompasses a large marsh and small forest at the head of Wallace Bay. Although primarily of interest to birdwatchers – this is an important migration and breeding habitat for waterfowl – a 4km loop trail along a raised dyke makes a pleasant and easy wander.

One of the world's greatest astronomers, Simon Newcomb (1835–1909) was born (and grew up) in Wallace.

Wallace Area Museum (*13440 Hwy 6;* ✆ *257 2191; www.wallacemuseum.ns.ca;* ⊕ *Jun–Sep 09.00–17.00 Mon–Sat, 13.00–16.00 Sun; off-season 09.00–16.30; admission free*) Housed in the restored c1840 home of a local shipbuilder, offering local history, plus changing themed displays and also 4km of walking trails on the museum grounds.

AROUND WALLACE

Wallace is a good base for a visit to the Malagash Peninsula, where lush green farmlands roll down to the red sandy shore. Two sites are worth a visit:

JOST VINEYARDS (✆ *257 2636, T/F 1 800 565 4567; www.jostwine.com;* ⊕ *May–Christmas 09.00–17.00 Mon–Sat, 12.00–17.00 Sun; Christmas–Apr 09.00–16.00 Mon–Sat; free tours mid-Jun–mid-Sep 12.00 & 15.00*) This vineyard was created by the Jost family from Germany's Rhine Valley – the first vines actually came from the agricultural research station at Kentville (see page 215). The most common grapes grown are French and German varieties (Marechal Foch, Vidal, Muscat, Baco Noir and L'Acadie). Smaller quantities of other grapes are grown on a more experimental basis. Most harvesting takes place in September and October.

MALAGASH SALT MINERS' MUSEUM (*1926 North Shore Rd;* ✆ *257 2407;* ⊕ *mid-Jun–mid-Sep 10.00–17.00 Tue–Sat, 12.00–17.00 Sun; admission CAN$2*) Canada's – and the British Commonwealth's – first salt mine operated here between 1918 and 1959. The salt here was particularly pure owing to long slow crystallisation, and despite a large amount of unmined salt, the mine was closed as the harbour here was too shallow for larger shipping. Operations moved to Pugwash (see page 266) which has a deeper harbour.

WENTWORTH

Although best known as the largest of the province's few downhill-skiing destinations, Wentworth and the Wentworth Valley are popular year-round with lovers of the outdoors – when the snow has gone, the hilly region is ideal for hiking and biking. In autumn, the high proportion of maple trees contribute to a fine display of colours.

GETTING THERE Wentworth is on Highway 4, 24km/15 miles from Exit 7 of Highway 104, 28km/17 miles from Exit 11 of Highway 104 and 22km/14 miles from Wallace (via Highway 307).

⌂ **WHERE TO STAY AND EAT**

⌂ **Wentworth Valley Inn** (14 rooms) 14962 Hwy 4; ✆ 548 2202, T/F 1 877 548 2202; e paisley@istar.ca; www.home.istar.ca/~paisley/; ⊕ year-round. A traditional-style single-storey motel offering simple, but perfectly adequate, accommodation. There is a pub (⊕ 12.00–midnight daily) & restaurant (⊕ 12.00–14.00 & 16.00–18.30 Wed–Sat, 12.00–17.00 Sun; $$). $

⌂ **Wentworth International Hostel** (2 family rooms, 2 dorms) 249 Wentworth Station Rd: ✆ 548 2379; e wentworthhostel@ns.sympatico.ca; ⊕ year-round). A former c1870s' farmhouse with fully equipped kitchen, shared bathrooms, common room, laundry facilities, & large patio deck. Snowshoes & cross-country skis to rent. Dorm CAN$20, private room CAN$40. $

FESTIVALS
October
Fall Colours Festival Take a ski-lift up a mountain to see the glory of the autumn colours. Held on (Canadian) Thanksgiving weekend.

WHAT TO SEE AND DO There is a network of over 25km of trails all centred on the Wentworth Hostel and nearby Wentworth Provincial Park, which lies about 4km off Highway 4, just past the entrance to Ski Wentworth if you're coming from Truro or Halifax. Tough but not too long – and very rewarding if it is clear – is the 2km Look-off Trail from the hostel. In addition, an easy, short (400m return) trail starts 0.5km south of the Wentworth Valley Inn and leads to the picturesque Wentworth Falls.

Ski Wentworth (*14595 Hwy 4;* \ *548 2089; www.skiwentworth.ca*) has the highest vertical in the province at 250m and the largest area of downhill skiable terrain in the Maritimes.

A quad-chair, T-bar and two rope tows get you to the top of the 20 trails, three of which are open for skiing after dark. Learn-to-ski or snowboard schools are offered. There are numerous packages and offers, but a basic one-day lift pass is CAN$38. There is also a rental shop, bar and cafeteria. Snowmobilers can purchase a trail pass to explore over 170km of groomed trails.

TATAMAGOUCHE

This pretty community at the confluence of the French and Waugh rivers has become a popular stop for visitors. Its name evolved from the Mi'kmaq *takamegoochk*, meaning 'meeting of the waters'.

Some fine Victorian homes still stand and you'll also find a couple of museums (one housed in the old railway station), and interesting dining and accommodation choices.

The **Trans Canada Trail** offers a great opportunity for hiking or biking along the coast, and the old railway bed passing through the village has been converted to a trail popular with hikers, cyclists – and cross-country skiers in winter. The trail begins at **Sunrise Mercantile** (see page 271) and stretches from Nelson Park over the French River and along the shores of the Waugh River.

GETTING THERE Tatamagouche is on Highway 6, 84km/52 miles from Amherst and 49km/30 miles from Pictou.

TOURIST INFORMATION

🅵 Fraser Cultural Centre 362 Main St; ☎ 657 3285; ⊕ Jul–mid-Sep 10.00–17.00 Mon–Sat, 10.00–16.00 Sun. This c1889 former Canadian Red Cross building also houses an art gallery.

WHERE TO STAY AND EAT

🏠 **Balmoral Motel** (18 rooms) 131 Main St; ☎ 657 2000, T/F 1 888 383 9357; e stay@ balmoralmotel.ca; www.balmoralmotel.ca; ⊕ Apr–Oct. A traditional motel overlooking Tatamagouche Bay comprising 2 single-storey buildings. B/fast inc. $$

🏠 **Train Station Inn** (10 rooms & suites) 21 Station Rd; ☎ 657 3222, T/F 1 888 724 5233; www.trainstation.ca; ⊕ Apr–Oct. See box below for further information. The licensed restaurant (*reservation only*; $$) is open daily for lunch & dinner. Cont b/fast inc, full b/fast available for a surcharge. $$

🅰 **Poplar Grove Campground** (30 sites) 758 Willow Church Rd; ☎ 657 3034; ⊕ mid-May–mid-Oct. Open campground 6.5km from Tatamagouche. $

✖ **Big Al's Acadian Restaurant and Lounge** 9 Station Rd; ☎ 657 3341; ⊕ year-round 08.00–23.00

Mon–Sat, 12.00–22.00 Sun. Good portions of pub-style seafood. Licensed. The kitchen closes at 20.00 Mon–Wed & Sun, at 21.00 Thu–Sat. $

✖ **Chowder House on Main** 265 Main St; ☎ 657 2223; ⊕ year-round 07.00–19.00 daily (summer to 21.00). An excellent family-style restaurant offering a broad menu that leans towards seafood. Having said that, the spare ribs are great! Licensed. $

✖ **Sunrise Mercantile** 1631 Hwy 6; ☎ 657 1094; www.sunmerc.com; ⊕ Jun–Aug 08.00–20.00 Mon–Sat, 13.00–20.00 Sun; Sep–May 10.00–18.00 Mon–Sat, 13.00–18.00 Sun. Gourmet food & gift shop with funky café (with deck) overlooking the sea 2km west of town. Soups, sandwiches, wraps, desserts, etc. $

SHOPPING

Raven Gallery 267 Main St; ☎ 657 0350; ⊕ Jul–Sep 10.00–19.00 Mon–Sat, 12.00–16.00 Sun, Oct–Jun 10.00–17.00 Tue–Sat. Craft shop.

Sara Bonnyman Pottery 326 Maple Av; ☎ 657 3215; e sara.bonnyman@ns.sympatico.ca; ⊕ Jun–Sep 10.00–16.00; off-season by appointment. Craft shop.

FESTIVALS
September

Oktoberfest (☎ *657 3030; www.nsoktoberfest.ca*) Over the last weekend in September, Tatamagouche also hosts eastern Canada's largest Oktoberfest, attracting over 3,000 revellers. Think beer garden, dances, polkas and oom-pah music. Food is a mix of Canadian and German, with lobster rolls, sausages and schnitzels. German and local beers are served, and there's a schnapps bar.

OTHER PRACTICALITIES

$ **Scotiabank** 243 Main St; ☎ 657 2440; ⊕ 10.00–17.00 Mon–Fri

📧 **Post office** 236 Main St; ⊕ 08.00–17.00 Mon–Fri, 09.00–13.00 Sat

🖥 **Tatamagouche Branch Library** 237 Main St; ☎ 657 3064; ⊕ 11.00–17.00 & 19.00–21.00 Tue & Thu, 13.00–17.00 Fri, 09.00–13.00 Sat

---

TATAMAGOUCHE CHOO-CHOO

The c1887 railway station was scheduled for demolition in the 1970s but was acquired by an enterprising teenager, Jimmy LeFresne. At first he used it to house a farmers' market, but later purchased seven (1911–78) railway carriages and converted them into comfortable suites. A 1928 dining car became the restaurant (soups, salads, sandwiches at lunch, salmon and steak for dinner). His ambition created a unique, fun place to stay and eat (see above).

WHAT TO SEE AND DO

Creamery Square Heritage Centre and Farmers' Market (*39 Creamery Rd;* ✆ *657 3500; www.creamerysquare.ca/heritagecentre;* ⊕ *mid-Jun–Aug 09.00–17.00 daily; off-season by appointment*) A former c1925 creamery now houses a fascinating interactive museum with a varied collection including exhibits on Acadian, Mi'kmaq and European settlement, butter production, and Anna Swan (see box above). You can also see the Brule Fossils, discovered nearby in 1994, and the only example of a 285 million-year-old fossilised *Walchia* (primitive conifer) forest ever been found in its original growth position. With genealogical and historical archives (closed Sun).

A new performing arts centre is due to open next door in 2009, incorporating the old Ice House. Plans include a 160-seat theatre, performance space, and large outdoor stage.

The site also hosts one of the province's longest running and most vibrant Farmers' Markets (⊕ *Feb–Dec 08.00–12.00 Sat*).

AROUND TATAMAGOUCHE

BALMORAL GRIST MILL (*660 Matheson Brook Rd;* ✆ *657 3016; www.museum.gov.ns.ca/bgm/;* ⊕ *Jun–mid-Oct 09.30–17.30 Mon–Sat, 13.00–17.30 Sun; admission CAN$3*) A photogenic three-storey c1874 mill off Highway 311, approximately 10km from Tatamagouche, in a delightful riverside setting. Although originally a water mill, electricity now supplies the power. That apart, wheat, oats and barley are still ground using 19th-century methods.

SUGAR MOON FARM (*Alex MacDonald Rd, Earltown;* ✆ *657 3348, T/F 1 866 816 2753; www.sugarmoon.ca;* ⊕ *Sep–Jun 09.00–17.00 Sat–Sun; Jul–Aug 09.00–17.00 daily; admission free*) A working sugar maple farm just off Highway 326, approximately 35km from Tatamagouche. Learn about maple syrup production. Buttermilk pancakes with lashings of maple syrup are served in the pancake house: maple products are available in the gift shop. Hiking trails and snowshoe rental in winter. Very popular are regular Chef's Nights featuring top guest chefs from around the province.

SUTHERLAND STEAM MILL (*Hwy 326; Denmark;* ✆ *657 3016; www.museum.gov.ns.ca/ssm/;* ⊕ *Jun–mid-Oct 09.30–17.30 Mon–Sat, 13.00–17.30 Sun; admission CAN$3.25*) On Highway 326, 17km from Tatamagouche, see the workings of a c1894 lumber mill powered by steam generated from a huge boiler.

COASTAL SPIRIT EXPEDITIONS (☏ *351 2283; www.coastalspiritexp.com*) Based at Cape John, 6km off Highway 6, 28km from Tatamagouche and 40km from Pictou, Coastal Spirit offers sea-kayaking instruction and half- and full-day guided sea-kayaking trips.

PICTOU *(Population: 4,000)*

The harbour town of Pictou is one of the largest communities on the Northumberland Shore. Although just 8km from the terminal of the car ferry service (to and from Prince Edward Island), it is largely bypassed by the provincial highway system.

Only in the last 10–15 years has Pictou – derived from the Mi'kmaq name for the area, *Piwktook* ('exploding gas') – become a popular destination for visitors: the redevelopment of the waterfront, and, in particular, construction of a replica of an 18th-century ship, have been instrumental in putting the town firmly onto the tourist map.

The principal attractions, main museum, restaurants, and historic accommodations are found on or close to the waterfront, but there are also some lovely old houses in the residential streets further back. Granite was imported from Scotland and used to build several town edifices – you'll see fine examples of Scottish vernacular, New England Colonial, Gothic and Second Empire styles.

The local paper mill – which on rare occasions apparently wafts unpleasant odours over the water – shipbuilding, and one of tyre-manufacturer Michelin's three factories in Nova Scotia are major employers, and there's lobster fishing.

HISTORY In an effort to boost Nova Scotia's population, an agent named John Ross was sent to Scotland to try to attract disgruntled Highlanders (see page 8).

Ross placed a notice in the *Edinburgh Advertiser*, promising any family prepared to move to Nova Scotia (which he portrayed as a rich paradise with the most fertile of soil) free passage, their own farm land, and one year's provisions. In total, 189 Highlanders, including 71 children under eight, took up the offer.

Ross had chartered an old Dutch cargo ship, the *Hector* (said to be in poor condition), and she set sail from Loch Broom, Ross-Shire, in July 1773. It took the *Hector* 11 weeks to cross the ocean – 18 of the passengers died *en route*, most from smallpox. When she limped into Brown's Point in Pictou Harbour on 15 September, the land didn't seem to live up to the promises. Those on board were greeted by miles and miles of thick, unbroken forest right down to the shoreline and the nearest settlement several days' travel away. But the industrious new arrivals – 33 families and 25 single men – pulled together, set to work, felled trees and began to build a town on the site of an old Mi'kmaq village.

The almost ubiquitous stands of pine were put to good use, and less than a year after the *Hector*'s arrival, a ship laden with lumber sailed for England. This business boomed, and before too long shipbuilding also became established.

BURNING QUESTION

Look out across the Northumberland Strait after dark and you might be able to add yourself to the list of those who have seen a three- (some say four-) masted ship ablaze. The spectral burning vessel has also been seen from Prince Edward Island.

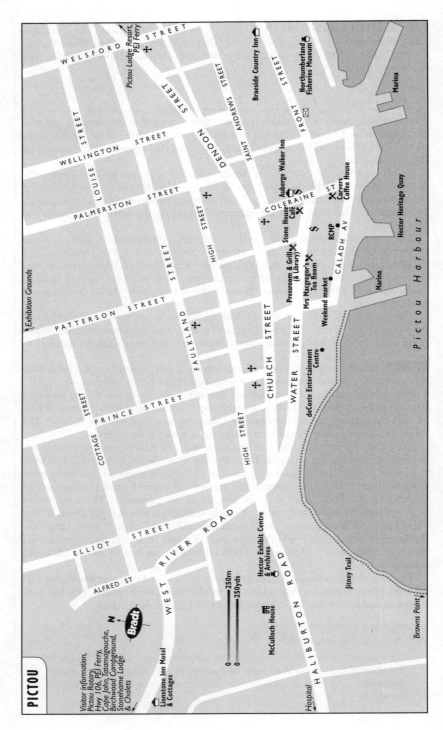

PICTOU

Visitor information,
Pictou Rotary,
Hwy 106, PEI Ferry,
Cape John, Tatamagouche,
Birchwood Campground,
Stonehame Lodge
& Chalets

Lionstone Inn Motel
& Cottages

Exhibition Grounds

WELSFORD STREET

Pictou Lodge Resort,
PEI Ferry

Braeside Country Inn

Northumberland
Fisheries Museum

Marina

WELLINGTON STREET

SAINT ANDREWS STREET

DENOON STREET

FRONT STREET

Auberge Walker Inn

PALMERSTON STREET

LOUISE STREET

Stone House
Café

COLERAINE ST

Carvers
Coffee House

$

PATTERSON STREET

HIGH STREET

Pressroom & Grill
(& Library)

Mrs Macgregor's
Tea Room

RCMP

$

CALADH AV

Hector Heritage Quay

FAULKLAND STREET

Weekend market

Marina

PRINCE STREET

CHURCH STREET

WATER STREET

deCoste Entertainment
Centre

Pictou Harbour

COTTAGE STREET

HIGH STREET

ELLIOT STREET

WEST RIVER ROAD

Hector Exhibit Centre
& Archives

Jitney Trail

Browns Point

ALFRED ST

250m
250yds

0
0

McCulloch House

HALIBURTON ROAD

Hospital

N

Bradt

In the 18th century, the Mi'kmaq who lived in the Pictou area had a particularly hostile reputation and were said to be fearless. However, they fled in terror at the sound of bagpipes.

The *Hector*'s voyage marking the beginning of a massive wave of Scottish immigration through the port over the next century, Pictou quickly became known as the 'birthplace of New Scotland'. Many of the Scots then dispersed along the Northumberland Strait shore, or to Cape Breton Island.

In 1817, Thomas McCulloch, a Presbyterian minister who was a great believer in equal access to education, established the Pictou Academy. For many decades it was said that any eastern American university worth its salt would have at least one professor who had graduated at Pictou. The original Pictou Academy was torn down in the 1930s.

GETTING THERE

By car Pictou is at Exit 3 of Highway 106, 10km/6 miles from the ferry terminus to Prince Edward Island (see page 39), 75km/47 miles from Truro, 169km/105 miles from Halifax and 183km/114 miles from Amherst. 14km/9 miles north of Exit 22 from Highway 104.

By bus The nearest Acadian coach stop is in New Glasgow, CAN$20 from Pictou by taxi.

TOURIST INFORMATION (*350 West River Rd;* ✎ *485 6213;* ✆ *daily early May–mid-Oct 08.30–18.30; mid-Oct–Nov 08.30–16.30*). Just off the Pictou Rotary, where Highways 106 and 6 meet.

⌂ WHERE TO STAY

⌂ **Braeside Country Inn** (18 rooms) 126 Front St; ✎ 485 5046, T/F 1 800 613 7701; www.braesideinn.com; ✆ year-round. A tastefully renovated c1938 inn on a hillside. Most guest rooms have harbour views. There are also some family rooms & a restaurant (see page 276). Continental b/fast (with a few extras) inc. $$

⌂ **Pictou Lodge Resort** (102 units) 172 Lodge Rd, Braeshore; ✎ 485 4322, T/F 1 800 495 6343; e guest.services@pictoulodge.com; www.pictoulodge.com; ✆ mid-May–mid-Oct. The lodge's main building was built of logs in the 1920s: for 3 decades this was a Canadian National Railways resort, welcoming royalty & Hollywood stars.

Under private ownership since 2007, thus far things are staying on track. There is a wide range of accommodation, from standard rooms to 3-bedroom executive chalets, in a quiet location overlooking the Northumberland Strait. Restaurant (see page 276). Not over many on-site activities are available, but it does have a heated outdoor pool (seasonal), mini-driving range & putting green. Bikes are available. $$

⌂ **Stonehame Lodge & Chalets** (27 units) 310 Fitzpatrick Mountain Rd, Scotsburn; ✎ 485 3468, T/F 1 877 646 3468; www.stonehamechalets.com; ✆ year-round. A lovely hilltop retreat beside a working farm 12km from Pictou. Overlooking

Local legend has it that an 18th-century Pictou County resident was one of the illegitimate sons of Britain's King George IV. The resident, who died at the age of 33, was reportedly buried in Pictou's Laurel Hill cemetery. The story resurfaced as a song, 'Prince of Pictou', recorded in 2004 by local musician Dave Gunning.

farmland, forests & Pictou Harbour. Accommodation comprises 10 1–3-bedroom chalets, 5 lodge rooms, & 12 rooms in new building (drive-up entrances, private decks, whirlpool baths). Nearest restaurants are in Pictou. For self-caterers, chalets have fully equipped kitchens. Scenic trails, heated pool (seasonal), mountain bike & snowshoe rental. Continental b/fast available. $$

🏠 **Auberge Walker Inn** (11 rooms) 78 Coleraine St; ☎ 485 1433, T/F 1 800 370 5553; www.walkerinn.com; ⊕ year-round. A comfortable c1865 4-storey Registered Heritage Property with 10 rooms & 1 ground-floor 1-bedroom suite with

private entrance. Continental b/fast inc, full b/fast at extra cost. $

🏠 **Lionstone Inn, Motel and Cottages** (14 rooms, 13 cottages) 241 West River Rd; ☎ 485 4157; www.lionstoneinn.ca; ⊕ year-round. As you'd expect for the price, accommodation is simple & functional rather than sumptuous. Near Pictou Rotary but within walking distance of town. $

🏕 **Birchwood Campground** (55 sites) 2521 Hwy 376, Lyons Brook; ☎ 485 8565; www.birchwoodcampground.ca; ⊕ mid-May–Sep. Open & wooded serviced & unserviced sites 3.5km from Pictou Rotary: heated outdoor pool. $

✖ WHERE TO EAT

✖ **Braeside Country Inn** 126 Front St; ☎ 485 5046, T/F 1 800 613 7701; www.braesideinn.com; ⊕ late May–early Oct daily, dinner only. A highly rated restaurant offering indoor or alfresco dining: the focus is on seafood. Reservations required. $$$

✖ **Pictou Lodge Resort** 172 Lodge Rd, Braeshore; ☎ 485 4322, T/F 1 800 495 6343; e guest.services@pictoulodge.com; www.pictoulodge.com; ⊕ mid-May–mid-Oct for b/fast & dinner; mid-Jun–mid-Oct for lunch; Sun brunch mid-Jun–mid-Oct 11.00–13.30. The main dining room of this exclusive resort has a big stone fireplace & more importantly, serves very good food. Sun brunch (reservations required) is something of a local institution. $$$

✖ **Mrs Macgregor's Tea Room** 59 Water St; ☎ 382 1878; www.mrsmacgregors.com; ⊕ year-round 11.00–15.00 Sun & Tue–Wed, 11.00–15.00 & 17.00–20.00 Thu–Sat. Light lunches at this Scottish-themed tearoom include soup (eg: Scotch broth), salads, wraps, quiches. Dinner menu offers more substantial fare including pan-seared haddock, meat

pie, & turkey with trimmings. Desserts include traditional Scottish shortbread, & sticky toffee pudding. $–$$

✖ **Carvers Coffee House** 41 Coleraine St; ☎ 382 3332; www.carvers.ca; ⊕ year-round 09.00–21.00 daily (Oct–May 12.00–17.00 Sun). A cheery blend of coffee house, Scottish pub & wood-carving studio: rustic décor. On warm, sunny days, the waterfront deck & patio are a delight. Tuck into a bowl of clam chowder or grab a cappuccino & triple mocca (sic) brownie to take away. $

✖ **Pressroom Pub & Grill** 50 Water St; ☎ 485 4041; www.thepressroompub.com; ⊕ year-round 11.30–22.00 daily. Cocktails, over 30 types of domestic & imported beer & generally good upmarket pub food (salads, steaks, sandwiches, fish & chips, pan-fried haddock). $

✖ **Stone House Cafe & Pizzeria** 12 Water St; ☎ 485 6885; ⊕ Apr–Oct 11.00–23.00 daily. Reliable pizzas, including some topped with lobster & scallops, plus simple meals such as lasagne & steaks served in a relaxed atmosphere. $

FESTIVALS
July
Lobster Carnival (*www.pictoulobstercarnival.ca*) Music, parades, antique cars, races, a beer garden and many other activities mark the end of the lobster-fishing season.

August
Natal Day Expect parades, buskers, yacht races and more.

HECTOR #2

The replica of the *Hector* (which brought the first Scottish settlers here in 1773) towers above the Pictou waterfront. Built entirely on site by local craftspeople and volunteers, some of whom were descendants of the original *Hector* passengers, it was launched in 2000.

Hector Festival (✆ *485 8848; www.decostecentre.ca*) This five-day festival celebrates the original *Hector*'s arrival in Pictou. Watch – or participate in – Highland dancing, attend a daily ceilidh (see page 18), and don't miss the re-enactment of the historic landing on the final day.

September

New Scotland Days Held over three days, the festival celebrates the pioneer spirit of the Scots who shaped Pictou County and Nova Scotia.

OTHER PRACTICALITIES

$ **Royal Bank** 25 Water St; ✆ 485 4352; ⊕ 10.00–17.00 Mon–Fri

$ **Scotiabank** 70 Coleraine St; ✆ 485 4378; ⊕ 10.00–17.00 Mon–Fri

✚ **Sutherland Harris Memorial Hospital** 222 Haliburton Rd; ✆ 485 4324

✆ **Pictou Library** 40 Water St; ✆ 485 5021; ⊕ 12.00–21.00 Tue & Thu, 10.00–17.00 Wed & Fri–Sat

✉ **Post office** 49 Front St; ⊕ 08.30–17.00 Mon–Thu, 08.30–20.30 Fri

🚕 **Dime's** ✆ 485 6089

🚕 **Alf's** ✆ 485 5025

WHAT TO SEE AND DO

Hector Heritage Quay (*33 Caladh Av;* ✆ *485 4371, T/F 1 877 574 2868; www.townofpictou.com;* ⊕ *mid-May–mid-Oct 09.00–17.00 Mon–Sat, 10.00–17.00 Sun (Jul–Aug to 19.00 Tue–Thu); guided tours 10.00 & 14.00; admission CAN$7*) To most of the hundreds of thousands of Canadians of Scottish descent, the *Hector*'s arrival in Pictou (see *History*, page 273) was every bit as important as the Pilgrim Fathers' arrival in New England on the *Mayflower* over 150 years earlier. The story of the *Hector* is told in the three-storey Interpretive Centre, designed to resemble an 18th-century Scottish warehouse. Costumed interpreters answer questions or tell stories to a background of bagpipe music. Rigging, blacksmithing and carpentry demonstrations relate to shipbuilding in the 18th century.

But the highlight is the chance to explore the replica of the three-masted *Hector*. Go below deck and try to imagine what the voyage to a new life might have been like in the middle of the Atlantic for all those on board. The combination of the absorbing centre and the *Hector* replica – and the story they tell – make this one of Nova Scotia's most important heritage attractions.

McCulloch House (*100 Old Haliburton Rd;* ✆ *485 1150; www.museum.gov.ns.ca/mch/;* ⊕ *Jun–mid-Oct 10.00–17.00 Mon–Sat, 13.00–17.00 Sun; admission CAN$3*) A c1805 brick and stone house built for Thomas McCulloch (see *History*, page 275). See McCulloch's writings which give a picture of early 19th-century Pictou life, and local newspapers from the period.

Northumberland Fisheries Museum (✆ *485 4972; www.northumberlandfisheriesmuseum. com;* ⊕ *Jun–Sep 10.00–17.00 daily; admission: adult CAN$5*) The main museum (*71 Front St*) is housed in the red-brick former c1908 Canadian National Railway station, with over 2,000 exhibits on the heritage and culture of the fishing industry along the Northumberland Strait. Don't miss the live, multi-coloured, rare lobsters and other shellfish species in the tank. On the waterfront at Caladh Avenue is a fully operational lobster hatchery in a boathouse-style structure. Next door is a replica 1908-style lighthouse with information on the lighthouses of the province and Maritimes.

deCoste Entertainment Centre (*85 Water St;* ✆ *485 8848, T/F 1 800 353 5338; www.decostecentre.ca;* ⊕ *Mar–Dec*) The regional performing arts centre is an excellent modern venue with a busy calendar of generally high-class events. In July and August on Tuesday–Thursday evenings, the centre hosts informal ceilidhs (see page 39) under the Summer Sounds of Nova Scotia label.

Weekend Market (*New Caledonia Curling Club, Waterfront;* ❧ *485 6329; www.pictouweekendmarket.com;* ☉ *late Jun–mid-Sep 10.00–17.00 Sat–Sun*) The market offers crafts, fruit and vegetables, other food and much more.

Jitney Trail If you feel like a wander, the 3km each way Jitney Trail starts at the Hector Heritage Quay and follows the abandoned rail line west along the shoreline around Norway Point and under the causeway to Browns Point.

AROUND PICTOU

CARIBOU/MUNROES ISLAND PROVINCIAL PARK (*2119 Three Brooks Rd;* ❧ *485 6134;* ☉ *late Jun–early Oct*) From the park entrance, 11km north of the junctions of Highways 6, 106 and 376, 4km east of the Caribou–Wood Islands ferry terminal (see page 40), a trail leads along 2km Little Caribou Spit to a traffic-free 100ha island. Here you'll find saltwater lagoons, salt marshes, small, secluded barrier beaches and wooded areas, good for birding, swimming, hiking or camping: choose from 95 wooded or open sites on a hillside overlooking the sea.

NEW GLASGOW, TRENTON, WESTVILLE AND STELLARTON

Across the harbour from Pictou the towns of New Glasgow, Trenton, Westville and Stellarton make up 'Industrial Pictou County'. Coal mining has been an integral part of this area's history since the first commercial mine opened in Stellarton in 1807, and since then, industry has continued to dominate. As with most of the world's industrial areas, unspoilt natural beauty is not abundant in these communities. There is one major attraction for the visitor – Atlantic Canada's biggest museum – but otherwise I would recommend sticking to the coastal corridor. New Glasgow (population: 9,400) is the region's largest community.

In summer, Westville holds what is said to be the largest **Canada Day celebration** in Atlantic Canada. Although Canada Day is 1 July, this birthday party lasts at least five days, with parades, games, barbecues, community suppers and more, climaxing in a huge firework display.

GETTING THERE

By car New Glasgow is just off Highway 104 Exits 24–25, 2km/1.2 miles from Trenton, 4km/2.3 miles from Stellarton, 8km/5 miles from Westville, 22km/14 miles from Pictou, 69km/43 miles from Truro and 165km/103 miles from Halifax.

By taxi There used to be a water taxi service to Pictou but this no longer operates: a land taxi to Pictou will cost approximately CAN$20. Try **Central Cabs** (❧ *755 6074*) or **K&M Taxi** (❧ *695 4040*).

By bus New Glasgow is on the Acadian coach line between Halifax and Sydney (see page 52).

TOURIST INFORMATION (*Cowan St Rest Area, 2500 Old Truro Rd, Westville;* ❧ *396 2800;* ☉ *09.00–16.00 Tue–Sat. 18.00 in summer*)

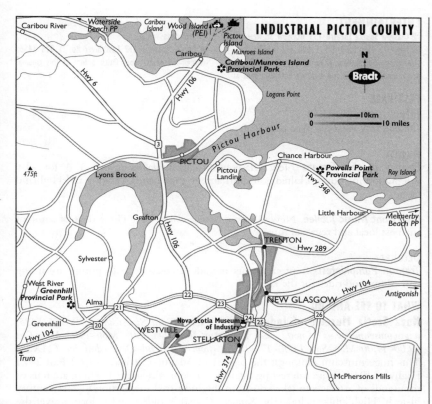

INDUSTRIAL PICTOU COUNTY

(Map labels:)
Caribou River, Waterside Beach PP, Caribou Island, Wood Island (PEI), Pictou Island, Munroes Island, Caribou/Munroes Island Provincial Park, Caribou, Logans Point, Hwy 6, Hwy 106, Pictou Harbour, Hwy 3, PICTOU, Chance Harbour, Pictou Landing, Powells Point Provincial Park, Roy Island, Hwy 348, 475ft, Lyons Brook, Little Harbour, Melmerby Beach PP, Grafton, Hwy 106, TRENTON, Hwy 289, Sylvester, West River, Greenhill Provincial Park, Alma, Hwy 22, Hwy 23, NEW GLASGOW, Hwy 104, Antigonish, Greenhill, Hwy 104, Hwy 20, Hwy 21, WESTVILLE, Nova Scotia Museum of Industry, Hwy 24, Hwy 25, Hwy 26, STELLARTON, Truro, Hwy 374, McPhersons Mills

Bradt

N

0 ———— 10km
0 ———— 10 miles

WHERE TO STAY

Country Inn and Suites By Carlson (65 units) 700 Westville Rd, New Glasgow; 928 1333, T/F 1 800 456 4000; www.countryinns.com/newglasgowns; year-round. An early 1990s' 3-storey motel with decent standard rooms & 1-bedroom suites. All rooms have mini-fridges; suites also have microwaves. Continental buffet b/fast inc. $$

Trenton Park Campground (43 sites) Park Rd, Trenton; 752 1019; mid-Jun–early Sep. Wooded & open serviced sites: pool, mini-golf, fishing & laundromat. 4km from New Glasgow. $

WHERE TO EAT

Hebel's Restaurant 71 Stellarton Rd, New Glasgow; 695 5955; www.hebelsrestaurant.ca; year-round 17.00–21.00 Tue–Sat. In the short time since opening this licensed restaurant, housed in a mid 19th-century sea captain's house & former inn, Peter Hebel has already impressed discerning foodies in the area. Start, perhaps, with seafood strudel or wonton-crusted shrimp: continue with the mixed grill or slow roasted rack of lamb, & round off with the 3-coloured Belgian chocolate mousse. $$$

Crofters Steak & Seafood 565 Stellarton Rd, New Glasgow; 755 3383; year-round 11.00–21.00 Tue–Sat, 12.00–20.00 Sun. The menu offers few surprises: daily specials are good deals, & the cooking generally reliable. Licensed. $$

Ming's Restaurant 211 Provost St, New Glasgow; 752 4102; year-round 11.00–22.00 daily. A good place to fill up on reasonably priced Chinese food. Cheap buffet (12.00–14.00 daily (also 16.00–20.00 Thu–Sat)). $

Pantry Kitchen 236 Foord St, Stellarton; 755 2292; year-round 07.00–19.00 Mon–Sat, 08.00–19.00 Sun. Simple unpretentious 'home cooking' at very good prices (many seniors are regulars). The roast turkey dinner & fish & chips are popular, & the daily special is very good value. $

ENTERTAINMENT

Glasgow Square Theatre 155 Glasgow St, New Glasgow; ℡ 752 4800, T/F 1 800 486 1377; www.glasgowsquare.com. A varied year-round programme of indoor and outdoor entertainment at this riverside venue.

Empire Studio 7 612 East River Rd; ℡ 928 3456; www.empiretheatres.com. Catch a film at this cinema.

FESTIVALS

July
Canada Day Westville (see page 278)

August
Festival of the Tartans New Glasgow (*www.festivalofthetartans.ca*) A four-day celebration including a kilted golf tournament, pipe bands, ceilidhs and Highland games.

Riverfront Music Jubilee, New Glasgow (*www.jubilee.ns.ca*) Three days of some of the best local and regional music.

October
Trenton Pumpkinfest Trenton Events include a costume ball, pumpkin-carving workshops and rides for the kids.

WHAT TO SEE AND DO

Nova Scotia Museum of Industry (*147 North Foord St, Stellarton;* ℡ *755 5425; www.museum.gov.ns.ca/moi/;* ⊕ *Nov–Apr 09.00–17.00 Mon–Fri; May–Oct 09.00–17.00 Mon–Sat, 13.00–17.00 Sun (from 10.00 Jul–Oct); admission CAN$8*) This huge museum (amongst the biggest in Atlantic Canada) just off Exit 24 of Highway 104 is more interesting than the name might suggest. There are tens of thousands of artefacts to take you from the Industrial Revolution to 21st-century hi-tech. Highlights include the *Samson*, Canada's oldest steam locomotive, the *Victorian* (the first petrol-powered car built in the Maritimes), a display of much-prized Trenton glass, and there's an abundance of interactive stuff which will keep kids of all ages happy.

Carmichael-Stewart House Museum (*86 Temperance St, New Glasgow;* ℡ *752 5583;* ⊕ *Jun–Sep 09.30–16.30 Mon–Sat; admission free*) This c1880 Victorian house with original hardwood floors and beautiful stained-glass windows was formerly owned by the Carmichael family, prominent New Glasgow shipbuilders. In addition to local history – particularly relating to shipbuilding – the collection includes old Trenton glassware and clothing from the late 1800s to the 1920s, including wedding gowns worn by some of New Glasgow's high society.

PITFALLS

The dangers of life underground are well known to miners and their families. On 9 May 1992, after only five months in operation, the Westray Mine in nearby Plymouth was destroyed by a huge gas explosion. All 26 men working underground at the time were killed, the youngest just 22. Fifteen bodies were recovered, but 11 remain underground. A memorial – 26 rays of light emitting from a miner's lamp, each bearing the name and age of one of the miners lost – was erected a year later at what is now the Westray Miners Memorial Park. Interpretive panels give details of the tragedy. The memorial is at the east end of Park Street, New Glasgow.

MELMERBY BEACH PROVINCIAL PARK (*Little Harbour Rd;* ⊕ *mid-Jun–mid-Oct*) 'The Merb', near Little Harbour, 14km from Highway 104 Exit 27A, 16km northeast of Exit 25 from Highway 104, is a very popular 1.7km beach on an isthmus. The left side (as you first walk along the beach) is generally more sheltered, whilst to your right is open ocean. In late summer, the water can be quite warm. Changing rooms are available.

ARISAIG PROVINCIAL PARK

Around 400 million-plus years ago, this area was covered by the sea, and as the layers of sediment built up on the sea bed, various creatures were buried.

Within the boundaries of the park, the erosion of shale cliffs has exposed a continuous record of conditions here from the late Ordovician period (448 million years ago) through the entire Silurian to Early Devonian (401 million years ago) periods. This is one of the only places in the world where such a long period of time is exposed in a single layered cliff line.

Fossils of brachiopods (shellfish), nautiloids (a type of shelled squid), trilobites (extinct spider or crab-like arthropods), snail-like gastropods, and crinoids (plant-like filter feeders) are among those that have been found and continue to be unearthed here.

In addition, experts can see differences in the geology of northern and southern Nova Scotia here with a major geological fault dividing the park. Cliffs on the east side expose dark grey shale layers, but very few fossils. On the west side, the shale layers are thinner, have more sandstone and contain abundant fossils.

An interpretive kiosk explains fossil formation. There is a picnic area, and 3km of trails, one of which leads down past observation platforms to the beach and cliffs.

Remember, you're not permitted to disturb fossils embedded in the cliffs without a permit (see page 32).

GETTING THERE The park is on Highway 245 near the village of Arisaig, 27km/17 miles north of Antigonish.

ANTIGONISH *(Population: 4,300)*

With a concentration of supermarkets, shopping malls, fast-food outlets, petrol stations and light industry along Highway 104 and (to a lesser degree) along the approaches to the town centre from Exits 31–34, this is yet another town where one could easily be put off if approaching from this direction. However, it is worth persevering to the downtown area of this bustling university town. Here you'll find a range of good choice of places to stay and eat, and some fine architecture. The Greek Revival-style c1855 **County Court House** (*168 Main St*), for example, survived a serious fire in the 1940s and still houses the county's Supreme Court – and the local jail.

About 20 sculptures (carved from dying elm trees) of life-size figures including a piper and a highland dancer – dot the town. Antigonish has a strong Scottish heritage and has been home to the popular **Antigonish Highland Games** (see page 285) for almost 150 years. The town also hosts an excellent summer theatre festival (see page 285).

In addition to the urban attractions, the town has a range of good beaches and hiking trails close by: its harbour borders a large tidal marsh where ospreys and bald eagles are commonly seen. Having said all that, first and foremost this is a working regional centre, with tourism further down the list.

HISTORY The name Antigonish probably derives from the Mi'kmaq *n'alegihooneech,* 'where branches are torn off' – a reference to a place where bears came to forage for beechnuts.

Post Expulsion settlement is said to date from 1784 when Irish Loyalists, led by Captain Timothy Hierlihy took up a large land grant surrounding Antigonish Harbour.

The majority of settlers who followed were Scots from the Highlands, who were predominantly Catholic, so whereas Pictou County's churches are in the main Presbyterian, here in Antigonish County the churches tend to be Roman Catholic.

GETTING THERE

By car Antigonish is just off Highway 104 by Exits 31–34, 55km/34 miles to the Canso Causeway, 74km/46 miles from Pictou, 123km/76 miles from Truro, 218km/135 miles from Halifax and 231km/144 miles from Amherst.

By bus Antigonish is on the Acadian coach line between Halifax and Sydney (see page 52).

MINI CABOT TRAIL?

Lovers of lighthouses, magnificent coastal scenery and hiking should include this detour (or side trip from Antigonish) in their itineraries. The '**Cape George Scenic Drive**' also gets labelled the 'mini Cabot Trail' (for the real Cabot Trail, one of the world's great scenic drives, see page 298): that's going a bit far, but this is still a delightful and scenic little diversion. The drive begins at **Malignant Cove** on Highway 245, 8km east of Arisaig (if you are starting in Antigonish, take Highway 245 north for approximately 21km). Turn onto Highway 337 and in less than 20km you'll reach Cape George Point. As you round the cape, watch for Lighthouse Road, a left turn onto a 1km unpaved road to the lighthouse (*www.parl.ns.ca/lighthouse/;* ⊕ *May–Nov – hours vary*). En route, you'll pass Cape George Day Park with picnic areas and a parking area for trailheads. From this lofty setting, Prince Edward Island (over 50km away) and the highlands of Cape Breton are often clearly visible. The **Cape George Hiking Trail** comprises over 30km of loops and point-to-point trails, some reaching over 180m above sea level.

Back on the road, just past Cape George, there is a striking view of a line of cliffs, which head off into the distance towards Antigonish, with the brightly painted homes of the pretty and predominantly tuna-fishing community of **Ballantyne's Cove** directly below. Learn about bluefin tuna fishing past and present at the cove's **Tuna Interpretive Centre** (⊕ *mid-Jun–mid-Sep 10.00–19.00 daily; admission free*).

With indoor dining and a deck overlooking St George's Bay, **Boyd's Seafood Galley** (*Cribbons Point Wharf;* ✆ *863 0279;* ⊕ *May–Sep 11.00–17.00 Tue–Sun;* $) is the obvious lunch spot.

You'll then pass the **Crystal Cliffs**, named for their whitish appearance (a result of their high gypsum content), and will then have a view of the narrow entrance to Antigonish Harbour.

Just past **Mahoney Beach** on Highway 337, several more hiking trails ranging from 3km to 13km allow you to explore beautiful Fairmont Ridge, which overlooks the harbour. From here it is just 9km to Antigonish.

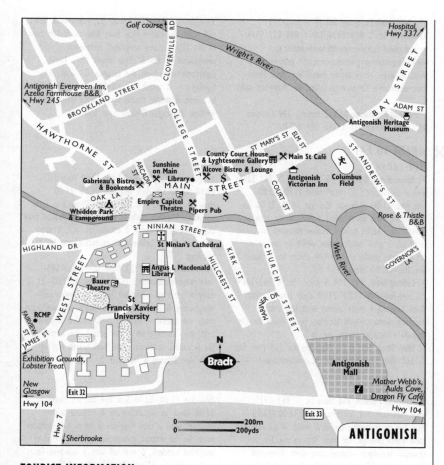

TOURIST INFORMATION

 Antigonish Mall complex Church St; ✆ 863 4921; ◷ mid-May–Jun & Sep–Oct 09.00–17.30 daily; Jul–Aug 09.00–19.00 daily. The mall is just by Exit 33 of Hwy 104. The tourist office isn't in the main mall buildings, but in a small building right by the highway.

WHERE TO STAY

🏠 **Antigonish Victorian Inn** (12 units) 149 Main St; ✆ 863 1103, T/F 1 800 706 5558; e victorianinn @ns.sympatico.ca; www.antigonishvictorianinn.ca; ◷ year-round. In the past, this fine (c1904) house, with 10 rooms & 2 apts. was a hospital, & a bishop's residence. Set on 2ha and conveniently located, it's a good blend of old & new. Full b/fast inc. $$

🏠 **Rose & Thistle B&B** (4 rooms) 4143 South River Rd; ✆ 735 2225, T/F 1 866 871 1440; e roseandthistle @eastlink.ca; www.roseandthistlebedandbreakfast.com; ◷ year-round. A purpose-built modern house on a hill outside the town centre with fine views over the harbour & surrounds. Guest rooms on the lower level. Large deck. Full b/fast inc. $$

⛺ **Whidden Park & Campground** (14 units, 174 campsites) 11 Hawthorne St; ✆ 863 3736; www.whiddens.com; ◷ mid-May–mid-Oct. These 2-bedroom well-equipped mini-homes might not be for aesthetes, but provide good value for those requiring more than 1 bedroom. The campground has serviced & unserviced sites. Outdoor pool (seasonal) & laundromat. Within walking distance of the town centre. $$

283

🏠 **Antigonish Evergreen Inn** (8 rooms) 295 Hawthorne St; ☎ 863 0830, T/F | 888 821 5566; e antigonishevergreeninn@ns.aliantzinc.ca; www.antigonishevergreeninn.com; ⏱ year-round. A pleasant, quiet single-storey motel less than 2km from downtown. Continental b/fast inc May–Sep only. $–$$

🏠 **Azelia Farmhouse B&B** (2 rooms) 309 Connors Rd; ☎ 863 4262, T/F | 866 309 0474; www.bbcanada.com/7409.html; ⏱ year-round. Quiet and rural but just 6.5km from Antigonish. This turn of the 20th century renovated farmhouse is surrounded by ash & sugar maple trees. Lovely, panoramic view from the veranda. Breakfast is a highlight – it could be buckwheat pancakes with hazelnuts & maple cream served with bacon, or perhaps asparagus & crab meat omelette. $

✕ WHERE TO EAT
Mid-range

✕ **Alcove Bistro & Lounge** 76 College St; ☎ 863 2248; www.alcovebistro.ca; ⏱ year-round 11.00–22.00 Tue–Wed, 11.00–midnight Thu–Sat, 16.00–21.00 Sun. This warm, lively bistro offers a Nova Scotia take on International fusion cuisine. Salmon fishcakes on Caesar salad are a good lunch choice, whilst for dinner try the Maritime paella or New York sirloin steak. Open late Thu–Sat for pizza. $$

✕ **Lobster Treat** Hwy 104 & James St; ☎ 863 5465; ⏱ mid-Apr–Oct 11.00–22.00 daily. Unpretentious 'fresh seafood & more' eatery with less than inspiring motorway-side location. Leave room for the legendary coconut cream pie. $$

✕ **Main Street Café at the Maritime Inn** 158 Main St; ☎ 863 4001; www.maritimeinns.com/en/home/antigonish/; ⏱ Jul–Sep 07.00–22.00 Mon–Fri, 08.00–22.00 Sat–Sun; Oct–Jun 07.00–21.00 Mon–Fri, 08.00–21.00 Sat, 08.00–20.00 Sun. Tasty, well-cooked dishes such as maple whisky-soaked pork chop with green apple & cranberry salsa, & apple cinnamon crème brûlée. Live entertainment Fri evenings. $$

✕ **Sunshine on Main** 332 Main St; ☎ 863 5851; www.sunshineonmain.ca; ⏱ year-round 07.00–21.30 daily. A great spot whether for a take-away coffee, imaginative & tasty sandwich or salad, or something more substantial – such as *pollo rustica* (chicken with spicy sausage on penne pasta). The bumbleberry pie & vanilla cheesecake are both worth leaving room for. Relaxed & informal. $–$$

Budget

✕ **Gabrieau's Bistro** 350 Main St; ☎ 863 1925; www.gabrieaus.com; ⏱ year-round 11.00–21.00 Mon–Sat. An extensive menu, & lunch in particular is good value (though the wine less so…). Try, for example, mandarin orange, camembert & roasted almond salad followed by jumbo shrimp & Italian sausage linguini. $

✕ **Mother Webb's** Hwy 104; ☎ 863 3809; www.motherwebbs.com; ⏱ year-round 11.00–23.00 daily. You'll see billboard advertising for this American roadhouse-style restaurant long before you get near to Antigonish. It manages to deliver hearty portions of reliable (if not gourmet) burgers, steaks, ribs & the like. Near Exit 35, approximately 6km east of the town centre. $

✕ **Pipers Pub** 33 College St; ☎ 863 2590; www.piperspub.ca; ⏱ year-round 10.00–02.00 Mon–Sat, 12.00–02.00 Sun. The kitchen closes at 21.00. Close to the university & popular with students, with a cosy fireplace & brook-side outdoor patio. Go for nachos, potato skins, fish & chips or pan-fried haddock, & cool off with a sub-zero Coors – or a portion of deep-fried ice cream! $

✕ **The Dragon Fly Café** Hwy 104, Lower South River; ☎ 863 2574; www.dragonflycafe.ca; ⏱ year-round 06.00–18.00 Mon–Fri, 07.00–18.00 Sat, 07.00–15.00 Sun. Approximately 6km east of the town centre, just east of Hwy 104's Exit 35, this place offers an imaginative menu, tasty well-priced food, very good coffee & – some say – the best oat cakes in the province. Sun b/fast/brunch menu. The occasional live music 'listen & dine' evenings are very popular & sell out quickly. $

SHOPPING The downtown area also has a couple of shops worth a quick browse, including:

Bookends 342 Main St; ☎ 863 6922; ⏱ 10.00–17.00 Mon–Sat. Not a bad second-hand bookshop.

Antigonish Mall The town's major shopping mall is out of the centre on Church Street by Exit 33 of Highway 104.

ENTERTAINMENT

🎭 **Empire Capitol Theatre** 291 Main St; ☎ 863 4646; www.empiretheatres.com. The town's cinema.

FESTIVALS
July
Antigonish Highland Games (☎ *863 4275; www.antigonishhighlandgames.com*) The games, a hit since 1863 and said to be the longest-running Highland Games outside Scotland, are held in the second week of July. Expect dancing, bagpipes and caber-tossing.

Evolve (*www.evolvefestival.com*) This three-day festival is held in Heatherton, about 25km from central Antigonish, and offers an eclectic mix of music genres. It is usually held late in July.

July–August
Music on Main (*www.antigonishmusiconmain.ca*) Free Wednesday evening concerts between mid-July and early August.

July–mid-September
Festival Antigonish (☎ *867 3333, T/F 1 800 563 7529; www.festivalantigonish.com*) Established in 1988, this festival is one of the province's biggest and best summer theatre programmes, with performances from early July to mid-September at the wonderful Bauer Theatre on the St FX campus.

End August/early September
Eastern Nova Scotia Exhibition (*www.ense.ca*) Held over five days, this festival has tug-of-wars, prize farm animals aplenty, live entertainment and much more.

OTHER PRACTICALITIES
$ **Royal Bank** 236 Main St; ☎ 863 0008; ⏰ 10.00–17.00 Mon–Fri

$ **Scotiabank** 255 Main St; ☎ 863 4800; ⏰ 10.00–15.00 Mon–Wed, 10.00–17.00 Thu–Fri

✚ **St Martha's Regional Hospital** 25 Bay St; ☎ 863 2830

📚 **Antigonish Library** College St; ☎ 863 4276; ⏰ 10.00–21.00 Tue & Thu, 10.00–17.00 Wed & Fri–Sat

✉ **Post office** 325 Main St; ⏰ 08.30–17.30 Mon–Fri

WHAT TO SEE AND DO
St Ninian's Cathedral (*120 St. Ninian St;* ☎ *863 2338; www.antigonishdiocese.com/ninian1.htm*) The bells of the c1870s' St Ninian's were cast in Dublin, Ireland, and slate for the roof tiles was imported from Scotland. High on the cathedral's façade you can see the words *Tigh Dhe* – Gaelic for 'House of God'.

St Francis Xavier University (*University Ave*) commonly known as 'St FX' or just 'X', was founded as a college by Roman Catholics in the 1850s, and gained university status in1866. No tours are offered but the landscaped grounds make for a pleasant wander.

Hall of the Clans (*Angus L Macdonald Library, St Francis Xavier University;* ☎ *867 2267; www.library.stfx.ca/index.php;* ⏰ *hours vary; admission free*) This contains one of the most significant collections of Celtic culture in North America. Comprising over 10,000 items including Scottish Gaelic, Irish- and Welsh-language resources, and Celtic literature, folklore and music.

Antigonish Heritage Museum (*20 East Main St;* ✆ *863 6160; www.parl.ns.ca/aheritage/;* ⊕ *year-round 10.00–12.00 & 13.00–17.00 Mon–Fri; admission free*) Housed in the restored former c1908 railway station, with two display rooms of photos and artefacts – including Mi'kmaq baskets – depicting the early days of the town and Antigonish County. Genealogical resource room (fee charged).

Antigonish Landing Trail This maintained 4.8km trail leads from the museum along part of the harbour and river estuary. Very popular with birdwatchers but just as enjoyable for walkers, joggers, and cyclists. You don't have to walk the whole way – just retrace your steps when you feel like turning round.

Lyghtesome Gallery (*166 Main St;* ✆ *863 5804; www.lyghtesome.ns.ca;* ⊕ *Jan–Mar 10.00–17.00 Wed–Sat; Apr–Dec 10.00–17.00 Mon–Fri; admission free*) Worth a visit for a range of works by artists from Nova Scotia and the Maritimes (and historic Scottish/Celtic art).

Antigonish Farmers' Market (*Exhibition Grounds, James St;* ✆ *867 7479; www.antigonishfarmersmarket.com;* ⊕ *late May–Nov 08.30–12.45 Sat*) If you're in town on a Saturday morning, pop along to this market.

POMQUET

You'll see many houses flying the Acadian flag in this village established in 1774 by five families originally from St Malo, France.

WHERE TO STAY

⌂ **Sunflower B&B** (2 rooms) 1572 Monk's Head Rd; ✆ 386 2492, T/F 1 866 904 2492; www.sunflowerbb.com; ⊕ year-round. This modern home offers panoramic views of Pomquet Harbour, best enjoyed from the sunroom or screened deck. Hearty full b/fast inc. $

WHAT TO SEE AND DO

Pomquet Beach Provincial Park Here the eponymous beach is backed by a series of 13 dunes stretching almost 4km. Boardwalks protect the dunes, while woods and both salt- and freshwater marshes attract a variety of wildlife: birdwatching is good, too. The park has changing rooms, loos, and interpretive panels explaining the dune formation.

AULDS COVE

This community is on the mainland side of the **Canso Causeway** (see page 294). Other than seeing a disproportionately high number of larger-than-life models – a big yellow sou'wester-clad mariner manning a boatwheel stands outside the Cove Motel (see page 287), and dotted about town are a big iceberg, a giant puffin, and a huge lobster in an even bigger lobster trap – and, if necessary filling up with petrol, eating and/or sleeping – there isn't much to delay you.

GETTING THERE

By car Aulds Cove is on Highways 104 and 4 and Highway 344, 5km/3.1 miles from Mulgrave, 10km/6 miles from Port Hawkesbury and 55km/34 miles from Antigonish.

By bus Aulds Cove is on the Acadian coach line between Halifax and Sydney (see page 52).

En route back to France from America in 1815, Father Vincent De Paul Merle of the Trappist Order was stranded in Halifax. He was given charge of the parishes of Havre Boucher, Tracadie and Cheticamp. In 1826, his house became the Monastery of Petit du Clairvaux, North America's first Trappist monastery. Although Father Vincent died in 1854, the monastery continued to blossom, and was 'upgraded' to an Abbey by Pope Pius IX in 1876.

It was struck by a couple of devastating fires, and in 1919, the Trappists returned to France. The property was abandoned until 1938 when the current owners, the Order of St Augustine, purchased and rebuilt the monastery. Late in 2007, the complex – now called Our Lady of Grace Monastery (*www.ourladyofgracemonastery.com*) became home to a group of Augustinian Contemplative Nuns, all of Filipino descent.

See the website for details of the Retreat House and service schedules, and the gift shop. To reach the monastery, take Exit 37 off Highway 104. Turn south onto Highway 16 and then right onto Monastery Road.

 ## WHERE TO STAY AND EAT

Cove Motel (30 units) Aulds Cove; ☎ 747 2700; e covemotel@ns.sympatico.ca; www.covemotel.com; ⊕ May–Oct. Choose from 18 motel rooms or 12 'chalets' at this reliable motel on a small peninsula jutting out into the Strait of Canso. The large licensed restaurant (⊕ *May–Oct 07.00–22.00 daily;* **$$**) can be busy with coach tours, but has a glassed-in patio with water views, an extensive menu & serves good food including lobster. **$$**

✕ Aulds Cove Lobster Suppers 13176 Hwy 104; ☎ 747 3368; ⊕ May–late Oct 11.00–19.00 daily. Despite the fact that the host is something of a loud, Acadian Basil Fawlty, the food is good. Acadian dishes are available in case you don't feel like the full lobster dinner. Just don't expect a quiet meal. **$$**

8

Cape Breton Island

Joined to the mainland since 1955 by the 2km-long Canso Causeway which crosses the narrow Strait of Canso, Cape Breton Island has a population of just under 150,000. Approximately 175km long and 135km wide, it covers 10,300km². At the island's core is the vast 260km² saltwater Bras d'Or Lake: to the northeast two natural passages connect the lake to the open sea, and in the southwest a short canal constructed in the 1850s and 1860s performs the same purpose. Cape Breton Island has the province's largest bald eagle population, many of which nest along the lake's shoreline.

Rugged highlands occupy much of the northern portion of Cape Breton Island: here you'll find the Cape Breton Highlands National Park, a region of deep, forested canyons, and magnificent coastal cliffs – and the best place in the province to see moose in the wild. This area of natural wonders is accessed by one of the world's great scenic drives, the 300km Cabot Trail. But don't just see it all through your car window – get out of your vehicle to hike, bike, kayak, play one of the superb golf courses, take a whale-watching trip or just relax on one of the beautiful beaches. Take a detour to remote Meat Cove, or wander the streets of the Trail's de facto capital, lakeside Baddeck, where Alexander Graham Bell was a summer resident for over 35 years.

Set on a magnificent harbour on the east coast, the port of Sydney is by far the biggest urban area: with the surrounding communities it makes up what is still called Industrial Cape Breton, a region largely built on coal mining and steel manufacturing which is home to over 70% of the island's population.

The island's major manmade attraction is in the southeast, a wonderful reconstruction of the Fortress of Louisbourg which played a major part in Nova Scotia's Anglo-French conflicts in the mid 18th century. In the southwest soak up the sleepy pastoral beauty and pretty backroads of Isle Madame.

But man has contributed another particular highlight of any visit to Cape Breton Island, part of the legacy left by the 50,000 Highland Scots who came here and settled in the late 18th and early 19th centuries – joyous Celtic music and dancing. Be sure to go to a ceilidh (see page 17) whilst in Cape Breton Island – or better still, try to time your visit to coincide with the Celtic Colours Festival (see box, page 293), a fantastic blend of traditional music, dancing and nature's splendour.

See for yourself why in 2008 *Travel & Leisure* magazine voted Cape Breton Island 'best island to visit in the continental United States and Canada', and why it took second place in the National Geographic *Traveler* magazine's list of the world's greatest destinations in 2004.

A century ago, Alexander Graham Bell said: 'I have travelled the globe. I have seen the Canadian and American Rockies, the Andes and the Alps and the Highlands of Scotland: But for simple beauty, Cape Breton outrivals them all.' He still has a case.

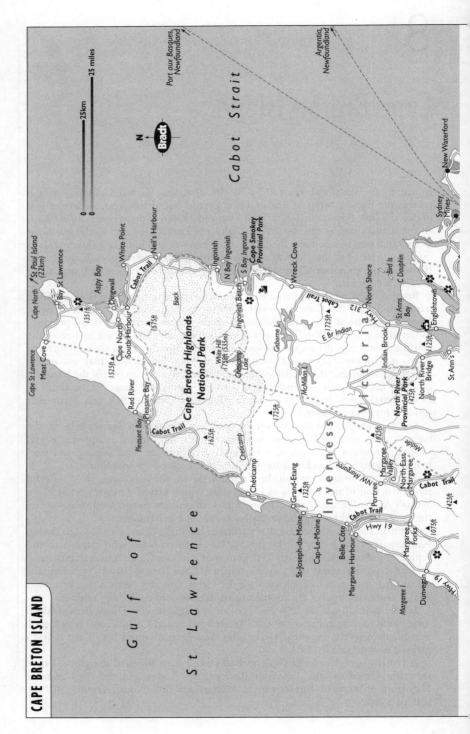

CAPE BRETON ISLAND

Gulf of

St Lawrence

Cape St Lawrence

Cape North   St Paul Island (22km)

Bay St Lawrence

Meat Cove

135ft

Aspy Bay

White Point

Dingwall

Neil's Harbour

Red River

Cape North

South Harbour

1525ft

Pleasant Bay

Black

1575ft

Cabot Trail

Ingonish

N Bay Ingonish

Pleasant Bay

Cape Breton Highlands National Park

White Hill 1738ft (535m)

Chéticamp Lake

Ingonish Beach

S Bay Ingonish

Cape Smokey Provincial Park

1625ft

Cabot Trail

Chéticamp

Wreck Cove

Chéticamp

Gisborne I

Grand-Étang

1325ft

McMillan I

E Br Indian

1725ft

North Shore

Bird Is

C Dauphin

St-Joseph-du-Moine

Inverness

Cabot Trail

St Anns Bay

Englishtown

Cap-Le-Moine

Hwy 19

NW Margaree

Margaree Valley

Middle

Indian Brook

Hwy 312

Victoria

Cabot Trail

125ft

St Ann's

Belle Côte

Portree

North East Margaree

1625ft

North River Provincial Park

North River Bridge

1425ft

St Ann's

Margaree Harbour

Cabot Trail

1425ft

Margaree Forks

1075ft

Dunvegan

Hwy 19

Margaree I

Cabot Strait

Port aux Basques, Newfoundland

Argentia, Newfoundland

New Waterford

Sydney Mines

N

Bradt

0   25km

0   25 miles

290

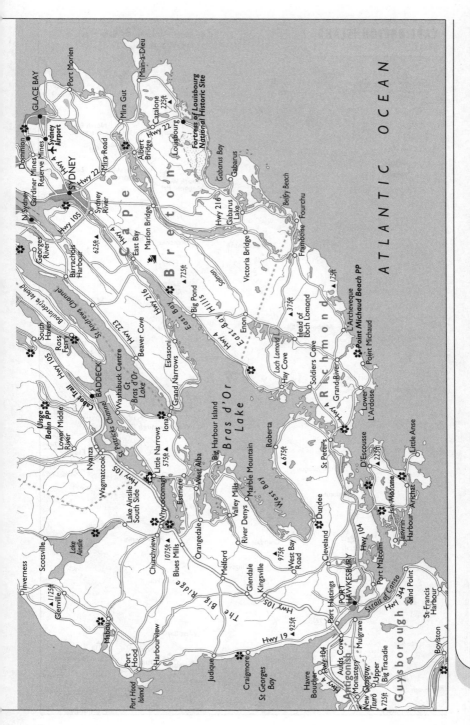

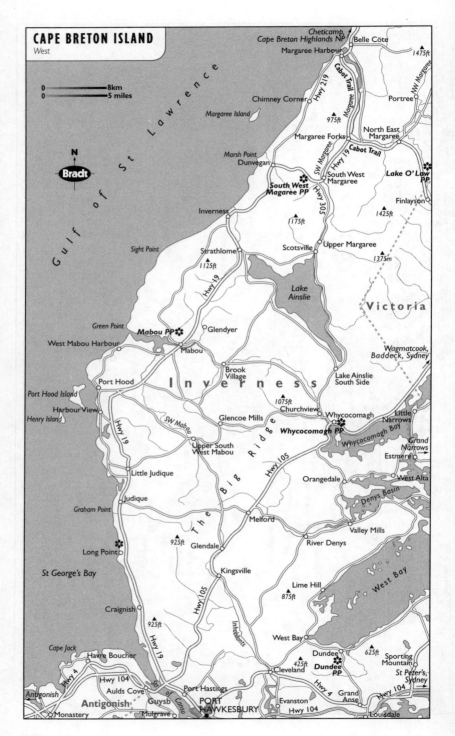

CAPE BRETON ISLAND
West

0 — 8km
0 — 5 miles

N
Bradt

Gulf of St Lawrence

Cheticamp,
Cape Breton Highlands NP   Belle Côte
Margaree Harbour   1475ft

Cabot Trail   Hwy 219   NW Margaree

Chimney Corner   Portree

Margaree Island   975ft   North East
                                                Margaree

Margaree Forks   Cabot Trail

Marsh Point   SW Margaree   Hwy 19
Dunvegan   South West   Lake O' Law
                    Margaree   PP

South West   Hwy 305   Finlayson
Magaree PP

Inverness   1175ft   1425ft

Sight Point   Strathlome   Scotsville   Upper Margaree
                    1125ft   1375m

Hwy 19   Lake
                    Ainslie   Victoria

Green Point   Mabou PP   Glendyer

West Mabou Harbour   Mabou   Wagmatcook,
                                        Baddeck, Sydney

Port Hood   Brook   Lake Ainslie
                    Village   South Side

Port Hood Island   1075ft   Little
                    Churchview   Whycocomagh   Narrows
Harbour View
Henry Island   SW Mabou   Glencoe Mills   Whycocomagh PP   Grand
                                                    Whycocomagh Bay   Narrows

Hwy 19   Upper South   Estmere
                    West Mabou   West Alta
                                    Orangedale

Little Judique   Denys Basin

Judique   Melford
Graham Point   River Denys   Valley Mills

                    925ft   Glendale   West Bay
Long Point   Hwy 105
                                    Kingsville
St George's Bay   Lime Hill
                                        875ft
                    925ft   West Bay
Craignish   Inhabitants

Cape Jack   West Bay   625ft   Sporting
    Havre Boucher   Mountain
                    Hwy 19   Dundee   St Peter's,
Hwy 4   Hwy 104   425ft   Dundee   Sydney
Antigonish   Auds Cove   Cleveland   PP
                    Port Hastings   Grand   Hwy 104
Monastery   Guysb   PORT   Evanston   Anse
    Mulgrave   HAWKESBURY   Hwy 104   Louisdale

Antigonish

The Big Ridge

Inverness

292

This section covers the region between Port Hastings (on the Cape Breton Island side of the Canso Causeway) and the village of Margaree Harbour 110km away on the Cabot Trail.

Scots first settled in this area in the 1770s, and their traditions are still strong. This part of Cape Breton Island seems to have produced a disproportionately high number of good dancers and musicians – Natalie MacMaster and her uncle Buddy, Ashley MacIsaac and the Rankins are amongst those who hail from the region. You get the feeling that a ceilidh is held in one community or another almost every evening. Music and dancing apart, there are some good beaches, the province's only whisky distillery, and some of Nova Scotia's best hiking.

PORT HASTINGS Port Hawkesbury (see page 342), 6km away, has accommodation and restaurants, so the only reasons to stop in this community at the Cape Breton end of the Canso Causeway are the well-stocked tourist office and the Gut of Canso Museum and Archives (see below).

Getting there Port Hastings is 51km/32 miles from Antigonish, 132km/82 miles from Cheticamp, 85km/53 miles from Baddeck and 171km/106 miles from Sydney.

Tourist information *(96 Hwy 4,* \ *625 4201;* ⊕ *daily May 09.00–16.00; Jun–Aug 08.00–20.30; Sep–mid-Oct 09.00–19.00; mid-Oct–early Jan 09.00–16.00)*

What to see and do
Gut of Canso Museum and Archives *(9 Church St;* \ *625 1295; www.porthastingsmuseum.org;* ⊕ *mid-Jun–mid-Oct 09.00–17.00 Mon–Fri (Jul–Aug also 12.00–16.00 Sat–Sun; admission free)* The museum is located in a century-old house with a collection focusing on life before, during and after construction of the causeway.

JUDIQUE Although most visitors come here for the Celtic Music Interpretive Centre, look out too for Judique's fine stone St Andrew's Church.

Getting there Judique is on Highway 19, 27km/17 miles from Port Hastings and 18km/11 miles from Port Hood.

What to see and do
Celtic Music Interpretive Centre (CMIC) *(5473 Hwy 19;* \ *787 2708; www.celticmusicsite.com;* ⊕ *year-round 09.00–17.00 Mon–Fri, 14.00–19.00 Sun; mid-Jun–Aug also 09.00–17.00 Sat; admission free; guided tours CAN$12)*, which collects the history and preserves and promotes the tradition of Cape Breton music.

CELTIC COLOURS INTERNATIONAL FESTIVAL

This nine-day festival (\ *562 6700; www.celtic-colours.com*) is a very good reason to delay your visit to Nova Scotia – or at least Cape Breton Island – until the second full week of October. It combines what traditionally is the best time to see nature's stunning autumn colours with Celtic music performed by the best musicians from Canada and further afield. Concerts are held each evening at venues of all sizes all around the island, there are several workshops, and numerous other events focus on Celtic heritage and culture.

Cape Breton Island **THE WEST COAST** | 8

The Canso Causeway connects Cape Breton with the mainland. Construction began in 1952: engineers blasted solid rock and fill from Cape Porcupine on the mainland side and began dumping it into the water. Slowly the roadway-to-be began to elongate. Locks were constructed on the Cape Breton side to allow shipping to pass through the barrier. Completed in 1955, the causeway is 1.37km long with a surface width of 24m. Ten million tonnes of rock fill were used in the construction, piled to a depth of 66m. On the Cape Breton side, a 94m swing bridge allows larger vessels to pass through the locks. The causeway's construction created one of the finest ice-free harbours in the world.

Fishermen say that this wall across the strait has killed off tuna fishing in the area. On the other hand, they say lobsters are much easier to catch as the crustaceans crawl back and forth under the sea looking for a way through.

Special events are held year-round – particularly during October's Celtic Colours Festival. In August, the town holds the **Kintyre Farm Scottish Concert,** an outdoor afternoon celebration of local music and dance.

PORT HOOD This pretty community – the self-proclaimed 'step-dancing capital of Cape Breton' – is the second largest on this route. For the non-terpsichoreal, step-dancing is a fast-paced dance which involves a lot of fast footwork, but little hand or arm movement: it is usually performed to traditional fiddle music.

There are fine views over **Port Hood Island** and if the weather is behaving, a few nice beaches to enjoy. The sea is very shallow, allowing the water to heat up early in the season and stay warm. There are days when the 'warmest water in Eastern Canada' claim seems justified.

What is now Port Hood Island was connected to Cape Breton Island until the turn of the 20th century when the effects of severe winter storms cut across the isthmus and created an island. Once one of the region's most important lobster-fishing bases, the brightly coloured houses amid meadows and high bluffs are now occupied only by those who come for the summer.

History Named Just-au-Corps by the French (after a garment popular at the time), much of the stone used to construct the Fortress of Louisbourg (see page 333) came from here.

With time, Just-au-Corps became Chestico (this name lives on as the name of the local museum and summer festival (see page 295).

Settling in the late 18th century, Catholic Highland Scots and New England Loyalists produced the Port Hood of today. It became an important port in the mid 19th century, and coal mining which began in the 1890s helped the town prosper over the next few decades.

Getting there Port Hood is on Highway 19, 45km/28 miles from Port Hastings and 35km/22 miles from Inverness.

 Where to stay and eat

Haus Treuburg Country Inn and Cottages (6 units) 175 Main St; ☎ 787 2116; e kargoll@ haustreuburg.com; www.haustreuburg.com; ⊕ May–Dec. 2 rooms & a suite are in the main house, but it's worth splashing out for 1 of the 3 cottages. The dining room (⊕ Jun–Oct 18.00–22.00 daily) offers a set 4-course dinner for CAN$44 (seafood, European & traditional German dishes); reservations recommended. B/fast not inc. $$

Other practicalities

$ **East Coast Credit Union** 138 Main St; ☎ 787 3246; ⏰ 09.30–16.30 Mon–Wed, 09.30–16.00 Thu

What to see and do

Chestico Museum and Historical Society (*Hwy 19, Harbourview;* ☎ *787 2244;* ⏰ *Jun–Aug 09.00–17.00 Mon–Sat; admission CAN$2*) Local history museum 3km south of Port Hood hosting several **Chestico Days** (a six-day festival in early August at Harbourview, near Port Hood) events including step-dancing demonstrations.

Port Hood Island View Boat Tours (*Shore Rd, Little Judique Harbour;* ☎ *787 3490; www3.ns.sympatico.ca/d_r/*) This company offers three-hour boat tours around Port Hood Island between July and October with possibilities to see dolphins, whales and bald eagles.

MABOU One of the most attractive villages on Cape Breton Island's west coast, Mabou (population: 410) is the province's centre of Gaelic education (the language is taught in the local school).

In summer, the town resonates to the sound of Celtic music with a Tuesday-evening ceilidh at Mabou Community Hall, the four-day **Mabou Ceilidh** in July, music at the **Red Shoe Pub** and **Strathspey Place**, and more. The beautiful surrounding area offers wonderful hiking.

Getting there Mabou is on Highway 19, 60km/37 miles from Port Hastings, 86km/53 miles from Cheticamp and 66km/41 miles from Baddeck.

Where to stay and eat

🏠 **Ceilidh Cottages and Camping Park** (10 units) 1425 New Rocky Ridge Rd, West Mabou; ☎ 945 2486, T/F 1 888 220 7977; www.ceilidhcottages.ca; ⏰ May–Oct. 10 1-bedroom cottages with fireplace & deck & a 17-site campground with tent & serviced motorhome sites. Facilities include laundromat, tennis court & heated pool (in season). $$

🏠 **Duncreigan Country Inn** (8 rooms) 11409 Hwy 19; ☎ 945 2207, T/F 1 800 840 2207; www.duncreigan.ca; ⏰ year-round. A lovely, comfortable c1990 harbourside inn, a blend of traditional & modern features with 4 rooms in the main house & 4 rooms in the 1996 adjacent Spring House. Full b/fast inc. $$

✗ **Red Shoe Pub** 11573 Hwy 19; ☎ 945 2996; www.redshoepub.com; ⏰ Jun–mid-Oct 11.30–23.00 Mon–Wed, 11.30–02.00 Thu–Sat, 12.00–23.00 Sun. Owned since 2005 by members of local singing favourites the Rankin Family & looking like a big-city coffee house. Offers sophisticated pub food & regular (& occasional spontaneous) live music performances: you're probably paying a couple of dollars extra for the celebrity connections. Food served until 21.30. $$

✗ **The Mull Café** 11630 Hwy 19; ☎ 945 2244; www.duncreigan.ca; ⏰ year-round late Jun–mid-Oct 11.00–20.00 daily; mid-Oct–late Jun 11.00–19.00 Sun–Thu, 11.00–20.00 Fri–Sat. Popular, unpretentious licensed restaurant: extensive menu. Eat inside or on the all-weather deck. $$

✗ **Shining Waters Bakery** 11497 Main St; ☎ 945 2728; call for hours. Locals value good, simple food & low prices more highly than fancy décor: they love this small place – but it was for sale at the time of writing. If things continue as they were, come for excellent sandwiches, homemade bread & baked goods. $

POSSIBLE DETOUR

For a scenic break from Highway 19, take the Colindale Road from the north end of town: unpaved for much of the way, it rejoins Highway 19 just south of Mabou.

Cape Breton Island **THE WEST COAST**

8

Entertainment

🎭 **Strathspey Place** 11156 Hwy 19; ☏ 945 5300; www.strathspeyplace.com; ⏰ year-round. A modern 500-seat theatre/performing arts centre with excellent acoustics and offering a varied programme.

Other practicalities

$ **East Coast Credit Union** 11627 Hwy 19; ☏ 945 2003; ⏰ 09.30–16.30 Mon–Wed & Fri, 09.30–18.00 Thu

✉ **Post office** 11541 Main St; ⏰ 09.00–17.00 Mon–Fri

What to see and do

Mother of Sorrows Shrine (*45 Southwest Ridge Rd;* ☏ *945 2221;* ⏰ *year-round daily; admission free*) A shrine (dedicated to Our Lady of Seven Sorrows and the pioneers of the Mabou area) enclosed in a miniature pioneer church.

West Mabou Beach Provincial Park This (usually quiet) park has a picnic area, good birding, ponds, sand dunes, old farm fields and marshes, and a beautiful 2km sandy beach. For walkers, the Old Ferry Road and Acarsaid (Harbour) trails are both worthwhile. To reach the park from Highway 19, take Colindale Road at Port Hood, or the West Mabou Road just before you get to Mabou Station.

An Drochaid (The Bridge Museum) (*11513 Hwy 19;* ☏ *945 2311; http://fortress.uccb.ns.ca/ historic/Mabou.html;* ⏰ *Jul–Aug 12.00–18.00 Mon–Fri, 10.00–16.00 Sat, 12.00–16.00 Sun; admission free*) Housed in a c1874 former general store, the museum focuses on traditional Cape Breton music and local history. Special events are held year-round.

INVERNESS Most visitors are attracted to the largest community (population: 1,800) along Highway 19 not by the town's mining history (coal was mined commercially here from 1890 to 1958), but for a huge, long sandy beach. An extensive boardwalk runs alongside the beach, and – compared with many other beaches further south – the sea can be quite warm.

At the wharf, depending on the season, watch fishermen unload lobster, crab or tuna.

In summer, there's a weekly ceilidh at Inverness Fire Hall on Thursday evenings.

Incidentally, Inverness is home to acclaimed author Alistair MacLeod, whose work includes the Cape Breton Island-set *No Great Mischief*.

A new golf course, Cabot Links, is planned for the area.

Getting there Inverness is on Highway 19, 80km/50 miles from Port Hastings, 57km/35 miles from Cheticamp and 153km/95 miles from Sydney.

MABOU HIKING

The Mabou area offers enough excellent trails to fill a book. Over a dozen well-marked trails through the beautiful highlands have been developed (and are maintained) by the Cape Mabou Trail Club, which produces an invaluable map, sold in various places in Mabou, including the general store.

If you'd rather stay on more level ground, one of several possibilities is to walk the Rail Trail from Mabou (near the bridge over the Mabou River) to Glendyer Station, approximately 4km each way. Old railway line it may be, but the views are stunning. West Mabou Beach Provincial Park (see above) also has good trails.

Glenville, on Highway 19, 9km north of Mabou, is home to **The Glenora Inn and Distillery** (↘ 258 2662, T/F 1 800 839 0491; www.glenoradistillery.com; ⊕ mid-May–mid-Oct; distillery tours (inc sample) daily; CAN$7) The highly regarded Glen Breton Rare, distilled here, is the only single malt whisky produced in Canada.

In 2001, the Edinburgh-based Scotch Whisky Association filed a suit against the Glenora Distillery, arguing that the use of the word 'Glen' in the distillery's main product, *Glen Breton Rare Single Malt Whisky* misled consumers to believe the spirit is a 'Scotch', a designation that can only be used by whiskies made in Scotland. Although Glenora Distillery makes no references to 'Scotch' anywhere in its marketing, in 2008, the Federal Court of Canada ruled that the company cannot register a trademark including the word 'Glen' in the name of its whisky. A bit ironic for a whisky made in 'New Scotland'…

Where to stay and eat

🏠 **Inverness Beach Village** (41 cottages) 50 Beach Village Rd; ↘ 258 2653; e village@macleods.com; www.macleods.com; ⊕ Jun–late Oct. The 1- & 2-bedroom cottages are OK: what keeps people coming back here is the magnificent beach location. There's an open & wooded 50-site campground on the same site, plus laundry facilities & tennis court. $$

✘ **Coal Miners Café** 15832 Central Av; ↘ 258 3413; ⊕ year-round 07.00–21.30 daily. This friendly eatery offers quite a sophisticated menu, though on occasions can't quite cope with it. Live entertainment Jul–Aug Thu evenings. $$

✘ **Tommycat Bistro** 15643 Hwy 19; ↘ 258 2388; ⊕ year-round 11.00–22.00 daily. Yet another Nova Scotia eatery where the uninspiring appearance belies a rather good eatery. Seafood, pasta, steak. Licensed. $$

Festivals

July

Broad Cove Scottish Concert Broad Cove, near Inverness. The largest outdoor Scottish concert on Cape Breton Island is held on the last Sunday in July.

Other practicalities

$ **Royal Bank** 15794 Central Av; ↘ 258 2776; ⊕ 10.00–15.00 Mon–Wed & Fri, 10.00–17.00 Thu

✚ **Inverness Consolidated Memorial Hospital** 39 James St; ↘ 258 2100

✉ **Post office** 16 Railway St; ⊕ 08.30–17.30 Mon–Fri

What to see and do

Inverness Miners' Museum (62 Lower Railway St; ↘ 258 2097; http://fortress.uccb.ns.ca/historic/invmm.html; ⊕ Jun–Sep 09.00–17.30 Mon–Fri, 12.00–17.00 Sat–Sun; admission CAN$2) Housed in the former c1901 railway station with information on the region's mining history & a tea room in an old railway caboose.

Inverness County Centre for the Arts (16080 Hwy 19; ↘ 258 2533; www.invernessarts.ca; ⊕ year-round 10.00–17.00 Mon–Fri; (also mid-Jun–mid-Sep 13.00–17.00 Sat–Sun); admission free) This good gallery features local and international artists: occasional live music performances.

Inverness Raceway (Forrest St; ↘ 258 2648; www.invernessraceway.net; horse-harness racing Jun–Sep Sun afternoon; Jul–Aug Wed evening)

MARGAREE HARBOUR This quaint village with a cluster of shingle and clapboard houses wraps around a once-bustling harbour flanked by two c1900 lighthouses. The busy old-fashioned general store is the hub of village life.

Getting there Margaree Harbour is at the junction of Highway 219 and the Cabot Trail, 112km/70 miles from Port Hastings, 27km/17 miles from Cheticamp and 60km/37 miles from Baddeck.

Where to stay and eat

Duck Cove Inn (24 rooms) 10289 Cabot Trail; 235 2658, T/F 1 800 565 9993; e info@ duckcoveinn.com; www.duckcoveinn.com; Jun–late Oct. Motel overlooking Margaree River, just a short walk from Margaree Harbour. Laundry facilities. The licensed dining room (Jun–late Oct 07.30–10.00 & 17.30–20.00 daily; $$) offers good-value family dining. $$

THE CABOT TRAIL

The Cabot Trail is the official name for a road which loops around northern Cape Breton Island. This region is justly renowned for its spectacular unspoiled beauty and regularly features high on lists of the world's best scenic drives.

The most spectacular stretch of the approximately 300km trail is the 115km between Cheticamp and Ingonish Beach, much of which passes through the Cape Breton Highlands National Park. From early summer well into autumn, pilot, minke, fin and humpback whales come to feed in the Gulf of St Lawrence and off the northern tip of Cape Breton Island. Whale-watching tours depart from Cheticamp, Pleasant Bay, Bay St Lawrence, and the Ingonishes.

The national park apart, there are many other beautiful sections of the Cabot Trail, such as the drive through the Margaree Valley. There are also some beautiful side trips such as the one from Cape North to Meat Cove.

This is not a drive to be rushed: ideally plan to stay a couple of nights (ideally more) *en route* to have time to walk some trails, appreciate the look-outs, take a side trip or two, look round Baddeck, try your hand at sea kayaking, go whale watching, cycling, or just relax on the beach.

As no public transport operates here, you'll need your own vehicle or to join a tour.

One-day Cabot Trail tours are offered by Sydney-based **Tartan Tours** (see page 337) and Baddeck-based **Bannockburn Discovery Tours** (see page 319).

Guided and self-guided bike tours of the entire Cabot Trail are offered by **Pedal and Sea Adventures** (see page 35) and **Sea Spray Outdoor Adventures** (see page 309). There are several strenuous climbs, and no paved hard shoulders. Not for the novice! Sea Spray, in my opinion, offer the best activity tours of the northern Cabot Trail and vicinity – including possibilities to cycle some of the best sections of the Cabot Trail. For other tour operators, see pages 33–5.

BELLE COTE Just north of the Margaree River, the wharf at the fishing village of Belle Cote tends to be busy with fishermen returning with their catches in the

---

A WORD OF WARNING

The first time I drove this route it was through thick fog and although I suspected that I was passing magnificent scenery, I could just make out the trees by the side of the road. I tried to make the best of it, and did a couple of 'atmospheric' forest trails, but felt quite down. Luckily, the fog lifted on the second morning, and I saw what all the fuss was about. Keep your fingers crossed!

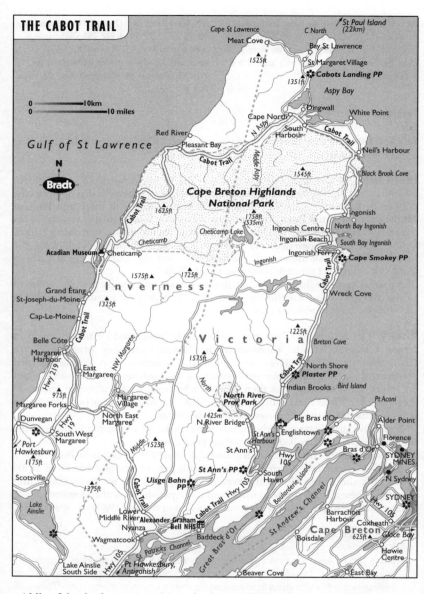

THE CABOT TRAIL

St Paul Island
(22km)

Cape St Lawrence
C North
Meat Cove
1525ft
Bay St Lawrence
St Margaret Village
Cabots Landing PP
1351ft
Aspy Bay
Dingwall
White Point
Cape North
South Harbour
Cabot Trail
Neil's Harbour
Red River
Pleasant Bay
Cabot Trail
1545ft
Black Brook Cove

Gulf of St Lawrence

N

Bradt

Cape Breton Highlands
National Park
1758ft
(535m)
Cheticamp Lake
Ingonish
North Bay Ingonish
Ingonish Centre
Ingonish Beach
South Bay Ingonish
1625ft
Cabot Trail
Cheticamp
Ingonish
Ingonish Ferry
Cape Smokey PP
Acadian Museum Cheticamp

I n v e r n e s s
1575ft
725ft
Wreck Cove
Grand Étang
St-Joseph-du-Moine
1325ft
Cap-Le-Moine
Cabot Trail
V i c t o r i a
1225ft
Breton Cove
Belle Côte
1575ft
North Shore
Cabot Trail
Plaster PP
Margaree
Harbour
East
Margaree
NW Margaree
Indian Brooks Bird Island
Hwy 219
Pt Aconi
975ft
Margaree
Village
North
Big Bras d'Or
Alder Point
Margaree Forks
Hwy
19
North East
Margaree
1425m
N River Bridge
St Ann's
Harbour
Englishtown
Florence
Dunvegan
South West
Margaree
Middle
1525ft
St Ann's
Bras d'Or
SYDNEY
MINES
Port
Hawkesbury
1175ft
North River
Prov Park
Hwy
105
South
Haven
N Sydney
Scotsville
St Ann's PP
Boularderie Island
SYDNEY
*Uisge Bahn
PP*
Cabot Trail Hwy 105
Hwy 105
Barrachois
Harbour
Hwy 105
Lake
Ainslie
1375ft
Lower
Middle River
Alexander Graham
Bell NHS
Nyanza
Baddeck
St Ann's Channel
Coxheath
Wagmatcook
St Patricks Channel
Baddeck
Great Bras d'Or
Cape Breton
625ft
Glace Bay
Boisdale
Howie
Centre
Lake Ainslie
South Side
Hwy 105
Pt Hawkesbury,
Antigonish
Beaver Cove
East Bay

middle of the day between spring and autumn. Wander the beach on the other side of the breakwater, and, in season, buy a fresh-cooked lobster at the pound.

Getting there Belle Cote is just off the Cabot Trail, less than 4km/2.4 miles from Margaree Harbour and 23km/14 miles from Cheticamp.

Where to stay and eat
Island Sunset Resort and Spa (18 units) 19 Beach Cove Rd; ☎ 235 2669, T/F 1 866 515

2900; www.islandsunset.com; ⏰ year-round. The very comfortable, well-decorated cottages overlook the beach, with wonderful sea views. The licensed restaurant (🕐 Jun–Oct 16.00–21.00; $$$) serves good, fresh food: start perhaps with the mussels, whilst the chicken breast stuffed with apple & brie is delicious. $$$

🏠 **Ocean Haven B&B** (2 rooms) 49 Old Belle Cote Rd; 🔾 235 2329; T/F 1 888 280 0885; www.oceanhaven.ca; 🕐 Jun–mid-Oct. Choose a room with en-suite or private bathroom at this restored farmhouse on 40ha overlooking the ocean. Full b/fast inc. $$

Festivals
July
Belle Cote Days Five days of concerts, dances, barbecues and competitions, including a golf tournament.

CHETICAMP
(*Population: 1,000*) Cheticamp – the largest Acadian village in North America – is a busy fishing village set along a protected waterway that opens to the Gulf of St Lawrence. Just 5km from the western entrance to the **Cape Breton Highlands National Park**, the community has long been regarded as a centre for the craft of **rug hooking**. It is also a departure point for **whale-watching** cruises to the Gulf of St Lawrence, and home to a good golf course overlooking the harbour. Virtually all attractions, places to stay and eat, and services are strung along the main road through town, the Cabot Trail.

A road along a sandbar leads to Cheticamp Island, where you can walk (or drive) to the Enragee Point Lighthouse. The island's large cow population probably accounts for large amounts of flies.

History The history of Cheticamp was strongly influenced by fishermen from Jersey, Channel Islands, particularly the Robin Company which came to Cheticamp in the late 1760s to exploit the fisheries. Two families settled permanently in 1782, and they were joined by 14 Acadians from St John's Island (as Prince Edward Island was then known) who became affectionately known as 'Les Quatorze Vieux', and many other Acadians who had spent the post-Expulsion years looking for somewhere new to put down roots.

Formerly called Eastern Harbour, following the influx of impecunious Acadians the community was labelled *cheti camp*, or 'poor camp'.

Construction of the imposing Romanesque-style c1892 Eglise St-Pierre was a team effort: parishioners donated a day's work per month, and blocks of stone donated by the Robin Company were dragged across the ice from Cheticamp Island by horses. In addition to man-hours, the parishioners also donated all the lumber. The Baroque-style interior – redecorated in the late 1980s – is spectacular,

---

MASKS

In the Middle Ages, the French took a one-day respite from the rigours of Lent to enjoy themselves. Disguised from head to toe, locals went from house to house getting people to try to guess their identity: they were known as *mi-carêmers*. They then removed their masks and were offered treats. This tradition has largely died out in most French and Acadian regions but remains strong here and in Cheticamp (see above). Festivities take place in the third week of Lent (usually March) and last a week. The celebration has led to the revival of carnival mask-making as a folk art. A new purpose-built **Centre de la Mi-Carême** (*51 Harbour Rd, Grand Etang;* 🔾 *224 1016; www.micareme.ca;* 🕐 *mid-May–late Oct 09.00–16.00 daily; admission CAN$5*) opened in the summer of 2009, displaying over 100 masks crafted locally for the annual festival.

with four plaster columns looking remarkably like marble: the 1904 Casavant organ is still in excellent working order.

Getting there Cheticamp is on the Cabot Trail, 88km/55 miles from Baddeck and 115km/71 miles from Ingonish Beach. If you continue more than a few kilometres past Cheticamp, the Cabot Trail passes through the national park (see page 303), and – even if you have no intention of stopping or using facilities – park entry fees are payable.

Tourist information In Les Trois Pignons Museum (*15584 Cabot Trail;* ✆ *224 2642;* ⌚ *mid-May–mid-Oct 08.00–19.00 daily*). See page 302 for further information.

Where to stay

🏠 **L'Auberge Doucet Inn** (11 rooms, 2 suites) 14758 Cabot Trail; ✆ 224 3438, T/F 1 800 646 8668; e doucetinn@ns.sympatico.ca; www.aubergedoucetinn.com; ⌚ May–mid-Nov. In pleasant grounds, the rooms feel a bit more 'motel' than 'inn', but are clean & quite spacious. Full b/fast inc. $$

🏠 **Cheticamp Outfitters Inn B&B** (6 rooms) 13938 Cabot Trail, Point Cross; ✆ 224 2776; www.cheticampns.com/cheticampoutfitters; ⌚ Apr–Nov. Wonderful views from this modern cedar home set on a hillside approximately 3km south of Cheticamp. Rooms with private or (cheaper) shared bathroom. The Acadian hosts know the area very well. Full b/fast inc. $

🏠 **Merry's Motel & B&B** (10 rooms) 15356 Cabot Trail; ✆ 224 2456; e merrysmotel@capebretonisland.com;

www.capebretonisland.com/cheticamp/merrysmotel; ⌚ mid-May–mid-Oct. 2 rooms in the main house (shared bath) & 10 traditional motel units (private bath). Clean, friendly & good value. Light b/fast inc. $

🅰 **Plage St-Pierre Beach & Campground** (94 sites & 50 seasonal) 653 Cheticamp Island Rd; ✆ 224 2112; www.plagestpierrebeachandcampground.com; ⌚ mid-May–mid-Oct. Open & wooded serviced & tent sites, laundromat & canteen. On Cheticamp Island, with a long stretch of beach frontage. $

🅰 **Cheticamp Campground** (162 sites) Cape Breton Highlands National Park western entrance, Cabot Trail; ✆ T/F 1 877 737 3783 (reservations); www.pccamping.ca; ⌚ year-round: sites can be reserved for late Jun–early Sep. Open & wooded campground with serviced & unserviced sites. Note: national park entrance fee payable (see page 310). $

Where to eat

❌ **Le Gabriel** 15424 Cabot Trail; ✆ 224 3685; www.legabriel.com; ⌚ early May–late Oct 11.30–22.00 daily. This large licensed restaurant, incorporating a mock lighthouse is about as upmarket as things get in Cheticamp. The seafood (eg: shrimp & scallop kebabs, broiled fillet of haddock, or sole stuffed with scallops & crab) is good. Lounge, billiard table & a regular programme of live Acadian/Celtic music. $$

❌ **Restaurant Acadian** (contact details as Cooperative Artisanale, see page 302) ⌚ daily mid-May–mid-June 11.00–19.00; mid-Jun–mid-Sep 07.00–21.00; mid-Sep–late Oct 08.00–20.00. It might not look much, but – with traditionally dressed serving staff – this is a great place to try authentic Acadian dishes such as chicken fricot. The lobster salad is a good choice & the butterscotch pie divine. Licensed. $–$$

Cape Breton Island **THE CABOT TRAIL**

8

✗ **Aucoin Bakery** Rue Lapointe 14, Petit Etang; ↘ 224 3220; ⊕ year-round 07.30–17.00 Mon–Sat. Take-away energy-boosting calorific treats between Cheticamp & the national park. $

✗ **Restaurant Evangeline** 15150 Cabot Trail; ↘ 224 2044; ⊕ year-round 06.30–21.00 daily. A simple, unsophisticated diner dishing up reliable fish & chips, pizzas & the like. $

Festivals
July–August
Festival de l'Escaouette (*www.festivallescaouette.com*) Event-packed festival celebrating Acadian culture and heritage.

Shopping
A stop that seems to be on every coach-tour itinerary is **Flora's** (*14208 Cabot Trail; ↘ 224 3139; www.floras.com; ⊕ May–Oct 08.30–18.00 daily*) but this big, often-busy craft and souvenir shop isn't a tourist trap: whilst there are few real bargains, in general, prices are fair.

Other practicalities
$ **Royal Bank** 15374 Cabot Trail; ↘ 224 2040; ⊕ 10.00–17.00 Mon–Fri
✚ **Sacred Heart Community Health Centre** 15102 Cabot Trail; ↘ 224 1500

✉ **Post office** 15240 Cabot Trail; ⊕ 08.45–17.15 Mon–Fri

What to see and do
Les Trois Pignons Museum of the Hooked Rug and Home Life (*15584 Cabot Trail; ↘ 224 2642; www.lestroispignons.com; ⊕ mid-May–mid-Oct 09.00–17.00 daily; Jul–Aug to 19.00; admission CAN$3.50*) The collection links Cheticamp's history with the development of rug hooking. The Elizabeth LeFort Gallery has a unique collection of hooked rug masterpieces by Ms LeFort, Cheticamp's most famous daughter, and, some would say, the country's best rug hooker – her works have graced walls in Buckingham Palace, the White House and the Vatican.

Cooperative Artisanale (*15067 Cabot Trail; ↘ 224 2170; www.co-opartisanale.com; ⊕ mid-May–late Oct 08.30–20.30 daily; admission free*) Started in the 1930s as a rug-hooking co-operative, this has expanded into a centre for displays on the history of wool in the area, with hands-on demonstrations of weaving, carding and spinning. There is a good craft shop (eg: locally made hooked rugs).

La Pirogue Museum (*15359 Cabot Trail; ↘ 224 3349; www.cbmuseums.tripod.com/id58.html; ⊕ May–Oct 09.00–20.00 daily; admission CAN$5*) A purpose-built waterfront museum celebrating the area's ties to the fishing industry, past and present. See an old Acadian homestead and watch how a lobster trap is constructed.

Whale watching Local operators offering 2.5–3-hour boat trips two–three times a day for approximately CAN$35 include:

> ### OMM
> Turn off the Cabot Trail onto Pleasant Bay Road, and within five minutes you'll come to the remote community of Red River. As you'd expect, there are weathered houses and fishermen's shacks: less predictable is a Tibetan Buddist Monastery. If you wish to look round **Gampo Abbey** (↘ 224 2752; www.gampoabbey.org; tours are generally offered mid-Jun–mid-Sep 13.30–15.30 Mon–Fri). It's best to ring ahead to check.

Love Boat Seaside Whale Cruises ❯ 224 2400, T/F
1 800 959 4253; www.loveboatwhalecruises.com.
Tours mid-Jun–mid-Oct.

Whale Cruisers ❯ 224 3376, T/F 1 800 813 3376;
www.whalecruisers.com. Tours mid-May–early Oct.

Le Portage Golf Club (*15580 Cabot Trail;* ❯ *224 3338; www.leportagegolfclub.com*) A
6,751yd par-72 course and one of Cape Breton Island's top courses. Green fees
CAN$57.

Little Pond Stables (*103 LaPointe Rd, Petit Etang;* ❯ *224 3858, T/F 1 888 250 6799; www.horsebackcapebreton.com*) Wooded trail, beach and mountain rides of 90 minutes
up to three hours, plus short pony rides for little kids.

PLEASANT BAY The Cabot Trail leaves the park just before Pleasant Bay, a working
fishing village which bills itself 'Whale Watching Capital of Cape Breton Island'.
Whales come closer to Pleasant Bay than they do to Cheticamp (see page 300), so
tours from here tend to be shorter. For a list of tour operators, see below.

Getting there Pleasant Bay is on the Cabot Trail, 42km/26 miles from Cheticamp
and 73km/45 miles from Ingonish Beach.

 Where to stay and eat

🏠 **Highland Breeze** (3 rooms) 42 Harbour Rd;
❯ 224 2974, T/F 1 877 224 2974;
e highlandbreezebnb@yahoo.ca;
www.bbcanada.com/highlandbreeze; ⊕ year-round.
Moose are often seen from the deck of this modern
chalet-style home with outdoor hot-tub & seasonal
pool. Country b/fast, evening dessert, & entry to the
Whale Interpretive Centre inc in rate. $$
🏠 **Midtrail Motel & Inn** (20 rooms) 23475 Cabot
Trail; ❯ 224 2529, T/F 1 800 215 0411;
www.midtrail.com; ⊕ mid-May–mid-Oct. Choose from
the inn or (cheaper) motel rooms at this pink
complex with wonderful views on 12ha on the
waterfront. The licensed restaurant

(⊕ mid-May–mid-Oct 08.00–20.00 daily; $$)
isn't bad, & the seafood is recommended. $$
🏠 **Cabot Trail Backpackers** 23349 Cabot Trail;
❯ 224 1976; email; hostel@cabottrail.com;
⊕ Apr–Oct. A clean & friendly hostel with 14 beds
in dorm rooms & 1 private room. Shared bathrooms,
2 kitchens. Dorm CAN$27, private room CAN$59. $
✗ **Rusty Anchor Restaurant** 23197 Cabot Trail;
❯ 224 1313; ⊕ May–Oct 08.00–22.30 daily. Set
on a hill with a fabulous view & a deck overlooking
Pleasant Bay, this is a great spot. The menu is a bit
more creative than many, & once again fresh
seafood the best choice. Save room for dessert, too.
$$

What to see and do

Whale watching Choose between a conventional boat (*C; CAN$25–35*) or Zodiac
type (*Z; CAN$45*). It's worth booking in advance for July and August trips.
Operators include:

Cabot Trail Whale Watching ❯ 224 1976;
www.cabottrail.com/whales/. Z available.
Captain Mark's ❯ 224 1316, T/F 1 888 754 5112;

www.whaleandsealcruise.com. C & Z both available.
Fiddlin' Whale Tours ❯ 1 866 688 2424;
www.fiddlinwhaletours.com. C available

Whale Interpretive Centre (*104 Harbour Rd;* ❯ *224 1411;* ⊕ *Jun–mid-Oct
09.00–17.00 daily; admission CAN$6*) Ideal place to learn more about whales – and
see a life-size model of a pilot whale.

CAPE BRETON HIGHLANDS NATIONAL PARK

(❯ *224 2306; www.pc.gc.ca/pn-np/ns/cbreton;* ⊕ *year-round daily, reduced services late
Oct–mid-May; admission CAN$7.80*) Established in 1936, the Cape Breton

8

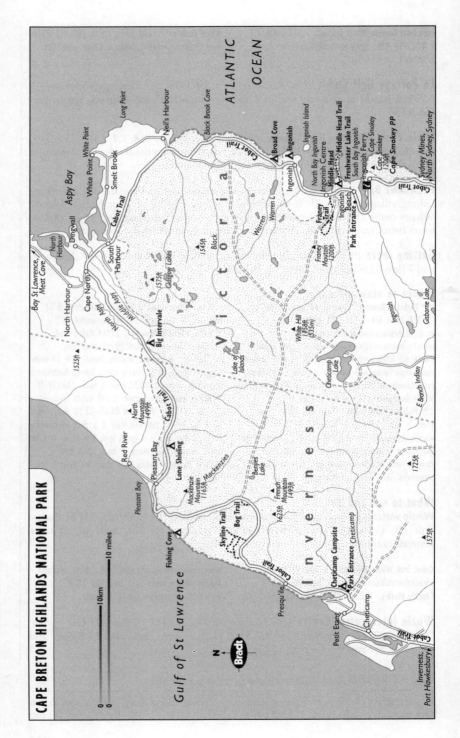

CAPE BRETON HIGHLANDS NATIONAL PARK

Gulf of St Lawrence

ATLANTIC OCEAN

Aspy Bay

Victoria

Inverness

Highlands National Park (CBHNP) was the first national park in the Maritime Provinces. The largest protected wilderness area in the province, it encompasses 950km² of the Maritime Acadian Highlands, one of the 39 natural regions of Canada. In addition to the magnificent forested highlands and deep river canyons, large sections of northern Cape Breton Island's stunning coastal wilderness fall within the park's boundaries. Wildlife is plentiful, with moose top of most visitors' 'want to see' lists. If you drive the western part of the Trail in late afternoon or early evening, you're very likely to see moose standing in the roadside ditches: drive slowly and carefully. From the Trail's look-offs, you might see whales just offshore.

The Cabot Trail is the only road through the park: along the road are two-dozen scenic roadside look-offs, many with interpretive panels: if the weather is clear, enjoy magnificent breathtaking views of the Highlands, the Gulf of St Lawrence, and, on the eastern side, the Atlantic. Pass soaring cliffs, rocky shorelines, fabulous beaches – and one of the world's top golf courses. Although I strongly advise you to get out of your vehicle as often as possible to walk a few trails, enjoy a picnic with an awesome view, or just wander a deserted beach, this is a park that *can* be enjoyed by those much happier doing their sightseeing without having to undo their seat belts.

With all this and sandy beaches, mountain trails, old-growth forests, waterfalls and highland barrens carpeted in rare wild flowers, this national park is one of the finest in Canada – and that's saying something.

The Cabot Trail dips in and out of the park: this means that those who do not wish to camp can stay very close to all the natural beauty, albeit just outside the park's boundaries.

GEOGRAPHY The CBHNP protects a spectacular portion of the largest remaining wild area of the Maritime Acadian Highlands. The dominant feature is the forested high plateau, which encompasses White Hill, the province's highest point at 535m. Extensive bog systems on the plateau are drained by numerous streams, stained the colour of tea by tannins leeching from the vegetation. After heavy rain, or during the spring snow melt, these in turn feed plunging waterfalls. There are also deep, forested canyons, and magnificent coastal cliffs which tend to be steeper to the west and more gently sloping on the park's eastern side.

A unique mix of Acadian, Boreal and Taiga forest regions co-exists as a result of the rugged topography and cool maritime climate.

GEOLOGY The park's plateau is part of the worn-down Appalachian mountain chain which stretches from Georgia to Newfoundland. Part of the park belongs to the Blair River inlier (an area, or formation of, older rocks completely surrounded by a more recent formation), formed 1,500 to 1,000 million years ago, and the oldest rocks in the Maritime Provinces.

FLORA AND FAUNA The most common tree species include balsam fir, white and yellow birch, white and dwarf spruce and sugar maple – there are over 750 vascular plant species, the vast majority native. These include Arctic-Alpine species such as dwarf birch (*Betula nana*) and southern temperate plants such as Dutchman's breeches (*Dicentra cucullaria*).

The park is also home to white-tailed deer, moose, black bear, beaver, mink, red fox, snow-shoe hare, Gaspe shrew, rock vole and lynx, and over 200 bird species, including eagles and red-tailed hawks.

Wildlife can be seen offshore too, with pilot and minke whales, and harbour seal the most commonly seen marine mammals. Humpback whales and grey seals are spotted less frequently.

TRAILS Walkers and hikers can choose from 25 trails which range from ten minutes to six hours. A short summary of each trail is given on the park map obtainable at the information centres, or on the website (see page 303). Mountain biking is permitted on four of the trails.

Suggestions include the 10–15-minute **Bog Trail**, where a boardwalk – with interpretive boards – leads through a highland plateau bog: flora includes pitcher plants and wild orchids. Or try the well-hiked (and well-liked) 9km **Skyline Trail**, which despite its name, doesn't involve a huge amount of climbing: it leads to a headland clifftop high above the sea. On this trail, look carefully for moose which often lie down in the undergrowth very close to the path: the majority of walkers pass them by without noticing them. Many people visiting the park stay at the Ingonishes (see page 310), and that area has some good, but understandably popular trails, such as the 2km wander around Freshwater Lake (look for beavers towards dusk). Very hard work but worth it for the view is the 7.5km **Franey Trail**, which involves an ascent of over 300m. And despite starting behind a resort, the 4km **Middle Head Trail** is very enjoyable, with fine coastal views, and the possibility of seeing whales from the end of the peninsula.

It is definitely worth talking to the information centre staff and listening to their hiking suggestions.

Winter visitors should see the website for details of groomed cross-country ski trails and charges.

TOURIST INFORMATION The park has information centres (⊕ *mid–May–Jun & Sep–mid–Oct 09.00–17.00 daily; Jul–Aug 08.00–20.00 daily, rest of year ask for information at the park offices* ⊕ *08.00–16.00 Mon–Fri except holidays*) at both entrances: **Cheticamp** (✆ *224 2306*), and **Ingonish** (✆ *285 2691*). The centre at Cheticamp is by far the larger and in addition to exhibits on natural history, sightseeing and hiking opportunities, also houses a well-stocked bookshop, **Les Amis du Plein Air** (✆ *224 3814*).

 WHERE TO STAY The park has seven campgrounds, six accessible by road (and ranging from ten to 256 sites), and one hike-in. Reservations are only accepted at two: Cheticamp and Broad Cove.

The campgrounds at Cheticamp, Broad Cove and Ingonish are described in the respective sections.

Suggestions for non-campers are shown under the appropriate area (or see page 303).

OFF-SEASON Although the park is open all year round, between late October and mid-May, few services operate. Offices at both entrances can provide you with information (⊕ *08.00–16.00 Mon–Fri except holidays*) and camping is possible at Cheticamp, Ingonish and the Black Brook ski area. Other than at the Cheticamp entrance, you'll have to make do with pit toilets. The park is popular with cross-country skiers.

FESTIVALS
End May/June
Lobsterpalooza (*www.lobsterpalooza.ca*) The festival takes place in numerous Cabot Trail coastal communities. It comprises five weeks of events which celebrate seafaring traditions – and seafood.

September
Hike the Highlands Festival (*www.hikethehighlandsfestival.com*) The festival takes place in numerous Cabot Trail coastal communities. It comprises five weeks of events, including guided hikes in the Highlands of Cape Breton Island.

The Cabot Trail community of Cape North is the launching point for a beautiful side-trip to explore some of Nova Scotia's most stunning scenery and remote communities.

CAPE NORTH The small community of Cape North is about 30km from the eponymous geographic feature – which, as the name might suggest, is Nova Scotia's most northerly point.

Winter visitors may be tempted to don cross-country skis – the North Highlands Nordic Ski Club is based here.

Getting there Cape North is on the Cabot Trail, 71km/44 miles from Cheticamp and 44km/27 miles from Ingonish Beach.

Where to stay and eat

Markland Coastal Resort (25 units) 802 Dingwall Rd; ☎ 383 2246, T/F 1 800 872 6084; e markland@canada.com; www.marklandresort.com; ⊕ mid-Jun–mid-Oct. Close to the quaint fishing village of Dingwall, 5km from Cape North, the Markland offers log rooms & 1- & 2-bedroom chalets. Less of a luxury activity-packed resort, more a simple place to stay & enjoy the outdoors, there is a heated outdoor pool, & private beach in a magnificent, scenic location. In my opinion, it is a bit overpriced. Its restaurant (**$$$**) is good – fresh, local ingredients, seafood, organic vegetables, etc – but again, not cheap. **$$$**

Oakwood Manor (4 units) 250 North Side Rd; ☎ 383 2317; www.capebretonisland.com/oakwood; ⊕ May–Oct. A c1930 manor house on a 80ha estate, with 3 rooms & a suite. If you like old wood, you'll love the beautiful interior. Full b/fast inc. **$**

Hideaway Campground, Cabins & Oyster Market (4 cabins, 37 campsites) 401 Shore Rd, South Harbour; ☎ 383 2116; www.campingcapebreton.com; ⊕ mid-May–mid-Oct. Rustic camping cabins & well-spread open & wooded sites approximately 5km from Cape North, overlooking Aspy Bay with laundromat. Canoe & kayak rentals, & boat launch. Oysters sold. Recommended for campers. Cabins CAN$40. **$**

What to see and do

North Highlands Community Museum (29243 Cabot Trail; ☎ 383 2579; www.northhighlandsmuseum.ca; ⊕ late Jun–late Oct 10.00–18.00 daily; admission CAN$5) Displays tell of pioneer days in the Cape Breton Highlands, and more recent history. See, too, artefacts from the *Auguste*, wrecked in Aspy Bay in 1761 *en route* from Quebec to France. Of the 121 on board, only seven reached the shore alive. Traditional skills – eg: net mending, weaving, ropemaking, quilting and boatbuilding – are demonstrated in July and August. There is also a settlers' garden.

Arts North (28571 Cabot Trail ☎ 383 2732; www.arts-north.com; ⊕ Jun–Oct 09.00–19.00 daily) The work of over two-dozen surprisingly-gifted resident artisans is displayed at this venue 2km west of Cape North village, including handmade pottery, wood turning, jewellery, quilting and basketry.

Octagon Arts Centre (Markland Coastal Resort – contact details as above; ⊕ late Jun–mid-Oct; check website for schedule and ticket prices) Chamber music concerts and weekly ceilidhs in season are held at this centre, with superb acoustics.

Eagle North (299 Shore Rd, South Harbour; ☎ 383 2552; www.kayakingcapebreton.ca) A family business renting canoes and sea kayaks and offering 90-minute, three-hour and full-day guided sea-kayaking trips exploring the region's beautiful coastal waters.

Cape Breton Island THE FAR NORTH

8

Consider a beautiful, scenic side-trip from Cape North to **Bay St Lawrence** and **Meat Cove**, the province's most northerly community.

Follow Bay St Lawrence Road along the lovely Aspy Bay shore to Cabot Landing Provincial Park. This picnic park has a long red sand beach – tinged white in places by naturally occurring gypsum – facing Aspy Bay, and a cairn commemorating the supposed landfall of John Cabot in 1497 (see page 5). If the weather is clear, you'll have a good view of St Paul Island (see below). For those who feel like burning off some calories in return for amazing views, the park is also the starting point for a hike up the 442m Sugar Loaf Mountain.

St Margaret's Village has a lovely setting, and a right turn leads to **Bay St Lawrence**, another pretty fishing village (crab is a speciality). Whale-watching, and other boat trips depart from the wharf with some of the province's most remote and stunning coastal scenery as a backdrop. Fin whales – the second-largest whale species after the blue whale – are often seen. Local operators include **Oshan Whale Watch** (T/F 1 877 383 2883; www.oshan.ca; Jul–Oct) who can also arrange birdwatching boat trips, deep-sea fishing charters, and (with notice) trips to St Paul Island. There's also **Captain Cox's Whale Watch** (383 2981, T/F 1 888 346 5556; www.whalewatching-novascotia.com; mid-Jun–Oct). Very fresh seafood can be purchased at the village's Victoria Co-op Fisheries. There are two decent take-outs, and a café and laundromat in the Community Centre.

Continue to **Capstick**, and then on a 7km unpaved road: virtually all the way, you will enjoy spectacular views from high above the sea. Whilst drivers will want to concentrate on the road, passengers can look out for pods of whales in the bays below. The road descends to (and ends at) remote **Meat Cove**. Here, you'll find a Welcome Centre (Jun–early Oct 09.30–16.30 Mon–Fri), which houses a tea room, a couple of simple places to stay – the rustic **Meat Cove Lodge** (383 2672; Jun–mid-Sep), the **Meat Cove Ocean View Lodge** (383 2562; www.meatcoveoceanviewlodge.com; May–Nov), and the amazingly located clifftop 26-site **Meat Cove Campground** (383 2379; mid-Jun–mid-Oct), which also rents kayaks. Attached to the campground is the **Chowder Hut** (mid-Jun–mid-Oct, hours vary) which is actually rather good. There are some very good hikes and Meat Cove is a place for those who appreciate nature and the great coastal outdoors: ironically, this is also a popular hunting area in the hunting season.

ST PAUL ISLAND The rocky shores of St Paul Island – 22km offshore between the tip of Cape North and the Ingonishes (see page 310) – have accounted for over 350 recorded shipwrecks.

The Graveyard of the Gulf lies directly in the path of marine travel to and from the Gulf of St Lawrence, and in an area prone to thick fog in the spring and early summer and squalls and snowstorms in the autumn and winter.

Very hilly, the 4.5km by 1.5km island is covered with stunted spruce. Two lakes feed several streams. In season, there are abundant wild flowers but no animal life. The only relatively safe landing areas are Atlantic Cove, and Trinity Cove on the island's opposite side.

In the early days, each year, when fishermen came to St Paul in spring, they would find the frozen bodies of shipwreck survivors who had managed to scale the island's cliffs only to perish from exposure and starvation.

For decades, demands were made for a lighthouse: in just one stormy 1835 night, four ships were wrecked on the island's shores.

Finally in 1837, construction of two lighthouses, one at each end of the island, began. A building was also put up to house shipwreck victims. Subsequently there were still occasional tragedies, but far less loss of life.

Getting there Visits to the island can be arranged through, eg: Oshan Whale Watch (see box on page 308) and you'll need a permit from the Real Property: Safety and Security Department of Fisheries and Oceans Canada (↘ *426 3550; www.dfo-mpo.gc.ca*).

What to do The island's shipwreck-dotted waters are popular with divers – if you'd like to join them, Terry Dwyer (↘ *830 7898; www.wreckhunter.ca*) may be able to help.

THE EAST COAST

Beautiful though the Cabot Trail is, at the start of the next section of the Trail, a simple detour will yield rich rewards. Further south is a popular resort area known collectively as 'The Ingonishes' at the southeastern boundary of the Cape Breton Highlands National Park. Just a few kilometres further on is magnificent Cape Smokey before the scenery eases down a gear or two from the highs further north.

NEIL'S HARBOUR This busy working fishing community has a sandy beach bordered by high cliffs. On a hillock is a pyramid-shaped white wooden lighthouse with a square base, topped by a red light. In the summer the lighthouse is home to an ice-cream shop.

Getting there Neil's Harbour is just off the Cabot Trail, 28km/17 miles north of Ingonish Beach.

Where to stay and eat

⌂ **Seymour Harbour View B&B** (3 rooms) 31 Seymour Lane; ↘ 336 2543; www.capebretonisland.com/northernhighlands/seymour/; ⊕ year-round; off-season by reservation. This good-value place offers fine views of the harbour & beach, & has a lovely deck. There are fridges in the guestrooms. Full b/fast inc. $

✘ **Chowder House** Main Rd; ↘ 336 2463; ⊕ May–Sep 11.00–20.00 daily. Once again, forsake sophistication, fancy décor & waitress service & your reward will be decent portions of well-cooked fresh seafood. The chowder is a favourite, of course, but most other things – fish & chips, for instance – are good, too. $

SUGGESTED DETOUR

For a spectacular alternative to the next stretch of the Cabot Trail, turn off at Effies Brook and follow White Point Road. *En route*, look out for the excellent **Sea Spray Outdoor Adventures** (↘ *383 2732; www.cabot-trail-outdoors.com;* ⊕ *year-round: hours vary*) which offers a wealth of local knowledge, cycle hire and a range of guided and self-guided tours from hiking, cycling, sea kayaking and trail running in summer to snow-shoeing and back-country skiing in winter.

Along White Point Road you'll pass high cliffs and a photogenic sheltered lagoon before a long descent to the picturesque and beautifully situated village of **White Point**. See the colourful fishing boats protected by the little harbour, and be sure to wander down the track towards the point (the site of the village during the Age of Sail). Watch for whales, sit in the meadow and tuck into a picnic, or just soak up the coastal scenery. Rejoin the Cabot Trail at Neil's Harbour.

THE INGONISHES On the shores of two lovely large bays (North and South), separated by the ruggedly beautiful Middle Head Peninsula, are the communities of (from north to south) Ingonish, Ingonish Centre, Ingonish Beach, Ingonish Harbour and (16km from Ingonish) Ingonish Ferry. Offshore is Ingonish Island.

Ingonish Beach is the eastern gateway to the Cape Breton Highlands National Park: within this region are a range of fine accommodations, excellent eateries, beautiful beaches (offering swimming in both fresh and salt water), and a relaxed resort atmosphere. Many will be drawn by the chance to play one of the world's best golf courses, others for the hiking. You can camp here, but it is also a good base from which non-campers can explore the national park and Cape North area.

Dotted about the Ingonishes are a couple of convenience stores, a liquor store, a bank and a laundromat.

Many people come and stay for a week or more – even if you're on a tight itinerary try to give yourself a couple of nights at least. Demand for accommodation can exceed supply in July and August, so book well ahead.

Getting there The Ingonishes are on the Cabot Trail, 110km/68 miles east of Cheticamp and 100km/62 miles north of Baddeck.

Where to stay

☗ **Keltic Lodge Resort and Spa** (82 units) Middle Head Peninsula, Ingonish Beach; ☏ 285 2880, T/F 1 800 565 0444; e keltic@signatureresorts.com; www.kelticlodge.ca; ⊕ mid-May–mid-Oct. This Ingonish institution is in a magnificent setting on the peninsula dividing North & South bays. There are 32 rooms in the main lodge, 10 2–4-bedroom cottages & 40 upmarket-motel-style rooms in the inn at Keltic (probably the best choice). For restaurants, see page 311. Facilities include a bar, outdoor heated pool, tennis courts & Aveda spa, but the *pièce de résistance* is the golf course (see page 311). Various packages are offered. $$$$

☗ **Seascape Coastal Retreat** (10 cabins) 36083 Cabot Trail, Ingonish; ☏ 285 3003, T/F 1 866 385 3003; www.seascapecoastalretreat.com; ⊕ May–Oct. Comfortable 1-bedroom cottages in a wonderful location aimed at couples rather than families, & not ideal for self-caterers (small kitchen area with microwave). For restaurant listing, see page 311. Use of kayaks & mountain bikes. Recommended. Full b/fast and snacks inc. $$$

☗ **Castle Rock Country Inn** (17 rooms) 39339 Cabot Trail, Ingonish Ferry; ☏ 285 2700; T/F 1 888 884 7625; e castlerock@ns.sympatico.ca; www.ingonish.com/castlerock; ⊕ year-round. A modern Georgian-style inn on a cliffside high above the Ingonishes with magnificent views. Rooms are on 3 levels (basement rooms are smaller but still have ocean views). For the on-site Avalon Restaurant, see page 311. Continental b/fast inc. $$

☗ **The Point Cottages by the Sea** (6 cottages) 2 Point Cottages Lane, Ingonish; ☏ 285 2804; www.thepointcottages.com; ⊕ Jun–mid-Oct. 3 1-bedroom, 2 2-bedroom & 1 3-bedroom cottage in a group of 12 in a great location virtually on the beach. A 1-week minimum rental applies Jul–Aug. $$

⬠ **Broad Cove** (256 sites); ☏ T/F 1 877 737 3783 (reservations); www.pccamping.ca; ⊕ year-round but services & showers operate late May–early Oct only. A large open & wooded campground with serviced & unserviced sites. Only a short walk to the sea approximately 5km north of Ingonish. $

⬠ **Ingonish** (90 sites) Ingonish Beach; ⊕ year-round but services & showers operate late May–early Oct only. Open campground, unserviced sites 10mins' walk to the lake or beach. $

FEES PLEASE

As parts of Ingonish and environs (eg: the Highland Links golf course, the Keltic Lodge and the Broad Cove and Ingonish campgrounds – and the campground at Cheticamp) are officially within park boundaries, national park entry fees are payable.

✕ Where to eat

✕ **Keltic Lodge Resort & Spa** Middle Head Peninsula, Ingonish Beach; ☎ 285 2880, T/F 1 800 565 0444; e keltic@signatureresorts.com; www.kelticlodge.ca. Keltic offers 2 dining options: the modern **Atlantic Restaurant** (⊕ early Jun–mid-Sep 11.00–20.00 daily; $$), offering casual family-style dining (predominantly seafood), & the fine-dining gourmet **Purple Thistle** (⊕ mid-May–mid-Oct 18.00–21.00 daily; $$$–$$$$). Reservations recommended; dress code – smart casual – applies.

✕ **Seascape Coastal Retreat** 36083 Cabot Trail, Ingonish; ☎ 285 3003, T/F 1 866 385 3003; www.seascapecoastalretreat.com; ⊕ Jun–late Oct, daily 11.30–14.30 & 17.00–21.00. Specialising in seafood & also very good with al fresco dining when the weather permits. $$$

✕ **Castle Rock Country Inn** 39339 Cabot Trail, Ingonish Ferry; ☎ 285 2700; T/F 1 888 884 7625; e castlerock@ns.sympatico.ca;

www.ingonish.com/castlerock; ⊕ year-round 17.00–20.00 daily; Nov–Jun by reservation only. The on-site licensed Avalon Restaurant shares the inn's views & offers alfresco dining when the weather permits. The limited menu focuses on seafood, but might include, eg: grilled chicken breast served with lobster sauce. Dessert fans will enjoy the tarte tatin. Considering the panorama & food quality, prices are reasonable. $$

✕ **Coastal Waters** 36404 Cabot Trail, Ingonish; ☎ 285 2526; ⊕ May–Oct 08.00–22.00 daily. Dependable family dining with the emphasis on seafood. Patio. Licensed. $$

✕ **Main Street Restaurant & Bakery** 37764 Cabot Trail, Ingonish Beach; ☎ 285 2225; ⊕ Sep–Jun 07.00–20.00 Tue–Sat; Jul–Aug 07.00–21.00 Tue–Sat. Good-size portions, well-cooked food & friendly service: another place that does superb seafood chowder – & a lot more. $$

Other practicalities

$ **Scotiabank** 37787 Cabot Trail, Ingonish Beach; ☎ 285 2555

☼ **Victoria North Regional Library** 36243 Cabot Trail; ☎ 285 2544; ⊕ 12.00–17.00 & 18.00–20.00

Tue–Thu, 09.00–12.00 & 13.00–17.00 Fri, 10.00–12.00 & 13.00–17.00 Sat

✉ **Post office** 37813 Cabot Trail, Ingonish Beach; ⊕ 08.00–17.00 Mon–Fri, 10.00–14.00 Sat

What to see and do

Whale watching Ingonish whale-watching tour operators seem to come and go.

Keltic Express Zodiac Adventures ☎ T/F 1 866 688 2424; www.capebretonwhaletours.com; ⊕ May–Oct. A 2-hr tour costs CAN$50.

Golf

Highland Links Ingonish Beach; ☎ 285 2600, T/F 1 800 441 1118; www.highlandslinksgolf.com. One of Canada's top courses, which features on most 'World's 100 Best Courses' lists, this 6,592yd par-72 course was designed by Stanley Thompson, who was also responsible for the Digby Pines course (see page 194). The setting is truly magnificent. Note that there are walks of up to 500m between holes. Green fees CAN$103 in high season (2008).

CAPE SMOKEY From Ingonish Ferry, the Cabot Trail climbs steadily to the crest of 360m Cape Smokey, named for the white cloud that often sits atop the red granite promontory. You're no longer within the national park, but nature is just as stunning here.

A turn-off leads to the **Cape Smokey Provincial Park** (⊕ late May–early Oct; admission free) which provides magnificent vistas of the mountainous coastline. There are several picnic areas, and a moderate to difficult 10km return trail leads past several look-offs to the very tip of the Cape. Bald eagles and hawks can often be seen soaring the updrafts and moose are plentiful in this area: on my last visit I saw three by the roadside between the Cabot Trail and the parking area.

From the top of old Smokey, the steep and twisting road descends, offering views of the offshore Bird Islands (see page 314).

Getting there Cape Smokey is on the Cabot Trail, 13km/8 miles south of Ingonish Beach, and 87km/54 miles from Baddeck.

WRECK COVE TO INDIAN BROOK The Cabot Trail continues along the coastal plain passing little fishing communities and a couple of beaches.

The **Plaster Provincial Park** has a day-use picnic area and a great little 1.5km trail passing gypsum deposits and giving fine coastal views. Buy lunch at the Clucking Hen (see below) and enjoy it here.

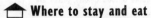
Where to stay and eat

⌂ **English Country Garden B&B** (4 rooms) 45478 Cabot Trail, Indian Brook; ↘ T/F 1 866 929 2721; e ipgreen@ns.sympatico.ca; www.capebretongarden.com; ⊕ year-round. Penny & Ian have created a luxurious B&B on 15 lakeside hectares. There are 3 themed beautifully decorated suites in the main house, & an open-plan private cottage down the path. A 3-course set menu is offered for CAN$52 in the (reservation only) dining room (⊕ Oct–Apr 19.00 Thu–Sat – year-round Thu–Sat by advance reservation for guests): the main course might be maple baked salmon, or perhaps filet mignon with hunter sauce. Full b/fast inc. $$
⌂ **Wreck Cove Wilderness Cabins** (2 cabins) 42314 Cabot Trail, Wreck Cove; ↘ 929 2800, T/F 1 877 929 2800; www.capebretonsnaturecoast.com; ⊕ year-round. Cosy, fully equipped 2-bedroom cabins ideal

for lovers of the outdoors, just 5mins' walk from the sea & close to highland walking trails. $$
✕ **Clucking Hen Café, Bakery & Deli** 45073 Cabot Trail, North Shore; ↘ 929 2501; ⊕ early May–mid-Oct 07.00–18.00 daily (Jun–Sep to 19.00). A homely, laid-back licensed eatery. The fish chowder is very good, & the pan-fried haddock dinner recommended. There's an outdoor eating area, or grab a coffee & a cinnamon roll, blondie (trust me!) or wedge of homemade pie & eat it at Plaster Provincial Park (see above), just 500m away. $
✕ **Wreck Cove General Store** 42470 Cabot Trail, Wreck Cove; ↘ 929 2900; www.wreckcovegeneralstore.com; ⊕ year-round, in summer daily. This well-stocked old-fashioned store is worth a stop: excellent lobster sandwiches in season, pizza by the slice, oatcakes, and in summer, ice cream. $

NORTH RIVER Shortly after Indian Brook, the Cabot Trail turns inland before reaching North River. With an excellent place to stay and eat, beautiful provincial parks nearby, several artisans' shops and galleries to visit, and a good kayaking company just up the road, this is worth considering as a base from which to explore the Cabot Trail and the Bras d'Or Lake area.

Winter visitors looking to do some wilderness Telemark skiing should check out **Ski Tuonela** (↘ 295 7694; www.skituonela.com), between North River and St Ann's (see below).

Getting there North River is on the Cabot Trail, 20km/12 miles from Exit 11 of Highway 105, 55km/34 miles from Ingonish Beach and 36km/22 miles from Baddeck.

Where to stay and eat

⌂ **Chanterelle Country Inn** (12 units) 48678 Cabot Trail, North River; ↘ 929 2263, T/F 1 866 277 0577; www.chanterelleinn.com; ⊕ May–Oct. 'Green' inn set on 60ha overlooking the North River estuary: 9 simply decorated guest rooms & 3 well-equipped nearby cottages. Very comfortable &

homely. Don't expect TVs or AC. The menu in the rather good licensed dining room (⊕ May–Oct 18.00–20.00; $$$) changes nightly & always includes a vegetarian, non-vegetarian & seafood main course & freshly baked artisan bread. Imaginative buffet b/fast inc (room, not cottage). $$

What to see and do
North River Provincial Park Popular with anglers and hikers, this small riverside picnic park gives access to the North River Wilderness Area. A moderate-difficult (9km each way) trail leads to the 31m North River Falls.

North River Kayak (☎ 929 2628; *www.northriverkayak.com;* ⊕ *mid-May–mid-Oct*) Kayak rentals, lessons, courses, and guided half-, full- and multi-day trips around the region's lovely waters.

ST ANN'S At 17km further along the Cabot Trail from North River is St Ann's: home to the **Gaelic College of Celtic Arts and Crafts**, the community is considered the centre of Cape Breton's Gaelic culture. St Ann's Provincial Park has a picnic area and a short walking trail that leads to a vantage point overlooking the beautiful harbour.

Getting there St Ann's is on the Cabot Trail and just off Highway 105 Exit 11, 74km/46 miles south of Ingonish Beach and 17km/11 miles from Baddeck. It is 17km/ 11 miles from North River.

 Where to stay and eat

⌂ **St Ann's Motel** (8 rooms) 51947 Cabot Trail; ☎ 295 2876; e stannsmotel@ns.aliantzinc.ca; www.baddeck.com/stannsmotel; ⊕ Apr–Oct. A traditional-style motel right on the waterfront with wonderful views. Rooms are simple but perfectly comfortable. Continental b/fast CAN$2. $$

✗ **Lobster Galley** 51943 Cabot Trail, South Haven; ☎ 295 3100; www.lobstergalley.com; ⊕ early May–late Oct 08.00–21.30 daily. Start with lobster-stuffed mushrooms, & move on to sautéed Digby scallops. Licensed. Next door to St Ann's Motel. $$

Festivals

August

Festival of Cape Breton Fiddling (*www.capebretonfiddlers.com*) Two-day event with concerts and workshops.

What to see and do

Gaelic College of Celtic Arts and Crafts (51779 Cabot Trail; ☎ 295 3441; *www.gaeliccollege.edu*) North America's only Gaelic college was founded in 1938 in a log cabin to encourage the study and preservation of the Gaelic language, arts and culture. Several musical and cultural events are held here during the summer: the campus shop sells a wide range of Celticana (tartans and kilts are predominant), Gaelic-language books, music books and supplies. The **Great Hall of the Clans Museum** (⊕ *Jun & Sep 09.00–17.00 Wed–Sun; Jul–Aug 09.00–17.00 daily; admission*

ANOTHER TALL STORY

Angus MacAskill was one of 14 children and as a baby was so small that few thought he would survive. He was six when the family came to Nova Scotia from the island of Harris in the Scottish Hebrides, and 14 before anyone began to notice his unusual size and strength. He grew to be 2.36m tall and weighed 193kg and became known in Gaelic as *Gille Mòr St Ann's*, ('The St Ann's Big Boy'). An entrepreneurial tradesman met him by chance and took him on tour to show off his size and strength. He often performed with a tiny midget, who, it is said, would dance in the palm of MacAskill's huge hand. Like all good giants from Nova Scotia, he went to England to meet Queen Victoria. Her majesty is said to have commented that he was the tallest, strongest and stoutest man ever to have entered her palace, and the *Guinness Book of World Records* listed him as 'the tallest true (non-pathological) giant'. When he tired of showbiz, he returned to a simple life as a St Ann's storekeeper, and passed away in 1863 aged 38. He is buried in the local cemetery. Learn more at the Giant MacAskill Museum (see page 314).

Reverend Norman McLeod (or MacLeod), originally from Scotland, arrived in Pictou (see page 273) in 1817 and quickly established and ran a church there. Having earned a good reputation, he was offered a church in Ohio (USA) to minister to other Highland Scots who had settled there. He accepted on the condition that all the members of his congregation who wished to join him could come too.

McLeod and his flock sailed out from Pictou in the *Ark*, bound for America. As luck would have it, before the ship had lost sight of Nova Scotia's shore, the Ark was caught in (not a flood but) a big storm, and – in darkness – the ship's captain took refuge in the nearest safe water, St Ann's Bay.

When the new day dawned, the passengers cast their eyes on a landscape very similar to their old Scottish homeland, and decided that they'd done more than enough travelling. They dispensed with all thoughts of Ohio and made their new homes here. They were rewarded with severe winters and crop failures.

McLeod's son sailed off to take cargo to Glasgow, but was not heard from for eight years. Finally, word came from him in Australia, suggesting that his father (and, of course, the entire congregation) come to join him. By now, there were too many parishioners for one ship, and so between 1851 and 1858 seven shiploads of McLeod's followers sailed almost halfway across the planet.

Incidentally, McLeod was less enamoured with Australia than his son had been, and led his followers across the Tasman Sea to New Zealand instead. It was from there – in his late eighties – that he went to meet his maker.

CAN$7) displays Scottish pioneer artefacts, an art gallery tells the Reverend McLeod saga (see box), and interactive exhibits portray the cultural and linguistic contribution of the Gaels to the social fibre of Cape Breton Island, Nova Scotia and Canada.

ENGLISHTOWN In addition to taking a boat to the Bird Islands (see below), you can visit a museum commemorating another of Nova Scotia's larger-than-life characters.

Getting there Englishtown is on Highway 312, 10km/6 miles from St Ann's.

Where to stay

Å **Englishtown Ridge Campground** (73 sites) 938 Englishtown Rd; ☏ 929 2598, T/F 1 866 929 2598; www.englishtown-ridge.com; ⊕ mid-May–mid- Oct. The campground offers good facilities, serviced & tent sites, and overlooks St Ann's Bay & Harbour. $

What to see and do

Giant MacAskill Museum (*Hwy 312, Englishtown;* ☏ *929 2925;* ⊕ *mid-Jun–mid-Sep 09.00–17.00 daily; admission CAN$2.50*). See box on page 313 for full information. Incidentally, there's also a Giant MacAskill Museum at Dunvegan on the Scottish Isle of Skye.

THE BIRD ISLANDS Birdwatchers (and others) will want to take a boat trip around Hertford and Ciboux islands, much more commonly known as the Bird Islands. You won't land on either island, but the boat goes close enough to get a good view, though binoculars and/or telephoto lenses will enhance the experience of the thousands of seabirds that nest here. Depending on the time of year (June and July are probably best), expect to see black guillemots, razorbills, black-legged kittiwakes, great cormorants and Atlantic puffins. Grey seals and bald eagles are also often seen. Contact **Donelda's Puffin Boat Tours** *(Hwy 312, Englishtown;* ✆ *929 2563, T/F 1 877 278 3346; www.puffinboattours.ca;* ⊕ *mid-May–mid-Oct; 2.5–3hr boat trip CAN$35–40).*

En route are good views of Cape Dauphin: according to Mi'kmaq legend, somewhere at the cape (the exact location is kept secret to protect the site) is Glooscap's Cave – sometimes called Fairy Hole – where the man-god was supposed to have lived for several winters.

BADDECK With a beautiful setting on the shores of the sparkling **Bras d'Or Lake** and well located on the Cabot Trail but in relatively easy reach of many of Cape Breton Island's highlights, Baddeck (population: 1,100) is understandably popular. There are numerous activities, ranging from ceilidhs to kayaking, within walking distance for the visitor, and one must-see museum.

Learn about the ecology of the area's lakes in a late 19th-century former post office, and be sure to get out onto the water (Baddeck's yacht club is the sailing centre of the Bras d'Or Lake). Take a trip on a classic yacht, a conventional boat tour, or in a kayak. In summer, have a swim in the lake from an island beach. A top golf course and beautiful waterfall hike are in easy driving distance.

History The name Baddeck derives from the Mi'kmaq *abadak*, 'place near an island' – referring to what is now called Kidston Island (see page 319). European settlement began late in the 1830s when an Irish and a Scottish family made their homes here. Within 50 years, Baddeck was home to several hotels, a post office, a library, three newspapers and numerous other services. A well-known celebrity, Alexander Graham Bell, arrived to settle with his family (see box on page 317).

In 1908, Baddeck was struck by an outbreak of cholera which claimed over 30 lives, and there was more tragedy in 1926 when fire destroyed almost two-dozen buildings along Main Street.

Getting there
By car Baddeck is just off Highway 105 Exits 8 or 9, 85km/53 miles from Port Hastings, 77km/46 miles from Sydney and 111km/69 miles from Louisbourg.

By bus Baddeck is on the Acadian coach route between Halifax and Sydney (see page 52).

Tourist information *(454 Chebucto St;* ✆ *295 1911;* ⊕ *late May–mid-Oct 09.00–17.00 daily, to 19.00 in Jul–Aug)*

⌂ Where to stay and eat
⌂ **Castle Moffett** (10 rooms) 11980 Hwy 105; ✆ 756 9070, T/F 1 888 756 9070; e info@ castlemoffett.com; www.castlemoffett.com; ⊕ late May–mid-Oct. If you were looking for a slightly over-the-top c1993 faux castle overlooking the Bras d'Or Lake, you've found it, at 19km west of Baddeck towards Whycocomagh. Expect antiques, canopy or 4-poster beds, a grand piano in the great hall & 80ha of grounds. Dinner is a no-choice set menu served at 19.00, with reservations required (⊕ *late*

May–mid-Oct Tue–Sun; $$$). B/fast offered but not inc. $$$$
⌂ **Crown Jewel Resort Ranch Guest House** (8 rooms) 992 Westside Baddeck Rd, Big Baddeck; ✆ 295 1096; e info@crownjewelresort.com; www.crownjewelresort.com; ⊕ year-round. A working ranch approximately 8km from Baddeck with a private airstrip on 320ha grounds. Fly-fishing, horseriding, dog sledding (in winter!) & more. Bar & restaurant. Various room & meal options & packages. $$$$

BADDECK

Alexander Graham Bell National Historic Site of Canada

Bell Bay Golf Club ▶

Auld Farm Inn,
Hwy 105 (East)

Boardwalk

Baddeck Bay

DUNTULM ST

JONES STREET

Dunlop Inn

Bras d'Or
Lakes & Watershed
Interpretive Centre

● Yacht Club

GRANT STREET

McKAYS LA

$

Library ●

● The Water's Edge
Inn, Café & Gallery

Yacht Club

Yacht hire △

Baddeck Wharf

✠ Lighthouse

St Michael's
(Roman Catholic)

CAMERON
ST

QUEEN
STREET

BUCHANAN
STREET

✠ Knox
(Presbyterian)

QUEEN ST

PRINCE ST

$

CHEBUCTO STREET (MAIN ST)

Boardwalk

WATER STREET

Kidston Island Ferry

Kidston Island

TWINING ST

✠ Greenwood
United

Telegraph House ⌂

Highwheeler Café ✕

TWINING STREET

✠ Victoria County
Memorial Hospital

Baddeck Gathering
Ceilidhs (live music) ●

Lynwood Inn ⌂

✠

Baddeck
Lobster Suppers ✕

ROSS STREET

The Worn Doorstep
B&B ⌂

OLD MARGAREE ROAD

CAMBELL ROAD

Inverary Resort ⌂

SHORE ROAD

✠

Hwy 105, Uisge Bahn Falls,
Crown Jewel Resort ◀

Hwy 105 (West), Castle Moffett,
Bras d'Or Lakes Campground,
Herring Choker Deli ◀

N

Bradt

200m
200yds

0
0

Inverary Resort 368 Shore Rd; ☎ 295 3500, T/F 1 800 565 5660; www.inveraryresort.com; ⊕ May–mid-Dec. This lakeside resort on over 4ha offers a spa, various activities, & 9 types of accommodation. As you'd expect, the higher cost rooms & units are better, with some of the cheaper ones less than inspiring. Food at the **Lakeside Restaurant** (⊕ mid-Jun–Oct 11.00–22.00 daily; $$) may not be spectacular, but it is above average & prices – considering the fantastic waterfront setting – pretty reasonable. When the weather's good, dining on the deck is a delight. Licensed. $$–$$$

Dunlop Inn (5 rooms) 552 Chebucto St; ☎ 295 1100, T/F 1 888 290 1988; www.dunlopinn.com; ⊕ May–Oct. A very comfortable centrally located Victorian inn with individually decorated rooms right by the water. With 2 waterside decks, sunroom & private beach. Continental b/fast inc. $$

Lynwood Inn (31 suites) 441 Shore Rd; ☎ 295 1995, T/F 1 877 666 1995; e lynwood@ baddeck.com; www.lynwoodinn.com; ⊕ year-round; off-season by reservation. 3 rooms in this c1868 original house, 28 suites (some with balconies) in the 2002 addition. The elegant licensed Victorian-style restaurant (⊕ mid-Jun–mid-Oct 07.00–21.00; daily; $$) has a casual atmosphere, & is one of the better ones in Baddeck. Fresh, local ingredients are used where possible, the lobster platter is good value, & the desserts very good. Live local entertainment most evenings. $$

Telegraph House (39 units) 479 Chebucto St; ☎ 295 1100, T/F 1 888 263 9840; www.baddeck.com/telegraph; ⊕ year-round. In addition to rooms (some up a couple of flights of stairs) in the grand c1861 main building – a former telegraph office – there is also a modern motel section & 4 cabins. Alexander Graham Bell (see box below) stayed here several times in the 1880s (Room 1). The dining room (⊕ for b/fast, lunch & dinner daily; $$) is good without being outstanding. $$

The Water's Edge Inn, Café & Gallery (7 units) 18–22 Water St; ☎ 295 3600; e stay@ thewatersedgeinn.com; www.thewatersedgeinn.com. Tastefully decorated, stylish & comfortable rooms – some with lake view – are on the 1st or 2nd floor, above an art & crafts gallery. The café (⊕ Jun–mid-Oct 11.00–17.00 daily; $) has an outdoor patio & harbour views. Very tasty snacks, light meals (eg: chicken quesadillas) & scrumptious desserts (eg: chocolate hazelnut torte). $$

The Worn Doorstep B&B (4 suites) 43 Old Margaret Rd; ☎ 295 1997; e hunter.baddeck@

LET'S HEAR IT FOR THE BELLS

Alexander Graham Bell (AGB) was born in Edinburgh, Scotland in 1847. By 1885, he had already invented the telephone and was living with his American wife in the US. Travelling via Nova Scotia to Newfoundland, the Bells passed through and fell in love with this area. In 1885, AGB bought land across the inlet from Baddeck and had a summer home built (Beinn Bhreagh).

Although best known for inventing the phone, Bell's major interests were flight and aerodynamics. Financed by his wife, he formed the Aerial Experiment Association. Experiments with man-carrying kites led to the creation of the *Silver Dart*, and this craft, piloted by Baddeck native Douglas McCurdy, took off from iced-up Baddeck Bay on 23 February 1909. Flying 9m in the air for a distance of about 1.4km, this was the first heavier-than-air flight in the British Empire.

In 1919, AGB (aged 72), his wife and his estate manager invented a prototype hydrofoil: the *HD-4* smashed the then world water-speed record, travelling at 114km/h.

Bell had many other interests – including the pastoral. For example, he experimented on raising multi-nippled sheep for 30 years. In addition to providing financial support and input for her husband's work, Mabel Bell was instrumental in the development of one of Cape Breton Island's traditional crafts. Rug hooking had always been popular, but Mrs Bell hired a teacher of the art to come over from Washington, and this revolutionised the colours and designs that the rug-hookers used.

AGB died in 1922, and his wife the following year: both are buried at Beinn Bhreagh. Still owned by the family, the estate is not open to the public.

ns.sympatico.ca; www.baddeck.com/worndoorstep; ① year-round. Spacious, comfortable rooms overlook the water: all have private entrances. Rate includes full b/fast which the very friendly hosts serve on your patio or in your room. Highly recommended. $$

🏠 **Auld Farm Inn** (8 rooms) 1817 Bay Rd, Baddeck Bay; ☏ 295 1977; www.baddeck.com/auldfarminn; ① mid-May–Oct. A renovated farmhouse 7km east of Baddeck with en-suite or shared bathrooms. The free breakfast is enough for most people, but a full breakfast is also available for an extra CAN$5pp. $

🛖 **Bras d'Or Lakes Campground** (95 sites) 8885 Hwy 105, between Exits 7 & 8; ☏ 295 2329; www.brasdorlakescampground.com; ① mid-Jun–Sep. 5km from Baddeck, with open serviced & unserviced sites are set back from over 100m of lakeshore. Pool, store & laundromat. $

✕ **Baddeck Lobster Suppers** Ross St; ☏ 295 3307; www.baddeck.com/lobstersuppers/; ① Jun–Oct

11.30–13.30 & 16.00–21.00 daily. The lunch menu is short & simple (lobster rolls, mussels, seafood chowder, etc): dinners are the big draw. Not a good choice for an intimate, romantic meal, but fun & reasonable value. Most come for lobster served with all-you-can-eat mussels, seafood chowder, etc, but salmon or ham are possible substitutes. Set dinner CAN$34.

✕ **Herring Choker Deli** 10158 Hwy 105, Nyanza; ☏ 295 2275; www.baddeck.com/herringchoker/; ① Apr–Oct 07.45–18.00 daily. Café/deli/bakery 10km west of Baddeck with deck overlooking the lake offering a range of freshly made wraps, paninis, soups, salads, sandwiches & baked goods. An ideal spot for breakfast or a light lunch. $

✕ **Highwheeler Café** 486 Chebucto St; ☏ 295 3006; ① May–mid-Oct 06.30–19.00 daily. Superb coffee, friendly service, great sandwiches, snacks & baked goods. Also does a good-value packed lunch to take away. $

Festivals
July–August
Baddeck Gathering Ceilidhs (*St Michael's Parish Hall, Main St;* ☏ *295 2794; www.baddeckgathering.com; admission CAN$10*) Not only are several events held in the town during the Celtic Colours Festival (see page 293) but you can enjoy Cape Breton fiddle music and dancing every evening in July and August as part of the Baddeck Gathering Ceilidhs.

August
Bras d'Or Yacht Club Regatta Seven days of races during the first full week of August.

Other practicalities
$ **Royal Bank** 496 Chebucto St; ☏ 295 2224; ① 09.30–17.00 Mon–Fri

✚ **Victoria County Memorial Hospital** 30 Old Margaree Rd; ☏ 295 2112

📖 **Baddeck Public Library** 526 Chebucto St; ☏ 295 2055; ① 13.00–17.00 Mon, 13.00–17.00 &

18.00–20.00 Tue & Fri, 17.00–20.00 Thu, 10.00–12.00 & 13.00–17.00 Sat

✉ **Post office** 485 Chebucto St; ① 08.00–17.00 Mon–Fri, 08.00–12.00 Sat

What to see and do
Alexander Graham Bell National Historic Site of Canada (*Chebucto St;* ☏ *295 2069; www.pc.gc.ca/lhn-nhs/ns/grahambell/;* ① *May–mid/end Oct 09.00–17.00 daily; Jun 09.00–18.00 daily; Jul–mid-Oct 08.30–18.00 daily; Nov–Apr by appointment; admission CAN$7.80*) An absorbing museum dedicated to Baddeck's most famous resident on a 10ha site with lovely views of the Bras d'Or Lake. Working models, photographs and multi-media exhibits; several children's programmes. There is also a full-size replica of the *HD-4* hydrofoil.

Bras d'Or Lakes and Watershed Interpretive Centre (*Chebucto St;* ☏ *295 1675; www.brasdor-conservation.com;* ① *Jun–Aug 09.00–19.00 daily (limited hours in Sep); admission free*) Housed in a c1885 former post office, six interactive exhibits detail the history, geography, geology and ecology of the lake.

One of the delights of a visit to Baddeck is getting out onto the water. For many years trips were offered on the *Elsie* – a 55ft yacht built by Alexander Graham Bell and launched in 1917 – but these were not offered in the 2009 season. Alternatives include:

Amoeba Sailing Tours ☎ 295 2481; www.amoebasailingtours.com; ⊕ mid-May–mid-Oct. 3–4 90-minute sailing trips daily on a 67ft schooner. Costs CAN$25 per person.

Ship Harbour Boat Tours ☎ T/F 1 800 565 5660; www.harbourtours.ca. 90-minute tours on the (motorised) *J Franklin Wright* depart mid-May–late-Sep at 10.00, 14.00 and 16.00 (subject to a minimum of 4 passengers) and cost CAN$30 per person.

Paddledog Kayak Tours ☎ 295 3363; www.paddledog.ca; ⊕ Jul–Aug. 90-minute beginner-friendly sea-kayak tours on the waters around Baddeck and Kidston Island. Costs CAN$44 per person.

Uisge Bahn Falls Provincial Park There is a 1.5km (each way) trail to these photogenic falls (*Uisge Bahn* is Gaelic for 'white water'). To reach the park, take Margaree Road from Baddeck, or Exit 9 of Highway 105, to Baddeck Bridge, then turn right towards Big Baddeck and Baddeck Forks. After 6.5km turn left onto North Branch Road. The park is approximately 16km from Baddeck.

Kidston Island Just 200m across the water from Baddeck, wooded Kidston Island has short walking trails, a beach with supervised swimming, and a lighthouse dating from 1875. Reach it by a free ferry, every 20 minutes (*Jul–Aug 10.00–18.00 Mon–Fri, 12.00–18.00 Sat–Sun*).

Bell Bay Golf Club (*761 Hwy 205;* ☎ *295 1333, T/F 1 800 565 3077; www.bellbaygolfclub.com*) With excellent facilities and fabulous views over the Bras d'Or Lake, this 7,037yd par 72 course is one of Cape Breton Island's best. Ask about play-and-stay packages (*May, Jun & mid-Sep–Oct*). Green fees CAN$79 plus tax.

Bannockburn Discovery Tours (☎ *295 3310, T/F 1 888 577 4747; www.bannockburntours.com*) 6- to 8-hour Cabot Trail tours to/from Baddeck from CAN$85.

MARGAREE RIVER VALLEY The Margaree River is divided into two main channels: the Northeast Margaree, which rises on the plateau of the highlands, and the Southwest Margaree. The two branches tumble over rapids and waterfalls, through deep salmon pools and verdant forested floodplains before merging at Margaree Forks and then flowing into the Gulf of St Lawrence at Margaree Harbour.

The valley is peaceful, pastoral and beautiful in any season, though at its most spectacular when ablaze with autumn colours.

From Margaree Forks, choose the road on either bank of the river to reach Margaree Harbour (see page 298) or Belle Cote (see page 298). The official Cabot Trail follows the west bank, but East Margaree Road also offers wonderful river views.

The Margaree River is renowned for its fishing, particularly salmon and trout, and the valley offers good hiking.

Getting there
By car The Margaree Valley is easily reached from Inverness via Highway 19, or from Highway 104 via the Cabot Trail. Margaree Forks is 27km/17 miles from Inverness, and 50km/31 miles from Baddeck.

Cape Breton Island **THE EAST COAST**

8

On a 17ha hillside site with a magnificent view of the Bras d'Or Lake and surrounding countryside, the Highland Village Museum (*4119 Hwy 223, Iona;* ☎ *725 2272, T/F 1 866 442 3542; www.museum.gov.ns.ca/hv/;* ⊕ *Jun–mid-Oct 09.30–17.30 daily; admission CAN$9*) is North America's only living-history museum for Gaelic language and culture. The museum is 24km east of Highway 105 Exit 6, via the Little Narrows ferry (CAN$5), and 61km from Sydney. The complex includes a visitor centre and 11 historic buildings (some original, some replicas). Costumed staff, activity demonstrations, language, stories, music and song bring to life the culture and lifestyle of the Gaels who settled in Nova Scotia from the Highlands and Islands of Scotland in the late 1700s and early 1800s. Be prepared for a lot of walking.

Tourist information (*7990 Cabot Trail, Margaree Forks;* ☎ *248 2803;* ⊕ *early Jun–early Oct 09.00–17.00 daily, to 19.00 in Jul–Aug*)

🏠 Where to stay and eat

🏠 **Old Miller Trout Farm Guest House** (1 cottage) 408 Doyles Rd, Margaree Forks; ☎ 248 2080, T/F 1 800 479 0220; e oldmiller@ns.sympatico.ca; www.oldmiller.com; ⊕ mid-May–Oct. A well-equipped, quiet 2-bedroom cottage by a pond on a working trout farm: approximately 2km off Cabot Trail. 3-night minimum stay. $$$

🏠 **Normaway Inn** (26 units) 691 Egypt Rd, Margaree Valley; ☎ 248 2987, T/F 1 800 565 9463; www.normaway.com; ⊕ mid-Jun–mid-Oct. 9 rooms (inc 3 suites) in an old-fashioned c1928 main lodge 3km off the Cabot Trail, & 17 1- & 2-bedroom rustic cabins spread out over a 100ha estate which would benefit from renovations. Guided fishing trips can be arranged. Food in the dining room (⊕ mid-Jun–mid-Oct 07.30–10.00 & 18.00–21.00 daily; $$$) is generally good without being great, & seems a touch overpriced. $$

🏕 **Scottish Crofters Campground** (32 sites) 51 Acadian Rd; ☎ 248 2304; e scotcroft2@ns.sympatico.ca; ⊕ Jun–Oct. Open serviced & tent sites & laundromat located 400m off the Cabot Trail. $

✕ **Dancing Goat** 6335 Cabot Trail, Margaree Valley; ☎ 248 2308; ⊕ year-round 10.00–17.00 Tue–Sun. Not very big, but very, very good. Excellent coffees, sandwiches & wonderful desserts. Try the cranberry almond scones. $

What to see and do

The Margaree Salmon Museum (*60 East Big Intervale Rd, Northeast Margaree;* ☎ *248 2848;* ⊕ *mid-Jun–mid-Oct 09.00–17.00 daily; admission CAN$2*) Angling, salmon fishing and local history housed in a former schoolhouse.

AROUND BRAS D'OR LAKE

In addition to Baddeck (see pages 315–19) and apart from the ever-changing views of the beautiful bays, islands and yachts and pleasure boats on the tidal waters, the lake shores offer several other points of interest. A scenic drive (look out for signs with a bald eagle motif – the shore and surrounding areas are a major nesting area for hundreds of these majestic birds) runs all the way around the shore of this vast lake, but most people just choose a section depending on their interests and itinerary.

WAGMATCOOK The best reason to stop in Wagmatcook is to learn about the Mi'kmaq at the culture and heritage centre (see page 321).

Getting there Wagmatcook is on Highway 105, 15km/9 miles from Baddeck and 25km/16 miles from Whycocomagh.

What to see and do
Wagmatcook Culture and Heritage Centre (*10765 Hwy 105;* \ *295 2999, T/F 1 866 295 2999; www.wagmatcook.com;* ⊕ *daily May–Oct 09.00–20.00; off-season 09.00–17.00; admission free*) The centre tells the story of the Mi'kmaq through multi-media presentations, slides and live demonstrations of crafts. The on-site restaurant's menu includes some traditional Mi'kmaq options.

WHYCOCOMAGH Located just east of the Skye River, Whycocomagh's name comes from the Mi'kmaq *We'koqma'q*, 'Head of the waters'. Wrapped in mountains on three sides, the community's 'open' side fronts the Bras d'Or Lake. Its main claims to fame are the fact that Alexander Graham Bell once described it as 'the Rio de Janeiro of North America', and the view from trails in its eponymous provincial park (see *Where to stay*).

Getting there
By car Whycocomagh is on Highway 105, 50km from the Canso Causeway, 30km/19 miles from Baddeck and 115km/71 miles from Sydney.

By bus Whycocomagh is on the Acadian coach route between Halifax and Sydney (see page 52).

⌂ Where to stay and eat
⌂ **A Moeller's Lake View Cottage, B&B** (3 units) Portage Rd, South Side Whycocomagh Bay; \ 756 2865, T/F 1 877 756 2865; www.capebretoncottage.com; ⊕ May–Oct; off-season by reservation. With 2 ground floor B&B rooms with private entrance in a modern house, or a well-equipped, comfortable 1-bedroom cottage close by. Bald eagles often nest on this 15ha forested lakeshore property. Full b/fast inc. $

⌂ **Bear on the Lake Guest House** 10705 Hwy 105, Aberdeen; \ 756 2750, T/F 1 866 718 5253; www.bearonthelake.com; ⊕ mid-May–Oct. 7km east of Whycocomagh. Dorms & private rooms, shared kitchen, laundry facilities & good lake views. Cabot Trail shuttle service offered. Dorm CAN$30, private room CAN$75. $

⌂ **Fair Isle Motel** (21 units) 9557 Hwy 105; \ 756 2291, T/F 1 877 238 8950;

e fairislemotel@ns.sympatico.ca; www.fairislemotel.com; ⊕ mid-May–Oct. A traditional-style motel on the hill above the main road, overlooking the lake, offering standard rooms, a couple of suites & some larger rooms. Laundry facilities. $

⋀ **Whycocomagh Provincial Park** (62 sites) \ T/F 1 888 544 3434 (reservations); ⊕ late Jun–early Oct. Sites on grassy slopes or tucked into the forest on a hillside less than 500m east of town. 3 short but steep & challenging trails lead up Salt Mountain, 240m above sea level. If it is clear, views from the mountaintop are sensational. $

✗ **Vi's Restaurant** 9381 Hwy 105; \ 756 2338; ⊕ year-round 07.00–20.00 Mon–Sat, 08.00–20.00 Sun. This institution recently celebrated its 50th birthday. Nothing fancy or pretentious, just reliable home cooking. $

Other practicalities
$ **Royal Bank** 72 Village Rd; \ 756 2600; ⊕ 10.00–16.00 Mon–Wed, 10.00–17.00 Thu–Fri

✉ **Post office** 115 Main St; ⊕ 08.30–17.00 Mon–Fri, 08.30–12.30 Sat

ORANGEDALE This little community is worth a short stop for those with an interest in railway history.

Getting there Orangedale is just off Orangedale Rd, 7km/4 miles south of Highway 105 Exit 4.

What to see and do
Orangedale Railway Museum (*1428 Main St;* \ *756 3384;* ⊕ *late Jun–late Aug 09.00–17.00 Wed–Sun; Sep–mid-Oct 09.00–17.00 Sat–Sun; admission CAN$3*)

Housed in the restored c1886 station which was in operation until 1990. Several good displays inside and outside, and an interpretive centre in a replica freight shed.

DUNDEE On West Bay on the southern shore of Bras d'Or Lake, Dundee has a small provincial park with a sandy beach, and a resort with one of Cape Breton Island's finest 18-hole golf courses.

Getting there Dundee is 51km/32 miles from Orangedale and 24km/15 miles from St Peter's.

Where to stay and eat

⌂ **Dundee Resort and Golf Club** (98 units) 2750 West Bay Hwy; ☏ 345 2649, T/F 1 800 565 5660; www.capebretonresorts.com/dundee.asp; ⏰ mid-May–Oct. With 60 hotel rooms & 38 1- & 2-bedroom cottages. Facilities include tennis, indoor & outdoor (seasonal) pools, spa, hiking, canoe & pedal-boat rental. On my most recent visit, this resort was looking a bit worn. There is a restaurant serving breakfast, lunch & dinner, and a pub on site. You can also eat in the golf

clubhouse. Various packages are offered. $$$
⌂ **Kayak Cape Breton and Cottages** (2 cottages) 5385 Dundee Rd, Roberta; ☏ 535 3060; www.kayakcapebreton.com; ⏰ May–Oct. 2 well-equipped 2-bedroom cedar-log cottages are tucked between the trees by the lakeside. Min stay applies: 2 nights May–Jun & Sep–Oct, 3 nights Jul–Aug. Kayak lessons, guided trips & rentals are all offered. 12km from the Dundee Resort and 16km from St Peter's. $

What to see and do

The Dundee Resort Championship Golf Course (☏ 345 0420, T/F 1 800 565 5660; www.dundeegolfclub.com; ⏰ May–Oct) This course is absolutely beautiful, but you'll really need to concentrate and play hard, particularly on the front nine. Expect a lot of hills! Various stay-and-play packages are available, and the course is open to non-resort guests. Green fees CAN$63 including tax (2008).

ST PETER'S One of Nova Scotia's oldest communities, pleasant St Peter's (population: 735) is situated on a narrow strip of land separating the Atlantic Ocean and the Bras d'Or Lake. The largest community on the southern part of the lake shore and the service centre for Richmond County can almost be described as bustling in summer. The eponymous canal is one of two access points for boats entering Bras d'Or Lake and there are picnic areas on the canal's grassy banks.

History Founded by Nicolas Denys (see box on page 323) as Saint Pierre in 1650, the French later built a fort on this strategically important portage between the Atlantic and the Bras d'Or Lake.

They seriously considered establishing their capital here, but that honour went to Louisbourg (see page 333). In 1745, the British attacked the fort and torched the buildings, and in 1793, built Fort Grenville on the site.

Work on the construction of an 800m canal, now a National Historic Site (☏ 733 2280; www.pc.gc.ca/lhn-nhs/ns/stpeters; ⏰ year-round; admission free), began in 1854 and was completed in 1869. Its opening saved over 120km of sailing for vessels wishing to enter or leave the southwest of the lake.

Getting there

By car St Peter's is on Highway 4, 55km/34 miles from Port Hastings, 24km/15 miles from Isle Madame, 38km/24 miles from Big Pond and 87km/54 miles from Sydney.

By bus St Peter's is on the Acadian coach route between Halifax and Sydney (see page 52).

Tourist information *(10259 Granville St;* ☎ *535 2185;* ⊕ *early Jun–mid-Oct 09.00–17.00 daily, to 19.00 in Jul–Aug)*

⌂ Where to stay and eat

⌂ **Bras d'Or Lakes Inn** (19 rooms) 10095 Grenville St; ☎ 535 2200, T/F 1 800 818 5885; e info@brasdorlakesinn.com; www.brasdorlakesinn.com; ⊕ year-round. A red cedar-log building in a lovely lakefront location. Rooms are comfortable & well equipped. Wood features strongly in the décor of the licensed restaurant & lounge (⊕ 07.30–16.30 & 17.00–20.00 daily; $$$): large picture windows look out over the lake. The restaurant offers Canadian cuisine with a French influence: try eg: crab & scallop-stuffed crêpes followed by sautéed Cajun-style tilapia. Dinner reservations recommended. There is a lounge with ceilidh & square dances, a

patio, exercise room, private dock. Kayaks, canoe & bicycles for guest use. $$$

⌂ **Canal House B&B** (5 rooms) 9329 Pepperell St; ☎ 535 2049, T/F 1 866 419 9266; e info@canal-house.com; www.canal-house.com; ⊕ year-round. Rooms with shared or en-suite bathrooms & a good-sized garden in this friendly B&B. Full b/fast inc. $

⌂ **Joyce's Motel & Cottages** (24 units) 10354 Grenville St; ☎ 535 2404; www.joycesmotel.com; ⊕ Jun–Sep. 6 simple motel rooms & 18 basic 1- & 2-bedroom cabins/cottages (some with cooking facilities) across the main road from the lake. Laundromat & outdoor pool. $

Festivals

End July–early August
Nicolas Denys Days Events include auctions, a parade, ceilidhs, and chowder lunches.

November
Festival of Trees Get festive with a display of decorated Christmas trees.

Other practicalities

$ **Royal Bank** 9955 Grenville St; ☎ 535 2001; ⊕ 10.00–15.00 Mon–Fri

✉ **Post office** 9981 Grenville St; ⊕ 09.00–17.00 Mon–Fri, 09.00–14.00 Sat

---

NICOLAS DENYS

Born in Tours, France, in approximately 1598, his name crops up throughout Nova Scotia and Atlantic Canada's early history. Denys first came to Nova Scotia as part of an expedition led by Isaac de Razilly in 1632. He settled on the LaHave River (see page 156), and after a spell in France returned to these shores as Governor of Canso and Ile Royale (what is now Cape Breton Island). He established various settlements, including one here at Saint Pierre (St Peter's) in 1650. Trading extensively with the Mi'kmaq and other settlers at that time, he constructed a track on the isthmus between the sea and the lake to allow teams of oxen to haul boats onto skids and across the portage.

In 1654, Denys obtained a concession from Louis XIV to work all the island's minerals in return for a 10% royalty.

In the years that followed, he ran many businesses here (eg: fishing, lumber, and farming) but in 1669, his home and business were destroyed by fire. In financial ruin, he moved to Nipisiguit (now Bathurst, New Brunswick) and began writing about the lands he had lived in and visited, and their peoples. He died in 1688 and legend has it that he is buried near what is now the 15th hole of Bathurst's Gowan Brae Golf Course.

What to see and do

Battery Provincial Park (✆ 535 3094; *www.novascotiaparks.ca/parks/battery.asp;* ☻ *mid-June–early Sep; admission free*) Walking trails lead to the c1883 Jerome Point Lighthouse, and a short but steep section to the site of Fort Grenville (see *History*, page 322). Both of these offer lovely views.

Nicolas Denys Museum (*46 Denys St;* ✆ 535 2379; ☻ *Jun–Sep 09.00–17.00 daily; admission CAN$1*) The world's only museum dedicated to this important historical figure (see box on page 323).

Wallace MacAskill Museum (*7 MacAskill Dr;* ✆ 535 2531; ☻ *mid-Jun–Aug 09.30–17.30 daily; Sep–Oct by appointment; admission free*) This c1850s' house with period furnishings is the restored birthplace and childhood home of perhaps the world's best marine photographer, Wallace MacAskill (1890–1956). In addition to a good collection of his works – many in their original frames – one room is dedicated to a display of vintage cameras.

Ship Harbour Boat Tours (✆ 227 5456; *www.harbourtours.ca*) Boat trips through the canal and to Cape George in the summer. Call ahead to check schedules/prices.

EAST BAY East Bay offers the chance to play golf between spring and late autumn, and to hit the slopes when the snow comes down. Bald eagles are often seen in this area.

Getting there East Bay is on Highway 4, 27km/17 miles from Sydney and 54km/34 miles from St Peter's.

 Where to stay and eat

🏠 **Birches at Ben Eoin Country Inn** (12 units) 5153 Hwy 4; ✆ 828 2277, T/F 1 866 244 8862; www.thebirchescountryinn.ca; ☻ year-round. Here you can choose from 10 luxurious modern rooms or 2 suites. Outdoor jacuzzi. $$

✗ **Malcolm's** ☻ Feb–Dec 17.00–21.00 Tue–Sun. The Inn's licensed restaurant offers fine dining in elegant & intimate surroundings. Try, for example, lobster bisque or scallops Florentine. $$$

CHAPEL ISLAND

The Chapel Island First Nations Reserve (CIFN) is known to the Mi'kmaq as *Potlotek* and is sometimes described as the Mi'kmaq 'capital'. It is named for the island (*Mniku* to the Mi'kmaq) just offshore. The first missionary priest to visit this region lived among the Mi'kmaq and settled with them on Chapel Island in the 1740s: he built a church here in 1754. This is the longest continuous mission in Canada.

Held over the weekend starting on the third Friday in July, the Chapel Island Pow Wow is an important social, cultural, and spiritual event for the Mi'kmaq and gives an opportunity for them to share their culture and heritage with others. In addition to daily feasting, there are dancing demonstrations, story telling, traditional games, and masses. Authentic arts & crafts are sold.

The CIFN encompasses the island itself, and a strip of land from the lakeshore back across Highway 4 which was granted to the Mi'kmaq in the 1830s.

There isn't a huge amount for the casual visitor to see but the island still holds great spiritual significance for the Mi'kmaq. To visit the island, turn from Highway 4 onto Chapel Island Road (10km east of St Peter's) or onto Mountain Road (1km further east along Highway 4). Ask around near the shore, and someone will probably take you across by boat (make sure that they wait around to take you back) for a few dollars.

Big Pond, on Highway 4, halfway between St Peter's and Sydney, is best known as the home of Rita MacNeil, acclaimed singer, songwriter and recording artist. Rita's fans, and other hungry travellers, will want to stop at **Rita's Tea Room** (*8077 Hwy 4;* ✆ *828 2667; www.ritamacneil.com;* ☉ *Jul–mid–Oct;* **$–$$**) to see a collection of Rita memorabilia, and to tuck in to soup, salads, sandwiches, sweet things and more: it is good stuff, but prices seem a few celebrity-connection dollars higher than the norm. Rita pops in sometimes and (most summers) performs a few concerts at the local community centre.

What to see and do

The Lakes (*Hwy 4;* ✆ *539 6494: www.thelakesgolfclub.ca*) Play a round or two at Cape Breton Island's brand-new (Aug 2009) 6,973yd par 72 Graham Cooke-designed golf course. Green fees CAN$89.

Ski Ben Eoin (*Hwy 4;* ✆ *828 2804; www.skibeneoin.com*) Take to the snow in winter at this place, which also rents snowshoes.

SYDNEY

With a past in which the words 'steel' and 'coal mining' feature prominently, those who are not industrial historians could be forgiven for wondering if they should include Nova Scotia's second (and Cape Breton Island's) largest urban centre in their itineraries. In fact, Sydney is no longer a city, but since 1995 has been part of the Cape Breton Regional Municipality (population: 104,000) which also includes communities such as North Sydney, Sydney Mines and Glace Bay.

Like Halifax (and its namesake in Australia), Sydney lies on a magnificent harbour, and the downtown area occupies part of a peninsula jutting out into the water. Despite the setting, with the exception of a pleasant historic district and a nice waterfront boardwalk, it isn't the most attractive of places. For most visitors it is only a bit of an exaggeration to say that once you've walked along both the **Esplanade** and parallel **Charlotte Street** (just one block inland) between Townsend and Amelia streets, you've done Sydney.

There are, of course, some other attractions, including a good art gallery at **Cape Breton University** and a **casino**, and for those who like an urban base, Sydney is well placed for day trips to Louisbourg and many of the Bras d'Or Lake communities.

The 3km waterfront boardwalk buzzes with activity on nice summer days and by the time you read this, work to redevelop **Wentworth Park** just south of downtown back into an attractive green space – with duck ponds, walking paths and picnic areas – should have been completed.

ESKASONI

Less than 4km northeast along Highway 4 from East Bay, Highway 216 leads 26km west to Eskasoni (the name comes from the Mi'kmaq for 'still waters'), the biggest Mi'kmaq reserve in the province. Although the setting is scenic, unlike Wagmatcook (see page 320) or Bear River (see page 197), there isn't a centre where one can learn about Mi'kmaq life and culture here – in fact Eskasoni is bereft of services for the visitor.

Cape Breton Island SYDNEY

8

North Sydney's former railway station, now housing offices, at 1 Station Street, is worth a look for its fine Victorian architecture.

Neighbouring **Sydney Mines** is more attractive: its red sandstone c1904 Gothic-style former post office is now used as the **Town Hall**, and the c1905 railway station now houses a heritage museum.

Sydney Mines is one of the province's important fossil sites, particularly for plant fossils.

HISTORY Previously known as Spanish Bay, Sydney was founded in 1785 by Colonel DesBarres, a Swiss-born Huguenot. It was first settled by Loyalists from New York State: a garrison, in use until 1854, was constructed. The settlement was named for Lord Sydney, the British Home Secretary. Immigrants from the Scottish Highlands began to arrive in the early 1800s. For 35 years, until the island was reunited with mainland Nova Scotia in 1820, Sydney was the capital of the colony of Cape Breton. As industrial development increased, so did the population. Sydney became home to the largest self-contained steel plant in North America, fed by the area's numerous coal mines. One pit – Princess Colliery in Sydney Mines – operated continuously from 1875 to 1975.

Sydney ranked as Canada's third-largest steel producer through World War II, a time when its harbour was an important staging point for Europe-bound shipping convoys. Post-war came decades of economic decline, not least for Sydney's iconic mainstays: both the coal and steel industries had completely dried up by the end of 2001.

GETTING THERE

By air Sydney Airport is 14km/9 miles northeast of the city centre. A taxi from outside the arrivals area to downtown Sydney costs CAN$14. For flights within Nova Scotia, see page 48, for flights further afield, see page 38, and car rental, see page 49.

By car Highway 105 connects North Sydney with Port Hastings and the Canso Causeway: Highway 125 links North Sydney, Sydney River and Sydney. Highway 22 heads from Sydney to Louisbourg, and Highway 4 to Glace Bay. Sydney is some 400km/249 miles from Halifax, a drive of about five hours (without stops).

By bus/coach Three Acadian coach services a day connect Sydney with Halifax (see page 52) the Acadian terminal is at 99 Terminal Road (564 5533). Some services also stop in North Sydney and Sydney River. Several shuttle services (see page 53) also make the run.

By sea For those travelling to and from Newfoundland, the ferry terminus (see page 39) is on the North Sydney waterfront.

GETTING AROUND
By taxi
Kings Taxi 564 4444   City-wide Taxi 564 5432

By bus
Transit Cape Breton (539 8124; www.cbrm.ns.ca/portal/community/transit/default.asp) offers limited bus services (Monday–Saturday only) between Sydney and nearby communities including North Sydney, Sydney Mines and Glace Bay.

There is also an accessible Handi-Trans service (539 4336) which provides transportation for those unable to use the normal buses, but note that pre-registration is required to use the service.

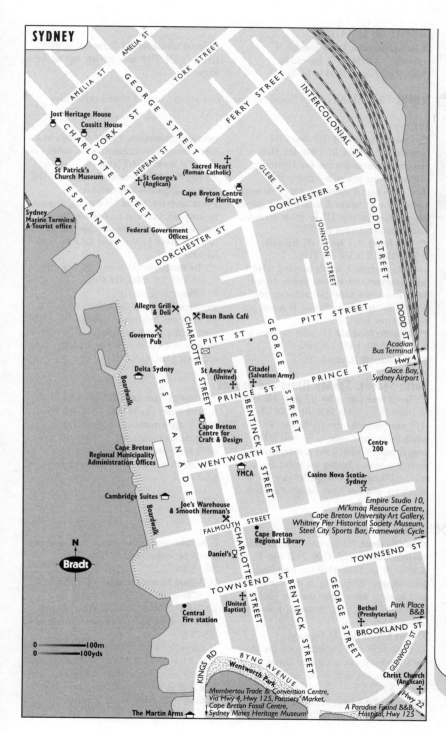

TOURIST INFORMATION

ⓘ Tourist information Marine Terminal, 74 Esplanade; ☏ 539 9876; ⏲ Jun–mid-Oct 09.00–17.00 daily, to 19.00 in Jul–Aug.

ⓘ Tourist information 299 Commercial St, North Sydney; ☏ 794 7719; early Jun–late Aug; call for hours.

🏠 **WHERE TO STAY** All places listed are open year-round unless stated otherwise.

Sydney

🏠 **Cambridge Suites Hotel** (147 suites) 380 Esplanade; ☏ 562 6500, T/F 1 800 565 9466; www.cambridgesuitessydney.com. Fine Esplanade location, with free parking & a rooftop fitness centre. These clean & comfortable modern suites are a good choice for families & those who like spacious accommodation. See page 329 for on-site restaurant, Goody's. Continental b/fast inc. $$$

🏠 **Delta Sydney** (152 rooms) 300 Esplanade; ☏ 562 7500, T/F 1 800 268 1133; www.deltasydney.com. A recently renovated c1988 8-storey waterfront hotel with free parking. Exercise room, sauna, heated indoor pool with waterslide. See below for on-site Highland Mermaid Restaurant and Moose & Crown pub. $$$

🏠 **A Paradise Found B&B** (3 rooms) 62 Milton St; ☏ 539 9377; T/F 1 877 539 9377; e paradisefound@ns.sympatico.ca; www.paradisefoundbb.com. A lovely old house on a quiet tree-lined residential street within walking distance of downtown. Full b/fast inc. $$

🏠 **Park Place B&B** (3 rooms) 169 Park St; ☏ 562 3518; e parkplacebandb@eastlink.ca; www.bbcanada.com/81.html; ⏲ May–Oct; off-season by reservation. Convenient for downtown, this Victorian house built for the steel company has some nice period features. Shared bathroom. Good full b/fast inc. $

🏠 **The Martin Arms** (62 rooms) 100 Kings Rd; ☏ 567 3311, T/F 1 866 999 6700; e 100kingsroad@gmail.com; www.themartinarms.com. Don't expect too much & you might even be pleasantly surprised. The c1960s' motel building doesn't look great, & it's virtually on the main road, but prices are low for Sydney. Light continental b/fast inc. $

North Sydney, Sydney Mines and beyond

🏠 **Gowrie House Country Inn** (10 units) 840 Shore Rd, Sydney Mines; ☏ 544 1050, T/F 1 800 372 1115; www.gowriehouse.com; ⏲ May–Oct. 6 individually decorated rooms in the main c1820 Georgian house, 4 others (more contemporary in décor) in a separate building just behind. Also a deluxe c1870 caretaker's cottage. See page 329 for Country Inn restaurant listing. Full b/fast inc. $$

🏠 **Chambers' Guest House B&B** (4 rooms) 64 King St, North Sydney; ☏ 794 7301, T/F 1 866 496 9453; e cheryl.chambers@ns.sympatico.ca; www.bbcapebretonisland.com; ⏲ May–Oct. A lovely c1880 former sea captain's house with shared or en-suite bathrooms & a veranda & pleasant garden. Full b/fast inc. $

WHERE TO EAT

✕ **Sydney**

✕ **Joe's Warehouse** 424 Charlotte St; ☏ 539 6686; www.joeswarehouse.ca; ⏲ 11.00–22.00 Mon–Fri, 10.00–22.00 Sat, 16.00–22.00 Sun. International Italian-influenced family dining. To my mind, prices are a couple of dollars higher than they should be. Expect lobster, steak, pasta, ribs, nachos & the like. Licensed. $$$

✕ **Crown & Moose Pub** 300 Esplanade; ⏲ 11.00–02.00 daily. The Delta Sydney (see above) hotel's British-style pub is a popular spot for locals & hotel guests. Live music Fri–Sat evenings, patio in summer. $$–$$$

✕ **Governor's Pub & Eatery** 233 Esplanade; ☏ 562 7646; ⏲ 11.00–22.30. An upmarket restaurant, café

& the rather good Bunkers Peanut Bar. Harbour views & – if the weather permits – patio dining. $$–$$$

✕ **Highland Mermaid Restaurant** 300 Esplanade; ⏲ 07.00–11.00 Mon–Sat, 07.00–14.00 Sun; Jun–Sep 17.00–21.00 daily. The Delta Sydney (see above) on-site restaurant has fabulous harbour views. $$–$$$

✕ **Allegro Grill & Deli** 222 Charlotte St; ☏ 562 1623; ⏲ 11.00–15.00 Mon, 11.00–22.00 Tue–Sat. The imaginative menu & healthy freshly made food helps liven up the downtown dining scene. $$

✕ **Goody's** 380 Esplanade; ⏲ year-round 07.00–22.00 Mon–Sat, 17.00–22.00 Sun. The casual on-site restaurant of the Cambridge Suites Hotel (see page 328) is reasonably priced, with a varied menu. $$

✕ **All Star Grille** Casino Nova Scotia (see page 331) ⊕ 11.00–midnight Mon–Thu, 07.00–02.00 Fri–Sat, 07.00–midnight Sun. Not *haute cuisine* but good meal deals – especially if the CAN$10 pp discount offer for visitors staying in approved accommodation

in town (ask at the promotions desk) is still running. $

✕ **Bean Bank Café** 243 Charlotte St; ☏ 562 5400; www.beanbank.ca; ⊕ 07.30–17.00 Mon–Fri, 08.30–17.00 Sat, 11.00–16.00 Sun. Conveniently located & offering excellent coffee & good snacks, sandwiches & baked goods. $

North Sydney, Sydney Mines and beyond

✕ **Gowrie House Country Inn** (10 units) 840 Shore Rd; ⊕ May–Oct daily. The dining room of the Country Inn hotel (see page 328) serves 4-course dinner at 19.30 (reservations required). Although

limited (soup, appetiser, choice of 2 mains, choice of 3 desserts) the menu changes daily & the standard is very high. CAN$62

NIGHTLIFE In addition to the Crown & Moose Pub (see page 328) at the Delta Sydney and Bunkers Peanut Bar at Governor's (see page 328), try:

♀ **Daniel's** 456 Charlotte St; ☏ 562 8586; ⊕ 10.00–2.00 Mon–Sat, 12.00–02.00 Sun.
♀ **Smooth Herman's** 424 Charlotte St; ☏ 539 0408; ⊕ 12.00–03.30 Wed–Thu, 17.00–03.30 Fri, 11.00–03.30 Sat. Part of the Joe's Warehouse

complex (see page 328), offers cocktails, live music and DJs & tends to attract a younger crowd.
♀ **Steel City Sports Bar** 252 Townsend St; ☏ 562 4501. Jumps on Wed & Thu nights.

ENTERTAINMENT

Centre 200 481 George St; ☏ 564 6668; www.centre200.ca; ⊕ year-round. Home to the Cape Breton Screaming Eagles ice-hockey team from mid-Sep to mid-March, this large modern facility hosts big-name concerts.

🕱 **Membertou Trade and Convention Centre** 50 Maillard St; ☏ 539 2300; www.membertoucc.com. Concerts, performances, comedy shows and more.
🎬 **Empire Studio 10** Prince St Plaza, 325 Prince St; ☏ 539 9050; www.empiretheatres.com. The cinema offers 10 film choices.

FESTIVALS
May
PierScape Week-long eclectic arts and food festival.

August
Action Week (*www.actionweek.com*) Includes concerts, a Busker festival, a Caribbean festival and more.

Cape Breton County Exhibition (*www.eans.ca/Cape Breton County Exhibition.htm*) The terminus for ferries to and from Newfoundland (see page 39) is around the harbour in North Sydney, where horse shows and events – the biggest of which is this festival – are held in the summer at the Exhibition Grounds on Regent Street.

SHOPPING Shoppers looking for something more than Charlotte Street offers should head for the **Sydney Shopping Mall** (*272 Prince St*), or (further out) the larger **Mayflower Mall** (*800 Grand Lake Rd*).

OTHER PRACTICALITIES
🚲 **Framework Cycle and Fitness** 273 Townsend St; ☏ 567 1909, T/F 1 866 567 1909;

www.frameworkfitness.com; ⊕ 10.00–17.00 Mon–Fri, 09.00–13.00 Sat. Bike hire; daily or weekly rentals.

✚ **Cape Breton Regional Hospital** 1482 George St; ✆ 567 8000

📚 **James McConnell Memorial Library** 50 Falmouth St; ✆ 562 3161; ⏱ 10.00–21.00 Tue–Fri, 10.00–17.30 Sat

✉ **Post office** 269 Charlotte St; ⏱ 08.00–17.00 Mon–Fri

WHAT TO SEE AND DO

St Patrick's Church Museum (*87 Esplanade;* ✆ *562 8237;* ⏱ *Jun–Aug 09.00–17.00 Mon–Sat, 13.00–17.00 Sun; admission CAN$2*) This small c1828 Pioneer Gothic-style building is Cape Breton Island's oldest standing Roman Catholic church. Some stone used in the building's construction came from the ruins of Louisbourg (see page 333). Displays focus on the city's history.

St George's Anglican Church (*119 Charlotte St*) Much added to since its construction (1785–91) as a garrison chapel, this was the first Anglican church on Cape Breton Island. The adjoining graveyard has several interesting sandstone and limestone grave markers.

Mi'kmaq Resource Centre (*Beaton Institute, Cape Breton University, 1250 Grand Lake Rd;* ✆ *563 1660; www.mrc.uccb.ns.ca;* ⏱ *year-round 09.00–16.30 Tue–Wed, 09.00–12.00 Thu; admission free*) A repository of documents relating to the Mi'kmaq.

The Cape Breton Centre for Heritage and Science (*225 George St;* ✆ *539 1572; www.oldsydney.com/museums/centre.html;* ⏱ *Jun–Aug 09.00–17.00 Mon–Fri; Sep–May 10.00–16.00 Tue–Fri; admission free*) On the ground floor of a c1904 Colonial Revival-style former theatre, displays focus on the social and natural history of eastern Cape Breton.

The Cape Breton Centre for Craft and Design (*322 Charlotte St;* ✆ *270 7491; www.capebretoncraft.com;* ⏱ *10.00–16.00 Mon–Fri, 12.00–16.00 Sat; admission free*) An overview of the work of some of Cape Breton Island's best artisans.

Cossit House (*75 Charlotte St;* ✆ *539 7973; www.museum.gov.ns.ca/ch/;* ⏱ *Jun–mid-Oct 09.30–17.30 Mon–Sat, 13.00–17.30 Sun; admission CAN$2*) Proudly billing itself as Sydney's oldest house, this c1787 manse was home to the town's first Anglican minister, a Rev Ranna Cossit. The house has been restored almost to its original condition, and several rooms have been furnished based on an 1815 inventory of Cossit's estate. Costumed guides give tours.

WHERE'S THE OPERA HOUSE

In 2002, a British couple, both 19, booked their flights on the internet and flew here via Halifax. Before too long, they realised that although there was a big harbour and the name was the same, this wasn't the Sydney they were expecting. They didn't get to climb the Harbour Bridge, sunbathe on Bondi Beach or have a drink in a Paddington bar, but a kind and sympathetic Air Canada employee took them under her wing. She drove them to see many of Cape Breton Island's delights, and invited them home for dinner. The couple were particularly impressed with the friendliness of the local people. Sydney (Nova Scotia) airport staff said that although on occasion the odd bag turned up here instead of Australia, this was the first time it had happened to humans.

Jost Heritage House (*54 Charlotte St;* ✆ *539 0366;* ⏰ *Jun–Aug 09.00–17.00 daily; Sep–Oct 10.00–16.00 daily; admission CAN$3.75*) Parts of this building also date from 1787, but unlike the nearby Cossit House, there have since been additions in several different architectural styles. Each part of the house has been furnished in keeping with the era in which it was built.

Cape Breton University Art Gallery (*1250 Grand Lake Rd;* ✆ *563 1342; www.capebretonu.ca;* ⏰ *year-round; admission free*) Cape Breton Island's first (and only) full-time public art gallery has a diverse permanent collection of historical and contemporary Canadian and international artwork.

Casino Nova Scotia–Sydney (*525 George St;* ✆ *563 7777; www.casinonovascotia.com/ sydney/home.aspx;* ⏰ *year-round 11.00–03.00 daily*) Slot machines plus (*Wed–Sun 17.00–02.00*) table games. For 19s or over only.

Whitney Pier Historical Society Museum (*88 Mt Pleasant St;* ✆ *564 9819; www.whitneypiermuseum.org;* ⏰ *Jun–Oct 09.00–12.00 & 13.00–17.00 Mon–Fri; off-season by appointment; admission free*) Staffed by enthusiastic volunteers and housed in a former synagogue, this unusual hands-on museum tells of the multi-cultural (in close proximity are the Holy Ghost Ukrainian Church, Polish St Mary's Parish Church and St Phillips, the only African Orthodox Church in Canada) community which developed around the steel plant and coal piers.

Cape Breton Fossil Centre and Sydney Mines Heritage Museum (*159 Legatto St, Sydney Mines;* ✆ *544 992; www.cbfossil.org;* ⏰ *mid-May–mid-Oct 09.00–17.00 Tue–Sat; off-season by appointment; admission CAN$5*) Get two museums for the price of one. Numerous 300million-year-old fossils have been found over the years in the area's coalfields: fossil hikes are also offered three+ times weekly for an extra CAN$10. In the adjacent former railway station is a museum telling the story of the community of Sydney Mines – with emphasis of course on coal mining and steel manufacture.

Sydney Marine Terminal In season, large cruise ships are regular visitors to the Sydney Marine Terminal (also home to a tourist office and what is said to be the world's biggest violin – the fiddle is of course a vital part of Celtic music). Many passengers jump into waiting taxis and zoom off in the direction of Louisbourg or Baddeck.

Cape Breton Farmers' Market (*340 Keltic Drive, Sydney River; www.sfm.cb-ns.org;* ⏰ *year-round 08.30–13.00 Sat*) Though well out of town, this market is worth a visit between late spring and the end of autumn.

AROUND SYDNEY

GLACE BAY Glace Bay is the former heart of Cape Breton Island's once-flourishing coal industry. Mining apart, the town has another claim to fame as the place from which in 1902, the first west-to-east transatlantic wireless message was sent by **Guglielmo Marconi**.

Despite the death of the mining, Glace Bay is very much alive. For the visitor, in addition to the excellent mining museum (more interesting than it sounds!), there's a very good heritage museum, the beautifully renovated c1920s' **Savoy Theatre** (*116 Commercial St;* ✆ *842 1577; www.savoytheatre.com*) – a wonderful live music venue – and the Marconi site.

Getting there

By car Glace Bay is on Highways 4 and 28, 21km/13 miles northeast of Sydney.
By bus An hourly bus #1 *(Mon–Sat; CAN$2.25)* connects Glace Bay with downtown Sydney.

✗ Where to eat

✗ **Miners' Village Restaurant** (see below for contacts) ◷ mid-Apr–late Oct 12.00–20.00 daily. Located at the Miners' Museum (see below), this licensed restaurant offers a varied menu & reasonable prices. Try, the seafood casserole or prime rib. **$$**

What to see and do

Cape Breton Miners' Museum *(42 Birkley St;* ℡ *849 4522; www.minersmuseum.com;* ◷ *Jun–late Oct 10.00–18.00 daily; Nov–May 09.00–16.00 Mon–Fri; admission CAN$5)* Displays on the history of coal mining both in Cape Breton and internationally, and a recreation of a mining village between 1850 and 1900, with a miner's home and company store. Well worthwhile (an extra CAN$5) is the guided tour of the Ocean Deeps Colliery, over which the museum has been built. Don hard hats and overalls and be guided deep underground, to where the coal was extracted manually, by retired miners. A summer bonus is weekly concerts by the Men of the Deeps, a choir of working and retired Cape Breton Island miners *(late Jun–late Aug 20.00 Tue – book in advance)*.

Glace Bay Heritage Museum *(14 McKeen St;* ℡ *842 5345;* ◷ *Feb–Jun & Sep–Dec 14.00–16.00 Tue, Thu & Sat; Jul–Aug 10.00–17.00 Tue–Sat, 13.00–18.00 Sun; admission free)* This interesting museum occupies two storeys of the restored c1903 former town hall. A large mural depicts both mining and another pursuit popular in Glace Bay in days gone by, sword fishing. See also the old court room and council chambers. There's also a gift shop with a good selection of books on Cape Breton Island, and a secondhand bookstore.

Marconi National Historic Site *(Timmerman St, Table Head;* ℡ *295 2069; www.pc.gc.ca/lhn-nhs/marconi;* ◷ *Jun–mid-Sep 10.00–18.00 daily; admission free)* On this site in 1902, with use of a 400-wire antenna suspended from four 61m wooden towers, Guglielmo Marconi sent the first west-to-east transatlantic wireless message. In addition to displays on Marconi's life on Cape Breton Island and his experiments and achievements, there's a model of the original radio station: the foundations of the huge transmitting towers are visible outside.

THE SOUTH

By far the biggest attraction in the southeast of Cape Breton Island is the reconstruction of the fortress at Louisbourg. Much of the island's south coast is rugged, remote and sparsely populated, even by Nova Scotia standards. You won't see many people, or many (if any) shops, eateries and places to stay. Somewhat harsh – even bleak – for much of the year, it is best enjoyed in good weather by those who enjoy pottering along on quiet roads, taking side-trips to pretty fishing villages, and soaking up an atmosphere of days gone by.

Highlights of this comparatively little-travelled trail include an opportunity to explore the beautiful coastal waters by sea kayak at Gabarus, gorgeous beaches at Belfry and Point Michaud, and the delightful Isle Madame.

PORT MORIEN This pleasant, quiet little seaside lobster-fishing village has a wide sandy barrier beach and a migratory bird sanctuary. It's not a bad choice for those who want a quiet base from which to explore the larger old industrial urban centres, and Louisbourg (see below), a 45-minute drive away.

Getting there Port Morien is on Highway 255, 10km/6 miles from Glace Bay, 30km/19 miles from Sydney and 50km/31 miles from Louisbourg.

🏠 **Where to stay and eat**

🏠 **Port Morien Rectory B&B** (2 rooms) 2652 Hwy 255; ☏ 737 1453, T/F 1 888 737 1453; e pmrectorybb@seaside.ns.ca; www.bbcanada.com/pmrectorybb; ⊕ year-round. Housed in a c1885 former Anglican Church rectory, both guestrooms offer ocean views. Full b/fast inc. $$

✗ **Dock Y'ur Dory Tea Room** 2845 Hwy 255; ☏ 737 1832; ⊕ Jun–Sep 11.00–19.00 daily. A licensed ocean-side restaurant/tea room with a large deck. The fresh ocean-caught 'catch of the day' is always good. $–$$

MAIN-A-DIEU (*Population: 235*) The name Main-à-Dieu is a French corruption of the region's Mi'kmaq name, *Menadou*. This is the largest fishing village on the coast between Port Morien and Louisbourg.

Getting there To reach Main-a-Dieu from Port Morien, continue south on Highway 255 then turn left onto Main-a-Dieu Road, a total distance of approximately 28km/17 miles. The village is 17km/10.5 miles from Louisbourg, via Main-a-Dieu Road.

What to see and do Look out for tiny **St James Cemetery**, dating from 1768. Stop off first at the **Coastal Discovery Centre** (*2886 Louisbourg – Main-à-Dieu Rd;* ☏ *733 2258; www.coastaldiscoverycentre.ca;* ⊕ *Jul–Aug 10.00–18.00 daily; Sep–Jun 09.00–17.00 daily*), which houses the Fishermen's Museum, a seasonal café and a public library (☏ *733 5708*). Then wander the sandy beach or the boardwalk just behind. A short but worthwhile shoreline hike is the **Moque Head Trail**.

LOUISBOURG Although best known for its wonderfully impressive reconstructed historic site (see page 337), the small fishing town of Louisbourg (population: 1,250) has a few other attractions too.

These include a lighthouse with a spectacular setting, shipwrecks in the harbour for divers to explore, a railway museum, an Elizabethan-style theatre and some good beaches a short ten-minute drive away along the unpaved Kennington Cove Road.

History Around 1719, the French began a huge project to construct what was not to be just a military fort, but a fortified town that would be a prestigious centre for commerce, culture and government, the capital of Ile Royale (as Cape Breton Island was then known). Home to 2,000–5,000 French soldiers, fishermen, merchants and their families and children, it was just about ready when New Englanders attacked by land in 1745, supported by a large British naval force. The fortress fell in seven weeks.

The victors' success was tempered by the reality of the severe winters here: food (particularly fresh food) was scarce, shelter limited – owing to damage caused by

DIB DIB DIB

The first Boy Scout troop in North America was established in Port Morien in 1908.

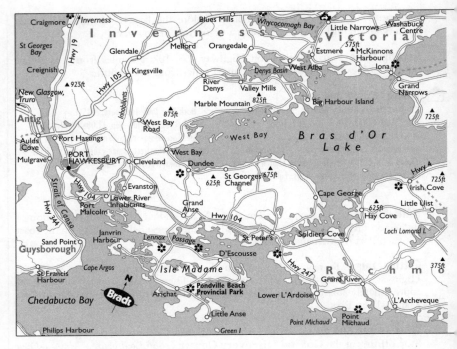

the assault – and sanitary conditions awful. Ten times more New Englanders died of the cold, disease or starvation than had been killed in the fighting.

In 1748, the Treaty of Aix-la-Chapelle returned the fortress to France, and back under French control, it thrived again. Fortifications were repaired, strengthened and added to. But the second assault came in 1758, when a huge British force led by General Wolfe once again took the 'impregnable' fortress after a six-week siege.

In 1760, the British totally demolished the fortifications and outer works: in later years some of the stones were recycled and used in the construction of new buildings such as Halifax's Government House (1800), and Sydney's St George (1785) and St Patrick's (1828) churches.

As mines boomed in the Sydney area, the need for transport to connect that area with an ice-free port, so that coal could be shipped year-round, grew. As a result, the Sydney and Louisburg Railway was constructed in 1895.

Two centuries after the British had laid Louisbourg to waste, the Canadian government approved a plan to rebuild the fortifications and parts of the historic fortress to how they would have looked in the 1740s. Where possible, traditional

LIGHTHOUSE HISTORY

The second-oldest lighthouse on the North American continent, and the first in what is now Canada, was built by the French at Louisbourg in the 1730s, and destroyed (though later rebuilt) when the British besieged the fortress in 1758. The current version, on a volcanic rock outcrop, was first lit in 1924: enjoy the views! Trails currently under development lead from the lighthouse along the coast in both directions. To get there, follow Havenside Road from Main Street.

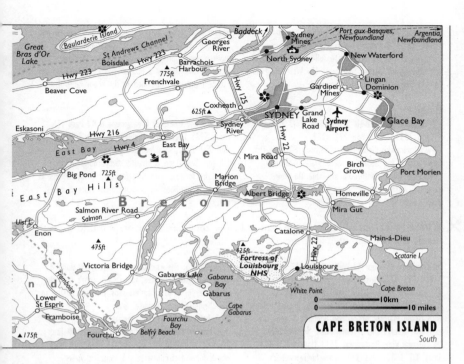

CAPE BRETON ISLAND
South

French construction methods – and many of the original stones – were used in the painstaking reconstruction.

Getting there Louisbourg is on the coast in the southeast corner of Cape Breton Island, 32km/20 miles from Sydney via Highway 22. It is 111km/69 miles from Baddeck and 207km/129 miles from the Canso Causeway. No scheduled public transport comes this way.

Tourist information *(7495 Main St; ⍭ 733 2321; ⊕ early Jun–early Oct 09.00–17.00 daily, to 19.00 in Jul–Aug)*

Where to stay
Luxury
⌂ Louisbourg Resort Golf & Spa
www.louisbourgresort.com. The grand opening of this resort with 420-plus luxurious 1- to 4-bedroom homes, 3–4 restaurants, a clubhouse, beachhouse, private airstrip, European-style spa, conference centre & Nick Faldo-designed 18-hole golf course is scheduled for 2010–11. $$$$ (estimate)

Mid-range
⌂ Cranberry Cove Inn (7 rooms) 12 Wolfe St; ⍭ 733 2171, T/F 1 800 929 0222; www.cranberrycoveinn.com; ⊕ May–Oct. A fine inn with individually themed guestrooms. For restaurant, see page 336. Full b/fast inc. $$
⌂ Louisbourg Heritage House B&B (6 rooms) 7544 Main St; ⍭ 733 3222, T/F 1 888 888 8466; www.louisbourgheritagehouse.com; ⊕ Jun–early Oct.

Each of the rooms in this centrally located c1886 former rectory have lovely wood floors & private balcony. Full b/fast inc. $$
⌂ Point of View Suites (& Campground) (16 units) 15 Commercial St Ext; ⍭ 733 2080, T/F 1 888 374 8439; www.louisbourgpointofview.com; ⊕ mid-May–mid-Oct. Bright, modern, well-designed deluxe suites & apartments – many with kitchen facilities –

335

in a great location on a 1.6ha peninsula with private beach & fortress views. Motorhome campground (no tents) with 36 full-service sites. $$
🏠 **Wolvespack Cottage** (2 rooms) 157 West Shore Rd; 🕿 733 2062; e wolvespackcottage@

ns.sympatico.ca; ⊕ Jun–Oct. Choose from a room with private or en-suite bathroom at this quiet, relaxing modern oceanfront home approximately 5km from the historical site. Borrow a bike or kayak to work off the excellent breakfast (included in the room rate). $$

Budget
🏠 **Spinning Wheel B&B** 5 Riverdale St (3 rooms) 🕿 733 3332, T/F 1 866 272 3222; www.spinningwheelbedandbreakfast.com; ⊕ May–Oct. Don't expect big bedrooms or a grand mansion. Private or shared bathroom available. Do, however, expect a warm welcome, huge breakfast (included) & good value. $

🅰 **Lakeview Treasures Campground & RV Park** (75 sites) 5785 Louisbourg Highway; 🕿 733 2058, T/F 1 866 233 2267; www.louisbourgcampground.com; ⊕ Jun–Sep. Open & shaded campground 10km from the fortress with lake frontage & motorhome & serviced sites. Pool (in season), small store & take-out. $

✗ Where to eat
In addition to the listings below, there are also restaurants and a café inside the historic site (see page 337).

✗ **Cranberry Cove Inn** 12 Wolfe St; 🕿 733 2171, T/F 1 800 929 0222; www.cranberrycoveinn.com; ⊕ Jun–Sep 17.00–21.00 daily. This inn has a relatively short menu, but the food (eg: seared halibut with Grand Marnier, or seafood linguini) & wine are excellent. Reservations recommended. $$–$$$
✗ **Fortress View Restaurant** 7513 Main St; 🕿 733 3131, T/F 1 877 733 3131; www.fortressview.ca; ⊕ mid-May–mid-Oct 07.00–20.00. Seafood & more, plus an on-site bakery. Dependable without being overexciting. Fish can be grilled or poached on request. $$
✗ **Grubstake Restaurant** 7499 Main St; 🕿 733 2308; www.grubstake.ca; ⊕ late Jun–mid-Oct

12.00–20.15. The varied menu includes seafood & other interesting choices, too: steaks aren't bad, the barbecue pork has countless fans, but I'm partial to the shrimp/scallop flambée. $$
✗ **Lobster Kettle** 41 Commercial St; 🕿 733 2723; www.lobsterkettle.com; ⊕ daily 16.00–20.00 Jun; Jul–Aug 11.30–21.00; Sep–Oct 11.30–20.00. With a wonderful waterfront setting & fantastic views, generally, this licensed restaurant dishes up food to match. Seafood is very good (eg: the chowder, or lobster dinner) but there are also options for carnivores. Accompanying vegetables can be the only weak point. $$

Entertainment
🎭 **Louisbourg Playhouse** 11 Aberdeen St; 🕿 733 2996, T/F 1 888 733 2787; www.louisbourgplayhouse.com; ⊕ late Jun–mid-Oct. Based on London, England's

(Elizabethan) Globe Theatre, Louisbourg's version opened in 1994. The programme focuses on live theatre and Cape Breton music.

Festivals
August
Feast of St Louis Recreation of an 18th-century celebration honouring French monarch Louis IX. Cannon salutes, musket firings, dancing, children's games and music.

Other practicalities
$ **Royal Bank** 7509 Main St; 🕿 733 2012; ⊕ 10.00–15.00 Mon–Wed, 10.00–17.00 Thu–Fri
📚 **WW Lewis Memorial Library** 10 Upper Warren St; 🕿 733 3608; ⊕ 14.00–17.00 & 18.00–20.00

Tue & Thu, 14.00–17.00 Wed & Sat, Mon–Fri, 11.00–14.00 Sat
✉ **Post office** 7529 Main St; ⊕ 08.30–17.30 Mon–Fri, 09.30–13.30 Sat

What to see and do
Louisbourg Scuba Services (🕿 733 2480; www.louisbourgscuba.com; ⊕ year-round) Offers a range of services, including courses and charters to dive wrecks such as the *Celebre*, which sank in 1758.

Paradise Kayaks (*200 Byrnes Lane, Catalone;* ✆ *733 3244; www.paradisekayaks.com*) Based 8km north of Louisbourg, Paradise offers kayaking lessons, guided kayak tours, and guided hunting trips. One-hour group kayak lessons cost CAN$25 per person (min 4 people); individual lessons start at CAN$50.

Tartan Tours (✆ *578 4501; www.tartantours.guided-tours.ca*) Half- and full-day tours (leaving from Sydney) to destinations such as Baddeck and the Cabot Trail. Prices vary depending on numbers.

Sydney and Louisburg Railway Museum (*Main St;* ✆ *733 2321; www.fortress.uccb.ns.ca/historic/s_l.html;* ⊕ *Jun 09.00–17.00 Mon–Fri; Jul–Sep 10.00–19.00 daily; admission free*) Appropriately housed in the former c1895 Sydney and Louisburg railway station, exhibits for train fans include two passenger carriages from 1881 and 1914, and a working model of the line in an original freight shed.

Fortress of Louisbourg National Historic Site of Canada (✆ *733 2280; www.pc.gc.ca/louisbourg;* ⊕ *Jun–mid-Oct 09.30–17.00; Jul–Aug 09.00–17.30; mid/end May & mid/end Oct access by pre-arranged guided tour (daily 10.00 & 14.00); Nov–mid-May visitor centre closed, buildings closed but grounds open; admission May & Oct CAN$7.30, Jun–Sep CAN$17.60*) To say that this is the largest reconstructed 18th-century French fortified town in North America doesn't really begin to give an idea of the scale of the 6,700ha site.

Park (for free) at the visitor centre, buy your ticket and take the seven-minute bus ride to the fortress area. The reconstructed area alone sprawls across some 10ha, with over 50 buildings to visit and numerous activities to entertain you.

Theme centres and exhibits abound, each of which offers insight into a different part of the history and everyday life of the fortress in the 1740s. Whereas in many other living museums you'll see a few interpreters demonstrating a few traditional techniques, Louisbourg seems alive with men, women and children in costume, only too prepared to interact – in character – with visitors.

See building techniques demonstrated, nail making, open-hearth cooking and lace making. Observe military exercises and musket firing. Haggle with street vendors, or watch a video on a soldier's life. Herbs and vegetables are tended in tidy back gardens.

Strikingly obvious is the class difference at the time, with both fine houses on cobbled streets for the gentry, and simple spartan dwellings for the have-not's.

Join a guided walking tour (check in advance for tour times), or use the site map to explore on your own. Be prepared for windy and/or wet weather, and a lot of walking. Allow far more time than you usually would for a 'standard' historical site or living museum. Get in the mood, and go back over two-and-a-half centuries!

✕ **Where to eat** If you work up an appetite whilst exploring, your options include a café and a couple of restaurants, themed either for humble soldiers, or officers and gentlemen.

✕ **Hotel de la Marine** ⊕ Jun–mid-Oct 10.00–17.00 daily. Here you are given a spoon with which to eat 18th-century-style rustic French cuisine served in a wooden bowl & prepared to authentic recipes. The menu isn't overlong but includes at least 1 fish, meat & vegan option each day. With period décor & waiting staff in costume, it is a fun experience. Licensed. **$$**

✕ **L'Epee Royale** ⊕ Jul–Aug 11.00–17.00 daily. The 3-course set menu is the upper-class choice. Your finer dining is served on china crockery – & you also get a knife & fork. Licensed. **$$**

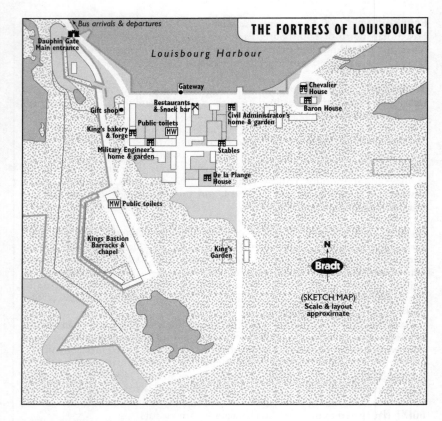

THE FORTRESS OF LOUISBOURG

Bus arrivals & departures

Dauphin Gate
Main entrance

Louisbourg Harbour

Gateway

Chevalier House

Baron House

Gift shop

Restaurants & Snack bar

Civil Administrator's home & garden

Public toilets

King's bakery & forge

MW

Military Engineer's home & garden

Stables

De la Plange House

MW Public toilets

Kings Bastion Barracks & chapel

King's Garden

N

Bradt

(SKETCH MAP)
Scale & layout approximate

✗ Café Destouches ⊕ Jun–Aug 09.00–17.00 daily.
Offers period desserts, baked goods, sandwiches &
wraps. $

MARION BRIDGE This small community is named for the bridge which crosses the
Mira River. Services are limited with the focus a gift shop/tea room.

Getting there Marion Bridge is on Highway 327, 15km/9 miles from Sydney,
31km/19 miles from Louisbourg and 25km/16 miles from Gabarus.

✗ Where to eat
✗ Tigger's Treasures and Tea Room 3850 Gabarus
Hwy, ☏ 727 2653; ⊕ May–Dec 11.00–17.00
Tue–Sat, 11.00–18.00 Sun. During the week, pop in
for snacks (eg: toasted sandwiches); on Sun there's
a set meal (eg: roast turkey plus trimmings,
beverage & dessert) for CAN$17.95.

What to see and do
Two Rivers Wildlife Park (*Grand Mira North Rd;* ☏ 727 2483; f 727 3153;
www.tworiverspark.ca; ⊕ *late Oct–Apr 10.00-16.00 daily; May–mid-Jun & Sep–mid-Oct
10.00–17.00 daily; mid-Jun–Aug 10.00–19.00 daily; admission CAN$6*) This peaceful
200ha wildlife park at the confluence of the Salmon and Mira rivers 8km west of
Marion Bridge displays wildlife native to the Maritimes (with a couple of exotic
extras such as emus).

GABARUS This is a truly picturesque fishing village. Before you reach the breakwater, turn left onto Harbour Point Road past the **Harbour Cemetery** which has lost several graves to the sea, to reach the c1950s' lighthouse. A pity that there is nowhere to stay or eat.

Getting there Gabarus is on Highway 327, 45km/28 miles from Sydney, 56km/35 miles from Louisbourg and 88km/55 miles from St Peter's.

What to see and do If you feel like a coastal hike, at the breakwater turn right onto Gull Cove Road, and follow it to its end. The walking trail (6km each way) leads to what was the fishing community of **Gull Cove**. After about 1km you'll reach **Harris Beach**, and have a wonderful view over Gabarus Bay.

Kayaking
Rising Tide Expeditions Hwy 327; \ 884 2884, T/F 1 877 884 2884; e info@risingtideexpeditions.ca; www.risingtideexpeditions.ca. Guided sea-kayak trips (Jun–Sep) from half-day paddles around the beautiful Gabarus Bay to five-day trips in three different regions of Cape Breton Island, some camping, some inn-based. Rising Tide does not rent out sea kayaks.

BELFRY BEACH Don't be surprised to have this magnificent long stretch of sand – backed by Belfry Lake – to yourself. This is a remote and very sparsely populated corner of Cape Breton Island, and the beach itself is easily missed by the casual tourist. Long may it stay that way! Enjoy the solitude and natural splendour, and wander for miles. You might see harbour or grey seals in June and July, you'll definitely see a range of seabirds, and – in spring and summer in particular – migratory shorebirds.

Getting there Belfry Beach is at the end of Belfry Road, off Fourchu Road approximately 8.5km/5 miles south of the tiny community of Gabarus Lake.

POINT MICHAUD A fine beach – which attracts surfers and birdwatchers – justifies Point Michaud's inclusion in this book – there's not a lot else going on.

Getting there Point Michaud is 21km/13 miles from St Peter's and 67km/42 miles from Gabarus.

What to see and do **Point Michaud Beach Provincial Park** encompasses a glorious 3km curve of sand backed by marram grass-covered dunes. The beach is popular (perhaps that is the wrong word to use – it rarely gets at all busy) with surfers and windsurfers.

ISLE MADAME

Despite the name, this is actually a cluster (measuring approximately 16km by 11km) of islands separated from Cape Breton Island by the narrow Lennox Passage.

Arichat is the most significant of the main communities, and several tiny hamlets such as picturesque Little Anse and Samsons Cove fringe secluded inlets and coves. Acadian heritage is still strong here, and you will often hear French being spoken.

Once again, specific sites are few, the attraction being beautiful coastal scenery, genuinely friendly people, and a very relaxed atmosphere. With a wooded interior, relatively gentle terrain, virtually no heavy traffic, a lovely beach, a fine hiking trail and a few good places to stay and eat, this is a delightful area to motor (or better still, cycle) around, especially when the sun is out.

On the Lennox Passage waterfront, Martinique has a picnic park, the c1884 Grandique Point Lighthouse and a small beach, but the best beaches are on **Janvrin Island** and at Pondville, where the sandy 1km-long strand is backed by dunes and a lagoon.

Probably the best of Isle Madame's numerous trails is the **Cape Auguet Eco Trail** which begins near Boudreauville, offering over 10km of loop trails, both coastal and through hardwood forest.

HISTORY European contact with Isle Madame goes at least as far back as the early 16th century, when Basque and Portuguese fishermen took refuge from storms at Petit-de-Grat, the oldest fishing village in the area. The name is a combination of French and Spanish/Basque and means 'little fishing place (station)'.

Initially, Isle Madame was named Sante Marie. The name change was in honour of Madame de Maintenon, second wife of French monarch Louis XIV.

One of the oldest communities in Nova Scotia, Arichat had strong business ties with Jersey in the Channel Islands during the mid 1700s, not least because that was where most of its early inhabitants, many of whom were French Huguenots, had come from. The red-petalled Jersey lilies visible in many of the island's gardens were brought over three centuries ago. In the late 18th century in particular, the harbour teemed with commerce and shipbuilding. When tall ships ruled the seas, it was a booming Atlantic seaport with 17 consular representatives.

Previously connected to Cape Breton Island only by water transport, a bridge across Lennox Passage was completed in 1919.

The economy was built around fishing, and fishing and fish processing are still hugely important. Shellfish, and to a lesser degree, mackerel, predominate now.

GETTING THERE The bridge across to Isle Madame is 5km/3 miles from Exit 46 of Highway 104, 35k/22 miles from Port Hastings, 24km/15 miles from St Peter's, and 109km/68 miles from Sydney.

FESTIVALS
August
Acadian Festival Petit-de-Grat. Five-day event celebrating Acadian culture and heritage.

 WHERE TO STAY AND EAT

⌂ **L'Auberge Acadienne Inn** (17 rooms) 2375 Hwy 206; Arichat; ✆ 226 2200, T/F 1 877 787 2200; e inn@acadienne.com; www.acadienne.com; ⊕ year-round. Friendly, comfortable, modern – but traditional Acadian-style – country inn. There are 9 rooms in the main building & 8 roomy drive-up motel-style units. Laundry facilities. The licensed dining room (⊕ daily year-round 07.30–10.00 & 17.00–20.00, to 21.00 mid-Jun–mid-Oct; **$–$$**) specialises in Acadian dishes & seafood and is excellent. **$$**

⌂ **Robin's Harbour View Cottages** (3 cottages) Robin's Rd, Arichat; ✆ 226 9515; e robinscottages@ns.sympatico.ca; ⊕ mid-May–mid-Oct. Overlooking the harbour, these well-equipped 2-bedroom cottages are good for those wanting extra space. **$$**

⌂ **Vollmer's Island Paradise** (6 units) 1489 Main St, Janvrin's Harbour; ✆ 226 1507; e info@vipilodge.com; www.vipilodge.com; ⊕ May–Oct. Hand-built log cabins on lovely Janvrin Island really allow you to get away from it all. Canoes available, boat trips & scuba diving offered (Jul–Sep). B/fast not inc. **$$**

⌂ **Vina Motel** (4 rooms) 2354 Highway 206, Arichat; ✆ 226 2662; ⊕ year-round. Simple, basic motel rooms with small fridge & microwave. **$**

You'll see them on many menus, in tanks in restaurants and supermarkets, and the contraptions used to capture them in a multitude of fishing villages.

A lobster has a long body and five sets of legs, including two large front claws, one of which is large and flat while the other is thinner and smaller. The body, tail and claws are protected by a hard shell. Lobsters grow by moulting, or shedding their shell. After a moult (typically in summer), the lobster is soft-shelled and filled with the sea water it has absorbed in the process. Up to two months pass before the absorbed sea water is replaced by new flesh. The shell hardens again in the cold sea before the cycle repeats.

Although live lobsters range in colour from brownish-rust to greenish-brown, all lobster shells turn bright orangey-red when cooked – traditionally by being immersed in a pot of salted water that has been heated to a rolling boil. Lobsters die within moments when immersed in boiling water. They have very primitive nervous systems, and the jury is out on whether they experience anything similar to the concept of pain. Often called the 'King of Seafood', though it can be messy to extract (especially for novices), the lobster's white flesh is firm and dense with a rich flavour.

Lobster fishers use small boats to fish with baited, wooden-frame or plastic-coated steel-mesh traps which are weighted and lowered to the sea bottom. The traps are hauled by ropes attached to buoys which mark their location.

Atlantic Canada's waters are divided into specific fishing areas, each with its own season, varying in length from eight weeks to eight months. These are staggered to protect summer moults.

If you're wondering how fresh lobster manages to appear on menus year-round, the answer is lobster pounds. In the past, these were large, fenced areas of the ocean where captive lobsters lived until required, new technology has meant huge dry-land holding facilities being built. One of the biggest of these is owned by Clearwater Seafoods, and is on Isle Madame at Presqu'Ile Cove.

Here, around one million lobsters usually reside in individual containers stacked over 30 levels high. Their environment makes the crustaceans lose all inclination to moult. Lobsters caught all over the Maritime provinces are brought here, and, when required, shipped all over the world.

Although no scheduled tours are offered, in the past staff at the pound have been happy to show visitors around. If you'd like to see the facility, it might be worth phoning ahead For various reasons, you may choose not to eat it during your time in Nova Scotia, but be prepared to be offered lobster frequently (and, more often than not, for the offerer to be surprised if you decline).

SHOPPING Nearby, major seafood distributor **Premium Seafoods** (*449 Lower Rd;* ℡ *226 3474; www.premiumseafoods.ns.ca;* ⊕ *year-round 08.00–17.00 Mon–Sat*) has a retail outlet.

OTHER PRACTICALITIES
$ **East Coast Credit Union** 9 Cap La Ronde Rd, D'Escousse; ℡ 226 2722; ⊕ 09.00–16.00 Mon–Wed & Fri, 09.00–18.00 Thu

⬚ **Petit-de-Grat Branch Library** 3435 Hwy 206; ℡ 226 3534

✉ **Post office** 2451 High Rd, Arichat; ⊕ 08.00–17.00 Mon–Fri, 10.00–13.00 Sat

WHAT TO SEE AND DO
Notre Dame de L'Assomption (Our Lady of the Assumption)
Overlooking the harbour is this large, wooden c1837 cathedral. In 1858, the then bishop imported a

pipe organ – now considered to be one of very few of its kind in North America – from Philadelphia, USA. Just by the cathedral, **Cannon Look-off** offers fine views and has interpretive displays detailing the region's history.

LeNoir Forge Museum (*Lower Rd;* ✆ *226 9364;* ⊕ *early Jun–Aug 10.00–17.00 daily; admission free*) The c1789 forge down on the waterfront was built in the French Regime style. It was used more recently as an ice house, and in 1967, restored as a working museum.

PORT HAWKESBURY

A short drive from Port Hastings (see page 293) Port Hawkesbury is a commercial and industrial pulp mill, power plant and oil centre on the Strait of Canso. As at Mulgrave across the water, construction of the nearby Canso Causeway has created an ice-free deep-water port capable of accommodating the largest ships in the world.

GETTING THERE
By car Port Hawkesbury is on Highway 4, 6km/4 miles from Port Hastings and 7km/4.3 miles to the Canso Causeway. It is 43km/27 miles from St Peter's and 165km/103 miles from Sydney.

By bus Port Hawkesbury is on the Acadian coach route between Halifax and Sydney (see page 52).

🏠 WHERE TO STAY
🏠 **Maritime Inn Port Hawkesbury** (73 rooms) 717 Reeves St; ✆ 625 0320, T/F 1 888 662 7484; www.maritimeinns.com. A comfortable mid-range hotel with indoor & seasonal outdoor pools, & a fitness centre. See below for Millers Café and Millers Tap & Grill restaurant listings. $$

🏠 **Home Again B&B** (3 rooms) 308 Prince St; ✆ 625 3076; e homeagain@aliantzinc.ca; www.homeagainbandb.com; ⊕ year-round. Housed in a centrally located, recently renovated c1870s' home.

There are plans to offer suites. Delicious full b/fast inc. $$

🏠 **Harbourview B&B and Motel** (9 units) 209 Granville St; ✆ 625 3224, T/F 1 877 676 6886; www.harbourviewbb.com; ⊕ year-round. There are 3 rooms in the c1880 main house (built for a ferry captain), & 6 motel rooms with fridge & microwave. Watch the modern-day water traffic from the large deck. Full b/fast inc. $

✖ WHERE TO EAT
✖ **Millers Café** 717 Reeves St; ⊕ 06.30–14.00 Mon–Fri, 07.00–14.00 Sat–Sun all year. Maritime Inn Port Hawkesbury's (see above) on-site restaurant. $$

✖ **Millers Tap & Grill** 717 Reeves St; ⊕ 14.00–midnight Mon–Sat, 14.00–22.00 Sun all year; food served until 21.00 (Jul–Sep until 22.00). Maritime Inn Port Hawkesbury's other on-site restaurant is licensed. The food – the closest you'll come to fine-dining in these parts – is good value. $$

✖ **China King** 825 Reeves St; ✆ 625 7000; ⊕ year-round 11.00–22.00 daily. Food from the fixed-price buffet or standard menu is well presented & tasty. The crispy calamari & hot pepper squid are both recommended. $

✖ **Fleur-de-Lis Tea Room and Dining Room** 634 Reeves St; ✆ 625 2566; ⊕ year-round 07.00–19.00 Mon–Sat. An easy-to-miss little gem tucked away in the Gateway Plaza shopping mall. There's no deep-fryer, & very few processed ingredients are used. All-day breakfast, seafood, Scottish & Acadian cuisine & more. Start with maple nut salad, then go for Acadian fishcakes or the grilled haddock dinner. Desserts are homemade & usually very good. Recommended! $

✖ **Shindigs Pub** 510 Granville St; ✆ 625 0263; www.shindigspub.com; ⊕ 16.00–late Tue–Sun. Waterfront pub with good atmosphere & decent pub food. Regular live music. $

ENTERTAINMENT Summer evenings bring regular Tuesday ceilidhs (*www.ceilidhs.ca*) and free outdoor concerts on Sunday at **Granville Green** (*Granville St;* ✆ *625 2591; www.granvillegreen.com*). Incidentally, the town had a weekly Artisans' Market, but this closed in 2008: there was, however, talk of reviving it.

FESTIVALS
July
Festival of the Strait (*www.festivalofthestrait.ca*) Four-day festival with activities including sailing, canoe races, outdoor concerts and dances.

OTHER PRACTICALITIES
$ **BMO Bank of Montreal** 634 Reeves St; ✆ 625 1250; ⏱ 10.00–16.00 Mon–Wed, 10.00–17.00 Thu–Fri
✚ **The Strait Richmond Hospital** 138 Hospital Rd, Evanston; ✆ 625 3100. 11km east of Port Hawkesbury at Exit 45 of Hwy 104

☞ **Port Hawkesbury Branch Library** 304 Pitt St; ✆ 625 2729; ⏱ 15.00–20.00 Mon–Fri, 11.00–14.00 Sat
✉ **Post office** 25 Pitt St; ⏱ 08.30–17.00 Mon–Fri, 08.30–12.30 Sat

WHAT TO SEE AND DO
Ship Harbour Boat Tours (✆ *227 5456; www.harbourtours.ca*) Offers harbour and Strait of Canso tours in the summer.

9

Eastern Shore

Stretching for almost 350km from Lawrencetown to the Canso Causeway, this is the least visited of any of the mainland tourist regions of Nova Scotia.

Ask those who live in other parts of the province about the Eastern Shore and 'always foggy' or 'no infrastructure' will probably be the most common answers.

To a degree, they have a point in terms of infrastructure. There are no sizeable towns, and accommodation, shopping and services are limited and public transport is non-existent.

So why come here?

This region offers some of Nova Scotia's wildest and most scenic coastal landscapes. Along the length of much of the coast, dozens of forested finger-like peninsulas protrude out into the Atlantic. The so-called main highway – in reality, for all but the first 35km of its length just a quiet two-lane road – cuts across the base of the peninsulas but from time to time be sure to turn off onto one of the side roads to get to a small fishing village, beautiful beach or wild rocky headland with a view of a lighthouse on a nearby island.

Much of the region is forest-covered, with spruce, fir, birch, larch and maple predominant. This is also one of the province's most rewarding destinations for viewing the beauty of the autumn colours.

There aren't any luxury hotels, but the relatively few – but delightful – B&Bs and inns, a few motels, some lovely campsites and one 'nature lover's' resort do the job.

The restaurants are also widely spaced, but although you may have to drive for a while there are some excellent dining opportunities, especially for lovers of seafood.

The sea is cold but the beaches are uncrowded and beautiful with the province's best surfing and windsurfing, and the hundreds of uninhabited, forested islands, many of which contain ruins of long-abandoned dwellings or fishing camps, and inlets make for ideal sea kayaking.

Birdwatchers will be in their element, and in addition, there is some wonderful riverside, forest and coastal hiking, and a history of gold mining. There's also an abundance of folklore, with seafaring traditions and legends still very much alive, and a very popular annual music festival.

There are, of course, foggy days, but wandering along a beautiful deserted beach, watching the sea mist roll in, and hearing the moan of a faraway foghorn can be very atmospheric.

Here, perhaps more than anywhere else in Nova Scotia, you'll feel like a traveller rather than a tourist. Come and enjoy the pace of life – slow – and the proximity to virtually untouched nature. It is no surprise that most of the Eastern Shore's manmade attractions celebrate days gone by, a life pre-electricity and pre-modern technology.

If you headed out to sea for approximately 170km from Tor Bay (see page 361) you would reach intriguing Sable Island (see pages 368–71) – though virtually all

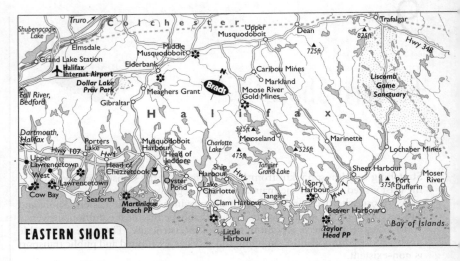

EASTERN SHORE

of the limited number of people who visit this long, narrow, storied strip of sand fly from Halifax Airport.

LAWRENCETOWN

Lawrencetown has little to offer service-wise – **MacDonald House**, the building on the right at the top of the hill, has a gallery, antique shop, a tea room and a basement surf shop. The principal attraction is the **Lawrencetown Beach Provincial Park,** renowned for offering the province's best and most consistent wave breaks for surfers.

The waves are best for surfing in the autumn and winter, in particular between September and May, but whatever time of the year people surf, wetsuits are a must – this isn't Hawaii. And the closest you'll get to a pina colada is a coke from the (summer-only) canteen.

For those who merely want to watch, the beach is well worth a (breezy) stop, look and stroll. Lifeguards are on duty in season, and the park has changing rooms, showers and toilets.

Far quieter, and usually surfer-free, is Conrad Beach, at the end of Conrad Road, 6km east of Lawrencetown. Here your only companions are likely to be birds – and birdwatchers. Boardwalks connect the small parking area with the (especially at low tide) huge, fine sand beach.

GETTING THERE Lawrencetown is on Highway 207, 18km/11 miles from Dartmouth, 20km/12 miles from Halifax and 24km/15 miles from Musquodoboit Harbour.

WHERE TO STAY AND EAT

🏠 **A Moonlight Beach Inn** (3 rooms) 2 Wyndenfog Lane; 🕾 827 2712; www.moonlightbeachinn.com; ⊕ year-round. In a magnificent location virtually on Lawrencetown Beach, each guest room has a sitting area, fireplace, dining nook, private entrance & deck overlooking ocean. Lobster dinners in season. B/fast inc (eg: eggs Benedict 'Maritime Style' with crab or smoked salmon). $$

🏠 **Beach Niche** (1 unit) 5 Wyndenfog Lane; 🕾 827 4011; e bettyhoughton@eastlink.ca; www.beachniche.ca; ⊕ year-round. Less than 100m from Lawrencetown Beach is this comfortable, spacious, 2-bedroom, 2-bathroom ground-floor apartment suite which can sleep up to 8. Private entrance & well-equipped kitchen. Continental b/fast inc. $$

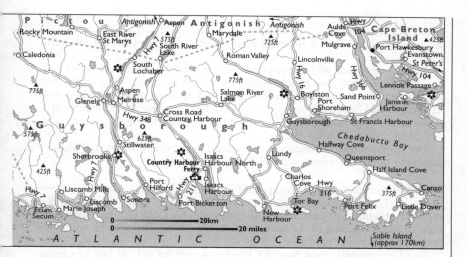

🏠 **Ocean Dream B&B** (2 suites) 86 Spruce Court, Three Fathom Harbour; ↘ 827 5295, T/F I 866 301 9857; www.oceandreambb.com; ⏰ year-round; off-season on request. A Swiss-Canadian-run oceanfront property just over 2km from Lawrencetown Beach. Both suites have small fridge & complimentary fruit basket; decorated with a mix of modern & antique furniture. 2-night minimum stay applies. B/fast inc. 💲💲

Å **Porter's Lake Provincial Park Campground** (80 sites) 1160 West Porter's Lake Rd; ↘ 827 2250, 424 5937; www.novascotiaparks.ca/parks/porters.asp. Beautifully located & virtually surrounded by water, 10km from Lawrencetown. 💲
✕ **Heron's Nest Tea Room** 4144 Lawrencetown Rd; ↘ 434 7895; ⏰ mid-May–early Oct 11.00–17.00 Tue–Sun. Salads, soups & sandwiches & an enticing array of baked goods. 💲

FESTIVALS
End August–September
Kite Festival A one-day event with kite-flying demonstrations and competitions, and a BBQ.

SHOPPING Surfing shops in the area include **DaCane Beach Store** (↘ *431 7873; www.hurricanesurf.com; ⏰ Jun–Sep*) right in the provincial park, and **Kannon Beach** (*4144 Hwy 7;* ↘ *471 0025; www.kannonbeach.com; ⏰ year-round*) at the top of the hill.

SEAFORTH

The only reasons to break your journey in this small community would be to rent a canoe or bike, or to visit the wildlife rehabilitation centre.

GETTING THERE Seaforth is on Highway 207, 9km/6 miles east of Lawrencetown.

WHAT TO SEE AND DO
Captain Canoe (*5336 Hwy 207;* ↘ *827 3933; www.captcanoe.com*) This company rents kayaks, canoes and bikes; staff can provide maps, charts and advice on worthwhile routes in the area. Kayaks cost CAN$30 per day; canoes CAN$45.

Hope for Wildlife Society (*5909 Hwy 207;* ↘ *481 2401; www.hopeforwildlife.net*) Specialising in the care, treatment and rehabilitation of injured or orphaned native mammals and birds. Call in advance if you would like to visit.

THE CHEZZETCOOKS

West and East Chezzetcook are pretty villages dotted along the Chezzetcook Inlet's shores.

On the eastern side of the inlet a road offering more lovely harbour views leads to East Chezzetcook. Ask local residents the best things about their community and most will mention the Acadian roots and heritage, fishing history, wild Misener's Head (further down the road), and Chad Doucette. East Chezzetcook is home to young Mr Doucette who reached the Top 4 in the 2006 series of reality pop talent contest *Canadian Idol*.

The neighbouring communities of Grand Desert, Gaetz Brook and Porter's Lake offer more accommodation and dining choices.

HISTORY *Chezzetcook* is a Mi'kmaq word for 'running waters divided into many channels'. The first permanent Acadian settlers arrived in 1764. They befriended the local Mi'kmaq and joined them in harvesting clams and fishing. Dykes were built to enable farming of the marshland. In the 1870s, Chezzetcook was Nova Scotia's biggest oyster producer.

West Chezzetcook's Saint Anselm Church was founded in 1740, but the current (brick) version was built in 1894. Each local family was asked to pay for 400 bricks to help meet construction costs. The church remains the major focus of the area's communities.

GETTING THERE The Chezzetcooks are on Highway 7, and between Exits 20 and 21 of Highway 107. Some 23km/14 miles from Dartmouth, and 14km/9 miles from Musquodoboit Harbour.

 WHERE TO STAY

🏠 **Changing Tides B&B** (2 rooms) 6627 Hwy 207, Grand Desert; ☎ 827 5134; www.changingtides.ca; ⏲ year-round. A modern house 3km from West Chezzetcook with lovely views over the ocean, wetlands & islands. Fireplace in lounge; deck & sun room. Full b/fast inc. $$

🏠 **Elephant's Nest B&B** (3 rooms) 127 Pleasant Dr, Gaetz Brook; ☎ 827 3891, T/F 1 866 633 6378; e info@elephantsnestbnb.ca; www.elephantsnestbnb.ca;

⏲ year-round. A comfortable lakefront house less than 4km from Head of Chezzetcook, 7km west of Musquodoboit Harbour, with en-suite bathrooms. Swim, enjoy free use of kayaks, canoe & pedal boat, relax on one of the decks, in lovely gardens or the outdoor hot tub. Full b/fast inc (eg: baked peach with hot berries & yoghurt). $$

🏠 **The IN House Musical B&B** (2 rooms) 5315 Hwy 7, Porter's Lake; ☎ 827 2532, T/F 1 866 236

0597; www.inhousemusicalbnb.com; ⊕ year-round; off-season by reservation. A Victorian-style country house, 5km from Head of Chezzetcook, decorated with hostess's art work. There are candlelight evening concerts of mostly original music with a musician host who delights in his alter-ego soubriquet, *The Cosmic Surfer*. Continental b/fast inc. $

✖ WHERE TO EAT AND DRINK

✖ **Tin Roof Mercantile and Café** 6321 Hwy 7, Head of Chezzetcook; ✆ 827 5313, T/F 1 877 827 5313; www.tinroof.ca; ⊕ summer 09.00–16.00 Tue–Sun; winter 10.00–14.30 Thu–Fri, 10.00–15.00 Sat–Sun. Sit by the big open fire & tuck into good home cooking. Organic, local ingredients used where possible. Popular with Halifax/Dartmouth residents for weekend lunches. $$

✖ **Porter's Lake Pub** 5228 Hwy 7, Porter's Lake; ✆ 827 3097; ⊕ year-round 10.00–21.00

Mon–Wed (pub until midnight), 10.00–21.30 Thu–Sat (pub until 02.00), 12.00–21.00 Sun (pub until midnight). This relaxed, quaint & popular pub offers a full menu – scallop bubbly bake is a standout – & entertainment Thu–Sat evenings (plus summer Sun). $–$$

✖ **Nan Myatt's Family Restaurant** 5191 Hwy 7, Porter's Lake; ✆ 827 5959; ⊕ year-round 08.00–20.00 daily. Good simple food, pleasant service & family-friendly atmosphere. $

OTHER PRACTICALITIES

$ **Royal Bank** 5228 Hwy 7, Porter's Lake; ✆ 827 2930; ⊕ 09.30–17.00 Mon–Wed & Fri, 09.30–20.00 Thu

✉ **Post office** 5 Keizer Dr, Porter's Lake; ⊕ 08.30–17.15 Mon–Fri, 08.30–12.00 Sat

WHAT TO SEE AND DO

Acadian House Museum: L'Acadie de Chezzetcook (*79 Hill Rd, West Chezzetcook;* ✆ *827 5992;* ⊕ *Jul–Aug 10.00–16.30 Tue–Sun; admission varies by event*) Built in 1850, the museum retains the character of a typical Acadian home from the period. On show are clothes, documents, tools, photos and artefacts – including a mid 19th-century-style outdoor oven.

MUSQUODOBOIT HARBOUR (*Population: approx 1,000*)

Musquodoboit (pronounced 'Muska-dobbit') Harbour pips Sheet Harbour (see page 355) as the largest community between Dartmouth and Canso, a distance of some 200km. Unless you're sure that you'll reach Sheet Harbour when the relevant shops or services are open, stock up here.

The Mi'kmaq name was *Moosekudoboogwek* – 'suddenly widening out after a narrow entrance at the mouth'. The harbour itself is sheltered from the Atlantic Ocean by a long barrier beach system and is an incredibly productive estuary. The varied coastal scenery includes sandy beaches, salt marshes, saline ponds, dunes, eel grass beds, mudflats and mature coastal coniferous forest.

Large numbers of birds flock to this region every year to feed and rest during their long migration, and in 1987, Musquodoboit Harbour was added to the official 'List of Wetlands of International Importance' in recognition of its importance as a habitat for diverse waterfowl populations. Birds apart, there's a railway museum and good hiking.

GETTING THERE Musquodoboit Harbour is on Highway 7, approximately 45km/28 miles from Halifax and 69km/43 miles from Sheet Harbour.

TOURIST INFORMATION In the former Waiting Room of the Railway Museum complex (*Main St, Musquodoboit Harbour;* ✆ *889 2689;* ⊕ *mid-May-late Oct 09.00–16.00 daily, 09.00–18.00 in Jul/Aug*)

WHERE TO STAY AND EAT

⌂ **Old Riverside Lodge B&B** (3 rooms) 98 Riverside Av; ☎ 889 3464, T/F 1 877 859 3674; www.oldriversidelodgebnb.com; ⊕ May–Oct; off-season by reservation. A c1853 lodge with original hardwood floors. Continental b/fast inc. $$

⌂ **The Tourist Trap** (3 rooms) 8384 Hwy 7; ☎ 889 3791; e info@thetouristtrap.ca; www.thetouristtrap.ca; ⊕ year-round. A lovely (though less than enticingly named) guesthouse: rooms share a bathroom. There is a common room with microwave, fridge & complimentary coffee. Also on site is a café (⊕ late Jun–mid-Sep 08.00–19.00 daily; mid-Sep–Dec 08.30–18.45 Wed–Sun; Jan–mid-Jun 08.30–18.45 Thu–Sun; $), specialising in province-grown organic food (burritos, salads, sandwiches, good coffee & desserts, & more substantial fare). $$

✗ **Bear Den Café** 7955 Hwy 7; ☎ 889 3003; www.accesswave.ca/~beardencafe/; ⊕ year-round 07.00–19.00 daily. A small yellow shack offering unpretentious standards (burgers, simple salads, sandwiches & milkshakes) plus seafood chowder, (salt cod) fish cakes & steamed mussels. $

✗ **Harbour Fish 'N' Fries** 7886 Hwy 7; ☎ 889 3366; ⊕ Apr–mid-Dec 11.00–19.30 daily. Again, not the most exciting of exteriors. Cheap seafood eatery with a few tables in & outside a simple building. The fried clams & fish & chips are very good but you're quite limited if deep-fried is not for you (in which case, choose the lobster roll). That aside, quality is high & prices low. $

OTHER PRACTICALITIES

$ **Royal Bank** 7907 Hwy 7; ☎ 889 2626; ⊕ 09.30–17.00 Mon–Fri

📚 **Musquodoboit Harbour Public Library** 7900 Hwy 7; ☎ 889 2227; ⊕ 11.00–16.00 Tue, 17.00–20.00

Wed–Thu, 12.00–18.00 Fri, 10.00–15.00 Sat

✉ **Post office** 7901 Hwy 7; ⊕ 08.30–16.30 Mon–Fri, 08.30–12.00 Sat

WHAT TO SEE AND DO

Musquodoboit Railway Museum (*Main St, Musquodoboit Harbour;* ☎ *889 2689;* ⊕ *mid-May–late Oct 09.00–16.00 daily (Jul/Aug 09.00–18.00); admission free*) Housed in the beautifully restored – and brightly painted – c1916 Canadian National Railways Station and three vintage rail cars. You don't need to be a train buff to enjoy a brief visit: there is a caboose and a huge old snowplough, and reader-friendly exhibits of the history of Nova Scotia's railways. Railway enthusiasts will also find photographs, maps, posters, tickets and artefacts relating to the history of the railway in the province and, in particular, this region.

Rail Trail The death of the province's railways (see box below) has brought some benefits – a section of the old line has been converted into the splendid 14.5km Rail Trail, part of the Musquodoboit Trailways network. Leading off the main trail are worthwhile side-trips, such as the Admiral Lake Loop, Bayer Lake Loop, and Gibraltar Loop. The trail crosses the Musquodoboit River on a long

BLUEBERRY EXPRESS

In 1916, the 'Dartmouth Branch Extension of the Intercolonial Railway' opened, linking Dartmouth with Musquodoboit Harbour. Prior to its construction, to reach the city people had a choice of travelling by sea, stagecoach or ox-drawn wagon over rough roads – or walking. The rail service was nicknamed the Blueberry Express: this may have been because of the copious amounts of the fruit that farmers took to the capital during the season, or perhaps because stops were so long that passengers could get off, pick their berries, and reboard the train before it moved on. There were plans to continue the line to Guysborough (see page 367) but despite some construction, the extension never came near completion. The last train ran in 1982 and the tracks were dismantled in 1985.

trestle bridge and then follows an old stagecoach road before reaching the shore of Bayer Lake. Access the trail from the museum car park.

MARTINIQUE BEACH

A worthwhile side-trip (12km each way) from Musquodoboit Harbour will take you along the shoreline of beautiful Petpeswick Inlet. You'll pass little jetties, fishing boats and neatly stacked lobster pots *en route* to the province's longest sand beach, much of which lies within the **Martinique Beach Provincial Park**. This has picnic tables and small parking areas at regular intervals along the first 1,500m from which boardwalks lead between the dunes to the stunning 5km beach.

Across the access road is a large wetland, popular with canoeists and kayakers. Part of the beach and wetland is a bird sanctuary, teeming during the spring and autumn migrations and attracting wintering Canada geese, black ducks, herons and osprey. The endangered piping plover nests on the beach and entry to sensitive areas is restricted during nesting season.

GETTING THERE Take East Petpeswick Road from Musquodoboit Harbour.

MEAGHERS GRANT

Highway 357 leads north (inland) off Highway 7 along the lovely, fertile Musquodoboit Valley, one of the province's principal farming areas. The country villages, rich rolling green farmlands and forested hills make this a very pleasant drive: in the autumn, the colours are breathtaking. Among these villages is Meaghers Grant, a small community which offers a few reasons to stop.

GETTING THERE Meaghers Grant is on Highway 357, 22km from Musquodoboit Harbour.

 WHERE TO STAY AND EAT

River Oaks Country Lodge (8 rooms) 3856 Meaghers Grant Rd; ☎ 384 3033; www.riveroaksgolfclub.ca; ⊕ mid-May–mid-Oct. The only other option in town, this motel is right by the golf course: some units have kitchenettes. Deck, pool (in season), & licensed restaurant (⊕ mid-May–

mid-Oct 08.00–20.00 daily; $) where the menu includes soups, pasta & seafood. $

Å Dollar Lake Provincial Park (119 sites) 5265 Old Guysborough Rd; ☎ 384 2770; www.parks.gov.ns.ca; ⊕ mid-Jun–mid-Oct. For further details, see page below.

WHAT TO SEE AND DO

River Oaks Golf Club Meaghers Grant is home to 18- and 9-hole courses, whose designs are one of the more successful attempts at blending fairways, greens and nature. Bird sightings (including bald eagles) are common, and you might be lucky enough to see otters, beavers, muskrats, deer or even moose. Green fees CAN$40–45.

Meaghers Grant Canoe Rentals (☎ 384 2513) In addition to the Musquodoboit, both the Stewiacke and the Shubenacadie rivers are easily accessible, and all three are excellent for canoeing. This company will drive you to your chosen put-in spot so that you can paddle downstream to your vehicle. The best time of year is late spring, while the waters are still high and the weather has warmed up a bit. Be prepared – you will pass through virtual wilderness.

Dollar Lake Provincial Park Just north of Meaghers Grant, a left turn onto Highway 212 will quickly bring you to this 1,200ha park. The eponymous lake has a white-sand beach, and the park offers picnic and camping facilities (see page 351). The park is criss-crossed with logging roads and tracks, offering a good variety of lakeside and forest walking trails.

OYSTER POND

The Mi'kmaq called Oyster Pond *Pajedoobaack* – 'wave washed'. In days gone by, bivalves were abundant, hence the current name. A sawmill was built on the water's edge, a dam constructed across the 'pond's' mouth, and the water was channelled with the intention of powering the mill. The good news was that this all worked well, and the mill's owners sawed their way to prosperity. The bad news was that playing with nature prevented salt water from entering the pond at high tide. As a result, Oyster Pond had plenty of freshly cut lumber – but no more oysters. The community is now home to a small, yet fascinating museum.

GETTING THERE Oyster Pond is on Highway 7, 68km/42 miles from Halifax, 13km/8 miles from Musquodoboit Harbour and 50km/31 miles from Sheet Harbour.

WHERE TO STAY AND EAT

Auberge Salmon River House Country Inn (8 units) 9931 Hwy 7, Salmon River Bridge; 889 3353; www.salmonriverhouse.com; ⊕ May–Oct; off-season by reservation. 7 charming guest rooms in this c1850s' inn at the mouth of the Salmon River, & a separate cottage. There are 2 justifiably highly regarded licensed restaurants: The **Lobster Shack** (⊕ daily May–Jun & Sep–Oct 11.00–19.00; Jul–Aug 11.00–21.00; $$) offers fine-dining without too much formality & an extensive wine list: start with steamed blue mussels, & follow with lobster thermidor, Acadian chaudree (seafood stew), or seafood chowder. Reserve in advance to secure a

window table overlooking the river. The **Bistro** (⊕ dates/ hours as above; $) serves lighter fare. Stop by for kaffeeklatsch (coffee & chatting). $$
Jeddore Lodge and Cabins (12 units) 9855 Hwy 7, Salmon River Bridge; 889 3030, T/F 1 888 889 3030; www.jeddorelodgecabins.blogspot.com/; ⊕ May–Oct. 2 B&B rooms (b/fast inc) & 10 1- & 2-bedroom cabins, some with fireplaces & verandas overlooking the river & harbour. Outdoor pool (seasonal). The licensed dining room (⊕ May–Oct for lunch & dinner; $$) offers salads, sandwiches & seafood. $

A SEAFARING SPECTRE

In 1817, a William Kent built a house on Kent Island, and always claimed it was haunted. The house was torn down in 1903, and a lighthouse constructed on the site in 1904. For many years, Kent's descendants operated their house adjacent to the lighthouse as a B&B, and there were several reports of supernatural activity in and around the lighthouse. A few years ago, a medium staying at the B&B announced that not only was the lighthouse haunted, but the haunter was the ghost of Admiral Horatio Nelson. The remarks were taken with a pinch of sea salt, but a couple of years later, when researching the family history, the current Kents discovered that William, who built the house, had sailed with Nelson, serving as navigator aboard Nelson's HMS *Victory* at the Battle of Trafalgar in 1805 when Horatio met his death.

The lighthouse is not open to the public. You can see it by turning onto Ostrea Lake Road from Highway 7 at Smith Settlement 4km east of Musquodoboit Harbour and following the road along the eastern side of the water, then turning onto Kent Road. It is worth continuing to Pleasant Point for lovely views of the harbour mouth.

Ⓐ Webber Lakeside Resort (66 sites) 738 Upper Lakeville Rd; ☎ 845 2340, T/F I 800 589 2282; www.webberslakesideresort.com; ⊕ mid-May–mid-Oct. Full hook-ups, lake swimming & canoe rental; 7km from Salmon River Bridge. ⑤

FESTIVALS
September
Pirate Days Festival (*www.novascotiapirates.ca*) A day of pirate-themed fun for all the family.

WHAT TO SEE AND DO
Fisherman's Life Museum (*58 Navy Pool Loop;* ☎ *889 2053; www.museum.gov.ns.ca/flm/;* ⊕ *Jun–mid-Oct 09.30–17.30 Mon–Sat, 13.00–17.30 Sun; admission CAN$3.25*) In the early 1900s, the tiny house and small farm that now make up this museum comprising restored farmhouse, garden and outbuildings. were home to an inshore fisherman, his wife and 12 daughters. The Myers family lived a simple life, supplementing their meagre fishing income with a small farm operation. Inside the house, guides in period costume hook rugs, prepare food using the old wood stove or tell stories about the land, the sea and life a century ago.

LAKE CHARLOTTE

This community was named in honour of Princess Charlotte Augusta of Wales, who died in 1817 shortly after the area was settled.

GETTING THERE Lake Charlotte is on Highway 7, 15km/9 miles from Musquodoboit Harbour and 50km/31 miles from Sheet Harbour.

FESTIVALS
June
Antique Car Show See a range of antique vehicles at the Memory Lane Heritage Village (see below).

WHAT TO SEE AND DO
Memory Lane Heritage Village (*Clam Harbour Rd;* ☎ *845 1937, T/F 1 877 287 0697; www.heritagevillage.ca;* ⊕ *mid-Jun–mid-Sep 11.00–16.00 daily; off-season by appointment; admission CAN$6*) This community-owned attraction takes a nostalgic look at rural village life in the 1940s. Most of the 15 c1894–1949 buildings – including the outhouse – were 'rescued' from around the region, restored, and moved here. There is also a general store, homestead relocated from Oyster Pond, one-room schoolhouse and more. Activity programmes might include a pump-organ accompanied choir practice in the church, or a forestry day with axe-sharpening lessons. Eat in the replica 1940s' cookhouse.

CLAM HARBOUR

Clam Harbour boasts one of the province's prettiest beaches, which – as a result of a warmer-than-average tidal stream – is usually the best swimming beach on the Eastern Shore.

The beach park has a hiking trail, a life guard and canteen (weekends in season), showers and changing rooms. There is also a picnic area with tables tucked between trees: to reach it, turn right at the end of the access road. The beach is unlikely to be crowded for 364 days of the year. However, several thousand visitors (incredible considering both the Eastern Shore's population and tourist numbers) stop by for the August one-day **Clam Harbour Beach Sandcastle Sculpture Contest** (*www.halifax.ca/sandcastle/; CAN$20 to enter, free-to-enter children's competition*). Competitors enthuse about the beach's 'perfect' sand in the same way skiers rave about 'champagne' snow. Not only can designs have minute, perfect features, but the sculptures remain in place for hours without collapsing or weathering.

This area is one reputed to have a larger than average number of foggy days, but fingers crossed that the sun will shine on the broad crescent of sand for your visit.

GETTING THERE Follow Clam Harbour Road for about 8km/5 miles from Lake Charlotte.

TANGIER *(Population: 115)*

This small community once serviced several gold mines. It is now home to an excellent sea kayaking company, a factory producing arguably the province's best smoked fish, and – just off Highway 7 at Mason Point road, the simple Prince Alfred Arch, erected to commemorate the (1861) visit to the local gold mine by Queen Victoria's son.

GETTING THERE Tangier is on Highway 7, 47km/29 miles from Musquodoboit Harbour and 20km/12 miles from Sheet Harbour.

⌂ WHERE TO STAY AND EAT

⌂ **Paddler's Retreat** (4 rooms) 84 Mason's Point Rd; ☎ 772 2774; e info@coastaladventures.com; www.coastaladventures.com; ⏰ mid-Jun–mid-Oct; off-season by reservation. Under the same management as Coastal Adventures (see below), this laid-back c1860s' old fisherman's home is the obvious choice for anyone on a kayaking course. 3 rooms share a bathroom, 1 has en suite. Outdoor hot tub. Full country b/fast inc. $

Å **Murphy's Camping on the Ocean** (40 sites) 308 Murphy's Rd, Murphy Cove; ☎ 772 2700; www.murphyscampingontheocean.ca; ⏰ mid-May–mid-Oct. Located on a headland just off Hwy 7, 7.5km west of Tangier, with open & wooded campsites (serviced & unserviced), boat rentals, scenic boat tours & numerous other activities including the host's entertaining storytelling evenings. Another great base for sea kayakers. $

SHOPPING A couple of unprepossessing buildings house **Willy Krauch and Sons** (*signposted just off Hwy 7*; ☎ 772 2188; ⏰ *year-round 08.00–18.00 Mon–Fri, 10.00–18.00 Sat–Sun*). Krauch was a Danish immigrant who settled in Tangier in the 1950s and brought with him a traditional Danish method of smoking fish: his sons continue to use this process. The smokehouse's shop stocks smoked eel and different varieties of salmon and mackerel. Pack prices range from around CAN$5.

OTHER PRACTICALITIES

✉ **Post office** 17276 Hwy 7; ⏰ 07.30–15.00 Mon–Fri, 07.30–12.00 Sat

WHAT TO SEE AND DO

Coastal Adventures (*84 Mason's Point Rd*; ☎ 772 2774; *www.coastaladventures.com*) One of Nova Scotia's top sea kayaking companies – and one of the only places offering kayak rental along the entire Eastern Shore. Come for expert advice, half- and full-day kayak excursions which include visits to uninhabited islands, and a range of longer (multi-day) packages.

TAYLOR HEAD PROVINCIAL PARK (⊕ mid-May–mid-Oct)

This beautiful park occupies a narrow 6.5km peninsula, jutting into the Atlantic like a huge rocky finger. It encompasses 16km of unspoiled and virtually untouched coastline, varied habitats rich in flora and fauna, and fascinating geology.

In season, the park offers unsupervised swimming, changing rooms, several picnic areas, interpretive panels and vault toilets.

The west side of the peninsula is rugged and windswept: as a result of the salt spray and almost constant winds, white spruce and firs are stunted, almost flattened to the rocky ground. The more protected east side has sandy coves lapped by calmer waters. Several rocky barrens covered with dwarf shrubs and lichens are found in the southern portion of Taylor Head, and peat-filled open bogs are scattered throughout the park.

This is one of only a few locations in Nova Scotia where these sand volcanoes (small cone-shaped geological features) are found. Other special features, called flute marks, appear as ripples in the bedrock and indicate that strong ocean currents once moved large volumes of sediment rapidly across what was the sea floor. Parallel northeast–southwest quartzite ridges that show the direction of bedrock folding can still be seen at Taylor Head, and the beach and sand dunes at Psyche Cove were formed by sand deposits from the erosion of glacial till and bedrock.

The park is home to a variety of mammals including white-tailed deer, raccoons and muskrats. Seals have been spotted on nearby rocks, and there have also been sightings of pilot whales and dolphins offshore.

For most, though, it is the park's walking and hiking trails that are the big draw: many people rate them among the finest coastal trail systems on North America's eastern seaboard. Possibilities include the 2km Beach Walk, and the Headland Trail, a wonderful 8km figure-of-eight hike taking in boardwalks and bogs, forest dripping with moss, and of course stretches of the shoreline.

A 5km unpaved road from Highway 7 hugs the west side of the peninsula before crossing to sheltered Psyche Cove. At the end of the road is a series of small parking areas with beach access.

GETTING THERE The park is just off Highway 7, 14km/9 miles from Tangier and 12km/7 miles from Sheet Harbour.

SHEET HARBOUR (Population: 825)

Roughly halfway between Halifax and Canso, the town lies between the outflows of the West and East Sheet Harbour rivers at the head of a long narrow bay. After Musquodoboit Harbour it is the biggest community along the Eastern Shore. If you're heading east and need anything, stock up here: further along don't expect more than the sporadic general store.

HISTORY Sheet Harbour was founded in 1784 by Loyalist refugees and British veterans of the American Revolution and became a prosperous centre for the lumber industry and consequently as a shipbuilding centre.

In recent years, the government has made an effort to make Sheet Harbour into a major port and chief supply depot for the gas platforms off Sable Island (see page 368).

GETTING THERE Sheet Harbour is on Highway 7, 120km/75 miles east of Dartmouth and 65km/40 miles west of Sherbrooke.

TOURIST INFORMATION In the MacPhee House Museum (*Hwy 7 at the West River Bridge;* ☏ *885 2595;* ⏰ *summer 10.00–19.00 daily*)

 WHERE TO STAY AND EAT

🏠 **Back In Thyme B&B** (2 rooms) 22960 Hwy 7; ☏ 885 2352; www.backinthyme.ca; ⏰ year-round; off-season by reservation. A c1885 sea captain's house set on a 1.2ha riverside property with fruit trees. 1 room has a small en suite, 1 a shared bathroom. Canoes & bicycle for guest use. Full b/fast inc & served in the sun room overlooking the East River. $

🏠 **Fairwinds Motel & Restaurant** (10 rooms) 22522 Hwy 7; ☏ 885 2502; www.fairwindsmotelsheetharbour.ca; ⏰ year-round. A traditional single-storey motel; some rooms have sea views. The restaurant (⏰ year-round 07.00–20.30 daily; $) offers good service & reliable food (splendid fish & chips) & is a better choice than the Sheet Harbour Motel across the road. Deck overlooks the sea. $

🏕 **East River Lodge Campground** (42 sites) 200 Pool Rd; ☏ 885 2864; ⏰ May–Oct. Serviced & unserviced sites. $

FESTIVALS

August

Seaside Festival Two-week festival with a range of events including parades, Fun Day and Kids Activity Day.

OTHER PRACTICALITIES

$ **Scotiabank** 22540 Hwy 7; ☏ 885 2310; ⏰ 10.00–17.00 Mon–Fri

✚ **Eastern Shore Memorial Hospital** 22637 Hwy 7; ☏ 885 2554

✉ **Post office** 22526 Hwy 7; ⏰ 08.00–17.00 Mon–Fri, 09.00–12.00 Sat

WHAT TO SEE AND DO

MacPhee House Community Museum (*Hwy 7 at the West River Bridge;* ☏ *885 2595;* ⏰ *late May–Sep 09.00–17.00 daily; off-season by appointment; admission free*) Life before Plastic exhibit illustrates Eastern Shore life in the days before modern technology. You're unlikely to spend overlong here, but there are some interesting objects and curios that may intrigue and challenge young and old alike.

LISCOMB GAME SANCTUARY

From Sheet Harbour, Highway 374 heads north for 130km to Stellarton (see page 278). For much of the way, this remote road passes through a game sanctuary established in 1928 to protect wildlife, particularly moose and woodland caribou. We are not talking safari parks here, but over 43,000ha of remote forest, logging roads, rivers and lakes and no services.

The rugged landscape is dotted with ancient drumlins (see page 207) and dips that have filled with water. The 'protected area' was cloaked in old-growth boreal forest, but sadly much of it has been logged as the legislation which created the sanctuary protected the animals themselves, with little thought for their habitat.

In recent years, environmentalists and conservationists have campaigned to extend the sanctuary's boundaries right up to the Atlantic coast and, more important, to change the designation to 'wilderness area' (see page 28). Not only has this met with little success thus far, but there have been reports that logging activity has actually increased.

Within the sanctuary boundary, four small wilderness areas have been established, including Boggy Lake Wilderness Area, where a chain of lakes are ideal for extended canoe trips.

Just east of the Moser River Bridge on Necum Teuch Harbour, the **Bay of Islands Centre Association** (*Hwy 7;* ☎ *347 2602; www.bay-of-islands.org*) maintains walking trails at the former site of an 18th-century forge and lumber mill. On one side of Highway 7, the trail follows a short railway track on which lumber was transported to the harbour.

On a 120ha farm property the centre offers special events and periodic workshops in sustainable rural living and 'back to basics' life skills such as low-impact forestry. WWoofers (willing workers on organic farms) and volunteers are welcome to exchange work for room and board – contact the centre in advance. Centre staff can also arrange boat trips, guides or advise on self-guided tours of the region, with many spots rarely seen by tourists.

PORT DUFFERIN

This small community was named for the Marquis of Dufferin, Governor-General of Canada 1872–78. It offers beautiful views out to sea from the Salmon River Bridge area. If you turn along the waterside just by the bridge, there's a small look-out: continue on this road (signposted Smiley's Point) and a 2km drive will bring you to a small jetty and parking area also offering tranquil coastal vistas.

GETTING THERE Port Dufferin is on Highway 7, 13km/8 miles east of Sheet Harbour and 18km/11 miles west of Moser River.

WHERE TO STAY AND EAT

⌂ **Marquis of Dufferin Seaside Inn** (9 units) 25658 Hwy 7; ☎ 654 2696, T/F 1 877 654 2696; f 654 2406; www.marquisofdufferinmotel.com; ⊕ early May–late Oct. A delightful inn. Guest rooms with private balconies & beautiful views over the fishing village, Beaver Harbour & its islands. Bikes & canoes available for guest use. Licensed dining room (⊕ early May–late Oct 07.00–21.00 daily; $$) in a c1859 building overlooking the water. The food is excellent, especially the seafood chowder & scallops. The sticky apple pudding is a personal favourite. $$

BAY OF ISLANDS

Many of the next stretches of Highway 7 offer wonderful views of wooded peninsulas and tiny coves, and a sea dotted with dozens and dozens of uninhabited wooded islands. The region between Beaver Harbour and Ecum Secum is known as the Bay of Islands.

Small fishing communities dot the highway and in autumn the forests are ablaze with red maple and birch, the brilliant colours reflected in the rivers, lakes and coves.

MOSER RIVER Moser River's waterfront park on the estuary is a favourite spot for birdwatchers. Seaward, you'll see hundreds of small islands, popular with sea kayakers and yachtsmen. The Moser was once famous for its abundance of Atlantic salmon, which the old timers will tell you, could 'be scooped up in buckets' as they travelled upstream to spawn.

Getting there Moser River is on Highway 7, 18km/11 miles east of Port Dufferin and 35km/22 miles west of Liscomb.

✕ Where to eat

✕ **Trail Stop** Hwy 7, Moser River; ☎ 347 2602; www.trailstop.ca; ⊕ summer daily: hours & seasons vary — call ahead or try your luck. Part of the Bay of Islands Centre (see page 357), the Trail Stop is primarily a take-out, but there are 3 tables inside an adjoining rustic building. Or take your food down to one of the riverside picnic areas. **$**

LISCOMB MILLS

This isn't a community as such, more some fine hiking trails and a resort. Accessed from the parking area and trailhead immediately east of the Liscombe Lodge's entrance are a couple of relatively challenging hikes. The 9.6km return **Liscomb River Trail** follows the river's edge upstream to a swinging suspension bridge which spans a 20m waterfall. Near the waterfall is a fish ladder comprising 15 pools separated by concrete weirs, designed to aid salmon in their annual migration. The best time to see them 'climbing' the ladder is from early June to October (peaking in July). Return to the trailhead along the river's other bank. From the same trailhead, the rugged 2.9km loop **Mayflower Point Trail** heads to the mouth of the river opposite Rileys Island before returning along and above the riverbank.

GETTING THERE Liscomb Mills is 47km/29 miles east of Sheet Harbour, and 7km/4 miles west of Liscomb. Liscomb is 18km/11 miles east of Sherbrooke.

WHERE TO STAY AND EAT

🏠 **Liscombe Lodge Resort & Conference Centre** (52 units) 2884 Hwy 7, Liscomb Mills; ☎ 779 2307; www.liscombelodge.ca; ⊕ late May–mid-Oct. One of Nova Scotia's few resorts is located not on a beach but in a lovely riverside setting. Rather than 1 of the 5 cottages or 30 lodge rooms, choose a riverfront chalet & wake to the sound of birdsong. Complimentary use of good-size indoor pool & sauna, canoes & bicycles. Breakfast is available in the restaurant (**$$$–$$$$**). Ask about packages. The lodge is famous for its 'Planked Salmon Dinner' — the fish is cooked over an open fire. Arrive early to secure a coveted window table. If the restaurant prices are steeper than you'd like, Sherbrooke (see page 359), 24km along Hwy 7, offers cheaper dining. B/fast not inc. **$$$**
🏠 **Birchill B&B & Guest House** (4 units) 5254 Hwy 7, Liscomb; ☎ 779 2017; www.birchillbb.com; ⊕ year-round. If resorts don't do it for you, try 1 of the B&B rooms (b/fast inc) or a 1- or 2-

---

NECUM TEUCH AND ECUM SECUM

Necum Teuch — the name derives from the Mi'kmaq and means 'sandy river bottom' — is 5km past Moser River on Highway 7. It was home to Angella Geddes, author of several popular children's books, most famous of which is *Necum Teuch Scarecrows*, which has been translated into German and French. In addition to writing about them, she created a large collection of articulated scarecrows — many of which represented local people — which adorned her house and garden. Sadly Geddes passed away in 2006, but her figures still live in the garden of 'Aunt Mary's House', a simple private museum representing life in the early 1900s. It may be possible to arrange a tour of the house (*29451 Hwy 7, Necum Teuch*) — it is on the left as you drive through Necum Teuch — if someone is in attendance when you visit.

If you thought that Necum Teuch was an odd name, the next community, 5km further east, is Ecum Secum (this name derives from the Mi'kmaq *Megwasaagunk*, and means 'a red house'). At Ecum Secum Bridge, turn right and follow the side road to Mitchell Bay, where there is a beautiful Anglican church and cemetery overlooking the water. Stay on this road and it will take you back to Highway 7.

bedroom cottage 7km east of Liscomb Mills. Free use of kayaks (the property is on the Liscomb Harbour waterfront): boat tours & diving trips can be arranged. $

SHERBROOKE

This town on the St Mary's River has a hospital, a few places to stay and eat, a bank, post office, convenience store and a little supermarket. Most visitors come to see the living museum (see page 360), or to fish.

Every year, hundreds of fishermen come to try their luck on the river, though salmon numbers have dramatically reduced. The river was a favourite fishing spot of baseball legend Babe Ruth and many other famous celebrities and anglers.

HISTORY Sherbrooke was founded in the early 1800s at the farthest navigable point of the St Mary's River. Gold was discovered in the area in the late 1860s and was mined until 1890. Lumber was processed and exported, and there were shipbuilding operations.

The mines closed and shipbuilding ceased. By the late 1960s, there were few visitors apart from anglers. The town was beginning to die until ambitious locals, with help from the Nova Scotia Museum, began a big restoration project. The result is the Eastern Shore's most popular attraction.

GETTING THERE Sherbrooke is on Highway 7, 80km/50 miles from Sheet Harbour, 209km/130 miles from Halifax and 60km/37 miles from Antigonish.

TOURIST INFORMATION At the entrance to Sherbrooke Village (*7975 Hwy 7;* ✆ *522 2400;* ⊕ *Jun–mid-Sep 09.30–17.00 daily*)

WHERE TO STAY AND EAT

⌂ **Sherbrooke Village Inn** (19 units) 7975 Hwy 7; ✆ 522 2235, T/F 1 866 522 3818; www.sherbrookevillageinn.ca; ⊕ year-round. Cottages, a family house, a B&B suite (b/fast inc) & motel-type units. The licensed dining room (⊕ *07.30–19.30 daily, to 21.00 in summer;* $$) focuses on seafood & most dishes are made without use of a deep-fryer. $$

⌂ **Daysago B&B** (3 rooms) 15 Cameron Rd; ✆ 522 2811, T/F 1 866 522 2811; www.bbcanada.com/daysago; ⊕ year-round. A c1920 house in a rural setting with fine views of the St Mary's River. 3 guestrooms share 2 bathrooms. Kayaks for guests' use; stained-glass workshop on the premises. Full b/fast inc. $

⌂ **St Mary's River Lodge** (8 units) 21 Main St; ✆ 522 2177; www.riverlodge.ca; ⊕ Apr–Oct; off-season by reservation. Under Swiss management, the lodge itself — across the road from the river and right by the museum — has 7 guestrooms (full b/fast inc), all with private bathrooms. Across the river on a beautiful peninsula is the Lodge Residence, a 2-bedroom 2-bathroom suite with kitchen facilities. $

Å **St Mary's Riverside Campground** (24 sites) 3987 Sonora Rd; ✆ 522 2913; ⊕ mid-May–mid-Oct. Open sites, laundromat, pool (in season). $

✗ **House of Jade** 8164 Main St; ✆ 522 2731; ⊕ Jun–Sep 11.30–19.45 Tue–Sun; Oct–May 12.00–19.00 Wed–Sun. Canadian & Chinese standards. The won ton soup is a stand-out. $

SHOPPING

St Mary's River Smokehouses 8000 Hwy 7; ✆ 522 2005; www.thebestsmokedsalmon.com; ⊕ 08.30–17.00 Mon–Fri. At the western end of town. This shop's oven-smoked salmon nuggets, flavoured with garlic & maple syrup, are particularly good.

FESTIVALS
November
Old-fashioned Sherbrooke Christmas Tree lighting and procession, Christmas crafts, concerts, dinner theatre, Victorian tea and more.

OTHER PRACTICALITIES

$ **Royal Bank** 6 Main St; ☎ 522 2800;
🕐 10.00–15.00 Mon–Fri
✚ **St Mary's Memorial Hospital** 91 Hospital Rd;
☎ 522 2882

📖 **Sherbrooke Library** 11 Main St; ☎ 522 2180
✉ **Post office** 15 Main St; 🕐 08.30–17.00
Mon–Fri, 09.00–13.00 Sat

WHAT TO SEE AND DO

Sherbrooke Village (*Main St;* ☎ *522 2400; museum.gov.ns.ca/sv/;* 🕐 *Jun–mid-Oct 09.30–17.00 daily; admission CAN$10*) This unusual living museum reflects Nova Scotia as it was during its industrial boom in the late 1800s/early 1900s and comprises more than 80 restored buildings, 29 of which are open to the public, which are integrated with the town itself. It is the largest Nova Scotia Museum site and unlike (say) Memory Lane (see page 353), the buildings here are on their original sites.

Every morning at 09.30, this part of the town is closed to traffic, and the clock goes back a century. Period-costumed, knowledgeable guides help maintain the feeling that you have indeed been transported back in time as they tend to the crops, stroll through the town, staff the buildings and demonstrate such skills as pottery, weaving, candle making, blacksmithing and wood-turning.

Eat at the Sherbrooke Hotel's tea room – the menu is unpretentious, and – bearing in mind that it caters to something of a captive market – offers good value. Be sure to follow the Sonora Road on the east bank of the river for a few hundred metres from the main restoration area to hear the rush of water and smell the scent of lumber freshly cut by the village's authentic, photogenic water-powered sawmill.

Across the street in the stamp mill, you can see how gold ore was mined, crushed and processed during the gold rush.

If you visit out of season, this is still a nice place to wander even when the village is not officially 'open'.

St Mary's River Education and Interpretive Centre (*8404 Hwy 7;* ☎ *522 2099; www.geocities.com/stmarysriverassociation;* 🕐 *Jun–mid-Oct 09.00–17.30 daily; admission free*) The centre has exhibits relating to fishing, river enhancement and stabilisation projects, and the history of fishing. There is also a small aquarium.

PORT BICKERTON

Lighthouse fans will want to break their journey in this small community, just west of the Country Harbour ferry. As with much of the Eastern Shore, expect little in the way of services.

GOLDEN TALES

History books state a farmer, Nelson Nickerson, found gold in 1861 while he was haymaking. The story locals tell is that a woman picking wild flowers was attracted by a shiny piece of quartz which she took home. A passing traveller later saw the quartz, recognised its significance, and casually asked the woman where she'd found it. Armed with this information, he took his leave, found himself a pick and shovel and put Goldenville (on Highway 7, 5km west of Sherbrooke) on the map. The tiny community's c1900 Presbyterian Church now houses the **Goldenville Gold Mining Interpretive Centre** (*Goldenville Rd;* ☎ *522 4653;* 🕐 *Jun–mid-Oct 09.30–17.30 daily; admission free*), which tells of the history of gold mining in Nova Scotia.

Just offshore from Drum Head, which is on Highway 316 between the Country Harbour ferry and Tor Bay, is Harbour Island: its southern end is named 'Saladin Point' after a vessel which ran aground here in 1844. More interesting than the fact that the *Saladin, en route* from Chile to London, was carrying a cargo of guano, copper and silver is that the vessel beached because her captain, officers and many of the crew had been butchered by mutineers who had overlooked the fact that they had not spared any skilled navigators. The four mutineers were rescued – and sent to the gallows.

GETTING THERE Port Bickerton is on Highway 211, 29km/18 miles from Sherbrooke and 90km/56 miles from Canso.

WHAT TO SEE AND DO
Nova Scotia Lighthouse Interpretive Centre (*630 Lighthouse Rd;* ✆ *364 2000;* ⏰ *mid-Jun–mid-Sep 09.00–17.00 daily; admission CAN$3*) A 2km unpaved road leads to two lighthouses standing on a windswept, often fog-enshrouded bluff at the end of the headland. The newer of these is a fully automated working lighthouse dating from 1962. The older, built in 1930, is now a lighthouse museum with an original foghorn and well-laid-out display about the province's 170-plus lighthouses. A secondary building houses a collection of miniature replicas of some of the better-known lighthouses in Nova Scotia. Climb up the narrow staircase for a panoramic view of the wild and beautiful coastline and walk to a sandy beach.

The Country Harbour Ferry (*On Hwy 211, 7km from Port Bickerton*) For the princely sum of CAN$5, you and your vehicle can enjoy a pleasant – albeit just seven-minute – boat ride on the Country Harbour ferry. The ferry operates year-round, 24 hours a day: it departs the east side (Halifax side) of the bay on the half hour and the west side on the hour. If you are going east, it is well-worth checking that the ferry is running before heading this way – ask at a local tourist office. The alternate route via Country Harbour Cross Roads is longer of course, but you would also have to add on the 30km backtrack from the ferry dock.

TOR BAY

Originally named 'Port Savalette' after a French fisherman, Tor Bay is well worth a stop for its provincial park (see below).

GETTING THERE Tor Bay is just off Highway 316, 22km/14 miles from Guysborough, 33km/21 miles from Country Harbour and 52km/32 miles from Canso.

WHERE TO STAY AND EAT
🏠 **Seawind Landing Country Inn** (14 rooms) 1 Wharf Rd, Charlos Cove; ✆ T/F 1 800 563 4667; www.seawindlanding.com; ⏰ year-round. On Hwy 316, about 15km east of Tor Bay, the picturesque Acadian fishing village of Charlos Cove is home to this establishment, which occupies a 8ha peninsula with over 900m of ocean frontage, including a couple of lovely secluded beaches. Most of the rooms offer sea views. The inn has an excellent dining room open to non-guests by reservation (⏰ summer 07.30–10.00 & 18.00–21.00 daily; off-season 18.00–21.00 Fri–Sat; $$$), with a regularly changing menu of fresh locally sourced ingredients. Try, for example, bourbon-glazed pork tenderloin or scallops in a vermouth cream sauce. The lemon loaf is a delicious dessert. $$

WHAT TO SEE AND DO

Tor Bay Provincial Park (*off Hwy 316*) The park is situated on an isthmus along a peninsula that forms the southern boundary of the bay. Within the small day-use park, a boardwalk leads to a sandy beach, from which a short trail leads to a rocky headland where covered interpretive boards describe the geology of the region. There are other (almost always empty) beaches on the other side of the headland. The park also has picnic facilities.

CANSO

Situated at the entrance to Chedabucto Bay, Canso is sheltered from the ocean by round Grassy Island (see page 364). The town is located at the extreme eastern point of mainland Nova Scotia and – were it not for a little bit of Labrador – would have the honour of being the closest point on the North American mainland to Europe. For a while Canso has been in need of a cash injection, but work to revitalise the waterfront's old Whitman Wharf is now well underway.

The surrounding waters make another great sea-kayaking destination: however, unless your accommodation offers kayak loan or rental – and very few do – you'll need to have rented one back in Tangier (see page 354).

Take Union Street to its end, then follow a rugged unpaved road to **Glasgow Head**. *En route* enjoy wonderful views of the mouth of Canso Harbour, lighthouse and islands. When you reach the road end, choose between a swim in a manmade pond sheltered from the direct coastal waters by a rock barrier, and the spectacular cove on the other side of the barrier. If it's not too windy, the sandy knoll which separates the two areas is excellent for a picnic.

Two other lovely local beaches (you'll need a car or bike) are those at **Fox Island**, just off Highway 16, 11km from Canso, and at **Black Duck Cove Day Use Park** (*1609 Dover Rd;* ☺ *mid-May–mid-Oct*), approximately 18km from Canso.

HISTORY There is evidence that the French and the Basques were making annual visits to fish in the Canso area perhaps a century before 1605, the 'official' year of Canso's first permanent settlement. They built temporary shelters and came ashore to salt and dry their abundant cod catches. In any case, Canso is thought to be the oldest fishing village in the Maritimes, and one of the oldest settlements in Nova Scotia.

It was one of the most coveted anchorages for the cod-fishing industry during the 16th and 17th centuries, offering shelter and a relatively ice-free harbour well positioned for markets in western Europe and the Caribbean.

From the 1680s on, New Englanders used the area for trade and fishing with increasing frequency. They decided to establish and fortify a community on Grassy Island (see page 364) in 1718. Soon after, the wood-and-earth Fort William Augustus was constructed. The settlement met its end quite suddenly in the summer of 1744 when a French expedition from Louisbourg (see page 333) attacked and burned all the buildings to the ground. The following year, New

Englanders used the island as a staging point for their attack on Louisbourg. After the fall of Louisbourg, the French threat faded and Grassy Island was abandoned. It lay virtually untouched until reclaimed as a Canadian National Historic Site in 1977.

In the 18th century, there was talk that Canso, a thriving commercial centre and major fishing port, would become Nova Scotia's capital but this did not happen, partly because of its somewhat remote location.

GETTING THERE Canso is at the eastern end of Highway 16, 46km/29 miles from Guysborough, 105km/65 miles from Aulds Cove, 114km/71 miles from Antigonish and 320km/199 miles from Halifax.

TOURIST INFORMATION In the Canso Museum (*Whitman Hse, 1297 Union St;* ✆ *366 2170;* ⊕ *early May–early Oct 09.00–17.00 daily*)

WHERE TO STAY AND EAT

⌂ **Last Port Motel** (13 units) 10 Hwy 16; ✆ 366 2400; e hanhamsf@ns.sympatico.ca; ⊕ year-round. A clean, old-style standard motel outside the town centre. You wouldn't call food at its licensed restaurant (⊕ *07.00–21.00 daily;* $) gourmet, but prices are reasonable & the fish & chips reliable. $

⌂ **Whitman Wharf House B&B** (3 rooms) 1309 Union St; ✆ 366 2450, T/F 1 888 728 2424; e emeasures@rogers.com; www.whitmanwharf.com; ⊕ May–Oct. A lovely Victorian house with deck overlooking the sea. Shared bathroom & communal kitchenette. Light supper on request. Delicious gourmet b/fast inc – think fresh lobster crepes, or wholewheat waffles with pecans, maple syrup & wild summer berries. $

⋏ **Cape Canso RV Park** (33 sites) 1639 Union St; ✆ 366 2937; ⊕ Jun–Oct. Geared to motorhomes (sites are serviced) there are a few grassy spots on which to pitch a tent. $

⋏ **Seabreeze Campground** (74 sites) 230 Fox Island Rd; ✆ 366 2532; e seabreeze.camp@ns.sympatico.ca; ⊕ mid-May–mid-Oct. A quiet, beautifully located site overlooking Chedabucto Bay, approximately 10km west of Canso. Wooded & open serviced & unserviced sites. $

✗ **AJ's Dining Room, Lounge & Pub** 237 Main St; ✆ 366 2281; ⊕ 10.00–midnight daily. Decent pub food, the closest Canso comes to nightlife, & occasional live music. $

FESTIVALS
July
Stan Rogers Folk Festival See box on page 365.

August
Canso Regatta Boat races, dances, parades and concerts held over an August weekend.

OTHER PRACTICALITIES
$ **Bank of Montreal** 28 Main St ✆ 366 2654; ⊕ 10.00–15.00 Mon–Fri

✚ **Eastern Memorial Hospital** 1746 Union St; ✆ 366 2794

≋ **Canso Branch Library** 130 School St; ✆ 366 2955; ⊕ for hours, call or see www.ecrl.library.ns.ca

✉ **Post office** 1315 Union St; ⊕ 08.00–17.00 Mon–Fri, 11.00–15.00 Sat

WHAT TO SEE AND DO
Canso Museum (*Whitman Hse, 1297 Union St;* ✆ *366 2170;* ⊕ *Jun–Sep 09.00–17.00 daily; admission free*) Housed in the magnificent three-storey Whitman House (see box, page 364), local history exhibits cover Canso and eastern Guysborough County, with period furniture. Many works by Canso folk artist Mel Schrader. There are wonderful views of the town, harbour – and fuel tanks – from the widow's walk atop the corner tower.

Canso Islands and Grassy Island Fort National Historic Sites of Canada (*Union St,* ☎ *295 2069; www.pc.gc.ca/lhn-nhs/ns/canso;* ⊕ *Jun–mid-Sep 10.00–18.00 daily; admission & boat fare by donation*) The waterfront visitor centre describes the region's history: here you can see a scale model of the island before the French attack, a short video, and life-size dioramas of three island properties.

Park boats leave on demand (weather permitting) from the adjacent wharf for the 15-minute trip to Grassy Island where you can wander around, or take a self-guided (or free guided) tour of the ruins of 18th-century fortifications and remains of a colonial New England fishing station. Most traces of the church, fort, gun batteries, barracks and houses have gone, leaving just foundations and a few flattened remnants of the 18th-century fortifications. Go prepared: the only on-island services are pit toilets.

Hiking Follow the signs from town to take the Chapel Gully Trail (Chapel Gully is actually a saltwater inlet), a well-maintained easy 10km loop hike through diverse forest, over rocks and on long boardwalks. You'll find picnic tables, lookouts and numerous bird-feeders. There is also a shorter loop but offering fewer coastal views. Both loops take you across a 40m footbridge that spans the gully. This is also a popular area for birdwatchers.

HALF ISLAND COVE, QUEENSPORT AND HALFWAY COVE

These three tiny communities on Highway 16 offer a couple of attractions and a good place to stay. Queensport has a beach and picnic area just off Highway 16: just offshore on Rook Island is the photogenic c1937 Queensport Lighthouse.

South of Highway 16 and carved by glaciers millions of years ago, the 10,000ha Bonnet Lake Barrens Wilderness Area is dotted with lakes, marshes, granite barrens and coastal spruce-fir forest.

You won't find a restaurant along this stretch of Highway 16 – head back to Canso, or on to Guysborough.

GETTING THERE On Highway 16 between Canso and Guysborough. Half Island Cove is 17km/11 miles from Canso, Queensport 23km/14 miles and Halfway Cove 34km/21 miles from Canso and 15km/9 miles from Guysborough.

 WHERE TO STAY

🏠 **Barrens at Bay Coastal Cottages** (3 cottages) 6870 Hwy 16, Halfway Cove; ☎ 358 2157; www.barrensatbay.com; ⊕ year-round. A spacious, peaceful property comprising an old renovated 1-bedroom house & 2 new 2-bedroom cottages, all with very well-equipped kitchens in a wooded setting close to the water. Lovely location by deserted beaches. $$$

WHITMAN HOUSE

In 1885, wealthy merchant and businessman Clement H Whitman supervised construction of a rectory for the Baptist minister. However, the building work went so far over budget that the Baptist congregation withdrew from the project. Undeterred, Whitman poured more and more of his own money in, using the best materials he could find. When the house (one of the costliest in the province) was completed, he moved in – and generously gave his old, far more modest home to the church for use as a rectory. The house was sold following Whitman's death in 1932, and after that resold many times. Apparently, if you'd come along at the right time, you could have picked it up for less than CAN$500. It now houses the Canso Museum.

Over the first weekend in July, thousands of music fans descend on Canso for the **Stan Rogers Folk Festival** (↘ T/F 1 888 554 7826; www.stanfest.com), or, more simply, Stanfest.

Born in Ontario, Stan Rogers spent many of his summers in Nova Scotia's Guysborough County when growing up. His songs often had a Celtic feel, and some were in the style of sea shanties. Following his death in an air accident in 1983, he was nominated posthumously for a Juno (the Canadian equivalent of the Grammy) Best Male Vocalist award.

Since the decision in 1997 to hold a festival in Canso in his memory, the event has been a roaring success. The ever-growing outdoor event features around 50 acts from around the world performing on six stages. It may have 'folk' in the title, but expect to hear just about every main musical genre.

There is limited accommodation in the area, so most visitors camp at the special festival campground. In 2009, a camping pass cost CAN$50 and entry to the concert CAN$90 for the entire weekend.

WHAT TO SEE AND DO Lighthouse fans will want to pop in to the **Out of the Fog Lighthouse Museum** (*Hwy 16, at Half Island Cove;* ↘ *358 2108;* e *keepers_of_the_beacon@hotmail.com;* ⊕ *late Jun–mid-Sep 10.00–18.00 Thu–Mon; admission CAN$3*) Here, a varied and extensive collection of lighthouse- and fishing-related artefacts and memorabilia can be seen. Displayed in two rooms of a former schoolhouse, exhibits include working fog horns and numerous lenses.

GUYSBOROUGH

Lying at the head of lovely Chedabucto Bay, Guysborough has a few things going on including some excellent places to eat, a brew pub, marina, golf course and fine hiking/cycling trails in the area. On the main street, several businesses are located in beautifully restored historic buildings backing on to the waterfront. The **Old Court House**, which houses the tourist office and a museum, is one block up the relatively steep Queen Street from Main Street.

HISTORY First European settlement dates from 1636 when Nicolas Denys (see page 323) established a fishing station here and called it 'Chedaboutou', after *Sedabooktook*, the Mi'kmaq name for the area, meaning 'running far back, or deep extending harbour'. Fort St Louis was built, and by 1683, the community had become home to over 150 Acadians.

Some people – many of whom are members of The Prince Henry Sinclair Society of North America – believe that Prince Henry Sinclair landed at Chedabucto Bay in 1398. In 1996, they erected a monument in the pretty picnic area at Halfway Cove to commemorate their belief. The Prince – whose other titles included 1st Earl of Orkney, Baron of Roslin, and Lord of Shetland – is thought by some to have undertaken voyages of discovery in the late 14th century to what is now Greenland, Nova Scotia and the US. Some claim that the Mi'kmaq deity Glooscap is none other than Sinclair. We do know that his grandson, William Sinclair, was the builder of Rosslyn Chapel, just outside Edinburgh, Scotland, well known to Freemasons and fans of The Da Vinci Code.

Eastern Shore **GUYSBOROUGH**

9

In 1690, the fort was sacked by privateers from New England: the last Acadians left as a result of the Expulsion (see page 7) in 1755.

Subsequently, the largest group of settlers came at the end of the American Revolution when lands were granted to Loyalists. Guysborough was named in honour of Sir Guy Carleton, commander-in-chief of the British forces in America and the Governor-General of Canada during the 1780s.

GETTING THERE Guysborough is on Highway 16, 46km/29 miles from Canso, 59km/37 miles from the Canso Causeway, 70km/43 miles from Antigonish and 281km/175 miles from Halifax.

TOURIST INFORMATION In the Old Court House (*106 Church St;* ✆ *533 4008;* ⊕ *early Jun–late Sep 09.00–17.00 Mon–Fri, 10.00–17.00 Sat–Sun).*

🏠 WHERE TO STAY AND EAT

🏠 **DesBarres Manor Inn** (10 rooms) 90 Church St; ✆ 533 2099; www.desbarres.com; ⊕ year-round. Built for a Supreme Court judge in 1837, this beautifully restored mansion is set in immaculate landscaped grounds. Rooms are large & furnished with antiques. In the restaurant (⊕ *May–Nov from 17.30 daily;* **$$$**) you can sit on the lovely outdoor deck when the weather is clement, or inside by the fire. The menu gives a Maritimes twist to contemporary Canadian cuisine: the pan-seared pheasant breast, served with a spiced apple glaze is sublime. Or try the 5-course tasting menu. Although short, the wine list is well chosen. A true fine-dining experience. All in all, this is the region's best upmarket accommodation. Full gourmet b/fast inc. **$$$**

🏠 **Osprey Shores Golf Resort** (10 rooms) 119 Ferry Lane; ✆ 533 3904; T/F 1 800 909 3904; www.ospreyshoresresort.com; ⊕ May–mid-Oct. As the name suggests, the motel-style rooms are most popular with golfers. Outdoor pool (seasonal). Ask about 'Stay & Play' packages. The licensed clubhouse lounge ⊕ *May–mid-Oct 08.00–19.00 daily;* **$**) serves sandwiches & beverages. Continental b/fast inc. **$$**

Ⓐ **Boylston Provincial Park campground** (35 sites) Hwy 16; www.novascotiaparks.ca/parks/boylston.asp;

⊕ late Jun–early Sep. 5km north of Guysborough, this site offers exceptional views of the harbour & Chedabucto Bay from a hillside above the wide Milford Haven River with picnic facilities & a basic 35-site wooded campground & occasional concerts in season. Prince Henry Sinclair (see box on page 365) is once again commemorated, here by a wooden prow-shaped monument. **$**

✕ **Days Gone By Bakery & Restaurant** 59 Main St; ✆ 665 7886; www.daysgoneby.ca; ⊕ Jun–mid-Sep 07.00–19.00 daily; mid-Sep–May 07.00–17.00 Mon–Fri, 08.00–17.00 Sat–Sun. Buy fresh-baked bread & pastries to take away, or sit at one of the pine tables to enjoy healthy salads, soups & excellent-value daily specials such as chilli con carne or vegetable lasagne. Licensed. **$**

✕ **Rare Bird Pub** 80 Main St; ✆ 533 2128; www.rarebirdpub.com; ⊕ Jun–mid-Oct 11.00–22.00 Mon–Fri, 11.00–23.00 Sat, 11.00–21.00 Sun. A tastefully restored c1866 heritage building offering good pub fare, including burgers, salads, chowders & surprisingly good pizzas. All-day all-you-can-eat Sun brunch buffet. Patio looks out over the water. Quench your thirst with one of the pub's own Chedabucto Bay ales. Occasional live music. **$**

SHOPPING There's a small Save Easy Supermarket in the **Chedabucto Centre** (*9996 Hwy 16*) on the south side of town.

OTHER PRACTICALITIES

$ **Royal Bank** Main St; ✆ 533 3604; ⊕ 10.00–15.00 Mon–Fri

✚ **Guysborough Memorial Hospital** 10560 Hwy 16; ✆ 533 3702

📚 **Cyril Ward Memorial Library** 27 Pleasant St; ✆ 533 3586

✉ **Post office** 120 Main St; ⊕ 08.30–17.00 Mon–Fri, 10.30–16.00 Sat

WHAT TO SEE AND DO

Old Court House (*106 Church St;* ✆ *533 4008; www3.ns.sympatico.ca/ Guysboroughhistoricalsociety;* ⊕ *early Jun–late Sep 09.00–17.00 Mon–Fri, 10.00–17.00*

Sat–Sun; admission free) This c1843 church-like building now houses the local museum. Serving as both courthouse and town hall for 130 years until 1973, this is one of the country's oldest preserved courthouses. Displays include information on early Acadian and black settlements in the area, a collection of domestic tools and early photographs. Reading room with historical and genealogical information.

Hiking Whereas the entire 44km Guysborough Nature Trail which connects Guysborough with Cross Roads Country Harbour (on Highway 316 25km northwest of the eastern terminal of the Country Harbour ferry) might be too daunting, a walk along the first part of this trail, which follows the path of a railbed that never became a railway, is still worthwhile. Pick up the trail opposite the Fire Station on Queen Street (*Hwy 16*).

Golf At the magnificently situated **Osprey Shores Golf Resort** (see *Where to stay and eat*, page 366), green fees are CAN$28 for 9 holes. There are wonderful Chedabucto Bay views from every hole.

Boylston Provincial Park (see *Where to stay and eat*, page 366) is also worth a visit.

PORT SHOREHAM

Between Guysborough and Mulgrave, Highway 344 follows the western bank of the Strait of Canso. At Port Shoreham, a small provincial park features a boardwalk to the 1.5km sand and pebble beach, picnic tables overlooking the sea, changing rooms and toilets.

GETTING THERE Port Shoreham is on Highway 344, 19km/12 miles from Guysborough.

MULGRAVE

Other than a tourist office, neighbouring heritage centre, library and a look-off, there is little to delay you in Mulgrave.

At the south end of town the **Scotia Ferry Look-off** offers a good vantage point from which to watch the Strait of Canso shipping. Interpretive boards tell of the pre-Causeway ferries (see below).

On the north side, Venus Cove Marine Park has a picnic area, playground, boardwalk and floating dock on a small cove. It is also the location of the **Mulgrave Heritage Centre** (see page 368).

HISTORY In 1833, ferry services were established, carrying passengers from Mulgrave to Port Hawkesbury. Following the completion of the eastern extension of the Inter-Colonial Railway in 1882, passengers got off the train here to board a ferry across to Cape Breton Island. Mulgrave saw great prosperity and became one of the region's principal commercial hubs. That all changed when the Canso Causeway was completed in 1955: almost immediately, rail and much of the road traffic by-passed the town, severely hitting the social and economic life of the community.

But things have improved in recent times. One consequence of the causeway's construction was the creation of the deepest ice-free harbour on the coast of North America, and a superport has been constructed at Mulgrave.

GETTING THERE Mulgrave is on Highway 344, 5km/3 miles from Aulds Cove, 54km/34 miles from Guysborough.

TOURIST INFORMATION In the Mulgrave Heritage Centre building (*54 Loggie St;* ☎ *747 2788;* ⏰ *early Jun–early Sep 09.00–17.30 daily*).

 WHERE TO STAY AND EAT As well as the listing below, try eating at Auld's Cove (see page 286), five minutes' drive away.

🏠 **Mulgrave Mill Street B&B** (2 suites) 115 Mill St; ☎ 747 2532, T/F 1 800 546 5553; www.millstreetbedbrkfst.com; ⏰ late May–mid-Oct.

A traditionally decorated Cape Cod-style house just a 5min drive from the Canso Causeway. $$$

FESTIVALS

July

Scotia Days Festival Five days of dances, dinners, races, music and more, culminating in a last-night firework display.

OTHER PRACTICALITIES

📚 **Mulgrave Library** 390 Murray St; ☎ 747 2588; www.ecrl.library.ns.ca; ⏰ Jul–Aug 10.30–12.30 & 14.00–20.00 Mon, 14.30–20.00 Tue–Wed, 13.00–16.00 Thu; Sep–Jun 10.30–12.30 &

14.00–18.00 Mon, 14.30–18.00 Tue–Wed, 13.00–16.00 Thu, 13.00–16.00 Sat
✉ **Post office** 433 Main St; ⏰ 08.30–17.15 Mon–Fri, 08.30–13.00 Sat

WHAT TO SEE AND DO

Mulgrave Heritage Centre (*54 Loggie St;* ☎ *747 2788;* ⏰ *early Jun–early Sep 09.00–17.30 daily; admission CAN$2.50*) The centre is housed in an edifice built to resemble one of the old ferries. Displays on the Canso Causeway (see page 294), World War memorabilia, railway and fishing industry history.

Highway 344 continues on to Aulds Cove (5km from Mulgrave) and ends there at the junction with Highway 104. Choose to follow Highway 104 to the west, or cross the Canso Causeway to explore Cape Breton Island.

SABLE ISLAND

One of Nova Scotia's most fascinating parts is one of the most difficult (and costly) to visit.

Not to be confused with Cape Sable Island in the southwest of the province, Sable Island is a 40km-long windswept treeless and rockless crescent of land a maximum of 1.5km wide in the Atlantic Ocean approximately 300km southeast of Halifax.

Some of the island's many dunes approach 25m in height, and shift slowly towards the east. In the centre of the south side of the island lies brackish Wallace Lake which floods and recedes continuously as waves break over the beach head and cause the lake's waters to burst through the sand and drain back into the ocean.

In winter and spring, the only obvious vegetation is marram grass, but in summer and autumn the island becomes almost lush with wild flowers and berries.

Sable Island is close to one of the major shipping routes between Europe and North America. Because it lies directly in the path of most storm systems that track up the Atlantic coast, it is often hit by strange weather patterns. Being low-lying and treeless, it would have been very difficult for mariners to spot the island before it was too late – even more so in foggy conditions or after dark.

HISTORY There are disputes over the 'discovery' of the island with three unsubstantiated claims by the French and Portuguese in the early and mid 16th century.

In 1598, the Lieutenant-General of New France landed on Sable Island, leaving some 50 or 60 convicts with a few provisions whilst he sailed off to find a safer place to anchor. Strong winds made it almost impossible for him to return to the island and instead he made a brisk journey back to France. It is hard to imagine how anyone survived on the treeless windblown island without proper shelter or provisions: incredibly 11 castaways were picked up by a relief expedition in 1603.

Access to the island was first restricted in 1801 (and has been ever since) to try to stop the plunder of shipwrecks, and later to protect the island's unique environment. It wasn't until the 1870s that the government decided to erect a couple of lighthouses at each end of the island – it has been necessary to move these several times due to the constantly shifting shoreline.

The lighthouses are now automated, and the only permanent residents are four scientists, monitoring the weather and environment, and studying the wildlife.

GAS Vast reserves of offshore undersea gas were found off Sable Island in the 1990s. In 1999, the first wells were opened – the drilling platforms can be clearly seen from the island (when it is not foggy) – and the gas is transported to the mainland via a 225km pipeline. Scientists and environmentalists keep a close watch on any unwelcome side effects – and keep their fingers crossed.

SHIPWRECKS AND GHOSTLY TALES The cool Labrador Current flows into the Atlantic Ocean and meets the warm Gulf Stream flowing from the southeast. Not only does this result in a far higher than average number of foggy days, but is also thought to be the cause of an immense whirlpool. The Gully, the largest undersea canyon in eastern North America, might also be a contributing factor.

Since the early 17th century, there are records of over 500 vessels which have come to grief on and immediately around Sable Island. It's impossible to estimate how many others failed to be recorded. Not without reason has it long been known as the 'Graveyard of the Atlantic'.

Today, with modern navigational equipment, few boats run aground on Sable Island: the last wreck recorded was a luxury yacht in July 1999. But remains from centuries of shipwrecks are buried in the sand, appearing and disappearing as the wind shifts the grains.

SABLE ISLAND'S HORSES

Seals are quite common on the beach and in the surrounding waters, and over 300 bird species have been sighted, but the island's most famous residents are equine. There is speculation over how they first came here, but 300–400 wild horses now run free on Sable Island.

One of the world's few truly wild horse populations is naturally controlled by the island's food and water supply. The horses fatten up on the relatively lush and plentiful summer vegetation: in winter they rely on marram grass.

Isolated, windswept and frequently foggy, and with restricted access: not much might grow on the Graveyard of the Atlantic but it has proved fertile for those who like to tell a good yarn, and although they might not admit it, many a Maritimer believes the island to be haunted.

Stories circulated that pirates and bandits used the island as a base from which to lure ships into trouble, allowing the buccaneers to steal anything of value from the stricken vessels, and those on board. Almost as many ghost stories are told about the island as ships that have been wrecked there.

For example, it is said that a dead mother was washed ashore, clutching a baby which somehow still clung to life, albeit very weakly. The baby was taken to the nearest house, and the mother buried on the beach. No-one was surprised when the baby died a day or two later. After that there have been many reports of sightings of a sobbing female spirit wandering the beach as if looking for something.

Some survived wrecks, others were not so lucky. From time to time, bodies would be washed ashore on a strip of Sable Island's shore that became known as the 'haunted beach'. Those living on the island would regularly check the beach for bodies: if any were found, the corpse would be sewn up into a bag made from old sailcloth, and then left on the shoreline to be picked up on the supply boat's next visit – the shifting sand was too unstable for permanent burials.

In the mid 1990s, a scientist reported hearing the sound of piano music floating across the dunes. He knew that no-one else on the island would be playing a radio or CD, and also knew that although there had been pianos on the island in the past, there certainly weren't any at that time.

GETTING THERE During an average year about 50–100 people visit Sable Island: visits are only permitted with permission of the Director of Marine Programs (Canadian Coast Guard, see Contacts, below): requests must be made in writing (emails are acceptable): the request must include the purpose of the visit, mode of transportation to/from the island (eg: type of aircraft or vessel), the number of people in the party and their names and addresses, the anticipated arrival and departure dates, and requirements for logistical support on the island.

In reality, transport options and logistical support requirements should already have been checked out before applying.

The vast majority of visitors contact **Maritime Air Charter** (↖ 873 3330; www.maritimeair.com), Environment Canada's contracted airline. No permanent landing strip exists on the island – landings and take-offs are carried out on the southern beach.

Chartering a helicopter is also a possibility – try **Cougar Helicopters Inc** (↖ 873 3611; www.cougar.ca) or **CHC Canadian Helicopters International** (↖ 873 3778; www.chc.ca). All of these operate from Halifax International Airport. In addition to the aircraft charter, there are landing charges to pay: if you wish to stay overnight or longer, you will have to pay again for the aircraft to come back to get you. All in all, you'll do well to organise a day trip for under CAN$5,000 (though this could be split between up to six people): stay overnight and you're looking at almost double that amount.

Once permission has been obtained and the logistics sorted, weather problems can still play havoc with air and sea travel to and from the island. In general, August to October offers the best likelihood of suitable flying conditions. However, be aware that some of those who arrived by air found themselves staying a few days longer than expected as their aircraft could not return to pick them up. No-one will be permitted to go to the island unless they are adequately supplied and equipped to look after themselves completely.

GETTING AROUND No vehicles are available for rent, but visitors may be able to charter a Station vehicle and driver, subject to availability. To arrange services, contact the Operations Manager, Sable Island Station (see *Contacts*, below).

WHERE TO STAY Camping is not permitted and overnight visitors must arrange to stay at the Sable Island Station administered by the Meteorological Service of Environment Canada – the cost is currently CAN$150 per person per night.

CONTACTS AND RESOURCES Director, Marine Programs, Canadian Coast Guard (✆ *426 9022, 426 3550 (media relations);* f *426 6207;* e *simont@mar.dfo–mpo.gc.ca*). Operations Manager, Sable Island Station (✆ *482 8600;* e *gforbes@ca.inter.net*). To arrange accommodation and/or transport on the island. See also www.sabletrust.ns.ca and www.greenhorsesociety.com.

Appendix

FURTHER INFORMATION

BOOKS Note that many of these titles are out of print but often pop up in (real or online) used bookshops.

Autobiography

Haines, Max *The Spitting Champion of the World* Penguin, Canada, 2007. Growing up in Antigonish in the 1930s–50s.

Maclean, Angus Hector *God and the Devil at Seal Cove* Petheric Press, 1976

Architecture

Archibald, Stephen and Stevenson, Sheila *Heritage Houses of Nova Scotia* Formac, 2003

Penney, Allen *Houses of Nova Scotia: An Illustrated Guide to Architectural Style Recognition* Nova Scotia Museum, 1989

Fiction

Buckler, Ernest *The Mountain and the Valley* New Canadian Library, 1989

Eaton, Evelyn *Quietly My Captain Waits* Formac, 2001

Fitch, Sheree *The Gravesavers* Doubleday Canada, 2005. Based on the SS *Atlantic* disaster – for readers aged ten plus.

Haliburton, Thomas Chandler *The Clockmaker* BiblioLife, 2009

MacLeod, Alistair *No Great Mischief* Vintage, 2001. Cape Breton Island-set Scottish family saga.

Raddall, Thomas Head *The Governor's Lady,* Nimbus, 1992

Folklore

Creighton, Helen, & others *Bluenose Ghosts, Bluenose Magic, Traditional Songs from Nova Scotia* Nimbus, 2009

History

Bradley, Michael *Holy Grail Across the Atlantic* Hounslow Press, 1988

Bruce, Harry *An Illustrated History of Nova Scotia* Nimbus, 1997

Campey, Lucille H *After the Hector: The Scottish Pioneers of Nova Scotia and Cape Breton 1733 – 1852* Dundurn Group, 2008

Choyce, Lesley *Nova Scotia: Shaped by the Sea* Pottersfield, 2007

Finnan, Mark *The story of Sir William Alexander* Formac, 1997. The story of the first Nova Scotian.

Goodwin, William B *The Truth About Leif Ericsson and the Greenland Voyages* Kessinger, 2007

Hannay, James *The History of Acadia (1605 – 1763)* J&A McMillan, 1879. Very rare.

Kitz, Janet *Shattered City: The Halifax Explosion and The Road to Recovery* Nimbus, 2008

Ledger, Don, Style, Chris & Strieber, Whitley *Dark Object: The World's Only Government-Documented UFO Crash* Dell Publishing, 2001

MacNeill, Blair H *Ferry Tales: Stories of Village Life* Pronto, 2000. Stories from Digby Neck.

Mann, William F *The Knights Templar in the New World: How Henry Sinclair Brought the Grail to Acadia* Inner Traditions Bear and Company, 2004

Perkins, Charlotte *The Romance of Old Annapolis Royal* Historical Association of Annapolis Royal, 1985

Pohl, Frederick *Prince Henry Sinclair: His Expedition to the New World in 1398* Nimbus, 1997

Raddall, Thomas Head *Halifax, Warden of the North,* Nimbus, 2007

Raddall, Thomas Head *The Rover: Story of A Canadian Privateer* , MacMillan, 1966

Mi'kmaq

Choyce, Lesley and May, Rita (eds) *The Mi'kmaq Anthology* Pottersfield, 1997

Lacey, Laurie *Micmac Medicines Remedies and Recollections* Nimbus, 1993

Paul, Daniel N *We Were Not The Savages* Fernwood Publishing, 2006. Nova Scotia's history from a Mi'kmaq perspective.

Spicer, Stanley T *Glooscap Legends* Nimbus, 2007. The life history of Glooscap.

Natural history

Ferguson, Laing *The Fossil Cliffs of Joggins* Nova Scotia Museum, 1988

Maybank, Blake *Birding Sites of Nova Scotia* Nimbus, 2005

O'Connor, D'Arcy *The Secret Treasure of Oak Island* The Lyons Press, 2004

Parker, Mike *Guides of the North Woods: Hunting & Fishing Tales* Nimbus, 2004

Sibley, David *The Sibley Field Guide to Birds of Eastern North America* Knopf Publishing, 2003

Thurston, Harry *Dawning of the Dinosaurs: the story of Canada's oldest dinosaurs* Nimbus, 1994

Zinck, Marion (ed) *Roland's Flora of Nova Scotia* Nimbus, 1998. Two volumes.

Poetry

Bishop, Elizabeth *The Complete Poems (1927–79)* Chatto and Windus, 1983. A number relate to her time in Nova Scotia.

Clarke, George Elliot *Whylah Falls* Raincoast Books, 2001

Joe, Rita *The Poems of Rita Joe* Abanaki Press, 1978

Sports
Hiking

Dill, C *Canoe Routes of Nova Scotia* Canoe Nova Scotia Association, 1983

Haynes, Michael *Hiking Trails of Nova Scotia* Goose Lane Editions, 2002

Smith, Andrew L *Paddling the Tobeatic: Canoe Routes of Southwestern Nova Scotia* Nimbus, 2004

Cycling

Conrod, Gary *The Nova Scotia Bicycle Book* Available from Atlantic Canada Cycling (✆ 423 2453; *www.atlanticcanadacycling.com*), 1995. The accommodation listings are out of date but the rest of the book is still very useful.

Watt, Walter *Nova Scotia By Bicycle* Available from Bicycle Nova Scotia (*www.bicycle.ns.ca*), 2004

Paine, Albert Bigelow *The Tent Dwellers* Kessinger, 2005

Travel writing

Bird, Will R *This Is Nova Scotia* and *Off-Trail in Nova Scotia* Ryerson Press, 1950 and 1956 respectively. Motoring around Nova Scotia in the 1950s.

Crowell, Clement W *Novascotiaman* Nova Scotia Museum, 1979

Day, Frank Parker *Rockbound* University of Toronto Press, 1998. Based on East Ironbound Island near Blandford.

Dennis, Clara *Down in Nova Scotia* and *More about Nova Scotia* Ryerson Press, 1946 and 1937 respectively. Motoring around Nova Scotia in the 1930s.

Howe, Joseph *Western and Eastern Rambles: travel sketches of Nova Scotia* University of Toronto Press, 1973

Richardson, Evelyn *We Keep a Light* Nimbus, 1995. Set on Bon Portage Island near Shag Harbour.

Spicer, Stanley T *Masters of Sail* Ryerson Press, 1968

WEBSITES

Facts

www.clean.ns.ca, www.ecologyaction.ca and www.nsen.ca Environmental groups.

www.destinationhalifax.com/rainbow and gay.hfxns.org Useful information for gays.

www.nsgna.ednet.ns.ca Genealogy.

www.weatheroffice.gc.ca Five-day weather forecasts for locations all over the province.

Travel information

www.bbcanada.com Inns and B&Bs across Nova Scotia.

www.cbsa-asfc.gc.ca Canadian Border Services Agency – customs and immigration.

www.novascotia.com Official Nova Scotia tourism site.

www.peisland.com/triustours/line.htm Trius Tours coach schedule.

www.smtbus.com Acadian coaches schedules and prices.

www.viarail.ca VIA Rail Canada schedules and prices.

Natural history

www.maybank.tripod.com/BSNS/BSNS.htm Birding sites of Nova Scotia.

www.nsbs.chebucto.org The Nova Scotia Bird Society.

www.nswildflora.ca Nova Scotia Wild Flora Society.

Sport and outdoor activities

www.atlanticcanadacycling.com and www.bicycle.ns.ca Cycling.

www.ckns.ca and www.swpaddlers.com Canoeing and kayaking.

www.geocaching.com and www.maritimegeocaching.com Geocaching.

www.golfingns.com and www.nsga.ns.ca Golf.

www.novatrails.com and www.trails.gov.ns.ca Hiking.

www.scotiasurfer.com and www.surfns.com Surfing.

Bradt Travel Guides

www.bradtguides.com

Africa

Access Africa: Safaris for People with Limited Mobility	£16.99
Africa Overland	£16.99
Algeria	£15.99
Botswana: Okavango, Chobe, Northern Kalahari	£15.99
Burkina Faso	£14.99
Cameroon	£15.99
Cape Verde Islands	£14.99
Congo	£15.99
Eritrea	£15.99
Ethiopia	£16.99
Gambia, The	£13.99
Ghana	£15.99
Johannesburg	£6.99
Madagascar	£15.99
Malawi	£13.99
Mali	£14.99
Mauritius, Rodrigues & Réunion	£15.99
Mozambique	£13.99
Namibia	£15.99
Niger	£14.99
Nigeria	£17.99
North Africa: Roman Coast	£15.99
Rwanda	£14.99
São Tomé & Principe	£14.99
Seychelles	£14.99
Sierra Leone	£16.99
Sudan	£15.99
Tanzania, Northern	£14.99
Tanzania	£17.99
Uganda	£15.99
Zambia	£17.99
Zanzibar	£14.99

Britain and Europe

Albania	£15.99
Armenia, Nagorno Karabagh	£14.99
Azores	£13.99
Baltic Cities	£14.99
Belarus	£14.99
Bosnia & Herzegovina	£13.99
Bratislava	£9.99
Britain from the Rails	£17.99
Budapest	£9.99
Bulgaria	£13.99
Cork	£6.99
Croatia	£13.99
Cyprus see North Cyprus	

Czech Republic	£13.99
Dresden	£7.99
Dubrovnik	£6.99
Estonia	£13.99
Faroe Islands	£15.99
Georgia	£14.99
Hungary	£14.99
Iceland	£14.99
Kosovo	£14.99
Lapland	£13.99
Latvia	£13.99
Lille	£9.99
Lithuania	£14.99
Ljubljana	£7.99
Luxembourg	£13.99
Macedonia	£14.99
Montenegro	£14.99
North Cyprus	£12.99
Riga	£6.99
Serbia	£14.99
Slovakia	£14.99
Slovenia	£13.99
Spitsbergen	£16.99
Switzerland Without a Car	£14.99
Tallinn	£6.99
Transylvania	£14.99
Ukraine	£14.99
Vilnius	£6.99
Zagreb	£6.99

Middle East, Asia and Australasia

Bangladesh	£15.99
Borneo	£17.99
China: Yunnan Province	£13.99
Great Wall of China	£13.99
Iran	£15.99
Iraq: Then & Now	£15.99
Israel	£15.99
Kazakhstan	£15.99
Kyrgyzstan	£15.99
Maldives	£15.99
Mongolia	£16.99
North Korea	£14.99
Oman	£13.99
Shangri-La: A Travel Guide to the Himalayan Dream	£14.99
Sri Lanka	£15.99
Syria	£14.99
Tibet	£13.99
Turkmenistan	£14.99
Yemen	£14.99

The Americas and the Caribbean

Amazon, The	£14.99
Argentina	£15.99
Bolivia	£14.99
Cayman Islands	£14.99
Chile	£16.95
Colombia	£16.99
Costa Rica	£13.99
Dominica	£14.99
Grenada, Carriacou & Petite Martinique	£14.99
Guyana	£14.99
Panama	£14.99
St Helena	£14.99
Turks & Caicos Islands	£14.99
USA by Rail	£14.99

Wildlife

100 Animals to See Before They Die	£16.99
Antarctica: Guide to the Wildlife	£15.99
Arctic: Guide to the Wildlife	£15.99
Central & Eastern European Wildlife	£15.99
Chinese Wildlife	£16.99
East African Wildlife	£19.99
Galápagos Wildlife	£15.99
Madagascar Wildlife	£16.99
New Zealand Wildlife	£14.99
North Atlantic Wildlife	£16.99
Peruvian Wildlife	£15.99
Southern African Wildlife	£18.95
Sri Lankan Wildlife	£15.99
Wildlife and Conservation Volunteering: The Complete Guide	£13.99

Eccentric Guides

Eccentric Australia	£12.99
Eccentric Britain	£13.99
Eccentric California	£13.99
Eccentric Cambridge	£6.99
Eccentric Edinburgh	£5.95
Eccentric France	£12.95
Eccentric London	£13.99

Others

Something Different for the Weekend	£9.99
Weird World	£14.99
Your Child Abroad: A Travel Health Guide	£10.95

WIN £100 CASH!

READER QUESTIONNAIRE

Send in your completed questionnaire for the chance to win £100 cash in our regular draw

All respondents may order a Bradt guide at half the UK retail price – please complete the order form overleaf.

(Entries may be posted or faxed to us, or scanned and emailed.)

We are interested in getting feedback from our readers to help us plan future Bradt guides. Please answer ALL the questions below and return the form to us in order to qualify for an entry in our regular draw.

Have you used any other Bradt guides? If so, which titles? . . . .

. . . .

What other publishers' travel guides do you use regularly? . . . .

. . . .

Where did you buy this guidebook? . . . .

What was the main purpose of your trip to Nova Scotia (or for what other reason did you read our guide)? eg: holiday/business/charity etc. . . . .

. . . .

What other destinations would you like to see covered by a Bradt guide?

. . . .

Would you like to receive our catalogue/newsletters?

YES / NO (If yes, please complete details on reverse)

If yes – by post or email? . . . .

Age (circle relevant category) 16–25   26–45   46–60   60+

Male/Female (delete as appropriate)

Home country . . . .

Please send us any comments about our guide to Nova Scotia or other Bradt Travel Guides. . . . .

. . . .

. . . .

. . . .

Bradt Travel Guides

23 High Street, Chalfont St Peter, Bucks SL9 9QE, UK
☏ +44 (0)1753 893444 **f** +44 (0)1753 892333
e info@bradtguides.com
www.bradtguides.com

CLAIM YOUR HALF-PRICE BRADT GUIDE!

Order Form

To order your half-price copy of a Bradt guide, and to enter our prize draw to win £100 (see overleaf), please fill in the order form below, complete the questionnaire overleaf, and send it to Bradt Travel Guides by post, fax or email.

Please send me one copy of the following guide at half the UK retail price

Title	Retail price	Half price
... .	....	....

Please send the following additional guides at full UK retail price

No	Title	Retail price	Total
...	....	....	....
...	....	....	....
...	....	....	....

Sub total ....

Post & packing ....
(£2 per book UK; £4 per book Europe; £6 per book rest of world)

Total ....

Name . . . .

Address. . . . .

Tel . . . .   Email . . . .

☐ I enclose a cheque for £. . . . . made payable to Bradt Travel Guides Ltd

☐ I would like to pay by credit card. Number: . . . .

Expiry date: . . . / . . .   3-digit security code (on reverse of card) . . . . .

Issue no (debit cards only) . . . . .

☐ Please add my name to your catalogue mailing list.

☐ I would be happy for you to use my name and comments in Bradt marketing material.

Send your order on this form, with the completed questionnaire, to:

Bradt Travel Guides NS1
23 High Street, Chalfont St Peter, Bucks SL9 9QE
✆ +44 (0)1753 893444   f +44 (0)1753 892333
e info@bradtguides.com   www.bradtguides.com

Index

Entries in **bold** indicate main entries; those in *italics* indicate maps